"Khaki Letters" from ....
"My Colleagues in South Africa."

CORRESPONDENCE FROM THE

POST OFFICE TELEGRAPHISTS

OF THE

24th MIDDLESEX (P.O.) RIFLE VOLUNTEERS

(*Royal Engineer Reserves*),

ON ACTIVE SERVICE.

THE BOND THAT BINDS US—FRIENDSHIP—COMRADESHIP.

Published fortnightly for the Postal Telegraph Service.
Conducted by COLOUR-SERGEANT R. E. KEMP, *Central Telegraph Office, London.*

The Naval & Military Press Ltd

in association with

The National Army Museum, London

Published jointly by

The Naval & Military Press Ltd
Unit 10 Ridgewood Industrial Park,
Uckfield, East Sussex,
TN22 5QE England

Tel: +44 (0) 1825 749494
Fax: +44 (0) 1825 765701

www.naval-military-press.com
www.military-genealogy.com
www.militarymaproom.com

and

The National Army Museum, London
www.national-army-museum.ac.uk

In reprinting in facsimile from the original, any imperfections are inevitably reproduced and the quality may fall short of modern type and cartographic standards.

Presented with No. 21.

Khaki Letters.

With the Season's Greetings.
Yours heartily,
R. E. KEMP, "Colours."

From a photo taken by himself on Christmas Morning, 1900.

"Khaki Letters" from . . . .
"My Colleagues in South Africa."

CORRESPONDENCE FROM THE
POST OFFICE TELEGRAPHISTS
OF THE
24th MIDDLESEX (P.O.) RIFLE VOLUNTEERS
(Royal Engineer Reserves),
ON ACTIVE SERVICE.

THE BOND THAT BINDS US—FRIENDSHIP—COMRADESHIP.

Published fortnightly for the Postal Telegraph Service.
Conducted by COLOUR-SERGEANT R. E. KEMP, *Central Telegraph Office, London.*

No. 1.   MARCH 9TH, 1900.   PRICE ONE PENNY.

Central Telegraph Office,
London, E.C.

LAUNCHED! See how she rides! Note her fair lines—fair but frail. Fair to those who gladly welcome her—frail to those who know her best. How gallantly she breasts the waves, how proudly she displays her pennant! Her snow-white sail is set, and all eyes eagerly watch her. "She's a picture," says one. "She's a trim little craft, as spick and span as I've seen for many a day." "Ah! and she's the right sort too! Did you notice her name?" "No!" "What! you haven't heard it? I'll tell ye, m'boy. She's a little bit of a thing, but she's taken a big name, and what's more, every bolt and plank in her is as true to it as can be. She's called the 'Friendship-Comradeship,' and mark ye what I say: she's true from keel to topmast, from stem to stern." "Is she strong?" She may encounter some nasty squalls. "Is she taut and tight?" She may find dirty weather. In a word—

"WILL SHE LIVE?"

I'm an amateur, and a poor amateur at that. I have very little literary merit, but a large lump of love. Love for the boys out yonder—love begotten of a very high esteem, an unlimited admiration for the lads who have laid aside their civvy's life and right royally gone forth for Queen and country—taking risks they might have avoided, enduring trials they could easily have escaped—willingly, gallantly, loyally and lovingly lending their labours and lives for a nation's duty.

I can make no apology for introducing my little booklet to you—my fellow clerks. Such is the custom I am fully aware, but can we not dispense with formalities and come straight to the point?

WILL SHE LIVE?

'Tis a pertinent question, but you can make the response, YES. For she's only intended to run during war-time.

Time and labour have been lavishly spent in collecting, copying and sending letters for publication to the *Telegraph Chronicle*. And I heartily thank that organ for its help in bringing them before your notice. That journal assures me it has done its best; and as a man, I believe what its Editor says. But its best is not enough, not half enough, to satisfy the longings of our Staff in this matter. The opportunity has been offered, and refused. Suggestions for occasional extra issues or pages have been made and rejected: more important matter has crowded us out bit by bit, and in a few weeks' time, would almost extinguish our light altogether—so pressing is the other matter. I'm driven to take action—I've done so for you, for you only, for you that you may enjoy letters from your own fellow-clerks; and again I ask—

WILL SHE LIVE?

The little barque is afloat, but the clouds are hovering round. My circular letter has been mis-read, misconstrued, and misapplied by some who are biased against the project—biased by fear, biased by an indecision—a blue fever, dog-in-the-manger attitude—a reluctance to give adequate space in their own paper, and an apparent abhorrence to the finding of space elsewhere. Friends, my letter was calmly worded, very calmly worded, if you only knew how intensely earnest I feel my—OUR—duty to our bonny boys afar. Never has the semblance of a thought entered my mind to injure the editor, his staff, or his paper. Never has the remotest germ of ill-will to anybody ever entered—much less found a welcome—in my thoughts, and never will I be at enmity with my fellow-officers. I speak now in solemn earnest. Those who prefer to dub me an enemy of theirs, will find I am no such thing. Moreover, I wrote for the *Chronicle* up to the very hour of its going to press on Tuesday last, supplying it with what I might have used for this little booklet; thus it will prove I have done my duty to that paper.

Cast aside the cause of war! that's not the question. Every true Britisher hates war—the killing of fellow-men; but that's not the question. Nearly 140 Telegraph clerks are engaged in this special yet awful duty. They are men we know, they are men we have worked with, men we are hoping to see again, men who are constantly thinking of their loved ones at home, men who are communicating with us week by week. The little booklet is the vessel by which those consignments of experiences, letters of friendship and mutual attachment can be conveyed to and fro, and the large Postal Telegraph Staff can seal the verdict.

WILL SHE LIVE?

Again I thank the *Telegraph Chronicle* for all it has done. I heartily thank the band of workers who have responded so nobly to my invitation. There's one thing more to be done, and that is all. Send your copy away to your friend, make it widely known throughout the entire service, remembering that not half the offices have heard of this; and the answer will undoubtedly be—

SHE WILL LIVE.

Work well, work cheerfully—all for the boys, and success will crown your efforts with honour and gladness.

Yours very heartily,

Tuesday, March 6th, 1900.   R. E. KEMP.

MARCH 1st, 1900.

COLOUR-SERGEANT KEMP,

If you like to copy the enclosed for your Booklet you are at liberty to do so. Then please post it in time for to-morrow's mail.

(*Signed*) S. RAFFLES THOMPSON,
Colonel.

❖ ❖ ❖ ❖ ❖ ❖ ❖ ❖ ❖ ❖ ❖ ❖ ❖ ❖ ❖ ❖

HEAD-QUARTERS,
24TH MIDDLESEX (P.O.) RIFLE VOLUNTEERS,
GENERAL POST OFFICE, LONDON,
March 1st, 1900.

SERGEANT-MAJOR TEE,

I was much gratified to hear of the safe arrival at Capetown of yourself and comrades of "L" Company. Others sailed yesterday, so that altogether about 140 of our Telegraphists are in, or on their way to, South Africa, and I am sure that they will all do credit to the Regiment, and we hope to welcome them all home again safe and sound.

It was a great satisfaction to me that my representation to the War Office secured the recognition of the N.C. rank of all the Sergeants, especially of those who had volunteered to go on service even as Sappers.

The excellent spirit shewn by them was most creditable.

Now that affairs are taking a turn for the better, I hope the end of the fighting may be hastened, although I think the campaign will not be over for a long time.

COLOUR-SERGEANT KEMP keeps a most interesting record of all your doings, which is pleasant reading to your friends, who constantly think of their absent comrades.

I shall be glad if you will remember me most kindly to all your comrades, and tell SERGEANT MILLER I was much pleased to hear from him.

(*Signed*) S. RAFFLES THOMPSON,
Colonel.

COPYRIGHT.—" Khaki Letters" must not be used without permission.—
R. E. KEMP.

Khaki Letters.

No. 21,410, Sergeant **J. H. Nelson**, Modder River, Dec. 21st (delayed), says:—" . . . . Matters are rather quiet here now; the 1st Division resting upon their arms, with the exception of a few shots from the long range naval gun now and aga n, to let the Boers know we are not asleep. Now and again also the enemy reply with their 'Long Tom,' and one or two of their shells have fallen too close to the camp to be comfortable, although without damage, consequently the work is rather light for the Wheatstone Staff, although the long hours of duty continue.

"To-day one of our party (Sapper Quinn) was sent down in the hospital train to Capetown, suffering from some form of strain in the abdomen. It is sincerely hoped his trouble will not incapacitate him from duty very long, for his Irish geniality will be much missed. His duties as Assistant Cook are now being performed by another 'disthressed patriot' from the Emerald Isle.

"Our rations are being varied in very agreeable fashion, about our only trouble being the very stale bread and hard biscuits. Yesterday the cooks turned out a very creditable suet pudding, which we disposed of at tea-time with much gusto, with the aid of jam. Several times we have enjoyed a respectable portion of boiled rice and condensed milk for supper. Every other day or so lime juice is served out, and twice a week a tot of rum is available for those who care for it. On two or three occasions potatoes for dinner have been our fortune, but usually we take our vegetables in compressed preserved form. Nearly every day jam takes the place of butter for breakfast and tea, and when it doesn't the bread or biscuit goes down dry.

"Now that the Colonial railway people have substituted permanent wire for the T.B.'s air-line, the working capacity has increased appreciably, and we are able to work Wheatstone Duplex at 200 words per minute comfortably.

"According to accounts which have reached us, there is another batch of the 'L' Company very near their destination at the present time, but nothing definite as to their whereabouts is known either here or at De Aar.

"According to information supplied on the wire, Colour-Sergeant Kemp has sent each man of the party an Xmas card; we haven't yet had the pleasure of seeing a copy, but we are nevertheless grateful in anticipation, hoping that our reciprocal photo card safely reached him.

"Although our party was undoubtedly booked for Kimberley, there is a doubt abroad as to our reaching there after all, it being asserted in some quarters that we shall shortly get orders to get back to De Aar, and from thence to Naauwpoort, to form part of General Buller's division f)r the advance on Bloemfontein in the Orange Free State. Nothing definite is known here, however, excepting the great probability of no further advance taking place from here for some time to come. In the meantime things appear to be quite settling down again—the railway authorities having taken over the station from the military, and this afternoon I notice the hotel refreshment bar outside the station has been re-opened (for the benefit of a select few only). A cricket match and other sports are being arranged for Xmas Day."

KHAKI LETTERS—*continued*.

No. 21,410, Sergeant **J. H. Nelson,** writing from Modder River, South Africa, January 3rd, 1900, gives us the following interesting notes *re* Christmas there :—" DEAR KEMP,—Many thanks for welcome Christmas cards and good wishes, and also for news in general supplied through different correspondents. Sapper Jenner is also writing you by this mail, but he has left me to furnish a few particulars of our doings on Christmas Day, so am giving you a short account :—

Christmas Day with Lord Methuen's Kimberley Relief Force.

" The 'advanced Wheatstone Section' dine in a dust storm at Modder River. Neither carols, waits, nor peals of bells broke the stillness of the Camp to usher in the Christmas of 1899, the only sounds to break the utter silence being the occasional challenges of sentries, and the sounder clicks and the buzz of the vibrators. Daylight dawned with its usual brightness, and the promise of another hot day was soon in evidence. Lack of material made it very difficult to indulge in decorations, but a number of our party celebrated the day by discarding their very much soiled khaki for the new suits which had previously been sent up in their kit bags from De Aar. The compliments of the season were freely exchanged, and cheerfulness befitting the occasion inspired the hearts and lighted the faces of all. By special arrangements all the Military Telegraph Offices were closed from 6 till 8 p m., and so it was decided to utilize the opportunity of general relief from duty during these two hours by combining our forces with those of No. 3 Section in the formation of a grand Christmas party. And thus it happened, while most of our kinsfolk in Dear Old England were on the eve of onslaught on roast beef, turkey, Christmas pudding, and mince pies, we were satisfying the more pressing claims of anatomy at 1 p.m. with a frugal snack of bread and cheese and cooled boiled water. As the afternoon wore on, the great heat was succeeded by the gathering of heavy black thunderclouds, and a gale of wind sprang up, bringing blinding clouds of sandy dust from the west. The messing arrangements were in the hands of No. 3 Section, under the direction of T.Q.M.S. Lowe and Sergeant Shergold, and right good use they made of the limited resources at their command, the table arrangements being unique, and the cooking excellent. At 6 p.m. prompt our office was closed, and the party of twenty with mess tin, knives and forks in their hands, trooped across to No. 3's quarters—about 400 yards away—towards the north bank of the River. Here we found all ready for the repast, and down we sat shoulder to shoulder, and soon the rattling of dining utensils and the clashing of elbows evidenced the commencement of operations. The menu consisted of hot roast ribs of beef and potatoes, beetroot and salad, and a pint of beer per man (for those who desired), concluding with Christmas pudding and fresh peaches. Unfortunately, the Christmas pudding gifts from England for the troops had been miscirculated to Natal, and it was only due to the kindness of Lieutenant Moir, who supplied not only a private pudding but also the spirit illuminant, that our Christmas feast was blessed with a taste of the season's delicacy at all. Injudicious feeding was impossible, for obvious reasons, and temperate in all things (for same reasons), the troops' digestive organs underwent no undue strain as the result of Christmas festivities. A word of description is due to the ingenious arrangement by which the diners were able to avoid taking their meals squatted amidst the sand and dust. The table, at which about forty guests were seated, was about thirty feet long, supported by the familiar air-line poles, the top being

KHAKI LETTERS—*continued.*

made up of G. S. (general service) wagon sides strongly secured by three-strand wire. The seating accommodation was made up of ladders resting upon air-line drums. Doubtlessly there is good foundation for the statement that in certain peculiarly constituted households the exigencies sometimes demand curious domestic contrivances; so considering the conditions under which our Christmas fare was disposed of, it was excusable that our table-cloths during the day formed part of the bed-clothes during the night—in fact, they were waterproof sheets. As the dinner progressed, so, likewise, did the duststorm, while vivid and frequent flashes of lightning darted from the threatening black clouds, but fortunately rain held off, and ultimately the dinner concluded without the marring incident of a downpour. Sergeant Nelson was then called upon for a speech, and in a few words he acknowledged with much pleasure the successful efforts of No. 3 Section to provide such entertainment under awkward conditions, concluding by leading three cheers for Lieutenant Moir and non-commissioned officers and men of the Section. (Kindly excuse blunders, my attention being continually drawn away to surroundings, which just now are somewhat bustling, a De Aar train having just steamed into Station.) A rough-and-ready smoking concert followed, and although the ever-present dust, and nearly always absent lubricant, made the top notes somewhat difficult of easy attainment, general enjoyment prevailed until 9 p.m., when song and jest were abruptly terminated by the rigidity of Camp regulations, and, wending our ways to respective quarters, Christmas Day on active service in South Africa came to a close. Boxing Day came and went with no departure from the normal for us, the only incidents of the day being a dust storm worse than that of the 25th—lasting about eight hours—and a furious fusilade from the Boer trenches and kopje guns in the evening, owing to an impression that our forces were moving forward for a night attack. In connection with the remark *re* the miscirculated puddings, it may be added they are still *non est*, while the Queen's chocolate and promised public gifts would appear to have gone in search. Heavy strain upon transport no doubt accounts for much of the delay, but we shall be quite content if the goodies turn up in time for wholesome consumption. Although there is a Mission Hall (formerly a school) in Camp, martial veto prevented the holding of a watch-night service on New Year's Eve, and 1900 was ushered in by a vigorous tinkling from the staff quarters, apparently brought about by means of a saucepan and iron rod. This was immediately followed by a scene of mild excitement, two clerks being warned to parade in full marching order at once, and two to report for duty in the Vibrator Office. The former couple, however, were taken from No. 3 Section, and went off for cable-cart duty with a flying column then starting for reconnaissance work, while the other two were supplied from our own detachment for buzzer operations in Camp. A good proportion of our second party has been distributed at the several offices between here and De Aar, so we have not yet had the pleasure of greeting any of them in person, though the wires have been made use of for fraternal enquiry. The health of our detachment at Modder remains very satisfactory, although we regret our friend Quinn is still absent from us at—as we believe—Wynberg Hospital, Cape Town. The *Telegraph Chronicles* continue to arrive with welcome regularity, the Home news being followed with an interest never felt to the same extent before.

"Further advance towards Kimberley is still delayed, and the troops are getting a bit tired at the long inactivity. Commencing with the 1st of January, the monotony has been considerably relieved by the carrying out

KHAKI LETTERS—*continued.*

of a gymkhana, which extends throughout the current week. Sapper Poole (of Inverness) is down to play for the R.E.'s in the football ties, but nobody else of 'Ours' is taking part in the sports.

"January 4th—At six o'clock this morning we removed all our Wheatstone apparatus to the platform outside the office, and the party at work were cinematographed by the P. M. O. Scots Guards. The same officer previously photographed us as a group outside the Crown and Royal Hotel, and by arrangement we are having enlargements made from the negatives by an old friend at Southsea.

"News is just about exhausted, especially as others' letters doubtless contain all else I could touch upon. So will draw to a close, with kind regards and New Year wishes, hoping you will not have occasion to lament lack of intelligence from the front."

No. 2,342, Lance-Corporal **S. G. Davis** (of LV), Modder River, January 7th, 1900, writes as under :—

"DEAR COLOUR-SERGEANT KEMP,—I know not hardly how to express my sincere gratitude to yourself for so many, and in so many ways wishing us true joys of campaigning, *i.e.*, God-speed, safe return, and a happy re-union; those words have filled me—since reading them in the train down to Aldershot—many and many a time. Again, that beautiful card, which I may tell you has been sent home to be framed.

"This sort of thing I never experienced during the whole of my twelve years with the R.E.'s. You also seem to take more than a comrade's interest in our welfare and doings, and I very pleasingly can say your very great thoughtfulness has won everyone over, and each and all swell your praises.

"Well, I don't know that I can say very much but what you know already. Of course, you will know by now that all are safe and well, except poor Quinn. . . . We have made friends with Surgeon-Major Beevor, of Scots Guards. He informed me if any of our men were ill to go to him personally. This is great kindness, especially seeing he is P.M.O. of our (1st division) hospital. He has taken us by the cinematograph. So suppose a 'stiver' a time will show telegraphists at work under fire. This would not be untrue, for during the 2½ minutes three shots were fired from two 4.7 in. naval guns about one and a-half miles from here.

"We are anxiously waiting to shake hands with the telegraphists at Kimberley. We shall then go round to Naauwpoort, I hear, and move up with staff, moving by night generally (as they drop for night we close up). The Wheatstone has to be at the extreme front at all times, so suppose we shall punch and rush through the glad 'peace'—news that will gladden many a heart. The worst experience that I have had yet was as corporal of guard of ration train from Orange River to Klokfontein. We well knew Boers were on the journey somewhere. Proof of this was obtained the very next night, when they cut wires and broke up line behind us, but only stopping wires and line for about ten hours, so well are the telegraph sections organised. I enclose as a curio the orders issued on that memorable night. With many thanks again. Kind regards to self, Sergt.-Instr. Graham, and Sergt.-Major Hoy."

[NOTE.—Most of the above letter was published in the *Telegraph Chronicle*. The first two paragraphs, however, were deleted. I insert it here in order to show how such small efforts as mine are appreciated by "our boys."

KHAKI LETTERS—*continued*.

This is only one of the very many expressions of a similar character, and such acknowledgments of my desire to keep them in touch has encouraged me to continue in my self-imposed task. My readers will kindly note that I am not asking for praise in any shape or form; I believe I am doing but a comrade's duty.—R.E.K.]

Lance-Corporal **W. B. Ruffell** (of TS), writing from De Aar, Jan. 8th, says:—". . . . I am afraid there is no news to tell you, everything is at an absolute deadlock here; Methuen seems to be resting on his arms reversed. For my own part I do not think he will move till there has been a big battle at Ladysmith and they have driven them back there, then Methuen may take action on the supposition that some of the opposing force may be withdrawn to help Joubert. There is no sign of our moving from here yet, and we are all getting a wee bit 'fed up' with it. The dust storms here are terrible and a change would be welcome, also we want to see more of the country now we are here. . . . . You have seen the account of the Douglas 'scrap'—those prisoners they took came through here this morning, they are Colonial Dutch, and a real scratch lot; I think they will swing or be shot as rebels. A train of refugees from Port Elizabeth, *en route* to Cape Town and England, passed through last night, and it was pitiful to see the distress some of them are in. One poor woman had two little chicks, and had lost her husband (in the Imperial Light Horse)—killed at Molteno; the only compensation the Government offered was a free passage to England (steerage, too). I got her some tea and a bite, and managed to rake up a quid among the chaps for her, and I can tell you she was very thankful. . . . . I enclose a sort of diagram and sketch of De Aar, just to give you an idea of the place. . . . . Have not been able to get a selection of relics yet, the game is not far enough advanced for that, but have picked up two or three little curios. Some of the chaps at the front have made off with Mauser rifles, but they will find some difficulty in holding on to them, as they are cumbersome to take about when on the march or move. . . . . Remember me to all friends—I include their names in spirit if not lettered. . . . . Those puddings and Queen's chocolate for the troops are still visions of the future. I shall keep my 'duff' as an interesting 'petrified relic of ages past,' and ask the British Museum to accept it. 'By gad, sir,' won't it have a beard when it gets there!"

No. 27,844, Sapper **John Fallon,** Green Point Camp, January 10th, writes:—

"MY DEAR COLOURS,—Most of our *confrères* at home—yourself included—must think that 'the absent-minded beggar' element is asserting itself very strongly amongst some of us, at least, so far as the members of the 2nd detachment of the reserve is concerned, for, with the notable exception of our old friend Miller (whose voluminous despatch we all seemed to look upon as representing *our* views, &c.), I'm afraid you've found very poor subscribers to your 'Records.' . . . . We are just beginning to get a bit 'fed up' with Cape Town after three weeks' sojourn, and begin to look both with envy and pride upon our more fortunate comrades who have gone 'up country.' . . . . Speaking of the latter pastime (fishing), some of our chaps are getting quite adepts, and seem to have collared the knack

KHAKI LETTERS—*continued.*

of luring the fishes and sea monsters from their native element. One of them succeeded in capturing an octopus the other day, and he was certainly looked upon as the hero of the hour. Others captured minor specimens of the piscatorial tribe, but one man set his teeth hard, and murmured, ' I won't be beaten.' Neither was he, for only a day or two later did he succeed in landing a shark fully 4ft. 6in. in length Accordingly, Sappers Thomas (Polegate) and Tovey (Croydon), the captors, wrested the palm from the Octopus King, and conveyed their prize into camp to the strains of ' See the Conquering Hero(es) Come !' Great, indeed, were the rejoicings, in which our officers shared, and if there were any dry eyes, there certainly were no dry throats in the R E. camp that night. We were all dumbfounded and annoyed at the rumour concerning Jenner, in which, of course, there isn't a word of truth. . . . Quinn left Wynberg Hospital last week, and has gone back to duty at De Aar. . . . All 24th men desire me to thank you most heartily for the beautiful Christmas cards which, up to now, are the only reminder of home some of us have had, as it appears our letters travel all over South Africa before reaching us. Yours, however, was an exception, and was delivered the day after Christmas. The *Telegraph Chronicle* also arrives, and we read with pleasure the doings of our good friends at home. In fact. our life since arriving here has been so uneventful that it seems hard to believe we are not in England. . . . The night guard has instructions that, after dark, if three whistles are heard, it means ' camp alarm,' and if three guns, a ' general alarm.' Well, on Sunday, the 31st ult., we retired at the usual hour, and happening to be one of the guard not on sentry, I was sleeping peacefully, when the Corporal shook me up, and, half awake, I heard the ominous words, ' Three guns gone ! Out you get !!' We fell in outside the tent to find the whole camp in a state of silent activity. Anxious whispers could scarce be heard above the roar of cannon, and it was n't until the sentry came round and reminded us of the fact that the New Year was being heralded in, that we breathed freely again. There are only a few of us left here now, 24th men being Miller, Milton. Samuel, Storm r, Hawkins, Dellbridge, Bannister (MR), Bouriay (SY), Andrews (NN), Austen. Brooks, Poole (BS), and myself, all others having gone to De Aar and Modder River."

In another letter, of same date, John writes to his brother, saying :— " Three weeks have passed, and we are still ensconced as above, still waiting anxiously to be sent up country, and still without any letters from home or anywhere else. The only ones I've had since arrival being one from you, which was addressed Queenstown, and had been all over the world pretty well, including Queenstown, South Africa ; a card from Mick, and a letter and card from Kemp. I'm sure there must be hundreds of R E. letters knocking about somewhere, but they've not yet found their way here.

" Considering events which have occurred in the last few days, and that Roberts and Kitchener are expected to-day, it is most probable that before you receive this we may be many a mile from here. During the last ten days we have had to go to the C.T.O. here to get an insight into the Colonial system of working ; none of us, strange to say, were particularly impressed with it, and most of the fellows displayed a decided apathy to learn anything, if anything were to be learnt. So up to now we all prefer the home method to the Colonial. Then, again, the commissariat arrangements are a bit uncertain, for, being a small body of men, the stores are irregularly delivered, with the result that very often we should have to go without breakfast or tea if we didn't have enough money to purchase the same, and I can tell you

KHAKI LETTERS—*continued.*

one or two of us have been mighty near to that. Even when the full rations are served out there is always something to buy, such as butter, milk (condensed), &c., which is never served out. Jam is *supposed* to be served out, one tin to each tent every other day, but if we get it twice a week, we're lucky. Dinner is the only time you get a real belly-full, and that is invariably potatoes and shackles, *i.e.*, stew, same as you've seen us have at Aldershot. It's all right, but, like other things, it gets a bit 'mono.' However, independent of these odds and ends, we manage to get some good feeds down us. Fellows in the Cape Office have asked several of us to dinner on various occasions, and have never met with a refusal; then, again, the various churches vie with one another to see who'll give the biggest spread to 'Tommy,' with the result that the latter always scores. So, taking one thing with another, we don't do so badly, and there are, no doubt, worse places to live in than Cape Town. .... Lewis sails, so he says, for home by to-day's mail, and I believe several other refugees are following his example—whether wisely or not, I don't pretend to say. But one thing I have been told . . . that when the war is over it won't take long for a fellow to make his 'brads' in the Transvaal. .... They've not overburdened us with 'oof' since leaving England—all we've had since 29th November being £2 10s. 2d. up to date. Our reserve pay is still held back or gone astray, and some of the fellows are getting near the end of the tether. Have just heard, tho', that they are going to weigh out to-morrow, so there will be merriment in the camp to-morrow night. .... I'm a bit tired—washing day to-day. ..... We have to wash our own things. Have done two pairs socks, undershirt, ordinary woollen shirt, pants, towel, and two handkerchiefs. Shall always do my own washing when I return (?) I nearly forgot Charley Quinn was in hospital about ten miles from here, but I didn't know of it until he was released, so didn't see him. He has now gone to take duty at De Aar. With best wishes to all."

No. 25,362, Sapper **G. W. Bannister** (of MR), writes the following interesting letter from Green Point Camp, January 11th:—

"DEAR COLOUR-SERGEANT KEMP—Many thanks for nice card, verses, and two letters to hand. I shall treasure the former, you may be sure. It were better, I think, at least for our friends at home that you have not received an account of our voyage. The food was very poor indeed, and often wretchedly cooked. Don't think I am complaining for myself, as I did very well the whole voyage—thanks to friendly stewards. Well, we had an uneventful voyage, with the exception of a death on board. We buried the poor fellow about on the Equator. He was wrapped in a Union Jack and dropped overboard, the ship's engine slowing down meanwhile. We had a very pleasant passage from a meteorological point of view, and very few were sick. Coaling at St. Vincent provided a bit of diversion for us all. It was fun to see the nigger boys diving fearlessly among the sharks for coppers thrown into the water. I daresay you will have had an account of the voyage from abler pens than mine, so I need not dwell any further upon it, excepting that we amused ourselves watching schools of porpoises gambolling around our ship. Some of them would try to keep well ahead of us, but they would give it up after a while. Our ship went on an average eleven or twelve knots an hour. We also saw a few dolphins, and once a young whale. Flying fish were very plentiful when we reached the Equator.

KHAKI LETTERS—*continued.*

For the rest it was rather monotonous. Nothing but sea every day. For days together we never sighted a passing ship. We were all very glad to see Table Mountain stand out boldly in front of us. It was 2.30 a m. before we marched from the landing stage to our camping ground, and you may guess we were all fatigued. Then came our first taste of foreign service. No tents were waiting for us, and the Captain gave the command, 'Lie down, men!' Everyone cheerfully obeyed, and we were soon all fast asleep in our great coats, with the Southern Cross and other constellations strange and new and wonderful shining down upon us, with now and then a sweep of light from the Lighthouse near by, lighting us all up with a weird, will-o'-the-wisp light. The murmur of the sea breaking on the shore 200 yards in front of us, and Table Mountain looming out, dark and shadowy, in the starlight, like some grim, giant sentinel. behind us, added to the strangeness of it all. We are encamped in a very nice spot – a 3d. ride from Cape Town on the electric car. A number of our men went up to De Aar on Christmas Day. Then Catling, Woolley, and Bishop left us to take duty at Wynberg, just the other side of Cape Town from here; two more men were sent to De Aar a few days later, and then six more. We have heard from two of the boys. Ferguson, of LV, wrote me on New Year's Day from Belmont; he is there with Eglinton (DY), Collins (Salisbury), and Porter (Woolwich); they have all been over the battlefields. The main body has pushed on from there, taking two sappers with a buzzer along with them, so that our boys are in touch with the front. Fallon has also had an interesting letter from Ray. who is now in Arundel with French's column. All the boys who have gone to the front had a comfortable railway journey of two or three days, some of them travelling second-class, and dining *en route* in first-class waiting room, table d'hôte. I think that is due to the influence of our officers. The men at De Aar went up under Captain Acworth, R.E.; he is a perfect gentleman, as, indeed, are the two of them in charge of us— Captain Fowler, D.S.O., and Second Lieutenant Hepper. The former treated us to cake on Christmas Day. It wasn't much like Christmas to us, something like 70° or 80° in the shade. A party of carol singers visited our Camp on Christmas Eve. Some of us were sleeping outside our tents in preference to the stuffy interior—seventeen men in a tent up to then. We got up, pulled our blankets round us, and joined heartily in good old Christmas carols. It was a treat. I got a piece of pudding from somewhere, but unfortunately it had gone musty. Everything is very dear here. Nothing less than 3d., which they call a 'tickey.' We could all do with a rise (mim.). The Cape Town Highlanders (Volunteers) garrison Cape Town at present; they have been called out a few months now; those of them who hold Civil Service appointments draw full pay from the office, and all get 7s. 6d per day. Everyone is most kind to the soldiers, and there is always a free tea or entertainment going on at some place or other for us. We go for a route march at 6.45 every morning, and return for breakfast about 8. Twelve of the men go to Cape Town office every day. . . . The idea is to get us into the Cape style of working, which is something like Stock Exchange working at home. A sender goes 'through,' timing messages with his left hand as he sends them. The lines won't carry our style of working either. The sending out here is very heavy like cable sending. They don't trouble much about spacing. Stormer, Samuel, and myself obtained leave on Sunday last, and ascended Table Mountain with a CT clerk acting as guide. We started 6 a.m. It took us three hours' hard climbing to reach the top. Cape Town water supply comes from the

KHAKI LETTERS—*continued*.

top, and we followed the water course for a considerable way through lovely dells and rocky gorges. The scenery was very fine. I came across a Zulu assegai, which I hope to bring back with me as a curio. It came in useful eventually, when a snake (a puff adder, very venomous) crossed Stormer's path. We promptly despatched it, and Stormer has the skin with him. I caught a beautiful butterfly, measuring six inches across. Wild flowers grow on the mountain in profusion : arum lilies (known as South African weeds, so thickly do they grow), heliotrope, geraniums, gladioli, and many other varieties strange to us. We also met with plenty of the prickly cactus bushes. We fell in with a party of four young fellows—refugees from the Johannesburg mines—and they had a camp kettle with them, also coffee, sugar, and condensed milk. We filled the kettle at a beautiful spring on the top and soon had a fire, whereon we prepared the most delicious coffee I ever tasted. Our other viands consisted of modest bread and cheese, and a sandwich, and I must say it was a most sumptuous repast. After a long rest we commenced the descent by another route, which took us four hours altogether ; we had quite a picnic that day. Some of our men killed a young shark on the beach last week, and we have caught two small octopus (perhaps I should say octopi) at our bathing place a few days ago, and went out armed with our bayonets prodding for a larger one which we had seen. However, the brute got away minus one of his tentacles. On New Year's Day we were all warned not to leave Camp, and each man had twenty rounds of ammunition served out to him. Don't know what was in the wind, unless trouble was feared from the natives, who make a lot of fuss on New Year's Day, and get drunk on what they call 'tickey beer'—vile stuff, I believe. Will give you an account of our system when I have a chance of seeing it in working order. At present we are waiting for stores preparatory to moving up country. I received a bit of welcome news from home to-day, notifying my appointment as sub-engineer in the North-Western district ; I sat for the exam. some weeks before coming out. Not heard any confirmation of the news *re* Jenner. Thanks for cutting. Hope I shall get a copy. All the boys are well, and send kindest regards to you, joining me in best wishes for this New Year of 1900.

No. 24,305, Sapper **F. T. Stimpson,** Modder River, January 15th, writes :—". . . . The rumours that have been, floating about *re* some of us being shot, dying of dysentery, &c., is causing us to be very down in spirits, especially in Jenner's case, where some kind pal informed his wife. . . . I hope news of this description does not reach my mater, or I think it would be the death of her. . . . . Jack Hall was also supposed to have been ' done in,' but I am pleased to say we are all very much alive. Quinn has been at Wynberg hospital for the last fortnight, and the doctors there have not been able to diagnose his case. I think he has ruptured himself internally ; we went swimming, and he ricked himself getting out. He is still in bed, and writes to say he is well in himself. . . . . The bread that is served out to us is just like a brick—have to put it in soak sometimes before we can touch it, but the living under the circumstances cannot be complained of. . . . . We have a ration of rum served out twice a week, also lime juice occasionally ; jam three times a week in place of butter, and fresh meat every day for dinner, with a portion of cheese to make up the meat ration. Jenner does the cooking, and turns out some dishes quite ' Parisienne ' Few days ago he made us some plum duff for tea, and you can just imagine our anxious

KHAKI LETTERS—continued.

eyes watching the Assistant Cook, O'Sullivan, bringing it over from the cook-house, when suddenly he caught his foot in the railway line and the pudding was no more. A search party was immediately sent out to find the plums, and it is reported that only about half-a-dozen have been found up to the time of writing (plums 1s. lb.). We have been having Quaker Oats as a first course for supper, but owing to high living we have had to give it a rest—the troops becoming bilious. . . . . 'Tisn't all lavender, although it is 'seeing life,' and this is the best section to be in, as we expect to be at the front all the time. The chaps at De Aar must be ' fed up '; they get a lot of slip writing and have more circuits to look after than we—also a Telephone Exchange in their office, connecting all the ports and redoubts. We get very big rushes when the Kimberley or Mafeking despatch riders come in. . . . . The men from H.M.S. Doris work the searchlight from here to KB from dusk to midnight. . . . . It is funny to see the blacks walking about in bits of uniform ; they delight in getting a pair of trousers with a red stripe. . . . . We are not allowed to wear anything but khaki. . . . . I was on duty one night about 11 p.m , and our guns put them in one or two shots ; the whole of hill where the Boers are encamped, some five miles distant, belched forth with shot and shell ; I thought my number was up until I went to the office door and found they were still there—it sounded as if they were attacking our camp. . . . . They are sending us out winter serge—khaki colour—so they don't appear to be in a hurry to finish matters. . . . [Describes Christmas festivities, &c.] We come across fresh TS men about every week . . . . and we have a big batch of them to dig up at KB. . . . . I hear all the TS men in the second batch have gone to Natal, bar W. C. Smith.

No. 23,653, Sapper **J. F. Metcalfe**, Gatacre's Division, Sterkstroom, January 16th, writes :—

"I have now got settled down to my duties in the telegraph office in camp. . . . Am sorry that General Gatacre failed to storm the Heights of Stormberg. . . . We might have stood a chance of receiving a bar. . . . . We had a plum pudding, 12 of us in the tent paid 6d. each, and Cook's mate made us a couple, so we came off O.K in that respect. On Boxing Day we had military sports (not much like active service, eh ?). All kinds of racing, horse-and-man, tent pegging, and various other events. I, unfortunately, was in the losing team of tug of war, losing to Sherwood Foresters, the Royal Scots being winners, Kaffrarian Rifles second. New Year passed with boxing competition—feather, light, middle and heavy weights—lasting three days ; very exciting, especially the two latter, as several knock-outs were made. On each occasion the town and country ladies and gentlemen from a radius of twenty miles received an invitation from the General to attend ; ladies in white, and other bright colours, straw hats, etc., and Kaffir men and women dressed up in cast-offs of their more fortunate brethren, and there were some comical sights, I can assure you. Kaffirs also took part in driving mule competition, obstacle races, etc. . . . . It is no great pleasure to be on duty at night alone half a mile from everywhere, in a tin shanty without door, and ventilated all round, so you can best imagine what it is like by candle light, and sometimes an oil lamp. . . . We are now being visited with myriads of locusts, flying over in great clouds, resembling a snowstorm when the sun is shining on their wings. . . ."

The Relief of Ladysmith.

The Central Telegraph Office has witnessed many scenes of excitement on many occasions. The staff has been filled with enthusiasm at some national event, but never before —never in the "memory of the oldest inhabitant "— Jubilees and Diamond Jubilees included — has it given vent to its pent-up feeling with such outbursts of joy and harmony. At every hour from 3 p.m. did the well-known "Soldiers of the Queen" ring out; the efforts of those in charge were fruitless to stop it, and not until the Day Staff were leaving at 8 p.m. did the office settle down to its usual order and decorum. The Staff at that hour rose and most lustily sang—

"GOD SAVE THE QUEEN,"

and we will add, "and Bless her Soldiers, too."— R. E. K.

Never Yield.

Arise, ye Sons of Albion,
  For danger lurketh near !
Bestir yourselves and hasten,
  To scatter ev'ry fear,
We love our dear old homeland,
  It's honour we must shield.
Let ev'ry foe to Britain know
  We'll never, never yield.

Chorus—What ? never, never yield ?
  No ! never, never yield ;
  We will combine with "th'
    [thin red line,"
  And never, never yield.

All glory to our Army—
  The bravest of the brave—
Their noble hearts are burning
  For vict'ry or the grave.
With courage, dash and daring,
  Their swords they fiercely wield,
Till ev'ry foe to us shall know,
  We'll never, never yield.

Chorus—What ? never, &c.

Our ships are ever watchful
  To guard our coastbound land —
Our Volunteers and Army
  Are linked both heart and hand.

Should evil days befall us,
  Our strength shall be revealed ;
Then ev'ry foe that comes, shall go—
  We'll never, never yield.

Chorus—What ? never, &c.

Let ev'ry loyal subject
  This day his duty do—
Enrol beneath our banner,
  The red, the white, the blue.
May God preserve and help us
  In peace or on the field,
Then ev'ry foe shall surely know
  We'll never, never yield.

Chorus—We'll never, &c.

The fame of mighty Nelson,
  The Iron Duke as well,
And hosts of British heroes,
  With pride their deeds we tell.
But bygones will not aid us,
  That fact lies unconcealed.
Stand for the Right ! prepare to fight
  'Till death, and never yield.

Chorus—What ? never, &c.

R. F. Kemp, Col.-Sergt.,
  24th Middx. R.V.C.

"Khaki Notes."

IDENTIFICATION.

It may appear strange to some that such complete and accurate lists of killed, wounded and missing, are so quickly forwarded to the Homeland by those at the Front. One would imagine this to be an impossibility, when such confusion and excitement reigns around our gallant soldiers, but—as in all well organized businesses, so in the dreadful work out yonder—a means has been provided by which the identity may be known. Here we have a true copy of what is known as the " Identification Card."

Army Form B. 2067.

DESCRIPTION CARD FOR ACTIVE SERVICE.

No. and Name

Rank and Regiment

Nearest of Kin

Residing at

Signature of Officer }
   Commanding Troop, }
   Battery or Company, }

H W V 50,000 8—99.

KHAKI NOTES—*continued*.

It is a glazed linen ticket of the size represented, and is sewn to the soldier's tunic, or jacket, just under the left flap below the belt. If the poor owner is found on the field dead, it will answer his name for him, the ticket is removed and a full description of him is in hand. If he is wounded and unable to answer enquiries, his ticket will bear record ; and if he gets into the enemies' hands and objects to give his name, his ticket will give all the information they require concerning his personality. Is it a wonder, then, that our casualty lists are so quickly compiled, or is it strange that we should hear of the enemy publishing in their newspapers the names, etc., of the prisoners whom they have taken from the British?

✣ ✣ ✣ ✣

THE BIG LETTER "I" Unfortunately—Ah ! yes, *very* unfortunately—I am not yet in a position to use the Editorial WE. The letter " I "—that personal pronoun so often used with an emphasis of pride by those who desire to bring to the notice of others the deeds they have done—is necessarily too apparent in this, the first number of " Khaki Letters" from " My Colleagues in South Africa." I admit it, but nevertheless it is true, for no other person here, there, or anywhere. has given a hand, or a suggestion, as to how this little booklet should be brought out. Many a man has said, " Let's have the letters in book form," but so vague have been the ways and means put forward, that the ideas have proved almost unprofitable. Many have said, " *You* bring it out and *we'll* buy it," and in this respect I will urge my friends to use every endeavour to make it most profitable. Pardon me, then, my colleagues at home, if I claim to have put this little brochure before you as the work of my own hands, and mine alone. It may be full of imperfections, errors, and all sorts of dreadful things, but it is also very, very full of friendship and love.—" Love," says one, " what does that mean by that ? " I mean, fellow-clerks, that this venture is not aimed at any person, place, or thing ; it is not intended to be aggressive or offensive to anyone, and never in its pages shall a sentence appear which I know would wound the feelings of others. Love, because I feel so keenly on the matter of keeping up our reputation, a reputation inbred with that enthusiasm, admiration and esteem which soars to such a height that it reaches the region of love.

✣ ✣ ✣ ✣

THE CHOICE OF A TITLE. It will be noticed that I have called the little paper containing a list of names of men who have gone to the front, " My Colleagues in South Africa." There is a peculiarity about this. It is here. Should I call it " Our Colleagues " or " My Colleagues " ? This question I asked myself when the idea first came to my mind. I reasoned it out—all alone again, you know—and the line of thought was something like this :—It is quite true that those men are *our* colleagues, for we can each and all of us claim them as such, collectively ; they come from many offices, and no one has a bigger right than another to call them theirs. " My Colleagues " is another way of putting the same thing. I am going to sell these card-lists, the staff will buy them, they will put them into their pockets and bring them out occasionally, and when their eyes catch the title they will be reminded in a more personal manner that those friends at the front are *theirs*, worthy to be counted in a special manner amongst those whom

KHAKI NOTES—*continued*.

they personally esteem and own. No one will suggest that the word "my" applies to any particular person, much less do I (R. E. K.) intend it to be taken as mine only.

✤ ✤ ✤ ✤

THE "KHAKI" CIRCULARS. In order to let people know you have something to sell, you must needs go in for a little judicious advertising, especially when you cannot display the commodities you wish to dispose of in a manner that will catch the public eye So with my little Scheme. I had to tell my friends of the Telegraph staff that something was going to happen, and the only way to make it known was by circular letter. Only one man was "in the know," and this was my good friend A. E. Knowles. There are many Knowall's about, but this time A. E. was the only one. (Excuse that nonsense, I'm so excited.) He readily fell in with my idea, took up the matter heartily, and set himself the task of "doing" TS, while I did the Provinces. He has done his work well I have done mine as well as I could, but it was a very big order single-handedly. My ammunition was very limited, and my time was even more so. The canvass has been very imperfect, many offices not being touched at all, and those that were have been asked to do an almost impossible thing, being requested to reply in so short a space of time. It had to be so, you know ; I could not well avoid it. I am going to ask you, every one of you, to make it *more* perfect. Make it known to your friends in other offices. Send this copy to them, tell them to order the next three numbers, and order another for yourself. I am very gratified with the response I have already had, but if we all put our shoulders to the wheel we shall have nothing to fear. Don't lose sight of the fact that we want it to flourish ; and, if there is anything left over, every penny piece shall go to a good object. I am not working for gain, not even for commendation.

✤ ✤ ✤ ✤

LETTERS FROM THE FRONT. Friends will very greatly assist this bijou booklet by forwarding to me from time to time, letters - or extracts from letters—that have come from the front. TS is most strongly represented out there, Edinburgh, Manchester, Cardiff, Liverpool, London Districts, etc., etc., all send contingents, as well as many other offices too numerous to mention. We have considerably over 120 men in the field, and I feel sure we can get very interesting matter from so large a number. I would ask you to write very clearly on one side of the paper only. One or two friends have already done so, enclosing them in the orders for my book. I heartily thank them. This is practical assistance. As a guide to what is required, kindly note this. Give the correspondent's name, number, place where written, and date of writing. This is most essential. Omit all personal matter—matter of a private nature. If there are any remarks in your letter that you consider doubtful, mark it conspicuously, and I will decide whether it may go in or not. Don't leave the letter by you until it gets stale, for by so doing it will lose its current value. Also give your name and address as a guarantee of good faith.

✤ ✤ ✤ ✤

REPETITIONS IN THE LETTERS. Every effort has been made to avoid unnecessary repetitions, but I beg readers to suffer them if they occur. Listen. A man at the front writes home. Picture his difficulties. He has no cosy corner, or quiet room as you have. He knows not where he may be called, or what duty he may

KHAKI NOTES—*continued.*

have to do. but it is all rough, every bit of it. He has a moment or two to spare, he writes home, he tells us all he can, and that in his own way. Such letter, I take it, is vastly more valuable compared with a letter the same man might write at home. Others write. They say the same as Tom said, and Bill says the same as Sam said, etc., etc. These letters are similar because those particular men are at the same place. Now, I select Tom s letter. How do you think the other writers will feel? I take *all* the letters, and cut them all down ; they see them, and very naturally say, " What's the use of writing to him ?"—Another view, Tom left the Z division, and the Z division looks out for *his* letters. Fred was attached to the Q group, and the Q group thinks there is not a letter like his. Joe can't write much, but what he dots down he does with a good heart ; every word is already known, but for the sake of his goodness and his comradeship we just put Joe's in as well.—Another instance. Rumours are rife. Sapper Buzzer is ill. The men from different places write home. One says he is sorry to inform us that Buzzer is in hospital suffering from dysentery. No. 2 says he's suffering from enteric fever, and is at Wynburg Hospital. No. 3 assures us he has taken an overdose of chlorodyne. No. 4 was with him when he caught a chill through swimming, when in a heated condition. And "so they ran." But who is correct? I cannot say, I was not there. No. 5 says Buzzer left hospital on the 9th, and Buzzer, himself, writes from the hospital on the 10th. It shows this, my readers, that the men are separated and know little of each other. You can't call these untruths. If they don't know much about their chums out there, we can help them by our printed letters in such a book as this. I can't cut such sentences out.

"KHAKI LETTER" DISTRIBUTORS. Every Group, Division, and Section in the CTO, as well as the offices to which my circular was sent, have been asked to choose their own representative, and, in the case of large sections, an assistant for him. In no instance have I selected, or asked, a man to do the duty. This fact will be sufficient to prove I have no clique of any kind whatsoever, but that I am ready and willing to work with anybody for the general welfare of this object. To those whom the staff have so selected, and to all the workers in this cause, I would say just one word—say it that others may see it too, it may help us over many a bit of lumpy ground. Work well, boys, bend to the oar and make the little craft go. Set your sail and run up your flag. Its motto is Friendship—Comradeship. You may at times' find the water choppy, or an undercurrent that may cause a little annoyance, but a little skilful handling will bear you over the crest of all the big billows. Keep the flag unsullied, and treat your critics as is most becoming a gentleman. My old schoolmaster once said to me, " Don't forget—it takes two to make a quarrel—always do your best to be the one that is out of it." That's my maxim ; if you help me, make it yours too. These remarks may strike one as being out of place in a magazine, but they are very pertinent and necessary, since some who have read my circular seem to think that the new venture is going to attack the *Telegraph Chronicle,* its editor, its agents, and goodness knows who. My word for it ; it is going to attack nobody. It shall live in peace, and if you don't support it—well, why it will die in peace, too.

KHAKI NOTES—*continued*.

HELP GRACIOUSLY OFFERED. Reader, do please excuse me. The big "I" will come in in this note. After reading my circular, a certain gentleman—I withhold his name—caught me by the shoulder and looking me straight in the face, said with great emphasis, "Sergeant, I DO admire you ; your enthusiasm is marvellous. I like it. Your pluck in running a book of your own is just what I really do admire. If you want a bit of money you know where to come," and suiting the action to the word, he put his hand into his pocket and continued, " I'll give you a couple of pounds now to start with." I have not asked for help, I don't know whether I shall want it, but I replied with a full heart, " G——, you are one of the best men I have met to-day. I'll make a note of your very kind offer. If I find myself in a hole I shall come to you, but I believe the Telegraph Service throughout the country will support me." In explanation, I may say he was waiting for me to arrive on duty ; I had seen hardly anyone else that day. The next night he repeated his offer, and I could not help relating it to a superintendent with whom I was conversing on my proposed scheme, and he immediately said, "And I'll do the same." Since that, I have heard the remark from others, who add, "And so will many more." How glad I am to know this ! I won't trouble anybody if I can help it. But, reader, take the tip, take the example for your own special course of action, and support the little pamphlet by increasing its circulation near and far.

"KHAKI LETTERS" FOR OUR BOYS. There are so many friends who have told me I have made a mistake in charging only one penny for this book, and assure me that they know "any amount" who would gladly give twopence, I am persuaded that I can meet you by giving you an idea. The men at the front must have a copy each, and there are just 127 of them. Who would like to pay the penny per copy for them every issue ? And who would like to pay the postage ? Answer this question in a practical way, and another load will be off my shoulders. Those who will so gladly pay twopence per copy for my little book will be pleased to know that I am not too proud to take it. Tell your distributor that you will give him twopence instead of a penny—double it for each copy you receive. If you don't like to do this, make your order two copies instead of one. You won't find the " Khaki Letter" subscribers grumble at you. Your cash will not be wasted. Send a copy away.

1st TEL. DIV. ROYAL ENGINEERS. The 24th are attached to the Royal Engineers—indeed, they are Engineers in every sense of the word. They work shoulder to shoulder with them in the most enthusiastic manner. Feelings of the most intense goodwill have always been sustained between them, and it was with regret that a day or two ago a paragraph was shewn me which would tend to upset such a bond of brotherliness. Others may have seen it ; it put the 24th men first, the R.E.'s next. I was surprised, and no wonder a well-known R.E., stationed in England, wrote me saying he took umbrage at it. I will give the credit to where it is due, and say that, in my opinion, where we hear expression of certain units being the "eyes" and the "ears" of the Army, the Royal Engineers are the " brains." Our own reserve men are associated

KHAKI NOTES—*continued.*

with their elder brethren—the regular R.E.'s—and they know full well that from them they can learn many things. I trust nothing in my notes or letters that have appeared in the *Telegraph Chronicle* has ever touched the susceptibilities of my ideal corps—the Royal Engineers. *Esprit de corps* often leads us on to dangerous ground—my contributors will please take the warning.

LETTERS TO THE FRONT. If Telegraphists who receive letters will make it a rule to let me know from where and by whom they are posted, I shall be able to help the whole Service here, the Army Post Office Corps in South Africa, and benefit the men out there in the bargain. I propose to devote a page of my book for the purpose of giving a list of men at the front and the place they were last known to be stationed at. Readers must send me a postcard in the following form; address it 12, Jerrard Street, Lewisham, S.E.

Received a letter to-day (date)..............................
From (name in full)....... ....
Dated.....................Stationed at....................
In it he mentions (other men)..............................
Who were, at the time of posting, quartered at..............

Then give your own name and address. By this means my special envelopes will be invaluable. You will add to your letters the name of the town or place where your friend was last known to be, the A.P.O.C. will have its work lessened, and your letter will travel all the quicker. By the help of my readers I can furnish such a page—not without.

CLEARING ALL DOUBTS. A friend sends the following cutting from the *Western Morning News* of March 1st. It will be read with much interest, especially as it refers to a family the name of which is very familiar to us all. "Poor Fred Ruse did good service in the Royal Engineers, after which he joined the 24th, and soon afterwards again entered the R.E Reserves, in which capacity he remained until his call to the great majority. Corporal E. Adams, R.E., mentioned for his gallantry in having swam the Tugela River with the telegraph wire, has quite a family connection with the Royal Engineers. He is the son of the late Quartermaster-Sergeant George Adams, R.E., Chatham, grandson of Mr. W. Ruse (Tonbridge), late sergeant R.E., nephew of Lieutenant Ruse, R.E. (Weymouth), and great-great-grandson of the late Mr. Charles Ruse, of Launceston."

CUTTINGS from various papers will be very welcome; they will add to the brightness of the pamphlet. Contributors must quote source and date fully.

ARTICLES by some of our comrades at home will be gladly received. Select a suitable subject—write brightly. My own contribution on "Army Signalling" I hold over.

LATEST. The s.s. "Oriental" called at Queenstown, March 2nd. The s.s. "Cephalonia" left St. Vincent on Sunday, March 4th, 1900.

COLOURS.

All posted letters containing Orders, MSS., &c., must be addressed to R. E. KEMP, 12, JERRARD STREET, LEWISHAM, S.E.

Printed by E. G. BERRYMAN & SONS, *Blackheath Road, London, S.E.*

"Khaki Letters" from ....
"My Colleagues in South Africa."

CORRESPONDENCE FROM THE
POST OFFICE TELEGRAPHISTS
OF THE
24th MIDDLESEX (P.O.) RIFLE VOLUNTEERS
(Royal Engineer Reserves),
ON ACTIVE SERVICE.

THE BOND THAT BINDS US—FRIENDSHIP—COMRADESHIP.

Published fortnightly for the Postal Telegraph Service.
Conducted by COLOUR-SERGEANT R. E. KEMP, *Central Telegraph Office, London.*

No. 2.   MARCH 23RD, 1900.   PRICE ONE PENNY.

Central Telegraph Office,
London, E.C.

SAILING, Sailing, o'er the ocean wave, admired by many a matured mariner who, with others, were awaiting her approach to pass their opinions on her build. A little dot on the horizon—just a speck—and there, just round the headland, sparkled the snowy sail on the sunlit sea. "Strange sail!" says one. "That can't be the boat we're looking for." "No," says another, "I guess she'll be a clumsy creature, without figure or comeliness." "And," adds a third, "more like one of Her Majesty's gunboats, armed stem, stern, and at every point capable of bearing a quick-firer or a Gatling. I don't like the thoughts of her at all, and I'll be bound she carries a crew of scallywags who'd stop at nothing." Up went the glasses, and levelling them towards the east'ard a somewhat closer acquaintance was made. "'Tis she!" gasped one, "I can just discern her name," and all eyes were strained to drink in the information of the more favoured spectator. "She's going splendidly, by Jove, she cuts her way in a masterly manner, and the foam seems to kiss her a welcome all along. I can see the men aboard. Quick! quick! out with the launch, we'll run out and meet her, and perchance hail her, and who knows but what we may find that all our apprehensions have been but vain."

So runs a picture—only in words, poorly put, but full of metaphor. In plain language, the question has received its answer, and we can all bear witness to the fact that

SHE LIVES!

My subscribers, I thank you, most heartily thank you, for your spontaneous reply, your magnificent support, your readiness to help in this little venture. I asked for a big number of subscribers; I was told I was too sanguine; I was informed I should never get them, but—

WHAT DO I FIND?

The number exceeded by far. I am not worthy to be at the helm in so large an affair. I am much less capable of guiding and controlling a huge concern, but I am doing, and will do my utmost to keep the barque buoyant and brave, bearing the news to and from Our Boys. The letters containing words of cheer have been very numerous, and such missives are most gratifying to me. From all sides I have heard nothing but praise, and I am entirely at a loss to convey to you how such flattering words have encouraged me. But we don't want to talk about that. There's other things to be done.

KEEP UP THE ENTHUSIASM

that is aroused within you. Take the spirit of the "Khaki Letters," and be determined that they shall continue. Don't budge an inch, don't go back a pace; keep pressing onward, determined to see it through. Oh, what a mighty master is Friendship; how he compels one to work, and work to win. Our men out yonder will be gladdened, their spirits will be cheered, and their very hardships will appear lightened when they know they have comrades by the thousand, eagerly watching their toil and talent in sandy South Africa.

What a thrill of delight fills one's breast when one finds there are so many who think the same, feel the same, and are willing to work the same, and all for one cause—the

COMMON CAUSE OF COMRADESHIP.

There are many things I could tell you, and many reasons I could give you, but I refrain from troubling you with more than just this—I hope you will support my "Khaki Postage Fund." It will then in reality be

YOU SENDING COPIES TO THE BOYS.

Also, respecting the next numbers. I have so much copy on hand, and I was so handicapped at the commencement by the block on the line, that I am cramming as much as I can into this number; but that won't help me sufficiently. I want to get up level with the times; I want to bring my letters nearer up to the day of receiving them, and the only way to do so—to increase their freshness and to serve you better—is to have

A DOUBLE NUMBER NEXT TIME.

Two numbers on one day, or call it a double one if you like. It can be made more varied, and it will clear the copy that is on hand. After that we will go back to the ordinary number again.

In proposing such a thing it looks very much like asking for more money, but it is not. You will get your money's worth, and you will not regret it. I trust my subscribers will continue to feel that we are all of one mind, all of of one sympathy, and all willing to own, recognise, cherish, and support the work that is on hand

FOR OUR COLLEAGUES IN SOUTH AFRICA.

Kindly make this known. Continue your subscriptions all along the line, and we shall be able to look our boys straight in the face when they return, and say— We've kept the little craft afloat,

SHE HAS LIVED;

we have admired you, stuck fast by you, and owned you during your absence from amongst us. Hurrah! Again thanking you, Dear Readers,

I am, yours most heartily,

Tuesday, March 20th, 1900. R. E. KEMP.

Central Telegraph Office,

London, E.C.

DEAR COMRADES, ONE AND ALL,

Greetings ! The above office is still in the same place and there are a few clerks remaining, but what a number there are amongst them burning to be with you. The spirit of the men is most marvellous, so many regret they are not eligible, and quite a number are rushing into our ranks eager to get through to the coveted position of "an efficient Volunteer." Others argue that drill is not wanted, skill should put them through. One can't help pitying them, for "it seems hard" such enthusiasm should be of no avail.

At the present moment the Depôt Company, the Company through which you all have passed, and the Company to which I have the honour to belong, stands stronger than it ever did, *i.e.*, 137. I believe every man that leaves it for the L. Co. is replaced by two recruits or re-enrolments. You've got a magnificent lot of fellows in the Volunteer Company, who, at a word, would spring up as one man and run to rub shoulders with their comrades at the Front. It makes one proud to be a Britisher.

There are many of your old chums rejoining. They can't leave it alone, you know. On Friday last, March 16th, we gave them a right royal send-off at Waterloo by the 2.45 p.m. train. "Soldiers of the Queen," "Auld Lang Syne," and "God Save the Queen," were lustily sung, and so we parted in the good old English fashion.

I will give you the names. You will recognise the boys of the Old Brigade. There's one of them they couldn't weigh. The scales were only able to show 16 stone, and when a certain gentleman placed himself upon it, down it went bang, and the Doctor had to confess that he couldn't say how much he weighed, but he was sure it was over 16 stone. Well, well ! You can recognise the boy, I'm sure. He's afraid he will get hung up in the same way that poor Metcalfe did, but we hope he won't, for he writes from Aldershot and says they are such "a jolly nice lot of fellows; should feel it keenly to get stranded from them."

Here are the names :—Friday, 16th, H. Barber, W. F. Frew, E. J. Ash, W. Bell, W. G. Carter, D. Semple, W. W. Pearce, H. J. Jackson, L. Sorenson, D. Leitch, E. P. Neate, W. Dadswell, H. J. Harrison, T. W. Stevenson, J. Davis, L. D. Page and C. H. Jones. Saturday, 17th : G. E. Plumridge, W. H. S. Marshall and B. Walton. A. H. Morse and J. MacMurtrie, who were put on furlough, are also now at the H.Q., Aldershot. All of TS.

Our Provincial men may recognise friends of theirs amongst the following :—At Aldershot up to time of writing on Monday : W. Foster (CV), E. A. Hunter (PR), J. P. Flanagan (MC), B. F. Warburton (NG), H. Baxter (CF), D. G. Davies (CF), W. P. Walker (MR), J. Heigh (EH), and H. J. White (LV). The London Districts are represented by E. A. Thrift (SWDO) and W. N. Kelly (Aldgate), our famous camp *chef.* They are anxious now to know the date of embarkation. Will send further details in my Weekly Circular Letter. Meanwhile I trust you all are in the very best of health and the pink of perfection.

Yours very heartily,
R. E. KEMP,
Colour-Sergeant.

To the L. Co. in South Africa.

Tuesday, March 20th, 1900.

COPYRIGHT.—"Khaki Letters" must not be used without permission.—R. E. KEMP.

Khaki Letters.

No. 23,653, Sapper **J. F. Metcalfe,** Gatacre's Division, Sterkstroom, writing on January 17th, says:—

". . . . Since our defeat at Stormberg, nothing in extent has been done here, only scouting skirmishes at Molteno, Cyphergat and Dordrecht, and on each occasion our troops are sent out. I am doing alternate day and night duty, our pay is 3s. 1½d. per day. We rise every morning at 4 a.m., lights out at 8.45 p.m. I am still isolated from the rest of the 24th Middlesex men, who are at De Aar and Modder River. Rations are improving daily now. Every morning we get some extras, either jam, preserved bacon, cheese, etc. For dinner we have stewed beef, and vegetables boiled with it. Since I left England, I have only had, as yet, three small Bass's, and that was on board; could do a drop occasionally, but not allowed to have it, even the publicans have been cautioned against serving us. Bass's here is 2s. 6d. per pint bottle, I don't suppose I should buy much at that price. I will wait till I return, and make up for lost time, what ho! We get tobacco at 1s. 4d. per lb.—cake tobacco. . . . I am getting the *Chronicle* O.K., and am pleased to see that the holiday scheme is being put forward, and hope it is adopted for next holidays. . . . The weather is very hot during the day, but cold and windy during the night. We are nearly 5,000 feet above the sea level here, and we get some good old-fashioned wind and sand storms, followed by very heavy rains. The evenings are spent playing football, cards, concerts (Kaffirs doing a bit as well), and last, but not least, religious services of every denomination take place nightly. Kindly remember me to the boys. I might mention that I have lost my corpulency, having lost over 20lbs. in weight. Several cases of enteric, but self been O.K. Boer spies and prisoners are being continually brought into camp."

✦ ✦ ✦ ✦

No. 460, Sapper **P. A. Milton,** Rensburg Camp, January 19th, says . . . . " I am now with Fallon and Samuels right clean bang up the front. We left Cape Town on Sunday last and called at De Aar and saw the office and Wheatstone sets, etc., and Hamer and Willis and several others, they had a bottle of whisky for us, we had a fine time, and then got the train for Naauwpoort, and changed there for Rensburg. This part of the country is grand for cavalry, and we have General French and the best cavalry in the world, *i.e.* 10th Hussars, 6th Dragoons, Lifes, and Carabineers, and several other regiments, and the Old Berks (they are at present—the Berks—on a kopje giving the Boers a tying up). We are only about seven miles from Colesberg, and that is in Boer hands, but the 'O' Battery, R.H.A., are on an immense kopje dropping Lyddite shells into the

KHAKI LETTERS—*continued.*

enemy, therefore they have had to quit their camp. We have got any amount of stray ponies here, and I commandeered one for myself and some grub for it and go out riding. I can tell you life here is worth living—we commandeer everything. Yesterday it was a dozen pineapples, a pig, and a goose, which we promptly despatched. We have been dished out with Dr. Jim hats and look like a lot of scouts and no mistake. . . . I think we are the nearest to the fighting line . . . . and can see their shells drop, but the majority of them don't burst, so there is not much danger. Our cable carts go out and take up positions on the different hills, namely Slinger's Farm, Maeder's Farm, Kloop Camp, Porter's Hill, Coleskop, and several other shows, and send in reports. . . . As soon as the enemy are driven through Colesberg we shall advance. I have hopes of ultimately going right through the Free State, we are only 15 miles from the border now, so there will soon be a change in affairs. . . . To-day we are expecting two howitzers so they will 'give them socks.' No mistake, we live very well, jam and coffee for breakfast; dinner, fresh meat; for tea we get jam and tea, and cocoa at night, rum and lime juice alternate days, so you see we DO live, and with what we manage to commandeer we get on a treat. . . . I am in excellent health, only wish I was with the Dragoons and could have a cut at them. French has got them hemmed in, and if they retire the cavalry will cut them up, so we expect some exciting times. . . . We have any amount of money and can't spend it, so we shall be all right for the nut brown ale when we return. . . ."

✤ ✤ ✤ ✤

No. 2,543, Sapper **Geo. Bishop,** writing from Wynberg Camp, Jan. 24th, 1900, says :—

"DEAR COLOUR-SERGEANT KEMP,—Another mail goes out to-day, and I will at last let you have an epistle. First of all let me thank you very much indeed for the splendid 'I' Company's New Year Card and also for your two most welcome letters. . . . Humm and Brooks were in my tent at Greenpoint, but I believe they are now at Naauwport. . . . By your letter I guess some more of the boys are on the way out here. As I am so close to Capetown I shall be over there soon to make enquiries. . . . I believe all the boys are well ; at any rate the second lot were up to last Thursday. I am in grand fettle myself. I hear Jimmy Miller is now a Sergeant. One hardly knows what to write to you about, for I reckon you have pretty well all the news from your more regular correspondents. Of course, you know the history of our stay at Green (I would rather say Sandy) Point. We pitched our tents there at 5 a.m., on 21st December. On the 25th, W. C. Smith (C group), together with nine provincials and several linemen, under Captain Ackworth, proceeded to De Aar. . . . . On the 30th, Catling (Euston B.O.), Woolley (I. Divn.), and myself were sent here. That day it poured with rain. By the way, the inhabitants here are much surprised at getting several heavy showers recently, and say the firing at the front accounts for it. After we had been here a fortnight, Catling and Woolley were ordered back to Green Point, and I am now in charge with a Royal Munster Fusilier (to which regiment I am attached), who used to be a lineman at LK, as assistant. We have two orderlies, a K.R.R. and a Gordon Highlander, as messengers, and they negotiate some tidy trots during the day. I forgot to say that whilst at Greenpoint we worked four hours per day at Capetown head office. Catling spoke to me from there last Wednesday, and said all the remainder of our men were going to Naauwport

KHAKI LETTERS—*continued*.

the following day, the 17th. Ray, Adams, Birch, and, I think, Wyatt (GY), had already gone there. Wynberg is a pretty little town, ten miles from Capetown on the Simonstown line. The camp is a mile from the station and occupies a lot of ground at the back of Table Mountain. There are two big General Hospitals here; one permanent (wooden huts), and the other temporary (tents), capable of accommodating about 2,000 patients. Then we have two Officers' Hospitals, Nursing Sisters' Quarters, A.S.C. Stores, R.A.M.C. Stores, R.E. Yard, a big Military Prison, and a Convict Prison also in our delivery. We work a Morse Printer to Cape Town. We are the terminal station with Wynberg station, Kenilworth and Rondebosch (where No. 3 Hospital is situate) as intermediate stations. The system of working is slightly different to that in vogue at TS. No 'up-and-down' here. When a station calls up I have to clear him out before I can send one of my own. They give one no time to fill in, but rush straight on until clear. I have just taken half a dozen, and out of those three are wrong numbers. Oh, they don't gain much by their rushing tactics. The amusing part of it comes in when *we* start a batch. It's ' Send A B C' then after each message (mim). I think the Capetown staff are somewhat overrated. I know plenty of better men in my old Division. The Cape service is now being principally recruited from Australia. They can get men for £120 from there. . . . I don't think many more C.T.O. men will find a haven at Capetown. A number of native learners are now being worked into the staff gradually. There is plenty of red tape here. Our 'Guide' is a counterpart of the home article, and the other publications are almost word for word as we have them at home. The rate here is 1d. per word for Inland, with minimum charge of 1s. Sundays, double rates. We are open 8 a.m.—8 p.m., Sundays included. We accept private messages, but our work is principally official. We seldom see a message shorter than 40 words. I'm getting well into the military terms now. Although we are so near to Capetown we have to adjust independently for each station on the line. Iron poles and cross pieces are in use here, as the wooden poles could not withstand the attacks of the ants. We have electric light here and electric trams to Capetown. It appears Quinn was in hospital here when I first came; he left before I knew about it Pretorious, the Boer Field Cornet, is here, and has had his leg amputated. I have spoken with several Boer wounded prisoners, and they don't seem particularly unhappy. The first one I spoke to came from London !! The wounded are cared for splendidly here—both Boer and Briton alike, and the rich folks around are constantly sending all manner of presents for use in the wards. Three drafts have left for England since my arrival. The hardest working woman in camp is Mrs. Dick Chamberlain (report says she is Joe's sister-in-law). She is very free with her money, too. Hundreds of pounds' worth of soda, lemonade and other stores have been purchased by her, and she has placed a miniature library in each ward. She reads to the men, writes and stamps their letters, in fact some term her a second Florence Nightingale. Her husband is dead. We have an English officer here who is mentally deranged; his friends say it is the effects of the sun, which is excessively trying at times to all. The wounds caused by the Mauser bullet are really wonderful. In the majority of cases, the men soon get better and return to the front, The bullet seems to travel at too great a speed to do much damage, and the wound soon heals. Men are here who have been shot through the head, lungs, groin and legs, but are all doing well. Last Saturday 25 men arrived here sick from a transport just come in from England. It's no wonder, if they had the same fare as allotted us. The dry canteen saved us. Perhaps

KHAKI LETTERS—*continued*

they had no money. I reckon you get more war news than we do ourselves. You see there is a strict press censorship here, and a good thing there is. The colony is swarming with disloyal Dutch, and we all have ammunition in case we have an outbreak. That fear is, however, now over, as we are not likely to experience another defeat at the front. I saw Lord Kitchener and Lord Roberts. The latter is staying at Capetown. Just opposite this office there is a convict prison surrounded by large eucalyptus trees. Most of the convicts are black; they work in gangs round here, each ganger carrying a loaded Winchester or a revolver. One prisoner made off the other day and got a ten minutes' start. Two mounted police soon brought him back, and cries coming from the 'Big House' told us plainly that the poor chap was receiving a flogging. He was afterwards put in irons. Had he got away the ganger would have forfeited £5. Flogging is a frequent mode of punishing certain crimes out here. The majority of the blacks here seem very loyal. They know which side their bread is buttered. They outnumber the whites and increase rapidly, although their death-rate last month was 52 per 1,000 in Capetown—nearly three times as much as the European death-rate. Things are very dear here. Taking the moral and material worth of money here I reckon £280 is worth no more than £90 or £100 in London. Oranges are 4d. each, bananas are very poor and are 1d. each, lemons 2d., peaches 2d., tomatoes 1d., apples and pears 1d. and plums (like our cherries) 4 a penny. Good milk is unobtainable. Fleas, mosquitoes, flies and cockroaches are plentiful (mim.), especially in my sleeping quarters. There are a tremendous lot of doves in the woods round here. There is plenty of vegetation round about the camp, but I have not seen a field of grass yet. As far as the eye can reach inland is sand, sand, sand, with some more mountains in the distance. There are some nice vineyards between us and Table Mountain. Barbed wire is very much *en evidence* here, though (mim). I saw a pretty sight last week, when the woods were on fire. All the undergrowth was burnt completely away. I won't trouble you any more this time, Colours. Hope you have not gone to sleep. Write again, please, if you can. Should not like to be left out in the cold, although I am now separated from the other boys. I trust you and all the 'I' are in good health. . . . Remember me very kindly to all. Kindly accept my best wishes for 1900."

✦ ✦ ✦ ✦

[PRIVATE S. E. STERLING, *of " I" Company, 24th Mr.R.V., joined the City Imperial Volunteers. He was a most enthusiastic Volunteer, and could not wait his turn to be enrolled in the R.E. Reserve, so anxious was he to go to the Front.*]

Private **Syd. Sterling**, No. 551, " C " Company, C.I.V., on board the S.S. " Gaul," off North Africa coast, writes on January 24th:—

". . . . We simply paraded every morning at London Scottish Headquarters or Wellington Barracks, and they never told us what we were going to do the next day. Last Thursday we went to the Tower for the arms. No mistake, the rifles are O.K., Lee-Enfield, Mark I, all the latest improvements, and the bayonet with the war point on it. From there we went and got the Freedom of the City. Friday we marched to Guildhall, got kit, back to London Scottish, and dressed in them; marched to St. Paul's, then to Lincoln's Inn. . . . Free port, claret, whisky, cigars, beer, lemonade, soda water, game pie, beef, Christmas pudding, custard, &c. . . . We were waited on by lawyers, counsel, Q.C.'s, &c. As I was going out one of them shook hands with me, and said I was young for this job, and gave me a box

KHAKI LETTERS—*continued*.

of cigars. Reveille at 4 a.m. Saturday at Wellington Barracks; breakfast—ham, beef, eggs, and coffee. . . . On first getting aboard this boat I was surprised; now I find we have plenty of room, except for hammocks, and they are a bit close. No drill aboard here; plenty to eat. Have four pounds of tobacco, 500 cigars; they also gave me two pipes, and something they call tobacco; the sailors like it, so I shall give it them to do my washing for me. We live like fighting-cocks, meat at almost every meal. We have had a very smooth passage up to now, and, though it is only four days out, it is nice and hot, and a splendid sunshine. Sorry to cut it so short, but they have just told us that letters are to be landed at Teneriffe, and they must be in very soon."

In another letter Sterling continues :—

"January 26th, 1900.

" . . . . Nothing happened since 24th, except that in afternoon they served out boxing gloves, and I managed to catch two very decent hidings. . . . . Last night we sighted a lighthouse about ten miles off Teneriffe, and just after that (7 p.m.) went to bed, or rather hammock. The next thing I remember was hearing a sailor shouting out, ' You with bananas, keep away from the propeller.' That was good enough for me, so I slipped out and up on the deck, and by jingo it was a lovely sight; it looked too fantastic, too much like a big transformation scene at Drury Lane pantomime; in fact, it regularly beggars description. I found we were anchored off a town lit by electricity—just fancy an out-of-the-way hole like Santa Cruz being lit by it. The mountains start right down from the water, and when you look towards the town the mountains on the right are fearfully rugged, and the tops seem awfully pointy. There was a splendid moon, and it illumined the place nicely. Most of the houses are painted white or a brilliant yellow, only a few of them being a dirty sort of a red, and when the sun rose it did make it look fine All the bare tops of the mountains were touched up by it, and looked like a pale pink coral, except one over to the left, which was covered with snow and glistened just like a diamond. The place was more picturesque by daylight, because the colours were so brilliant, and the housetops being red and so clean. The natives were what Captain Kettle would call Dagos, and I don't wonder at him despising them, for a smaller, uglier, dirtier lot I never saw. I don't think the average darkey would own up to them as a man and a brother. On looking at the mountains it seemed as if the sloping sides were covered with sheep, but on taking a peep through the glasses you could see they were snip villas with balconies along the front. . . . About ten minutes ago I looked at the log and found we had gone seventy-six miles from Santa Cruz, that's fifty-six miles from nearest part of island, and that big snow covered peak can be seen quite plainly above the clouds that hang round it. It makes a fine sight, because the rest of the sky is such a deep blue, and the cloud would look snow-white if it wasn't made so dull by the sun glistening on the snow. By George! it is hot here. I've just moved (been sitting at side of ship on the stern facing the wheel house), and I find the pi ch, or whatever it is, has melted, and striped the lower part of jacket and legs like a zebra, so I'll knock off for present as I shall have to get it off somehow. January 27th.—Up at six o'clock; bath on deck. It was rather cold in morning, but warmed up during the day. In the evening we had a quarter pound of tobacco given us each, and a pint of lemonade for me, or beer for those who preferred it. Organised a concert, but it wasn't very good; a

KHAKI LETTERS—*continued*.

clique of fellows, mostly from the—————, seemed to shove themselves forward, and you know the sort of things they sing—Marie Lloyd's songs—'You've got a long way to go,' and those depressing sentimental songs, like ' Bid me good-bye for ever,' &c. We had one or two decent, however, ' Let me like a Soldier fall,' ' The Bandolero,' ' The Soldier's Song,' ' Mona,' ' Winds that blow from the South,' ' Only another day to Roam,' and also one or two good recitations. We broke up by ten o'clock, and bed by eleven. Up this morning (Sunday, 28th); bath at six. We are to parade for Divine Service 10.15—boots, putties, khaki drill suits, and those terrible felt hats. . . . Just come back from parade. Here we are to be asked if we will be inoculated. I'm going to have it done ; saw some of the fellows done one afternoon. They wash the skin just below the ribs, and insert a needle three inches long with a syringe attached. The operation knocks you up for from 24 hours to six weeks if you cop it bad. . . . January 29th.—Fearfully hot to-day. Makes one feel inclined to use very unparliamentary language to be so hot, and to see the water so close. and looking so deliciously cool and clean. I had my hair cut by one of the sailors to-day. I say ' cut' ; the others say it's a nice clean shave, but, of course, that's only green envy on their part. Oh ! it's a fearful lazy time on board here. Only half hour to one hour's drill a day, and that's standing still nearly all the time. I started playing nap—thought I could do a bit at it too—but I find it comes too expensive a luxury considering the princely salary they force us to take. We took two niggers aboard at Teneriffe ; they're about the only pastime we have, bar cards. You could watch 'em for hours, scratching themselves. You'd think at first they were contortionists, and good ones at that ; see them scratch themselves in the small of the back with their big toes ! They were sent away from Teneriffe for borrowing potatoes and the inevitable chickens. We had a nice little impromptu concert on deck this evening. January 30th.—Another scorcher to-day. It was fearfully hot during the night. I was fairly bathed in perspiration, though I only had my pyjamas on. Got up at four o'clock and had half-an-hour's lay in the bath they rig up on deck. I've got to do twenty-four hours' guard, starting at noon to-day. . . . This evening whilst on deck it started to get cloudy. I was off sentry go at six, and on from midnight till 2 a.m. By jingo, it was dark ; I've never come across such a pitch black. The instructions they gave me made it worse, too. I was informed that there were four Boers, at anyrate pro-Boer Germans on board ship as spies ; I was armed with a cutlass, and had to guard the wheel-house, as they are afraid these men will endeavour to tamper with the rudder, and thus put us out of our course, most probably ashore. Just fancy being told this on a jolly dark night. It didn't make you feel as comfortable as you might like, and the sudden passing out of the light as you passed the stern lantern made you see all manner of shapes dodging after you. I used to regularly funk turning the corner for fear of coming on some of the jokers suddenly. . . . Went to bed at 9 p.m. It was very close down below, and some blinking jackass put some biscuit and cheese in the rack over my head, and, of course, that brought the rats. Twice during the night one fell on me, and it's not over-pleasant to have to kill rats with your fingers. I have to post ; just at St. Helena. Kind regards to all."

✣ ✣ ✣ ✣

No. 198, Sapper **F. H. Woodrow** (of SO), writes from De Aar, January 26th, as follows :—

"Dear Sergeant,—I read with deepest regret the sad news of poor

KHAKI LETTERS—*continued.*

Jummy (Harry Lankstead, R.E.K.); the whole of 24th out here are with me in expressing their sorrow. Will you kindly, on behalf of my comrades here, express our deepest sympathy with the family in this sad bereavement, and we trust that God will give the widow strength to bear this terrible trial. It gives us great pleasure, Sergeant, to know that you are pleased with our small gift. I am afraid that my letter from De Aar, which should have reached you Christmas must have gone astray, because in it I asked you on behalf of Section to accept photos as a small token of our esteem and regard. Your thoughtfulness in every way since being called up will ever remain uppermost in our thoughts, and I must also include our comrades in 'I' Company. I hope that you are still receiving full account of our doings, but I must beg to be excused. . . . . as I could not do our experiences sufficient justice in comparison with those already in print. All the Section is going strong, and our Corporal Nelson has now received confirmation of his promotion to Sergeant. I believe Sergeant Miller has gone to Naauwpoort, and Tee to Rensberg. There are a good few of 'B' Section still at De Aar waiting to be distributed to different offices. Our chocolate has just arrived here, but has not been distributed. We have not yet received Christmas puddings, and I think it is not very probable that we shall. I have met several old TS men, who have looked after us where possible. The majority of us are very disappointed at the Colony, and, from what I can see, postmasterships, that we hear so much about, are a myth, and what is generally described as a town (?) is nothing more than a Kaffir village, with one or two whites. . . . . I am pleased 'I' Company is also to be represented. Well, I am afraid I make a very bad letter writer, so please don't insert mine in *Chronicle*, although a notification *re* what I have said herein would give tip to rest of Section scattered over Colony that your Christmas photos have arrived O.K. I think I have now exhausted my small stock of news, so must now conclude. Hoping everybody is in best of health, and with kindest regards to all."

[The gift referred to was duly received and acknowledged. It consisted of a double-mounted photo of the first party, and is much appreciated in its oak and gilt frame.—R.E.K.]

No. 447, Sapper **C. J. Jenner,** sends a post-card from Modder River dated January 27th :—

"DEAR KEMP,—All quiet here. Don't expect we shall be long though before we make an advance. Thanks for letters—All delighted with them.

"Health of all here splendid, except Quinn (No. 17 Block, No. 1 General Hospital, Wynberg), but he feels well. Only strain. Regards to all."

No. 23,610, Sergeant **R. C. Luttrell,** sends the following :—

"s.s. 'St. Andrew,' at sea.

" DEAR DICK,—Herewith extracts from my regimental diary.

Saturday, 27th January—We paid 2½d. for each letter, but the officer of the boat that came out from H.M.S. 'Furious' at Las Palmas would not take it, said they must be paid for in England. We were pleased to catch a glimpse of land. We got into the bay at 6 a.m. and were well away at 8 a.m. We didn't see much of it, especially as we kept a mile off shore.

KHAKI LETTERS—*continued.*

Bumboats with fruit came round but were not allowed near the ship. Only one bunch of bananas for the officers was allowed. We were very disappointed, especially the sick. The latest telegrams also came on board, and we were sorry that Ladysmith had not been relieved, but hope to hear better news at Cape Town. Our rations have greatly deteriorated. No fresh meat now. Salt junk and potted meat, biscuits, with bread occasionally. We get plum pudding twice a week and look forward most eagerly to it. Waghorn is one of the cooks' mates of my mess and a capital pudding maker. Wright and Govier also do for the other messes. Most of the chaps have had terrible colds, and one R. E. has been in hospital up till February 5th. Orwin also went into hospital, temperature 100. He has been ailing ever since we were called up.

Sunday, 28th—Church service under the captain of the ship at 10 a.m. Tinned beef and biscuit for dinner.

Monday, 29th—Heat increasing. We are gradually discarding our clothing and decency will soon forbid us to leave off any more. The bath on deck gets well used. The 18 men of the K. O. S. B. were sent to sea without money. We collected £2 14s. from the R. E.'s for them for 'bacca, etc.

Tuesday, 30th—Everyone turns up for sunrise and sunset, both of which are glorious. The sea at night is quite phosphorous. At 9 p.m. we saw the two lighthouses of Cape Verde Islands. We were sorry it was night as no more land will be seen till Cape Town.

Wednesday 31st—The trumpeter overslept. The doctor inoculating against enteric fever, but has only 27 tubes. *Ergo*, we do not get a chance. Dead horse overboard, also Driver Hindle of the ammunition column, married, four children, died of malarial fever, pneumonia, etc. He passed away at 3 p.m. and we buried him at 5.15. The captain read the service, and sewn in his hammock and weighted with iron he quickly disappeared under the water. The ship's way had been stopped, but after the trumpeters had blown 'Last Post' and 'Reveille,' we proceeded on our way. We made a collection for the widow and children, R. E.'s £3. I must say my mob are a most decent lot and ever ready to put their hands in their pockets.

Thursday, February 1st—Another horse dead. Terribly hot. All sick on deck. Got three men in No. 1, Cpl. Rodway, Sappers Roberts and Orwin, all high temperatures. Flying fish numerous. Lime juice served out. It tried to rain, but failed. Decks crowded at night with sleeping men.

Friday, 2nd—Another horse dead. Crossed the line, Neptune came aboard at 4 p.m. The usual spree commenced, but only three officers were tackled. It ended abruptly by the captain jumping into the bath and stopping the free fight that had commenced. The fact is that someone lost his temper. Had a concert in the evening. Forth, of Leeds, stopped the ship this afternoon. He was filling the bath but couldn't turn off the water, which flooded the upper deck and steering deck shed. The ship made a complete circle, and the sick had to beat a hasty retreat. The boatswain who came to the rescue soon put matters right, but his language was truly sulphurous or at least equatorial. Forth has now to put up with a lot of friendly remarks, such as 'who stopped the ship,' chorus 'Forth.'

Saturday, 3rd—Another horse overboard. Sharpening swords all day, varied by revolver practice.

Sunday, 4th—Lovely day. Divine service 10 a.m. The boys passed evening singing hymns on deck.

KHAKI LETTERS—*continued.*

Monday, 5th—Cpl. Rodway discharged from hospital. Orwin still there; Govier attending with swollen ankles.

Tuesday, 6th—Passed one ship and two flying fish. One horse dead.

Wednesday, 7th—Lot of meat and poultry, that had been allowed to go bad, thrown overboard, whilst we descended to our usual salt junk. No one grumbled, of course. Fancy the poor beggars in hospital, longing for something tasty, but not allowed anything but their salt junk, while this beautiful grub is decaying in the refrigerator. Orwin discharged from hospital.

Thursday, 8th; Friday, 9th; Saturday, 10th—Ship rolling like a porpoise, and you have to hang on by your eyebrows.

Sunday, 11th—Divine Service at 9.50 a.m. Gave in embarkation reports, etc. We expect to get into Cape Town late to-night or early to-morrow. It's plum duff day to-morrow. They have just served out the flour and raisins. We are making it into a cake instead, to eat to-day, in case we are not on board at dinner time to-morrow. Well, the voyage is nearly over. Am glad to say the sick are all nearly well, and that the remainder of the fellows are in splendid condition and looking forward to a change of scene and work. We hope also to hear good news at Cape Town. With kind remembrances from us all to the old Regt. and TS fellows. Trusting all's going well with you as with us."

No. 1,546, Sapper **R. W. Eglinton (DY)**, writing on February 1st from Belmont, Griqualand West, says:—

"DEAR KEMP,--Your card and letter duly received. We all deeply appreciate your splendid efforts to keep us in touch with what is going on at home. News of the service is naturally hard to come by here. It is weeks since I saw our Journal's green cover, and then the news it contained had an ancient and fish-like odour.

"The 'Canada' reached St. Vincent just a week after leaving LV, coaled there, and after a splendid passage entered Table Bay 4 p.m., 19th December. The 'Canada' is a splendid boat, but the commissariat was off. We spent Christmas Day at Greenpoint Camp, Capetown, but there was little to remind us of the festive season, and the party for up-country fell in at 7 p.m. that day for their long journey to De Aar, about 600 miles, which we reached early on the 27th, and where we met some of the first detachment of the 24th. We were told off next morning for our respective stations. Hurdle, Jones, Fenton and Wilson, going to Orange River; Williams of Cardiff, Witteputts; Porter, Fergusson, Collins and myself, Belmont; Loosemore and Smith, of TS (the only TS man in this party), going to Enslin. Leaving at once we reached our several destinations the same day, and Porter took over the office on the 31st. We are more fortunate than some in not having to work in a tent, the office being in a room of the station buildings, which is preferable when the frequent sand-storms are raging. Belmont is no worse than any other place on this line of communication, and that is the best word that can be said of it. Besides the station buildings there is only one other house in the place, a Boer store or hotel, as it calls itself, the rest of the place is sand, stones and sage brush. The Colonial Volunteers (Canadians and Queenslanders), Munster Fusiliers and Cornwalls, are encamped here. The Colonials are mostly well-to-do, rolling in dollars, which they scatter lavishly, helping to keep up the prices

KHAKI LETTERS—*continued*.

of things, which is bad for us who are ill-provided with the needful.

"We have two single current sets here, one working to Modder and Enslin, the other to Orange River and De Aar, and two vibrators, one to Enslin, Honeynestkloof, Graspan and Klokfontein, and the other to Witteputts and De Aar, besides a temporary vibrator office to the Flying Column which operates against the Douglas rebels. We are not overtasked with work just yet, just sufficient to keep us fairly going.

"There is little excitement here, except when the alarm is raised of Boer parties coming to smash the railway, when patrols are sent out and come back emptyhanded, or when a cock fight, or a tarantula and scorpion fight comes off. The latter are unpleasantly plentiful on the camping ground, getting into the men's bedding. Their sting is painful and dangerous.

"We are anxiously waiting for Methuen to make a move, Spytfontein is said to be very strongly entrenched and will give our troops some trouble. We hear that we are likely to remain here till the end of the war. The Queen's chocolate was dished out the day before yesterday. Empty tins are being bought at £5 each at Modder. Besides slight attacks of dysentery we are all well, although enteric fever cases are occurring amongst the troops.

"I think that P. O. Circular, *re* Reservists, can scarcely refer to us. Our letters from home tell us that our P. O. pay is received by our nominees in full regularly. So our minds are at ease. Wishing you a very prosperous New Year."

No. 25,362, Sapper **G. W. Bannister,** writing from Zoutpan's Drift, Orange River, February 3rd, says :—

"DEAR COLOUR-SERGEANT KEMP—Yours of December 22nd.—Think I have already acknowledged it, but as there is an hour or so before the bag closes here goes for a few more lines. We are all split up now and I don't know where half the boys have got to. Your last letter reached me at De Aar where we were stationed for about a week. During the stay there, our section went out before breakfast each morning practising on air line. The director of Army Telegraphs has his headquarters at De Aar. Whibley has a job in the Cleaning House, this is equivalent to paybill man in Provincial Superintending Engineer's Office. I was also employed in the office there for a few days in the stores department. Then Catling, Hawkins, and myself, had orders to leave for Orange River station, which is rather an important advance base. From there I got orders to take charge of Zoutpan's Drift office, here I am. We—a lineman and myself - left Orange River 3 a.m., 27th January. We had to travel in a forage waggon drawn by a team of 10 mules. The convoy consisted of 6 waggons carrying provisions to the troops stationed here. It was all right so long as the mules kept on a steady trot, but when they were whipped up and commenced to gallop we had great difficulty in keeping our seats, what with having to hold our kit bags, carbines, and stores on, in addition. The journey was a very pleasant one however. We saw the sun rise over the veldt, and passed one or two Dutch farm houses on the way, to say nothing of innumerable ostriches, which raised their long necks and stared at us defiantly as we passed them. Zoutpan's is very pleasantly situated on the banks of the Orange River, about 11 miles from Orange River station to the east. It is an advanced post and the troops here are supposed to be in action. We have not seen anything of the Boers up to now, though I hear scouting

KHAKI LETTERS—*continued.*

parties of the Scots Greys have exchanged shots with them last week. As a matter of fact, I believe there is a small party of Boers in laager about 6 or 8 miles away on the Orange Free State side. They are deserters from the Commandoes round Kimberley, and have come in to protect their farms, etc , against our probable invasion. It is extremely improbable that they will attack us, as we are numerically stronger. On this side of the river there is a detachment of the Cornwalls, also 2 guns and a party of Cape Garrison Artillery—with a hospital manned by the Australian Medical Corps. On the north bank of the river (Orange Free State) there is a squadron of Scots Greys with a detachment of Shropshires and a party of R.A., with 2 old 9-pounder muzzle-loading guns. The bridging battalion R.E. have fixed up a flying bridge which is worked by the current. I have been across to the O.F.S. once or twice, and am probably the 1st 24th man to set foot in that country this journey. The river is nice and handy for a dip and to wash our clothes in. It is also the only water we've got to drink. In colour it resembles coffee more than anything, and this is due to the enormous quantity of sand it contains. There is a lineman here with me—Sapper J. Gant, from Maidenhead—and we get along together a treat. Sleeping on the ground is quite impracticable here owing to the number of insects prowling around in the night-time. Many varieties of beetles, scorpions, centipedes, mosquitoes, etc., pay us visits. We also get a few varieties of lizards paying us a call occasionally, but we have grown so accustomed to them all now that we sleep peacefully—a case of ' let 'em all come!' Two sheep's heads are better than one. We put ours together and rigged up a couple of bedsteads with the aid of some tree stumps, and broken telegraph poles, then I suggested lacing the framework across with G.P. wire (some we captured on the way to the Transvaal, and known as ' Kruger wire,' by the way). Then we bound this again with 3 strand G 1, and obtained as a result what Gant is pleased to term ' Bannister's Patent Spring Mattress'—they certainly are very comfortable and quite a novelty on active service. We get good food and take it in turns to do the cooking, some days we have steak and onions and at others Irish stew. Jam is served out to us every other day, rations of tea and coffee every day. We boil our water in an old corn beef tin. Often for breakfast we have Quaker Oats. One of the neighbouring farmers comes in every morning with milk, 6d. per pint bottle, eggs 2d. each, and occasionally fresh churned butter 4s. per lb. Owing to the bad water all troops served out with rum rations every other night—one 64th of a gallon per man. Not quite enough to cause trouble, eh? Gant patrols the line (air line. light poles, wire 3 strand G 1, No. 18 gauge, resistance about 74^w p.m.) armed with his trusty carbine and 30 rounds of ammunition. My Kruger pills are in my pouch slung up on the tent pole, with one in the emergency hole. I hope to bring them all back with me. Somebody raised an alarm in camp that the Boers were marching on us *in force* yesterday. It transpired that one of the Scots Greys patrols sighted a party of 40 or 50. They had entered our lines, but quietly retreated driving some of their own sheep and goats in. On the first alarm, the Scots Greys all saddled up and the infantry all stood to arms. The latter stand to arms at 4.30 every morning. . . The instrument here is an ordinary sounder complete with key, galvo and relay on base, army pattern, it is also fitted with connections to work as translators if required. We work to Orange River (ORM—our code is ZPM), ORM works to De Aar (DAM), and the latter works to Cape Town (CT). The buzzer is used extensively in conjunction with the sounder, but I hav'nt one on this cct—post time now—thanks for news. Kind regards to all old friends."

✤ ✤ ✤

KHAKI LETTERS—*continued.*

No. 23,653, Sapper **J. F. Metcalfe**, writing from Sterkstroom, January 31st, says :—

'DEAR KEMP,—Yours of the 22nd of December and January 5th received O.K. on the 26th and 27th of January respectively, the former evidently had been all over the Colony, as it bears no less than nine postmarks, hence the delay. I was more than pleased to have a few lines from you, but sorry indeed that they carried the sad news of no less than three of our colleagues' deaths. Poor old Chichester was always respected by all who came under his supervision. Cosier's death was also painfully sudden, and last, poor old Jummy, who was always very smart on parade, and always liked to see others neatly dressed, and ever ready to take a part in anything military ; I was pleased to see that our last respects for him were so kindly and thoughtfully carried out by you, during the absence of his past comrades. I am certain the enthusiasm at home must be very great during the mobilisation of our Volunteer forces for the front. I was pleased to see so many come forward, and trust that the 24th is well represented. Thanks for the cutting. We do not get so many English newspapers as you may suppose, but the most is made of them when we do; I can assure you that the *Telegraph Chronicle* is anxiously looked for, and I venture to say that the articles and letters under the heading, 'Where are our Boys?' take predominance, but I still have a sneaking regard for the 'TS Chronicles,' from which we have the workings and doings of the office, and all pertaining to the same, in a nutshell. A letter received from Hamer, at De Aar, reported that our friend Quinn had been sent down to hospital in Cape Town, suffering from some stomach ailment, but nothing about Jenner or Bishop ; trust the rumour is incorrect. Am pleased to hear that the whole of the ' L ' Company are now out here, and also hope that ' Bob ' will retain his stripes. No doubt you will be surprised to hear that I have lost no less than two stone, but have felt O.K. with the exception of a slight attack of dysentery. There are several cases of enteric fever in camp, mostly brought from Penhoek and Bushmanshoek. This, 12th Company, R.E., has lost one sapper, and a driver lies in hospital in a critical condition from this fearful malady. A military funeral was given to the former, who was interred at Sterkstroom Cemetery. On the 5th of January, Troop-Sergt.-Maj. Foote, of 1st T.B.'s, with Sappers Smith, Kimber and Willis (linemen), arrived here from De Aar, with 20 miles of stores and supplies for three offices. I thought perhaps there would be then a chance of getting away from this 12th Company, but up to the present we have heard nothing further than that the officer commanding the T.B.'s refused to transfer our accounts over to the 12th. Since the arrival of the above we feel more at home, although the 12th are not a bad lot of chaps. We share their tent, the party are only six, all told, an improvement on the tent of twelve men. You will in all probability have noticed that we have been rather quiet here since our disastrous defeat at Stormberg, with the exception of several skirmishes by Montmorency's Scouts, Brabant's Horse, C.M.R., C.M.P., and our Mounted Infantry, assisted by the Royal Scots and Derbyshires. Hope by the time this reaches you we shall have made a successful attack upon their strong position. Apparently we are not having it all our own way out here, as the enemy are so strongly fortified, and refuse to show themselves in the open, but I have no doubt as to the final result. I hope the memo. *re* half-pay does not include us of the ' M ' and ' L ' Companies. I shewed your letter to Sergt. Marshall, of the ' M ' Company, and he is of the same opinion as myself as regards our special conditions of pay, etc. The ZM continues

KHAKI LETTERS—*continued*.

very hot during the day, but fearfully cold at night, making it rather unpleasant for myself and Tough, who are still performing alternate night work. We have had several visits from the locusts, when the wind blows from the Equator they appear in the sky in great clouds. New Year was recognised by a boxing competition, open to all the camp, on January, 9th, 10th and 11th, viz.: feather, light, middle and heavy weights. Several knock-out blows were given, and finally the honours fell to the A.S.C., Kaffrarian Rifles, Royal Scots and Derbyshires. Much excitement was caused by a stick or spear fight between two of the Kaffirs, the one who gets the first hit on any part of the body loses. These muleteers also have their religious services, the sermon being interpreted by Dutch and Kaffir. We have several religious meetings all over the camp in large marquees, where we can spend a pleasant hour or so in the evening. We are still on bread rations and fresh beef or mutton, and preserved vegetables, jams, cheese, etc., occasionally getting some preserved bacon, which is warmed for us in camp-kettle lids. Excuse hurried letter, as I am rather busy in office, and find pencil most convenient. Trusting you have received letters dated December 2nd, from Durban, December 16th and January 1st from Sterkstroom. With thanks and best wishes to you and all enquiring friends.

✧ ✧ ✧ ✧

No. 220, Sergeant **J. W. Miller,** 1st Tel. Div. R.E.'s, Mil. Tel. Office, Naauwpoort, February 5th, writes as under :—

"DEAR OLD DICK,—Not having written to you for some time, I thought a few lines might be acceptable once again. But what about the book? You seem to be getting such an abundance of correspondence that it appears to me you will have to make it into volumes, or people who read it will never get through. Don't allow it to wear right out, as there are many who would like the pleasure of seeing the trouble you have so heartily taken in all our doings for the honour of the 24th. There is not much news to let you have from my quarter. Since the departure of the remainder of the section from Cape Town, many of us have separated to different offices. On arrival at De Aar we saw several of our men of the first batch, who greeted us in the kindest manner possible, but the stay was only short, several departing to different stations in a very few days. Sergt.-Major Tee and myself were sent to Rensburg and Naauwpoort, respectively, to take charge on the first day. Rensburg is about 28 miles distant from Naauwpoort, and a busy office, more so than this, having about 10 operators to my five. Those under my charge are Adams, Austen, and Birch from TS, Poole, from Bristol, and Andrew, from Newtown, Montgomery (commonly known as "Monty"). We are doing at the present time between 300 and 400 messages a day, whilst Rensburg does about 500. Both stations have two wires. On one we are the intermediate station with De Aar and Rensburg. The other goes *via* Arundel (where Ray from TS is stationed) on to Rensburg (R.G.M.). I am pleased to say all are in the best of health, and working 10 hours a day. One is on all night in case of emergency. Naauwport is rather a better place than any of the others—a nice cool office on the platform of the station, where trains are continually running through with war material, regiments and horses, mail trains, etc., a sight which passes many a few spare moments when off duty. The place is almost surrounded by very high hills, and we are not allowed to go very far away from the camp, as it is considered unsafe. Lord Roberts and all his staff contemplate coming here next week to try and do something extra at Colesberg, where General French has hemmed the Boers all round. But I

KHAKI LETTERS—*continued*.

expect you will have had the result by the time this letter reaches you. All of us are *not* getting the *Chronicle*, but I am pleased to say I often get mine all right. I don't think half the papers sent ever reach us, it is only a matter of chance whether you get them or not. On the platform just outside our office to-day are about 50 large baskets full of grapes supplied gratis to the troops by a gentleman. I believe there is a ton. We can purchase them here at 3d. a lb. (a luxury). In fact we have been very fortunate to what others have, by the kindness of those at home. The other day each man stationed here received three wooden pipes, a quarter lb. of Navy Cut (Player's), and a tin box of matches by Bell. Three or four days after yet another gift arrived for the troops, each man receiving five boxes of cigarettes, containing 10 each, and three sticks of hard tobacco, with a sentence pasted round it thus :—'**Dear Tommy Atkins,—That victory may always attend you, and that all your troubles may, like this tobacco, end in smoke, is the sincere wish of your Glasgow Friend,— R. D. WADDELL.**' So we are well provided for the present.

"In your last letter received you mention that Sergt.-Instr. Jackman is slowly improving. I hope that be the case, for I am sorry to say we had rumours that he was dead. I should like to know how he was getting on, and if you live near I would ask you to give my very kind regards, and hope he will pull through successfully. I don't know that I have much more to tell you this time. I believe that there is to be another big staff to go to the Modder River district, as all offices are being asked if any clerks can be spared. I wish I was going that way, as I have a brother in the Naval Brigade at Modder, and another brother at Ladysmith—one from H.M.S. *Monarch*, another from the *Forte*, so being three from one family is not a bad average. My other brother left the Carabineers some years ago; they are now at Rensberg.

"I send kindest regards to all enquiring friends, wishing you every success with your book, and with my kindest regards.

"P.S.—All in the office join me in sending kindest regards to *the* Colour-Sergeant."

✢ ✢ ✢ ✢

No. 1274, Sapper **W. F. Adams**, Naauwpoort Military Telegraphs, February 5th, writes :—

"DEAR SERGEANT KEMP,—Am sorry I haven't written before, but must admit I've had plenty to do. You've heard all the news of the boys, but perhaps one or two little adventures might interest you. On our way up to De Aar some of us stayed too long over breakfast at Matjesfontein, and so our train went on, and we were practically stranded on the Karoo. However, the Major of the 20th Battery R.H.A. kindly took us along on his train, and we arrived at De Aar about six hours behind the rest. No notice was taken of it.

"The next little excitement was when Austen and I went out for a walk one day. Unconsciously or otherwise, we got beyond the picket, and wandered on till we got hungry. On our way back we were observed and captured. The officer took a lenient view of it, but it was only our innocent faces and identification cards which saved us. Thanks very much for the Christmas card. I am endeavouring to keep it as a memento of probably the most exciting and novel part of my life.

"Jimmy Miller makes an excellent sergeant, and we find him a jolly good fellow, who doesn't mind a bit of work, of which, I may add, there is plenty. Must now close, hoping all is 'Kif' at TS, and that you are well.'

"Khaki Notes."

ON DUTY AGAIN. I had the intense pleasure of welcoming Sergeant-Instructor Jackman on his return to duty on Monday, March 12th. He had been on the sick list since December 18th, suffering from acute pneumonia. As he improved he went down to Devonshire for a stay of three weeks and returned to town again on February 22nd, having derived great benefit from the change. I asked him if he had got a word for the boys in S. A., and he said "Certainly. Remember me to every one of them. Thank them for their kind enquiries. Tell 'em I thought my number was up this time, but I've got through it all right. They used to call me a 'Terror,' I don't feel much like a Terror just now." And so the old soldier is back with us and we are happy again. "*What* are you going to do now?" "Is *that* how you hold your rifle?" "*Who* taught you that?"

❖ ❖ ❖ ❖

A FINGER IN THE PIE. Several orders were sent me last week requesting that copies of "K. L.'s" should be sent to men at the Front. This I had already done. Every man has had one posted to him. I believe in sending them addressed individually; it ensures delivery, as they are always changing their stations. To let my friends into a secret I will tell the cost of doing this. 127 men. 127 " K. L.'s " at 1d. = 10s. 7d. 127 ½d. stamps = 5s. 3½d. 127 printed wrappers (about), 1s. Total, 16s. 10½d. We *must* do this, and I am sure such a course will meet with the approval of all my subscribers. Now, I wish to suggest something. More men are going out, more " K. L.'s " will be sent, consequently more expense will be incurred in sending to " Our Very Own." I will put my scheme before you at once. It is this. Let every Division, Group, and Section of the C.T.O. (including the Stock Exchange, Commercial Sales Rooms, Schools, T.S.F. Delivery, &c.) contribute one penny per subscriber between now and the 31st inst. Such fund to be called the " Khaki Postage Fund." Keep it clear of all other matters whatsoever, and hand it over to Mr. George Costello, of the " L " Division, who will sit at the receipt of custom for that purpose. This amount will carry us over many issues of " K. L.'s "; it will lighten our burdens; it will clinch our friendship in a practical manner; it will please the boys out yonder, for they will know you are doing such a noble deed, and you will enjoy the pleasure of having a "finger in the pie" in the bargain. My Provincial friends need not respond. I will call upon them when the C.T.O. Fund is running out. Your turn will undoubtedly come, and I know you will be eager for it to do so. Did I hear somebody say 127 "K. L.'s" do not cost 10s. 7d.? One man said he would not take half-a-crown for his copy! I am giving you twenty pages again!

❖ ❖ ❖ ❖

KHAKI NOTES—*continued.*

'DEAR COLOUR-SERGEANT.' Some friends who head their letters thus, make a mistake. They should commence "Cheap Colour-Sergeant," for they thoughtfully enclose one penny stamp and expect a penny book, a wrapper, a halfpenny stamp, and the labour of addressing thrown in. Instead of me remaining in the workshop, friends, you'll transfer me to the workhouse in "double time." Kindly note that postage is extra, please. 1d. the book, ½d. the postage, and I don't mind finding the wrappers.

✤ ✤ ✤ ✤

2d. PER COPY. Some of my subscribers prefer to pay twopence per copy and the postage as well. Their generosity I appreciate quite as fully as they on their side appreciate my efforts. May their numbers increase.

✤ ✤ ✤ ✤

POSTAGE AND CARRIAGE. I prefer to make no hard and fast rule about carriage yet. I am content to see how my subscribers go. I would, however, point out that I am giving you a very full measure—even to running over, *i.e.*, sixteen pages was my promise, twenty I have given you. I have many supporters who gladly pay all expenses; they have entered fully into the spirit of the "K. L.'s" We will wait a wee, and live and learn. Meanwhile, kindly note that I can't pay for *all* the letters, &c., that may pass, unless I reduce again to sixteen pages. Less than a halfpenny, locally, now and then, would easily clear your Distributor.

✤ ✤ ✤ ✤

KEEPING THE BOYS IN TOUCH. Quietly, yet persistently, without flourish of trumpets, or boast and brag, have I worked for our colleagues at the front. I've not told you before, I am not telling you now, so that praise may be bestowed. I tell it you as an ordinary fact; I've done what my enthusiasm and regard has prompted me to do. Every Friday since October last —when the first batch of "Ours" left— I have sent twelve, twenty, thirty, and sometimes very many more hektographed letters to Our Boys. Letters semi-official, up-to-date, regimentally, and C.T.O.-ally (that's a good word), and every man, London or Provincial, known or unknown to me personally, has received them in turn. These communications are headed "CIRCULAR LETTERS" in large print, with the request, "Will you kindly endeavour to let every man see this, please?" And thus the men are always kept aware of the doings, the enrolments, &c., &c. of their regiment at home. Other letters have supplemented these. Keep on writing to them. They value it.

✤ ✤ ✤ ✤

V. E. GRAY, "I" Company, being so anxious to go on service has joined "Paget's Horse" (a corps of Sharpshooters), dated March 16th, 1900. He left the C.T.O. on the 19th inst., and proceeded to Aldershot the following day. Others contemplate doing the same.

✤ ✤ ✤ ✤

SERGT. W. M. KNIGHT, "I" Co., is still on sick leave, suffering from a severe attack of bronchitis. He is being well cared for at Hayes, Kent. We all wish such a popular Non-Com. a speedy recovery and a return to duty.

KHAKI NOTES—*continued.*

SAPPERS W. O. WILLIAMS, of the C.T.O. (1,548 R.E.), and **J. R. JONES,** of Shrewsbury (1,559 R.E.), being found medically unfit have been struck off the strength of the L.Co.

SAPPER A. W. HAWKINS, 1st Tel. Div., R.E., died of enteric fever at Orange River, March 13th, 1900. His No. is given as 458 in the Casualty List instead of 488, but we fear the slight discrepancy will not remove the sad fact that TSF has lost the first man of the P.O. Telegraphists in S.A.

Since writing the above par. I have received a letter, written by the unfortunate young fellow to a friend, dated Orange River, February 17th. It is very bright and cheery. No word referring to any illness. A footnote says :—" My number is 458, not 488."

Referring to letters I find the number is given as printed in my lists, showing the discrepancy occurred elsewhere. His letter will appear in the next issue of " K.L."

W. L. V. BAKER (Commissionaire 3,983, Night Collector TS), 2nd Battalion Seaforth Highlanders, died of wounds received at Paardeberg, March 1st, he was only married a fortnight before being called for service.

GEORGE HAWKINS, C.T.O. Night Check, died March 16th, 1900. Known to many of the L.Co.

F. W. CLARK, who was struck off the "I" Company roll, February 25th, 1899, owing to failing health, and proceeded to South Africa, has seen many of Our Boys during the last few months. He received a bonus, and the best wishes of his numerous friends; little improvement, however, was effected. He was given a passage to England, but it was seen he was too ill to endure the journey, and was put back, entered the hospital at Cape Town, and died eight days afterwards. (*Information by last mail.*)

PRIZE DISTRIBUTION, March 24th. Owing to the presence of so many men at the Front, the " I," " L," and " M " Companies' Prize Lists cannot be compiled.

" CEPHALONIA " letters from St. Vincent report "all well on board. The usual sea-illnesses have been and gone."

" ORIENTAL " correspondence from St. Vincent to hand to-day (March 21st) reports " All well." See next issue of " K.L."

ABSURDITIES. Quite a domestic affair. Mrs. Kruger (in a fit of passion) : " Paul, I'm sick and tired of trying. The Dutch ovens won't work at all."—Mr. Kruger : " Never mind, dearie, we shall soon have a real English Kitchener here."

A Vocalist, anxious to " catch on," requested a friend to alter the music of " Soldiers of the Queen." Asked in what key he would prefer it, he replied, " *Khaki*."

COLOURS.

All posted letters containing Remittances, Orders, MSS., &c., must be addressed to R. E. KEMP, 12, JERRARD STREET, LEWISHAM, S.E.
Postal Orders should be made payable at Loampit Vale, Lewisham, S.E.

Printed by E. G. BERRYMAN & SONS, *Blackheath Road, London, S.E.*

"Khaki Letters" from ....
"My Colleagues in South Africa."

CORRESPONDENCE FROM THE
POST OFFICE TELEGRAPHISTS
OF THE
24th MIDDLESEX (P.O.) RIFLE VOLUNTEERS
(Royal Engineer Reserves),
ON ACTIVE SERVICE.

THE BOND THAT BINDS US—FRIENDSHIP—COMRADESHIP.

Published fortnightly for the Postal Telegraph Service.
Conducted by COLOUR-SERGEANT R. E. KEMP, *Central Telegraph Office, London.*

No. 3.   APRIL 6TH, 1900.   PRICE ONE PENNY.

Central Telegraph Office,
London, E.C.

DEAR COMRADES, ONE AND ALL,

Greetings! It is possible that by the time this is in print, the first number of my little booklet will be in your hands. Of course, you will be rather surprised to see it, and you will doubtless be as eager to know "how she goes," as many a man here. Well, it is going "all Sir Garnet," and by what I can learn—and I am always open to do that—she seems to be a little favourite. One can generally judge how things go when they have opportunities of doing so, and fortunately, I have had those opportunities, for nearly every letter that comes in speaks well of the booklet, and not a few pay a very great tribute of respect to, and interest in, you. It is very encouraging that it is so. Others, whom you have probably never seen, or never heard of, claim you as theirs, for they have got hold of the words "Our Boys" with such a gusto, it makes one really all aglow to think that such friendship was lying latent, and only wanted, as it were, the poker to stir the smouldering embers. This done, out burst the big flame and enthusiasm went up to a white heat. And we're going to keep it there, too. There's many a man who will put his hand to the plough and make her go, and so it should be, for they recognise that you are ours, and we are yours, and why should our interest in each other wax and wane, the few months we are separated? "Out of sight, out of mind," is not our motto. I prefer to say ours is "Absence makes the heart grow fonder."

Buck up, my boys! you're doing well. You've got a harder task than people predicted, but you can do it. You have gone into real hard and tough work, but stick to it. We know it. All of us know it, but——

IS THE SPIRIT OF THE BRITISHER BROKEN?

NO!—Not nearly; for we find that with our knowledge, with our experience of the tussle so far, we have boys eager, willing, and ready to break loose and join you at your arduous work—boys who know more than you knew when you started, hastening to be at your side to share your trials and troubles, to reinforce and encourage you, to give their all for the flag that floats and shall ne'er be furled, sacrificing their all for Old England. And then there are those who would like to go but cannot. They are just as warm as the rest. Letters convey all kinds of expressions. Here's one: "We at Aldershot (P.O.) are all interested in the doings of 'Our Boys' in South Africa. Some of them will, no doubt, knock against some of our 'Aldershot Boys' who are now in the Cape Government Telegraphs. They number ten, and no less than five were in Kimberley during the siege. With best wishes for

THE SUCCESS OF OUR LITTLE BOOKLET."

Then Glasgow chimes in and says," Your publication is a splendid idea for keeping us in touch with those at the Front—eight of our Clerks are leaving here for Aldershot." Other offices speak in the same tone, saying," We all find them most interesting." So keep up you correspondence, my lads; we all want you to do so, and I am sure the 198 subscribers at Leeds wish it.

Now a word about the party that have just started to help you. The "Featherweight" writes me from Aldershot, saying," We have the best of times down here, all jolly good fellows, and we get along splendidly with them all. We have had a couple of smoking concerts, ably assisted by the following singers: Stevenson, Ash, Jones, Carter, Ben Walton and others, Bell accompanying, and your humble servant in the chair. We are living like fighting cocks—the food being of the best, and the cooking grand. We have been treated with the utmost kindness and consideration by Captain Powell, Sergt.-Major Ferrett, Sergt.-Instructor Walker, and other non-coms.; they exercised the utmost patience with our drill, and I think we are benefiting by it. Some of us old crocks require a lot of licking into shape. We have technical instruction on the rifle 8.0 to 8.45, and squad drills from 9.0 to 9.45, 10.15 to 11, and 11.30 to 12.15. In the afternoon we have technical instruction on the Army telegraphic apparatus. We have several double increment men here . . . Theory is a grand thing, but when it came to the 'practical,' most of them found they were 'up the pole.' The foreign service envelopes are going well, everyone agrees how advantageous they are to use . . . . Thanking you so much for 'Khaki Letters,' which are greedily read. We heartily thank our colleagues for the grand send-off on Sunday evening, and regretted not seeing you."

The detachment, which is the fifth the 24th have sent with the Royal Engineers, left H.-Q. early on Sunday, April 1st, headed by the band of the Royal Irish as far as Aldershot Station. Here they received an enthusiastic send-off, and proceeded to Southampton, where they embarked on s.s. "Winifredian" in the afternoon, and sailed shortly afterwards.

The following are the regimental numbers of the detachment :—

4307 J. P. Flanagan	4360 E. J. Ash	4371 L. Sorensen
4315 J. Morse	4361 H. Barber	4372 L. D. Page
4316 J. McMurtrie	4362 W. Bell	4373 T. W. Stevenson
4338 D. G. Davies	4363 W. G. Carter	4374 D. Semple
4341 E. A. Thrift	4364 W. Dadswell	4375 C. H. Jones
4342 W. Foster	4365 J. Davis	4376 W. W. Pearce
4350 B. F. Warburton	4366 W. F. Frew	4377 F. J. Jarvis
4351 W. N. Kelly	4367 H. J. Harrison	4378 W. H. S. Marshall
4353 W. P. Walker	4368 H. J. Jackson	4379 G. E. Plumridge
4354 H. J. White	4369 D. Leitch	4380 W. S. Thomas
4355 E. A. Hunter	4370 E. P Neate	4381 B. Walton
4356 J. Heigh		

The transport also carries drafts for the 1st Yorkshire Regiment, 2nd Dorset, 2nd Middlesex, Army Service Corps, altogether 735 officers and men. She will call at Queenstown to embark 303 officers and men of the Royal Munster Fusiliers and a number of remounts, and will sail thence for the Cape.

J. P. Flanagan has been appointed Sergeant, and is in charge of the men.

We are all deeply grieved to hear about poor Hawkins, and also to see in to-day's papers that McLaren is seriously ill. One or two other men are not quite up to the mark. We wish them every good wish that they may soon be up and doing again.

In closing, I must say how pleased I am to insert in No. 3 the letter which follows.

Yours most heartily,
R. E. KEMP,
Colour-Sergeant.

To the "L" Co. in South Africa.
Tuesday, April 3rd, 1900.

GENERAL POST OFFICE,
March 29*th,* 1900.

DEAR COLOUR-SERGEANT KEMP,

I was very glad to read the interesting communications in your "Khaki Letters," and am very much obliged to you for the opportunity of sending a word of greeting to old comrades in "I" and "L" Cos. who are now in South Africa. I take the warmest interest in the old Companies, and am very pleased that they have the chance of doing such good service, and am very proud that they are doing it so well. It will be a great favour if you will convey to them my warmest good wishes for their welfare and safe return.

Yours sincerely,
(Signed) A. M. OGILVIE,
Major.

COPYRIGHT.—"Khaki Letters" must not be used without permission. —R. E. KEMP.

Khaki Letters.

No. 2,336, Sapper **E. J. Samuel,** writing from Rensburg Mil. Tel. Office, January 24th, 1900, says:—". . . . I consider myself a very lucky young fellow to have so many kind pals to think of me and write to me, and only wish that I had time to write to you all individually. . . . . You have no idea how we all look forward to the mail-day here. It is so different to being on your holidays at home (not that this is a holiday, but still try and persuade myself that it is), and some of the unfortunate chaps with few friends get a little remorse—which lasts a long time--when they see others with bunches of letters. . . . . Am glad you are all well and doing plenty of work still. . . . . Had any skating yet? I could really enjoy a game of snow-balls just now. You will see I have made a move up country at last. This is General French's base, and I came here on January 9th, after three weeks' stay at Cape Town, where, on the whole, we enjoyed ourselves very much. Three of us were sent here, J. Fallon, Milton and your humble, and we were sent into this office to work with three Royal Engineers—fine fellows. There is nothing here but camp, kopjes, veldt, and work. The fighting line is about ten miles off—towards Colesberg—and we work through to all the outlying camps, and De Aar, where a lot of our fellows are. But they have a tame time compared with us here. . . . We see the real side of war. . . . After I had been here three days I had orders to proceed to Kleinfontein, the farthest off of the camps, to take charge of the office. I went. I sha'n't forget it. Do you know what a Scotch cart is? Perhaps you've seen them at Aldershot. A 'contraption' without springs. I don't know why they call them *Scotch* carts, but I imagine they are no joke. I had to go 32 miles over the veldt in one. Do you remember the Bourley Road at Aldershot? Well, try and conceive something a thousand times worse, and you will have a faint idea what our road was like. As this column was nearly all cavalry, our position was very extensive, and Kleinfontein was an advanced post on the opposite road to Rensburg. Before I had gone a mile I was nearly jolted to death, and when we reached our post my condition was pitiable in the extreme. I can hardly look at a chair now without thinking of it. We had a team of six mules, and of all the obstinate, stupid creatures God put upon this fair sphere, those six mules took the biscuit. If you kept the ten-foot whip still one minute three or four of them would be looking at you in the cart. . . . When I reached Potfontein (half way) I had my first bit of loot, for we discovered a deserted Boer farmhouse. It was near the spot where those sixteen N.S.W. Lancers were captured, and the owner had

KHAKI LETTERS—*continued.*

been run in. We got a lot of useful things, but no cash, alas! We captured some poultry and a lamb, which we killed and ate when we reached our journey's end. It was splendid fun, and this and the dead horses make one realise what war really means. On reaching Kleinfontein another deserted homestead was our quarters, and my 'buzzer' was fixed up in the larder—empty, unfortunately. I was quartered here with about 300 Rimington's Guides, and was only about 1,000 yards off the Boer position and thought I was in for a rough time. There was plenty of skirmishing, and I could see the Boer shells drop on the veldt a short way off. *It was great.* We lived on the fat of the land (rather lean fat, by the by), for there were hundreds of commandeered cattle. I commandeered a pony I found straying on the veldt and sold it for a quid to an officer, and we commandeer any mortal thing we see. I was standing near some signallers at work on a kopje, and I went to the top to see if I could get a glimpse of the enemy. I hadn't been standing on the ridge a minute, when ping, ping, came a couple of Mauser bullets from somewhere, and I was promptly ordered to lie down. It gave me a funny feeling, and I promptly sought the shelter of a farmhouse. Saw plenty of wounded prisoners. They only let me stay there a few days, and then I was ordered to return to Rensburg, as all the 24th men were to be kept together. I was sorry to come back, as the Guides are a fine lot of men and the excitement was very enjoyable. Still, I flatter myself I have been as near the front as any of the TS men, and the experience was well worth all the roughing it, and the journey. We had stray shots at ostriches and springbok on the road home, and captured another pony. We are all in excellent health, and I'm writing this at 3 a.m., it being my turn on night duty, and I've just finished a 3,000 word Press message. We work 16 hours a day in the office. . . . W. C. Smith, from C group, is in hospital with sunstroke, but climate suits me splendidly, and I've got a lovely (!) beard. We can't get much water, as it has to be brought from Naauwpoort, so washing is out of the question. With regard to our shirts, etc., we just follow the advice of a famous General and 'brush them.' I'm going to volunteer for the first job that will take me up country. It's too tame here. . . . I get my letters regularly, which is a blessing, and to hear that all is well cheers me up, for I tell you it makes you think of your home when you see all these homesteads desolated and our poor chaps coming in in the ambulance wagons minus arms and legs. . . . I must close now, as it is breaking day and I want to see the sun rise over the kopjes—a splendid sight. Hope to hear again soon, as we do appreciate letters out here. Please give my kindest regards to all the boys and my love to all the girls (mim)."

No. 2,543, Sapper **Geo. Bishop,** writing from Wynberg Camp, January 30th, says:—" . . . . I managed to write a little volume of stuff to Kemp last mail. . . . . It looks as if I'm here for some time, for I was sworn in as 'a Military Telegraphist, dealing with private telegrams,' on Saturday. You see, we accept private messages here, but the bulk of the work is Imperial (no charge—only entered). It makes a lot of work with accounts, etc., though to-day I have taken over £3 in private messages, but I have to hand it over to the town office to-morrow morning. Seems hard!! . . . . Catling (N.W.D.O.), Woolley ('I' Div.), and myself, were sent here. We found a civvy and a Munster Fusilier in charge on our arrival. The civvy cleared out, and a fortnight afterwards Catling and Woolley were

KHAKI LETTERS—*continued*.

withdrawn also, leaving me in charge, with the Munster. Catling, Woolley, and the others from Greenpoint, afterwards went to De Aar, the headquarters of our Battalion. . . . No one knows anything here, not even the papers, and I reckon you are as well informed as we are. This is a very pretty village, between Cape Town and Simonstown. The weather is certainly hot, but the firing up front has resulted in several heavy showers, and as there are a multitude of trees here the heat is not felt. I find khaki very comfortable. Our serge clothes lie in store at the docks. I am attached to the Munsters, but am sleeping in a tin hut with the 'details'—servants of officers who are in hospital and men with staff appointments. To illustrate the mixture we have here I will give a few regiments which are represented in my dormitory:—The Seaforths, Gordons, Argyle and Sutherlands, K.O.Y.L.I., Shropshires, Warwicks, Glosters, 1st and 2nd Dragoons (Scots Greys), K.R.R., 5th Lancers, R.A., R.H.A., R.E. (mim.), Dublin Fusiliers, W.R. Yorks, 2nd Life Guards, H.L.I., Devons and Black Watch. I am doing all right here, but things get very dull at times as I am the only 24th man for miles around. At Church Parade on Sunday, one of the military prisoners (a Pte. D.C.L.I.) knocked a warder down and got away; that made me pretty busy, but he was recaptured and brought back to-day. Our rations are bread and butter with coffee for breakfast, gipper (everlasting) for dinner, and dry bread and tea for tea. It's rather a nice feeling to be in charge of one's self. . . . It's my opinion the Cape Colony service is played out. It would have been a bitter revelation to me had I come here as a clerk from TS. . . . Undoubtedly the fellows at CT slave, and they always will, because they can never be united. Too many nationalities are mixed up there. I'd rather have £80 at home than £160 out here. Of course, when the Transvaal opens up things may be brighter for the TC. At present he is little above the black, and *that* means a good deal. Things are dear here. Labour *at present* is cheap. A Rand refugee begged a loaf of bread from me yesterday. Grass is an unknown luxury, we have sand instead; it's very handy for washing up after dinner. Milk is also an almost unknown luxury; and even the patients in hospital use condensed milk. Butter is principally imported from Australia. There are several Australians in hospital here, and very nice fellows they are. So are the Canadians I have met. The Boer prisoners I have seen are a sturdy lot. They don't seem sorry they are captured. Eucalyptus trees are exceedingly plentiful, so are doves and some smaller live things that roam around one at night time. A jackal somehow or other got in the woods last week and kept me awake with his unearthly cry. There are several vineyards about here. I don't think much of Cape Town. I am told Natal can lick Cape Colony into fits. . . . . I hope Baden-Powell will be able to hold out. He is a brave man and a useful one too. . . . I suppose I shan't be back in time to meet you at camp this year. I am in very good health."

NOTE—A splendid letter, necessarily cut down owing to repetitions. See previous one. No. 2 K.L.—R.E.K.

[*The three following letters have been delayed. They are inserted by request.*]
No. 2,547, Sapper **A. McAulay**, writing on board the s.s. "St. Andrew," January 26th, posts from Las Palmas the following :—

"s.s. 'St. Andrew,' January 26th.

"DEAR KEMP,—Our luck has been in so far—a good ship, calm passage, and plenty of provisions. Plenty of good meat on board, and numerous other things, which inclines one towards a holiday trip rather than a business

KHAKI LETTERS—*continued*.

one with Kruger. We left the dock at 4 a.m., so we were told, for when we woke up the vessel was slowly gliding down the Thames. We had many cheers and recognitions before we reached the sea. One fisherman shouted out, 'Give Kruger a big bump for me.' The pilot left at Dover, and the ship kept near land, and Dungeness was passed as the sun went down, and darkness stopped our view. Tuesday found us still gliding down Channel, the sea being rather rough, and towards evening some retreated to the ship's side rather unsettled. As we retired to our hammocks we received the disquieting news that we had entered the 'Bay.' It was not very noticeable while in our hammocks, except for the constant clatter of the horses' hoofs. Next morning the ship was rolling more, and sea-sickness became more noticeable; but still, it was fairly calm for the 'Bay.' Many turned in early that night to escape the turnings and twistings of the boat. The trumpet-call brought quite a revelation to the scene. We were told that the ship had left the 'Bay' at 2 a.m. that morning, and an appearance on deck showed a calm sea and prospects of an enjoyable time. As day went on, the sky became cloudless and the day bright, and everybody felt in the best of spirits. No serious cases of sickness amongst our men, only petty ailments. There are 491 men and about 400 horses, so plenty of work to do. Some of the fellows have had to do stable work, such as leading horses round for exercise. All have some fatigue to do, as we are rather short of men, on account of the large number of horses that need so much attention. But still, we must not grumble, as we are out on active service, and must put up with it."

No. 23,610, Sergeant **R. C. Luttrell,** s.s. "St. Andrew," Las Palmas. January 27th, writes :—

"DEAR DICK,—Glorious weather; getting quite hot; awning being fixed over the decks, and two baths erected for a flounder. We lost a horse this morning with inflammation of lungs. Pitched him overboard at 10 a.m. We are getting near Las Palmas. Has been a lovely trip up to the present. Plenty of fatigues, but also plenty spare time. I gave a lecture this morning on joining up, double current, duplex, and Wheatstone, &c. As no officer, have to do the best I can. We are anxious to get some news of the fighting, and so shall be pleased to see Las Palmas. We still feel pleased at the reception we met with from Waterloo by all hands. We have our sea-legs by now, and thoroughly enjoy it. Most of the troops aboard are Section D (married men, too). The horses—remounts, 'bus horses, &c. Being a cattle boat, not much room for physical exercise, &c. All 24th men well and jolly. Appetites getting quite alarming. Love to the boys."

✣ ✣ ✣

No. 21,066, Sapper **Chas. Jones** (WOL), sends the following letter :—

"s.s. 'St. Andrew,' nearing Las Palmas,
"Saturday, January 27th, 1900.

"DEAR COLOUR-SERGEANT KEMP.—This is my second attempt to write you. The first epistle near its finish was completely spoiled, myself with it almost, by an amateur deluge through the port hole on to the mess table. If that is my only contribution to the casualty list I sha'n't grumble. We were all heartily glad to see you and other friends at the dock on Sunday, but sorry, too, that you could not see the vessel off. It was 5 a.m., Monday, 22nd, before we got into the river; dropped the pilot at Dover in the afternoon with many letters of farewell he kindly took for us, and settled down on the dark deck for a quiet smoke and happy recollections of the places we could see marked out on the coast. Alas, those memories! Everything

KHAKI LETTERS—*continued.*

went well, and on Tuesday night Ushant flashed its warning light marking the entrance to the Bay, which meant a day or so of misery for some of us. However, the passage through this noted part was fairly smooth, and soon we were off Cape Finisterre, realising brighter skies and smoother seas. The weather has continued to improve until to-day. We are all in khaki, and find that quite warm enough. Several patients in the hospital with pneumonia are pulling round, as well they might in this beautiful climate. By the way, there is not much doubt that this illness was caused by the awful fog and damp at the docks on Saturday and Sunday, as we all started with colds more or less serious, although every man is as fit as possible now, and looking forward to cigars *ad lib.* in a few hours. This ship is said to be the best on the line, and it cannot be far from that. There is plenty of air space and good food, bar a little salt junk and biscuit, which brings on a raid on the dry (very dry) canteen. From the latter sufficient little luxuries can be obtained to eke out other things. We feel that we are unfortunate in having 400 horses on board without sufficient men (so we were told on complaining) to look after them. This means that our time is spent in exercising horses for two hours per day round the stuffy horse deck, while others of us clean their stalls out, in addition to the ordinary ship fatigues. Certainly we asked for working pay, and were promised it; let us hope we may get it. However, having had our growl, we obey, and are happy. Thanks so much for your visit on Sunday, and to all other friends for their happy send-off."

✢ ✢ ✢ ✢

No. 802, Sapper **A. Ray,** writing from Arundel on February 10th, says :—

" . . . . They mess about with our letters and parcels, and goodness knows where they go. We never receive them. There's nothing particularly stirring, or hasn't been till the past week. Up till then the usual few prisoners and wounded used to come through. We worked the wire, and used to go out shooting or looking out for live-stock in the way of tortoises and hedgehogs every day. This week, however, the troops have all left the positions round Colesberg, and been replaced by fresh troops, but a much smaller number. The soldiers going up and down the line made it a bit more lively just here; but now the Boers have found out that French's cavalry has gone, and are beginning to move. For the last few days we had warning that the Boers were trying to move on the north-east, and to look to our entrenchments. Yesterday we were told they were trying to get round us, so all our pickets were doubled, cavalry patrols went out, the artillery were turned out, and mules inspanned. In the afternoon some fellows came in and told us how they had been attacked by an ostrich, and had had a desperate fight. Eventually they killed it, but thought they might get into trouble about it, so hurried away.

"As soon as we heard it, we decided that I should go to this place, about three miles out, and bring in the feathers. I started about 4 p.m., in shirt-sleeves and Boer hat, and with a walking-stick. I stepped out across the veldt, and after half-an-hour found myself near the place I wanted. On looking up, I saw in the distance two men coming down the kopje. At first, in the distance, I thought they were niggers, but as they came nearer, I saw one had a long beard. Both were dark, had bandoliers, and rifles slung over their backs.

"I thought I was in a pretty mess, as I was quite unarmed, and run

KHAKI LETTERS—*continued*.

ning, as I supposed, up against two Boers. At first I thought of trying to slip, but came to the conclusion that they couldn't possibly help hitting me, so I determined to walk on. I turned half right, and tried to pass, but as they approached they opened out, unslung rifles, and presented at me.

"I did the only thing I could—walked up to them. I found one a white and one a nigger. The former asked me where I was going, to which I replied, ' Looking for feathers. " Well,' said he, 'you'd better get back, for if you get across those kopjes you'll get into Boer hands.' I questioned him, and he told me he belonged to the 26th Company of Engineers, had been driven in from Slingersfontein (22 miles away), and that our troops had to retreat. His mules had stampeded, and he narrowly escaped being taken. He shot a Boer, and had his Mauser carbine and bandolier on, and had been walking since nine. At first I thought he was a Boer trying to get information, so I questioned him.

" There happened to be some of the same Company at Arundel, so after a lot of enquiries, which he answered correctly, I asked him to give me his carbine. He did so, and I at once thought he was all right, as a Boer wouldn't be likely to give me his loaded gun. After walking a bit, I suggested we should run to warn camp, but they were so evidently done up, and they said they couldn't walk much farther, let alone run. Declining to take his gun, as it was such scrubby ground, I set off at a run for camp. I went for about two miles, when in the distance I saw a train just preparing to leave with half our garrison ; so took a turn left, and ran for the railway to stop it, as the train would have to pass the place where the Boers were reported to be advancing. I reported to the Commanding Officer, and he had the train backed to the station, and in turn reported to the Camp Commandant. I had a couple of patrols sent out to help the refugees, and they were brought in about half-an-hour later. There was considerable excitement. I was dead-beat with running and dry as possible, and the two refugees were nearly dead.

" We could hear firing on the kopjes, but apparently they knew we were warned, and didn't attempt to tear up the line. They burnt a farm near us, but although we expected attack all night, we were not disturbed. We entertained this chap, and next morning he left us to go back to Rensburg, but he left me a slide of Mauser ammunition from the Boer whom he killed.

" Up till now (Sunday, February 11th) we have been constantly expecting attack, as the Boers have fought our patrols only two miles away, and we know they are all around us. If you should hear of me being taken up to Pretoria handcuffed, I shall be glad to hear about the 'B' group there, as I expect it will be a bit monotonous. They are going to put us through to De Aar soon, so I suppose I shall work with Mr. Woode. Hope he won't want to fight me. It's impossible to get anything at all here, so to oblige the troops we had some jam, condensed milk, and cigarettes sent down, and now we've quite a shop here. Quite a new *rôle* for me, dispensing groceries to soldiers. Mr. Gamgee wrote once with all the 'B' group news up to January 4th, but I haven't heard since ; but should be glad to hear it all, and in detail, too. Mr. Woode joins me in kind regards to all our friends in the group, and to yourself.

" P.S.—I wasn't exactly frightened when I saw the supposed two Boers, but I didn't feel exactly happy.

" *Monday Morning.*—I've just opened this to give the latest bit of news. Last night we were suddenly warned that three trains were to leave Naauwpoort for Rensburg, and return in the middle of the night. No lights

KHAKI LETTERS—*continued.*

were to be carried, and no whistles blown. On the return journey one was to stop here for half-an-hour to load. Of course, there could only be one reason, viz., that our troops were being beaten, and had to get out of all these positions. We packed our kits and got ready, but little later heard they had better news, and Boers were retiring. At 4.30 this morning the alarm was sounded in our camp—six guns. Some Colonials were being driven in, but the Boers did not attack. Now the three trains, each 40 empty trucks, are waiting a bit higher up in case they're wanted, so I may be gone from here next time I write."

No. 27,844, Sapper **John Fallon,** writing from Rensburg (Military Tels.), February 9th, says :—

"MY DEAR COLOURS,—Your persuasive letter received about a week ago. Rather vague, you will say, but really we have no official record kept of days and dates, and we only record things by current events, such as 'Oh! I received the girl's photo the same day as the Major shaved!' (N.B. He hasn't done so for three weeks)—or, 'I got Bill's letter the day Jim said he *would* have a bath, but didn't'—or, 'Well, I wrote to Liz the day they served out the beer.' However, as nobody shaved, washed, or drank beer on the day I received your last, you can understand why no record was kept of it. Suffice it to say that it was received, and the contents greedily devoured by all 24th men. . . . Very little of note occurred since last writing you, beyond the fact that all the second draft of R.E. Tel. Battalion have been shifted from Cape Town after a month's rest there. C.S.M. Tee, Milton, Samuel, Wyatt (GY) and myself, represent the 24th at Rensburg (Mil), the remaining staff being comprised of 2nd division men, viz. : Sappers Chapple (SO) and Buckingham (PY). Tee is, of course, in charge, and we consequently get rid of the work—which is, as a rule, plentiful—in the usual expeditious manner. We had one night alarm, which was unproductive on either side, tho' many of us thought, 'Well, whatever will become of the accumulating shekels at home, if I get signed off.' However, the morning sun and a sumptuous breakfast (cooked in Sapper Milton's well-known style) helped to dispel our fears of the previous night, and we settled down to our day's work as if the enemy were a thousand miles away instead of five or six. I heard from De Aar yesterday that Sergt. Nelson had been invalided to Cape Town, suffering from sunstroke,* and Willis was also down with an affection of the throat ; otherwise the health of the troops is excellent. I don't think there's anything more to say at present, except to thank you heartily on behalf of 'our boys' here for the great and unflagging interest you take in our doings, and to say that you are at liberty to publish the whole or any portion of this incongruous epistle you may think proper. With kindest regards to yourself and all 24th men at home."

* See " Notes."

No. 220, Sergeant **J. W. Miller,** writing from Naauwpoort, January 29th, says :—" . . . . I am very pleased indeed to tell you and all the lads that I am having the very best of health up to the present. Not had an ache, barring, of course, the feathers in the bed seem inclined to be somewhat harder than they do at home ; that's about the worst—at least, that and the blinking dust storms. Ah ! and another thing, too, I was nearly forgetting,

KHAKI LETTERS—*continued.*

and I'm sure I ought not to, for whilst I'm penning this lot I have to keep stopping to smack my arm or neck. The flies are a perfect pest, and you should see our tent at night!—well, the only comparison that I can make is that it's just like our faces in the morning after a sandstorm has been blowing all night. It's lovely, especially at breakfast, either blowing flies off your bread and jam or else covering up your pot of tea with your fist. Well, we had a delightful trip in the train up country, only two nights in the train. Took a tour up and through the mountains; after leaving them there was scarcely any alteration in scenery the whole 500 miles, only like Aldershot and the Long Valley all the way. The only redeeming feature was the occasional sight of the Duke of Edinburgh's Own Volunteers, guarding all the bridges over which we had to pass—out away miles from nowhere. They must have felt very lonely. Sometimes we saw a few ostriches mopping it across the sand, making a deuce of a dust. I'm hoping I shall get up a bit higher. I want to take a pal and coax one of these dickie birds up to the fence, have a big bit of string, chuck it over his head and hold him tight, whilst the pal eases him of some of his laborious weight. . . . When we reached De Aar I thought I might have had a chance to go up to Modder River, where I unexpectedly found, while at Cape Town, that one of my brothers was stationed in the Naval Brigade off H.M.S. 'Monarch.' I had a letter from him, and he also tells me of another brother who is round Ladysmith, off H.M.S. 'Forte,' so our family is well in it. Hope we all get home together! The one at Modder says he has got plenty of oof. I don't know if he has done a bit of looting. Says his guns are overlooking Kimberley. So I, of course, was disappointed to get three-parts of the way up to him after absence of about six years, to have to come on in charge of this office and seven men; only got three from TS—Austin, Birch and Adams; remainder provincials. Don't do much—about 300 a day, but shocking long 'uns, all Ordnance, Commissariat, etc. Still, I'm safe up to the present, but don't get anything extra for being in charge, as the P.O. next door take all paid messages, so we get no revenue to bring me in a bit. . . . Was very sorry to hear about Jummy Lankstead going home Christmas Day. It's a bit hard getting letters at all out here. There's not half the fun here there was in Egypt; still, up to the present we're not in civilisation, only a few old Kaffirs looking like nobs of coal, and ugly mugs, yapping at each other all day. Some of 'em got lovely trousers on, half black, half white—think themselves howlers. Well, give my kind regards to all on the rounds. I am sorry to say I nearly forget the way to play cards, that my heart sometimes yearns for bygone days. They don't seem to have only just enough posh to get a few tins of jam and condensed milk at 9d. per tin; butter, 2s. per lb.; BEER—BASS, 2s. 6d. per bottle (mim.). What Oh! Not much chance for poor little 'Willie.' He would have to do the same as I do, treat himself to a pound of grapes, 3d., and a big bunch too. Only don't swallow the skin (mim.)."

No. 1,457, Sapper **H. J. Hayden** (LS), sends the following diary notes:—

"On board s.s. 'St. Andrew,'
" 8th February, 1900."

"*Sunday, 28th January*—Wake up to find ourselves just entering the harbour at Las Palmas; most charming place and lovely scenery. The

KHAKI LETTERS.—continued.

Commander of H.M. gunboat 'Furious' came alongside with despatches and for letters. We were disappointed at the officers not allowing any fruit to come on board. Steamed out of the harbour at 8 a.m.

"*Monday, 29th*—Much sea-sickness amongst the horses, several brought up on deck; also several men in hospital suffering from slight attacks of pneumonia. Artillerymen at revolver practice. Smoking concert in the evening.

"*Tuesday, 30th*—Splendid day and much warmer. Five of us told off to stock the canteen with mineral waters (also stock ourselves). This is the first work I have done on board, having been bad with sea-sickness. Now quite well again.

"*Wednesday, 31st*—Horse died this morning; carcase thrown overboard. Had a dip in the large canvas sea-bath; also washed underclothing, socks, &c. At 3.30 p.m. a bombardier died from malarial fever. Body sewn up in canvas, weighted with large sheets of iron and wrapped in the Union Jack. At 5.15 we were all paraded for the Burial Service. The captain of the ship met the body as it was borne up on deck, and read the Service. Amidst grim silence the body was thrown into the sea. At the same time the trumpeters sounded the 'Last Post,' and at the end of the Service the 'Reveille.' Thus ended a most impressive sight. The poor fellow was a reservist from Preston, and leaves a wife and four children. We all subscribed a shilling each. The money, amounting to £40, will be forwarded to his widow on our arrival at Cape Town.

"*Thursday, 1st February*—Very hot to-day. Seen several flying fish. Most of us going about bare-footed. This saves washing socks.

"*Friday, 2nd*—Another horse died. To-day we cross the Equator. Several of crew paraded the ship in comic costume, the chief character being Father Neptune. Several fellows were down to be shaved and ducked in the sea-bath, including eight young lieutenants of the Artillery. The officers were taken first. Number one got out of it by paying half-a-sovereign; number two wouldn't pay, so he was shaved with a tar brush and dipped. The third officer lost his temper when the tar brush was shoved into his mouth, and began to fight. He was promptly seized, and in being thrown into the water he dragged two of the men with him. The captain, seeing things were getting lively, jumped into the bath and stopped the proceedings.

"*Saturday, 3rd*—Nothing of any note beyond two horses dying.

"*Sunday, 4th*—Being Sunday, not much stirring. Paraded for Church Service at 10 a.m., which was conducted by the ship's captain. Had a luxury for dinner—'boiled potatoes.'

"*Monday, 5th*—We have a dry canteen on board of grocery store, managed by the under-steward. To-day, until the end of the voyage, I am his assistant. It's all right weighing cheese, butter, bread, biscuits, cake, jams, &c., and can always get plenty to eat. Another horse died.

"*Tuesday, 6th*—A nice breezy morning. Several sharks seen.

"*Wednesday, 7th*—A bullock and two sheep slaughtered. Smoking concert in the evening.

"*Thursday, 8th*—Do nothing, only lounge about smoking and reading.

"*Friday, 9th*—Artillery sharpening their swords. Another horse died.

"*Saturday, 10th*—Preparatory to disembarking, we have an entire change of underclothing. Wash dirty clothes. Concert in the evening.

"*Sunday, 11th*—Church Service at 10 a.m. Pack our South African field kit. Transport No. 62 passed us, homeward bound. She signalled 'Situation unchanged.' Ship rolls very much to-day.

KHAKI LETTERS—*continued.*

"Since leaving England the food has been very much the same. Get up at 5 a.m.; coffee served out 5 to 5.30; lime juice at 10.30; dinner at noon. Bully beef and biscuits one day, the next salt junk, bread, and preserved potatoes. Another day corned beef, preserved potatoes, and ship biscuits. Tea at 4 p.m., same as breakfast; also tea served out at 8 p.m., and lights out 9.30 p.m. The owners of the ship have given to each man one pound of hard tobacco, writing paper and pencils, and one pair of socks.

"*Monday, 12th*—Arrived Table Bay at 2 a.m. Docked Cape Town at 3.30 p.m. We are ordered to disembark here to-morrow, and proceed up to De Aar for further orders. We were all disappointed to hear that Ladysmith is not relieved, and of General Buller having to retire across the Tugela."

[NOTE.—Although this ground has been covered by another correspondent, it is thought the above is sufficiently varied to warrant its insertion. The "one horse" incident cannot be overlooked.—R.E.K.]

✣ ✣ ✣ ✣

27,483, Sapper **Frank Clark,** B Section, 1st Tel. Div., R.E, writing from De Aar, February 12th, says:—

"DEAR COLOUR-SERGEANT,—Just a line to thank you very much for your Christmas card, and to tell you that your weekly letters are much appreciated. To-day we received the news of Lankstead's death. It hardly seems possible that a man of his splendid physique should have been taken away by consumption. There is not much to report on here. Plenty of work just lately. . . . Some of the City Imperial Volunteers passed through last Sunday morning. They looked very serviceable in their rig-out—what a time they had before leaving ! . . . . We don't know how much longer we are likely to remain here. Hope to get a change soon, but as we have been expecting a change for the last month it is best to wait and see what turns up. I believe the last party have arrived at Cape Town, and that they are expected up here in about two days. . . . I expect they will soon be shifted from DAM. We have had our Queen's chocolate, and are all very pleased with it. You no doubt have heard that Sergeant Nelson has had sunstroke and gone down to Wynberg.* Do not think I have any more to say now, except that I wish to be remembered to all the boys.

"P.S.—Whibley wishes to be remembered to you. Thomas ditto. Will write soon.

* See "Notes."

✣ ✣ ✣ ✣

15,734, Trooper **V. E. Gray** (of "I" Company), 79th Company Rough Riders, Imperial Yeomanry, Aldershot, April 1st, says:—

"MY DEAR KEMP,—I trust a few lines respecting my movements since joining the Troop may not prove uninteresting to your readers, especially those of my own division, with whom I regret being unable to individually correspond. We came here on Saturday, 24th ult., and are quartered at the West Cavalry Barracks. We were at once set to work drawing bedding, blankets, and the necessary kit. On Monday, the real work commenced. Reveille at 5.30 a.m.; stables, 6 a.m.; breakfast, 7.45 a.m.; parades, 8.30 a.m., 11 a.m., and 2 p.m.; and stables again from 5 p.m. till 6 p.m. The evenings in barracks are passed very pleasantly. In our room we have a piano, and singing and music are indulged in until 'lights out.' We have plenty of hard work, but our officers are experienced soldiers and gentlemen, which makes service under them a pleasure. We are expecting to sail on the 10th inst., and one and all will not be sorry to leave this, the least loved of all military centres. I hope in my next letter to give you more interesting details of our doings in South Africa. With kindest regards."

Alfred William Hawkins.

THE untimely death of Sapper **A. W. Hawkins** was a shock to the C.T.O., especially to the members of the 24th Mx.R.V. and his friends in the Cable Room. Letters received from him gave no indication that anything was amiss, and it was hard for his colleagues at home to realise the fact when his name appeared in the Casualty List. It, however, proved only too true,—our comrade succumbed to that fearful scourge, enteric fever, on Tuesday, March 13th, at Orange River.

ALFRED WILLIAM HAWKINS was 22 years of age. He entered the Central Telegraph Office on December 12th, 1893, being posted to the Cable Room, and forming, with eleven others, the first reinforcement of the old Submarine Staff. He proved himself to be one of the most promising Baudôt & Hughes manipulators. He was enrolled as a member of the 'I' Company in December, 1894, and was transferred to the Royal Engineer Reserve ('L' Coy.) on January 15th 1897. Always a bright and enthusiastic Volunteer, always cheery and well disposed, always a friend whom one could feel was of the genuine kind, he was one who most willingly offered his services for Queen and Country in the War in South Africa. He sailed with the second detachment of Ours on board

the s.s. "Canada," which left Liverpool on December 1st, 1899, and arrived at Capetown just before Christmas.

He was mostly connected with the Signalling Department in the 24th, and on several occasions was accompanist at the Signallers' Annual Dinner; and was a Solo Bass in the Choir at St. Matthew's, Bayswater, W.

The photo reproduced here was taken last year while staying at Torquay. In this number will also be found two letters that have been received from him, and probably they are his last.

IN MEMORIAM.

✠

Sapper A. W. Hawkins, C.T.O., London.

Died Orange River, March 13th, 1900.

✠

Little we thought as we said " Good-bye ! "
   Returning the clasp of your hand—
That you went, for the sake of the old flag, to die,
   Away in the unknown land ;
You went with the light-hearted soldier-host
   That answered the War-god's call—
You yielded the hopes that you valued most,
   And gave to your country—all !
But the hand of the War-god smote you not—
   No victim of shot or shell—
Though you died—and death is the soldier's lot—
   At the stroke of disease you fell !
And hence, from the Homeland by wide-rolling wave,
   Go thoughts from old friends to your far distant grave.

TSF.   W. H. F. WEBB.

The following letter has been received by a Colleague in TSF., where **A. W. Hawkins** was known as "'Enery" :—

"Orange River, February 17th, 1900.

" I was very pleased indeed to have your letter, and must also thank you very much for sending me out the programme of your concert (TSF Patriotic Concert, in aid of *Daily Telegraph* Fund). I daresay you thought of little ''Enery' that night, and wondered what he was doing. Well, on referring to my diary—I have kept one since leaving England—I find that I was down at a friend's house—or, rather, the friend of one of our fellows—and after having a swim in Table Bay, went to supper at his house. Well, since that date, I have spent a week at De Aar (awfully sandy), and for the past three weeks have been at Orange River. I have spoken many times to Con (O'Sullivan), who is still at Modder, but before long may be in Kimberley. Of course, by the time you get this letter the news of the relief of this place will have become quite stale. This morning we had information from the officer commanding at Zoutpans Drift (a place about ten miles from here) to the effect that firing was heard there, or, rather, north-east of it, and that the mounted patrols were retiring ; so that it would not be at all improbable that we might have the Boers down here yet. We have several prisoners here, and among them, unfortunately, one of the Civil Telegraphists, who had been rather indiscreet on the wires; although I don't suppose for one moment anything was intended in what was said. At any rate, the result is that a military TC has to be in the Civil Office night and day to prevent or take notice of and report any conversation which may take place. To-day I have done duty from 6 a.m. to 4 p.m., and from 6 to 11 p.m., 'Policeman' in the Civil Office! We have had a hard time of it with the work, which, owing to the presence of the 7th Division for about a week, made us very busy. Now we manage to work a ten-hour day, but you see that has been prevented, owing to this little affair. We used to go down to the Orange River for a swim every evening, and if a train was going there 'commandeer' it. Last night we had the pleasure of coming back in a truck. Still, anything will do for us now, even a TS steak, which at times we are wont to think about. We get chronic sandstorms here—almost blind you. Hoping all friends are well in TSF, with kind remembrances to all, and same to self,

"Yours very sincerely,
"'ENERY.

"P.S.—My number is 458, not 488."

The following letter, written by No. 458, Sapper **A. W. Hawkins**, Orange River, February 24th, has been received by C. W. Hawkins, of "I" Company, a relative :—

"DEAR CHARLIE,—Thank you so much for sending me out that parcel, and thank ———, too, for the 'pudden,' which, of course, went round the office, and was a fair treat. I received it last Monday, and also half a pudding from ———, which was jolly fine, and both of them reached here in fine condition. I got my Queen's chocolate last Monday, and shall probably send it home untouched. We are getting along here very well, and now that Kimberley is relieved, and the work becoming quite slack, we are all hoping to push further up country. The first train, consisting of trucks, came down from Kimberley last Tuesday, and the engine, which had been shut up in the town the whole time that the siege lasted, together with the driver and stoker, was covered in front with a large 'Union Jack.' When I saw it I cut off sharp, made for the flag, and jolly soon ripped a piece of the flag off, as a souvenir, you know. Shortly afterwards the whole of the lower part had gone, and if someone had not stopped them the poor flag would not have stood an earthly chance. After a little while, one of the A.M.C. corporals came along with his camera, and off I went with two or three others to assist him in carrying it. I got on the front of the engine, and Bannister, from Manchester, and Catling, from Euston, got on the other side, and we had a fine photo taken. I have bought one, and shall send it home, so that you can just have a glimpse of Your Humble in a lovely auburn, flowing beard ! We are having lots of wounded down every day, and hospital trains are in great requisition. We have got the rainy season just starting here now, and regularly, almost every afternoon, we get a terrific sandstorm, which you cannot stay out in, and when the wind ceases, down comes the rain like a sheet, and lightning and thunder, which makes you pretty well quake. There is so much iron in the kopjes and ironstone, and the lightning plays round these little hills marvellously. Next morning up comes the sun, scorches the ground, and 2 p.m. sees another sandstorm, followed by the same rain, and this occurs almost as regularly as clockwork. We have had two alarms since last I wrote you, as there is a big commando of Boers and rebels knocking about here; and a patrol which went out last Thursday at 8 a.m. did not return until the next day, although it was expected back about midday. The Boers evidently want to have a shot at the bridge here, which, once blown up, could not be repaired for some months, owing to the rainy season starting the rivers, which will soon begin to swell up. I had to attend a Court-martial yesterday (23rd) as a witness in the trial of one of the Civil Telegraphists for divulging official news of movements of troops to a T.C. at Strydenberg, where they are all disloyal Dutch. It is a matter of chatting on the wires, and the fellow at Hopetown, intermediate station, tapped it, and let his tape run, so that all remarks were reproduced yesterday at the Court. He will get off all right, as he was once postmaster at Douglas before the Boers came there, and has splendid testimonials from Sir A. Milner and others. It is very funny here. Did you ever 'watch' for your breakfast? We have any amount of chickens next door to the office, and we sit outside in the morning early, talking (?), and when we hear certain sounds which tell us an egg has been laid we 'commandeer' it immediately. We are all splendid foragers. . . . Well, ta-ta, Charlie; take care of yourself. With love to all, and also the 'Wanderer in Egypt' when you write.

"I remain, yours very affectionately,

"ALF.

"P.S.—Am night duty as policeman in the Civil Office. . . . We have got two niggers to look after us here. One of them has a coat of many, many colours. Fancy a sack with a hole for the head and arms, patched all sorts of colours!"

The following cutting is taken from the *Essex Weekly News*, March 23rd, 1900. It may perhaps be read in conjunction with the above:—

TRAITOR SENTENCED AT ORANGE RIVER.

Captain Fred Taylor, commanding one of the two Chelmsford Companies of the 2nd V.B.E.R., has received a letter from Private R. Soffe, of the C.I.V.'s, formerly of Chelmsford, dated from Orange River. After a reference to the journey up from Cape Town, the writer says:—" This is said to be a very healthy place; we are camped close to the railway, and about half-a-mile from the Orange River. We have all had our bandoliers filled with 100 rounds of ammunition, which we always have to carry with our rifles and sidearms when on drill. Yesterday we marched out to a 'bathing parade' in the Orange River; one half guarded the banks while the other half bathed. The water is very muddy, but it is wet, and that is the chief thing! We have 45 Boer prisoners here. They are kept within a wire fence, with sentries posted round. They are a very mixed lot. There is also a telegraphist in with them who was at the station here, and was caught giving information to the enemy. He has been tried and found guilty, and we hear he is to be shot this evening. A firing party has gone off somewhere."

"Khaki Notes."

DUKE OF NORFOLK IN KHAKI. The Duke of Norfolk, Postmaster-General, left for South Africa on Saturday (March 31st), in the "Carisbrooke Castle." His Grace, who is honorary lieutenant-colonel of the 2nd V.B. Royal Sussex Regiment, is going to the front as an officer in the Sussex Mounted Infantry. His only brother, Major Lord Edmund Talbot, M.P., is A.D.C. to General French. When the first call was made for Volunteers the Duke of Norfolk made an urgent application to the War Office to be sent to the front, but his application was refused. The orders he has now received to join the Sussex Mounted Infantry have naturally given the Duke considerable satisfaction.—*Daily Mail.*

It was stated last night (March 28th), in the Parliamentary Lobby that the Duke of Norfolk sent in his resignation of the Postmaster-Generalship four days ago. Mr. Balfour made a statement on the subject in the House on March 29th. In reference to the Postmaster-General, Mr. Balfour answered simply and tersely, "The Duke of Norfolk has resigned." "Has the Government accepted his resignation?" asked a Member—a point that this curt answer had left unsolved. Mr. Balfour simply nodded.

Major the Duke of Norfolk, attached to the 69th (Sussex) Company Imperial Yeomanry, left Arundel Castle on Saturday morning for Southampton, where he embarked on the "Carisbrooke Castle." The inhabitants dressed the town with bunting, while a large crowd assembled at the station to wish his grace "God speed."—*Daily Mail,* April 2nd.

The Marquis of Londonderry, K.G., is the new Postmaster-General in succession to the Duke of Norfolk. It was officially announced on April 2nd that the Queen had signified her approval of the appointment.

✣ ✣ ✣ ✣

"PONIARD, LONDON." Wm. Payne, Esq., Supt., Moorgate Buildings, E.C., has registered "Poniard, London" (*via* Eastern). If every "L" Co. man will forward to either him or myself the address of their relatives, such information will be booked and kept for reference. As soon as a cablegram is received, he (Mr. Payne) has undertaken to advise those at home. The man referred to in this "Emergency Cable" will be considered as the one whose name is given as the sender. Example: "Poniard London Fever Wynberg Atkins." It will be understood that Atkins is down with fever, is now at Wynberg Hospital, and the friends of Atkins will be informed. There may be many occasions where Emergency Cables may be useful; the comrades could then wire home at a great saving in cost, besides being put into telegraphic communication and avoiding delay. Mr. Payne sent for me, laid his scheme before me, and I could not but thank him—in your name—for his great kindness and thoughtfulness.

✣ ✣ ✣ ✣

THE B. GROUP (C.T.O.) has received a box of Queen's chocolate from Sapper C. J. Woode, with the request that a taste of the contents may be given to each "B-ite" (hardly a bite each), while the box itself is to become the property of the lucky "Mistress of the Group." All are delighted.

KHAKI NOTES—continued.

STATIONERY. Our boys are writing home on all kinds of paper. It is interesting to read letters written on Press flimsies headed "Orange Free State" (printed in blue), and then posted stampless in a Service envelope addressed "Den Postmeester te ———"; "Postkantoor" being in the left lower corner. Others snap up and use paper on which is a red cross and the words : "A Gift from the British Red Cross Society," as the head-line ; while others prefer the note-paper bearing crossed flags (in colours) and headed " Young Men's Christian Association—Canadian Contingent, on active service with British Forces, South Africa." They own the flags by illuminating them with the much-admired initials " R.E." (Mr. Printer, don't make an error : R.E. please, *not* R.E.K.) The more shoppy chums prefer the ordinary Cape telegraph forms. But we like them all. Keep the pot a-boiling, boys. You're doing well, and your stay-at-home colleagues are all eager to hear from you.

✤ ✤ ✤ ✤

20 VERSUS 16. I know there are a great many telegraphists who enjoy a few figures. I don't think the following set will mystify any reader, nor will it be "giving the game away." On the other hand, it will go to prove how much the subscriber gains, and how beneficial the 20-page booklet is for him all round. An example :—

5 issues of " K.L." each of 16 pages = 80 pages, and cost 5d.
4 " " " 20 " = 80 " " 4d.

What do we find ? We find the readers gain one penny, besides receiving their 80th page a fortnight earlier than if they waited for No. 5 with its 16 pages. This prevents delay on our " Letters," and when I ask for voluntary assistance in the way of carriage to be borne by my subscribers, it is not such a big item for them—individually—as it seems. At the same time, the issue of 20 pages in place of 16 costs me over £2 ; or, for the four issues, £8 won't cover it. In return for such an outlay I am asking much less from you, and it won't amount to the penny you have saved. I am convinced my friends prefer the extra four pages. We will still have the matter " under consideration." In the meantime, do just as you like.

✤ ✤ ✤

KHAKI POSTAGE FUND. Mr. George Costello has, I am pleased to say, now resumed duty. He is, however, not now in the " L " Division, but on the Special Staff. If my readers will kindly turn up page 38, No. 2, " Khaki Letters," they will find something that I am sure they will like to have a finger in. Every Division, Group, etc., should arrange for an Assistant Distributor, so that when one is on early duty the other is on late ; this will overcome some little inconvenience that may arise. The Assistant Distributor could then arrange such a small duty as collecting for the " Khaki Postage Fund," and he could also note the names of those who are sending copies out to our men. I have learned that several do this, and they like to do it—well and good. We don't want to send two copies to one man. Give his name, and I will erase it from my list and give the honour of supplying him with " K.L.'s" over to you. But when you write him, don't forget to mention the reason he does not get a copy from me. He may think " Colours " is slighting him. This done, hand over to G.C., who will be pleased to see you, and in our next number we hope to give the result. Make Monday next, April 8th, Khaki Day, and see that every subscriber is given an opportunity.

KHAKI NOTES—*continued.*

3d. SUBS. With the present number our 3d. subscribers have had their supply. In other words, we have completed our contract. We must now start again, and I ask you, my good friends, to see your Distributor and hand him another 3d., so that we may continue supplying you with "K.L.'s" that will carry you up to No. 6. There were some prophets abroad who thought the 3d. subs. would not all be inclined to continue, but I have no fear of that. EVERY ONE of you MUST go on. You must "see us through," you know. I hardly know why I should mention this, for I am persuaded there is no one—if he or she thinks a moment—who will drop it. The spirit of the booklet must not be lost sight of; the literary merit, I know, is not what it might be; but that's not the point. Keep up the enthusiasm, don't break rank; if you want to change at all, get another subscriber, and if you all do this we shall double our circulation. It is easier to all concerned to have the 3d. payment system. You pay once and you are supplied three times. Your Distributor doesn't annoy you so often, you know. And as regards myself, well, I'm not building houses, but I'm paying my way, and I know how to go on. I know what to say to my printer, and I know how many copies I want printed To see 2,000 on my mantelpiece might be pretty, but what an eyesore! Yes, friends, 3d. for the next three, please. Thank you.

SAPPER C. J. WOODE (1,275) sends a cabinet photo home, but no one would recognise him in his Boer hat and beard.

SERGEANT J. H. NELSON (21,410) is, I am pleased to say, at work again, fully recovered. He was not at Wynberg Hospital with sunstroke, as stated in some of the letters to hand, but was suffering from low fever in the Rondebosch Hospital.

SAPPER L. ORWIN (1,547) writes from the General Hospital, Naauwpoort Junction, saying he is in bed "knocked up."

SAPPER D. McLAREN (2,340), of EH, is reported by the General of Communications, Cape Town, to be seriously ill.

SAPPER W. R. WILLIAMS (852), 1st Tel. Div., R.E. (son of Assistant Superintendent), is also reported by General of Communications, Cape Town, to be seriously ill.

SERGEANT T. WATSON (241), A.P.O.C., died of enteric fever at Modder River, March 17th.

SERGEANT C. E. MINARDS (283), A.P.O.C., died of enteric fever at the base hospital, Maritzburg, March 24th.

F. W. G. WHITE, Senior Telegraphist, after an illness of only eight or nine days, died on April 1st, of rheumatic fever.

VERY INTERESTING LETTERS have had to be held over. They are from Adams, Bourlay (SY), A. J. Brooks, Catling, Corkill, Forth (LS), Hayden (LS), Metcalfe, Minors, Sterling, Stimpson, Woodrow (SO), Woolley and York. Also those received by last Cape mail from Abbott (BM), Ferguson (LV), Jenner, Luttrell, Orwin and others.

COLOURS.

"KHAKI LETTERS," One Penny. By post, Three Halfpence.

All posted letters containing Remittances, Orders, MSS., &c., must be addressed to R. E. KEMP, 12, JERRARD STREET, LEWISHAM, S.E.
Postal Orders should be made payable at Loampit Vale, Lewisham, S.E.

Printed by E. G. BERRYMAN & SONS, *Blackheath Road, London, S.E.*

"Khaki Letters" from ....
"My Colleagues in South Africa."

CORRESPONDENCE FROM THE

POST OFFICE TELEGRAPHISTS

OF THE

24th MIDDLESEX (P.O.) RIFLE VOLUNTEERS

(Royal Engineer Reserves),

ON ACTIVE SERVICE.

THE BOND THAT BINDS US—FRIENDSHIP—COMRADESHIP.

Published fortnightly for the Postal Telegraph Service.
Conducted by COLOUR-SERGEANT R. E. KEMP, *Central Telegraph Office, London.*

Nos. 4 and 5.   APRIL 20TH, 1900.   PRICE ONE PENNY.

Central Telegraph Office,

London, E.C.

DEAR COMRADES, ONE AND ALL,
Greetings! I have to thank you for your letters again, written as they are—in many cases—under very trying circumstances. Nothing can please us more than a continuance of this correspondence in the same happy fashion as heretofore. I assure you most candidly that your fellow telegraphists are very eager to learn of your doings, adventures, and so forth. It forms most interesting food matter for us all. Robbie Burns is not on our Editorial Staff, neither is Charles Dickens one of our Correspondents at the front, but you need not fear for your notes and narratives being given due respect and honour. We look at your will, not at your way. No one outside the dignified (?) sphere of a Carpist has ever thought of pulling you to pieces. Patriotism, goodwill, friendship, and esteem smoothes your way and the judicious " Colours " puts them through the filter, should they need it. "The Sapper" says, in its April number, "KHAKI LETTERS is interesting from beginning to end. . . . We think this little book will *commend itself* to our readers, &c.," while an esteemed R.E. friend of mine at Chatham, puts his pen to paper and says "it is a *rattler*, and it is praised very much by all the Corps people here to whom I have shewn it. It is an excellent idea, and you deserve great praise for the trouble you are taking, &c." Tut, tut! never mind the praise. Tut, tut! never mind the trouble. I've set myself the task of taking the chain that might have been broken and forging a link to strengthen it, even such a golden link as the little book before you; and, Comrades, you and I, will see there's no fracture in it until we meet again (D.V.). There's one thing I might add. The booklet is becoming better known, and it seems to be speaking for itself.

Now a little news for you. Am sorry I must curtail it so.

A Special Army Order has been issued, from which the following extracts are taken:—

The Secretary of State has approved of the period for which Volunteer infantry brigade camps are held being extended, for 1900, to 28 days; and the Commander-in-Chief trusts that all ranks will attend in large numbers and remain as long as possible in camp, so as to avail themselves of this opportunity of gaining instruction.

The training of units will be mainly directed to—

Securing increased musketry efficiency by firing whilst in camp the special course laid down in the appendix. The annual allowance of ammunition will be increased this year, from 90 rounds to 150, for each member of a Volunteer infantry corps firing the special course before November 1st, 1900. Camps will only be formed at places where suitable and ample rifle range accommodation is available.

Ceremonial drill will not be practised on more than two days of the 28 spent in camp.

A special grant of £2 2s. will be allowed to the corps for each member who attends in camp during the above period for at least 14 full days, 12 of which must be week days, and fires, whilst in camp, the whole of the special course of musketry.

The special grant will only be granted provided that at least 50 per cent. of the members of the corps comply with the above conditions.

Pay will be issued to all ranks at Army rates for the actual days in camp, including the days of arrival and departure. Travelling expenses will be met by the issue of the usual allowance under the Volunteer Regulations.

Leave on full pay, at the rate of two days a week (of which only one shall be a week day), will be allowed to all who actually attend camp for 14 days or more. No leave will be allowed during the days devoted to musketry.

Separation allowance will be paid to the families of all married Volunteers who earn Army rates of pay for not less than 14 days.

Special musketry course to entitle efficients to the additional grant. Nature of practice:—Deliberate volleys at 300, rapid volleys at 300, rapid independent firing at 300, rapid volleys at 500, deliberate volleys at 600, and rapid volleys at 600 yards; 7 rounds each. Also, at the discretion of the commanding officer, 18 rounds. Total 60. An officer must be present at each of these practices.

Officers commanding units may, with the approval of the officer commanding the brigade, expend 21 rounds of the above in attack practice or battalion field firing. In such cases three of the above practices will be omitted from the course.

This course will be fired whilst in camp, and is additional to the usual class firing courses. Where time admits, and range accommodation is available, units may also fire, whilst in camp, the usual course of class firing. Recruits who have not fired their course prior to going into camp, may similarly be allowed to do so while there.

Now, just briefly, our new **Prize Scheme.** It will interest you.

Battalion Prizes. For highest individual scores made in trained soldiers' course. 51 Prizes, as follows:—1st, a Special Prize for Best Shot of Battalion, and £5; 1 at £4, 2 £3, 5 £2, 10 £1, and 20 at 10s., 12 Prizes at £2 to the "Best Shot" of Companies. Battalion Shot cannot take both Battalion and Company Prizes. The latter going to second best Shot in the Company. No man can take a Prize unless he has fired his Individual Course by July 31st, and Efficient in Drill by Inspection, and fired in collective practice before the end of the year. Only Scores to count that are made on Regimental Musketry Parades.

Surveyors' Cup. For Recruits who have attended at least 32 drills before Annual Inspection. Class Firing being added to drills above 32 attended before the Annual Inspection. One point for each drill over 32. 1st Prize, CUP and 30s., and 11 others.

Aldershot Cup. To be fired for during the Annual Training. ONE PRIZE:—CUP, and Section Commander, £1. 10 men, 10s. each.

Colonel's Cup. (Sergeants' Prize). For the highest score in the trained soldiers' course. ONE PRIZE:—CUP and £5. Should the winner also be Battalion Shot, the money Prize will go to the next best Shot, and so on, provided that no Sergeant receives a Prize of value more than £5. The money Prize will only be given to Sergeants who have performed the duties of Register Keeper on at least Six Musketry Parades. Every Parade beyond six to count One point in addition.

Officers' Prize, Fyer's Cup, Cuca: Cocoa Challenge Cup, etc.

☞ **N.B.—Any man returning from South Africa before October 31st, will be allowed to compete for Prizes.**

The C.O. informs me there is nothing definitely decided as to our duties, etc., yet. Our Camp time will be from July 21st to August 18th. Probably the usual number of men will be arranged for by the L.P.S. We are likely to see Salisbury this year. More anon.

A week or so ago the papers published the intimation that 60 more Telegraphists were required. This at once caused a stir. I really think a good number of the aspirants for the front must have had ready-written letters in their pockets, for I received no less than six, by post, the same afternoon. They only had to insert the date, you know, seal it up, and drop it in the post, forgetting, of course, in their haste, to enclose a stamp for reply. I'm sure a good many people think your old Colour-Sergeant is a millionaire. However, the news was unreliable, or if not so bad as that, our Colonel, whom I interviewed a few days afterwards, knew nought of such requirement.

You will notice your Company is increasing still, and of course they go from mine, but strange as it may seem, the more you take the more there are remain. "I" Company now stands over 150 men, and the battalion itself goes beyond 1,500.

In addition to the men whose names I gave you in my letter published in No. 3 KHAKI LETTERS, the following men have joined the "L" Company and are at Aldershot waiting for "G.":—

4382 C. N. Bateman,	NG	4392 W. Gilmour,	GW	4609 H. A. J. Foster,	TS
4383 S. H. Haycock,	LV	4393 J. J. McSweeney,	MR	4610 A. E. Stevens,	,,
4384 H. T. Roberts,	,,	4399 J. H. E. Walker,	LV	4611 W. W. Tozer,	,,
4385 J. F. McPherson,	GW	4402 R. D. S. Norman,	SS	4612 F. Somerville,	EES
4386 T. Hamilton,	,,	4603 R. Robson,	NT	4613 W. J. Hargreaves,	TS
4387 J. Y. Fox,	,,	4604 J. W. Lincoln,	,,	4614 F. R. White,	,,
4388 J. McQueen,	,,	4605 J. J. Bramwell,	,,	4615 R. W. E. Lasham,	,,
4389 A. E. Gibson,	,,	4606 A. Walkley,	BS	4616 W. E. Burden,	SO
4390 W. Kyle,	,,	4607 W. H. Butt,	DO		
4391 T. R. Stevens,	,,	4608 E. J. Allen,	TS		

462, H. F. Picker (LV), who is now fit, is at Aldershot with the rest. Among the men mentioned above there are four in waiting, and naturally they are very anxious to know when they will leave Old England's shores. Their names are Burden, Walkley, Norman and Butt. Their only chance for the next batch is, apparently, the illness of their more fortunate comrades.

The first and second Divisions are mostly kept up to full strength, and when that is attained they number about 173 and 165 respectively, or close upon 340 in all. At the present time, however, owing to their ranks being swelled from so many sources, they stand at no less than 540 on active service in South Africa, or on their way there.

A Third Division is in the course of formation, and already some 30 linemen and operators have left Chatham for Aldershot, where they will form the nucleus of the new Division.

Owing to the Easter holidays and the fact that people *will* run away from work, I am compelled to go to press earlier than usual. Another item that adds to the necessity for such a course is the fact of this being a double number. In it you will find another of my songs, which, when Jimmy Miller has time, he can sing to you. He knows the tune.

I with others am very sorry to hear of the further casualties in the TB's, coming as they do from amongst those we so well know. I would call your attention to the splendid photo that is inserted in this number, and you will be pleased to know that you were not left out of the reckoning when good old "Bob" decided to put it in your representative booklet.

Trusting you are all well, happy, and cheerful,

Yours most heartily,
R. E. KEMP,
Colour Sergeant.

To the "L" Co. in South Africa.
Good Friday, April 13th, 1900.

COPYRIGHT.—"Khaki Letters" must not be used without permission.—R. E. KEMP.

Khaki Letters.

No. 1,449, Sapper **L. A. Bourlay** (SY) (1st Tel. Div. R.E.), Rensburg, in a letter dated about February 10th, writes :—

"DEAR CHUMS,—After a six weeks' sojourn in the Cape Colony, I consider myself entitled to give you my impressions of the country.

"We landed in Cape Town on the morning of December 20th, about two o'clock, and marched through the outskirts of the town to a place called Green Point Common, where we passed a most uneventful though pleasant month. The loyal proportion of the citizens vied with each other in showing us kindness—feeds, smokers, and free letter writing were of daily occurrence. About December 29th a feeling of uneasiness pervaded the camp, and orders from our Colonel *re* guards, pickets, outposts, &c., became very numerous. Every man was instructed to sleep on his arms, and the sentries were ordered to keep one round in the 'emergency hole' of their pouches, so that in the event of a surprise no time would be lost in loading. The reason for this was that a rising of the disloyal Cape Dutch (of whom large numbers were known to be in Cape Town) was hourly expected. On New Year's Eve at midnight, as we lay asleep, we were suddenly aroused by all the vessels in the harbour hooting like mad, and immediately three guns from the Castle boomed out. Now, the signal for a general alarm was to have been three shots from the quick-firer at the Castle, and in the general confusion it was not noticed that these three shots were not from a quick-firer, so in about one minute the whole camp was under arms waiting orders. In about three minutes we got the order to turn in again by order of the Camp Commandant. It was then that it dawned upon us that it was only the shipping in the harbour welcoming the New Year. All the clerks of the division who were not sent up country at once were detailed for duty in Cape Town office. I was amongst that most unhappy number.

"I venture to assert that to any well-regulated home superintendent their method of working would be fatal in five minutes. You never saw such a state of affairs in your lives." [Goes on to describe method of working.] "The first day I was in attendance I noticed *a week's* delay. However, it was noticeable that after a few days the delay steadily decreased. You ought to see the skins the poor chaps get ; five or six errors in one message is common. The worst of it is that they keep the tape running all the time, so there is no getting out of the consequences of your misdeeds. Well, enough shop. Our whole section proceeded up country to De Aar about a

KHAKI LETTERS—*continued*.

week ago, through the Karoo Desert, and a more desolate piece of country I never want to see. Nothing but ostriches and a few springboks to be seen. From De Aar a TS man, one of the R.E.'s, and myself were ordered to Rensburg, with General French, where we are now. From my tent door I can see our gunners dropping lyddite into the Boer position. There isn't much danger for us in the office, but the cable-cart job is really an exciting one, as the Boers know exactly what it is, and consequently, whenever it is exposed, it becomes the target for a hundred bullets. Several of our chaps have had a feeding-up of it, and don't wish for any more.

"It's all right charging with a troop of cavalry against odds, for then there is a chance of getting your own back ; but sitting in a jolting cart, drawn by ten kicking mules, and the bullets whistling round you, sending 'R.D.'s' ain't all lavender ; at least, so our chaps say. Anyway, I shall know for myself when we make an advance, as the R.E. who came with me from De Aar and myself are attached to the cable section. It don't worry me much, though, for the danger, in my opinion, would be amply compensated for by the novelty. This is the railway terminus. Beyond here the railway is in Boer hands.

"The trains here are very speedy, some of them rushing through the country at the alarming speed of twenty miles an hour. We came from Naauwpoort here in open trucks under a blazing sun. The climate is all that can be desired if only a man had enough money to quench his thirst. What with 130 to 140 degrees of heat and dust storms a careful man can develop about forty first-class thirsts per diem. I have seen Lord Roberts, Kitchener, and Colonel Hector Macdonald, the latter of whom did me the honour to use my back as a writing-desk. All troops, except just enough to hold enemy in check, have left here to-day for the Modder ; so don't expect a forward move from here for some time. Have lots more to say, but no time to say it. With kind regards to you all."

No. 23,764, Sapper **C. T. Catling** (EUS), in a letter dated Orange River, February 12th, says :—

". . . I am getting on A1 and in the best of health, which is a great deal to say when you live under the conditions which exist here. I am on night duty this week, or I might say eighteen hours out of twenty-four. Plenty of overtime, but no extra pay for it. I go on at 6 p.m., and at 6 a.m. the next morning I wake my reliefs. I then help the orderly to prepare breakfast. We have to go a quarter of a mile for well water, or we have to drink that which comes from the Orange River, which is very muddy indeed. Then we have to find wood to make a fire to boil the water. The orderly in the meantime has drawn the meat for the day, over a pound for each man, generally a leg of mutton and some chops. The chops we have for breakfast at 7 a.m. We are able to buy twopennyworth of Quaker oats (cooked), so you see we are living in grand style. After breakfast I help the orderly to tidy up the tent and wash up. We can now get some grapes very cheap. Yesterday I got a double bunch for threepence. It weighed quite two and a half to three pounds, and I may tell you that they were soon demolished with the aid of a few of the boys. This place is much better than De Aar, as there is not so much dust and sand flying about, and the living is much better. Last night thousands of locusts were flying about, and the office got

KHAKI LETTERS—*continued*.

quite uncomfortable through them, flying everywhere and into every crevice they could find; also striking one in the face and alighting on our clothing. I caught about thirty yesterday. I'm not used to luxuries, so I'll be generous and send a few home to my friends in London. Yesterday, whilst the Horse Guards and 2nd Life Guards were crossing the Orange River in a train, they ran into an ox span, consisting of sixteen oxen drawing a cart. Several of the oxen were killed, and the train had a very narrow escape of being wrecked and thrown into the river. The driver jumped off his engine, and was badly hurt. The stoker stuck to his post, and no doubt saved them all. Nevertheless, it was a bad thing for the cows, for within an hour of the accident the troops were cooking steaks, kidneys, &c., so you see 'It's an ill wind, &c.' The work here is very heavy. We have four circuits, two stations on two of them, De Aar and Belmont—Modder River and Modder River Siding—Zoutpansdrift—and one to Witteputs. The messages are very long ones, some of which are in cypher. The De Aar circuit never ceases all day long, and we have five and six hours' delay on our work. Troops have been passing through here all the week by train, not mentioning those who marched all the way. Before this letter reaches you no doubt you will have read of a great battle having been fought. When on duty night time I manage to get about two hours' sleep, in doses from fifteen to thirty minutes at a time. It is too hot to sleep in the daytime, because when I lie down it is just like having a Turkish bath, the perspiration soaking my clothing through. We never steal or annex anything; but one of our men commandeered a tin of bovril. I was once on duty for over thirty-six hours at a stretch. This was caused through three of our clerks being sent to Modder River. The others had been doing eighteen and twenty hours right off. Oh, yes; we do enjoy ourselves sometimes; but 'all's fair in war.' You undoubtedly hear the news much quicker than we do here, and it seems strange to say so, but things get a bit monotonous at times, unless there is a diversion caused by ourselves. For instance, yesterday we commandeered a chicken, and it was plucked and trussed by your humble servant before it was cold, and we had it for supper in the evening. In spite of reverses and the conditions, which appear at this moment to be so much against us, everyone is cheerful, and believes, as I do, that the British will be successful, even if the war had to last for years. Kind regards to all enquiring friends."

NOTE.—See photograph of group.

✤ ✤ ✤ ✤

Private **S. E. Sterling** (late "I" Company), No. 551, "C" Company, C.I.V., continues his diary in a letter later as under:—

"s.s. 'Gaul,' two days south of St. Helena.

". . . . We arrived at St. Helena at six o'clock on Monday morning. It looks a very rugged sort of place from the sea, but it's just like England inland. They did not allow the men ashore; only the officers, sergeants, and officers' servants. I was taking the place of an officer's servant who was ill with inoculation, so I managed to get ashore. The town lays in the hollow of a valley, the sides being very steep. The barracks are right on top of the hill towards the left. There are on the Island seven girls to every fellow, and they are every colour, from black to a lovely cream. We sailed away at three o'clock Tuesday, leaving behind a passenger who's a Roman Catholic priest. I don't know if it's another case of St. Anthony, though. At five o'clock I was inoculated, and the bounder who invented it ought to

KHAKI LETTERS—*continued*.

be boiled in oil, for it's fearful torture, and makes you in a day as weak as a rat, and gives you fearful pains all over the body ; but I'm glad it's done, as it makes one feel more confident. Wednesday evening it made me so weak that I couldn't lift myself up to get downstairs, so I had to be carried, and that made me faint. This morning I felt a bit better, and was able to get on deck by myself, and have picked up a treat since then, so I managed to get better rather quick.

Friday, February 9th—Feel O.K. this morning. Only a pain like stitch in my side ; don't know how I shall wear a belt over it, though. We've seen nothing since leaving St. Helena, except a fearfully blue sea all day, and nothing has happened on board.

Sunday, 11*th*—Lovely day, but still nothing to see. Hear we reach Cape Town to-morrow, and land then or on Tuesday, but haven't heard what they are going to do with us yet.

Monday, 12*th*—Cape Town in sight. Expect to land about four o'clock. It's a fine looking place from the sea. The houses are built of grey stone, or are painted grey. We landed at 4.45 p.m. in the transport dock, and they marched us to this camp, which is called Green Point Camp. . . . They say we go up to the front in a day or two, and will try and write again before I go. . . . Good-bye for the present. Kind remembrances."

Taking up the thread again in another letter, dated February 19th, from Green Point Camp, Sterling says :—

"We arrived here Monday last, and marched to this Camp, which is about 500 yards from the sea. . . . Very close to the sea is Signal Hill, a fair blighter to go up ; it looks nice and smooth from the bottom, but after going a little way you find it is covered with small bushes, about two foot or so high, which smell of eucalyptus when you tread upon them. These bushes conceal stones about a foot across, which roll directly you put a foot on them, and it's a deuce of a roll if once you do start. When you get to the top there's an awfully pretty view of Table Bay and the town, and you can see a tremendous way round. They drill us very differently from the way they do at home—none of the wheeling this way, and then that, and no kneeling down carefully. In the first place we drill in shirt sleeves, and the hats are turned down all round. The fellows look very serviceable in this fashion, if they don't look smart. We also drill in extended order, single line six paces apart, and don't we get yelled at if we get near one another. They signal the orders by holding the hand in different positions, not by voice. One signal—hand straight up, halt, and down you have to go on the knee. Sometimes we are marching along the field or the road, and the officer will suddenly yell ' cover,' and you have to fling yourself flat on your face ; the face must be touching the ground too, or else he'll go for you. One or two blithering idiots started laughing when we did it first, and the officer got his rag out, so to speak, and said, ' That's right, laugh now ; wait a little while, and you'll be doing something else.' The town is crowded with wounded from the front, and they are all (or at any rate, all I've seen) wounded in more than one place. They say it's terribly hard up there, worse than anybody can imagine. They only give you one bottle of water a day, which they serve out at six p.m. ; that has to last till six p.m. the next day, and they put you in the clink if you don't keep off the water. I saw one guardsman who was wounded at Modder River in the head, through

KHAKI LETTERS—*continued.*

the chest, the wrist, and the ankle. He seems all right now, and the scars are very small. He says he doesn't want to go to the front again, though. There are a rare lot of Malays, Lascars, Hindoos, and such like in Cape Town, and they have plenty of sauce, too. I had to boot one the other day, and he followed me about threatening me till we got in a quiet street, and then he sloped when I tried to get at the brute. . . . Lots of fellows ask you to come home to tea. I went home with one fellow, only a youngster, and he gave me a regular fine time of it, rowing, &c. I went there several times, and was made very welcome, and he used to come up to the Camp with his sisters and father. They brought up pineapples, melons, and all sorts of fruit, but wouldn't let me pay for any of it. . . . I'm writing this in the train bound for 'goodness knows where.' They told us we weren't going up to the front until Wednesday (to-morrow), and this morning we had a parade through the town, but at three o'clock they said, 'get ready for marching order,' and we gave in our kit bags for storage at Cape Town, taking with us (in the clothing line) one shirt and towel, one pair of socks, and a holdall, with knife, fork, and spoon. I have not seen any of the telegraphists from TS yet, though I inquired for them at the G.P.O., the Castle, and the Main Barracks. I hope to see some of them when we get out of this train, which is a bit sickening. They put us eight in a carriage made for six, and warn us we shall be in the train two or three days. Regards to all."

No. 2,548, Sapper **W. C. Smith,** writing from Enslin, February 15th, says:—

". . . . A great change has come over this place. Thousands and thousands have stayed here for a day or two, and then gone forward to the front, viz., Ramdam and Waterval Drift, which lay about eight and fifteen miles respectively from here. Roberts and Kitchener were here also, and that, of course, made us busy. I have had to work twenty-one hours out of twenty-four, as there were two circuits, and one only supposed to look after them. Needless to say, with the troops here, it was impossible for one to do it. We now work to the front, and have a staff of twenty here. . . . An attack is expected to-night from 3,000 Boers, and as there are only 200 men left in the camp to mind the tents it will go hard with us if it comes off; but, there, you can never believe the rumours about the Boers. The armoured train is patrolling to-day, as there is a convoy passing, which in length is about six miles. . . . I posted my chocolate-box yesterday. Hope it will arrive safely, for it will be worth keeping in remembrance of 'roughing it.' . . . We are to sleep with arms handy to-night. I am down to work all night, but shall not, as the wire to the front is down. . . Letters are arriving a month or so overdue, but shall get them all, I expect, in time. It is generally thought that the war will be over in a month or two. As soon as the Boers have had a good hiding it will be all over. Kindly remember me to all friends at TS. When writing in future, please address 1st Telegraph Division, there being a Telegraph Battalion round at Natal."

No. 1,457, Sapper **H. J. Hayden** (LS), writing from De Aar, 17th February, 1900, says:—

". . . Just a line to let you know where I am for, and that I am in first class condition. I like the country very well. We disembarked last Tuesday

KHAKI LETTERS—*continued.*

and marched straight to Cape Town Station, and got in the train for De Aar. We were packed eight in a carriage (narrow gauge railway). It came on raining heavily, the water came through the tops of the carriages, and all soon got wet through, so had to make ourselves as happy as we could under the circumstances. We were thirty-nine hours in the train, reaching De Aar at one o'clock on Thursday. In case of an attack from disloyal Dutch, each man was served out with a hundred rounds of ammunition. All along the line fruit was very plentiful. Very fine grapes, about a penny per pound. Everything else very dear. Up to the troops coming here there was no less coin than the threepenny-piece, called here a 'tickie.' Great excitement prevailed here when the news came that Kimberley was relieved and Jacobsdal taken yesterday. Coming up country we passed several trains of wounded and refugees. To-day we entrain for Modder River, so have another long journey before us. Yesterday and this morning we had to get all the stores (air line poles, wire, &c.) ready for loading the trucks. Haven't much time for writing here. Kind regards to all."

No. 25,366, Sapper **Chas. Forth** (LS), sends a letter in diary form from Modder River (date about February 24th). as under:—

"Capetown. February 12th—On deck ('St. Andrew') before daylight. Grand scene. Table Mountains silhouetted against a clear sky like a dense cloud, counted over hundred steamers, mostly transports. Horse chews rope and chokes, another dies. At anchor outside until 3 p.m. before vacancy at wharf. Not allowed leave ship, but about 9 p.m. 'Bert' (Hayden) and I had a good stroll about town, returning about 12.30. No hammocks, doss where we can, get good supply cork life belts on floor and make spring mattress, too tired to undress.

Tuesday, February 13th—All bustle and work getting together stores and equipment. De Aar our destination. Leave ship 2.30 for station, only to find we cannot get away before night, marched off to Fort Knokke for refreshments. Grapes cheap, 1½d. a bunch. Steam away 10 p.m. No racks or cushions, cannot get comfortable position for sleep, keep waking with half dislocated necks, a couple try the floor, then I snooze soundly.

February 14th—Wake 6 a.m., find at Worcester station, breakfast, next stop De Doorns or the Thorns; train climbs mountains with plenty horse-shoe curves to save bridging over ravines, two engines, but ascent so steep in places, pace tortoise-like. Dine at Matjesfontein station, corned beef, biscuits. At 9.30 p.m. reach Prince Albert Road station. Tea. Terrific thunder, lightning and rain.

February 15th—Wake 5.30 a.m. to find our carriage far from rainproof, wet through. Victoria West next station. Still raining heavy, not one can find a place to sit or stand without being under a tap. Few ostriches seen at intervals. Last 80 miles good straight run. After 39 hours ride De Aar is reached at 1 p.m. Our train comprised 150 horses, 150 men of West Riding Mounted Infantry, and 58 of us. Our camp just outside station, pitch tents, then tea. Very dry fine deep sand, puff of wind and we are in perfect mist, glad of plunge in canvas bath. At 9 p.m. six of ours sent Modder River, open trucks, raining in torrents. Many 24th men come and greet me, but disguised in beards difficult make them out. Beer 8d. a quart. Little sleep last few nights, feel could slumber naked on a bed of thistles

February 16th—Fall in 6 a.m. Breakfast 7. At 8 divided parties for fatigue duty, my lot are removing 100 heavy iron poles, finish about 11, heat

KHAKI LETTERS—*continued.*

too great to work longer, now reclining, garden chair, at Soldiers' Home—a large marquee—eating grapes and drinking squash. Heavy rain at noon. Kaffir huts close to our tents, children, naked, are enjoying themselves in rain-pools. After tea again at work. At 10.30 we puff off, and although a dozen or so go on open trucks, we are tightly packed when laid down.

Sunday, February 18*th*—Reach Orange River 3.30, and do not get away until 7.30. Train off without warning, have to run for it and just manage to board guard's van. Pass Belmont, Gras Pan and Enslin, large camp latter place, can see mounted scouts out on plains. Armoured trains stationed here. Meeting our boys all along the line. Feed ostriches, extract few feathers in return, only poor birds already plucked. Few lizards and swarms of locusts. Miles of bullock wagons, with teams of 16, 18 and 20, trekking to Kimberley with corn, fodder, etc., they do about 15 miles a day under escort of mounted rifles. 4 o'clock when we detrain at Modder River—$17\frac{1}{2}$ hours to cover about 120 miles, thanks to single line railway. Off to river for a swim as soon as can slip away, return to find all tea cleared away pitch tents and retire.

February 19*th*—Begin day with a swim. Dozen bullock wagons bring in telegraph stores which we unload. Pure water precious, not able get any until noon to-day, no beer in our canteen—sold out—and no soldier (officers excepted) allowed in hotel. Whisky, 8s. ; jam, 1s. lb. ; condensed milk, 9d. ; Eno's, 4s. ; tobacco, 10s. lb. Seek refuge in our tents from sandstorm, cannot be much worse on the Sahara. Heat intense. Lay down literally bathing in our own perspiration and caked sand, longing for evening and the river. After tea wind goes down, plunge in the Modder, return, shake blankets and settle for night.

February 20*th*—Before sun is up am in the river, swim about only luxury here. Four of us go to take down wires, done with. Rum rations served out, also free issue of grapes. Another party sent off to find water. They came across a well at deserted bullet-ridden farm several miles out, all furniture intact. 5 p.m., another four (myself included) go off with mule team and eight Kaffirs to take down further portion of air line, meet no adventure. This trip robs me of a swim.

February 21*st*—Our Captain inspects carbines, etc. Loaves bread substitute hard biscuits, but still on tinned meat. A barrel of beer arrives, find a pint at bedtime very beneficial. Enjoy a swim. See cattle dealer branding bullocks, smells very savoury (mim).

February 22*nd*—Little to do but all try to shirk it. 1 lb. jam to four men served out. Fresh mutton dinner. Sand blowing chronic until 2 p.m. when heavy rain settles it. No bathing this evening, too wet.

February 23*rd*—A swim for a start, 7.30 to 12.30 working in the stores. 4 p.m. 'Bert' (Hayden) and I take duty in the office here. Mail goes this evening, so must draw my letter to a close, with kindest regards to all colleagues."

✤ ✤ ✤ ✤

No. 1,274, Sapper **W. F. Adams,** writing from Modder River, 20th February, 1900, says :—

" . . . Have had a very changeable time lately, and last week was sent down for several days to Enslin on a kind of race-meeting job. We were working in a marquee ; had eight wires with about fifteen stations and a staff of about

KHAKI LETTERS—*continued*.

twenty-two or twenty-three. We had a very busy time. The reason was the starting of Roberts's column. I don't know that it all went from ENM, but a large part of it, and also a large convoy of stores of all kinds, forage, and ammunition, which, by the way, was nearly all captured. Enslin was the worst place I've ever been in for sand. It was like that in the caves at Hastings, only the Enslin article was red. I'm sure some of our kit must have been buried in it. Lost my knife and fork, mess tin, and carbine. I 'found' another mess tin and carbine, but have had to buy a knife and fork.

"Owing to presence of 'slip on the line,' I was unable to continue this afternoon. I have now been for a swim, and nearly experienced the most unpleasant sensation one can possibly imagine, viz., that of drowning. Four of us went down to the river and accidentally my tobacco pouch went in and Stormer after it to bring it out. He was getting near it when I went in and succeeded in reaching it. Then I turned about and went for the bank. On the way back I had to pick up Bertie, or, rather, tried to. He grabbed me, and we went down together. Then we came up again and got nearer the bank. I freed myself and reached out for the bushes, and then succeeded in hauling him in, and the others on the bank hauled him up. Then I went for a quiet swim to steady my nerves. It was a horrible sensation being under water. Thank goodness, it wasn't serious. As it was, we both quenched our thirst.

"It is strange to say it, but we get little news here. We have heard nothing from Buller for a long time. We are well posted in Roberts's moves because we have a wire always in communication with him.

"There is a possible chance that we may go to Kimberley soon, but no one knows where they are going till they get there.

"We are all now enduring the agonies of mosquito bites. I've about a dozen on my hands and a few on my face. They give one a very gouty appearance, particularly when on the fingers.

"Please remember me to the Group, and say I'm very sorry indeed I can't write to all of them. We work twelve hours' duty and several hours' honorary overtime, so there is not much time to spare.

"Ta ta. Look out for me on the boat at Old Swan Pier."

No. 23,653, Sapper **J. F. Metcalfe**, 3rd Division, R.E., writing from Sterkstroom, February 21st, says :—

"DEAR KEMP,—Yours of January 19th just to hand, we were delighted to hear that all our Company had come forward to assist in this great campaign. I see they were more fortunate than the first party in many ways, having a respectable send off, etc. I will endeavour to comply with your request to keep the pot a-boiling. It is useless for me to preach on 'War,' as I know fully well that you are much more acquainted with and in receipt of the very latest rumours. We, 'the Two Macs' out here, being isolated, have to be content with what we can pick up from a semi-Dutch publication. With regard to our Division, we have been content to watch and wait since our terrible disaster at Stormberg, with the exception of several skirmishes, details of which would now come to you as very stale

KHAKI LETTERS—*continued.*

news. I might mention, though, that Montmorency and his scouts are doing splendid work amongst the hills surrounding us, by bringing in prisoners, rebels and their farm stocks to the tune of 1,500 sheep and 1,000 head of cattle at a time, so long as this continues we are sure of fresh meat daily, in fact it would appear as though we were getting too much of it, as the authorities sent one large seizure down to Queenstown for sale, realising £3,600. This is, I consider, quite equal to killing other kinds of beasts (Boers) B.P., and will carry weight towards bringing the war to a final issue, and there can be no doubt as to what that issue will be. On February 15th the whole camp received an invitation from Soldiers' Home people (who are doing splendid work towards making everything comfortable for the troops) to tea, cakes, buns, coffee, pineapples, melons, etc., every man had to help himself, and eat and drink as much as he wished to, this was to celebrate the inauguration of a new and large marquee for services, etc. An address was given by General Gatacre, and the band of the Fighting Fifth played during the evening, the most important of all, though, was a telegram read out to the troops by Mr. Howe, S.C.A., conveying the news of French's and Kelly-Kenny's successes in the O.F.S., capturing no less than five laagers, reaching Kimberley, occupying Jacobsdal, and shelling of Cronje's retreating column. This good news aroused everybody, and cheers after cheers were given for these, the General, and Mr. Howe, whilst the band closed with the National Anthem. We are pleased to receive the *Chronicle*, and I venture to say that the compilation of letters from various sources, with the addition of your authentic and most reliable notes pertaining to the same, increases the value of our official publication. I wish you would add 12th Coy., R.E.'s, to my address, I should then receive them a week earlier. Convey my congratulations to Mr. R. Furness on his recent success in heading the poll for the election of Secretary NH. I was pleased to read such a good account of poor Jummy's experiences; grieved to think that he should have been struck off the roll whilst just in his prime. We are now receiving Reuter's war news from Capetown, and since its introduction to our troops I have had some exceptionally busy nights, the number of words in one message alone was 1,934, this was giving the details of General Buller's affairs at Tugela, messages like the above added to the usual night's work, which is mostly in cypher, keep one from getting idle, considering that he is absolutely on his own from 9 p.m. till 7.30 a.m., but with its disadvantages I much prefer it to day duty, as the sun is so hot, and enables me to spend an hour or so in the Soldiers' Home, playing chess, draughts, reading or writing; there is every convenience and everything free, with the exception of postage, so there can be no excuse whatever for failing to write you a few lines. Enteric is still very prevalent amongst our division troops, funerals taking place almost daily. The interment of Col. Eager, R. I. Rifles, who was wounded and taken prisoner at Stormberg, was very impressive. We received him in exchange from the Boers for Commander Pretorius, a prisoner of war. We still continue to have sand storms, locusts, an thunder storms, the latter causing several casualties. The other day one man killed and three wounded by lightning at Bushman's-Hoek, of the Royal Irish Rifles. I fail to remember anything else of interest this mail. We are in health, all that can be expected considering we are existing principally on jams and jipper. Regards to all.

"P.S.—I have it on good authority that we are making a forward move this week end, February 25th, towards the O.F. State."

NOTE. S. C. A.—Soldiers' Christian Association.—R.E.K.

KHAKI LETTERS—*continued*.

No. 4,311, Sapper **C. J. Minors** (Telegraph Section, 2nd Div. Royal Engineers), on board the s.s. "Cephalonia," writes under date February 28th, and posts at St. Vincent the following :—

"Dear Kemp,—Many thanks for wire and good wishes. Our party for Natal, numbering 35, is made up as follows:—R.E.'s : Sgt. Knapman, PT, Cpl. Pope, NX, L.-Cpl. Lewis, BZ ; Sappers Purdue, GI, Smith (W. E.), CU, Maynard, CN ; Chowne, Bryant, Holland, Sargeant, Chatfield, Carter (Reservists). 24th Middlesex R.V. : Sappers Sinclair, Townshend, Mackness, Minors, Wheller, Ingram, Brown, Jeffrey, Leaver, Snow, Symonds, Collins, Chubbock, Consal (all of TS), Rowson, EES, Peters, TSF, Corkhill, TSF, Pocock, CO, Bevan, ACN, Mason, EDO, Milne, AB, Robinson, DY, Harvey, LV.

"The ' Cephalonia ' left Southampton about 2.40 p.m. on Tuesday. The *Daily Mail* A.M.B. Fund served out tea, coffee, cake, etc., to the men previous to embarking. We have two Militia regiments on board, 4th Scottish Rifles and 3rd Queen's West Surrey. Had a good send-off from Southampton. Couple of torpedo destroyers accompanied us a short distance, the crews, led by their officers, giving three cheers for Tommy Atkins. The 'Cephalonia' cannot be described as a greyhound of the ocean, but for rolling and pitching it would be hard to beat. We have to hold fast to our tins, dishes, etc., or they go flying off to the other side of the boat. Occasionally a large tin of soup, tea, or coffee comes clattering down the stairs, scattering its contents over all who happen to be underneath. Those who prefer sleeping on the tables to swinging in hammocks have anything but a quiet night. Quite a common occurrence to find themselves shot off the table on to the floor and then rolled away to the other side of the boat. The language used by the Militia on these occasions is very blue. Most of our party suffered from sea-sickness —some are still poorly. The sleeping arrangements are very bad. We are crowded in hammocks like herrings in a box. The height of sleeping quarters from floor to ceiling is about six feet. You can imagine what it is like on a warm night with about 1,600 troops on board. The food served out is very similar to that received by previous parties. Breakfast—coffee, porridge, soup, bread and butter. Dinner—soup, boiled beef, potatoes, rice, prunes, and plum pudding. Tea—tea, biscuits, bread and butter, jam, marmalade, etc. There is a canteen where tinned goods may be purchased (*no beer*). Food can also be bought from the kitchen staff, such as eggs, bacon, chops, steaks, soup, tea, coffee, pastry, etc. Had our first sea-bath yesterday morning, Tuesday, 27th. Sail-baths rigged up on deck, followed by feet, arms, and bared chest inspection. So far, we are having an easy time as regards parades, drills, etc. This boat will probably beat the record to the Cape for slow travelling by transports. Kindest regards."

No. 4,313, Sapper **S. H. Townsend,** on board the s.s. " Cephalonia," writing from St. Vincent, February 28th, says :—

"Just a line to let you know all is O.K. Have had a rough passage for 5 days, but after passing Madeira it suddenly changed for summer-like weather. We had several accidents on board. Broken arms and legs owing to the heavy gales. We are packed like sardines, but getting used to it now ; the grub is O.K. Our boat rolled a little extra on Friday morning and shot all the Scottish Rifles in the opposite mess on top of us. There were men lying on the floor all amongst the coffee, butter, rolls,

KHAKI LETTERS—*continued.*

and porridge. They even could not get up for the floor was well greased. We work it all right by the power of oof, to get a few extras, such as a chop or a steak for breakfast, etc. On board are two Militia Battalions, West Surreys and Scottish Rifles, nicknamed the 'The Jocks.' A stoker has died, also two horses during the voyage My appetite is grand, but although a large number have been seasick your humble has escaped it. I have just come off doctor's inspection, it is to guard against fever. This boat is 24 hours behind, and she bumps. A cruiser came up last night and after exchanging signals went off. Tell Bob —— no 11-2's allowed on this boat, also Sid. ——, no Barclay & Perkins allowed, but I have found where Bass is stored, but you have to go about like a burglar, it's worth it. This is all at present, as we are nearing St. Vincent. Kind regards to everyone."

No. 23,577, Lance-Corporal **Chas. M. E. Wilson,** sends the following letter from Military Telegraphs, Orange River, on March 15th :—

"Dear Colour-Sergeant Kemp,—Your circular letter, and complete list of names and numbers of men serving with the R.E.'s, to hand, for which we are very thankful. The list makes a splendid addition to our kit, and has proved very useful. Thanks, also, for the previous letters which you thoughtfully sent us. It's very good of you to take so much trouble, but it's characteristic of you. As to the *Chronicles*, we don't see any of them; they seem to get as far as head-quarters, and there stick. By the time this reaches you the sad news of poor Hawkins will have reached you. It was a terrible blow to us; he was a splendid fellow. It was very sudden; all within a week practically. Time he was in hospital he worried a great deal, which, of course, did not improve matters. The day previous to his death he seemed pretty well, but owing to the bursting of a blood-vessel he collapsed into a state of unconsciousness, from which he never recovered. He passed away very peacefully. Last night he was buried; we all attended the burial, and the firing party was detailed from the 29th Company R.E.'s. The chaplain gave a nice service; he also promised (as did the doctors) to write to his relatives. Sambells came from Hopetown to see the last of his comrade. With this letter I have enclosed a photo of staff at this office. I am sorry that poor Alf. was unable to be with us. The work is falling off greatly round this quarter, and we expect the office to be closed shortly. We are sadly in need of a change, I can assure you. Kind regards to you and all enquiring friends. Again thanking you for your kind letters."

[The photo referred to is reproduced on the next page. It was taken by a corporal of the 29th Co. R.E., who is a professional photographer in business at Cape Town, and at present stationed at Orange River. Every man represented there has signed his name on the back—including poor Reggie Williams, who has been so suddenly cut off—adding, "with best wishes for Colour-Sergeant Kemp." The background is the office where they are employed. Such enclosures as this are highly prized, and the "best wishes" are heartily reciprocated by, not only the recipient, but by all the Telegraph Service at home, I feel sure.—R.E.K.]

The Military Telegraph Staff.

AT ORANGE RIVER, CAPE COLONY.

Taken 5th March, 1900.

KEY.

    1.   2.   3.   4.   5.
      6.   7.   8.   9.

1. Sapper J. H. TOVEY, Lineman, R.E.
2. ,, W. R. WILLIAMS, Plymouth ("Bob").
3. ,, SAM WILLIAMS, Cardiff.
4. Private JIM CANN, 1st Bn. Scots Gds.
5. Sapper G. W. BANNISTER, Engr's. Dept., Manchester.
6. Sapper C. T. CATLING, Euston.
7. ,, C. M. E. WILSON, Yarmouth, Acting Lce.-Cpl. in charge.
8. ,, A. URQUHART, Inverness.
9. ,, W. A. DELLBRIDGE, C.T.O., London ("Ponto").

With Best Wishes for COLOUR-SERGT. KEMP.

Office Stamp, 13.3.00.

Khaki Sidelights.

The Telegraph in the Shooting Line.
McNeill's Zereba.

From **One of the Old Brigade,** an esteemed ex-R.E., now stationed at TS :—

"*To the Editor* KHAKI LETTERS."

"DEAR SIR,—In response to your request for articles of interest to telegraphists, and in view of the misconception existing as to employment of telegraphists in the fighting line, I venture to submit the following extract from the diary of a telegraphist at the battle of To Frek, Suakin (McNeill's zereba), March 22nd, 1885 :—

"'We paraded at 5 a.m. this morning with 16 Tel. Bn. N.C O.'s and men, under Major Turner and Lieutenant Lindsay. Wagon with ten miles of outpost cable on drums and a water barrel. The air-lines having been previously erected to the outskirts of the camp, the cable was joined on and the wire unreeled as the column advanced. It being impossible to bury the wire, it was laid in the ruts in the sand caused by the wheels of the wagon, some of the party following and kicking the soil over it. It was intended to work inside one of the squares, of which there were two (the leading column of British troops under General McNeill and the rear column, Indians, under Colonel Hudson); but, owing to their crowded state with heavy convoy of camels and mules, this was found impracticable, and we worked on the left of the columns, sometimes up close to the British and at others lagging behind the Indian column. We had orders to run for the nearest square in case of attack. Owing to the mimosa bush being somewhat dense in places, the work was very arduous and the advance slow, as may be judged by the fact that after five and a half hours' march the column had only covered five and three-quarter miles. The camels had become so exhausted that we could go no further, and General McNeill telegraphed to General Graham explaining matters and obtained sanction to form a zereba there instead of two miles further on. This breakdown of transport cost us heavy loss, as the spot where we now zereba'd was surrounded by bush, whereas the camp intended was an open plateau. The troops were now busily occupied in cutting the brushwood to form the zereba and partaking of a well-earned lunch of bully-beef and biscuit. The telegraph men were engaged in burying the wire near the zereba where the traffic was likely to injure it, when a few shots were heard, and, looking round, we saw some of the scouts flying for their lives with the enemy on their heels. Lieutenant Lindsay

KHAKI SIDELIGHTS—*continued*.

gave the order " Left about wheel. Charge ! " and we showed the enemy a clean pair of heels, being almost the last to get into the zereba. The opening was quickly closed by the Naval Brigade under Lieutenant Paget, and we manned the side of the zereba with the Marines. Fortunately for us the first rush was at the other end, where all the Naval men at a Gatling were killed, and the enemy broke into the square, but were quickly driven out or bayoneted by the gallant Berkshires. The enemy being driven off the zereba itself, now turned to those who had been cut off by the surprise and those who had been carried out by the stampeding animals. Small squares started by men standing back to back and gradually increasing in size fought their way in. The telegraph instrument was found trodden on and spoilt ; but a new buzzer being joined up, we were delighted to find ourselves through O. K. to Q. I. (Quarantine Island). Telegrams were sent reporting "heavy and sudden attack repulsed with great slaughter," and messages were sent to the *Times* and *Daily News*, the telegraphist having to leave the instrument to assist in repulsing fresh assaults several times whilst keying the press work. About 7 p.m., when offering another press message for the *Times*, the wire was found to be cut, and the signallers opened communication by lamp to the Right Water Fort. The Tel. Bn. escaped very luckily, Major Turner losing his horse ; but our comrades of the 24th Company R.E. lost fourteen men killed, and Captains Romilly and Newman, of the Indian sappers and miners, with many of their men, were killed. The enemy's loss was estimated at 1,500, ours about 300. The night passed with many alarms.' "Yours truly,
" March 19th, 1900. "Ex-R.E."

[N.B.—Major Beresford refers to this as "the first occasion on which the telegraph has been used in the 'shooting line' during an action by any European power."]

✣ ✣ ✣ ✣

The following excerpt is sent me from a Lincolnshire paper, and refers to a speech made early in March :—

" Earl Brownlow, late Under Secretary of State for War, addressing the officers and men of the 2nd Volunteer Battalion Lincolnshire Regiment, who had been selected for service in South Africa, at Grantham, a few days ago, made use of the following remarks, which may interest our readers :—

" I have no hesitation in saying that this evening we are inaugurating a new era in Volunteer history. This is the first time, or we may call it the first time, our Volunteers have been called to come forward for active service abroad. There is one small exception, and that was during the first Egyptian campaign. A small number of the London P.O. Volunteers were then enrolled to manage the P.O. and telegraph service. They went out, and although they saw very little fighting necessarily, being engaged in their duties, still, when they came back, they received their medals, and they marched through London with those medals on their breasts when Lord Wolseley entered London with the army. I remember seeing them then, and think that that was the first time they had been on active service and under fire, for although they were never exactly in the van, still they did see some little fighting, because when General Graham's camp was attacked, and as the shells came tumbling in, the men jumped up on boxes so that they could have a chance of being shot at. That, perhaps, was the only fire they were under. Now, of course, this is a much larger and more important and graver question. The Government has now called on the Volunteers, and they have come forward readily, and magnificently responded to the call of the Government."

KHAKI SIDELIGHTS—*continued.*

In reference to the foregoing cutting, it may interest K.L. readers to know that in 1882 the A.P.O.C. was raised. Two companies were formed. One proceeded to Egypt, per the *British Prince*, on August 8th, the other remaining as a reserve company. On the 24th of April, 1884, authority was given for the formation of a Field Telegraph Corps. At the end of that year, September 15th, twelve selected men joined the Royal Engineers at Aldershot, and proceeded with them to Egypt. On March 3rd, 1885, a detachment of the A.P.O.C. embarked for Suakin, per s.s. *Navarino*. Thus it will be seen the 24th have had the honour of being on active service twice before the general call of Volunteers. At the present moment there are over 500 at the front. If space permits, a fuller account of their services will appear in K.L.

The Volunteers, however, of to-day are becoming more recognised than ever before. The Country is awake to their work.

The Banner of Britain.

The Banner of Britain shall float on the breeze.
Our bulwarks we'll strengthen as oft as we please.
Our Army and Navy—stout-hearted and tried—
Shall know we—as Britons—stand close by their side.

    For we love our dear old Homeland—
        We'll dispel all doubts and fears (doubts and fears);
        We will prove to Queen and Country,
        We are earnest British Volunteers (Volunteers).

Our mission is peaceful, our motive is right,
Our Motto is worthy, our Union is Might—
" Defence, Not Defiance," we boast not nor brag,
We'll stand by our Comrades, the Army and Flag.
    For we love, etc.

Fierce conflicts are waging, that tend peace to mar,
Strong nations are boist'rous and threatening for war.
Old England shall stand fast and ever shall feel
Her " Third line " is ready—with hearts true as steel.
    For we love, etc.

Our hearths and our homes we have sworn to defend,
Our wives and our children we'll shield to the end;—
Usurpers may clamour, but soon have to learn,
The " Citizen Soldier " they never can turn.
    For we love, etc.

Three cheers for our standard—let none dare subdue,—
Three cheers for Our Empire—and hearty ones too—
May God still befriend us, may naught come between
The bloodbonds that bind us, our people, and Queen.
    For we love, etc.

                R. E. KEMP, *Colour-Sergeant,*
                            24th Middlesex R.V.C.

A tune, which requires very slight alteration, suitable for the above lines, will be found in the Revised and Enlarged Edition of "The Christian Choir," No. 132.

Khaki Letters—*continued.*

No. 4,333, Sapper **A. W. York** (2nd Div. R.E.), on board the s.s. "Oriental," nearing St. Vincent, March 8th, writes :—

"DEAR COLOUR-SERGEANT KEMP,—Nearly a month has elapsed since I received your bright and pleasant letter, but as we were such a numerous party I deferred my reply until we were thinned down a bit, a proceeding which took place when the first party left for Natal; and now we eight have also left, but our destination has not been vouchsafed unto us. We marched from the 'Shot in the murky darkness at 4 a.m. on the 28th ult., and after an eventful journey, the events consisting of the cheering, yelling, and flag-waving that greeted us as we steamed through London. Arrived at the docks, and embarked at 10 a.m. An hour later we drifted slowly down the river, leaving an enthusiastic crowd behind. The swell began to be felt towards the close of the next day, and the majority of us underwent our first dose of sea-sickness after tea. I am glad to add that, as far as my knowledge goes, this was the only occasion on which the 24th indulged in the little weakness. Six or seven hundred Jocks of the Royal Scots Militia embarked at Queenstown. We were swarmed with Jocks (Cameron Militia) at Aldershot, and now we have them again on the good ship 'Oriental.' Not that I wish to convey the impression that there is any ill-feeling; on the contrary, the best of good temper prevails, and we join in their sing-songs, they in ours, with great good-fellowship. We are somewhat crowded, especially the hammocks, but many will be sleeping on the upper decks now the weather is so delightful. If I sketch one day's routine it will do for the voyage, as there is a terrible sameness about everything on board, and one often hears the TS expression 'Fed up,' though it is a sin to complain, as we never had such delightful skies, such gentle winds, such glorious sunrises, nor such lovely sunsets as we have had lately. 'Reveille' is at 6 a.m. Turn out, stow hammocks, wash or bath, shave (?), and brush-up. Breakfast—oatmeal, coffee, and bread, 7 a.m. Physical drill 8 a.m. Roll-call, 11 a.m. Meanwhile mess decks are inspected. Dinner—fresh meat at first—now salt or bully—and potatoes or split peas, at 12. Then sometimes an afternoon parade. Supper—vile tea and bread, at 4.30. Sling hammocks 5.30, and out with the electric lights at 8.15 (sometimes later). We had a Church Parade and a prayer meeting by our own Lieutenant on Sunday. A batch of R.E.'s suffered two days' agony in hospital after inoculation against enteric this week; no more men volunteering. Kindest regards to yourself and all TS friends.

"Please note we are 2nd Division."

No. 4,327, Sapper **A. J. Brooks** (2nd Tel. Div. R.E.), writing on board the s.s. "Oriental," and posting at St. Vincent on March 9th, 1900, chronicles the following :—

"DEAR COLOUR-SERGEANT KEMP,—We are all having a fairly good time on board the 'Oriental.' Pickford, Hudson, George, York, and I are in the same mess together. There are sixteen in each mess, and we could not wish for a better lot of fellows than the R.E.'s who make up the remaining eleven. We left the Albert Docks with drafts for the Essex, Warwick, and Border Regiments, and with the Langman Hospital, with which is Dr. Conan Doyle. At Queenstown we picked up the 3rd Royal Scots (Militia). They are a decent lot of fellows taken all round, and are unmistakeably Scotch. Their lingo is as unintelligible to us as is that of the Lascars who form the

KHAKI LETTERS—*continued*.

crew and general slaveys of this vessel. The Lascars are an unwashed, ragged-looking lot. All are as thin as match-sticks ; some wear their hair long with plenty of oil and grease on it, whilst others are shaven quite bald. See them slap the dough about. Ugh ! We are rather pushed for room, and I daresay I shall lose half my kit before the journey finishes, owing to difficulty in putting things away after using. We sleep in hammocks when we can get them, but up to the present I have snoozed anywhere and almost everywhere. Tables, forms, floor, cells (when not otherwise required), sitting up to lying down—I have tried all, but had my best go last night on the hatch over the hold wrapped in my great coat (blankets always get collared). We live well, and buy plenty of tinned stuff at reasonable prices from the store. One can't grumble at butter 8d. per half-pound tin ; salmon, 6d. tin ; all jams, 6d. tin, etc., etc. Terrible job to get it, though, owing to the crowd. I think we have all got over our *mal de mer* by now, and everything is going swimmingly. That is to say, now that we have recovered from the effects of the anti-enteric fever inoculation. Most of us were done on Sunday afternoon (I am speaking of R.E.'s only). We afterwards attended a Bible Class on the hurricane deck. It was conducted by Lieutenant Sherrard, of our No. 8 Section, was very interesting, and well attended. He is very energetic in distributing note-paper and periodicals to the various messes. I rather wish I was in his section myself. We who were inoculated were very bad from Sunday afternoon until Tuesday morning, when we were obliged to crawl out of our hammocks. We had nothing to eat or drink the whole time, with the exception of a little water handed up when asked for. Those who went into hospital fared no better. There were about ten who went unconscious on Sunday night, and had to be taken below, hammocks and all, into hospital. They were not fed at all whilst there. One chap, a driver in R.E.'s, temperature 105, asked for a drink of soda-water. Three bottles were brought him, for which he was charged 1s. 6d. ! The inoculation, from all accounts, was much more effective than is usual. I certainly would not go through those two days again. The weather has been grand, and the sing-songs on deck in the evening are very enjoyable. A corporal of the Borderers is very strong on the clarionette, and one of the R.E.'s and a youngster of the Jocks do great execution with someone's cornet. Sentimental songs, those referring to home and ' mother ' especially, are great favourites. The bagpipes and drums play aft during officers' mess. I am getting to like the pipes. They're not half bad once you get hold of the tune. It has not been particularly warm yet, but hundreds slept on deck last night. We have physical exercise every day—very amusing when the vessel rolls. Sail-cloth sea-bath was started this morning, and we had a good splorge, drenching nearly all the onlookers with the hose-pipe. We do all parades from to-day until we land barefooted, trousers turned up to the knees, and in shirt-sleeves. We have not yet sighted land (Thursday, March 8th, 3 p.m.), and understand that we do not reach St. Vincent until to-morrow morning ; but all letters must be handed in this afternoon. We heard of the relief of Ladysmith when we reached Queenstown, from the Cork papers. I wonder what we shall hear at St. Vincent ! It's best not to speculate. We have been speculating enough over your mysterious references to your big surprise packet ; but whatever it is, we all hope that you will be amply recompensed for all your kindness and trouble you have taken. Brook (HF) read your letter just before we left Aldershot ; he said he would write you. Winkle is an ideal Sec.-Corporal. We in our mess, however, seldom have much to do with Brook, Nash, Gwill, or Winkle, as they are fixed in messes on the other

KHAKI LETTERS—*continued.*

side of the hatchway. We meet at parades, concerts, etc. We shall be glad to get off the water, as everything is so cramped and uncomfortable. No room for anything. The clean linen question will have to be solved somehow, as everything, from cough tablets to unwashed shirts, must be kept in the kit-bag. So roll on Cape Town and a little more room to live. Best wishes to all, and to yourself especially."

No. 28,866, Sapper **W. H. P. Woolley** (1st Tel. Div., R.E.), writing from De Aar, February 18th, says:—

"Dear Kemp,—I suppose you have been on the look-out for a line from me before now, to know how I have been getting on, and where I have been to. Well, when I landed at Cape Town, I had to go to CTO with the other boys, 4 hours a day, for a day or two, when I was ordered, with Catling and Bishop, to Wynberg Camp, and it didn't half rain when we left Green Point Camp, on the 30th December, we stayed there a fortnight, when Catling and I received orders to rejoin at the Camp, preparatory to coming to De Aar. It took us two nights and a day to get here, but, before leaving Cape Town, we had a lot of stuff given us, tea and buns to start with, from the people of Cape Town, and then tobacco, matches, bags of buns, and large melons; one melon to each compartment of train, eight in a compartment, 3rd class, to sleep best way we could, but some, being lucky enough to get into first and second class carriages, got sleeping bunks which could be projected from each side of the compartments. But let me say what Wynberg is like; well, we were in sheds there, with details, with beds, but they were full of fleas and bugs. Old Cat. and I had a hunt every morning for the lively jumpers, and I caught 27 one morning. The place itself is a very pretty place indeed, surrounded by firs, pines, and eucalyptus trees, with tremendous cactuses here and there, and mountains all round us outside. At night-time the place was illuminated with thousands of glowworms, a most magnificent sight, especially when the moon was not up. This is the place where most of the dangerous cases of wounded are sent to. Two days after I arrived at DA (De Aar) I was sent to Rensburg, where I was on the field cables, working buzzers. A week after this I was told off to Maeder's Farm, where I stayed a fortnight, then I was relieved and sent back here the next day. The Boers were in at that place and the two Sappers I left behind – Silver from SO and Woodcock from PY (Silver had only been there a few days from Potfontein, where he had to clear out, as the Boers were coming in in great force)—had to pack up and tramp their way back to Rensburg, a distance of about nine miles, with instruments and batteries, and their kits. I don't know how they managed to do it, though. The staff at Rensburg, under Colour-Sergeant Tee, have now had to fall back to Arundel, about 10 miles nearer Naauwpoort, where they are now. Jimmy Miller has gone from Naauwpoort to Modder River and we expect to go from here to Bloemfontein as soon as it is taken. Hope things are going on well at TS. Regards to all.

"How did the Relief of Kimberley go down in Town?"

KHAKI LETTERS—*continued*.

No. 1888, Sapper **W. G. Collins** (SA), sends the following acknowledgment. By noticing the date readers may get some idea of the way letters are travelling out there. Other men of the "L" Company received their cards at the close of 1899.

"Belmont, Cape Colony, 1st March, 1900.

"DEAR COLOUR-SERGEANT KEMP—Please accept my best thanks for your kindness in sending me the Christmas Card and also the list of names of Telegraphists employed with the S.A. Field Force, which is very much appreciated. The Card will be greatly prized."

No. 198, Sapper **F. H. Woodrow** (of SO), writing from Modder River, March 2nd, says :—

". . . . Things are looking much brighter now and it is the general opinion that the war will soon come to an abrupt finish.

I went up to Kimberley the day after its relief and met many old TS friends, including Fred Foote of the CGp, who came out about 3 years ago. He took me to his place where I had a cup of tea and some butter, the first they had tasted for 3 months. They insisted on my staying the night and for the first time since leaving home, I slept in a real bed. Can you imagine what a luxury this was? And it brought home very vividly what I had given up to serve under the Union Jack. Coming back I got out of the train near Magersfontein trenches and walked over the whole Boer line. I have never seen such a wicked hole in my life. For 12 miles there is a double row of trenches, one above the other, in front of which is barbed wire. All trenches are dug at the foot of kopjes or hills, so that the Boers could also fire from top and behind boulders on the sides. The Boers fired through loopholes made by piling up sandbags and leaving space for rifles so that they never exposed themselves. They lived in small huts made of branches of trees and sailcloth. I never saw such dirtiness before as I did there. They had apparently lived the same as pigs. Skins of sheep and bullocks were lying all over the place and the stench was indescribable. Our guns seemed to have fairly riddled their trenches with shrapnel and lyddite, and to have given them a warm time. In their retreat they left behind guns, revolvers, tons of ammunition, boots, blankets, and wearing apparel, all, barring the arms, being in the last stages of decay. Wagons of food were left behind which they endeavoured to hide in small caves.

"Judging by appearances, I should say the Boers are the dirtiest race on earth, bar none. Yesterday, 1st March, our troops brought in over 4000 prisoners and they looked more like tramps than anything else. Every consideration was shown them and they tell us candidly that they have received more kindness and good food since falling into our hands than they have done for years. They are splendid specimens of physique, but appearances make them look like tramps. Cronje was brought here in a cart accompanied by his wife, grandson, and secretary. They presented a sorry spectacle alongside our officers and men in khaki. Cronje was dressed in an old black suit now turning green with age. His wife resembles one of the ladies who live in the back courts of our towns, whilst his grandson, about 6 years old, without boots, looks like a mudlark at Portsea. His secretary and captain is a typical looking public house loafer—same as you see on the Hard (Portsea). The prisoners' camp is surrounded by wire fencing,

KHAKI LETTERS—*continued.*

guarded by two lines of armed sentinels outside and one inside. It is a picture to see them sitting on their haunches waiting for rations. At night the camp is a pretty sight, being played upon by a searchlight, and beacons are placed at intervals round the fencing. This combined with the sentries in overcoats with bayonets fixed, walking their beats, is extremely novel. Last night I watched it for quite an hour from a small hillock. They sleep 14 in a tent with a sentry at the door. We are sending them in batches of 500 down to Cape Town. Batches of them are taken to the river to bathe and they all seem pleased that their fighting is over. Their living is better than ours as they get fresh meat whilst we are only on tinned, but we don't envy them as they seem to be fairly broken up. I think this will give you a fair idea of how we are progressing and how prisoners of war are treated by us. Their loss has been very heavy during the last few days. Being at the counter now I get on A1 with some of the folks round, and yesterday was given a box of cigars that would have cost 6d. each to buy . . . . I am still keeping well."

No. 551, Private **Syd. Sterling** (late "I" Company), C.I.V., in a letter, dated "Fincham's Farm, near Witteputs, Griqualand West, March 2nd," says :—

". . . . We had three days and three nights in the train before reaching here. The country is very dreary; very much like Dartmoor, only more stony. . . . We stopped at De Aar, and I saw Humm, Charley Woode, Arundel, Woolley, and a few more 'L' Company men. We detrained at Orange River, where I met Dellbridge and a fellow from TSF.* We camped there for the night, and in the morning our Company entrained and came to this hole. It's the nearest post to the enemy behind the attacking column, and if a lot slip round they'll come on us, and we'll have a lively time of it. The first night we were here a body of horsemen were seen approaching, so we turned out and advanced towards them—forty of us, and 200 of them. When we got within about 800 yards of them they turned round and scooted off. They were captured by a mounted infantry patrol, and we found out they had been informed the Warwicks had left here, but not that we had replaced them; they thought they were going to loot the farm and cut the railway, but on seeing us didn't think it worth the trouble. Later on in the evening it came on raining, and it doesn't do it by halves either out here. I was out on patrol, and got soaked through. My only consolation being that I had a dry change when I got back. When I did get back our little camp (three tents) was in the middle of a fair-sized pond, and all our kits were lovely and wet. I wrung them out in the morning, but I had to lay in the pool to sleep. I took some quinine before doing so, and don't think it has made much difference to me up to the present. We are constantly turning out to stop rebels from getting through the lines. We haven't been under fire yet because they always scoot, and we mustn't fire after them if they go back, as it would alarm all camps back to De Aar, ninety-two miles away. Two of us on picket duty had a bit of a set-to with three niggers. They are not allowed out after dark, as the country is under martial law. We heard them coming up the kopje we were posted on, so the other fellow fell back, and I waited till they passed, and out on them with the bayonet, and he stopped them in front. They started to bolt, but on our threat to fire, stopped, and when the patrol came we handed them

* NOTE.—Undoubtedly Sapper Hawkins, who died on March 13th.

KHAKI LETTERS—*continued.*

over. They were taken back to camp, and imprisoned for two days for being out without a pass. I went down to the railway to see Cronje being taken down country. He looked rather a dignified old buffer; not the fierce-looking fellow I imagined he was."

Private **S. E. Sterling,** in another letter from Wigton Culverts, near Witteputts, March 11th, continues :—

"We arrived here last Monday from Fincham's Farm. We had a very rough time of it there : precious little sleep and food. During the ten days I was there I only had one night's rest ; the other nights I had from two to three hours, and sometimes we had an alarm in that time. . . . On Monday night I fired my first shot at a light that would not stop when I challenged. I managed to hit it, and whoever had it dropped it and bolted. When we got to it we found it was a railway lamp, which had been carried I expect by a nigger who didn't understand English and was too frightened to come near, as I hardly think Boers would come with a light. They do rush us here. When we go to a farm about two miles from us to get milk they charge us 6d. a half pint ; jam, 1s. a lb. pot ; small bottle of lime juice, 3s. ; small buns, 3d. each ; safety matches, which you get in London 1d. a dozen, they charge us 1s. a dozen for. . . . Whilst I was up at Fincham's Farm the storekeeper told me that he bought a sheepskin from one of the Munster Fusiliers, and when he came to examine it a day or so after he found his own brand on it. He also said his chickens had stopped laying since they've been there. I don't know how he will get on now, as very shortly he is going to have the Warwick Militia up there, and they are a tough crowd. They were encamped next to us at Capetown, so I can fully appreciate his anxiety on hearing of their approach. This is a hole for flies, ants, lizards, snakes, and scorpions. We get all these in our tents, so you can guess how gingerly we shake our blanket out in the morning. We have a good many impromptu ostrich hunts. The game is to go with some bad meat or bread, and stand behind a boulder and throw the meat near the ostrich, then gradually draw him on, and when he's almost up to you rush out, and as he turns round push your rifle between his legs and he trips over, so you can place a blanket over his head and pluck some feathers. . . . We have been getting very fair weather, considering it is winter here now, but the place is very quiet. The only variety is trains of wounded Boer prisoners going down, and more horses, oxen, artillery, and troops coming up. . . . "

No. 23,610, **Sergeant R. C. Luttrell,** writes from Colesberg Junction Camp, March 6th, as under :—

"DEAR DICK,—Just a few lines to go on with. The St. Andrew party landed safely at Cape Town and marched up to Fort Knokke, where we met Quinn at the hospital. He had got over his sprain and was nearly well. We moved off that same night for De Aar, slept as well as one can with four a-side in a 3rd class carriage filled with accessories for campaigning. Travelled all next day and next night, which was a wet one, and the roof leaking made it still more unpleasant. We all woke up cheerful, however, and arrived at De Aar about 12 noon. Here I was installed Acting

KHAKI LETTERS—*continued.*

Sergeant-Major of the camp, also Acting Q.M.S., and a multitude of other empty titles. We got up the tents, and, like good soldiers, immediately looked for something to eat and drink. The first comers welcomed us and told us how to go on. We stayed there two days when we got sudden orders to proceed to Modder River Camp. We raced on board a truck and were shunted into a siding at 5 p.m., we stayed there till 10 when we went to sleep, we must have started some hours because I woke up at 4 at Orange River. There was a big tank of boiling water here so we out with the camp kettles and made coffee. We were all standing round with our canteens, chewing the rag and also hard biscuit, when suddenly the engine whistled and the train began to move. You can guess the scramble. Canteens, waterbottles, camp kettles, went flying up, and the whole train was alive with arms and legs, hanging and kicking to get on board. We all got in somehow and proceeded. We passed by the battle fields of Belmont, Graspan, Enslin, and over the pontoon bridge at Modder, into the camp. Here we fixed up our camp on a sandy desert a foot thick. The pegs were an awful job to keep in, and heavy stones were used instead. Being very warm, however, its just as good to sleep in the open as in the tent. We had a lot of sickness here, which I put down to hard rations, and generally unsettled mode of living. However, a few days pulled the troops together. I had, also, some 40 linemen handed over to me here, two carts, and 8 mules. We had to go to a well, about two miles from Camp, because the Modder river was tainted by dead bodies of men and horses. One of the fellows stirred up a dead Kaffir, when he was bathing, he says it smelt awful. He ain't washed since. About 20 of the boys were taken for the Telegraph Office, which was being extremely well managed by Lance-Corporal Davis, in place of Sergeant Nelson, who was in hospital. The dust storms here were terrific. It was here we saw 800 wounded arrive from Paardeburg, also General Cronje and a lot of Boer prisoners. Stray horses are plentiful here, one chap captured 3 horses and 2 foals. One horse was saddled and bridled. He sold the saddled one for two cigars. No one would take the others, they eat too much. We went sailing comfortably on when, about 11.30 a m. one day, the Captain says, 'You must catch the 1 p.m. train.' Well, we did it somehow. I only took 15 clerks and 32 linemen, and away we went to De Aar, spent the night in empty truck, with a Sergeant of the 'Old and Bold,' we had met at Bisley. There were 3 of them at Bisley, now, there are only 2; one was left at Modder. It was 'Old Smiler,' too, poor chap. If you remember, we got to De Aar and stayed a day, when we loaded up a lot of telegraph stores, and away we started again for Naauwpoort, we got there at 7 p.m., ordered to proceed at 9 p.m., to Arundel and Rensburg. We got out and made some tea, just as it was boiling, the most awful thunderstorm that we have had, came on, and washed a bit of meat Rudd was frying, out of the pan. We got under the engine shed and eat the half cooked joint, without salt. It tasted good though, and tea is always palatable. After that we crawled under the tarpaulin of the truck, as it still poured with rain. We were so crowded. that, having got one arm in my overcoat, getting on the truck, I really couldn't move to get the other in. We passed the time singing hymns, etc., till 12 midnight, when we reached Rensburg, where Sergeant-Major Tee is located. I got out here and laid down on the floor of the Telegraph Office; I was sleeping peacefully when I heard a frightful crash, made sure it was a shell, but on looking up saw it was only the cook, shifting a beam from the roof to get dry wood for the fire. The Boers were here a few

KHAKI LETTERS—*continued*.

days ago and Tee had a lively time of it. Their laager is just outside, we got a bag of onions out of it. After breakfast we proceeded to Plecomann siding, mended the wire broken by the enemy, and left Creasey and Rudd as clerks. Then we continued the line to Colesberg, fixed up our instruments, but couldn't get through because a bullock wagon had knocked over one pole, and the wires down. I am still here with 12 clerks, etc., but the remainder have pushed on to Achtertang and Norval's Pont. Am drawing rations, etc., and as soon as the depôt is established at Norval's Pont, hope to go on. I saw General Clements' army go by, in skirmishing order, at Joubert Siding and it was a grand sight. We hear the big guns here occasionally, but have only seen dead horses up to the present. There are 8 poor brutes all of a heap, a little way off. Expect a shell found them. The bridge here was knocked about, but the R.E.'s soon put it right, and trains go to Achtertang. This is a lovely country, but very sparsely populated. One cabin every 20 miles Haven't spent a day in an office yet, am still Acting Q.M.S., and am getting a good judge of provisions. . . . . Love to Harry Rich, yourself, and the boys. Corporal Stevens is here, also Ray, Samuel, Little, and Fairall."

No. 199, Sapper **F. J. Sainsbury,** sends the following from Enslin, dated February 20th :—

"DEAR KEMP,—At last Kimberley is relieved, must have been after a well thought out plan on the part of French, Roberts, Kitchener and Co. Had it not been for them I would never have been here. I spent a good time at De Aar volunteering for the duties of 'cook's mate,' which I undertook to do until an order came out to the effect that clerks were no longer to be utilised for domestic purposes. My first shift was into a kind of detective agency, the military were evidently suspicious of the civil authorities in particular, of accepting questionable work or in 'giving the game away.' When Lords Roberts, Kitchener and Staff came up, this business, I believe, fell through, and at 3 a.m. one morning I was roused and warned to catch the 5 a.m. train for Modder. Our means of conveyance were rather unique, we had the choice of a cattle truck partially filled with stores, or an open truck with wood. About a dozen of us made the journey, we travelled fairly well until we reached Orange River where we were shunted, and hung about until 5 p.m. The water they gave us here was very bad indeed, coffee-coloured. Soon after leaving, the train crosses the Orange River, it is spanned by a fine iron bridge which commands a splendid view. The slopes of the river are dotted with trees, shrubs and tents. Horses and cattle are taken down the slopes to be watered. This is by far the best bit of scenery I've seen in Africa up to now. After passing the battle-fields of Belmont, Graspan and Enslin, we eventually arrived at our destination at 2 a.m., having been 21 hours on the road—a distance of 150 miles. We did not then detrain, we were shunted off on to the main line for Kimberley, then idle. Prior to this I had a blanket over me and had fallen asleep in the wood trucks; when the guard cleared out, several of us crouched ourselves down in the corners of his van to finish out our nap. We turned out about six and found ourselves not a very great distance from the ganger's hut, from which 'Long Tom' had already started shelling Magersfontein, the dust flew up in clouds. We then heard Lord Roberts address the Highland

KHAKI LETTERS—*continued*.

Brigade, they cheered him again and again. I was not at Modder long, I had time enough to have a look round, have a dip in the river Modder, see the graves of those who fell on December 11th, and was there to assist in the pressure due to Lord Roberts and his Staff. When they came here—Enslin—we came also, an armoured engine protected his saloon in front and our cattle truck in the rear. On arrival his Lordship and Staff joined the column. We put up a marquee and were not long before we were in communication with about a dozen stations including the column. A day or so later we had a wire to Jacobsdal from whence we heard the good tidings that French had got into Kimberley. Of course we could then hardly believe it, having heard so often the false rumours that Kimberley, Ladysmith, and even Mafeking had been relieved, all on good authority. The work now has been transferred to Modder, three of us remain. The work has now practically toned down into its normal state, one of us may shift again at any moment, but where no one knows. This place is quite a wilderness, nevertheless we might go farther and fare much worse. It contains one house, and a ruin at that, bearing testimony, as it does, to effect of shot and shell. The office was originally in one room, we are now in a bell tent—very cosy. For about a week we practically lived on Quaker Oats, and our rations, bread, meat and tea, with occasionally dripping done down from the meat; however, the stores have now a fresh stock, a few extras again will not be found amiss. Kind regards."

No. 2,336, Sapper **E. J. Samuel**, writing from the Military Telegraph Office, Arundel, February 24th, says :—

" . . . . Your admonition *re* the pencil is noted, and I've scoured the camp for some ink, and succeeded in obtaining some. I am pleased to hear you got the silver leaves O.K. We have heard terrible yarns about the new R.B. and the bicycle seats. You ought not to exceed your 30 mins. now. You will observe that I have changed my address. I little thought when I came out here that I should take part in a retreat of the British Army. A fortnight ago they withdrew a lot of our troops from Rensburg. They had not been away many days before the enemy was all round us, and our outlying camps in danger of being cut off. At Slingersfontein they were shelled out of the office for three days and had a rough time. The order was given to fall back on Rensburg, and on the night of the 12th they all came in after a rough passage. The Australians and the Worcesters suffered very heavily and the wounded were sent down to De Aar in open trucks. While they were waiting for the trucks the poor fellows were laid out on the ground beside the line and just in front of our office. It was a sickening sight. I was speaking to one of the Berks who had seven bad wounds ; he had three shots in one arm and two in the other, and he was ' cribbing ' because he couldn't brush the flies off his face. There was never a groan amongst the lot of them. Our main body left during the next day for Arundel. The Boers were all round us on the kopjes, we were almost the last to leave and had our line through until 12.30 p.m., and at 1 a.m. there was not a man left in the camp. Our rearguard was cut off and a lot killed and missing. This is a more comfortable office and the work has fallen off a lot, which enables us to pay a little attention to our personal comforts. I shall get a chance of washing my shirt, perhaps, now. I have worn it for five weeks now and I want to set an example to the rest of the troops and be *clean*. We've been having a lot of rain the last few days, and we hadn't trenched our tent, and were washed clean out. It was wicked, and so cold putting the tent up with no boots on and up to ankles in water. We had a lively day yesterday, for we were shelled from all directions, though luckily they all fell very short, but it got the 'breeze up' very successfully. There is a high kopje near here where we can see all that goes on round the camp. We have got two big Lyddite guns sent here from De Aar, regular 'Lengthy Thomas's,' and it was a treat to see the shells burst on the kopjes. The report is fearful. I wish you were here with your camera for there are some lovely subjects amongst the natives. Their costumes are most comical. If they can only get a pair of regimental trousers they are in the seventh heaven. We've got one attached to us who has the most remarkable pair of pants I ever saw. There are at least fifty patches on them. There's a native Kraal just here, and occasionally we have a look at them, but the girls are *not* lovely by any means, and a strong pipe is necessary to allay the odours from their houses.

" Did I tell you we had some STOUT issued to us? It was glorious, and as we have pals, we got an extra gallon. We have been presented with tons of grapes, and scoff them till we are bad. The remainder of ' L ' Company arrived last week at De Aar. There is a rumour that all the T.B.'s are to be kept out here from two to three years after peace is declared. What will poor Sam do if this is true, eh? What price the C.I.V. and their gloves? We hear one contingent of them were second in Kimberley. There was a scene here when we posted up the news about the relief of Kimberley, and the office was besieged with enquirers for news. We certainly seem to have the whiphand of them now. I don't know how we should have got on without the Colonials. We've three regiments of Mounted Infantry with us, and they have done magnificent work, and are the equals, if not the superiors, of our crack cavalry. Three batteries have just galloped out, so there's more work for the undertaker. It does one good to see them open out across the veldt at a stretch gallop with their escorts. I believe a few of our fellows at MO and DA are sick. Sergeant Nelson is reported to have sunstroke. Well, I hope you and *all* the others are well, and have no grievances. Have the holidays been settled yet? Pity a party of you can't take a trip out here, isn't it? for what a change from 10/8. Did you send me a *Times Weekly*? If so, many thanks. We haven't got our chocolate yet. Give my brotherly love to all. We may be in Colesberg this time next week, and on the road to Bloemfontein, and another bar to my medal. Ta, ta ; be good."

✣ ✣ ✣ ✣

No. 21,066, Sapper **Chas. Jones** (WOL), writing from Kimberley Station, Monday, February 26th, says :—

" DEAR COLOUR-SERGEANT KEMP,—Our little party has been subjected to such a hustling in various ways since leaving the 'St. Andrew' that we have had to be strangers to pencil and paper. The voyage out, as you have no doubt heard, could be summed up as a long dream of fierce sun, fairy-like nights, and unnatural horses, which for ever cried for grooming and feeding, all of which came to an end in Table Bay early on February 12th, in sight of the famous Mountain which kindly spreads its cloth in the usual style. There was too much preparation for our further journey to allow time to moralize on the beauties of the harbour and its background, however, and we had to leave at 10 p.m. on the 13th for De Aar without seeing into the town. Personally, the journey of 520 miles, with seven others, plus equipment, all packed in an inferior kind of L.C.D.R. carriage, minus racks, will remain as a horrible experience of discomfort, want of sleep and little food, to say nothing of the sun-baked hilly country, deserted by all living creatures, and almost devoid of green grass

KHAKI LETTERS—*continued*.

or shrubs. Still, hearts are trumps, and we arrived mid-day, 15th, with spirits enough to be curious about De Aar. Here we met some colleagues—Thomas (EH), Woolley (TS), Quarmby (HF), and others, all doing well, and with heaps of work, so on the latter account some of our party of fifty-eight remained at De Aar, the bulk going on to Modder River, starting on the 17th, and arriving on February 18th. Modder is a very busy office, worked by a little crowd of 24th ; the men are Stimpson, Stormer, Horton, Jenner (who is very much alive), &c., with Corporal Davis, of I.V, in charge. On the way to Modder several places of note were passed and eagerly scanned—Orange River (Catling and Pallett), Belmont (Porter, Collins, and Eglinton), Graspan, Enslin (Loosemore, CF ; Smith, TS). I can't remember half the boys I saw on the way, but most of the good old Company seemed to have pitched on this side of the country, and, anyway it was hard to recognise a colleague under the thick growth of beard which nearly everyone is developing. All were doing well despite the bad water at Modder, and the constant sand storms, and other such trifles. Here our party settled for the time being, and after a day or two on fatigues commenced office work. On February 21st a cct was got through to Kimberley, and a party of seven R.E.'s, including only Sergeant Miller and myself of the 24th, were sent there for duty. Up to the time of writing there is no prospect of any further change, unless the good news of Cronje's capitulation brings about a general exodus Westward. But it is good to be at Kimberley, although food is scanty, as there is so much to see in the signs of the recent siege, and the picturesque crowds of every nationality leaving and arriving. The postal arrangements seem to have gone astray somewhere, as bags for the last two or three weeks are being dumped into Kimberley, but letters are beginning to circulate now. Thanks to the kindness of Mr. Miller, of the Telegraphic Department (late of Dundee), we are quite comfortable here. With kind regards from all."

✧   ✧   ✧   ✧

No. 2,548, Sapper **W. C. Smith,** writing from Enslin, February 27th, says :—

"DEAR COLOUR-SERGEANT,—You must think that I am very ungrateful not to have written to you before, especially after the trouble you have been put to on our behalf. I thank you very much for the card and letter, which, although received rather late, came as a very pleasant surprise, and were very much appreciated. By the above heading you will see that I am stationed at Enslin, and have been since the 28th of December. From Enslin the Gordons signal to Kimberley by helio, and then transmit to Modder from KB, as the KB helio cannot be seen from Modder. Jacobsdal also works to 'Big Hill,' Enslin. When the Gordons were here it was possible to have a game of football, but since they left with the footballs I have had to mope round the camp. (The signallers were left behind, but no football.) The Australians have left here also, so there is no cricket. I think I shall go in for ostrich farming. Heaps of wounded are being brought down from the front. They all appear cheerful, and want to get back to their regiments again. Truck-loads of refugees from Kimberley and neighbourhood are passing through here on their way south. Boer prisoners to a great number, in trucks, prison vans, saloons, etc., are also being sent south. Most of them are pleased that they are captured. Like most places in the Karoo, there is plenty of dust. The last few days, however, we have had some rain—quite a Godsend. It was appreciated so much that I stood outside the tent to have the pleasure of it wetting me. Thanking you once more for your kindness to the poor wanderers."

Sapper W. R. Williams, R.E.

In the last No. of KHAKI LETTERS, you will remember, I had to chronicle the death of Sapper A. W. Hawkins, of TSF. This time, I regret to say, I have to announce that 852, Sapper W. R. Williams—a colleague of Hawkins—died at the same place, from the same cause, 19 days afterwards. Walter Reginald Williams was not a 24th man, but a Royal Engineer, he was, however, closely attached to the Corps, being the son of an old member, who has been in the P.O. Rifles since 1872, viz., Assistant-Quartermaster-Sergeant Williams, of TS, now Assistant Superintendent in charge of CLS. Sapper Williams, after a tuition at Mr. Ward's School, at Brixton, joined the Royal Engineers, at Chatham, March, 1897, removed to Aldershot, February, 1898, sent to Plymouth, March, 1899, where he remained until November, when he left with the R.E. Reserves, C.S.M. Tee, Sergt. Miller, Sapper Hawkins, and others, in the "Canada," for South Africa. He was well known to many TS men who were on the Salisbury Manœuvres, 1898. I have known him ever since he was a little boy—1882, I think, being the first year, when he was 5 years old.

At that time the 24th used Brown's Grounds, Nunhead, for class firing and drill, and nothing seemed to please Reggie better than to be there to watch the proceedings. Perhaps his most favourite amusement was the long distance signalling that used to be carried on there, for in those days heliograph work was possible from the top of Telegraph Hill (now built over) to very far away places. He would accompany us to either home or distant station, but this was not all, he was always pleased to be with the 24th in camp at Aldershot, and this gave him a great desire to become a soldier. He was 22 years and 8 months old when he died, and the only son. I am able to reproduce a cabinet portrait of him that was taken in October last at Plymouth, at his father's request—(he kindly bearing the expense) as so many, he feels sure, would like a portrait as a memento.

I have had the pleasure of seeing a good many of Reggie's letters. He was in constant communication with those at home, for he seems to have devoted almost all his spare moments in writing to his "Dear Father, Mother and Sisters," telling them all the news of his journeyings, adventures, and not the least, perhaps, his chums, both of the 24th and his own Royal Corps. This is significant, for it once again indicates the oneness of the men at the front. He appears to have been most anxious about his chocolate box, he mentions it so often. It has arrived.

Mr. Williams has given me permission to publish extracts from some of his son's recent letters, and this I am doing in order to show that almost up to the time of his death his health had always been "good"—in fact, the day before he was reported ill (which was the day he died—April 2nd), a long letter was received which ended as you will see--in the most effusive terms—"Health charming, delightful, awfully nice, etc., self and Urquhart healthiest here"—but the next letter (received 4 days after his death), which was dated March 18th, speaks of the death and burial of Sapper Hawkins, which cast a gloom over them—and that he had "been suffering from a severe cold, but am much better, hope to be all right to-morrow," he concludes with "Really no more to say, so will close———" and that is probably his last letter. No doubt some of his comrades at Orange River in their letters which may be on the way will give some details of his death and burial, as Reggie did of poor Hawkins.

"KHAKI LETTERS," *April 20th* 1900.

Walter Reginald Williams,
SAPPER, ROYAL ENGINEERS.

Born August 17th, 1877,
Died of Enteric Fever, at Orange River, while on Active Service, April 2nd, 1900.

"My Dear Kemp,—In reply to your request that I should send you some of my son's recent letters, I have great pleasure in doing so. In them you will notice my son mentions many of the 24th men, viz., Tee, Miller, Luttrell, Nelson, C. Wilson, Dellbridge, Jones (Cardiff), Bannister, &c. He was doing similar duty to Hawkins, *i.e.*, watching talking on the wires in the civil office. You will see by his letters how he said all along that his health was good. This made the shock all the worse for us to bear. It shews the suddenness of these attacks of fever. He was actually dead before we knew he was ill. That 24th men should take the greatest care of themselves is the earnest wish of

"Yours truly,

"April 12th, 1900." "W. R. WILLIAMS."

[Yes, truly a great loss, and the many to whom "Bob" is known—as well as others who have not had that pleasure—tender their sincere condolences to a father and his sorrowing family.]

IN MEMORIAM.

✠

A noble nature, fervent, strong and true,
    Honest, sincere; a mind alert and keen;
A faithful friend, a stubborn foe, a type
    Of England's gallant soldiers of the Queen.

He gave his life for England; Duty called,
    And for the land from whence he first drew breath
He sailed with others of Her valiant sons,
    And on Life's very threshold—met with death.

Happy the country that can send such men
    Prepared in Freedom's cause to play a part:
Glory will soften, though it cannot heal
    A father's grief, a mother's broken heart.

CLS, *April 11th.* R. W. HALL.

✠

Extracts From His Various Letters—(*All from Orange River*).

Dated February 13th, he says:—" I am now, as you will see, in a different part of the country. I left Kloof about 2 p.m. on Saturday, and rode in a cart to Rensburg, where I arrived about 5.45 p.m. I then had a drop of tea, and left by 6 p.m. train for De Aar. Arrived Naauwpoort 7.30; left again 11 p.m. Arrived De Aar 2.15 a.m., and slept on the platform till 6.30 a.m. Carried my blankets with me. I then reported myself at the camp, and was told to be ready to leave for Orange River at 9 a.m. Arrived here about 3 p.m., so that I was travelling for 25 hours. Plenty of work here. Have not yet received H.M.'s chocolate. In the office we have six circuits, to—(1) Modder River, for Honeynest Kloof and Klokfontein; (2) De Aar;

(3) Belmont, for Enslin and Graspan ; (4) Zoutpansdrift (O.F.S.) ; (5) phonophore circuit to Witteputts, and (6) spare circuit to De Aar."

Dated February 16th :—" Good news this morning. Kimberley has been relieved by General French, who left Rensburg to come up this way. . . . Tee, I'm told, had to make a hurried exit from there as the Boers advanced, the troops having for the most part withdrawn. Tee is now in charge at Arundel. Jimmy Miller has left Naauwpoort, and passed through here this morning. Sergeant Luttrell and party arrived at De Aar yesterday from England. . . . Still in best of health."

February 18th. ". . . A chap in Modder River Office went for a walk over Magersfontein battle-field. He found a beautiful little revolver ; another man in front of him picked up a gold watch and chain. . . . . I received a letter yesterday from Fred Cosier. He tells me he gave you a memorial card (of his brother) for me. I shall always prize it in memoriam of my best and dearest chum. . . . . He concludes : Health O.K. Don't fear. Now acclimatised I think. Keep writing. Letters most welcome. Love to all.— REG."

February 25th.—" My ambition now is to see Kimberley. . . . Have received H.M.'s chocolate, and eaten half. Remainder and box posted to you. It should arrive with this letter. Write immediately you receive it. I shall be anxious to hear. Of course, you may do what you wish with the contents. Boxes are exceedingly valuable—£5 being offered for a single one even out here. See back of it. This was done by Bannister. He's a clever man at this work. Done with a penknife. . . . Have been chatting to that carabineer who sat opposite us at the ' I ' and ' L ' Companies' dinner. You will remember, dad, he was wounded at Potfontein, near Rensburg, and has now been sent to join his regiment at Kimberley. Enclosed is part of the Union Jack which was on the front of the engine of the first train to come through from Kimberley after the relief. I can vouch for its genuineness. May send a photo of this interesting event later. The Post Office are very heavily taxed, it's a wonder they do it so well. . . . I sold those badges I had on my belt for £1, marvellous business that. Worth a shilling in England, but Colonials pay any price for British regimental badges.

March 4th.—In this he refers to a fire just behind the office in a building containing a large quantity of paraffin oil, they had to strike tents and hastily remove everything, a bicycle was burnt " beyond all recognition." He goes on to say " the troops call the C.I.V. ' come in vain' (mim.). Am still in best of health, I am glad to say. Hawkins, a 24th man from TSF has been admitted to hospital, we think with enteric. His temperature is 103 this morning. I fancy the cause is through drinking the river water which we get from the station. It is the colour of mud, and although it is said to be good, I am very shy of it . . . . I am making an attempt to grow a beard . . . .We can't look our best out here, though. I have hair an inch long with no prospect of getting it cut. One of the railway porters was cutting hair at 6d. a time with an old pair of lamp scissors which had been rescued from our late fire."

March 8th.—Replying to his mother :—" Your reference to my being made Corporal created a broad smile on my countenance. I can't understand what made you think that . . . . The Military Telegraph Staff had a photo taken on Tuesday evening last, and a splendid picture it turned out. Splendid picture of myself, too. Just five minutes before we were taken the chap who stands on my left, who is also a Williams (from Cardiff), laughingly told me that my beard was neither one thing nor the other, so I had a hasty shave. I am sending you all three copies . . . . Don't forget to write to me immediately on receipt of chocolate, also *re* photo of first Kimberley train. Am very anxious about chocolate, keep saying to myself 'I ought to have registered it.' . . . . I somehow fancy we (the 2nd TB) are out here for a long time to come. You see, all the offices in both the O.F.S. and the Transvaal will have to be manned by Englishmen after peace is proclaimed. I am sure they won't have any Dutchmen in the telegraph staff out here again. The offices, from Pretoria to Bloemfontein, were all manned by Dutchmen until war was proclaimed. You see what a pull it will be on the Englishmen."

"I am sorry you are so worried about my welfare; believe me, I never realize the fact that I am over 6,000 miles from home, except with the letters. I get plenty to eat, and, as they have opened up a well near here, we get splendid water. Will let you know immediately I receive either or all of the parcels. Don't think the authorities will give us any warmer clothing just yet. I have three shirts (two of them greybacks), two lamb's wool undershirts (rather worse for wear, but no matter), a suit of red at Capetown (which will be sent up, I expect, when the war is over), and an overcoat, not to mention a jersey; so if I can't keep warm it will be a mystery. I don't anticipate being under canvas by the time the bad weather comes along. All officers are in corrugated huts, and for the past week I have been sleeping in the civil office, which adjoins ours. Hope my letter from Kloof Camp did not upset you. No harm now in telling you that bullets whistled over our heads all day, with an occasional shell for a change. All now changed that way. British occupying Norvals Pont. Miller is now clerk in charge at Kimberley; wish I could get there with him. Fine place, I hear. Barnes has gone to Osfontein. You write in a down-hearted tone about affairs with Buller, and the war generally, but I trust by now you are more than agreeably surprised at 'Bobs'' doings. He, with French and Kitchener, has turned the tide all round. Only want to see Mafeking relieved (big force going that way) and then—Pretoria from two or three directions. 'Bobs' wants Buller to keep 'em in the Drakenberg Mountains all he can, so that he ('Bobs') can continue his northward march. The end will be a complete collapse of the enemy—demoralised. You see! My health? Charming, delightful, awfully nice, &c. Self and Urquhart, from Inverness, healthiest here. Much love to all. Remembrances to all enquiring friends.—REG."

Probably the following is his last letter, March 18th :—" Dear Mother, Father and Sisters,—Very little to tell you this week, the only excitement we get here is the trains passing through. We lost a comrade last Tuesday evening, and buried him on the following day. It was a very sad affair, and created a gloom over us for a day or two. Col. Hippesley, the D.A.G., wired the other day for names of clerks here, so we shall probably be getting an order to shift at any moment. No letters arrived yet, expect them every minute now. I have been suffering from severe cold for two or three days, but glad to say am much better this morning. Hope be right by to-morrow. Weather still warm, no signs of winter yet. Believe it comes on us suddenly. We have now a Militia battalion with a drum and fife band, so things are made somewhat livelier. Really no more to say, so will close. With love to all.—REG."

"Khaki Notes."

MUSKETRY FOR THE MILITIA. We cull from the *Naval and Military Record* a portion of its "Aldershot Letter," which reads as follows:—" We are quick in modifying our methods, and some of the lessons of the South African campaign are already being taught. As might be supposed, the attack practice in connection with musketry is the first subject to which attention has been officially directed. A modified course of procedure at the rifle ranges, although tentative, is rightly directed. The conditions under which firing will occur will more nearly approach to those of actual service. The troops will commence their firing exercise at the greatest distance that the range will allow, and the officers commanding will exercise entire discretion as to the character of the fire, the position of their men in executing it, and their general movements. Everything, however, will be governed by the effectiveness of this fire, as judged by the marks given at the butts. At the expiration of each range practice results will be tabulated, and a short lecture delivered to the men while the subject matter is fresh in their minds, thus ensuring an intelligent conception of the work they have to perform. What is known as vanishing black band practice is to receive careful attention. This is a firing exercise which demands alertness, as well as steadiness, and is a great advance on our previous musketry training. This target better represents the enemy than any other. It appears and vanishes at intervals of about ten seconds, and the targets are to be so distributed with regard to the sections of men firing that hits and misses will come home to those employed."

MORE BARRACKS FOR ALDERSHOT. The accommodation for troops at Aldershot is to be increased at once by the building at Ewshott of huts for eight infantry battalions and three batteries of artillery. A board of officers, of which Major-General R. H. Murray is to be president, assembled recently to report on the suitability of the plan and to facilitate these buildings.—*Daily Mail.*

THE FIELD TELEGRAPH. There is a branch of the service which is doing good work, and which deserves a word of praise. I refer to the Field Telegraph Department. When an engagement is being fought the Field Telegraph cart goes with the General, under the fire of the enemy's guns, if need be, leaving in its track the strand of wire by which the General is able to issue his commands to the forces in any part of the field of operations. That high hill two miles to the left is defended by four companies of the 2nd Berkshires, and yet to the very top of it, over boulders and through bushes, the endless coil of wire is taken, and the "tap-tap" of the instrument speaks in the Morse language whatever the General says. At night, while the camp sleeps, a picket guards the lonely hill. If danger suddenly threatens, a few taps of the magical

KHAKI NOTES—*continued*.

instrument speaks to the vigilant telegraphist far below, and in an instant the camp is standing to its arms, each man in his proper place. This brief sketch is sufficient to demonstrate the great value of the Field Telegraph Department.—*Daily Telegraph.*

A GOOD DRINK. The 1,000 bottles of Eiffel Tower Lemonade, which the War Office accepted as a present from Messrs. Foster, Clark, and Co., of Maidstone, to soldiers at the front—not being nearly sufficient—the firm makes known that they are prepared to send to any soldier in South Africa a sixpenny tin of the lemonade, each tin sufficient to make two gallons of good lemonade, on receipt of three penny stamps, from any wife or mother of a soldier at the front. The correct address, and the rank, name, number, and corps of the soldier must be sent.—*Daily News.*

THE C.T.O. A.M.B. CONCERT. A most successful Patriotic Concert was given at the Holborn Town Hall, on Friday evening, April 6th. Initiated and carried through by the staff of the Central Telegraph Department. There can be no doubt that the *Daily Mail* Relief Fund will receive a substantial addition to its splendid and useful scheme. Rudyard Kipling's "Pay, Pay, Pay," for the time was changed to "Give, Give, Give," as everything was given freely, not only by the artistes, but hearty and enthusiastic support was also given by those holding the "sinews of war," as the Greeks termed the "root of all evil." Upwards of fourteen pounds were collected by the fair ones with the Tambourines during the interval. The proceeds will amount to nearly £100.

A FRAMED PHOTOGRAPH of the late Duke of Teck has been received by Sergeant-Major Hoy and each of the eight colour-sergeants who acted as bearers at the funeral at St. George's Chapel, Windsor, together with H.R.H. the Duchess of York's thanks for the kind thought of the sergeants in sending a wreath.

SERGEANT J. C. HAVES, our old store-room sergeant, has been absent from H.-Q. with a severe cold since April 2nd. We trust "Jacob" may soon resume his duties. He has served every recruit with his kit, etc., for over 20 years, and the Orderly Room does not seem complete without him. Be quick, Jacob, and get well again. Every man in the Regiment admires an old soldier like you.

"JACOB" is an ideal Storekeeper. He has always at hand the article one requires. Go to him for a new pair of leggings, service cap, or whatever it may be, and Jacob's answer is the same: "There it is, my boy, I'd put it on one side for you." If you break your bootlace, chances are Jacob thought you'd do so, he's got one told off for you. Fitting a man with a busby is rather amusing. "Too small, Sergeant." "Then try this one," says Jacob, as he hands him another and receives busby No. 1 in return. "No, that's too tight, too." Meanwhile Jacob rummages about among the busbies and is ready with another. "Now, here's one, but I'm afraid it is slightly too big for *you*." It's tried, and the man is delighted. "It's just right, Sergeant, that'll suit me splendidly." And off he goes with the one he tried at first.

CORRESPONDENTS are constantly asking questions *re* pay, etc. The answer is 24th men of the R.E. Reserve enjoy their full P.O. pay plus that of their emoluments as a soldier.

KHAKI NOTES—*continued.*

COLOUR-SERGEANT J. W. SIBLEY (of "I" Company), who has for some time been in charge of the East London Volunteer Brigade Signallers, and has acted as teacher of telegraphy for the Post Office employees in the Northern District, is gazetted in the *P.O. Circular*, dated April 3rd, as Postmaster of Epping. Comrades at the front will be glad to hear of Sib.'s success.

THE "CEPHALONIA" sailed from Southampton Feb. 20th, and

THE "ORIENTAL" sailed from London February 28th, but they both came up smiling at Cape Town on the same evening, Wednesday, 21st March, reuniting, as it were, the separated Fourth party of "Ours."

OUR NEXT PARTY are expecting to leave by the end of this week, per s.s. "Montfort," from the Royal Albert Docks, London.

SERGEANT "BILLY" KNIGHT hopes to resume his official duties at the week-end. He has had a terrible time of it. Give him a winning welcome.

LETTERS HELD OVER for next issue are numerous and highly interesting. There is one strong point in them: The highest praise is accorded the non-com.'s of the Royal Engineers, who have dealt with our men while at Aldershot, for their "kindness and patience," says one writer, adding "I hope you will emphasise this."

SAPPER C. A. G. FAIRALL (28,865), of Mount Pleasant Engineers' Office, died at Naauwpoort of enteric fever, April 6th. In the Casualty Lists the name is given as C. Farrell, and the regimental number slightly differs, *i.e.*, 28,665, but official information received later puts it beyond doubt that the poor victim is another of "Ours."

SERGEANT P. CANEY, 238 A.P.O.C., died of enteric fever at Maritzburg, April 4th.

CORRECTION.—Sapper Morse's initials are A. H., not as shown in "K.L.," No. 3, page 43.

THE VOLUNTEER ACCIDENT FUND costs but 1s. per year. Every volunteer should join it. You never know what may happen.

I HAVE to acknowledge two postal orders for 3s. from G.S.W., who says "you can send a few ('K.L.'s) on to some of your splendid fellows who so well telegraph the news of Khaki to us civilians."

Also, for the same object, "A Supt.," 2s. 6d. Thank you.

CABLE ROOM BOHEMIAN, May 2nd, Champion Hotel, Aldersgate Street, E.C. Santley's setting of Mrs. Hemans' poem, "Son of the Ocean Isle," will be sung by Mr. George Bowthorpe in memoriam of our lamented colleague, A. W. Hawkins. 24th men and others are invited, and should make an effort to be there. Proceeds to the *D.T.* Fund.

☞ Divisional doings, group gatherings, interesting items, and other short, sweet, and suitable subjects should reach me by Friday if their senders desire them to appear in "Khaki Notes" the following week.

COLOURS.

"KHAKI LETTERS," One Penny. By post, Three Halfpence.

All posted letters containing Remittances, Orders, MSS., &c., must be addressed to R. E. KEMP, 12, JERRARD STREET, LEWISHAM, S.E.
Postal Orders should be made payable at Loampit Vale, Lewisham, S.E.

Printed by E. G. BERRYMAN & SONS, *Blackheath Road, London, S.E.*

"Khaki Letters" from ....
"My Colleagues in South Africa."

CORRESPONDENCE FROM THE
POST OFFICE TELEGRAPHISTS
OF THE
24th MIDDLESEX (P.O.) RIFLE VOLUNTEERS
(Royal Engineer Reserves),
ON ACTIVE SERVICE.

THE BOND THAT BINDS US—FRIENDSHIP—COMRADESHIP.

Published fortnightly for the Postal Telegraph Service.
Conducted by COLOUR-SERGEANT R. E. KEMP. *Central Telegraph Office, London.*

No. 6.   MAY 4TH, 1900.   PRICE ONE PENNY.

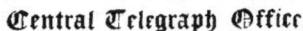

Central Telegraph Office,

London, E.C.

EAR COMRADES, ONE AND ALL.

Greetings! Thanks and congratulations for your numerous letters and their splendid words of cheer. Also the newspapers, especially the copies of *The Friend*—our keynote, by the way, and may it ever be so.

Your old regiment is now in the bustle of its drill season, and is going strong. We have had the opportunity of noticing that the men look prouder than ever, and why? For the very good reason that they are represented in South Africa by quite a small battalion of right royal worthy comrades, begetting honour to our name. No other Corps in the Kingdom can point to 600 of their men at the front, but had they the opportunity there is no doubt they would be forthcoming.

After the customary course of firing exercise, drill, etc., at Aldershot, the last portion of the 60 have sailed to join you. A worthy chum has favoured me with their "last moments in Camp." I will give it you in his own words, which will be a change for you. Writing on April 26th, re

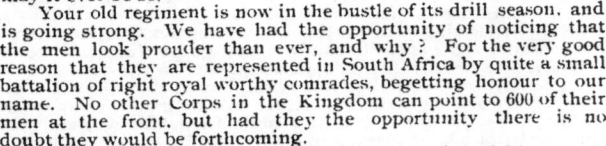

ANOTHER CONTINGENT OF TELEGRAPHISTS

for the front, he goes on to say:—

"The batch of 60 is now complete, 46 having arrived at the Cape and the remaining 14 left here this morning. There was a most enjoyable time here last night, when a farewell Concert was held to give a send-off to the draft. The company was a very mixed one, for besides the R.E.'s, who turned up *en masse*, there were representatives of a good number of other corps, including R.A.M.C., A.S.C., and R.H.A. The chair was taken by Sapper Newbury, one of the oldest R.E.'s. The programme was opened by a Corporal of the R.H.A., who sang

'Darling Baby' in good style. Sapper Tozer in his inimitable style then gave us a treat in the rendering of 'I should like to go halves in that.' Sapper Hargreaves was next called upon and sang 'The Drummer Boy' and 'Queen of the Earth' in fine style. Sapper Tozer again gave us a good turn in singing 'There'll be a hot time in the Transvaal to-night.' Corporal Sullivan of the R.E.'s gave us an original verse of this song (when Tozer had finished), which was received very enthusiastically, the words being very appropriate. Sapper Collins, another old R.E., also gave us a laughable song which was preceded by a very nice speech. Amongst other things he commented on the friendly feelings which existed between the Volunteers and Regulars, and said he felt sure that the feeling would continue, and if they were denied the pleasure of meeting them in South Africa, they would make quite certain of giving them a hearty reception on their return, which he hoped would be soon. (It should be here noted that the R.E.'s have indeed been brothers to us, and the bitter feeling said to exist between Volunteers and Regulars, has, in our case, happily, been absent.) The Chairman then spoke of the pleasure it had been to the R.E.'s individually and collectively to render any assistance to the Volunteers, for they knew such services were appreciated and returned when an opportunity offered. He also remarked that he gave voice to the general opinion when he said that the 24th boys would uphold the honour of the country either in working or fighting. He was heartily cheered for his kind words and Sergt. Walker, on behalf of the draft responded in suitable terms, and said that the only drawback was leaving such good and trusted friends behind them. The company then rose, and, joining hands, sang 'Auld Lang Syne,' and 'He's a jolly good fellow.' The party then came to 'attention' and sang the National Anthem. This concluded a pleasant and enjoyable evening. The draft were up betimes this morning and took the sea and service kit bags down to the Guardroom where the wagon was waiting. They were breakfasted in good style and paraded 7.15 a.m. We were marched down to the Square and inspected by the Captain. After this he addressed the draft, and in the course of his remarks said they would on embarking have a chance of being inoculated, but, as it was optional, they must choose for themselves whether or not they would have it. Continuing he said that if he had a friend going out he would use his utmost endeavours to persuade him to have it, and if he was allowed to go out himself he would most assuredly have it as a preventative of enteric fever. The waiting men were ordered to fall out (as none of the draft had been considerate enough to fall sick), and then wishing them a safe journey, success, and safe return, ordered Sergt.-Major Hall to march them off. The waiting men were alarmed at being kept back and feared we were not going to be allowed to bid our chums good-bye. Our fears were happily unfounded, for the Captain came and said we could go down to the station (Government Siding), and see our chums off. He said he had given orders to have us watched as he expected we should try to get away with them (mim). We promptly followed in the wake of 'Our Boys,' and although we lost sight of them at times, we could easily have followed them by the cheering, which was tremendous. On reaching the station the Provost would not allow us to go on the platform, this made us feel sick. If he thought that would prevent us he had very little idea of dealing with our lot, for, putting on dejected looks we turned away and went down the opposite platform, and on getting opposite our chaps, jumped on to the line and into the carriage and thence to the platform. All the men were in high spirits and very cheerful. Capt. Powell came on to the platform and made kind enquiries about their comfort, &c. As he moved away we raised three cheers for him, and although we gained a smile from him we received a frown from the Bandmaster of a band playing in front of us, for our cheers were so hearty that the music was lost entirely.

"By this time the train was ready to leave. and as it commenced to move, with flags flying, bands playing and cheers, we gave a last hand-shake and good wishes, and then stood by. This concluded the most enthusiastic send-off for such a small party it has ever been my good fortune to witness."

The detachment arrived at the Royal Albert Docks at 11 a.m., and were timed to sail at 3 p.m., but it was nearer 7.30 p.m. before a start was made, amidst renewed cheering. And so left the boys of the Old Brigade, who will bring the "L" Company up to nearly 170 men at the front. These are 3rd T.B.'s, but, it is believed, will be 2nd T.B.'s on arrival at Cape Town.

There are two promotions amongst the "Montfort" party. 4399 Sapper J. H. E. Walker (LV), who has seen considerable Volunteer Service, and was a Colour-Sergt.

in his late corps, was promoted Sergeant, April 12th. J. W. Lincoln (NT), who was a Sergt. in the 5th V.B.D.L.l., together with J. J. McSweeney and R. W. E. Lasham, who have both done their Service period with the Royal Engineers, were told off to attend Orderly Office where one had to be selected for Lance-Corporal. This was given to the former, in accordance to a rule from War Office, which states that N.C.O.'s must retain their rank as far as practicable. Lincoln is therefore Lance-Corporal from April 12th, 1900. Good luck to both of you.

Referring to Nos. 3 and 4 of KHAKI LETTERS, Sergeant Flanagan's party consisted of all the men whose names are shewn therein, up to and including 4392 W. Gilmour, the remainder—exclusive of the four waiting-men—sailed in the "Montfort," and are those referred to above.

There are at present at Aldershot or on furlough ten men who are anxious for their time of departure to be made known to them. They have had intimation that they may perchance be sent off when their numbers have increased to twelve. This will not mean many days, more than those required being already on their way, and it is possible that by May 10th we shall again say " Good-bye." Amongst them are the following :—W. E. Burden (SO), A. Walkley (BS), R. D. S. Norman (SS), W. H. Butt (DO), F. Robinson (LV), W. H. Turnbull (LV), T. M. Morris (NU), D. Armstrong (EH). C. W. Perkins (MR), and C. Bourdeaux (BM). It is expected they will be sent to Beira.

On April 25th, the new contingent of 82 men, for reinforcing the over-worked Army Post Office Corps now in South Africa, paraded for inspection at the Head Quarters of our regiment, Throgmorton Avenue, E.C., and were addressed by the new Postmaster-General, Lord Londonderry, who thus made his first public appearance in connection with the Post Office. He congratulated the detachment, who were all specially selected men, and complimented them on their thorough and soldierly appearance. He told them of the valuable work they would be able to discharge with the Army—in fighting for the reputation of the Post Office as well as for the cause of their country. He wished them God-speed and a safe return. The men were in full marching order, and had been very rapidly served out with all necessaries within a couple of days by the Permanent Staff—Sergt.-Major Hoy, Sergt.-Instructors Graham, Jackman, Slee, and Master-Tailor E. Bell—who had worked during the whole of Tuesday night in order to cope with the urgency of this case. The men arrived at all hours from various provincial offices. Amongst them are Overseers, Senior Telegraphists, Sorters, Sorting Clerks and Telegraphists, most of whom have seen more or less service in the Volunteer force. Amongst the men better known to 24th comrades are Colour-Sergt. T. Feldwick, " K " Company, from the S.E. District, who is Acting-Sergt.-Major and in charge of the men, Colour-Sergt. W. Williams, " F " Company, from the N.W. District, and Staff-Sergt. W. C. James from the F.B., G.P.O., London. Of the remainder, half are London men and half are provincials. All are enrolled as members of the 24th and are transferred to the " M " Company—otherwise A.P.O.C. The terms of the service under which they have engaged varies—some have enlisted for one year or during the continuance of the war, others for the usual six years. There is no doubt much care has been exercised in getting the best together, and it is hoped the Army will soon benefit by this addition to its Post Office contingent. Complaints against the Post Office administration at the front have appeared from various sources and in several newspapers, but all seem to forget the insurmountable difficulties with which our men have had to contend. The addresses at the front are constantly on the move, and some of your letters had informed us that there had been no less than nine postmarks on my envelopes, proving that the enormous quantity of correspondence has to be dealt with over and over again. People often tell what ought to be done but they omit to explain how to do it. This Company sailed in the same boat as their Telegraph Colleagues, the s.s. " Montfort," on April 26th.

We have read Mr. Hanbury's statement in the House re Camp, pay, &c., but nothing has been regimentally or officially communicated to us yet. We are waiting.

Trusting you are all well and going strong.

Yours most heartily,

R. E. KEMP,

Colour-Sergeant.

Tuesday, May 1st, 1900.

COPYRIGHT.—"Khaki Letters" must not be used without permission.—R. E. KEMP.

Khaki Letters.

No. 447, Sapper **C. J. Jenner**, writing from Kimberley, February 25th, says:—

"Salutations from the Diamond Fields. This is a splendid place and I would not mind living here, but the siege has been terrible and the sufferings of the people ditto. The Boers cannoned the whole town recently, and in a house where I visited they had a shrapnel through the roof. Another big house had been blown up and burnt by a hundred pounder, in fact, every house has a gruesome memento of some kind. Am feeling well again, although I had a touch of the prevalent complaint—diarrhœa. Kindly remember me to all friends. Am deeply grieved about Jack Cosier, poor fellow, I did not think it would be so soon with him. Isn't Bobs making this hum? You don't know half what he is doing. Things are indeed very hot. . . . . Off to Bloemfontein I expect, now."

In another letter from the same place, dated March 10th, C. J. Jenner says:—

"DEAR KEMP,—I had written you before, but a great change in the situation took place before I posted it, so I cancelled the letter, as the incidents of Camp life were quite eclipsed by the doings of Lord Roberts' Army, which reinforced us. I had the honour of taking in and despatching the telegram to London, communicating the joyful news of the Relief of Kimberley. A galloper brought the message in from Jacobsdaal at 2 a.m. We had heard the firing during the two previous days, telling us our army was advancing northwards, otherwise we were quite in the dark as to what was 'coming off.' Directly the news was brought in we could hear the Mounted Orderlies dashing off to the Supply Depôt and elsewhere, carrying orders for the gastronomic relief of KB. The next day brought full confirmation of Lord Roberts' brilliant victory, and also the intelligence that the Boers had, in a great hurry, evacuated Magersfontein, and the country between Modder and Kimberley. Then the first railway train, containing two Companies of R.E's and 200 natives, steamed out of the station to repair the line; the Engine was at the rear of the train, and on the cowcatcher of the engine was Jimmy Jones of CF, O'Sullivan, and myself, 'sneaking up to the front,' we got separated in a severe dust storm and I got sent back, but Jones and O'Sullivan got into the trenches and secured a lot of loot. Jimmy found Cronje's revolver and belt amongst other things. As we were delayed in proceeding to KB, a great many of us went

KHAKI LETTERS—*continued*.

there on a visit, insinuating ourselves into the guard's van of the KB train. Jimmy Miller had already gone on with a construction party, and was one of the first to enter the besieged town. Many of us visited the Boer position at Magersfontein on the return journey. It was a wonderfully fortified place and I am glad our troops were not again sent to a frontal attack. It surely must have proved disastrous.

"On March 8th we had the inexpressible joy of seeing Cronje and 4,200 of his army brought into Modder, as prisoners, together with 5 guns, one of which was the dreaded ' Pom-pom,' *i.e.*, the 1-pounder, quick-firing Vickers-Maxim. Cronje was taken, together with his officers (one of whom was Major Albrecht, the German Artillerist), to the Hotel, at Modder, which is the Chief Staff Office, and at 4 p.m. he was brought out, to proceed by special train, to Cape Town. The scene was like one from a comic opera, in front of the hotel a guard of honour of the R.H.A. was placed, and, as Cronje, his wife, grandson, and servant, emerged from the hotel, the trumpeter sounded the salute. We had a splendid view of the droll procession, everything seemed so shoddy, and Bertie Stormer got a fine snapshot of the affair. We did not move forward so soon as anticipated, one Wheatstone Staff was detailed for the 'front,' the others proceeding to KB to work WX from the advanced base. All the the men were greatly pleased with KB. Murch, late of the ' C,' is here, having stood the siege fairly well, although his health is far from being good. We were glad to get away from Modder, as we were all getting run down and were fearful of contracting camp fever, so many troops and horses had been encamped there.

"March 9th, Lord Roberts has so entirely routed the Boers (about which you will glean from the papers, which will also tell how he pursued them from KB to Paardeburg,) that our plans are likely to be changed, and we expect to move at once to Colesburg and work up through the Free State to Bloemfontein, and on to Pretoria (we hope).

"From KB we are, pending the arrival of the Wheatstone Staff at the front, working Quad. to De Aar, D.C. Simplex to Orange River and intermediate stations, and Dx to the front. We are working in KB Post Office.

"All the Boys wish to be remembered to any individual enquirer, and send their best thanks to you for letters and papers, and are getting hopeful of a return by June."

On a Postcard dated 17th March, Jenner adds :—

" Milton right to the front, and entered Bloemfontein with Roberts' Army. Sappers Poole, Stimpson, Horton, Hall, and others, have trekked to BFN with Wheatstone to work back to us at KB. Sorry poor Hawkins (TSF) died."

✥ ✥ ✥ ✥

No. 24,305, Sapper **F. T. Stimpson,** writing from Kimberley, February 27th, says :—

" . . . To-day has been a red-letter day in the campaign. Early this morning we had a message to despatch home that Cronje and all his men had surrendered unconditionally, and there was great rejoicing in the camp, and I expect there will be at home. I think this is the beginning of the end of the campaign, as Cronje is the man who has been keeping his men together by threats and false reports as to us being done in. He is coming

KHAKI LETTERS—*continued.*

in to-morrow night *en route* for (suggested) battle-ship at Cape Town. The railway people have got instructions to prepare for 3,000 prisoners. They have been pouring in for the last week, reinforcements being sent up from Ladysmith, and French capturing them. One cannot speak too highly of French's work throughout the whole campaign, but the change in the whole aspect of the campaign is like a dream. We all thought we were booked for another twelve months, but now we may be home in twelve weeks. It was a grand move of Roberts's to attack Jacobsdal, where all their provisions were stored, and hospitals also. Then, sending French on to Kimberley, Cronje retreated from Magersfontein, and tried to get back to Bloemfontein; but Kelly-Kenny was sent to chase him, and French instructed to chase him from the KB side. The move was successful, as they enclosed him in about a mile square in the bed and banks of a dry river, with our position on the surrounding hills, and about 100 guns pouring into them. As their reinforcements came up, French captured them. The position became untenable, and Cronje sent to Roberts saying he would surrender conditionally. Kitchener was going to interview him, and was met by a messenger, who said it was a mistake, and that they would fight on. Cronje has surrendered unconditionally with about 4,000 men, and horses to number of about 500. They lost a great number of horses; hundreds were seen floating down the Modder. They were practically starved out, and, with the great number of guns we had round them, their losses must have been terrible.

"February 28th.—There has been great excitement in the camp all morning, in anticipation of seeing Cronje brought in. He arrived about 12.30, with his wife, secretary, and little black boy, in a spider carriage, drawn by six artillery horses, escorted by 50 C.I.V.'s, which is a great honour. Well, we got a good view of the old rat. He is a fine, stern-looking man, but his wife is of the common or garden washerwoman type. They treated him in every way as a general by sounding the general salute when he arrived and departed from the Crown Hotel just opposite us. He looked as if he was going to the scaffold when leaving the hotel for the station. He went down in a saloon carriage, and had a plentiful supply of soda and whisky and cigars, also 'guards of honour' on the train.

"March 1st —To-day we still have excitement; the 4,370 prisoners were brought in. It looked a grand sight to see them on the opposite side of the river. They looked fairly fagged, having had a distance of 35 miles to walk in two days. The C.I.V. again had the honour of heading the procession, and the other escort was the 3rd Grenadiers, who also looked tired out. They have been on half rations for about a week, and had one or two wet shirts. I saw several of the leaders mounted on horses of the 82nd Battery of Artillery. There were not many mounted; in fact, horses are at a very high premium in Africa at present. Well, they were all encamped at the back of the station. There was a barbed wire fencing all round the camp and four companies of the N. Lancs. as guard at night time. There was a waste-oil lamp burning on each of the four sides of the camp. Our fellows had a chat with several of them, including myself, and they informed me that they were heartily sick of it, and very glad to be taken prisoners. They forced Cronje to surrender. We mentioned about them using the white flag and firing on the ambulance, and they said it was done by Free Staters. That's natural, of course. They had great respect for Roberts, but didn't think much of Methuen. We bought a lot of their money as relics, giving 18 shillings for a sovereign, and told them they would not be able to use them any more. They seemed very hungry, and, at a very high premium, bought golden syrup

KHAKI LETTERS—*continued.*

and condensed milk that the fellows had bought in the store, and wended their way back to the tents. I paid a visit to Kimberley a few days ago, and had the honour of travelling in the guard's van with Francis of Teck. They are not very particular out here ; in fact, some of the officers are fairly in rags and boots very much down at heel, and are very glad to get into Tommy's boots. Well, of course, we saw it at a great disadvantage. It was a few days after the relief, and they were still on rations. The town doesn't appear to have suffered much from the shells. There were one or two houses burnt down by the shells, but, of course, the 100-lb. gun was only playing on the town for eight days. The man on the conning tower used to give the signal when he saw the gun fire, by means of a bugle, and people used to take cover. They put the majority of women and children down De Beers Mines during the last week. It is wonderful how the place held out as long as it did by the number of traitors and guns. They had a mounted battery, four Maxims, and a few others, including the one that Labram made ; but they say it was always going wrong after firing a few shots. I met a great number of TS men, including George Hahn. There is some talk of us shifting up there, but we have been expecting to shift for so long that we don't take much notice of it. We are about sick of the Modder and the work, having done twelve and fourteen hours a day when Roberts was about here. Well, what do you think of ' Bobs' now ? Ladysmith was relieved this morning, and, in fact, the whole campaign will soon be relieved."

✤ ✤ ✤ ✤

No. 2,355, Sapper **Hv. H. A. Ferguson** (LV), 1st T.D., R.E., writing from Belmont, March 8th, says :—

"MY DEAR KEMP.—I must apologise for not writing you a line or two sooner, but still better late than never. I suppose great excitement has been caused in England at our successes this last week or two, viz., capture of Cronje and all his force, relief of Kimberley and Ladysmith. I must say it has given all the troops fresh courage to go forward, and at the moment of writing I hear Roberts and French has had them again round the neck. Most of the boys have been moved again. Several from Modder down country to Naauwport, some to Kimberley, two from here to Colesburg. Two of us now left at Belmont, Sapper Porter, of Woolwich, and myself. I expect they will keep us here for a bit yet as there are still signs of hostilities with the rebels out west from here. I hear there are about 800 who are busy entrenching themselves and intend to reoccupy Sunnyside. We have scarcely any troops left here, they have moved on to the front ; I think we have about 100 altogether, besides a few more stationed between this and Sunnyside, and with whom we keep up communication. The cable has been cut twice this last week so expect to have a rosy time of it shortly. We have a night alarm at times, but no damage has been done. We simply let them know we are awake and all is over.

"I think the Free Staters are pretty well fed up now. Train loads of Boer prisoners are passing down daily, some of them in horse boxes with iron bars across, the scene altogether resembling that of a wild beast show. They are treated with great kindness here in the way of a drink of water and a newspaper for them to read containing the news of the capture. They look as if they had never seen water, and altogether now quite tame.

"I think we will soon be into the Transvaal then *en route* for Johannesburg and Pretoria, and six weeks from now ought to see us on the briny ' sailing merrily home.'

KHAKI LETTERS—*continued.*

" We have been living very well here under the circumstances, Porter and myself are A1. . . . . We have not seen a *Telegraph Chronicle* since the day we landed, but both of us thank you very much for the kind manner in which you have kept us in touch with the things going on at home through the medium of your circular letters. Rest of the boys whom I have seen pass up and down are looking splendid.

" I will conclude now with best good wishes to yourself and rest of the boys of the old Brigade, the 24th, from Porter and myself."

No. 3,230, Sapper **W. Abbott** (of BM), writing on March 8th, from Jacobsdal, says :—

" DEAR COLOUR-SERGEANT,—I was very pleased to receive your letter dated February 2nd, with the list of 'Ours' who are here, which I received Wednesday, March 7th. Glad to see that all the fellows have so much interest in our doings, and I can assure you that everyone of us heartily appreciate your kindness in sending us a letter and paper, and all hope to be back again with you and have a hearty handshake. Well, you can see by the above that I am at Jacobsdal, a small village about 11 or 12 miles from Modder River, where I left most of my companions I came out with. There are two of us here in charge, Barham is my companion, a second division man, off the Reserves, and we get along splendidly together, and have fared very well up till last week, when the rations ran short, so had to put up with half rations, but there being a Store here we have been able to get a little more, but, cash supplies being short, one has to be careful, but, on the whole, I must say that we fare excellent compared with some, especially the line regiments at the front, who come in on the sick convoy with pitiful tales of short rations. The Office we are now occupying was, previous to our entry to the place, the Boer Post Office, and we still have all their books, but all the stamps and money were taken by the D.A.T. and the troops who got in first ; the C.I.V.'s, I am told, fared best, by their being the first to enter, and the behaviour, during the siege of the place, was reported by the General here, as excellent, and every man was as cool as possible.

" We get plenty of work here for two, in fact rather too much, as the office is open night and day, and we have had to work two days and nights at a stretch to get the work off, but since the 7th Division has moved towards the front and the Highland L.I. come in it has been much slacker. Most of the messages here average about 80 to 100 words each. Just heard that Dan Horton and two more have left Modder for the front. Modder now is nearly forsaken, only four left there, Kimberley now doing all the work to the front. News just come in of another brush with the Boers by good old Bobs at Poplar Grove on Wednesday, 7th, and said to have given them a good hiding and our losses very slight. Expect one more big battle and all over, and probably, by Lord Roberts' account, peace declared by the time you receive this. Glad to say I am in good health and hope all the rest are faring well. Don't hear much of them as being so far away. Best respects to all, hoping all well, and again thanking you for your kind letter.

" P.S.—Please excuse paper as have no other at present, and sorry cannot affix stamp as unobtainable here."

[The above letter is written on Press flimsies of the Orange Free State. The Code of the office is JDN.—R.E.K.]

KHAKI LETTERS—*continued.*

No. 23,610, **Sergt. R. C. Luttrell**, writes from Achtertang, near Norvals Pont, under date March 11th:—

"Have just taken over charge of this office, and so am able to write you a cuffer or two. Up to the present we have all been together and I have been Acting S.M. of camp, also Q.M.S., but now we are all split up into offices, and I got sent here. We are waiting to go on to Norvals Pont as soon as they clear the enemy from the other bank of the river. We first went to De Aar then on to Modder River. I left most of the 58 I brought out there and picked up 32 linemen and with 15 of our mob came on round this way. Half the linemen, however, have gone back round to Stormberg Junction and the remainder are up at Norvals Pont putting the main line wires through. They put in an office near the bridge yesterday, but the General sent them back as the enemy's guns could reach there.

" Am getting on all right myself and enjoying it as well as expected. Up to the present we have only been stationed at places in the great Karoo desert, which is something like the Fox Hill on a very big scale. You only see a tree wherever there is a watercourse, and they are about 4 feet high. Most monotonous kind of scenery. This place, however, is at the foot of a great hill, whilst in front is a deep ravine with a mountain torrent. Trees, too, of a decent size, grow on the banks. It's quite a treat after the other wilderness. We are very quiet here, the troops have pushed on and left us in the station house as a transmitting station. I had a slight shock yesterday. Was doing a bit of washing down at the waterfall. After washing I laid the clothes on the rocks and strolled up stream. I had just come from behind a big boulder when bang goes a rifle and I could hear the bullet sing overhead. Of course, I sat down and waited a few minutes. Just as I got up again, bang goes another. Thinking I wasn't wanted I crawled after my clothes and keeping well under the lee of the river made for home. In the evening I found out what was up. It appears that a sergeant of the Worcesters, who have a detachment just below to guard the railway bridge, drew the men's ration of rum and also scoffed it. Being in the rats in consequence, he got his rifle, and his eyesight not being improved by the rum he thought he saw the enemy, and let drive to make sure. He was made a prisoner last night, so I expect he won't get any rum for some time.

" I saw General Clements' army go by the other day at Joubert's siding, in skirmishing order. It was a grand sight. We can hear the big guns from Norvals Pont every now and again. It's very comfortable here as we live and sleep indoors, there being no one else but the two R.E.'s acting as stationmaster and shunter, and my mob of ten with a few black gents. One is outside now with his Sunday clothes on, consisting of a sack, with a hole for his head and two for his arms. They are a tired lot. Used to chase 'em at Modder, for if you take your eyes off they stop work. This is a paid office here. Fairall and Little and Poole are with me, otherwise no 24th. Creasey, Wright and Payne are at Head Quarters. We were at Modder when Paardeburg was fought and Cronje taken prisoner; saw about 800 of our wounded come in. Poor beggars, mostly wounded in arms and legs. I also saw Arnold, one of those three Northumberland sergeants we met at Bisley. Arnold is attached to Lord Kitchener's staff and has been mentioned three times. He is all right for a commission. Ted Way is the Sergt. Inspector of this line and Jack Hart is Corporal. Friends of Fred Ruse and Charley Peckham. The weather here is very hot, but bear-

KHAKI LETTERS—*continued*.

able, only the flies make life a misery. Millions of 'em. We had a fine passage out only the food was rather poor, should have starved, only one old soldier who I lent to the storeman used to collect all the officers' leavings and we made decent suppers at 2d. a time, which kept us alive. Out here one day, perhaps, you get a good feed, then you may go on bully for a bit. So I always eat whenever I get a chance. I left Stevens in charge at Colesburg. Tee has gone back to Nauuwport. Nelson was still at De Aar when I left, waiting instructions after coming out of hospital. Quinn was there, too, in the clearing-house. He came up from Cape Town, where he had been in hospital, and, on the way up, fell out of the train. He is a cough drop. You should see Jack Fallon's beard. Most of the boys are in the best of health and spirits. We hear a lot more of the fellows are coming out, but trust it will be all over before they arrive. We were cinematographed the other day, so look out for it at the New Hippodrome, in Leicester Square, or at the Music Halls."

✤ ✤ ✤ ✤

No. 1,547, Sapper **L. Orwin**, writing from the Naauwpoort Junction Hospital, Ward G 4, on March 12th, says :—

" DEAR KEMP,—Just a line thanking you for the list of 24th Middlesex men out here. I received it at Modder River last week. I was in the Field Hospital there for about a week, and on Wednesday last was transferred down here. We left Modder about noon, travelling saloon carriage. Some of the men went to Wynberg, others as far as De Aar only, and a third section down here. We travelled six in a compartment, two sleeping in the racks, and the others on floor and seats. We had several wounded Boers on the train. We reached De Aar early Thursday morning after passing Honeynestkloof, Belmont, Graspan, Orange River, and seeing several of the boys *en route*. The scenery from De Aar to Naauwpoort (75 miles) was veldt, covered with heather, with a chain of hills each side in the distance. We arrived here about three o'clock in the afternoon, and have been here in bed since that time, generally knocked up. When at Modder was in the office there, and saw Cronje, wife, grandson, and private secretary, rather an imposing ceremony, escorted by mounted C.I.V., Artillery, and Infantry, and accompanied by a General and one or two other officers. Two general salutes were given. Saw the 4,000 Boer prisoners brought in, and went and had a chat with them. One offered to sell me a pair of field-glasses for £1. Said he gave £2 10s. for them. I didn't take them. Another had a watch and gold chain to sell for 25s. I hadn't got 25s.; was unable to get any Kruger money from them, as I was a bit late. They kept a searchlight playing on their camp all night. Charlie Godden (late of Met. TS) ran down from Kimberley to see us. He looked very well, although he had been in Kimberley all through the siege. The only things out here at all plentiful are ostriches, and even they have been plucked. Bread 6d. a loaf here. It is 1s. farther up country. Owing to the fact that they had very little medicine or accommodation, the sick and wounded fared very badly at Modder.

"We had a terrific storm one night, and got wet through, and tents blown down. The next day we had a hailstorm. It may hardly seem credible, but some of the hailstones were as large as chickens' eggs. The men in the tent went out and collected a lot of them to suck as ice. You won't be surprised when I tell you that funerals averaged three or four a day. The dead bodies were simply put on a stretcher with a 'Union Jack over them, carried out by three or four men, and buried without any further

KHAKI LETTERS—*continued*.

ceremony. The camp here (Naauwpoort) lies each side of the railway, and is surrounded by hills, the scene of a lot of fighting. A couple of dozen corrugated iron shanties comprises the town. It it very cold here at night, and the wind blows into our marquee with surprising force. With kind regards."

✣ ✣ ✣ ✣

The following extracts are taken from Sergeant **J. H. Nelson's** letters. His illness has caused various rumours to float abroad. We will see what he says himself.

"Rondebosch, *February* 11*th*.—For the last four or five days in January I was going to the doctor night and morning with pains in my back and absence of appetite. .... Six or seven different kinds of medicine he tried upon me without apparent benefit, until at last he said I had better go into Hospital. Well, on the 2nd inst., I was admitted to the 1st Division Field Hospital, and placed on milk diet. Oh, dear! that milk—not fresh cow's milk mind you, but merely watered condensed milk, a mixture that didn't go down at all well with me. Lying on the hard floor with no more convenience than I had in my own tent did not help me either, and I used to sleep wretchedly. However, after a couple of days my temperature abated slightly, and on the 7th inst. I was placed aboard the Hospital Ambulance Train en route for Wynberg or Rondebosch (it wasn't known which). On the train my diet was improved upon, inasmuch as after passing De Aar I got soda water and fresh milk and a nice meal of milk-custard and corn flour. The inhabitants at the different towns on the way down are very kind towards the sick and wounded, and hand in all kinds of fruits, cakes, jellies, milk, &c. Well, on the evening of the 8th inst. we arrived at Rondebosch, but it then being dark we remained on the train until the morning, when ambulance waggons carted us up to the Hospital, about a mile and a-half from the station. Here we were distributed among the wards, and I was placed in the surgical section for the time being; and as my temperature was a bit up the doctor ordered me to bed, and placed me on milk diet. Next day my temperature had gone down to 98, so the doctor gave me permission to get up for a while. On the strength of my improvement, in addition to my milk diet, I have a lovely bunch of grapes, a piece of water melon, a couple of eggs, and a bath bun. All this looked rather formidable after my starvation diet, but no harm whatever came of it, and I found my appetite had commenced to reassert itself. My complaint was diagnosed as 'S.C.F.,' meaning slow continued fever. On the 9th inst. I was transferred to a ward in the medical section.

"*February* 12*th*.—I'm pleased to say I'm still progressing all right, and my strength is slowly returning. Of course, I can't expect to get strong again all at once, for 8 or nine days without solid food means a considerable loss of stamina, and requires a bit of making up, and thus I must not be a bit surprised if things go a bit slow at first. However, 'slow and sure' is the best after all.

"Fort Knokke, *February* 19*th*.— I am pleased to say that my health is all but quite restored again, and that but for a little weakness I am myself once more. The day before yesterday I was discharged from Hospital and sent on here previous to my returning to duty at Modder River, which I am expecting and hoping will be to-morrow. The hospital patients upon discharge are sent to one or other of the different camps about Capetown before rejoining their respective regiments, and as Fort Knokke is the spot

KHAKI LETTERS—*continued.*

appointed for Royal Engineers to finish off their convalescence at, here I am for a day or so. Although it is so nice and easy-going down here I'm anxious to get back to my duties, for otherwise I'm losing all the fun and experience.

"De Aar, *February* 25*th*.—I did not get away from Fort Knokke quite so soon as I expected and wished, but on Friday last I *did* make another move up country, leaving Capetown at 9 p.m. by the mail train. My railway warrant was only made available as far as De Aar, so am here awaiting instructions.

"Norvals Pont, *March* 18*th*.—My stay here will be very short as I'm only doing a bit of touring with stores and letters for officers along the line, viz., Naauwpoort, Colesburg, and Norvals Pont, and I start back for De Aar very probably to-morrow morning."

No. 797, Sapper **E. G. Loosemore** (CF), writing from Enslin, South Africa, March 15th, says :—

"DEAR COLOUR-SERGEANT KEMP,—Whilst at this place there is absolutely nothing of interest to write, our experiences having been fully chronicled by others, I feel it would be ungrateful not to acknowledge your kindnesses in forwarding card, letters, etc. I can assure you they have been very acceptable. There are only three of us here, W. C. Smith, of TS, and a R.E. lineman. Things have got very quiet, not doing a dozen messages a day now, so we shall surely be moved ere long. You, of course, have heard the sad news of A. W. Hawkins' death. It was a terribly hard and unexpected blow to us all. Hoping you are in good health."

No. 551, Private **S. E. Sterling** (C.I.V.), writing from Wigton Culverts, near Witteputts, March 18th, says :—

" . . . . Since I wrote you before I have been fired at twice. It makes one feel quite funny to be in the place where the target should be. I fired my first shot the Monday before last at a light which was coming towards the culvert I was guarding, and it would not stop when I challenged. I aimed a bit behind it to hit the man carrying it, but I only hit the lamp, which the fellow dropped and cleared off. The time we were fired at was two days ago. The sentry on the big culvert challenged some horsemen who promptly fired at him, but they missed him. The guard turned out six of us and corporal, and as we went along the railway embankment to reach a small stone fort we had built they fired two volleys at us, but in spite of their supposed good marksmanship very few of the bullets went close to us though quite close enough for me. When we were in the fort they started retiring towards Prieska. We gave them a volley, and a man and a horse went down but were up almost immediately. Soon after firing, the armoured train which patrols the line from Witteputts came along, and there was no more firing done. The morning's patrol found a dead horse about ¼ mile from camp with three shots in it. You can guess how this makes us fancy night guard, especially on the culvert 350 yards from our tent when you know that being on the railway embankment you are on the sky-line for the surrounding country, and form a lovely mark for anyone.

"Before we came here we were stationed at Fincham's Farm, 7½ miles farther up, only not on the railway. We were there for 10 days, during that time I only had one clear night in bed, the other nights I didn't get more than

KHAKI LETTERS—continued.

three hours' sleep. We have to be constantly on the alert here as the big culvert consists of two big spans, and if some of these detached commandoes of Boers did happen to do us in and blow it up it would cut off Roberts' supplies. We do guard one day, 12 noon one day to 12 noon next. and then the other day we do one afternoon patrol, one evening and one morning, each of us then go on guard again, and so on. . . . . When our train stopped at De Aar for tea, of course I nipped out and looked up our fellows in the telegraph office. I saw Charlie Woode, Arundell, Woolley, Humm, a fellow out of "G" Division named Swan, and a Manchester man, and also young Wilson. They seemed to be getting on all right, and didn't seem to be overworking themselves. At Orange River I saw Dellbridge. . . . Please remember me to all the fellows.

"P.S.—Just heard that our half Company at Witteputts has 13 down with dysentery. No one in our 16 here though."

No. 2,554, Sapper **E. C. Govier**, sends the following interesting account of a part of his work from Britstown, March 19th :—

"DEAR COLOUR-SERGEANT KEMP,—Your last letter duly received, the nominal roll you have had printed will prove most useful. I am enjoying the best of health out here. but some of our members are or have been very ill, I trust they will all recover. I am 'teed' on the civil wire from De Aar, and have Houwater, Omaraais Vlei. in cct, also the cable cart with the head of the column whenever they tap in. There is plenty of work for Lord Kitchener, but all goes smoothly, and I trust that this fair land will soon be rid of the blight of war and our return journey booked. I enclose you an account of our journey with the Prieska column, which you may find a bit out of the usual run. Trusting you are well, I close with best regards."

"Messrs. Govier, F. Clark and Swan, of TS, and Whitten and Hendry, of EH, formed the operative staff in connection with a Telegraph Section detailed for duty with Lord Kitchener's column, which had been formed to crush a rebel rising in the Britstown, Houwater and Prieska districts, and which was growing every day. Troops had several times been despatched from De Aar, our advanced base, to cope with the trouble, but without decisive result, the rebels invariably retiring, except on the last occasion, 6th March, when on a reconnaisance being made by the 'A' Co.,C.I.V.'s,with 44th Battery R.F.A., they were suddenly enfiladed by the enemy posted on hills either side, and had a very hot time. Llewellyn, R.E., late of BM, and Harris, were following our artillery with their apparatus when they were suddenly left on their own in the plain by the artillery who galloped away to a fresh position, bullets fell fast and thick around them, until finally extricated from their difficult position by some of the artillery bringing them horses enabling them to rejoin the main body without a scratch. At 4 p.m. on the 13th March, the above-mentioned section moved off from De Aar under convoy of Imperial Yeomanry, for Britstown, to join the expedition which was composed of 68th R.F.A., 7th Dragoons, Mounted Suffolks, and Imperial Yeomanry, some of whom proceeded via Carnarvon, with a probable flank movement in view, which quite nonplusses the Boers. The *personnel* of the section was as follows, Lieutenant Bannerman, R.E., Q.M.S. Kilburn, Sappers Bleach, Sandalls, Kenny, and Crowther, and a colonial carpenter, these acted in their various capacities as mounted linemen, drivers, etc., together with the above-mentioned operators. Four transport waggons

KHAKI LETTERS—*continued*.

were loaded with the usual Field Telegraph requisites, and a Scotch cart, converted into a cable cart, for use at the front.

"The whole party moved off from De Aar at 4 p.m. and formed a picturesque and striking spectacle. The large donkey and mule teams, driven by Cape Boys, with mounted R.E.'s alongside, to give necessary directions as to speed, route, etc,: the I.Y., with their bandoliers and excellent horses, and the 24th, holding on by its teeth, perched on bales of hay, cases of bully, and telegraph poles, the whole enveloped in a brown cloud of dust. The route lay chiefly between ranges of mountains, and it was with considerable interest that we watched the movements of our Scouts, some five or six miles in advance, on our right and left, passing at times behind large kopjes, then re-appearing to scan the plains ahead, always watchful and alert to guard against a surprise. The scenery was delightful, the mountain ranges showing up grandly against the clear Cape sky, the air is most invigorating, so the time passed, intermingled with chaffing salutes from waggon to waggon, and the sharp cries of 'ekk, ekk, ekk,' from the Cape Boys, driving the mules, accompanied with the dexterous cracking of enormous whips, the handles of which were quite 12 feet long, and with a proportionate length of cord and thong, the object of which being to give a little physical encouragement to the mules, who combine the strength of a horse with the playfulness of the kitten, being very partial to rolling on their backs and kicking out left and right, possibly to draw attention to a grievance; their gambols quite over, the journey is continued, broken occasionally with the excitement of crossing a stream or struggling up a hill, all hands to the spokes. Night coming on, we halted at a place called Spreeuwfontein, where, after feeding our cattle, a meal was partaken of, with hot cocoa made on our camp fires, after which we proceeded to enjoy a well earned rest. We slept under the waggons, the animals being tethered to the wheels outside, the stillness of the night being now and again broken by the iron tones of 'Halt, who goes there?' or a football match between the mules, accompanied by child-like cries, a draw being proclaimed, we would make another effort, to be again roused by a long warm breath on our faces from an inquisitive mule, probably to see if we were really asleep, the matter resting entirely with them. At last, however, dead to the wide world, and unconscious of our surroundings; reveille, at 4 a.m. was the next sound that greeted our ears. After preparing breakfast and feeding the animals, the journey to Britstown was cautiously resumed, and reached at noon, March 14th, without incident.

"We were agreeably surprised at the town, which contained some fair-sized buildings, and an excellent stone church which is quite up to some of ours at home, and the spire of which is visible nine miles off. The houses are mainly composed of red brick and plaster, with verandahs in front, under which their occupants discuss the war during the evening. After partaking of field refreshment I was instructed by Lieutenant Bannerman to proceed to the telegraph office, and was provided with the following emergency apparatus—batteries, two phonophores, military sounder set, P.O. sounder, relay and Dx switch, Dc key, and a phonophore diagram—and to be prepared to join up either when he and his party were out with the column. With this little lot, and the kind assistance of Messrs. Clarke, Swan, and Whitten, I advanced on the position, where I joined Llewellyn, the hero of Houwater. I was accorded a hearty welcome by the postmaster, an Englishman, and the town jailor, who is very good to us; sends us dinners and coffee, &c. He is Sergeant-Major of Cape

KHAKI LETTERS—*continued*.

Police. After joining up my phonophore I set to work on Lord Kitchener's dispatches, which kept us going till the small hours. We have to keep constant watch for the musical note of the cable carts vibrator, which comes in cct at any time. The last time I spoke to them I was informed by Sandalls that eighteen mounted Boers were on their West side, and that it was just getting dark. They were, however, instructed to fall back on Roorpoort, and encamp for the night with a guard of Suffolks. By the time you get this the whole operation will have been successfully carried out by Lord Kitchener of Khartoum, and we shall have returned to De Aar laden with sick men and prisoners, which is the penalty of Empire."

No. 4,376, Sapper **W. W. Pearce**, on board the s.s. "Winifredian," posts the following letter at Queenstown, April 3rd :—

"DEAR KEMP,—Perhaps you will think it unkind in not writing you before we left the 'Shot, but we had a lot of messing about and no furlough. We had a grand send-off from Aldershot yesterday ; the Royal Irish Militia played us to the station. The utmost enthusiasm prevailed, and a large body of Royal Engineers accompanied us to the station. We arrived at Southampton without incident. After shipping 300 horses and numerous drafts for various regiments, we got away about 7 p.m. after an enthusiastic send-off. Before going any farther I hope you will emphasise the kind and patient treatment we received by all we came in contact with of the Royal Engineers, and all look forward with pleasure to the time when we shall drill with them again.* We are not over elated with the 'Winifredian.' She is an immense boat and pretty steady, but the catering, what we have seen of it up to now, is not over grand. The smell arising from the horses, grease, cooking, and being overcrowded, is not 'all lavender,' and has been dubbed the 'Ocean K Division.' There is a decent swell on this morning, and its effects are somewhat disastrous to some of the boys. Last night some of us had our first experience in hammock slinging. Your humble servant held an inquest by himself for quite a quarter of an hour how to get into the tantalising thing, which would turn and twist in every direction to what you wanted it to. After a terrific struggle, I gave it up, and wished I was back again in the feather bed. At last, with the help of several friendly 'swaddies,' I made a plunge, and landed safe. Rather a peculiar sight to see three or four hundred men in hammocks. You would imagine that you were in an immense refrigerator with a lot of sheep in white cases slung lengthwise, and, by Jove ! it's like an ice-house at night. Flanagan has retained his stripes, and is sergeant, and his promotion has been very popular amongst us. We are now nearing Queenstown, where we take in several hundred more men and horses. Goodness alone knows how we shall be able to breathe then. Well, good-bye, old chap, thanking you for kind wishes and copies of KHAKI LETTERS, which are very popular with us. Will write again, and post at first stoppage."

---

*[NOTE.—With very great pleasure I call the special attention of "K.L." readers to Sapper Pearce's request. It goes to show the good feeling of friendship, sound to the core, is still existent between the R.E.'s and their Telegraph Reservists—a fact that has been attacked, but not overthrown, by some whose Khaki faces would index their internal state at the time they committed such insinuations to paper.—R.E.K.]

Sapper Charles A. G. Fairall.

TO the Metropolitan Districts has fallen the misfortune of providing the second victim on the Telegraph side to that dreaded scourge of South Africa, enteric fever, Charles A. G. Fairall having died from that disease at Naauwpoort on April 6th last, in his twenty-sixth year. He was appointed to the N.W. District in August, 1893, but, previous to that time, had served in an unestablished capacity for some years at Ryde and Seaview in the Isle of Wight. After a few months in London, he joined the 24th Middlesex R.V., Jan. 6th, 1894. He was most energetic in his new *rôle* as a volunteer, and his name was soon found on the list for the Reserve Company of Telegraphists. In this matter fortune favoured him somewhat. Barely out of his recruits' course, he was transferred to the Royal Engineer Reserves on the 22nd Feb. 1895, and year after year went through the special course of air-line and cable practice with the "Royals" at Aldershot. Most of his London service was at the Hampstead Green B.O., and whilst there he obtained the double increment for Technical Telegraphy. A few months back he was transferred to the Metropolitan Engineers' Office at Mount Pleasant on probation. He should have gone up for the recent examination, but, owing to a slight technicality, he failed to obtain a nomination, and almost immediately received his "marching orders" for South Africa. He sailed with the 3rd detachment of "Ours" on board the "St. Andrew," leaving the Royal Albert Docks, London, on January 21st, and arrived at Cape Town on February 12th, entraining almost immediately for the front. His letters—extracts of which are given—pointed to the fact that he was in excellent health and spirits. The last letter from him received in London was dated Achtertang, March 8th, and this gave no indication of any impending illness, so that the

news of his death caused consternation amongst his late colleagues, who vividly recalled to mind the parting farewell, when our comrade appeared to be fairly bubbling over with good health. It seems very hard to realise that he has really gone, and our heartfelt sympathy and condolence is extended to his bereaved parents and relatives in the very heavy blow they have sustained.

✤ ✤

IN MEMORIAM.

→✱ Sapper Charles A. G. Fairall. ✱←

Died at Naauwpoort, April 6th, 1900.

He came to us from England's southern isle,
    With open heart and hand,
To " dear old Hampstead "—'twas a little while—
    Then to the distant strand.

To serve his Queen ! the Flag ' with all the rest,
    A loyal Volunteer !
Britain's proud boast—she renders up her best,
    Their mem'ry we revere.

Not in the crash of battle was he slain,
    Disease soon laid him low,
Yet 'tis the one grand story o'er again—
    Facing a deadly foe.

A kind and genial comrade we shall miss,
    Who for his country died :
But what a noble death ! aye, think of this,
    After our tears are dried.

CBP.   J. H. W.

✤ ✤ ✤ ✤

Extracts from No. 28,865, Sapper **C. A. G. Fairall's** letters :—

" Modder River, February 25th, 1900.

" . . . . 'I ain't killed no brother Boers yet,' but otherwise, am enjoying myself a treat. The weather is rather hot, but to-day there is a cool breeze, and, after some rain yesterday, the sand doesn't blow about like it did for a few days, getting into eyes, ears, nose, mouth, and grub. It's all sand round here except just along the river bank, and our camp is on the site of the old Boer pitch. Magersfontein is about three or four miles, I should think, the hills show up plain enough, and some of the chaps have been rambling round there. I have a swim in the river occasionally, and ' it's a bit of all right,' although, one evening I struck a dead ' hoss ' in it (MIM.). He was really dead, downright and absolutely. Our trip up from Cape Town put you in mind of a Sunday League trip, only more so. Altogether we spent three nights in the train, two in carriages, and one in cattle trucks, lying down was a thing to be dreamt of. . . . . We stopped at De Aar for two days, met several of 'Ours' there and had some beer, but didn't care much for it. De Aar is sandy, and both there and here we get sandstorms sometimes. Had no chance to look at the village or town, but there was a Kaffir settlement close to our pitch and we were highly amused at their domestic arrangements (MIM.), although they were educated niggers. Saw Catling on the way up, at Belmont, I think it was, or Orange River, he was all serene. Jack Little has gone to the Office here, while the humble cook is yours truly. 'What O' the little mutton chop for lunch. You bet the cook ain't the worst fed. Fresh meat is going down well, we get it every day here, and enjoy it after a lot of tinned stuff; Beer is also to be had at tenpence a pot, but I'm saving my thirst for 'home, sweet home,' or somewhere where the liquid is more to my palate. They serve us out half a quartern of rum twice a week and quarter pound of jam once a week, so we are better off than a good many. Have seen some of the chaps who were shut up in Kimberley, they have roughed it and no mistake, they look it. . . . . Just heard that we shift up to the front to-morrow. Must look to the stew, so *au revoir.* . . . . "

" Modder River, February 26th, 1900.

". . . . Got on the trail all right now. Glad to say we aren't overworked, nothing much on, expected to trot on to to the front to-day but it has been countermanded. . . . . C. Jones, of Woolwich, has gone to Kimberley Office, Stevens, of Manchester, went up for a day and had a look round, Govier was left at De Aar. . . . , I've worked a jolly sight harder at Aldershot than here. One or two of our batch have gone sick, I'm much thinner but was never better in my little puff . . . . Niggers do hammer and jumper work when they are available, also fetching water and other odd jobs. Mules and oxen do the waggon pulling, it's not uncommon to see sixteen mules or twenty oxen on one cart . . . . Cook's job under a blazing sun is 'no cop.' . . . . Hope all are O.K. Kindest regards."

" Achtertang, March 8th, 1900.

" . . . . Many thanks for paper received yesterday. . . . The fruit is O.K. Sunrise and sunsets grand, but for scenery—why, the played-out old country knocks this show 'holler.' Achtertang is the prettiest spot I've seen since I landed, although Naauwpoort is a decent little town. This is the usual station : one house, one siding, one board, and, in normal times, about one man. The River Oorlog runs close here ; it's only a stream, but has miniature waterfalls, and is deep enough to have a soak in some places. The banks are well wooded just here, and big hills surround us, the effect at sunset being O.K. We have travelled about a bit, first to De Aar, then on to Modder (where we swam the river every day), back to De Aar (sand storms in both places were chronic), on to Naauwpoort, up to Rensburg, where I did my first bit of telegraphy at the headquarters, Jack Little and self, 'open always,' an apartment in a farmhouse 'unfurnished,' but well ventilated, and a stone floor. After two days there, we shifted up to Colesberg Junction, and thence here, which is about twelve miles from Norvals Pont, the Free State border, and expected scene of a big fight. The work is heavy—long messages, and plenty of code, but am in a perfect state, thank you, suffering only from thirst and commandeeria, which is general out here. Hope to get up to the front and see some fun in a day or so. . . . Kindest regards to all. . . ."

"Khaki Notes."

"THE FRIEND." Several copies of *The Friend*, edited by the War Correspondents with Lord Roberts' Force at Bloemfontein, have been sent me. It is printed partly in English and partly in Dutch. It gives proclamations by the Commander-in-Chief, and Notices by the Provost Marshal, etc., in both languages.' From it can be gathered the Produce Market opens at 6.30 a.m. daily at the Camp of the 6th Division, on the road west of Bloemfontein, near the old Toll Gate, military police being present to give all necessary protection. Then follows a list of prices of the various commodities

One proclamation referring to the Railway and Railway Telegraph Services, appoints Lieut.-Col. E. P. C. Girouard, D.S.O., Director of Railways, South African Field Force, administrator of the same in the occupied O.F.S. " And I do hereby order that the Railway and Railway Telegraph Services shall be resumed in the portions of the aforesaid Republic, already referred to, from the 19th day of March, 1900, under the existing Laws and Conventions of the Orange Free State, subject to such alterations as may from time to time be notified, and to the requirements of the Army. God Save the Queen.—ROBERTS, FIELD-MARSHAL."

Referring to the Proclamation reported to have been circulated throughout the Transvaal that London had been occupied by the Russians. etc., *The Friend* says: "It is painful to think that Lord Roberts is totally unaware that he is fighting for a country that has ceased to exist. That St. Paul's is now a Greek Chapel, that the Thames is called the Temsky River, that our beloved Queen is a prisoner at Moscow, and that Lord Salisbury is already trudging on the weary snow-bound way to the mines at Kara in Siberia. Why do you laugh? To us it seems awful!"

The Friend makes a request as follows:—"To correspondents.—Please do not write on both sides of your letter sheets when you contribute to *The Friend*. It's all right to take a kopje on both sides, but you should not send it in on both sides. Some of the editors are sufficiently profane already."

Here is a sample of their smart "Answers to Correspondents":—

"CATGUT.—You have wholly mistaken the purpose of this paper. Even the 'Pink 'Un' would turn purple if you were on the staff.

"H.A G.—It was only at the last moment that we saved you from the effects of your folly. If you were less attractive we should be more angry with you.

"R.D.N.—To clean khaki, do not wash, except in cold water, with a slight wipe of ammonia; but we cannot act as laundrymen to the force."

OTHER VOLUNTEER R.E.'s. The following sections of R.E. Volunteers, each composed of 1 officer, 1 N.C.O., and 24 sappers) 1st Middlesex, 1st Newcastle, 1st and 2nd Yorkshire, 2nd Tower Hamlets, 1st Durham, 1st Sussex, 1st Gloucesters, 1st Hants, and 1st London, have proceeded to South Africa, where they will

KHAKI NOTES—*continued*.

join the various companies and units of the Corps of which they will, at least for one year, form an integral part. These ex-volunteers—now, to all intents and purposes, they are *bona fide* regulars—had been attached to the School of Military Engineering for some weeks past. The instruction derived therefrom, together with the training already received at their respective headquarters, had moulded them into a very capable and efficient body of sappers, whose services at the front will be invaluable.—*The Sapper.*

SAPPER F. H. WOODROW—one of Ours—has performed the very kindly duty of carving a wooden cross, painting the same, and inscribing upon it the words "I.H.S. In loving memory of Sapper A. Hawkins, 1st Telegraph Battalion, R.E. Died March 13th, 1900. Erected by his comrades." I have received a photograph of the same. Such action speaks louder than words for the true friendship of Our Boys.

MR. GEORGE COSTELLO requests that those Divisions, etc., who have not yet completed their Khaki Postage Account will do so at once, please.

I have to acknowledge sums of 1s., 2s. 6d., and other amounts from nameless friends, for the Postage Account. Thank you.

BARKLY WEST, APRIL 21st. Telegraphic communication between here and Kimberley was stopped yesterday owing to a breakage in the wire. Mr. Harry Frew, the postmaster, has accompanied a patrol of yeomanry which is proceeding to locate and repair the breach.—*Reuter's Special Service.*

Mr. Harry Frew entered C.T.O. 1885; was transferred to Cape Government service 1889, and was stationed at Kimberley (where he joined the Scots Volunteers in August, 1891) until 1893, when he removed to De Aar. Was made postmaster of Barkly West 1898. He stuck to his post until the Boers occupied the town, and was complimented for so doing.

TO ORANGE RIVER. In a letter received April 28th from Thornton Heath I have been asked to "thank those gentlemen in South Africa who have so thoughtfully written, and tell them how much the kindness and sympathy they have shown has been appreciated." The comrades concerned will recognise by whom this request is made.

THE "WINIFREDIAN" arrived at Cape Town, April 23rd.

PRIVATE T. TAYLOR, 360 A.P.O.C., died on April 21st, at Ladysmith, of enteric fever.

PRIVATE F. W. RUSH, 299 A.P.O.C., died on April 15th, at Pietermaritzburg, of enteric fever.

FRIENDS who prefer to send "K.L.'s" to Our Boys at the front would oblige if they gave me their names, please.

ATTENTION is called to page 2 of cover.

COLOURS.

"KHAKI LETTERS," One Penny. By post, Three Halfpence.

All posted letters containing Remittances, Orders, MSS., &c., must be addressed to R. E. KEMP, 12, JERRARD STREET, LEWISHAM, S.E. Postal Orders should be made payable at Loampit Vale, Lewisham, S.E.

Printed by E. G. BERRYMAN & SONS, *Blackheath Road, London, S.E.*

"Khaki Letters" from ....
"My Colleagues in South Africa."

CORRESPONDENCE FROM THE
POST OFFICE TELEGRAPHISTS
OF THE
24th MIDDLESEX (P.O.) RIFLE VOLUNTEERS
(Royal Engineer Reserves).
ON ACTIVE SERVICE.

THE BOND THAT BINDS US—FRIENDSHIP—COMRADESHIP.

Published fortnightly for the Postal Telegraph Service.
Conducted by **COLOUR-SERGEANT R. E. KEMP**, *Central Telegraph Office, London.*

| No. 7. | MAY 18TH, 1900. | PRICE ONE PENNY. |

Central Telegraph Office,
London, E.C.

DEAR COMRADES, ONE AND ALL,

Greetings! May this find you cheerful and well. At the present moment the C.T.O. Staff are all excitement over the little town of Mafeking and its gallant defenders. Not only is our office anxious, but the whole of the British public are craning their necks and casting other topics aside to hear of the relief of Baden-Powell and his garrison. I wish I could say it was a *fait accompli*, we are expecting it every moment, perhaps it may be so ere this is published.

There is not much interesting news to record in connection with the Office. A few promotions have been notified to the lucky ones, and this has caused a little flutter. You will find their names in the Notes.

Regimentally, there has been a bit of excitement. I am informed that a further batch of some 18 or 20 more men for the A.P.O.C. are embarking on the 17th inst., per the s.s. "Monteagle," for the front. Our "waiting men" at Aldershot, who were left over when our last lot sailed, have been expecting to go by the same boat, but although they have been served out with kits, &c., most of them are on furlough with a liability of 12 hours' notice to rejoin. There is only one name to add to those given in No. 6 K.L., and that is Sapper A. E. Johnston, of LV. Up to the present, however, they have no instructions.

Sixty more telegraphists have been asked for, and the response has been very encouraging, the applicants far exceeding the demand. There is a slight difference in the conditions under which they are engaging. The six years service is no longer insisted on. Most of them are taking-on for one year, or until the close of the campaign. Again, they are not all Volunteers, although the majority are; but all will go out as "Royals." Shall be able to tell you more about them next time, I hope. This party will be pushed forward with all possible speed, and it is believed will be on their way about the end of this month. It may be that the "waiting men" and the 60 will sail together.

The next question is our Annual Camp. Although the papers have had it for some time past that we are going to Salisbury Plain, my information is that that is not yet decided. We may go there, we may not. It is just as likely that the old regiment will find itself this year in the Chatham District. That is another point that "no one knows" yet. Only one thing appears to be certain, and that is, we go to Camp on the 21st of July, and the course of instruction terminates on August 18th; half the battalion for one fortnight, and half for the other. The C.O. thinks he will in all possibility have 600 for the first contingent and 400 the second.

The Postmaster-General has, it is understood, decided as regards the attendance of Post Office Servants who are Volunteers at Camp this year, that it is undesirable to disturb in any way the annual leave arrangements which have been already made, and that as far as the requirements of the Service will admit, special leave, with full pay, is to be granted for the purpose of attending Camp. The period of attendance for the majority will be restricted to the minimum, viz., 14 days, except in those cases where additional leave can be granted to them without inconvenience or expense to the Department, or detrimental to their Colleagues who are not Volunteers.

The Volunteers will receive, while in Camp, full Army pay, according to rank, in addition to their Civilian pay.

Those men who are in Camp during the period of their ordinary annual leave will, in all probability, be allowed leave later on; but more about this anon.

We seem to be getting nearer the Volunteer Reserve movement now than ever before. The War Office has made its own stipulations, and invitations have gone out to ex-members of the 24th, for those not over 55, to register their names at 2, Throgmorton Avenue, E.C., before the 22nd of May. They must have been returned as "efficient" six times within the last ten years.

Men of the Volunteer Reserve will be bound to—(1) Rejoin the Regiment when called upon in a National Emergency ; (2) to parade once a year, in plain clothes, at Inspection for Review ; (3) to shoot at Regimental Ranges 21 rounds (supplied free of charge) once a year.

Doubtless you have heard of the disturbances in Ashanti, and how the town of Coomassie is threatened. You know also that one of our Sergt.-Instructors wears a medal that he won in a former scrimmage in that part of the world ; and perhaps you will be pleased to be reminded that the 24th are represented there also by Sir F. M. Hodgson, K.C.M.G., Governor of the Gold Coast, who was formerly a member of the Post Office Rifles. Joining as Ensign in 1869, he was made Lieutenant in 1871, and Captain in 1872, which rank he held until January, 1882, when he was appointed Postmaster-General of British Guiana. He was one of the most efficient and most popular Officers in the regiment, and left it to the great regret of all ranks. Previous to his departure from England, he was entertained by his brother Officers at dinner. He raised the Gold Coast Volunteer Corps in 1893, and is now Governor and Commander-in-Chief of that Colony. He has been seen by many of us since his appointment yonder, and a year or two back those of us who were under canvas at Aldershot had the pleasure of drilling with him again. It seemed like old times.

It is rather surprising to learn, and it may interest you to know, that under paragraph 55a Volunteer Regulations, 1898, and Army Order 39, 1898, no less than 28 Colonels, commanding Volunteer Corps in the Home District, retire during the year 1900, unless an extension is granted.

Paragraph 55a Volunteer Regulations is as follows : -" All appointments made to the command of Volunteer Corps will, subject to paragraph 111, be held for a period of four years, and any extension of tenure will be for terms not exceeding four years, but will only be granted on the recommendation of General Officers commanding Districts, who will submit their recommendations one month before the expiration of the tenure." Among the number named is Col. S. Raffles Thompson, whose time is in on September 28th, but we must not lose him. If we were all General Officers commanding Districts would we not send our recommendations in months before that time ? Why, certainly.

Paragraph 111 doesn't touch him yet. It says "all Officers (except Chaplains) are liable to retirement on attaining the age of 60, unless granted an extension of service." And these extensions are given not more than two years at a time, and not beyond 67.

A very large number of our boys at the front have done duty at the Bisley meetings of the N.R.A., and they will be interested to hear that the Council of the National Rifle Association has made a preliminary announcement of the principal alterations which are to take effect at the next meeting. Among changes in the regulations it may be noted that a winner at any meeting of the N.R.A. of a prize in kind or of £2 or upwards is not to be classed as a tyro. The regulated positions in future are to be: at 200 yards, standing; at 500 yards, standing or kneeling; at 600 yards, standing, sitting, kneeling, or prone; and above 600 yards, any. In the Queen's and St. George's competitions the limit of three representatives per company is omitted. In the third-class target, the central is to be 6-in., bull 12-in., inner 24-in., magpie 36-in., outer, rest of target, 4-ft. square. In the St. George's orthoptics are not allowed, and in the Wantage the target is to be colored khaki instead of blue.

It is announced that the Queen's Birthday will be celebrated in London alone on Wednesday, 23rd May, and at all other stations on Thursday, 24th. So the "24th" will be "all there" on Wednesday next, when they stream down the Strand and St. James', smart and smiling, with springy step, to go through the ordeal of their Official Inspection. We shall miss the good old "L" Company; they will not be "wheeled up, half right" on that day, in order that the flanks of the big battalion may hear the words of command and be seen by an admiring crowd in Hyde Park. But we'll make up for it, boys, when we get you back. We'll have a little "inspection" on our own, where the valise will not be necessary and kit-bags will be forgotten, and in the words of the forms some of you have so kindly sent me, may you get your "Order tot vertrek" from the "Oranje Vrystaatsche Telegrafen" right speedily. How's that, umpire? "Out," I expect—I shouldn't be at all surprised.

While writing thus, I am reminded of a Dutch letter that I received from one of you. As it was beyond my power to interpret it, and being curious to know its contents—perhaps the sender was just as much in the dark—I fortunately found a friend in the Cable Room who kindly gave all assistance, and it was most amusing to discover that it contained nothing more than the wife's information to her husband that she had written him three letters each post (and yet he complained—Oh, the rascal!) and that she had had several teeth drawn, and was hoping to have some more out soon. Why did he lose that letter? Ah! Perhaps he was in a hurry. How inconsistent men are!

We were all very sorry to hear that the 1st Division Telegraph Battalion had lost some of their men as prisoners, viz., 22,453 Sergt. C. Shergold, 29,234 Corporal H. Richard, 644 Corporal R. Williams, Sapper 29251 J. Hay, and Drivers 24,194 C. Preston, 342 G. Clarke, and 29,276 E. Davis. We trust they will soon be with you again, and that they and many many others are only lent for a very short space of time. We do not know whether they were out at air-line work, or cable-laying—that information was lacking. We know the duties of both sections, and can appreciate the work of each. We have seen something of it before. Everyone, however, is not so fortunate, as a little incident that has occurred recently will prove. Lord Roberts' rapid advance is being eagerly followed by all and sundry. Lately he has telegraphed home in the following fashion, from various places in the field:—"CABLE CART, Headquarters. Front, May 10th, 9 a.m. We are now across the Zand River. Enemy still holding a strong position, but we are gradually pushing them back." A certain newspaper complains as follows:—"Lord Roberts is still advancing. The maps do not enable us to locate 'Cable Cart'—for that matter, every step forward in the campaign requires a new map with place names before unheard of."

We are a dissatisfied lot, always were, and always will be, I suppose. "Cable Cart" could be easily marked on any map by using an old printer's method—who, not knowing where to insert the stops, used a pepper box for sprinkling them in. Such a practice might be just as effectual to mark the positions of the ever-shifting and numerous Cable Carts.

Now, boys, I'll close. Trusting you are all A1—or "all Sir Garnet," as we say—and that you can spare a little leisure to drop me a line.

Yours most heartily,

To the "L" Co., in South Africa.   R. E. KEMP,
Tuesday, May 15th, 1900.   *Colour-Sergeant.*

COPYRIGHT.—" Khaki Letters " must not be used without permission.—R. E. KEMP.

Khaki Letters.

No. 4376, Sapper **W. W. Pearce**, s.s. "Winifredian," nearing Las Palmas, 8th April, says :—

"DEAR KEMP,—**I want you to thank the Queenstown Post Office Staff for their kindness** in sending us a sackful of luxuries aboard, otherwise we should have sailed away empty handed. No one allowed ashore, and the only extra we could procure was pigs' trotters, 'Irish jaw breakers' as the bumboat women called them, some dirty looking whisky which turned out to be bad rum. We had a glorious send-off by the Queenstown people. They burnt bonfires, torches, coloured lights, and every window was manned by enthusiastic Royal Irish people, cheering and waving handkerchiefs, flags, &c. The 'Howe' man-of-war's band played 'Auld Lang Syne,' and ships of all nationalities dipped their ensigns and cheered lustily. We had very indifferent rations to start with, but through the kindness of Sergeant Flanagan, who saw C.O. and Chief Steward, we were allowed a separate mess by paying one shilling per day. We are living like fighting cocks. Here's a sample breakfast—tender steaks, vegetables mashed, tomato sauce, butter, condensed milk, and marmalade and jam, '*ad lib.*' Dinner—roast beef and spuds, soup. Tea—hashed meat and potatoes and the '*ad libs.*' Not allowed any intoxicants. The 'Winifredian' would make a good home for inebriates.

"Only a few of us have suffered from sea-sickness, and I think the majority of soldiers aboard are enjoying good health, so that will be something for the total abstainers to glorify in. We are on board a very unsteady boat; she rolls 25° even in a calm sea. One of the sailors told me that the cause of it was improper ballast, and as we have 500 horses aboard they convert themselves into a gigantic swing. When the ship lurches to the right the 250 horses that side naturally strain forward, and the 250 on the other side strain backwards : so the poor devils go on as regular as clockwork There is great credit due to the Army Service Corps in the way they have looked after them, as only two have died up to now. A post-mortem is immediately held on them, and then committed to the deep.

'Tommy Stevenson is in great request when we get in the dumps, loud calls for one of his quaint stories. Dick Frew is the father and handyman of the party, all consult him on anything serious or anything difficult to tackle. He is as of yore, a 'typical soldier.' The whole of our party took guard Friday morning, and on Saturday morning had four prisoners to march before the beak—one of them was caught lying on the hay smoking. . . . We were all pleased with Flanagan's promotion. Most of the old 24th men who have been under him at Aldershot well know what a considerate fellow he was, and he is still 'Hail, fellow, well met,' and is looking after our interests splendidly. Well, old chap, I will close this letter, and if anything

KHAKI LETTERS—*continued*.

of interest occurs will slip it in to-morrow at Las Palmas ; up to now we have had a glorious fine trip. Please send a KHAKI LETTER with the thanks in it to Queenstown staff.

" . . . . I think to-night we are to be allowed to sleep on deck, if so, thank God, as a thousand men sleeping between decks causes the atmosphere to be better imagined than described. Allowed our first bath of sea water this morning, and a lot of us promptly took advantage of it. Just sighting land, so will close."

✣ ✣ ✣ ✣

No. 24,305, Sapper **F. T. Stimpson,** writing from Modder River, March 8th, says :—

" . . . Letters from home are looked forward to as much as those from the front, I suppose. We have not been doing any too well up to the time of 'Bobs'' move, but it turned out to be a grand one, as all the world knows. The troops mobilised here, and took a circuitous route, via Enslin, to Jacobsdal, which they took with very little resistance. Jacobsdal is about ten miles from here. General French was then sent on to Kimberley with all mounted troops, including artillery and mounted infantry, numbering about 14,000. He fought two engagements outside KB successfully, and entered KB early on February 14th. It came as a dream to the people. I had a chat with several on the subject. They couldn't believe it was true. No sooner had he got there and sent information to Roberts than he was instructed to chase Cronje's mob. Well, after Cronje heard of the relief, he made tracks for Bloemfontein, but was too late. They completely surrounded him, and, after holding out for three or four days, he threw the sponge up. The victory was doubly important, as we revenged Majuba. Of course, Roberts made a desperate effort for this event, and it was due to the bayonet charge principally of the Canadians and Gordons. We have had a lot of wounded and sick Canadians, and they all say they are fed. They were very anxious to get in the firing line. They have done some good work, though. This move also led to the ultimate relief of Ladysmith, as a lot of them tried to reinforce Cronje. . . . [Describes Cronje's arrival.] . . . . He was a fine, determined-looking man, and looked as if he hadn't neglected his meals much ; but his wife was crying bitterly, and looked a miserable, thin, common or garden washerwoman type. He was only kept about four hours, then sent down to the Cape. The next day we had the pleasure of seeing the whole lot of prisoners marched in, escorted by the 3rd Grenadiers, and a bigger mass of rabble it was impossible to see. To think that a lot of rebels like these should have shot our good men down makes me wish I was in the firing line sometimes. . . . [Describes prisoners' camp.] . . . The captured guns were brought in yesterday. There are five— three Krupp 9-pounders, one 7-pounder, and a Vickers-Maxim quick-firing gun, which was practically done in by our shells. They were also sent down country. Last night we had a terrible thunderstorm. It does rain here when it starts. All the tents, with the exception of ours, were washed out, and the fellows had to sleep at the office, railway carriages, and railway station. The rainy season is starting, so expect we shall get one or two wet shirts. Quinn met with an accident coming up from the Cape. He fell out of the train, but I don't think he was seriously hurt. Several of our section have been queer ; I think it is due to stopping so long in one place. We expect to move to Kimberley in a few days. We are working quad. to De Aar, and they are fitting up another. They are making Kimberley the next

KHAKI LETTERS—*continued*.

base. I had a run up there a few days ago. Passenger carriages are very scarce just now. I saw poor old Murch, late of 'C' Division. The siege has brought him very low. He said he was feeling very well when he first went to KB after his rest at the Cape. We took him up a few bottles of Bovril as soon as K.B. was relieved. The people poured in here on bikes, traps, and Shanks's pony, and bought up nearly everything. Jimmy Miller is in charge of the military office at the railway station—a nice little job, too. Military law was in existence when I was there, and everyone had to be indoors by 9 p.m., and they were still on rations. It is a much better place to what I expected to find. There are some decent buildings, especially the Town Hall, and I should think was a very decent place at ordinary times; but I don't think they will get any of our chaps to remain in the country. We are all very deceived with the country this side. They say it is much better the other side, but there is a lot more fever there. The A.P.O.C. have lost a corporal on the other side from enteric. I did not see either of the Stevens' when I was at the Cape, but I met Sturman. He has a very decent berth in the Appointments Branch, I believe. We didn't get much chance of seeing round the place. We only had two days there, and were on fatigue unloading our stores from the boat the best part of the time, but we hope to get a night or two with the boys before we come back. We shall not be sorry to get away from here, as the smells about the camp are chronic. I hear this morning that Hawkins, TSF, is down with enteric. He is stationed at Orange River. Nearly all the fellows that came out on our boat were inoculated, including myself. Barham was here for a few days; he has gone on to Osfontein; wished to be remembered to the Bees when I was writing. We can do with plenty more clerks. We have a few Guardsmen at some of the smaller offices doing telegraph work. We had a football competition between the garrison here, but didn't have time to finish it. We played the 3rd Grenadiers, and had to play three times for a result, the Grenadiers winning eventually. We also had a boxing competition, which was 'great herbs,' several well-known military stars taking part. Well, remember me to all the lads.

"P.S.—Just off to the front again. Hall (TS), Horton (BM), Poole (IV), and self. Fifty-six miles' spin. Ta-ta!"

✧ ✧ ✧ ✧

In another letter from Kimberley, dated March 15th, Sapper F. T. Stimpson writes as follows :—

". . . . Have at last shifted from Modder, and not sorry either, as we were getting a lot of sickness in our camp. Have left four behind in hospital. It is quite by accident we are here. There were four of us at Modder told off for the front, and four from De Aar. We started off with four waggons to tramp it a distance of fifty-six miles across the veldt. We had not gone very far when, crossing the drift, our heaviest waggon got stuck in the middle of the river. We had ten mules to start with, and gradually increased them until we had eighteen in. They kept struggling and falling down in the water, and the officer said we should have to undress and unload the waggon. I thought this was a bit of all right for a start. Well, after struggling for some time, to our great joy they got it on the move, and pulled it out O.K. The stream was running fearfully strong at the time and washed the waggon off the drift. I thought some of the mules must be drowned. We started off again, and got well down the road, when the officer took us across the open veldt, and we had not gone far before we

KHAKI LETTERS—*continued.*

were well in a bog, and, after struggling with the mules for another two hours, putting them on back and front of the waggon, we had to unload a lot of the stuff. In the meantime, the officer galloped back into camp to say the roads were too heavy, and we had orders to return to camp, and go *via* KB. We left Modder about 11 p.m., and arrived at KB 1.15 a.m., and had to sleep in the railway carriages for the night. We hung on, waiting for a convoy, and were to have started on the Sunday night at 7, but Roberts cancelled it at the last moment, and said no more convoys were to leave here; so we are stranded here for the present. We are not doing any office work, but have to do guard every fourth night. At times of peace it would be a decent place, but most of the residents have gone down south, taking advantage of the free passes, to get a feed, things are still very scarce. We had a nice walk out to Kenilworth on Sunday morning, but no, 'Case is Altered' about there. It is about a three miles' walk. It is a pretty place, where all De Beers' employees live. You go right through the diamond fields, and get a view of the earth that has been put on the floors to dry, then it cracks, and they get some of the diamonds out this way. You can't get close enough to see any diamonds, there being a high barbed wire fence all round. None of the mines have started yet, on account of the water down them and no coal. Our fellows are working in the Kimberley Post Office, and they seem quite at home. . . . . [Refers to death of Hawkins.] . . . . We have about five hundred 24th men altogether out here, and they will look all right marching through Pall Mall for the next inspection. Well, as things are going, we ought to be home not later than June. Roberts is not far from Bloemfontein, and French has cut the railway off two miles north of Bloemfontein. Kruger sent a message to Salisbury suing for peace on his own terms and asking for independence, but he replied that they had lost their independence. They are losing a lot of their men; they are throwing their rifles down. Now the Transvaalers have got to do the fighting. It is principally Free Staters that have been doing the fighting up to Paardeberg. We expect to go by train when we move. To get to Bloemfontein we have to go to Naauwport, and then through the Free State; well, I want to have a look at Bloemfontein and Pretoria, then Southampton can roll on as soon as possible. It is their autumn out here now, and we are getting a lot of rain, and it is much cooler. We ran up against a Captain the other night, he bought us plenty of beer and ran us into his hotel to supper, finishing up with more beer, and Red Hussars took us out to Kenilworth and paid our tram fares back. We have struck a decent hotel, where we dine at 6 p.m. and get a very decent spread for 1/6 if you get there early. There is a big march past the Town Hall, this afternoon, of all the troops that took part in the defence of Kimberley, and a banquet afterwards. Let me know, as soon as possible, about our boys in green and white, they are 'good herbs,' and I can see the mob at the station to meet them; after doing the 'Wolves' in they ought to be in the semi-final with a bit of luck, and final with another bit. . . . . Well, ta-ta. . . . Kind regards to the Bees."

✧ ✧ ✧ ✧

No. 24,387, Sapper **E. J. Whibley**, 1st Tel. Div. R.E., De Aar, writing on March 18th, says :—

"My DEAR KEMP,—It is with very deep regret that I write announcing the death of one of our number. Sapper A. W. Hawkins, No. 458 (not 488, as shown in your list), fell a victim to enteric fever, and after lying a

KHAKI LETTERS—*continued.*

few days in the hospital at Orange River, passed away. Needless to say, this being the first casualty in the ranks of the 24th, it came as a great shock to us all, and his brother, who, so far as we know, is his *only* near relative, has our sincere sympathy. As regards the recent news from home, we all regret to hear of poor Lankstead's decease, although in his case it was not a very great surprise to many of us who were aware of his illness. It is gratifying to know that one or two of his old 24th Middlesex comrades were able to accompany him to his last resting-place in the Dover Cemetery. The last lot of our men who sailed by the 'Cephalonia' are expected at Cape Town daily, but at present their destination is unknown. I saw Captains Palmer and Price on the De Aar platform a few mornings ago. Both look as if the South African climate agrees with them. They left, I believe, with the intention of proceeding to the Free State Capital with the view of establishing an A.P.O. there. In saying that we at De Aar will welcome the proposed Magazine, I think I express the feelings of the whole of the 'L' Co. men out here, and personally I wish you every success in your undertaking. With kindest regards."

✤ ✤ ✤ ✤

Private **S. E. Sterling** (late of "I" Co.), 551, "C" Co., C.I.V., writes from Wigton Culverts, near Witteputts, on March 19th.

"As you see we are still kept here, but we hope to be moved up soon, as we have had our rifle sights made correct by a man of the Army Ordnance Corps. By the bye he told us a yarn about the Warwick Militia down at Orange River. He was sitting in a railway truck where there were two of them, and he heard one say : 'Jack, what does A.O.C. on his shoulder strap mean?' 'Why, Army 'Ospital Corps, of course.' The flies here are something fearful, they get in your food and crawl all over. Taking it all round I don't think guarding a railway is much catch, though it is a bit of a lark when a fellow finds a snake in his blanket or perhaps a scorpion. We get a lot of these and also a large kind of spider which is poisonous. . . . . The night before last a sentry on the culvert saw eight men on horseback approaching, and when he challenged they fired at him. He laid down quickly and fired back, and then the guard had turned out. The men fired twice more at us, but we were in the trenches round the culvert and they couldn't see us. The guard fired a volley at them and they cleared off. The morning patrols found a dead horse a quarter of a mile away. You can guess this sort of thing makes sentry-go very nice. It makes one fancy every bush or boulder is one of them."

Writing again on March 26th he continues :

"We've got fourteen of our Company in hospital with fever, pneumonia, etc., that's a good many considering there are only 123 in it. Two of them have got to be sent home as soon as they can stand it, as the doctor says they will never recover from dysentery while they are out here. There doesn't seem to be any chance of us moving yet. I think it's a shame to keep us here all this time without trying us to see if we are any good. We've just been told to stop any rebels crossing the line from Prieska, as Kitchener has smashed them up there. This job is the sort of thing that gives one the pip, we have more men go under with disease here than we should with disease and shot up at the front, and if the enemy take it into their heads to send about 200 men to smash the line, our little party (16) couldn't stop them, and we hear that 1,500 men and a Maxim are advancing on Belmont, 12 miles north, and we've only a very few troops there. We

KHAKI LETTERS—*continued*.

get a good deal of patrolling day and night. It isn't half bad when we go over the Free State Border, and along the Orange River it's very pretty, being much like the Dart now, as it has only about the same amount of water, and winds just like it, though the banks are not quite so steep. . . . . It will be a treat to get a stiff collar and shirt on, and to have room enough to lay out flat of a night. Just fancy, sixteen in a tent, and eight of them over 5ft. 10in., and also take into consideration we have to wear bandolier and sidearms, boots, etc., all day and night. Well, so long for the present. Kind regards."

✤ ✤ ✤ ✤

No. 1,274, Sapper **W. F. Adams,** Kimberley, March 19th, sends the following :

"I have made some dispositions from the parcel so kindly sent by the 'C' and 'E' Groups to Pallet, Miller, O'Sullivan and Jenner. I'm very pleased with the handkerchiefs, particularly as I had only two red ones and they perform all sorts of duties, including cleaning carbines and mess tins. I shall be quite respectable at church and in the park now. I went to the Presbyterian church last night and enjoyed it very much. The service was very musical, and instead of a sermon we had a lecture on the life of Ruskin. Next Sunday evening it is to be on the work of Ruskin, and I hope to go then as I fancy I'm a fixture here for some time. After the service we went into the park or gardens as they call it here. There is a fine band stand, and last night the combined bands of the KB Rifles and Lancs. Regiment were playing. They played selections from 'Gaiety Girl' and 'Belle of New York,' also 'Soldiers of the Queen,' etc., etc. It was most enjoyable. The band stand was struck by a shell during the siege, and a huge rent in the roof and flooring testify to the destructiveness of the 100-pounder. It is said that the Boers fired most of the big shells in and near the gardens because the people congregated there to escape the smaller shells which could not reach the gardens. One of the other men here and myself have adopted a novel way of bathing. Every night when it is not raining we get buckets of water and douche each other outside the tent, which has the effect of keeping us warm all night. Ordinarily one gets very cold towards morning, as the nights here are damp and very chilly. Pleased to say I am absolutely fit and going strong. Last week's mail not yet distributed owing to the 'business-like' manner in which the A.P.O.C. are doing their work. Well, ta-ta, hope you too are going strong."

Adams' No. 2. Warrenton Camp, March 29th.

"From the midst of shells, bullets, etc., I venture to pen (or pencil) a few lines and hope you are still all right. I am, I'm glad to say. You will see I have changed my address, and am now at the very front and find it rather warm. Yesterday morning we were shelled out of camp and I now occupy a position on the veldt, no tent, and up to this morning no blankets, waterproof sheet, or anything. Also, I'm in sole charge of this 'office.' I am enclosing a few botanical specimens gathered this morning. Thanks for the *Daily Mail.* Haven't had a chance of reading it yet owing to the unnecessary trouble given by the Boers. They hit only two men and killed a horse, though they fired all day. They're at it again to-day but have changed their position. That Corporal Adams at Tugela, needless to say, is not me. I wish it had been, but though the A.P.O.C. people send me his letters, I am still a sapper. Dinner is now on the table (mim.). Tinned rabbit, what ho ! Must now close as train is just going back, and I must give this to the guard. Kind regards to all."

KHAKI LETTERS—*continued*.

Adams' No. 3. Kimberley, April 6th.
"Just a short note to report all's well. Am back at KB, worse luck—dragged back on account of being on the Wheatstone staff—seems hard. T. B. George is up at KB so I'm not quite lonely now."

April 7th.—"Got very little more news and barely time to tell you so. Yesterday morning went for a walk round Kenilworth, and a kind civilian invited us to a drink at the De Beers Employees' Club and afterwards stood us a dinner. Then a terrible rain and hailstorm came on and we were weather-bound. We returned by tram. Distance, three miles. Fare, 6d. Drawn by four mules. At several places line was submerged and covered with stones and earth washed over it by the storm. Must close now or lose the mail. Please excuse brevity. Kind regards."

✢ ✢ ✢ ✢

No. 2,336, Sapper **E. J. Samuel,** writing to a "Quartette of Girls" from Colesberg Junction, March 25th, says:

"I'm on night duty and all my stationery is in the tent, so to avoid waking the rest of the troops I am using this paper, please excuse. It is very kind of you all to write me such nice letters and I can't tell you adequately how I appreciate them. It's a good thing though that I am aware of your 'kidding' propensities or otherwise I should be fearfully conceited when you tell me how you miss me! I've got no news much for you this time, for after the alarms and excursions of Rensburg and Arundel this place is very slow. What a change in the last three weeks! Then we were surrounded and expecting every minute to be our next, and now, thanks to 'Bobs,' there's not a Boer within fifty miles of us. All our troops have moved on and a few of us are left here with no work to do at all. Colesberg is not a bad place. Very prettily situated in the midst of a fearful nest of kopjes from which we could never have driven the Boers if they had seen fit to hold on. There are plenty of evidences of the struggle round about, scores of dead horses—Phew, and don't they talk!—and a goodly number of mounds of earth, the last resting place of our poor fellows and our opponents. The stores are just reopening and the people returning to the town now, for which we are very glad, for now we can obtain no luxuries, only our bare rations, for we can't afford 2s. a lb. for sugar and everything else in proportion. The rations are all right if you are 'fit,' but if you are off colour you sigh for the unobtainable extras, and one's thoughts fly back to home comforts, we call it the 'white tablecloth' feeling. Up to now I've not experienced it and have no desire to. There are some nice girls in the town, but what chance does a fellow stand who has a fringe round the bottom of his trousers and with several patches on them as well. Mine were rather small to begin with and after a time gave way every time I subjected them to extra pressure, but I'm growing accustomed to patching, and am a perfect snip at the 'featherstitch' (mim.). There was one redeeming feature about Colesberg and that was a splendid swimming bath. A natural bath, 18 feet deep all over, and filled by the overflow of the town supply. It was glorious, but that is denied us now a battalion of Militia was brought and is stationed here, and now persons with any regard for cleanliness don't swim there. We are under orders to move from here as this office can be dispensed with, so I hope the next letter I write will be from the Free State—Bloemfontein. I hope some of our men are there now. We are all anxious to see the green pastures of the Orange Free State, and are tired of the brown veldt and kopjes. Everything here is lean—horses, cattle and people, with the exception of the

KHAKI LETTERS—*continued.*

black girls who are very much inclined to what in the world of athleticism is called 'beefiness.' It's a pity they don't speak English, for some of them are 'erbus gigantum,' and dumb motions are not a very satisfactory medium of conversation. Dick Paddon told me in his last letter that you had sent me out a parcel and I'm still in a flutter of excitement over it. It has not put in an appearance yet and I am anxiously waiting the arrival of the shirt, etc. It will be a perfect Godsend to me, for on the strict Q.T. I made a mistake when washing my regimental shirts. I diligently and innocently scrubbed them, and to my horror discovered that it had caused them to shrink to an alarming extent, and————Well, no matter, they shrunk. The same with my socks which I now use for finger stalls (mim.). I haven't had much loot lately and haven't picked up many curios yet, for those in the front rank have the best opportunities, but I managed to get some ostrich feathers. I sent about twenty in a tin cylinder, which I hope you've received all right. I posted them on March 8th, they are small, but the birds are moulting at this season. Tell Dick Paddon that two days ago I had a conversation with Rudyard Kipling, and asked his opinion of Dick's parody on the A.M.B. His advice to Dick is that he should give up telegraphy and cultivate his undoubted poetic gifts. I hope you are all well, I am as well as my absence from you will allow me to be. Please give my kind regards to all, and hoping all of you will enjoy your holidays and have a good time generally, and that I shall be back before many more moons, yours to a cinder—SAM."

(This was written on Free State Telegraph Forms).

No. 27,844, Sapper **John Fallon,** Military Telegraphs, Naauwpoort Junction, 26th March, 1900, writes:

"MY DEAR OLD COLOURS—My duty is to heartily congratulate you on the pluck, perseverance and unselfishness with which you have faithfully portrayed the doings of your comrades abroad, and furthermore wish you every success in the publication which you propose taking on single-handed. I hope those comrades will now rally round you, supply you with plenty of copy, detail all their adventures, and in short give you the support of which you have proved yourself so deserving. Your circular letters arrive regularly and are transmitted CQ. It pains me to have to inform you of a gap in our ranks. Poor Alf. Hawkins died at Orange River, of enteric fever, on 14th (?) inst, and was given a military funeral by his comrades of the 24th. Although he had been in hospital for some weeks and was, so we heard, well on the road for recovery, his death came as a terrible surprise to us, and those of us who knew him more intimately felt as if we had lost a near relative. His gentlemanly yet unassuming disposition won him hosts of friends, indeed it was impossible to be otherwise than friendly with dear old Alf., while his soldier-like qualities which were many, made him one of the darlings of the regiment. On behalf of R.E.'s and 24th men on General Clements' column, I beg to tender our sympathies, on his untimely end, to his relatives. And now, perhaps, you'd like to hear a bit about the war. As it happens I've not seen to-day's paper yet, so must ask you to make up a bit of 'War Special' (mim. Fleet Street), and bung it in the Stop Press Column headed 'Latest from the Front.' It is the general opinion here that 'War Specials' will soon become a drug in the market, as its very possible that by the time you receive this some of the correspondents and their

KHAKI LETTERS—*continued*.

victims (telegraphists) may be packing their kits and making tracks for the nearest seaport, loaded with honour, loot and other vegetables. Talking of loot reminds one that our chaps, now in the Free State, are having the pull of some of us poor bounders at the base (another grievance), and would suggest a sharing-out after the march past. I believe Sappers Milton and Wyatt were amongst the first 24th men to reach Bloemfontein, so don't suppose there will be much left for those who arrived later, as their commandeering proclivities had, so it is said, got to the ears of Oom Paul some weeks ago, who warned his brother President of their approach, so *that* accounts for our rapid advance on Bloemfontein. I've heard that several pairs of spurs and riding breeches, as well as ammunition bandoliers, have been discovered in the neighbourhood of the Telegraph Office, and it is supposed these were left as a peace-offering to be equally divided amongst the operators. So now they only require riding whips, jack boots, and—— oh yes, horses. The Military Telegraphs here are still under the personal control and supervision of C. S. M. Tee, and a very large amount of work is daily despatched by himself and staff, especially in the culinary line. This is one of the largest junctions on the Cape Government Railways, but the population, exclusive of military, is not large, about a couple of dozen cottages, besides the station buildings, which consist of civil and military telegraph offices, stationmaster's office, railway staff officers' quarters, and a big refreshment bar. No, I've *not* been inside the latter (soldiers not served) 'But where there's a will,' etc. Well, my dear Colours, after struggling through this, I've come to the conclusion that there's no war news to hand. Some say there's no war, and that the Reserves are about to be called home. With fraternal greetings to yourself and the Rob-Roys, and wishing you every success in the journalistic world."

No. 23,653, Sapper **J. F. Metcalfe,** writing from Springfontein, on March 27th, says :—

"DEAR KEMP,—After a prolonged silence I will endeavour to favour you with a few more lines. In the first place I rejoice to inform you that I and Tough are now detached from the 12th Co., R.E.'s. This occurred owing to the evacuation of Stormberg, by Olivier, on Sunday, March 4th, necessitating a prompt move of the Field Corps to repair the railway lines, culverts, and bridges, which had been wantonly destroyed by the retreating force. We followed on Tuesday, the 6th, staying the night at Molteno, proceeding to Stormberg the following day. immediately the repairs were completed. The Military took over both the working of railways and telegraphs. Capt. Fowler, with a party of R.E.'s, Telegraph Battalion, arrived shortly after us, amongst whom was Sapper Eglington, of DY, he being the first 24th man I had met since leaving England ; leaving this party behind we moved still nearer the Free State, calling and leaving telegraphic communication at Burghersdorp, Knapdaar, and Bethulie (with a complement of clerks), through to the base of the Division. Owing to the manner in which this Division has been treated by the conspicuous absence of a Telegraph Section of R.E.'s, the C.O. of the Derby Regiment, was approached, the result being that we were supplied with 5 experienced telegraphists (Mr. Copeley, of NG Post Office, being amongst them). On our arrival at Bethulie Camp, which was pitched ½-mile this side of the Orange River, we were compelled to remain 3 or 4 days, as 5 out of

KHAKI LETTERS—*continued*.

the 8 spans of the railway bridge had been completely shattered, consequently, a temporary office was opened, a cable being run from the railway telegraphs (which had been repaired by a party of Linesmen, under T. S. M. Foote, R.E.) to the house of a Dutch farmer, who, presumably, had thrown in his lot with the enemy, or had made a hasty retreat, as part of his furniture had been left behind, several chairs, for instance, being very useful for our improvised office. On the 16th of March, however, the bridge had not, as yet, been repaired, consequently, we were obliged to march to our destination by way of the wagon or road bridge, which was saved only in the nick of time, from destruction by dynamite, the electrical fuse being cut by a small party, under a cross fire. The march through the Orange Free State was somewhat tedious under a hot sun, and the rough and rocky condition of the Veldt. Although the country is not so mountainous as the Colony, it is apparently devoid of vegetation. At nightfall we bivouacked at Providence Siding, and by 6 a.m. the following morning, we were ready to march off again, and arrived at the Camp about 4 p.m., having halted only once, for an hour's duration, to rest and partake of that appetizing bully beef and biscuits. Since our arrival here I have met Sapper McAuley, TS, and many other R.E.'s. I have, with great reluctance, to report the sickness of Sapper Tough, who is now in hospital suffering from bronchitis, trust my subsequent report will be most' favourable. Since I last wrote to you there have been many changes, and these in our favour, needless for me to repeat news which you have, in all probability, read of, months ago. I might mention that our Division has lost one of its bravest leaders in Capt. De Montmorency, V.C., of the Scouts, during one of the many reconnaissances and skirmishes, for which Stormberg has been responsible, he was, unfortunately, shot through the heart, on Rooi Kop. A most impressive funeral service, performed in the presence of General Gatacre and Staff, being their last tribute of respect for so gallant an officer, who gained his V.C. at Omdurman. Sir A. Milner has just passed through on his way to interview Kruger (so rumour has it). If it is a mission of peace let us hope that it will be a reasonable one. I am still enjoying the best of health, but my point is to keep off too much water. Thanks for the List of Names, and the interest you continue to show for the benefit of all your Comrades. Trusting you are well, and able to follow the doings of the L Company during the campaign.

"Since I have seen Stormberg, I venture to say that if the Boers had still kept their strong position, much loss of life would have been necessary before we could have routed them, and a repetition of the disaster of the 10th December has been averted by the Boers evacuating. Best wishes to all friends and yourself."

✣ ✣ ✣ ✣

No. 28,201, Company-Sergeant-Major **W. G. Tee,** writing on April 1st, from Naauwpoort, says :—

"MY DEAR DICK,—I have written to Peter King this post; perhaps he will allow you to peruse my letter. I need scarcely say we are very grateful to you for the interest which you have taken on our behalf, and for your letters, which we receive regularly each mail. I am sure we all feel indebted to you, and the kindness shown will always be remembered. You must excuse me writing a letter to each of you, as you must be aware that I have plenty to do. So take the word for the deed. Trusting you are enjoying the best of health.

P.S.—Enclosed are some of the forms left at Rensburg by the Boers."

KHAKI LETTERS—*continued*.

No. 1,275, Sapper **E. J. Woode,** writing from De Aar, April 2nd, says :—

"DEAR COLOUR-SERGEANT KEMP,—Thanks for your new book. It is very interesting to us here, and amusing to others. Willis, Proudfoot, Curnew, Whibley and myself are the only fellows who came out on the 'Gascon' who are still at De Aar. The Wheatstone has gone to Bloemfontein and Kimberley, and after the heavy rushes we had, with consequent long hours, we are not now anxious to follow that slip-running machine. At De Aar we are just now comfortable. For the last fortnight or so I have been cooking. I am only an amateur, so you can guess there was just a little grousing (not without cause). But still, I got on fairly well after a day or two. The fellows at De Aar are all in the best of health. We have received bad news from Orange River, two of Ours gone. One 24th, and the other an R.E., who is greatly connected to our regiment by family ties. All our fellows are much cut up at our loss. The last detachment of 24th, who came on the 'Cephalonia,' arrived here on Friday, and have now gone to Kimberley, and others to Bloemfontein, so we are still left at De Aar. You have to stay where they want you. Well, for present, ta ta."

No. 4,327, Sapper **A. J. Brooks,** 2nd Tel. Div., Bloemfontein Railway Yard, April 3rd, writes :—

"DEAR COL.-SGT. KEMP,—We were just going to settle down for awhile at De Aar, and Woode, Humm, and the 'old 'uns,' were jubilant at the prospect of moving up country, we, of course, to take their places. However, at 11 o'clock on Saturday morning the operators of No. 7 section, together with F. Clark, Lce.-Corpl. Thomas, Arundel, Swan, Greig, and Campbell, were ordered to parade at 11.30 for Bloemfontein. We ultimately got off at 2.30 p.m., and reached Naauwpoort Junction late the same night. At Naauwpoort were Tee, Little (SW), Payne, Warren, and several R.E.'s. They very kindly provided us with hot coffee for supper. We left Naauwpoort early next morning, and passed through the district where General French's Cavalry Division operated for so long, Arundel, Rensburg, Colesberg, Achtertang, Van Zyl, and on to Norval's Pont. We reached the latter place at 8.50 on Sunday morning, and found we had to wait there all day, so leaving our goods and chattels on the station platform, we walked down the line to see the Orange River, and to look across at the promised land. The splendid railway bridge was blown up by the Boers, and looked a terrible wreck, but the R.E.'s and the R.P.R. (Railway Pioneer Regiment) were making a good job of it. Alongside was the temporary 'bridge' of wood and ballast laid in the bed of the river, and across which a line of rails has been laid. Deep cuttings on either side connect it with the main line. Lower down the river was the pontoon bridge for ordinary traffic. We had a very enjoyable swim in the river. I had to wash all my clothes on the bank, as going down to the river side I unfortunately jumped into a bog. At Norval's Pont we found Jim Creasy, Luttrell, and the very much alive Alf. Rudd, of the R.E.'s. They are living in an abandoned house near the station, where I had the pleasure of having tea and bread and jam with Alf. It was a treat after eight days of bully beef and biscuit at every meal. We did not leave Norval's till 8 a.m. Monday morning, having spent the night in a coal truck, in which we travelled on to Springfontein, O.F.S. The first station over the border was Donkerpoort, where the Boers had had a large camp.

KHAKI LETTERS—*continued.*

All the farm buildings were in ruins, and the place for miles around was strewn with rubbish, sheep skins, tinned meat tins, &c. They had also left one of the Johannesberg 'werken comite's' water vans behind them. At Springfontein we changed trucks, and had an opportunity of going to see some Boer prisoners, who were confined in a house there. One of them had only been taken that morning. We were shown the holes in his garden from which our people had dug rifles and ammunition. Jim Metcalfe, not quite so stout as when I saw him last, but looking very well, was at Springfontein with Gen. Gatacre's Division; Tough is in hospital at Cape Town. Going up the line we passed great numbers of troops on the march to Bloemfontein. At several places on the way we picked up companies of the Scots Guards, who had been guarding the line. They have had a terrible time of it altogether, but still seemed as cheerful as crickets. They marched in the first place from Orange River, and went through Belmont, Graspan, Modder, Jacobsdal, Paardeberg, and on to Bloemfontein, fighting all the way. On reaching Bloemfontein, they had to hurry down the railway line to secure the various stations, and keep the line open. They are dressed in all kinds of rags, many of them with navvies' trousers and other civilian clothing. They have had nothing but what they stood up in since the campaign started. With their helmets smashed out of all shape, with armless jackets, and bare knees showing through, what is left of their trousers, they look a picture. We spent the evening and part of the night standing up in the coal trucks, arriving at Bloemfontein this morning at 2 a.m. Slept on the gravel platform until 7. Had a wash and more 'bully and biscuit,' and are now (10 a.m.) waiting for orders. Lord Roberts is operating about 30 miles from here. We are told that two batteries of the R.H.A. got a terrible cutting-up the other day. They were surrounded and shot down without mercy by the Boers. The men here are very bitter against the Boers altogether, and they will certainly give them no mercy when they get at them. We can only see a little of the town from here; it seems very prettily situated. I enclose a surcharged O.F.S. stamp. We must do our posting at the military office, so am not able to use it for the letter. Expect my letters are chasing me all over the country, have got none as yet. Hope everything is going on O.K. with you."

No. 198, Sapper **F. H. Woodrow** (of SO), writing from Kimberley, April 5th, says :—

"DEAR SERGEANT,—Your KHAKI LETTERS agreeably surprised all the Absent Minded Beggars of the 'L' Co., and we one and all wish you every possible success in your new undertaking. Those of our friends who have not received letters personally will find them a great boon, and will, I feel certain, appreciate your work. It would be impossible to write to all our friends however much we wished to, but by means of your journal everyone will get their share, and will know exactly how dreary South Africa is looking up.

"No doubt, by now, you have received the sad news of poor Hawkins, and, knowing him as I did, as one of the best, it fairly upset me. They told me on the wire that they would let you have full particulars, so that I will not repeat them, as they are painful to recall. Being a personal friend of his, I made inquiries as to erecting a cross in his memory, which I volunteered to finish off, paint, and carve, myself. I enclose photo of same.

KHAKI LETTERS—*continued*.

. . . . I have also, to-day, been informed that Bob Williams' son has succumbed to same complaint, for which I am, indeed, sorry. Will you kindly convey to his father my deepest sympathy, and tell him that I will, in my spare time, erect a similar cross over his son's grave, and write him on completion. It is, indeed, a sad duty to perform, but it will, no doubt, bring comfort to the loved ones at home to know that his comrades have placed it in his memory. . . . .

"It is perfect slogging from morning to night, but as long as we have successes to record, and keep in good health, we don't mind. Out of staff of 32, we had 10 in hospital at one time, but I'm pleased to say all are improving rapidly, and hope to be with us again soon. Roberts, McLaren, Alliston, Pallet, Sullivan, Stormer, Greenfield, Fenton, J. Jones, and Jenner, are still in Hospital. . . . . Hoping you are OK, and wishing you every success in new journal."

No. 1,457, Sapper **H. J. Hayden** (of LS), writing from Rondebosch Convalescent Hospital, near Cape Town, 10th April, 1900, says :

"We arrived at Rensburg on the 1st March. The Boers evacuated the place two days before we arrived. Rensburg was an awful place, the water was bad, and the whole place was absolutely rotten. Where the Boers had their laager were piles of dirty clothes, skins and entrails of sheep and goats which they had killed, and the stench was chronic. When the troops advanced on to Colesberg, Forth (Leeds) and I were left at Rensburg Telegraph Office. Forth in charge. After being there two or three days Charlie (Forth) was taken ill, I stuck to the office day and night for about six days, when I had a bad attack of diarrhœa, Forth was getting no better so we obtained reliefs and came down to Naauwport Hospital for treatment. Here they soon put us right again, we got plenty of good food and a bed to lie on. I stayed there a fortnight, when the doctor told me a week's rest would put me in good trim, so he sent me down to Rondebosch, about five miles out of Cape Town, to get my strength up again. Forth was under a different doctor so he didn't get sent down. Rondebosch Convalescent Hospital is a fine place. We have a splendid doctor. I get plenty of good bread and butter and tea for breakfast, roast chops and vegetables for dinner, eggs, bread and butter, for tea, and finish up with custard pudding. I have also whiskey and sodas allowed during the day. The place is pleasantly surrounded by plenty of trees and high rocks. Cecil Rhodes' estate is here, where he keeps a Zoo, and his band plays occasionally in the afternoon. I am now feeling first class again, and expect to go back up country in a few days, when I shall miss these little luxuries. Up country we consider ourselves lucky if we get dry bread, and we never get milk in the tea or coffee. The general order is bully beef and hard biscuits. I am very sorry to say one of the London men (Fairall) who was one of our party, died the other day from enteric fever ; there are more men dying from this disease and dysentery than from wounds, this is accounted for by the scarcity of water, which is also very bad. Myself, I am very careful, and have used myself to going a day without a drink. Forth is still at Naauwport Hospital, but he is all right again. I expect to join him early part of next week. Kind regards to all colleagues. Hope all well."

KHAKI LETTERS—*continued.*

No. 1,275, Sapper **C. J. Woode,** sends his compliments to "Colours" on the back of a photograph (which is reproduced below, giving the figures full size), representing

The Staff of Telegraphists at De Aar.

Most of the features are well known to us, but there are some we are doubtful of, owing to various adornments. Perhaps one of the men will identify them for us, and send a "Key" along bye-and-bye. Meanwhile K.L. readers will find some amusement in finding names for them all.

✤ ✤ ✤ ✤

To ..
the ..
Dear .
Ones.
Left. .

We've drunk the good health of the khaki-clad boys,
 Admiring the pride which inclined them
To sacrifice country, and home, with its joys—
 But what of the dear ones behind them?

The train as it leaves with its confident freight,
 And the transport which speeds thro' the foam,
Bear hearts apprehensive with shadows of fate—
 But what of the shadows at home?

We hear of our soldiers victorious, and cheer,
 And we think of their bodies decaying,
When we reckon the cost of the fight we hold dear—
 But Oh! it's their loved ones are paying.

So here's to the health of the ones that they left—
 Neglected in poem and story—
Who suffer in secret, bewildered, bereft,
 The heroes deserving of glory.

TSF.   S. A. COASE.

Khaki Sidelights.

Just a little space must be set aside in our booklet for such letters, or excerpts from letters, as the following, showing, as they do, that the boys out yonder are not forgetful of their sad duties to the bereaved.

Re REGGIE WILLIAMS.—The parents have received :—

From 23,577, Sapper **Charles M. Wilson,** Orange River, April 6th,
"Allow me on behalf of the staff here to express our deepest sympathy in your sad bereavement. We were very grieved at the loss of your son; he was very much liked by those that knew him. He was admitted into hospital 18th March. I visited him every day, and after eight days he appeared to get better. I certainly believed he would pull through, but he took a change for the worse, and died peacefully at midnight, 2nd April. Am pleased to tell you he had every comfort and was well cared for, and everything that was possible was done for him. He was very delirious the day prior to his death. All the staff attended his funeral. The firing party consisted of 6th Company, R.E.'s, and he had a nice service. It is our intention of placing a cross upon his grave, and having his name engraved thereon. I have sent you all his personal effects, as I thought you would be glad of same, these include his purse, which he gave me prior to going into hospital. Wishing you good health and strength to bear this terrible loss."

From 21,410, Sergeant **J. H. Nelson,** Bloemfontein, April 3rd :—
"The news of the death of your son has been received here with extreme regret, both by those who knew him, and also by those who know, or have known, his worthy father, and a large proportion of the staff now at Bloemfontein, R.E.'s and 24th, very sincerely sympathise with you and yours in your great trouble. The average R.E. of the T.B. is not called upon to share equally the war risks of his more militant comrades in the fighting line, but in the case of disease all are on a pretty level footing ; and so your boy died the brave soldier's death none the less heroically than others who have received the fatal wound ere barely conscious of the foe's presence. With kind regards and sincere condolence with yourself and family."

From the **Rev. H. J. Rose,** Chaplain and Hon. Major, Orange River, April 2nd :—
"I desire to express my sincere sympathy with the relatives of Sapper Williams in their recent bereavement. I saw him frequently during his last illness. To-day we laid him to rest in the quiet and well-ordered little Cemetery of this place. His comrades escorted the funeral, and with reverence performed the last honours. May God bind up the wounded hearts of those he has left behind, and soon bring this terrible war to a close."

Re A. W. HAWKINS.

No. 2,548, Sapper **W. C. Smith,** writing from Enslin, March 14th, refers to his late comrade, Sapper A. W. Hawkins, as follows :—
"The last time I saw him was when he, with another London man and myself, went to church on Christmas Eve, at Seapoint, near Cape Town, and made the place shake. It was only a small church. After the service was over we had a long chat with the clergyman, and many of the congregation. Hawkins then went to the organ, and we had the pleasure of listening to him for half-an-hour. Never did I imagine for one moment that that would be the last time that we should meet on this earth."

"Khaki Notes."

Absent-Minded Beggar Concert. — The Staff of the Central Telegraph Office are to be congratulated on the result of their Concert, given at the Holborn Town Hall on April 6th, 1900. The appended Balance Sheet will speak for itself.

RECEIPTS.	£ s. d.	EXPENDITURE.	£ s. d.
Guarantee Fund	27 15 0	Hire of Hall. Artistes, etc...	14 18 10
		Decorations. Refreshments, etc.	5 13 0½
		Printing	2 13 0
		Stationery	11 6
		Postage	5 5
		Fares, etc.	9 0
Balance in Hand	2 2 2½	Substitutes	1 2 0
			£25 12 9½

Proceeds of Concert.

	£ s. d.
Sale of Tickets	68 19 0
,, Programmes	12 9 8
A.M.B. Collection	14 8 11
Donations	2 0 2½
Balance from Guarantee Fund	2 2 2½
	£100 0 0

Audited and found correct.
R. PINNOCK, } *Auditors.*
C. G. JONES, }

May 8th, 1900.

C. A. MORGAN, *Chairman.*
R. J. TAYLOR, *Hon. Sec. and Treasurer.*

COPY OF RECEIPT.
Room 44, Harmsworth Buildings,
May 2nd, 1900.

DEAR SIR,
We beg to acknowledge the receipt of bank notes for £100, to be expended in relief for wounded and disabled soldiers.
THE DAILY MAIL PUBLISHING COMPANY.
A.M.B. RELIEF CORPS.

R. TAYLOR, C.T.O.

Subscribers going on annual leave would do well to hand to their Distributor an addressed stamped wrapper. Their booklets can then be posted to them, their Distributor will be clear, and they will have the pleasure of receiving them while away. Besides, what a number of friends you can introduce them to. Think of that!

Sergeant Haves resumed duty at his wonted post on Tuesday, 8th inst. The "L" Co. will be glad to know this. He doesn't look himself yet, but idleness would make the old soldier look worse. Well done, Jacob, hearty congrats.

KHAKI NOTES—*continued.*

The s.s. Montfort passed Las Palmas May 2nd, and up to that time "all the boys had dodged the sea sickness."

A passenger by the "Carisbrook Castle" on its voyage to the Cape, writes to a friend: "We have lots of Volunteers on board—Paget's Horse, Imperial Yeomen, Duke of Cambridge's Own, etc.—a fine lot of youngsters and men. The most distinguished of the Volunteers is the Duke of Norfolk. He has been having a real good time on board, going in for all the sports, fighting steerage passengers with pillows, riding on a rail, running obstacle races with youngsters, creeping through windsails, and under sails."—*Daily Mail.*

Parcels containing woollen hats, socks, handkerchiefs, and writing materials, have been sent out to some of the men at the front, by C and E Groups, as well as privately by members of the staff. The men have received them, as evidenced by the profuse thanks they have returned for the same.

Congratulations to the following on their promotions :—

2nd Class Assistant Superintendent F. W. N. Smith to be 1st Class Assistant Superintendent, dated October 30th, 1899.

Senior Telegraphists : F. Bragger, R. Young, G. Adams, dated October 30th, 1899, and W. A. Dering, dated March 14th, 1900, to be 2nd Class Assistant Superintendents.

Telegraphists: W. S. Priest, F. Morgan, E. Fulcher, dated October 30th, 1899; G. R. Salter, H. G. Kibblewhite, and J. Slade, dated March 14th, 1900, to be Senior Telegraphists.

Sapper J. Hall, 786, has received a chevron. Bravo, Jack ! That's the first step on the ladder for a General.

"Poniard, London," *via* Eastern, is our registered address for telegrams in cases of emergency. Send your relative's name and address to W. Payne, Esq., Moorgate Street Buildings, E.C., who will communicate with same on receipt of a cablegram.

Sergt. R. C. Luttrell, 23,610, universally known as "Our Bob" is, we are grieved to learn, on the Danger List, suffering from enteric. May our beloved friend and comrade be spared to return to us.

Sapper L. Orwin, 1,547, has written me: judge my surprise to see it headed "Herbert Hospital, Woolwich." He is the first man invalided home.

Sapper H. R. Alliston, 69. is on his way home, I believe, sick.

Private B. Baker, 453, A.P.O.C., died of enteric fever at Ladysmith, April 29th. This is the seventh fatality on the Postal side.

Mr. A. J. Knocker, of the "I" Division, C.T.O., died of pneumonia on April 28th, and his brother—

Mr. F. G. Knocker, of the Night Staff, C.T.O., succumbed to the same disease on May 9th. He was interred at Nunhead, May 15th. Both were married, the former leaves no children, but the latter, we believe, renders five fatherless, and ill-provided for, unfortunately. A collection was made by his colleagues for a wreath, but on learning the circumstances, the idea was very wisely put on one side for the better motive of giving a helping hand to the bereaved, which, however small, will prove more profitable. Good.

The Royal Military Tournament commences to-day, May 18th. "Defence not Defiance" is the title of the grand military pageant. Run up to the Agricultural Hall and help to swell the funds of that worthy object.

Very sorry, but I cannot undertake to supply binding cases.

☞ **See Page Two of Cover!**

COLOURS.

"KHAKI LETTERS," One Penny. By post, Three Halfpence.

All posted letters containing Remittances, Orders, MSS., &c., must be addressed to R. E. KEMP, 12, JERRARD STREET, LEWISHAM, S.E.
Postal Orders should be made payable at Loampit Vale, Lewisham, S.E.

Printed by E. G. BERRYMAN & SONS, *Blackheath Road, London, S.E.*

"Khaki Letters" from ....
"My Colleagues in South Africa."

CORRESPONDENCE FROM THE
POST OFFICE TELEGRAPHISTS
OF THE
24th MIDDLESEX (P.O.) RIFLE VOLUNTEERS
(Royal Engineer Reserves),
ON ACTIVE SERVICE.

THE BOND THAT BINDS US—FRIENDSHIP—COMRADESHIP.

Published fortnightly for the Postal Telegraph Service.
Conducted by COLOUR-SERGEANT R. E. KEMP, *Central Telegraph Office, London.*

Nos. 8 & 9.   JUNE 1st, 1900.   PRICE TWOPENCE.

Central Telegraph Office,
London, E.C.

EAR COMRADES, ONE AND ALL,
Greetings! Right Royal Greetings! What can we say, or what can we do, everyone's donning the red, white, and blue. Everyone's happy, all here is gay, we're quite different people since Mafeking day. Ah! what a relief *that* relief was. I can't describe it. The papers have tried and confessed—it isn't often they do, though—that they can't portray it. If they, with all *their* art, can't do so, how can I, with my poor pen, focus the desires of *my* heart so as to render you a picture of the passing and present popularity. Jubilee Day? No. Ladysmith Day? No; not in it. On Friday night the people began, all through the night they continued, as those of us on duty can testify. The early birds caught up the strain, and as I left the C.T.O., at 8 a.m., I strolled down to the Mansion House, and—dear, dear, what a mob. Flags of all kinds, as regards shape and size, but nearly all were Union Jacks. Frantically the crowd waved them as they sang "God Save the Queen," "Rule Britannia," "Soldiers of the Queen," etc. A young sailor came up, snatched a flag, climbed the electric light in the centre of the road, and hoisted the emblem on the apex of the lamp. It was a signal for a tremendous yell and three cheers. While everyone was gazing at the skyward sailor, a strong commando of the Charterhouse School came headlong down Cheapside and rushed madly through the starers, knocking several over, but all good-humouredly. A soldier in khaki appeared—he had been keeping Mafeking all night, to judge by his appearance. The mob espied him, snatched him up, and shouldered him to and fro amidst the madding crowd. Then they changed their tactics, and chanted "Lord Mayor, Lord Mayor," with a deafening din—one continued loud lullaby, indistinguishable to any but those who could catch an individual voice. But the Lord Mayor was not. A flunky appeared, and that pleased them—it was like the changing key on the barrel organ, it altered the hum to a popular song. And so it continued all day Saturday. The City police had to

be kissed, tickled with peacocks' feathers, and smothered with confetti, with the same grace that a tailor's dummy would display. Late into Saturday night, and on to Sunday morning, the jolly and jubilant people kept up the strain. The police had to "mind" 500 of them for several hours. They couldn't speak on Sunday evening, the stupid donkeys were so hoarse; they never thought of that.

Putting all nonsense on one side, we turn our attention to the C.T.O. and its doings on Mafeking day. The Staff had been warned on a previous occasion—Ladysmith day—that singing, cheering, etc., was out of order. Notices have been seen couched in persuasive terms, appealing to the clerks to preserve decorum and so forth, and so they do—always do; but who can bottle up one's feelings when the very soul and spirit of a man is flooded with joy? Who can hold up the hand in holy awe and say sh—s—s—s with any hope that they will be successful? Human nature is not made like that, our telegraphists are well disciplined, well conducted, and thoroughly British, and as a big body of between 3,000 and 4,000 strong leave little to be desired. But had they not been keenly waiting with bated breath the heralding of news that Baden Powell was free? Had they not felt as other Britons had felt—a deep seated anxiety enforcing itself within them? Who can wonder then that, when Britons freed Britons, and the relief was proclaimed to the world, that ecstacy and joy leapt to the front—discarding decorum in its thoughtlessness and its emotions—and gave three hearty cheers and sang "God save the Queen." This occurred principally at 11 a.m. Again, more modestly, at other hours, and lastly at 8 p.m. The electric gong gave the signal, and as they rose to leave duty both male and female voices blended in that grand old anthem. You can't help saying "God save the Queen" at such times, and "God save her Soldiers," too, every one of them.

The next item that will interest you is our Inspection. No doubt your thoughts have been with us, as you know what Queen's Birthday means for the "24th." The weather was changeable, and during the march from Charing Cross to the Piccadilly end of Green Park it came down in sheets and drenched us. In order to maintain my modesty I will let the *Daily Telegraph* tell you all about it.

"OFFICIAL INSPECTION.—The annual inspection of the fine body of men forming the 24th (Post-office) Middlesex Rifle Volunteers is invariably an occasion of keen public interest. This year, the interest manifested was even more marked than usual, owing to the fact that no corps in the country has temporarily parted with so many of its members in order to augment the ranks of the fighting force at the front. It speaks well for the 24th Middlesex that, while more than 500 men are accounted for with Lord Roberts and Sir Redvers Buller in South Africa, a splendid battalion of 900 men should muster on parade in Hyde Park yesterday. The exact numbers were—Present, 908; absent with leave, 39; sick, 8; absent in South Africa from the establishment, 24. Two reserve companies, numbering 326, are also at the Cape, together with one company R.E. Tel. Reserve, of 190; giving a total of 540 members actually taking part in the warlike operations against the Boers, and 1,493 as the effective strength of the regiment. Of those present opposite Knightsbridge Barracks yesterday, two companies, numbering 205, were recruits in plain clothes (52 of whom belong to "I" Co.).

"Colonel H. Ricardo, commanding the Grenadier Guards and Regimental District, who was the inspecting officer, was attended by Captain Earle, and among the many interested spectators present were the Marquis of Londonderry (Postmaster-General), who was accompanied by Lady Londonderry. Sir George Murray, Colonel Boyle, Mr. Badcock, C.B., Mr. F. R. Langton, etc. Colonel Raffles Thompson was in command of the 24th, and the officers of the regiment on parade included Colonel Hale, Major Ogilvie, Major Du Cane, and Captain and Adjutant Verner. In the march past the ranks presented a very creditable steadiness, and the subsequent evolutions, manual, firing, and bayonet exercise, were carried through in an eminently satisfactory manner. A few congratulatory remarks from the inspecting officer concluded an interesting function."—(Report condensed.)

Our Aldershot men are still preparing, as they are not yet fully complete. I will deal with them next time.

Owing to great pressure on space, I have given you short rations this time, but you will doubtless find some dainty bits in "Notes." Trusting you are all in good health and spirits.

Yours most heartily,

To the "I." Co. in South Africa.
Tuesday, May 29th, 1900.

R. E. KEMP,
Colour Sergeant.

The Land of the Lion-heart.

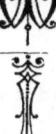
WHEN Britons of old among nations of earth
   Established their right to be free—
The spirit of wider dominion had birth,
   The dream of the Empire to be.
Their heroes, disdainful of indolent ease—
   Whose praises through centuries ring—
First bore Britain's name to the world overseas
   With Richard, the Lion-heart King!

When dark the horizon with ill-boding cloud,
   When anxious alarm banished joy—
When squadron on squadron in majesty proud
   Our liberty came to destroy—
The challenge was taken, the menace was met!
   Above us their flag never flew!
The star of the Spaniard for ever has set—
   For England then proved herself true!

When Time added laurels to England's fair fame,
   And years as they passed made her strong—
New nations arose with the old honoured name,
   A tribute to Right over Wrong!
Her sons never failed her on sea or on land,
   They carried her flag far and wide;
And where they have planted it, still doth it stand—
   The emblem of Liberty's pride!

But rivals grew stronger, and rivals grew bold—
   Harsh voices came over the sea;
"The Lion is feeble! the Lion is old!
   A tyrant shall fetter the free!
Long dead are their heroes! Long gone are their best!
   Behold how the mighty shall fall!"
But lo! from the north, and the south, east and west,
   True Lion-hearts answered the call.

Britannia! for Freedom thy flag was unfurled!
   Thy heroes are made at thy will!
And freemen shall keep thee the pride of the world—
   The Land of the Lion-heart still!

TSF.   W. H. F. WEBB.

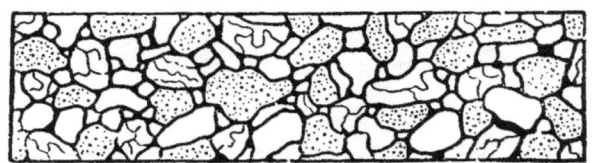

COPYRIGHT.—"Khaki Letters" must not be used without permission.—R. E. KEMP.

Khaki Letters.

No. 460, Sapper **P. A. Milton**, 1st Tel. Div., R.E., Lord Roberts' Headquarters, Bloemfontein, March 30th, writes:—

"Dear Colours,—Thanks very much for your very interesting letters. I see you were acquainted with my late address—'Rensburg.' Well, it wasn't much of a show, plenty of dust and very little water. The only reason I liked the show was the fact of its being at the front. J. Fallon and I used to watch our gunners on 'Coles Kop' giving the Boers their breakfast off Lyddite, etc. It was a marvellous performance to drag two field guns up this 'Kop,' similar to St. Paul's in shape only much higher. Well, what with one or two night alarms, everything was fairly quiet till it was decided to retire on Arundel, which we did in the middle of the night. I then stayed at Arundel for a day and was detailed with Wyatt of GY for Modder. We picked up J. Miller at Naauwpoort and then journeyed to De Aar. Stayed there a day and saw our old chums, the Third Detachment, come in—Bob Luttrell and Co. But we were not allowed to stay long at De Aar, just long enough to taste a pint or two of the 'Nut Brown Ale' of the village, after an enforced abstinence of two months. Then several of our late arrivals joined us, and we boarded a goods train loaded with iron telegraph poles and made ourselves comfortable on top; but as it rained all night we had rather a moppy time. Stopped at Orange River for breakfast and saw our late comrade, Hawkins, looking fit and well, little did I think I should so soon hear of his death, can assure you all the lads feel it very much. On our arrival at Modder we gave them a look up in the office and then bivouacked in a dust storm for the night, but not to sleep the sleep of the just. We were, (that is Sapper Evans of CF, and Wyatt of GY, and myself), roughly shaken at 2 a.m., and told to be ready to move at 4.30 a.m.; so we just got ready, not having the slightest idea of our destination. We reported ourselves at headquarters with our kit bags and had to leave hurriedly at 6 a.m., had to leave our bags outside the office, all we took was what we were wearing and one blanket and waterproof sheet. No time to get a change of linen or anything. We joined a convoy party to catch up Roberts' Column; well, it was simply trek from dawn till dusk, but thank goodness we were allowed to ride. Rations—four biscuits and bully. Water—dirty Modder River (extra special). It was very amusing to see the lads on the look out for loot. We came across a Boer laager recently evacuated, and I managed to find a few explosive bullets, tin of cocoa, a kettle and several other things, and a few Boer letters. Am enclosing one to you, not being acquainted with Dutch I am unable to read the contents, which I presume must be loving, as there were several locks of a lady's hair therein (mim).* After several days

*Letter is referred to in "K.L." No. 7.

KHAKI LETTERS—*continued.*

of weary marching, stopping at dusk and rising at 3 a.m., eventually we caught up the army at ' Paardeburg,' and had a very fair time on half rations —two biscuits and half pound of meat, and $\frac{1}{8}$ ounce of tea per man a day. Cronje's capture, of course, is stale news, so no need to dwell on that, merely to say that I was the only TS man present at the engagement, as I was sleeping in the open and awoke as soon as the 4·7 guns started and the 6-inch Howitzers. The firing was terrific, and we got as near the field guns as possible just to watch the fun. Judge our surprise when Cronje surrendered and came into our camp, officers shaking hands with the men, every one was highly delighted, no mistake, when he came into camp. Lord Roberts was having a chat with him, he looks the crafty, cunning beggar he is supposed to be, no mistake. After seeing him safely disposed of, our attention was next directed to the prisoners. I had a chat with a Free State Commander, he said we don't mind your rifles, but your big guns are too strong. One shell, he said, killed ten of my men. I told him it seemed very hard. He said he has never seen Cronje, who was always in a shell-proof case and never showed himself when the firing was going on, and his opinion was the war wouldn't last much longer. He was a decent chap, gave me some Kruger money, which I highly prize, coming from such a source and the history attached. The majority of the prisoners were a dirty, unkempt lot ; seemed very pleased to be well treated, they thought they were going to be shot or something. Our staff comprises about 20 men split into two sections, and we work in eight hour shifts, and when we trek, one party remains till the advanced party is through on the wire and then we follow on, so you see communication is through all the time. It's rare fun on the trek. Commandeering is a grand pastime. We have 12 C.I.V.'s for orderlies, and I manage to borrow a horse, and with a couple of pals we visit all the farms *en route* and commandeer chickens and ducks, etc. ; vegetables and fruit in abundance, pears, apples, melons, etc., and as I was cook on the march the old camp kettle was very busy. Had one or two exciting times after leaving Osfontein, we were fired on. You see our waggon was loaded up with chairs and tables, and I guess our chaps thought we were a Boer family on the trek. They put several volleys into us at about a 900 yards range, but their marksmanship was very indifferent. We put our mules to the trot and moved off very smart and came across a Captain of the Mounted Infantry, and he said ' Oh, they are my men over there.' ' Well,' says I, ' I wish they would shoot Boers, not pals.' So he dashed over for an explanation, and it appears they took our van load of stuff for ' partridges ' (mim.), made out they were shooting game. Most of the farms have been turned inside out. My pal found a box with £28 in it, so he will be O.K. on furlough ; I am always on the look out for boxes now. This experience has been grand, sleeping in the open at night, all day without food sometimes. But thank goodness my health is grand. I pity you in TS. Why, you don't know what life is. Must confess I am rather proud to think it was my good luck to be the only TS man to go right through from Modder to Bloemfontein, and I hear there will be a bar for Paardeberg, so I hope you will see me soon in TS with quite a ' list to port.' Now we are having a rest at Bloemfontein prior to moving up country. Am rather pleased, as we are getting two shirts, pants, socks, winter khaki. I look a fair ' Absent Minded Beggar ' now, no mistake ; trousers torn to shreds, tunic shrunk to blazes, lost my socks, boots falling off my feet, and an apology for a shirt, have to wear my overcoat every time I wash it till it's dry. ' What a life !' Food is dear here, 1s. for a small loaf, 2s. lb. butter, 6s. lb. tea, last, but not least, beer 4s. per pint, whiskey

KHAKI LETTERS—*continued*.

15s. Needless to say we are all teetotalers, at least we broke the pledge to drink Kipling's health; he gave us a bottle of Scotch, he is a decent chap, no mistake. Am sending you a copy or two of *The Friend*, edited by the War Correspondents, hope you will find them interesting, shall have to cut this SP short now. The Wheatstone Staff are here and will stop here I am told, but I do hope I shall go on to Pretoria, so look out for a letter from me from there. Trusting you will overlook all grammatical errors, etc., as I am writing this in the office between bits of sleep, etc. Yesterday we had our photos taken outside the office, with the Colonel and Captain, expect to see the proofs to-day. Rather a nice present for anyone, taken outside the office too. Well, I must conclude with best wishes for success of your enterprise, hope it will be a grand success.

"P.S.—Now going on the balcony to listen to the band in the Market Square and have a smoke. Don't mind, do you? Remember me to all chums, H. Richardson, Barber, and all the boys."

NOTE.—This was written on the printed flimsies of the Orange Free State Telegraphs. The word "Orange" being obliterated and "Now Defunct" substituted by the writer.

✤ ✤ ✤ ✤

No. 3,230, Sapper **W. Abbott** (of BM), writing from Content, near Warrenton, March 31st, says:—

"DEAR COLOUR-SERGT. KEMP,—Just a few lines to let you see that I am still in the land of the living and in good health. You can see by the above address that I have again moved, and this time nearer the scene of action. I am here within about four miles of Warrenton, where sniping is going on every day, and in all probability you have read of the artillery duels which have taken place there, it is situated much similar to Modder River, our troops on one side (South), and the Boers on the North side, and they have a Long Tom in action and several smaller guns, and our troops, under the command of Colonel Money, have done some fine work considering the small number he has to assist him. His troops only consist of about 300 Northumberland Fusiliers and a battery of artillery. Here we have three Companies of South Wales Borderers (Militia), and about 120 Yeomanry, who do most of the scouting for Warrenton and around Content. They have captured many prisoners; they had a great deal of trouble with one, who bit one of his escort and told them that all Yeomanry and Volunteers the Boers got hold of would have a very rough time, because they had no right out here, but Tommy (the Regular) was differently placed and that the Boers admired them (mim.), so we look like having a lively time if we get into their hands. I moved from Jacobsdal on the 14th March at 1 a.m., and marched into Modder River, about 12 miles, with the H.L.I. The evening previous it was reported that Commandant Lubbe had sent in to say that all women and children were to move out, as he intended bombarding the village, but cannot say if that was the reason we moved at night. We arrived at Modder River 6 a.m. and then went on to Kimberley, at which place I stayed until the 19th, when I again moved to Koodoo, and here I had the novel experience of sleeping in a ganger's hut with a baseboard for two nights by myself, as the troops all moved on with sudden orders and left me behind, but I managed to get some food from the 11th Co. R.E. Railway men who came up through the day to mend a culvert near by, which the Boers had blown up. On the 22nd I moved to Content, which is the railhead up to the present until we can drive the Boers away from the Vaal

KHAKI LETTERS—continued.

River, then I expect to go on that way. The country up here is very fine, very much better than down South, as the country is very fertile and no sand storms such as at De Aar and Modder River. Jones, of Woolwich, came up from Windsorton Road on the 29th, to give me assistance, and now we have a nice time together, and it is very much better to have one of your own men with you than being by oneself, although at present we have stopping with us two Railway men of the C.G.R. and also a Railway Frontier Officer who has supplied me with milk and jam nearly the whole time I have been at Content, we manage to get fresh butter and eggs from a farm close by, so you see that as regards food we do very well, but one big drawback is that we are unable to get any pay, so have to be careful of the little we have in stock. One of the R.E.'s, 11th Coy., was wounded (slight) at Warrenton (Sapper Deegan, a tailor,) got a Mauser which took the top of his right thumb off and his forefinger, which is very unfortunate for his trade. Glad to see that you have started another paper, and hope you will have every success, which you thoroughly deserve. No more at present, best regards."

No. 4,327, Sapper **A. J. Brooks**, writing from De Aar, March 31st, says:—

"DEAR COLOUR-SERGT. KEMP,—We left Cape Town on Wednesday afternoon at 5.20, arriving at De Aar Friday morning, 9 o'clock. Had a very comfortable journey in second-class saloons. Near Laingsburg we saw General Wauchope's grave. His body was being brought down country but was stopped at Laingsburg, on receipt of news from his wife to the effect that his wish was to be buried in the country where he fought. There are graves here and there all along the line, men who died on the way down and were buried at wayside stations. There are small detachments guarding all the bridges along the line. At Laingsburg the little nigger boys had been improving the shining hour learning the drill from the Lancashire Volunteers there. When the train pulled up, about a dozen or so of the little ragamuffins, dressed in very ancient toggery and armed with sticks, were drawn up alongside the line, standing 'at ease.' The youngster who acted as sergeant then gave the order 'shun—right dress,' and stepping just in front on the right of the line, dressed them up A1. 'Up a little on the left there,' 'Back in the centre,' etc. They then went through the whole of the manual and firing exercises, including a critical 'for inspection—port arms,' and examination of imaginary pouches, ending up with regulation 'dismiss.' They went through with a precision which would put the Guards to shame, and their seriousness made us roar with laughter. You have heard all about the Karroo from our predecessors; we laid in a stock of fruit at Paarl and managed to pass the time away very pleasantly on the platforms at the ends of the cars. At Beaufort West we stopped for supper, and were lucky enough to come across Teddy Milton, late of 'D' Division, who was just going off duty. He has been there a fortnight and gets on O.K. He wishes to be remembered to all old pals. There are still some of the old 'uns here at De Aar—Woode, Quinn, Woolley, Humm, Curnew, Willis, Frank Clark, Govier and Jones of Cardiff. I have just this moment got orders to parade at 11.45 to go to Bloemfontein. It is now 11.15, I cannot find any of the old guard at the moment of writing, so cannot find out exactly who is here. De Aar is not such a bad place as has been painted, but of course it's the best season now. Am now ordered to parade at 11.30, so must close up for the present. Pickford, York and Grant, are also going up. Best wishes to all.'

KHAKI LETTERS—*continued*.

No. 440, Lance-Corporal **A. Stevens** (of MR), writing from Bloemfontein, March 31st, says :—

"DEAR KEMP,—Your idea of publishing a paper to contain letters from South Africa is a very good one. . . . I will not trouble you with details of our life on board the 'St. Andrew,' except to say that our diet was varied. We had salt pork, salt beef, and bully beef in turn, varied with bread and biscuits. We were very glad to land at Capetown. I tried to see some of my old MR friends, one of whom is Chief Superintendent at Capetown, but was unable to see them. We started away from Capetown at 9.55 p.m. on February 13th, and reached De Aar at 2.30 p.m. on the 15th. Seven of us, with our kits, occupied an ordinary 3rd-class compartment, with no cushions on the seats, so you may imagine our discomforts when we came to try and get some sleep. On arrival at De Aar, six of our men were warned to leave for Modder River. They started at night in an open truck, accompanied by a nice heavy thunderstorm. On February 17th I entrained for Modder River at 4 p.m., but the train did not move off till 9 p.m. I took ill on the journey, and landed at Modder River about 6 a.m., quite prostrate. I learned there that a cousin, a Sergeant-Major, had been enquiring for me, but I was too ill to get out to see him, and as he could not leave his camp, owing to preparations for leaving that night, I did not see him, and have not seen him since. It is only 18 years since I saw him, so I can wait a little longer. At Modder I was on various duties of a non-telegraphic character, and on Friday, February 23rd, I paid a visit to Kimberley, went up the conning tower of De Beers Mines, saw three old MR friends, and had a very enjoyable time. You will read all about KB in the papers, so I will not attempt to describe my impressions of the place. At Modder I saw a great number of Boer prisoners, and crowds of sick and wounded. On Tuesday, February 27th, I started for De Aar, and on my going down saw Loosemore at Enslin, Fergusson at Belmont, and Bannister at Orange River. I stopped at De Aar for one day, and on 1st March I started for Naauwpoort, went through to Rensburg and saw Tee. I slept in the lobby of the telegraph office, and next day started for Colesberg Junction. Our train followed that of the railway pioneer regiment, who were repairing the culverts, all of which had been blown down, or up. Colesberg Junction was my first place for telegraph work, and I had it with a vengeance, for I did 13 hours on 8 hours off, 23 hours on and 4 off, then 36 hours on, and after that things assumed a more normal condition. Colesberg Junction consists of the station, station house, and a nigger shanty, so you may guess how lively it was. I parted with Sergeant Luttrell here, and I parted with regret, he and I having chummed together. I had Samuel Ray Dalton and some others on the staff, and our greatest excitement was to watch a train come in, or pay a visit to the town, which was three miles away over the kopjes. The town is a pretty place, but very quiet, many of the houses being shut up, owing to the residents being rebels, having shut up shop and gone to fight with the Boers. There is a nice open bath there, 18ft. deep, we used to enjoy a swim there. On February 28th, Colesberg Junction office was closed, our tents, instruments, and paraphernalia were packed in a truck, and we started *en route* for Bloemfontein. On reaching Norvals Pont I had to run after the RSO to see if our truck could go through, but found we could not get on that night, so I stayed the night with Sergeant Luttrell and others at Norvals Pont. Whilst standing by the truck, an artilleryman asked if I would have some tea, after partaking of which I found out he was a brother of Robey's. He did not

KHAKI LETTERS—continued.

know me in my slouch hat and beard. He has not seen his brother out here, but told me he was at Kimberley. I am writing this in the railway truck at Norvals Pont. I do not know when I shall get to Bloemfontein, but will keep this letter back till I get there. I have Dalton and Samuel among my men. After running about for information, I made a start for Bloemfontein at 10.10 p.m., and landed there next day. Finding Nelson, Milton, and a host of others there, who I expect have given you a description of the place, I will not attempt any myself.

"P.S.—Fighting is going on a few miles from here, we heard the guns firing."

✣ ✣ ✣ ✣

No. 1,547, Sapper L. Orwin, writes as follows from Ward A, Upper North, Herbert Hospital, Woolwich, May 13th:—

"DEAR KEMP. . . . You will see by above address that I have been invalided home. Going on all right here, only objection is, that being in the special ward (worst cases), it is difficult to get passes for one's friends to come and see one. Visiting days 2 to 5 in afternoon on Thursdays and Sundays. Can you tell me the names of TS men who went out with 4th Party? . . . . I herewith send you a few notes for KHAKI LETTERS.

"You may remember that I wrote from Naauwpoort Hospital saying I was generally knocked up. I had dysentery, fever, touch of rheumatism and acute palpitation of heart—this latter developed into heart disease. For over three weeks I lived solely on condensed milk which is not a pleasant diet, and, of course, kept in bed. At Naauwpoort I met Forth and Hayden (LS), who had both come in from Rensburg suffering from dysentery. Deaths were very frequent at Naauwpoort, mainly from enteric. Sir William Thompson, with Lord Iveagh's Irish Hospital, was here some time waiting to get through to Bloemfontein. Another morning Sir Alfred Milner came round the hospital. Every day there was a constant stream of trains going up to the front with troops and supplies. The usual cheering, yelling and waving of flags occurred every time. One afternoon I was told to get up and be ready to go to Capetown in half-an-hour. I was then put in hospital train, and a bag marked 'a gift from British Red Cross Society,' etc., given to each man. The bag contained a suit of pyjamas, shirt and a few smaller articles. Early next morning we arrived at Deelfontein, which is about 25 miles below De Aar, to our surprise we were all taken to the Imperial Yeomanry Hospital there. We had Volunteers from the Colonies, C.I.V.'s, Militia and Regulars, and they had wounds in every conceivable part of the body, still we were all cheerful and smiling. The hospital was situated just at the bottom of a long line of kopjes over which dozens of goats roamed. The Duke of Edinburgh's Own Volunteer Rifles were stationed near us, and used to keep us awake a good deal; every half-hour the sentries would shout 'No. 1, and all's well,' and so it would go on all round the camp. Two or three times a week concerts were organised at the foot of the kopje by moonlight, and they were very enjoyable. Yours obediently used to have an easy chair carried out, and stroll there in a Boer hat and blanket. I don't wish you to understand that I *only* had a blanket on. We were treated splendidly there, plenty of tobacco, cigarettes, notepaper, magazines, and anything you liked to ask for in reason. After, as near as I can remember, about a week there, we were put in the train *en route* for England as invalids. We had two nights in train, and we were supplied with hard biscuit and tinned meat to eat. Of course a great many of us could not touch it; however, at Town's

KHAKI LETTERS—*continued*.

River the loyal inhabitants turned out and gave us tea, milk, blanc-manges, fruit, cakes, sandwiches, etc. You should have heard the cheer we gave when our train steamed out of station. It was well we had a good meal that evening, as we got nothing at all the next day till about 3 in afternoon, when we arrived at Rondebosch Hospital more dead than alive. I met Hayden here, who was recuperating, but expected to get back to the front in a few days time. Rondebosch forms part of the estate of Cecil Rhodes, and is one of the prettiest parts of Cape Colony; we could see his house, and in front of us Table Mountain reared its head. I remained there nearly a fortnight, but the last week of my stay I was very queer, and the doctor didn't know what was the matter with me. Easter Sunday I spent in bed shivering, three days after (April 18th) we sailed for England in the White Star Liner 'Cymric.' Hayden was down at docks, at work apparently. I reported sick after being on board a few hours and was kept in bed on condensed milk. For first two or three days I was carried up the hatchways to the upper deck in a swing cot. I used to lie there all day for the benefit of the the air. I was then taken into hospital suffering from enteric fever, and remained there the rest of the voyage; kept alive on condensed milk and stimulants, and as helpless as a baby most of the time. We had an excellent voyage, losing only one man who was a sergeant in the Imperial Yeomanry. The civilian doctor who attended me the first week died very suddenly. We arrived at Southampton on Monday, 7th inst., and next morning I was carried ashore in a chair and lifted on to a bed in the hospital train, which ran us right through to Woolwich. We should have gone to Netley, but they were full up there. The Absent-minded Beggar Fund supplied us with shirts, socks, cigarettes, &c. Was put to bed when I got here and still remain there, but am progressing wonderfully. I was told at Deelfontein that my heart trouble was curable, so am hoping and trusting. Still I am not likeiy to see TS for a few months yet. I must ask you to excuse my writing this in pencil, but am too shaky for pen and ink yet. I only received one letter from wife during the time I was out in South Africa, so know nothing of TS news; all my other letters and papers went astray. Shall be pleased to hear from any of the boys. Kind regards."

No. 29,706, Sapper **C. H. Quinn**, 1st. Tel. Div., R.E., De Aar, April 2nd, writes to a friend :—

"Thanks, a thousand times, for your very welcome letter . . . . . I received the Dum Dum box and highly prize it, it goes to my mother to keep company with my chocolate box, so that both yours and the Queen's will have an equal share of my memory of South African travels. I had a letter from Syd. Barrett saying he was sending me out some 'fags' and I hope they will turn up O.K. Your letters were so cheering that I read them over and over again in order to instil my mind with happy thoughts of both of you. I'll stand each of you as big a half-pint as ever was drawn by an engine out of a barrel. . . . I often think of the happy times when doing night duty with them (Fraser and Dury). Remember me to them and also thank Geo. for the tobacco, I will appreciate it much. Good old Kemp is a fair brick, and *all* of us out here appreciate his works most highly, they are looked for as much as a letter from our dearest friends. I must write him thanking him for all his letters, etc., to me. We heard the results of the Grand National, Lincoln and Boat Race, in quick time. I backed Cambridge for two pots of beer and it comes off to-night; for goodness sake come and have

KHAKI LETTERS—*continued*.

a sup. I am tiptop again, feeling better than ever I did in my ' puff.' think my little sojourn at the hospital did me a wonderful lot of good Mother Seigel's Syrup Advt. could not say more . . . . . We had a horrible drenching the other night, tent was 1½ feet full of water, I took up my bed and walked. I slept on the carpenter's bench and rose like unto one refreshed in the morning. Did not upset one of us . . . . . Kindest regards to all."

✤ ✤ ✤ ✤

No. 23,764, Sapper **C. T. Catling** (EES), writing from Orange River, April 3rd, says :—

"DEAR COLOUR-SERGT. KEMP,—I have refrained from writing to you ere this as I thought anything I might say would only be an echo of other letters received from some of the boys in S. Africa. As I am, unfortunately, in hospital, I have plenty of time on my hands. I was admitted last Thursday, 29th March, as a candidate for enteric fever, my temperature was over 103; I asked the Doctor to make it something else by way of a change, as two of ours had already been admitted with it, he evidently complied with my request as I am now progressing favourably and expect to be discharged in a few days. Whilst the Seventh Division was passing through here the work was very heavy indeed, we were working 19 to 22 hours each day, and had as much as five hours' delay Dellbridge sat down to the Modder River wire for 18 hours and did not cease the whole of the time, the other fellows working equally as hard ; things are much quieter now, so that we are able to have an eight or ten hour duty. Food is fairly good but would be much improved if cooked better ; we have a Basuto for a cook who wants a lot of looking after, for instance, he will put the meat, etc., into the camp kettle, place it on the fire, and not go near it again till it is time to be served, the result is it is usually done to shreds or burnt. Three fowls at different times have found their way into the kettle, and one in the oven. the change of diet being fully appreciated by all, personally, I favoured the latter, although it wasn't stuffed, still commandeerers can't be choosers. A paraffin oil stove, a foot away from our tent, suddenly caught alight a little while ago, and would have burnt our tent and kits had they not been rescued by those off duty ; after it had been blazing for some time the Engineers came and put it out by throwing large quantities of earth and sand on it : on a search being made in the morning, it was discovered a bicycle (helical tubing) had been left there, and had withstood the terrible heat well, except the tyres and saddle. It is with deep regret I have to tell you poor Hawkins, of TSF, succumbed to enteric fever on 13th March last. We were all well aware of the grave nature of his illness, but no one anticipated a fatal termination, believing he would have strength enough to fight against it, and we all cherished the hope, each time we saw him, that we should soon have his companionship again. His case, however, took a change for the worse on the Tuesday morning, and it became apparent, later on in the day, that a fatal issue might result ; he had every care and medical comfort possible to give him, but, poor fellow, he passed beyond all human aid at 9 that evening ; his comrades were allowed to see him whenever they wished, and his death, occurring so suddenly, greatly grieved us. We all miss him, his kind disposition (for he was generous to a fault) and his heaps of other good qualities endeared him to us all. He was buried with full military honours, at 6 p.m., Wednesday, in the Cemetery under Mount ' Muckle Cheviot'; all off duty followed and acted as bearers, including Sambells, from Hopetown, and a lineman (Gant), from Zoutpans Drift. I also have, with deep regret, to

KHAKI LETTERS—*continued.*

inform you another of ours, son of Qr.-Mstr.-Sergt. Williams, died of enteric fever on Sunday, 1st inst., he was admitted nearly a fortnight ago, and was very bad from the time of his admission, and only occasionally recognised anybody who visited him. Although his case was bad from the first, nobody thought he, too, would become a victim. Although he was not personally known to many of us before our meeting at Aldershot, in November last, he very soon became one of us, and I can only say the same of him as I have said of our poor comrade, Hawkins. They both lie in the same Cemetery, and close to Colonel Keith-Falconer. A special wooden cross, made by the R.E.'s, was placed over poor Hawkins' grave, and one will also be placed over poor Williams.—Kind regards to all."

No. 23,610, Sergeant **R. C. Luttrell,** writing from Norvals Pont, April 5th, says:—"I was much pleased last week to see young Bell's face come inside the door. I didn't recognize him at first for, like myself, he has got very thin. Everyone else though is in the same boat out here, as extra food is a costly luxury. For instance, I got a bottle of whiskey for seven shillings as a great favour. Bell and I, of course, had a chat about the old choir, and wondered what the anthem would be for Easter, and how the Lent Services had gone off. He is acting as groom to one of his officers, and appears to be as well and comfortable as can be expected under the circs. He has been round Prieska way chasing rebels, but has not got to hands-grip with the beggars yet. Still, I think they are shortly moving on to Bloemfontein and will, no doubt, be in the thick of it before long. I daresay you folks think we ought to have such a lot to write about, but if you could only see the deadly monotony of this place, you would alter your opinion. Of course, there are plenty of troops passing, and we often get a little excitement when some half-a-dozen horses break loose on the platform of the station, otherwise, I can't think of anything worth writing. One thing that occupies our minds is water. We drink rainwater here; immense tanks being fitted to all houses, which are of galvanized iron and were, formerly, Boer hospitals. Well, our water is mighty low, and no signs of rain. The river water is just like water with mud stirred up in it. The natives say, 'It is all right, Boss, very good water,' but their digestive apparatus is of a special order. It hasn't rained for some considerable time. The sun rises at 6 a.m., is at its full heat about 7 a.m., and shines away all day till 6 p.m., when he disappears. Of course, we are at the end of their summer, and winter is approaching, but a stranger would hardly believe it. They are getting on splendidly with the bridge over the river. The three centre spans were blown up, so they built a low bridge by damming up certain portions by big stones and then bridging the remainder by immense baulks of timber, the rails being laid across the combination. This has been in use for some time now. The main bridge, a really fine structure, is also having attention. They are going to build us the one pier that was blown up, and then push the outer spans inwards, and so close the breach. The outer spans thus left open will be fitted with large baulks of timber till ironwork is ready. When you look at the wreck you think it would be impossible, but the Royal Engineers seem equal to all occasions. We have had very little news from the front, suppose they are keeping things quiet. At present, they are forming immense bases for stores of food, &c., and troops march from one to the other. Railway travelling here is not at all

KHAKI LETTERS—*continued*.

pleasant, mostly done, by Tommy Atkins, in open trucks. Suppose you want to go to Bloemfontein, you find a truck that is going, you get your gear up, but you may wait two days before it leaves. Everything gives place to the Supply Department, and you only go when the line is clear of supply wagons. Sir Alfred Milner and Lord Kitchener got through without waiting, but there are very few things that would stop Kitchener. Jews are very numerous out here, and, from what I can see of it, real Britons very scarce. The troops over the river had to stand to their arms last night, so expect a few desperate Boers are working round this way again. Thousands of troops have passed here to Bloemfontein, mostly mounted. Most of the Colonials were stopped here, but have since been ordered forward to Bloemfontein. No doubt we shall be leaving here shortly, but as they have already a staff at Bloemfontein, no doubt we shall have to go on to Kroonstadt, or up that way. We have to build two lines from Bloemfontein to Pretoria before we come home, so there is plenty of work in store; we would rather do anything than stand still, but suppose the guv'nor knows what he is up to. In the meantime we skirmish round for the larder, which is our main worry. People are gradually returning to their homes here, and we keep shifting from house to house. We shall shift into our tents again next time, as this is the last one available."

Again, writing from Sterkstroom Hospital, on April 18th, "**Bob**" says: "Am much brighter this morning. The night before last I had the shivers, it was terrible, my teeth rattled like hail. After twenty minutes agony the Sister fortunately came in, and gave me hot brandy and water, also water bottles at feet, and lot of blankets—was all right in the morning. The crisis takes place on the 21st day, but I don't know when to start counting from; at first I only got milk and barley-water, but now I get cocoa for breakfast and tea, and beef-tea for dinner, also two doses of brandy. The only thing is I can't sleep, haven't had a wink for eleven nights, otherwise, I feel as comfortable as can be; directly I am out of hospital I will wire you. Doctor says I am doing well, and I feel I shall soon be better. I hope my telegram will arrive before these letters. Our Sister is away to-day, we are so sorry, because she understands us.—Etc., etc."

No. 24,305, Sapper **F. T. Stimpson**, 1st Telegraph Division, Bloemfontein, writing on April 6th, says:—

"DEAR KEMP,—Having a few spare moments I thought I would take the opportunity of contributing an account of our journey across country from Modder. Well, now for a brief description of our journey. The original Wheatstone staffs being split up owing to sickness and increase of work, the staff with Roberts were canvassed, and they found with a few additions they could form a Wheatstone staff of those at the front. They asked for four volunteers from the Modder River staff, and Hall (TS), Horton (BM), Poole (IV), and myself volunteered. Four from De Aar joined us at Modder, viz.:—Quarmby (HF), Hamer, Wilson, and Corpl. Ruffell (TS), with Corpl. Fruchtnicht, mechanic. We were all very pleased to get away from Modder River, as the place was getting a hot bed of fever, we lost three from one tent in a week with fever, and I am sorry to say Roberts (TS), had rather a bad attack, but the last I heard he was pulling round O.K. We left Modder Friday, March 9th, with three light carts and one buck wagon, Lieut. Macfie being

KHAKI LETTERS—*continued*.

in charge. We had not gone far before our buck wagon got nicely fixed in the middle of the drift, and all efforts for about two hours proved of no avail. The three light carts and ourselves went across the pontoon bridge, the buck wagon being too heavy. After getting another start and proceeding some distance along the road we tried to cross the open veldt, leaving the main road to take the nearest route to join Roberts' Column, but another disaster befell us, our buck wagon sunk into a bog, and it looked as if this was our destination for the day; after struggling for some time to extricate it the Lieutenant galloped back to camp and brought back news that we were to return and go via Kimberley. We entrained same night and arrived at Kimberley about 1.30 a.m., sleeping in the railway carriage at Kimberley station for the night. After hanging on for a day, we were instructed that Lord Roberts had cancelled all convoys across country from KB, so we were doubtful as what was going to be done with us. Fortunately we only had to take duty (hurriedly) one night only, giving us about ten minutes notice to go on night duty from 11 p.m. to 7 a.m., but there was apparently some mistake. When we arrived the C. in C. informed us we were not required, and we resumed our sleep. The only duty we did was to guard every third night. We stayed in Kimberley until the following Friday, March 16th, having spent a very pleasant time. We met Murch, late of TS, who is working in the KB office, and the siege seems to have put him back in health a good deal. He told me after his stay at the Cape he went up to Kimberley much improved. We left Kimberley about 3 p.m. on the 16th ult. and bivouacked about 12 miles out for the night. We soon got the pot boiling, and after having satisfied ourselves we put a few more logs on the fire and amused ourselves by sitting round and singing songs. It was a glorious clear moonlight night, and everyone seemed to be in good spirits. After drawing lots for guard we retired for the night about 9.30, I being one of the fortunate ones. We started off soon after daybreak and reached Boshof about 3 p.m., where we were supposed to pick up an escort, but there was none available and we had to wait for one from Kimberley. We quite enjoyed our stay there. I tasted the first fresh butter since leaving England, nearly all the troops indulging in chops for breakfast, and fortunately we got our dinner baked by one of the inhabitants. We were encamped on the market green with four Companies of the Y.L.I., who, with two or three guns of the Diamond Fields Artillery, composed the garrison. In the evening the Yorkshires gave an open air concert, and invited a portion of the inhabitants, and a very good concert it was, too, one man in particular possessing a good tenor voice, and another sang 'On the road to Mandalay,' words by Kipling I believe, which was encored. There is a parody on this called 'On the road to Kimberley' being sung out here. Strange to say, this little place possessed an open-air swimming bath, which we were not long in sampling. It grieved me to see so many women and children in mourning, and I suppose it is the same at home, especially in Scotland. But I suppose no glory of defending the Empire can be attained without this terrible side of war. We left Boshof at daybreak on Monday, Lieut. Mackworth being in charge, but he left us to patrol the telegraph line, fault-finding before we had gone far, and we had the rest of the journey to ourselves. We had a good day's sport chasing fowls and ducks, with an occasional pot at a spring bok; nearly all the farms had been deserted, and everything in the shape of furniture taken away. We stayed at Ortles Farm for the night, this is the place where Kruger and Steyn tried to rally their men, but without effect. It had been raining all the afternoon and we were somewhat wet, the

KHAKI LETTERS—*continued*.

proprietor kindly lent us his coach-house to sleep in. After tea we retired for the night, as we were to push off first thing in the morning. I forgot to mention our escort consisted of 18 men and Lieutenant of the N. Lancs. M.I. as far as this place, then an escort of the Buffs M.I., but as we had orders to get to Bloemfontein as soon as possible, having the Wheatstone apparatus with us, the greater part of the Buffs were knocked up, and they could only muster eight men out of twenty-five, practically a farcical escort. Up to this point we had ridden on the buck wagon nearly all the way, but the roads being so heavy we had to walk some distance the next morning after the heavy rain, and it was not very pleasant walking up to one's ankles in mud; nothing of any moment happened that day beyond commandeering anything that was worth doing so. It is a splendid sensation to know that one can help himself to anything that is worth taking. We put up at an old post house for the night, our mules being done up. We soon got the fire going and after doing tea justice we put our spoil on and formed a cordon round it, and many a joke was passed about the fowls and ducks whilst they were cooking. We had a little surprise packet here, one of the M.I. was doing guard about a hundred yards from the house and was heard to challenge someone several times, when suddenly we heard the report of firearms, and immediately rushed off for our carbines and pouch, we all expected something to come off, or, in military language, 'we all had the breeze up,' but when we returned we found everything had passed off O.K., the man that was challenged had answered to the effect that he had a pass. We had a very lively time during the night, the place was swarmed with vermin. We pushed off again next morning at daybreak, and just outside Bloemfontein there was a large market garden, and we commandeered a good bag of vegetables and tomatoes, eventually arriving at Bloemfontein about noon, on Wednesday, March 21st. I might add that this road across country had only been open a few days and there were various rumours as to our safety during the trip We immediately fixed the Wheatstone apparatus up, this did not take long as all sets are on base boards, and the staff commenced work almost immediately, as there was about a day and a half's delay. At first our duties were 8 hours on and 8 off, they have since been revised, but we are still doing 12 hours a day, and the work is very heavy going day and night. The Boers have cut our wire via Boshof to Kimberley, so we have to work via Naauwpoort and De Aar, the line being about 250 miles long, but we have not been able to get any good results out of this line, earth faults being very frequent. We are in possession of the post office and work in their instrument room, but sanitation is very primitive and bad; fancy a large building like this without any water being laid on. The Colonel has taken a house close by for us, endeavouring to make us comfortable, but the same old tale—full of vermin. There are some good buildings in the town; Lord Roberts staying at Government House opposite the (Raadzaal) House of Parliament. There is very little to buy in the shape of food stuff, and they charge fabulous prices. Well, I must close now to catch post, kind regards to all."

✤ ✤ ✤ ✤

Khaki Letters continued on page 156.

" It don't look as if we are going to get any pay," said a downcast Soldier of the Queen. " Buck up, chum," replied a comrade, " or perhaps the Boers will give us a check."

Khaki Sidelights.

We have been favoured by the receipt of a letter from an old TS friend, **Mr. W. S. Costiff,** who has had a great deal to do with the construction of the Telegraph System in South Africa. It was written recently at Modder River, and some extracts will prove interesting at this period.

". . . You will no doubt be surprised at the heading of this letter, and I must first ask you to pardon all defects in it, as it is written on 'Active Service,' and the writer sitting on an empty milk case with the paper on his lap. How it came to be written under such circumstances I will describe later on.

"The past 18 months of my life has been spent, for the most part, under canvas, and it was for that reason that the festive season of 1898 passed without my sending my customary greetings. On my promotion to First Class Inspectorship of the Midland District of Cape Colony, I first of all had a thorough overhauling of all our most important sections of telegraph lines, and as the 'Midland' extends over many hundreds of miles, it was a lengthy undertaking. Some of the trips necessitated a stay under canvas of four or five months at a stretch. First of all I tackled the sections on the railway lines, and afterwards those across country, and I think I've got things in fairly good order all round, but not without a lot of privations and hardships, and plenty of good honest work.

"At Christmas time, 1898, I was away in the back country, some 230 miles from home, surveying and pegging out a new branch line, and, owing to the density of the bush, it took longer than I anticipated, and I was compelled to spend my Christmas dinner in the bush, and it consisted of a tin of corned beef and dry bread. We could not obtain even an egg or a cup of milk. We were 40 miles from a town, in a dense prickly pear country, and as they had had no rain there for over two years, you can imagine somewhat the state the country was in. We had to dig in the bed of the river, sometimes 10 or 12 feet before we touched water, and then it was hardly fit to drink.

"You can guess I was very pleased to say 'N N' to that trip, and I landed home, once more, on January 2nd, 1899. But not for long. You see our Financial Year ends on June 30th, and we get a certain amount of money voted for that year for Telegraph Works, and we try to crowd as much of it into the year as possible, and, consequently, the last six months are the busiest. I spent a few days at home, and then I was off again to build a new line in the Bedford district. Now this is one of the loveliest spots of my district, so I took my wife and family up with me and they stayed at an hotel whilst I went under canvas, but it had the advantage of my being able to run in to see them every week, and, as I got farther away from the town, Mrs. C. went to stay with some friends of mine on a farm, and she had a very enjoyable time.

"That trip lasted till the middle of March, when we went down home once more. We had only got nicely settled down, for less than a fortnight, when off I was packed again, and this time through an awfully cold and barren country, 123 miles, during which we had every conceivable kind of weather, rain, hail, sleet, snow, and frost, and you can guess under those circumstances life was not of the pleasantest. In fact, some days it was so cold that we were unable to start work until nine o'clock owing to the iron tools being so intensely cold as to blister the men's hands, that sounds rather paradoxical, does it not? but it is true, the tools were really hot with cold. As in the case of all things, this, too, came to an end eventually, and once more I saw my home on August 24th.

"In addition to Telegraphs, my work comprises the auditing of all Post Offices within the District, and, as soon as I got home on this occasion, I had to pay the usual quarterly inspection of some 70 odd offices, and that took me pretty well into September. Then my Chief got leave for a month from the 12th September to 12th October, and, during that time, I was acting for him in addition to my own work, so that my time was fully occupied during that period. In the home service the 'Surveyors' are a distinct branch from the Engineering Staff, but in this country the two are combined under the title of 'Surveyor and District Engineer,' and both branches of the service, postal and telegraph, are dealt with under this head. My next step will be 'Assistant Surveyor,' and then to the Surveyorship, so that you see one, at least, of the old 'Bees' is still buzzing away, and steadily climbing the ladder. It is the result of sheer hard work though, and I can look back and see that my efforts in the past, in no matter what direction they led me, have been appreciated by the 'powers that be' . . . .

KHAKI SIDELIGHTS—*continued.*

"Now I will tell you a little about how it is I'm a 'Tommy Atkins' *pro tem.*
"On the outbreak of this unfortunate war, and the invasion of Cape Colony by the Boers, much damage was done to the telegraph lines, mile upon mile of poles and line being wantonly destroyed. So our department, in conjunction with the military authorities, decided to send a party up with Lord Methuen's column for the repair of same, and fortunately or unfortunately (which remains to be seen) I was chosen, and in due course I started with 18 men for the base (De Aar). From thence we gradually pushed up, as you have read by the papers, towards the relief of Kimberley, until we reached Modder River (24 miles from KB), where we now are. We are attached to the Royal Engineers, under their control as far as military matters are concerned, and are in their lines.

"It is my first experience of soldiering, and I hope the last. It is indeed a hard life. We are rationed by the military, and one day's rations consists of the following:—Bread, 1lb. (or, in the absence of bread) biscuits, 1lb.; meat, 1lb. (fresh if procurable, but nearly always 'bully'); coffee, ⅓oz.; tea, ⅙oz.; pepper and salt, 1/32oz. This is served out to each man every day. Of course, I brought my own cook with me, but we have to jog along on the above rations just the same. It has been better since we got here though, as we are able to purchase a few luxuries—potatoes, 6d. lb.; condensed milk, 1s.; Quaker oats, 1s. 4d.; salmon, 1s. 9d., etc. so that by paying for it we are able to get a little variety. It was awful on the march up; one day's food, as a rule, consisted of bully beef and biscuits only. No time to serve out anything else. My idea of a British Army on active service was very crude indeed until recently. It is a wonderful organisation truly. The Army Service Corps is a huge concern, and when one takes into consideration that in this column alone there are 20,000 men, and each of those men have to be fed every day, one can imagine the amount of work to be done. But it moves with such clocklike precision, that one can scarcely imagine that it is more than a gigantic machine. Then, in addition to the men. there are thousands of horses, and tens of thousands of mules, also to be fed every day.

"Actual warfare, too, is a thing that one has to see to believe. One reads of wars in all their horrors, but the reading of it is one thing, and to be in any way associated with it is another. Some of the scenes I've witnessed in the last few months will remain in my memory as long as I have a memory. At Belmont, where we had, as you know, a splendid victory, the scene after the battle was terrible. The Boers, in their hurry to bury their dead, did not trouble even to dig a pit, but just covered up the bodies with stones, and I saw many of these rude graves, with the arms and legs of the dead sticking out between the boulders, and in one case the man had evidently been shot in the abdomen, for it had doubled him up, and he lay crouched as if for a spring, and there were his knees and arms both sticking out; and in another the long whiskers of some grey-bearded veteran were protruding, telling the tale of the death of some poor old father.

"Then again, bodies of quite beardless boys were found, side by side with those of old men, which proved that even the youths of the Boer Army were compelled to fight. At Orange River I saw amongst the prisoners an old Bloemfontein friend of mine, a decent fellow indeed, and as his eyes caught mine, they lit up with a pitying look of recognition.

"At Graspan the body of a little bugler was found. He could not have been more than 13 years old, and in his hand, clasped tightly in the clasp of death, was his bugle, evidently shot down whilst sounding the 'Rally.' But what was more pitiful still was the fact that in his pocket was a Testament and a letter signed 'Your loving mother,' saying how sorrowful her Christmas would be without her boy, and hoping that God would spare him to return to her soon.

"Alas, she was never to see that son again, and I can imagine the grief of that poor soul, when the news reached her in far away England. How many hundreds of such cases there will be in our dear 'Home Land,' recently and to come. War is indeed a terrible thing, and it makes one think of the necessity of being prepared for our future state. The hundreds of poor young fellows cut off in the prime of life, without a moment of preparation, without a chance of making their peace with God. It is terrible to contemplate, and makes us think that we should always have that beautiful little prayer on our lips, "Agnus Dei, qui tollis peccata mundi, miserere nobis" (Lamb of God, who takest away the sins of the world, have mercy on us).

"It was a very near thing for us at Graspan too. We were shifting camp to that spot, at 4 o'clock one morning, but owing to the "Ration Train" (which takes preference over all others) being very late, our train was not allowed to proceed, and

KHAKI SIDELIGHTS—*continued.*

after waiting 4 hours the "Ration Train" turned up and proceeded in front of us, but had not proceeded far when she backed into Belmont again, with the news that the Boers had blown up a culvert and were at Graspan in force.

"Had that train been up to time, she would have got through before the culvert was blown up, and we should have had our camp pitched at Graspan, and in all probability should be prisoners now, either at Bloemfontein or Pretoria. Providence was watching us then.

"The battle of Modder River, was a terrible affair too, after we had driven the Boers out of Enslin Koppies (small hills) they retreated to Modder River, where they had been entrenching and fortifying for weeks and had a splendid position. The country is fairly flat, with undulating ground for miles, and these flats were simply one mass of Boer trenches, and as our men marched on they were simply mowed down without being able to see a single Boer to fire at. Of course they had to lie down and with a scorching sun, without food or water, they lay for 13 solid hours. If a movement was made, a perfect shower of bullets was poured into them, and it was only when darkness came on did they retire.

"They retired to another splendid position that they had previously fortified, Magersfontein, and that is where the last battle occured, with such a disastrous effect, as you will have read. They still hold that position and since then we have made no effort to dislodge them, but content ourselves with daily shelling from the ridges commanding our own position. That was over a month ago, but we still seem to be in no hurry to make a forward movement, but I suppose the Generals know what they are about. Magersfontein is an almost impregnable position, and I think that they are going to surround them through the Free State and have given up the idea of attacking from this side only, it would in my humble opinion only be courting death.

"The 'Tommies' are getting very tired of this inactivity, and are eager to push forward, and, if they had their own way, I think we should have been in Kimberley long before this; but I suppose it is only a matter of time, although things are assuming a serious aspect there. They have now started eating horseflesh, and are only allowed a quarter of a pound of that per man per day, so that something will have to be done very soon. Another thing that occurs to me as to the delay here, is the repairing of the railway bridge over the Modder River, which was blown up by the Boers, and which, owing to the efforts of the Royal Engineers, is now nearing completion. You see, as soon as Kimberley is relieved an enormous quantity of stuff will come up, and that is the only means they have of crossing the river. I shall be glad, too, when we make a move forward, for I am tired of this inactivity and enforced idleness.

"Modder River is the pic-nic and pleasure resort of Kimberley, and, in its normal condition, is a pretty little spot, all grass, with a lovely river (but now owing to the traffic of the troops, it is a veritable desert, one mass of red sand, and we are treated to a dust storm every afternoon, which closely resembles a fog, and gets into everything, clothes, food, etc., and makes life generally unbearable, especially as the Thermometer stands at 108 in the shade. There is one redeeming feature about it though, and that is the river, where one can have a dip, and you can guess that I avail myself of every opportunity.

"I am afraid you would hardly recognise me now, in my khaki and putties—a regular Tommy Atkins. How little did we think in those old days, when I used to try and break the record in 'fives,' in the happy old 'B,' I should be writing to you on a battlefield. It has been an experience of a lifetime, and one I never want again. It will be something to look back upon as I grow into old age and recount the little incidents to my children. Of course, Mrs. Costiff does not like it at all, but I think she has got over her first alarm, and recognises now that only a modicum of danger is attached to my position, Of course, there is a certain amount of danger, but I'm not exactly in the firing line, so that the danger is greatly reduced; but still I've been as near as 300 yards to four bursting shells, and that is about as near as I ever want to get.

"I met two TS men up here, belonging to the 24th Middlesex; they are employed in the Military Telegraph Office, and have a Wheatstone fixed up.

"And now, with a word or two about TS, I'll close. . . . I wonder what they would say if they saw the transformation in me, now. From a little beardless boy who used to be petted with 'cakes' when the 'two slices and a mug of tea' came round, to the 'grim warrior,' ahem!! (mim.) of to-day. Please convey to any of them . . . . my kindest remembrances and regards, and say that in the wilds of the veldt a sweet remembrance of the old happy days comes to me, and I wonder how the world has been using them."

Mafeking Night and Ladysmith Day.

(The rejoicings in London over the Relief of Ladysmith began in the Daytime, and those over the Relief of Mafeking at Night-time—hence the expressions "Ladysmith Day" and "Mafeking Night.")

MAFEKING Night! and Ladysmith Day!
When was there ever so wild a display?
Words are too feeble the scenes to convey.
Who does not thrill as he thinks of the fray
Round the besieged in that land far away?
Hemmed and outnumbered our garrisons lay,
Boers all around us in battle array—
Cunning, and sanguine, and vengeful were they,
Bent on our capture and eager to slay.
Yet did we taunt them and keep them at bay,
Stinging them, too, when they ventured to stray
Rather more near than we thought was O.K.
Long the environment! bitter the stay!
Heavy the price we had often to pay.
Fell disease weakened us, famine held sway,
Marking the strongest and bravest for prey:
Deeply we mourned as we housed them in clay.
Then the Relief! and our skies that were grey
Burst into splendour no pen can portray:
Hearts that were aching grew festive and gay.

* * *

Let nations sneer, and deride us who may,
'Tis but in envy and malice they bray;
Ours is the progress, and theirs the decay.
Ours is the triumph they cannot gainsay.
Cheers for the brave, with a hip, hip, hooray!
Mafeking Night! and Ladysmith Day!

Ladysmith Day! and Mafeking Night!
Link them together with laurel bedight.
Who can, with justice, their history write,
Or tell how Old England went mad with delight
When the Relief long-delayed came in sight?
Bold Baden-Powell, and brave Sir George White,
How shall we honour them?—who can requite?
"Never surrender," and, "God and the Right,"
These were the mottoes with which they held tight.
Never betraying a spirit contrite,
Frequently showing the Boers they could bite,
Filling them oft with nocturnal affright,
Beating them back and inflaming their spite.
Cheerful, defiant, and ready to smite,
Even when hope of Relief seemed so slight.
Mafeking! Ladysmith! sad was thy plight.
Starvation rations and fever's dread blight
Thinning thy ranks with its pestilent might.
Keen were thy sufferings, grand was thy fight!
Empires shall crumble and foes shall unite,—
Mem'ries shall perish as Time wings its flight,—
Yet shall thy glory on Fame's topmost height
Shine with a lustre ineffably bright.
Britons unborn shall thy records recite
Ladysmith Day! and Mafeking Night!

C. T. O.   SYDNEY F. PARKER.

Khaki Letters—*continued.*

No. 3,224, Sapper **C. P. O'Sullivan**, writing from Kimberley on April 6th, says :—

"DEAR COLOUR-SERGEANT KEMP,—I must not be the 'outsider' of the crowd of 'our colleagues in South Africa,' for up to the present I've not written you a single line, though I have watched with interest the progress of your admirable work, and most heartily congratulate you on your undoubted success as an editor. In one way I am now having the most uneventful time during the whole campaign. Town life is not exactly active service, and when you come to think of doing your eight hours per day to and from the office it would be just as well, as far as we now see of the war, to be back in TSF. However, I'm not 'cribbing,' for the same crowd can't always expect to be in the front.

"The success of Lord Methuen at Boshof yesterday was very pleasant reading to some of us who worked for him up to Magersfontein. Personally, I was very glad, and only wished I was on the spot."

Con. O'Sullivan again writes from KB on April 22nd, as under :—

"DEAR COLOUR-SERGEANT KEMP,—Congratulations on your latest success—KHAKI LETTERS. As you say, she ploughs the waves nicely, and when she gets every inch of canvas set—50 pages of it—she'll be a daisy. All our lads are pleased with it, and everyone is anxious to have the first read. Occasionally some go astray, and a poor unfortunate colleague wonders 'why have I been forgotten?' After you with the KHAKI.'*

"The war fever which struck some of us so heavily at first, has been superseded since our arrival in Kimberley, and often it is remarked, 'Well, I'll chance my arm if I see a rough diamond, and do seven years.' The laws are very strict, and are carried out to the letter with regard to uncut diamonds. If you are found with one in your possession you are a dead cert. for seven years' hard. This is with the idea of keeping down I.D.B. You'll be surprised to hear that the streets are periodically dug up, and the dirt goes through the usual process of sifting, washing, etc., and many diamonds are found. It's a certainty De Beers would not have it done except it paid well. We were a bit taken back when we saw some black navvies fixing water pipes, as we thought, in Stockdale Street, screening the dirt, and washing it round the corner, where the Boss showed us a handful of the precious stones he had found in the morning's sorting. This has had a depressing effect on many a Tommy, and often our colleagues are seen walking along with bent heads, and eyes glued to the street. At home we should think a man with such an absent-minded expression should be 'inside'; here we simply shout 'Looking for 'em chum?' 'There'll come a time,' etc.

"I'm glad to see there's not so much hospital news published now in your booklet. It is almost certain to cause your friends at home some worry to see you've been in hospital ; especially when they are not aware you would be put in 'dock' for a slight attack of diarrhœa.

"Best regards, and wishing you the future success you undoubtedly deserve."

* Copies have been sent to *every* " L " Co. man.

[NOTE.—The less we hear of hospital cases the better we like it, but we think it is much better to have authentic information from the front than give ear to the many rumours that are constantly circulating. We would wish there were *no* cases. Comrades would do well to mention when chums " come out " as well as " go in."]

KHAKI LETTERS—*continued.*

No. 23,611, Sapper **J. A. Little** (of SW), writes from Naauwpoort, April 7th, to a colleague :—

"I daresay you have seen in the papers that poor Charlie is dead, and I have no doubt but that you would like to know a few particulars. He began to look queer about three weeks ago, while we were at Colesberg Junction. He got very thin, and went off his food, but it was only when we got to Norvals Pont a fortnight ago that he went into the Hospital. I saw him there twice, and he appeared to be getting on fairly well, and the Hospital orderly told me it was nothing serious. After keeping him there he was sent to the Base Hospital at Naauwpoort, so I lost sight of him. As it happened, a few days after I was sent back to take the place of a man who had gone sick here, so I at once made inquiries about Charlie, but could not get at him, though I made several tries to see him. About 9 last night we had a message handed in from Principal Medical Office to General, Capetown, notifying him of the death of Sapper Fairall from enteric fever. It was a shock to us all, you can guess ; and to make matters worse, on enquiry this morning I found that he was already buried. He died early yesterday morning, and was buried at 5 p.m. Poor old chap, I should very much liked to have seen the last of him. He was a good old chum of mine, and I miss him very much. We had kept together right up till he went into Hospital. This makes the second 24th man dead. Thank God, I am feeling very well indeed myself. A man has need to be thankful for good health out here. We see two or three funerals every day here, so I shan't be sorry when we make a move. I tried to get a few of his personal belongings for his friends, but they would give nothing up to me. Sentiment doesn't count in war. Do you know his people's address ? I would have written them, but I don't know it. Will you write them ? I feel so sorry for them ; I know what my own mother would feel. Everyone has to rough it a great deal here, though, of course, our fellows are not so badly off as the poor devils in the fighting line. The sooner it is all over the better for everyone concerned. With kindest regards to yourself."

No. 220, Sergeant **J. W. Miller,** 1st Tel. Div., R.E., writes from Kimberley, under date April 7th, as follows :—

"DEAR DICK,—Here's putting the pipe on first, you're the man that wants such a lot. Now to make a start. First of all I have to apologise for being so slow in answering the ever-welcomed letter from our renowned and hardworking 'Colours.' I'm sure you are doing your very best to let all our kind friends know what we are doing. I wish you every success in your excellent publication, and, in my opinion, if it has the support I should imagine it ought, it will run for a good time yet, for I see not the slightest possiblity of this trouble being over for some months. I daresay you would like to hear all that I have been up to since I was released from Naauwpoort office, owing to the Boers chasing Sgt.-Major Tee out of Rensberg, and usurping my post. I was sent on to De Aar to wait instructions, which did not keep me more than a day. I was told I was for Modder River, so off we went with a section and stores in an open truck, leaving De Aar at midnight. During the journey it came down in one of those lovely tropical showers, and we nearly all got drenched,

KHAKI LETTERS—*continued.*

so started drying our clothes as the morning sun made his appearance. Getting near Modder we passed through a storm of locusts, which almost resembled a snowstorm, and on our arrival at Modder the train had to stop because of a terrible dust storm that had commenced to blow, in fact, it was the heaviest dust storm I have ever seen. Something terrible. After getting our baggage to our camp, clerks were soon asked for for different places, and eventually it came to the last instrument clerk to be myself. I was then required to go by train to Railhead. That's as far as the Boers would allow the engine to travel, as they had broken rails and blown up bridges all along the railway line that divided the kopjes of Magersfontein. I took a vibrator with me and joined up to the wire that stood good to Modder. From there it was decided to build three lines of wire on to Kimberley. Next day a small air line section came out, and I accompanied them all the way till we met the Kimberley section of civilian workers building the line from that place. We joined up, and thus had a wire through to the Railway Military Telegraph Office, where we fixed our office a few days after the siege. The week on construction was a great change, and did me a world of good—although a bit rough, it was most enjoyable. During the journey, I wandered over the trenches of Magersfontein, and was struck with the grandeur of their fortifications and their laagers. The utensils and other things left by them on their departure pointed to it being of a very hurried one, for the potatoes, flour, onions, tobacco, Kaffir pots, boxes, ammunition, and other things too numerous to mention, were strewn all over the place. I then received instructions to take over charge of the Kimberley office at the station, and there, with five men, we got on fairly well and comfortable, but all of a sudden Lord Roberts starts getting on round Bloemfontein, and matters began to look so serious, that we had to shift our office over to the Head Post Office in the town, where we were to try to get through to the front. This we eventually did, and the outcome was the proposition of Wheatstone working, making Kimberley the transmitting station. Up came the staff from Modder, I should think bringing up a total of 34 clerks. So we worked on to different places where Roberts halted for each day, and the wire would be disconnected until they got to their destination for the day, and it would thus change its office of origin each time. At last it became known that Bloemfontein had been reached and taken without any opposition, and as soon as they settled on an office the work began to flow in. Since then we have been working very hard, and to make it so, permission was given for private work to be accepted, and it came in shoals from all parts of the Colony, so much that it flooded us, and so it goes on daily. The wire often goes wrong, doubtless a fault on the line, which seems to affect all our air lines, and causes lots of stoppages. The ground, I believe, has too much iron in it, that is why the wireless telegraphy was not a success at Modder. We are doing sometimes over 2,000 messages a day at this office, and have at the present time about 25 clerks. Several have gone sick, in fact, some of our best Wheatstone men from TS, Alliston, Jenner, Stormer, have all gone from Kimberley to Wynberg Camp, near Cape Town, for change and rest, and one or the other of those remaining seem to take turns in going sick for a day or so, principally dysentery. I am very sorry to tell you that poor Hawkins, of TSF, died at Orange River with enteric, some time ago, and then only last week we had the painful news that Bob Williams' son had been taken as well. The news was dreadful, and the whole sympathy of those who know his father, goes, I am certain, with the letter to him. Personally I offer my sincere condolence to Bob and his

KHAKI LETTERS—*continued.*

family, with whom I knew the son to be a rare favourite. The staff here of the 24th have had a beautiful cross made, and engraved by Woodrow, to be placed over the grave of poor Hawkins, who was a very promising young fellow. The TS men who are working here under my charge are not very numerous, however, they may give you some interest. O'Sullivan, Adams, Pallett, W. C. Smith, George— other 24th men, Roby, Fenton, Aird, Hurdle, Lang, Weir, Fergusson, two others from TS, F. Usher and Winkle. All are well at time of writing, and wondering if the next move will be Mafeking, or the railroad up to Pretoria, where I learn there are two sections to leave Cape Town for Boshof almost immediately, under the command of Captain Wright, who, I believe, has just arrived with a good number of linemen and clerks. I don't think I had better take up any more of your time, but close this with all my good wishes for the success of your fortnightly, and kindest regards for yourself. Am keeping in splendid health. Excuse pencil, writing in tent."

No. 26,866, Sapper **W. H. P. Woolley**, writes as follows from De Aar, April 9th.

"DEAR KEMP,—Before I start writing a letter to you, I must congratulate you and wish you many happy returns of your KHAKI LETTERS which must be of great interest in TS. I can just imagine the eager ones scrambling for a copy as they come out. I have just received a letter from Green (1 Div.), telling me how quickly the inadequate supply of 'K.L.'s had been bought up. Good luck, Dick, o.m., may success continue, and I hope letters will continue to roll in for you from the front and elsewhere, as there is not much news about, with the exception of a little reverse we had last Saturday from just outside Bloemfontein, which Lord 'Bobs' terms as of no consequence, and that everything otherwise is very satisfactory. I think if it had not been for French's cavalry horses not being done up so things would have been different.

"On Friday we heard Lord Methuen had scored a minor victory, out Warrenton way, over a party of Boers, commanded by a French individual, who, after showing a white flag, shot one of our officers, afterwards being shot dead by our little party of Yeomanry, and his commando being surrounded, had to surrender—about 80 of them.

"As there is not much news to tell you this time, I will endeavour to give you a description of De Aar. Well, to commence with, De Aar is a small place, generally called a railway camp, of about one to two hundred white inhabitants; it has one hotel and two general merchandise stores. One, with the hotel, is in the centre of the place, the other at the north end. Both, needless to say, are making their leg out of Tommy Atkins. De Aar is situated on the west of the railway, and its main street or road is about half a mile, running in parallel with railway, from south to north, there are also a couple of Kaffir kraals on the east of the railway—one south, the other north. Then there is a labour depôt, consisting of Kaffirs, Hottentots, Basutos, etc. These are employed by the military authorities, and are sent to different parts of the country in gangs, engaged chiefly in loading and off-loading trucks. De Aar, although a small place, is of great importance as to railway traffic, being the Clapham Junction of South Africa, as you would see if you could but take a walk down towards the south end of the place, where there has been special sidings laid down by the engineers for

KHAKI LETTERS—*continued.*

the ordnance and supply stores. These stores extend over several acres of ground, or rather sandy veldt. There are heaps and heaps of supplies of different kinds for man and horse, piled up and covered with huge tarpaulins —they look like great kopjes in the distance. Then there is a large square of general service wagons, small arms wagons, Scotch carts, and water carts, etc.—almost half a mile square. The place, however, is gradually diminishing, as they are sending all the stores round to Bloemfontein, which is to be the base instead of De Aar. When this was a headquarter depôt there were about 18,000 troops here.

"There is a base hospital here, and also a cemetery, but most cases of death are patients which have been brought down from up north, deaths being chiefly due to enteric fever or dysentery. There have been a good many funerals here since I came here, and we are all well accustomed to the slow funeral march, accompanied by the slow beat of the drum. Hawkins's death came as a great blow to us from Orange River. Likewise Sapper Williams (son of Quartermaster-Sergeant Williams, 24th, to whom I tender my sincere sympathies). Our staff here is reduced considerably. Corporal Thomas, Sappers Swan, Clark, Arundel, Greig, and Campbell left us last week for Bloemfontein. We are now left 12 in all.

"Some of the boys from the 'Cephalonia' arrived last week, very few from TS have come this way, others having gone round to Natal. Have only seen Hudson, George York, and Jemmy Brooks from TS, and Brook from HF.

"George York and Jimmy Brooks have gone to KB, I think. Again wishing you every success, etc."

No. 24,387, Sapper **E. J. Whibley**, writes from De Aar, April 9th, as under :—

"MY DEAR KEMP,—I regret once more having to report the death of one of ours. Poor Fairall, of Mount Pleasant, fell a victim to the dreaded enteric fever, and, after a very few days illness, passed away on April 6th.

"Nearly the whole of the original De Aar staff have left for Bloemfontein. A few have gone to Kimberley, and the remainder are still here, waiting patiently for the 'Gascon' to take them back, and 'oh! let it be soon.'

"Many thanks for your circular letter of the 16th ult., also the first number of KHAKI LETTERS and enclosure. The idea was grand, but the book is grander, and I for one shall keep the numbers safely as a reminder of the days the 24th spent under canvas in South Africa during 1899 and 1900. I wish you every success in your undertaking.

"The men who embarked on the 'Oriental' and 'Cephalonia' have reached South Africa, but unfortunately some were sent round to Natal, making it impossible for us to give them a welcome."

No. 1,888, Sapper **W. G. Collins** of (SA), writing from Bethulie Bridges, on April 10th, says :—

"DEAR COLOUR-SERGEANT,—I am somewhat late in the field with my little epistle, but I feel that I ought to write you, if only to show how much your labours on behalf of 'L' Company, 24th Middx., are appreciated by regimental number 1,888. Your movement to publish our letters in magazine form is one which I trust will meet with every success. I am writing

KHAKI LETTERS—*continued*.

this from Bethulie Bridges. There are two other operators here beside myself—Lance-Corporal Bulman, of the R.E.'s, and a military telegraphist Buffs (East Kent Regt.). I came round here from Belmont, some 5 weeks ago, after having spent ten pleasant weeks at that station. I was not sorry to have a change, however, as one gets 'fed up' (as Tommy says) after such a long period in one office, and nothing to break the monotony but an occasional stroll over the now famous battlefield, and a night alarm or two thrown in, and Staff officers rushing about with borrowed carbines (generally ours), and wiring for the armoured train, etc., when probably the nearest Boers were those at Magersfontein—anyhow, perhaps its a good thing for us they were not nearer. We are close to the Wagon Bridge here, which was so gallantly defended against a body of Boers by the Cape Police, after the Railway Bridge had been destroyed. It is not necessary to go into the history of its defence, as doubtless the full story has been described in the papers at home. General Gatacre's division is now at Springfontein, which is not far north, and from what I can hear they are having some excitement. It looks as if we are going to have some fun here, as a body of Boers, estimated by our scouts to number 5,000, are within a few miles of us. However, we have become so innured to these alarms that we shall feel ourselves quite safe until we find all the lines 'dis,' and hear the song of the Mauser bullets up against the walls of our hut—then, not till then (as we have too much work to attend to other matters) shall we turn out to 'do or die,' or, failing that, to show a clean pair of heels over the nearest kopje. Trusting that your new departure on behalf of the 24th boys 'Ordered South' will meet with the success which it deserves."

No. 4,314, Sapper **F. A. Mason,** writing from Ladysmith, Good Friday, April 13th, says:—

DEAR SERGT. KEMP,—It is some time since I have written to you, but I believe you have been kept informed as to the doings of the Natal section since that letter reached you ere we left England. In case it is not so, I will briefly recapitulate.

"As you know, we received sudden orders to embark on board the Cunard s.s. 'Cephalonia' from Southampton. We left Aldershot with snow on the ground, at 8.30 a.m., Tuesday, February 20th, and weighed anchor at 2.15 p.m., accompanied by ringing cheers from the spectators on the quay and the strains of a cornet playing 'Say Au Revoir, but not Good-bye.'

"I need not speak of the food on board. The Company supplied it and it was very good—much the same as previous lists. As for ourselves, we soon learnt the ropes and fared very well during the whole of the voyage.

"One thing made it very unpleasant—we were so dreadfully crowded; there were 1,600 men on board, consisting of the 4th Scottish Rifles Militia and the 3rd West Surrey Militia. The latter were awful—thorough rogues from the south-east of London; some of them boasted of belonging to the notorious 'Hooligans.' Still they left us pretty well alone and we got on all right. We did no duties except to parade at 10 a.m., which fell to the lot of all on board. A corporal of the R.E.'s also used to give us half an hour's lecture upon technical matters, but this was the whole day's work.

"When we got into warmer climates two baths were rigged up, but we were rather chary of using them unless we could get in first and have the hose turned upon us—yet we did not get dirty: Oh no! our knowledge of

KHAKI LETTERS—*continued.*

'the ropes' was of further use to us, and it was possible to obtain a fresh bath occasionally.

"We called at St. Vincent on our way, and stayed there three days coaling. H.M. cruiser 'Cambrian' was in the bay, and from them we heard of the relief of Ladysmith. You should have heard the cheer that went up and echoed and re-echoed from the surrounding hills. We bought heaps of fresh fruit here, which was very welcome. We passed the time of waiting in signalling to the cruiser and other transports as they came in.

"The delay in coaling frightened us a bit, and gave rise to a rumour that we were not wanted and were going back to England; we *were* despondent, I assure you.

"At last we sailed, and then ensued a time of wearisome monotony; nothing ever happened, we rose, had our meals, and went to bed. Day after day we seemed still to be in the same place—the same ship, the same sun, the same sky. There was nothing to mark any progress whatever, except that it became warmer and the stars shifted a little at night.

"Slowly we steamed along, lazily we did the little we had to; there was scarce any motion of the sea and boat, and scarce any of the sluggish blood in our veins. At last the wind got up, the sea was rougher, the boat pitched and rolled, and then we were happy in the sense of motion. It was really pleasant to do something, to exert one's faculties to maintain a perpendicular position to the deck, or grab something and hold on when the ship gave an extra big roll. It was a pleasure I say to move with life instead of slouching lazily along, only waking up and peering lazily out through our half-closed eyes and muttering deeply a sleepy apologetic 'sorry' when one cannoned dreamily against a fellow passenger.

"Well, at last it came to an end. We anchored under the shadow of Table Mountain, at 3.30, on Wednesday, March 21st, thus occupying 29 days on the voyage. We stayed in the bay three days, and then went alongside but did not disembark until two days later, when we transhipped on to the s.s. 'Antillian' bound for Durban.

"Whilst we lay out in the bay, indeed on the first evening, the s.s. 'Duke of Cambridge' passed close to us with a lot of Boer prisoners on board, bound for Simonstown; you may be sure they caused a great deal of interest to us. As the boat came along, the fellows cried 'Here's a transport, give 'em a cheer'; but the cheer died out into a growl as it approached nearer, and it was found what sort of a cargo was on board. The prisoners seemed contented and smiling enough, and apparently didn't care a rap what noise we made.

"We were a week getting to Durban by the s.s. 'Antillian,' calling at East London and Port Elizabeth on the way. We didn't fare so well on this boat as the other, being on Government rations. We had bully beef and biscuits and a little bread, also salt junk, and tea without milk and very little sugar. We worked much harder, too, doing our share of guards, fatigues, &c. It was whilst on one of the latter I got a touch of the sun and had wretched headaches the last three days on board. I would not go sick under the circumstances, but 'stuck it.'

"On Tuesday, April 3rd. we disembarked, got out our baggage, and departed to Ladysmith by train at 12.15 p.m. We *were* glad to be going there, I assure you. Of all the places in the theatre of war, I think Ladysmith is the most interesting.

"We received a hearty send-off from Durban, even the prisoners in gaol by the side of the line climbed up to the windows and waved their arms at

KHAKI LETTERS—*continued*.

the bars; also when we stopped, people came to our carriages with gifts of fruit, tea, &c., in fact we were treated splendidly.

"The journey was a long one of 17 hours. Although the direct distance is about 130 miles, yet we travelled nearly twice as far, for as we steamed up hill many curves were necessitated in order to avoid steep gradients. It was quite a Jacob's Ladder sort of a line. We did not go fast, but that was a pleasure rather than otherwise, for it afforded us excellent opportunities of viewing the magnificent vista of mountain tops and valleys bathed in sunlight and shadow; it was glorious, and when we journeyed along the edges of precipices and looked down into a tremendous depth below it took our breath away, but did not fail to impress us with the splendour of it all.

"We reached Maritzburg at 6.30, stayed there an hour for tea, and steamed on in the dark. No lamps were allowed us and this gave rise to a rumour Boers were about and would fire on us; of course that was absurd. We got candles somehow and passed the night in singing and playing cards —some of us got an uncomfortable sleep under the seats, &c. Ladysmith was reached at daybreak and breakfast was made on the siding. The men marched into camp; I stayed with baggage and then rode in on the waggon. Reaching there we formed up, the captain inspected us, and then the front rank were told they were for the front, and the rear rank (to which I belonged was to stay). The rear rank did not like it, I assure you, but since then they have departed in twos and threes for various places. I suppose we all shall eventually. Some of the latter men have returned, but expect to go out every moment. In the meantime duty is done at head-quarters, and plenty of work there is, too, as they are short staffed; in fact, men from other regiments having a knowledge of telegraphy have been requisitioned and are employed there.

"For my part I was urged to go into 'dock' when I arrived, which I did, and was found to be suffering with a slight touch of sun sickness; nothing much, indeed I was well in three days, but the doctor insisted upon my remaining longer in order to get thoroughly rid of it. It was very stupid, for, as a matter of fact, I've been more in the sun the last few days than I should have been on duty.

"After ten days I find I am going out of hospital, and very glad I am, too. It's exceedingly monotonous, although I have been very interestingly entertained by the patients here by stories of their troubles through the siege. Most are in with debility, and a poor, underfed, attenuated lot they look; nevertheless, they are treated well, and myself, too, getting chicken and jelly, Bass', port wine, whisky and soda, arrowroot, and every kind of nourishment possible.

"I went into Ladysmith town, yesterday, and was much struck with the evidences of destruction. Houses tumbling down, many showing interiors with tables, bed and bedding exposed, proving, I suppose, the inhabitants had departed ere the siege began. Ladysmith consists of one long street with a few offshoots containing a few houses. The buildings are nearly all of corrugated iron and a few of lath and plaster. There is one large stone edifice, the town hall, but that is battered. You will remember the Boers fired on it when the sick and wounded were there, and the red cross flag flying, killing two of the patients.

"The chief thing that strikes one is the means of transport. Teams of 10 to 20 oxen are yoked together and lazily draw their load behind them. The military use mules.

"April 16th. It is Easter Monday, to-day, and we are working fairly

KHAKI LETTERS—*continued*.

heavily in the head-quarter office. I came out of hospital Saturday, and commenced duty yesterday. We are a mixed staff—at present there are seven 24th men, several R.E.'s, an 18th Hussar, a West Kent man, and others. Our hours of duty are peculiar: one staff goes on 7 a.m. to 1 p.m., and 5 p.m. to 10 p.m.; the second staff fills up the gaps, viz., 1 p.m. to 5 p.m., and 10 p.m. to 7 a.m., several getting away during the night if the state of work permits. A change is effected each Saturday, when the 5 to 10 p.m. staff remains on, going early if work drops off. There is a free and easy style of working here which would be much appreciated by our friends in TS and the district. To get the work off is the main thing, never trouble about the delay. When a storm occurs a man puts his circuit to the earth and waits its termination with perfect *sang froid*.

"Communication with the outer world, as far as letters are concerned, seems almost closed to us; we have been here a fortnight and have only received about two letters for the whole section. .... Of course it may be the fault of the P.O., but if all letters for the Natal section were addressed to Telegraph Division R.E., Natal Field Force, they would be sorted out in London direct for Maritzburg, and then on to us at once.

"I should like to send you a list of the stations our men are at, but I fear 'tis impossible, they are constantly changing, owing to the varying positions of the forces. With me at HQ at present are Corkill (TSF), Harvey (LV), Milne (AB), Cousal, Wheller and Snow (TS), and myself of EDO, but I guess by the time this letter reaches you we shall probably be separated.

"There, Sergeant, I think I have concluded my budget of news. I wish it had been a little less personal. Probably my next will be more exciting; I hope so.

"With kindest regards and best wishes to friends in TS and the Districts.'

✣ ✣ ✣ ✣

No. 4,912, Sapper **F. Somerville** (EES), writing from Las Palmas, May 2nd (s.s. Montfort), says:—

"I heard we were going to anchor off Gravesend for the night, whether we did or did not I know not, as before we reached that place I had made the acquaintance of a hammock with a view to wooing sweet Morpheus. A hammock is a quaint creature, very erratic of temperament, and with a decided dislike to new acquaintances. I had to wrestle with mine for about half-an-hour before I overcame its shyness, and even then I had to be very circumspect with it; what with the peculiarity of the beast, the strangeness of the surroundings, and the restlessness of the horses (which were stamping about immediately above my head), my first night aboard a transport was not a thing to be looked back upon altogether without regret. The hammock difficulty is now, I am happy to say, a difficulty no longer. I had nine to ten hours beautiful 'shut-eye' last night. There is not the slightest doubt about our luck in being on the 'Montfort.' Messrs. Elder, Dempster & Co. are the owners, and they don't do things by halves. This paper is a portion of one of their gifts to us; the gift as a whole being a very natty stationery case, having inscribed on the front 'With the best wishes of Elder, Dempster & Co.,' and containing a copying ink pencil, penholder, several nibs in a small envelope, a lot of this writing paper, similar envelopes, and several sheets of blotting paper, got up in very good style, so that the case will make a very nice souvenir of our trip on the 'Montfort.' The following day we were each presented with a pound of jolly decent tobacco, made by the Richmond Cavendish Co., and had a pack of cards given us. If this were all they had done for us we should have good cause to remember them,

KHAKI LETTERS—*continued.*

but their great consideration for us is evident every time we sit down to a meal. You must know that we are not fed by the Admiralty or the War Office, the Company having it in their own hands, and they do the grubbing in great style. An ordinary 'trooper' does not give butter to the troops : Elder, Dempster give us butter and marmalade too, and pickles, and as much grub at every meal as we like, our instructions being 'if you haven't enough served out, go up to the galley and get some more,' which instruction we are not slow to follow, you bet. We are up to the present living like fighting cocks, with meat of some sort four times a day; bully beef as a rule for supper, some sort of curry for tea, soup, roast or boiled beef and potatoes for dinner, and a hash for breakfast. The only drawback is that the meat is as a rule rather tough."

"I learn that on account of the horses we skirted round the Bay of Biscay instead of going through it, only touching it at its southernmost extremity. The idea has apparently worked well, as we are having beautiful weather with the sea only rough enough to cause a slight roll, which we have got quite accustomed to now. There is absolutely nothing for our men to do with the exception of the two cook's mates, who have to look after the grub, wash up, etc. We have arranged spells of four days for the two cook's mates, my turn comes the day after to-morrow. As you may imagine from the foregoing we are having a grand time, rather lazy (perhaps 'restful' would be a better term, mim.), but eminently enjoyable and much more like a holiday than some of my 'annual leaves' in the winter have been. On Sunday we had a short divine service (no fancy religions recognised), after which an orange and banana were distributed to each man by the Company, who, in addition, served out rice and stewed prunes with dinner—good business that. I may mention that we soon discovered some bottled ale, but for fear of giving the game away will say nothing about ways and means. I hope you will be able to decipher all this, I'm not very sanguine of it myself, as I'm writing on deck with aforementioned case on my knees, and what with the roll and the awkwardness of the position and the playfulness of the wind, I am continually getting into difficulty.

"There is a noticeable lack of excitement on board, such little items as passing a derelict fishing smack and watching the flying fish amusing themselves, arousing quite a lot of enthusiasm. Some of the more energetic of us, apparently having had enough of the restfulness, started tugs-of-war, skipping. jumping and pickabacks, but each of these items aroused so much feeling, and incidentally such a devil of a row, that we were stopped at them by the officer, on the ground that the horses were being frightened. We have some very rough diamonds on board, the 'Montfort' carrying drafts of Worcester, A.P.O.C., Buffs, R.A., A.S.C., R.A.M.C., 10th Hussars, beside 14 of our men, and it is very funny to watch some of them at their little 'gambles' (not gambols). Banker and a variety of dice games being favorites. So far as I have seen and am able to judge, freedom of expression is the chief characteristic of Tommy Atkins. The samples on the 'Montfort' may, of course, be below the average, but their language is very cerulean. The way they dash for the grub as soon as it appears is also very amusing. A case in point : for tea on Sunday, herrings were brought round. and as soon as they were espied a tremendous yell went up, the men bringing them round were absolutely mobbed, and there was a regular pandemonium for five minutes ; they behave exactly like youngsters at a Sunday School treat, only their vocabulary is rather more extensive. As there is nothing more of interest at present I'll dry up now. No doubt in a few weeks' time I shall have something worth writing about."

KHAKI LETTERS—*continued*.

No. 4,613, Sapper **W. J. Hargreaves**, on board the transport "Montfort," nearing Las Palmas, writes on May 2nd as follows:—

"DEAR COLOURS.—The 14 boys left ACO at 7.15 a.m. on the 26th April, in charge of Sergeant Walker of LV. We had a good send off at Government siding, two bands vieing with each other as to which could play the loudest. All along the line we had a good reception, oranges and newspapers being thrown in at the carriage windows. On arriving at RFN, we were given a good breakfast of steak and kidney pie, tea, etc. (good portions too), then moved our trappings on board about 2 and we were free, but were not allowed off the boat, or any friend on, which was rather hard, especially for those that had come a long way to give us a farewell grip, as we did not sail till about 8.30. As we sailed down the river, hundreds of syrens were blowing, and captains shouting through their trumpets friendly greetings. All praise is due to the owners (Elder, Dempster & Co.) for the way in which they are feeding us—could not be better. We are indeed fortunate compared with others who have gone before. They have given us each 2½ lb. tins of tobacco and a nice writing case (filled). They also serve out bananas and oranges occasionally. Our boys are all fit and well. The ZM has been simply grand. All the boys have dodged the sea-sickness up to now. All send hearty greetings to you and KHAKI LETTERS wishing you continued luck.

The following letter was crowded out of last number of K.L., and is probably the last letter sent by our esteemed comrade.

. No. 23.653, Sapper **J. L. Metcalfe**, writing from Springfontein, on April 5th, says:—

"DEAR KEMP,—I received the first issue of your very interesting publication of KHAKI LETTERS, and List of Names of men who have left since my departure, and take the earliest opportunity of congratulating you upon your editorial skill. Our friend, Sapper Tough, of AB, I am sorry to say, is still in hospital with enteric, and has been sent down to Naauwpoort. Although Tough and I have been isolated from our comrades we have not, apparently, been forgotten by our friends in TS. on April 1st we were the recipients of a parcel containing 2 woollen helmets or Balaclava caps, sent out by Mr. E. T. Lock, of F. Division, and knitted by his sister, Miss Lock, of the "Met" Gallery, and her friends, accompanied by a most interesting letter describing the patriotism demonstrated by the staff on the receipt of the cable confirming the relief of Ladysmith. Although General Roberts has reached Bloemfontein and concentrating his troops to the tune of 100,000 men, it does not signify that the Free Staters have been subdued, the country around here is still in rebellion, they who have taken the oath of allegiance are not to be trusted, for, no sooner they see the backs of the British than they welcome the Boers, and replace the Union Jack by the Orange Free State flag, this occurred at Reddersburg, some few miles from here. The law requesting these people to lay down their arms appears to be misinterpeted, as, on Monday, April 2nd, two Free Staters, living close to our tent, and immediately opposite the station telegraph office, were arrested, their secret having been divulged by a native, whom they had been illtreating, to the effect that they had several Mauser rifles buried in their garden, this proved to be correct, as upon inspection a number of these rifles were found, 6 feet below the surface. The two men were promptly placed under arrest, causing their women folk to weep most bitterly. Previous to this incident they had been 'very loyal.' Since I have been

KHAKI LETTERS—*continued*.

stationed here I have had the pleasure of meeting a few of our boys, Sappers Fallon, Sainsbury, and Austin, and Sappers Arundel, Clarke, Swan, Brooks, and others, passing through from Naauwpoort and De Aar to Bloemfontein. There have been excitable times here these few days past, reports coming through to the effect that our small parties, who were guarding various districts, being surrounded, and that Springfontein was threatened, the telegraph office and station being in a state of commotion during the night, trains leaving at all hours with troops for their relief, after their departure the small party who were left behind, which consisted chiefly of the Headquarters Staff, their Clerks and Orderlies, were under arms all night in consequence of a reported attack upon this important Junction. General Brabant, in command of the Colonial Mounted Forces of this Division, was compelled to evacuate Smithfield and retire again into Aliwal North, being hard pressed by two large commandoes, who had the audacity to ask him to surrender if he did not want a repetition of the Stormberg disaster, in which so many lives were sacrificed, he despatched the messenger without any reply. Our small party here, under Sergt.-Major Foote, R.E., find that it takes us all our time to cope with the telegraph business, which necessitates an attendance of 13 and 14 hours a day for each man. We consist of 1 R.E., 2 men of the Derbyshire Regiment, and myself, with the Sergt.-Major in charge, and an R.E. lineman, to cook for us, and the dainty dishes which he has always ready at the appointed time assists us in keeping up the strain of heavy work. An order has just been issued to the effect that no private or press messages are to be accepted at this office owing to the heavy delay on military work. Another order is, that owing to the lack of railway transport, all troops for Bloemfontein must march the whole distance from Bethulie and Norvals Pont (distance about 130 miles), this will considerably reduce the number of railway messages, and so enable us to expedite the military work, as the former have priority over all except S.B.'s from Lords Roberts and Kitchener, and other Generals. The party of Royal Irish Rifles and Mounted Infantry who were surrounded at Reddersburg, which I have previously referred to, eventually surrendered after a stubborn resistance, losing 2 officers and 8 men killed, and 35 wounded, the whole 400 with 5 guns being ultimately captured by a strong Boer commando of 3,200 men. under the command of De Wet and Snyman. Captain Tennant, our Intelligence Officer, being amongst the prisoners. I am afraid that his case will go rather hard with him, as he is well known to the enemy under the guise of an Australian sheep farmer, agent for Remington Typewriters, and other disguises, during his term of Secret Service before the outbreak of the war. The winter is evidently approaching, there being a noticeable difference during the night and the heat not quite so intense in the daytime, the Colonials assure us that there is very little difference between the two seasons as regards heat, but now that the rains have finished, we may expect a few months of dry and bright weather. We have had no dust storms or high winds up here and locusts have failed to visit us, so taking all these into consideration there is absolutely nothing to grumble at. So with good health, good food, and plenty of work, we are as happy as anyone could wish to be under similar circumstances. Troops continue to pass through here both by road and rail, if by latter they are usually in open trucks night and day, the latest to pass through being the C.I.V.'s, who received such a magnificent 'send off' on their departure from London. Concluding with the usual best wishes to all."

Sapper James Lord Metcalfe.

THE Central Telegraph Office was thrown into a state of excitement on Tuesday, May 22nd, when the news was passed round that information had been received of the death of No. 23,653, Sapper J. L. Metcalfe, of the "L" Division C.T.O. A telegram to our registered address ran as follows :—"Cape Town, May 21st, 8 p.m. Poniard, London,—Metcalfe died dysentery, Sunday."

J. L. Metcalfe was born June 17th, 1867. Appointed Telegraph Messenger, August 22nd, '81 ; Parcel Post Assistant, July 16th, '83 ; S. C. and T., May 4th, '85, at Bolton, of which place he was a native. He was married there in 1887, and was transferred to the C.T.O. February 21st, 1891. He obtained two first-class certificates for Technical Knowledge, and consequently the double increment in 1898.

His Volunteer Service in the "24th" dates back some 12 or 13 years. Joining the "I" Company while at Bolton, on November 9th, 1887, with a view to the Res-

erves, he was ultimately successful in his wish, and was transferred to the "L" Company in March, 1889.

A fine, well set-up fellow of 6 ft., well liked generally, as a colleague in the office or as a comrade in the corps, he was looked upon as one of the best of our contingent. He sailed for South Africa, in the s.s. "Bavarian," November 8th, 1899, after he and his chum—Tough, of Aberdeen—had been detained at Aldershot awaiting uniforms. Being thus separated from their comrades, they were attached to the 12th Field Company, and it was only recently they could rejoin them. His letters have always been read with great interest.

One of our men, referring to the Springfontein Hospital, says, "it is in a little tin church, quite a cosy little place, and poor old 'Met' is occupying a bed up on the rostrum. He is pretty comfortable now (May 3rd), but for the first three days he was on the floor. He has got a touch of dysentery—and indeed he is very cheerful, considering, and as almost the whole of the hospital men are Lancashire Lads, 'Met.' gets on O.K."

He leaves a wife and three children to mourn his loss, and his late colleagues tender their condolences to them.

Sapper Alexander Milne.

SAPPER A. MILNE, of Aberdeen, whose death is reported as having taken place at Ladysmith, on Monday, May 21st, from dysentery, joined the "24th" on March 12th, 1886. In June, '86, he was transferred to the R.E. Reserve, where he remained until '98, having completed 12 years in "L" Co. Always anxious to see active service, he volunteered to serve with the Colours during the Soudan Campaign. Lately, many time-expired Reservists have been re-engaged, and, after repeated applications, "Sandy's" services were accepted, and he sailed for South Africa, per s.s. "Cephalonia," Feb. 20th, arriving at Capetown March 21st.

He was born March 1st, '66. Entered P.O. service as a Telegraph Messenger, Mar. 26th, '81, at Aberdeen. Appointed S.C. and T., June 22, '83; married, October, '91; and, in '92, was appointed to the *Aberdeen Free Press* special wire, a position which he most ably filled until his promotion to Provincial Clerk-in-Charge on April 9th,' 98.

He had the prospect of a very successful career, when he was unfortunately—as it turns out—accepted for service in South Africa, and has been cut off in the prime of life by the enemy which is working more havoc among our brave men than all the Boer bullets.

Milne was one of the first clerks in the Service to receive the treble increment for Postal and Technical qualifications. The Aberdeen staff and friends gave him a good "send off" at a "smoker," where "Sandy" was the recipient of several mementoes. Replying to the chairman's complimentary speech, he said: "In all probability he would not be called upon to join the fighting line, but, if necessity required, he would strive to do his duty." Duty was the guiding principle of his life. Straight-forward, honest, trusted by his superiors, loved and honoured by his brother officers, looked up to as a champion of justice and right, a true comrade in camp, a man of fine physique and an all-round athlete—golfer, cyclist, swimmer, and footballer (having played for his County), such was poor "Sandy," who leaves a sorrowing wife and two dear children. Friends in London join colleagues in Aberdeen in mourning the loss of so true a friend.

"Khaki Notes."

The Bloemfontein Friend for Monday, April 30th, publishes the following. From it will be seen that Our Boys can find a little time for amusement. The Reporter is a well-known contributor to the Corps paper. "The Sapper":—

A LOVELY GAME.—An Association Football Match. "Gonks" *versus* "Bastangos," was played on Saturday, on the ground outside "Gonkbird" Villa, the abode of the Field Telegraphists. Both teams (telegraphists) were in excellent fettle, and displayed some really remarkable and scientific form. It was apparent from the commencement that the "Gonks" were a strong team, and the "Bastangos" would have all their work cut out to "lick" them. The "Gonks" kicked off at 8.15 a.m., and succeeded in scoring a goal five minutes afterwards, which was due undoubtedly to the smart forwards, who, though having a formidable opponent in the "Bastangos" centre forward, succeeded by their sublime passing to get home many a shot. The goal of the "Bastangos" was rather weak, owing, possibly, to the fact that the ground in the immediate vicinity was interspersed with miniature kopjes: but then had not the "Gonks" to overcome these impedimenta too? A word of praise is due, however, to the "Bastangos" goal-keeper, who showed splendid pluck when harassed by the tricky opposition forwards. The "Gonks" full-backs and goal-keeper were the quintessence of perfection. The agility of the "Gonks" goal-keeper was positively surprising, and only one ball passed him into goal, and that was through the full back having the misfortune to trip over a bully beef tin. The near proximity of the sluit into which the ball seemed to have a partiality to wander, somewhat marred the game, but the vigilant linesman, "Shagrinoldo the Diminutive," soon recovered the delinquent bladder. At half time the game stood:—"Gonks" 5 goals; "Bastangos," 1 goal. During the second moiety an untoward accident happened to one of the forwards of the "Bastangos," who was making a tremendous charge for the "Gonks" full-back, when the latter, with a terrible kick from his No. 9 ammunitions, mark II., instead of lifting the ball, slightly elevated his opponent by delivering his daisy root clean on the "Bastango's" ankle. After anathematising the "Gonks" in general, and the full back in particular, the brave "Bastangos" (since gone sick) retired amidst the ringing cheers of the onlookers (2 Kaffirs and a half-starved mule). The "Bastangos," seeing that they were irretrievably beaten, endeavoured by super-human efforts to make up for lost time. But alas! 'twas all in vain. A well delivered kick from the "Gonks" centre forward caught the "Bastangos" ditto full in the face, knocking two of his teeth out and otherwise disfiguring his facial apparatus (he, too, has since gone sick). In despair the "Bastangos" played for all they were worth (which was not much, after paying exorbitant prices for grub in Bloemfontein), but they were unable to get through the "Gonks'" admirable stone wall of forwards. A scrimmage was at one time imminent on the edge of the sluit, but by a dexterous movement of the "Gonks" forward, the opposing force was quietly precipitated into the yawning abyss below, the mules giving vent to their feelings in hoarse cachinnations. This event incapacitated the "Bastangos" further participation in the game, and with a glorious score of 8 to 1, the game was closed. A Dhajiboy and its native driver, who were passing at the time, being over-interested in the game, came in sudden contact with a lamppost on the bridge, with the result that the lamppost was "downed" in fine style, and the horses tied up in inseparable knots.—"BLOBSWITCH." (R.E.T.D.)

N.B.—The "Gonks" challenge any team in Bloemfontein, but it is respectfully requested that the opposing party brings its own ambulance.

Poniard, London, *via* Eastern, is our registered address for telegrams in cases of emergency. Send your relative's name and address to W. Payne, Esq., Assistant Superintendent, Moorgate Street Buildings, E.C., who is keeping a list, and will communicate on receipt of a cablegram.

Poniard, London, brought the news of poor Metcalfe's death. Although the papers published a day or two after gave him as being dangerously ill, we cannot conceive our chums out yonder paying for, and sending on, a false alarm. Such action would be criminal, to say the least. Therefore, we must bow to the inevitable and take it that another of "Ours" has been promoted to the big majority.

KHAKI NOTES—*continued.*

No, No! BM is neither bugle-major, band-master, brigade-major, nor any such thing. When these letters occur after a man's name, they indicate from which office he is drawn. EH, "Eh?" No. Edinburgh. Fancy putting "Sapper So-and-so (AB)," down as an able seaman, when telegraphists know it is Aberdeen, abbreviated. But this is all excusable from friends not in the service. The codes are too numerous to be given here.

"Actions speak louder than words," writes a colleague who wishes to champion his section of the C.T.O., "and the acts of the 'G' Division have proved its rank and file to be far more patriotic than most. Not only has the Division sent five men to the front, but it has also, owing mainly to the unselfish labours of Mr. Francis Mead, sent 361 shillings to the *Daily Telegraph* Widows' Fund, £7 10s. to the *Daily Mail* A.M.B. Fund, and purchased £8 worth of concert tickets. Mr. Mead expects to continue collecting £5 monthly during the war. Other Divisions please copy."

Friends who have tried to guess the abbreviations in "K.L." will at once plump for this as being the GOOD Division. Well, so it is, for we have it on authority that they are doing a grand work, giving gladly, and going gloriously on. But we have heard of other Divisions who have also put their hands into their pockets, and are continuing to do so for various causes, one of which is the subscriptions to our less fortunate Reservists whose official pay is reduced during their absence. A little friendly rivalry between the Groups and Divisions is healthy—yes, and *wealthy* as well as wise. Meanwhile don't forget "K.L." has a claim, too. It is more blessed to give than to receive. The truth of this you experience every time you send your bobs to "Bobs'" boys, or to "Bobs'" boys' boys, or to "Bobs'" boys' boys' mothers and sisters. You also experience the joy of giving when you plank your pence down for your "K.L.'s," with the joy of receiving thrown in.

The "Khaki" Postage Fund.—The sums handed to Mr. George Costello are as follows:—

Divisions—A., 2s. 6d.; B., 4s.; C., 2s. 8d.; D., 5s. 9d.; E., 3s. 10d.; F., 3s.; G., 5s.; H., 4s.; I., 2s. 10d.; K., 4s. 10d.; L., 5s.; News, 3s. 2d.; Special, 4s. 3d.; Provincial Check, 5s.

Groups—A., 0; B., 4s. 6d.; C., 4s. 3d.; D., 0; E., 4s. 6d.; F., 0; G., 3s. H., 4s. 6d.; I., 2s. 3d.; K., 11d.; L., 1s. 2d.; M., 1s. Total, £4 1s. 11d. For which I heartily thank you. This, however, does not nearly cover the expense of posting to Our Boys out yonder. There are (roughly) 200 of them there now, and six issues—including one double—have been sent them. Reckon it up for yourselves, at a 1½d. each. That is, a book and postage to every man.

It may be of interest to readers to know that the much-debated penny postage stamp recently issued by the Cape Colony is the design of our old confrère, Jack Steven, another old 24ther, who left TS some years ago for the Colonial Service. The objection in patriotic circles arose from the fact that the Colony's coat of arms are shown instead of Her Majesty's profile. An excellent opportunity to show their loyalty to the Mother Country being thus lost.

Congratulations to the following on their promotions:—

2nd Class Asst. Supts.—G. W. Lucas, F. N. Druitt and H. R. Testar, to be 1st Class Asst. Supts.

Senior Telegraphists—E. Melvin, A. Burgoyne, E. Glass and R. Doree, to be 2nd Class Asst. Supts.

Telegraphists—W. J. Miell and J. F. Barnett, to be Senior Telegraphists. Dated 14th May.

Messrs. G. R. Salter, H. G. Kibblewhite and J. Slade's promotions are antedated to November 16th, 1899.

An Advertisement in "The Friend" calls the attention of no less than 160 regiments, batteries, and other units to the fact that heavy parcels are awaiting them at the Military Parcel Office, Bloemfontein, and adds, "a wheeled transport will be required to take them away." Besides this, over 340 soldiers are notified that parcels are there for them, and 10 unaddressed packages, containing officers' kits, a box of revolvers, 16 rifles, etc., all require claimants.

Mr. J. D. Smith goes to Moorgate Street Buildings as acting Senior.

KHAKI NOTES—*continued*.

Linemen are wanted at the Cape; 50 are being fixed up for this duty.

"The Invisible One," who sends me four pages of "Kimberley Chatter," should bear in mind that the publication of Skits might amuse a few, would hurt more, and would possibly be unintelligible to a vast majority. They are clever, and not intended to irritate, but they are better in writing than print, I think. Don't you?

"Ex-President Steyn," says "The Friend," "seems to be the real absent-minded beggar. He left his house door unlocked and bolted himself."

The P.M.G. has appointed Lieut. A. Maxwell, of "I" Company 24th Mx. R.V., to act as Asst. Director of Telegraph Messengers' drills during the absence of Captain Price, our esteemed officer, now serving with the A.P.O.C. in South Africa.

Mr. J. G. Davies, our old 24th comrade, Postmaster of Alford, Lincs., is, we hear, returning to London; the continued illness of his wife making this step imperative.

Pat Maguire of C. Div. and **F. N. Kelling** of the old F.G., have been invalided from the service.

Bob Luttrell's name is no longer seen in the lists. No reply to our telegram has yet been received. We have reason to hope that "no news is good news."

Sapper J. S. Tough (AB), has been ill for some time, and various rumours have been afloat concerning him. Enquiries have been made, and the W.O. will probably wire for information from South Africa.

Invalided Home and at Netley Hospital are the following:—Alliston, Roberts, McLaren (EH), and Williams (CF), and Sapper A. Ray is on the way.

Private E. F. Howes, 333, A.P.O.C., is reported to be ill at Bloemfontein, and is on the Danger List.

Sapper T. Robinson, 4335, 1st Div. Tel. Bn. R.E., died of dysentery at Ladysmith, May 23rd. There is evidently an error in the initials. It is undoubtedly F. W. Robinson, from Derby.

W. J. West, an old 24th man, who has also done a bit in the R.E. Reserves—"L" Company, died on Friday, May 25th, after being away about ten days. Consumption is said to be the cause. Interred, May 28th, at West Ham Cemetery.

"Casualty, Capetown," is the registered address of a Special Office in South Africa dealing with casualties, in case relatives wish to telegraph or write direct. (Circular from the War Office.)

Bisley Camp temporary B.O. was opened on May 26th, and will remain open until August 28th.

A temporary Field P.O. has been established at Bulford Camp, Salisbury, for all classes of P.O. business.

Letters from Tee, Townsend, Morse, Bannister (MR), W. G. Carter, Minors, York, Pickford, A. J. Brooks, Ray, J. A. Brown, Sinclair, Sorenson, Wheller, J. Fallon, Swan and others are crowded out.

"Well, I Never!" An old body who was on a visit to a garrison town for the first time was much startled by the sound of the evening gun. "Dear me," she exclaimed in terror, "are the enemy landing?" "It's only the sunset, ma'am," replied the landlady encouragingly. "Well, I never!" was the old lady's reply. "In London the sun sets as quietly as anything. But perhaps," she continued thoughtfully, "we don't hear the bang on account of the traffic." —*The Regiment.*

COLOURS.

"KHAKI LETTERS," One Penny. By post, Three Halfpence.

All posted letters containing Remittances, Orders, MSS., &c., must be addressed to R. E. KEMP, 12, JERRARD STREET, LEWISHAM, S.E. Postal Orders should be made payable at Loampit Vale, Lewisham, S.E.

Printed by E. G. BERRYMAN & SONS, *Blackheath Road, London, S.E.*

"Khaki Letters" from ....
"My Colleagues in South Africa."

CORRESPONDENCE FROM THE
POST OFFICE TELEGRAPHISTS
OF THE
24th MIDDLESEX (P.O.) RIFLE VOLUNTEERS
(Royal Engineer Reserves),
ON ACTIVE SERVICE.

THE BOND THAT BINDS US—FRIENDSHIP—COMRADESHIP.

Published fortnightly for the Postal Telegraph Service.
Conducted by COLOUR-SERGEANT R. E. KEMP, *Central Telegraph Office, London.*

No. 10.   JUNE 15TH, 1900.   PRICE ONE PENNY.

With Lord Roberts to Pretoria.
"Pretoria! Hurrah!!"

FALLON, PORTER, HAMER, SAINSBURY."

The above cablegram, dated Capetown, June 6th, 11.10 a.m., and probably one of the last sent from the Capital of the Transvaal just before the communications were cut, was addressed "Kemp, Poniard, London," and received on the 8th inst.

The second name was mutilated and rendered "Proler," but we believe Porter is the man intended.

Central Telegraph Office,
London, E.C.

DEAR COMRADES, ONE AND ALL.   GREETINGS AND CONGRATULATIONS.

All the boys are eager for the forthcoming fray at Camp, about which, however, there is a "marvellous uncertainty." It has been announced in one paper that we are going to Salisbury; in another, we are going to Aldershot; in a third inspired journal we are assured we are going to neither, but with buttonholed whisperings, it informs us we are down for Sheerness, certain. Why not go to all three, just to let them all see they were right. I am able to state—to ape the penny-a-liner—"on good authority," that the 24th will be encamped in the Chatham District. Exact spot, longitude, latitude, weather, &c., uncertain. Likewise, the attendance.

Uncertainties are prolific in this world. They come upon us when we least expect them. Applicants for Camp are referred to Par. 7 Regimental Orders, June 2nd, 1900, which reads as follows:—"The Regiment will go into Camp from the 21st of July to the 18th of August, at such place as may be notified hereafter. All Non-commissioned Officers and men should send in their names through their Colour-Sergeants before the 15th of June to the Orderly Room, stating, opposite each name, whether the man wishes to attend for the first 14 days or the last 14 days, or for any longer period, in order that the Post Office Authorities may decide for what period he can be absent. It is understood that men will receive, as far as the exigencies of the Post Office Service will admit, special leave for 14 days to attend Camp, with full pay. Any who can arrange to stay longer will receive Army pay only, unless they are on their annual leave. All ranks will receive Army pay while in Camp."

Those who have holidayed seem to be doomed to disappointment. The utmost business pressure is now upon the Staff. So many of you boys being away in South Africa, the civvy soldiers cannot be spared from our Department so well. But the end has not come yet. The matter is being considered, and we hope to hear pleasing results from the conferring officials later on. Once upon a time we prophesied the whole of I Company being in Camp this year. We prophesy no longer, we simply wish it may be so.

The troopship "Montrose" left the Thames yesterday for Capetown with 533 officers and men of various drafts. To-day she calls at Southampton and ships more troops, amongst whom are the following 24th men under the command of Lieutenant Elkington :—

4602 R. D. S. Norman,	4638 R. Watkins,	4658 J. R. Hewitt,
4606 A. Walkley,	4639 E. W. Crafter,	4659 C. Gibson,
4607 W. H. Butt,	4640 F. J. Morris,	4660 H. Clift,
4616 W. E. Burden,	4641 J. Houghton,	4661 J. Rendle,
4617 D. Armstrong,	4642 A. G. Watling,	4662 W. H. Lowe,
4618 W. H. Turnbull,	4643 J. P. Robson,	4663 F. P. Brown,
4619 F. Robinson,	4644 E. Sanderson,	4664 T. W. Jackson,
4620 T. M. Morris,	4645 J. H. Bell,	4665 W. J. Whelan,
4621 C. E. Bordeaux,	4646 J. D. Forster,	4666 W. H. Garland,
4622 C. W. Perkins,	4647 S. Webber,	4667 H. C. McBurney,
4628 A. E. Johnston,	4648 G. Barron,	4668 J. Gilchrist,
4629 C. F. G. Staines,	4649 A. D. Bennett,	4669 G. Tait,
4630 W. A. Pearson,	4650 A. G. Waters,	4670 W. E. Braybon,
4631 E. E. Bellwood,	4651 S. A. Deeble,	4671 G. Hulatt,
4632 G. E. Dodds,	4652 E. A. Turner,	4672 A. R. Revill,
4633 J. Lane,	4653 O. G. Pilley,	4673 H. E. Hughes,
4634 S. W. Wheatcroft,	4654 B. R. Howell,	4674 R. Dodd,
4635 J. J. Young,	4655 E. Whitworth,	4675 F. Harding,
4636 J. T. Thompson,	4656 W. H. Saunders,	4685 W. H. Turner,
4637 D. W. Jones,	4657 J. S. Lord,	4686 A. Dickinson.

Of the above contingent, some have remained in Aldershot 12 or 13 weeks, some on leave for a few weeks, and others stood on that time-honoured ground last Saturday for the first time in their natural. R. D. S. Norman and T. M. Morris mounted the first stripe on Saturday, others have been placed in charge of sections and expect one shortly. Up early yesterday morning, medical examination, plenty of little details to do, and so on, in heat that was intense (125° and 98° shade). In the evening they had the "usual"—a big Smoker—as a grand finale, accounts of which have just reached me (4 p.m.). "It was a mixed lot" they say, and those capable of judging give their verdict that "it was the best of its kind ever seen." Good. Let's see if we can't beat it when the lads return. Nothing would please your home chums better, Eh ? To-day they were fit and firm for the fresh fields and pastures new. Three are from the C.T.O., the remainder from the provinces, and a fine smart well-set-up lot they are. In letters to hand, and by word of mouth, I have heard tell—once again—of the kindness of the Royals, and the good times they have had together. I may mention that eleven of these are "short service men," the remainder are "one year or as required."

All these are coming to help you. May they, and you, all have the best of luck and health.

Yours most heartily,

To the " I," Co. in South Africa,   R. E. KEMP,
    Tuesday, June 12th, 1900.   *Colour Sergeant.*

COPYRIGHT.—"Khaki Letters" must not be used without permission.—R. E. KEMP.

Khaki Letters.

No. 1,546, Sapper **R. W. Eglinton** (of DY), writes from Reddersburg, O.F.S., April 11th, as follows :—

" . . . . After the Lord Mayor's Show comes a Corporation cart. I've been living like a lord at Fauresmith until the Boers, or rumours of their coming, drove out the garrison, which was composed entirely of our three brave selves, myself and two other R.E. telegraphists. Our retreat was solely for strategic purposes, otherwise wild horses, let alone Boers, would not have budged us. As it was, tame horses and two Cape carts sufficed for us and our belongings, and cost the Imperial Government a fiver to cart us the 40 odd miles between Fauresmith and Edinburg where we found the railway again. We started from Fauresmith about 4 p.m., passed through Jagersfontein, where the diamond mines are, about 5 p.m. (the troops had evacuated this place), and after being treated to whiskies and sodas by a loyal inhabitant, we pushed on, crossed several drifts in the dark and arrived at Edinburg at 11 p.m., seeing no Boers on the way. An attack was expected at Edinburg in the night, but we slept undisturbed in the telegraph office and went by train to a place called Bethany, a place that is little more than a name, where we bivouacked for the night. It was a night of disturbances. Stallions fighting close to our heads, fellows audibly grumbling about having to go on guard and being in a 'dirty' condition, and to crown all a thunderstorm with heavy rain : but I slept, somehow, in all my clothes, as I often have to sleep now. Next morning we loaded up, and with the 3rd Division (General Chermside's) marched by the side of the wagon to Reddersburg, about 11 miles tramp, in marching order, in rainy weather. We moved slowly and cautiously with scouts out in front and on flanks, but all was quiet, and we reached Reddersburg at 5 p.m. fairly clemmed, only had one biscuit since breakfast. The Boers have been aggressive in this district, and we hear rumour of disaster to our forces all about here. Heard that a British force is surrounded and likely to surrender through lack of ammunition at Wepener, but can get no authentic news whatever. Don't even know what this move of 3rd Division is, but hear that it goes on to Bloemfontein soon. At Fauresmith we held daily communication with Boers that had been out with commandoes, and fought against our men at Belmont, Magersfontein, etc., and they were quite friendly and even kind to us, and spoke well of our men and their shooting. I was sorry to leave Fauresmith ; had a pneumatic bicycle to ride nearly daily, which was not an unmixed blessing on these primitive roads, up to the chain in dust, but it was a pleasant break in my hardships. We also dined royally at the Hotel, off a tablecloth, and now, alas, I'm back again eating tough meat and drinking jipper out of a trossy canteen. Don't know whether I stop here or go on

KHAKI LETTERS—*continued*.

to Bloemfontein, and I don't care. This place has the reputation of harbouring the most fearful vermin in South Africa. There are some very decent chaps in the party. Wonder who got the English Cup. I'll have a guess—Notts Forest? Heard that Cambridge won the Boat Race by 20 lengths. That's all the English news I've had lately. Heard there was a parcel and letter lying at Bloemfontein P.O., but have no means of getting at them. Had to shake my shirt out well this morning. South African blood-sucking creepers dropped on me all last night from ceiling, as I lay on the floor listening to eternal rattle of instruments. Hope I don't stop here long. Say if you got my Chocolate Box, am a bit anxious about it. Good Friday tomorrow, but I shan't see any hot cross buns nor go to Matlock."

✤ ✤ ✤ ✤

No. 4,322, Sapper **T. H. Symonds**, writing from Buys Farm Camp, Natal, April 13th, says:—

" I expect all our doings are pretty well known to you. However, this letter may contain something that is news to you, and in that hope I will try and tell you (by the aid of a 3½d. Straker's Diary) what has happened . . . . (Describes start, sea voyage, and arrival. All very interesting, but previously chronicled by others.—R.E.K.) . . . . After a 16 hours' journey we arrived at Ladysmith. After duly admiring the show, armoured trains, damage, and the various positions, we were divided into two sections, one for the front and one for Ladysmith. Collins and myself found ourselves bound, with the rest of the HQ section, for the front that same night. They called it Sundays River Camp, which is about 20 miles beyond Ladysmith. We detrained at Elandslaagte Station, a place you may have heard of, and marched to the Telegraph Camp, attached to Clery's Brigade. Here we found we were in for a fairly soft time. Instruction in lineman's work, 6 a.m. for half an hour, 8 a.m. to noon, and 5 p.m. for half an hour. In the afternoons we would go down to Sundays River bathing and doing a little washing under a fine iron bridge which had been blown up by the Boers. Bevan, Chubbock, Leaver and Collins, had to leave us for various small offices of the camp. Our peaceful existence was destined to be speedily broken, however, only lasting for five days, for on the morning of the 10th the Boers started shelling the camp and made good practice, although some of their shells didn't burst. Thus, exactly a week from the day of landing I got my baptism of fire, a very small one though, according to some of the troops, who have had awful times. We paraded under arms immediately, struck camp, and took cover behind some rocks. As we were well advanced the shells passed over our heads, and we could see them bursting among the camps beyond. At first we ducked when the shells came, but after a little while we found it too much trouble. Soon after this I and a Provincial man got orders to go to the Sundays River Telegraph Office. As I went I noticed a 15 lb. shell strike the ground near, and instead of bursting it squirmed along for yards, throwing a cloud of smoke up, looking something like a firework. When I got to the office I found a shell had dropped a yard away and covered the instruments with dust. It didn't burst, and I think Leaver who was in the office is keeping it. It was rather awkward telegraphing, as less than a hundred miles—I should say yards—away, five 4·7 naval guns were working, and the Boers made a special target of them. Thus the duel went on until darkness set in. Our casualties, four killed, eight wounded, four of these being naval men. We then had orders to strike the tent, and the whole army, except outposts, retired to just near Elandslaagte. That

KHAKI LETTERS—*continued*.

night I slept in open air with nothing to cover me except what I stood upright in, and the nights are bitterly cold. Before dawn next morning I had orders to accompany a party of linemen with a cable cart to Buys Farm Camp, where Dundonald is in command. It was an awful ride. We had to go over rocks, ditches, railway lines and fields. We had a team of six mules with a couple of native drivers, and I ached all over before we finished, and part of the harness was smashed up. We passed dozens of dead horses, relics of Elandslaagte, all rotting as they lay. Well, we got here and put up a buzzer in one of these small tents, two poles waist high and open one end. We have had a busy time working half the night and all day. We had no rations and no kit, and only our belt and pouch to keep us warm. It is now Saturday and still in the same plight, and the nights are very cold. We have now shifted to a bell tent, but with the exception of more room are not much better here. In Sundays River there was a terrible amount of sickness, enteric fever and dysentery, and the drinking water was bad stuff. Here, with the Mounted Brigade, camp among the hills is supposed to be a healthy place."

✤ ✤ ✤ ✤

No. 28,201, Company Sergt.-Major **W. G. Tee**, R.E., writing from Naauwpoort, April 14th, sends the following :—

"I hope you received my last epistle safe, but I am rather doubtful, as it should have been on the 'Mexican,' the ill-fated mail boat, which went down 70 miles out of Capetown. I am writing this to you to ask if you will take extracts from a letter written to———, I really cannot find time to write to so many, as so much to do here and I have no doubt Dick Kemp would like a copy of it. I am sure Dick is working very hard for us and we all feel very grateful to him for his kindness and interest shown; his copies of KHAKI LETTERS are a decided success, and read with the greatest interest, many of the letters therein containing news which we are not able to get ourselves, not being in touch with all our comrades. I was exceedingly pleased to hear poor old Jackman was better again, and hope he may continue to improve and will be the same man when we return as when he saw us off at Waterloo. Bob Luttrell, I am sorry to say, is in Hospital, he passed down country the other day, and I trust he is progressing satisfactorily. Sapper Ray, I am pleased to say, is getting over his attack of typhoid, and is likely to be on 'solids' in the course of a day or two. I am pleased to say I am feeling very well, in fact, never felt better, the climate, I think, agrees with me. Speaking to Jimmy Miller this morning, at Kimberley, he said he was the same. We shall be pleased to meet the 60 additional men from England, no mistake, the old hands are turning up again. Trusting this will not be troubling you too much."

✤ ✤ ✤ ✤

Here are the extracts referred to. Letter written April 14th, Naauwpoort, by "Georgie" :—

"The contents of your letter were digested with very keen interest, and I can quite realise the rejoicings in London when the news of Ladysmith arrived, in fact the troops who have recently arrived state that Jubilee day was not to be compared with it. I need scarcely say all out here were overjoyed with the news, which was received soon after the relief, and exhibited outside our office, and the news soon spread throughout the camp, and flashed by heliograph to all outlying picquets and outposts. The relief

KHAKI LETTERS—*continued*.

of Kimberley, Cronje's surrender and the taking of Bloemfontein, has been a fatal blow to the Boers, and were it not for the fact that Kruger and Steyn are forcing all Burghers, under penalty of death, to join their Commandos, the fighting would soon terminate; it is thought here it will take some considerable time yet before it is settled. No doubt you are aware they are still causing us a deal of trouble in territory which we had already occupied, and the same ground has to be gone over again. The Jameson Raid did a deal of harm to the prestige of England, and the supposed loyal Dutch in the Colony have lost confidence in Rhodes'—who at one time they held in high esteem—and are, as is only natural, sympathetic with the Boers. Although there are nearly 200,000 troops in the Colony, the majority of these have to be taken for garrisoning disaffected areas and the keeping lines of communication; every town or village that has been the scene of disloyalty has to be left garrisoned by from two Companies to a Battalion of Infantry, and this, you will understand, in such a vast country, soon exhausts an army corps. The camp that Lord Roberts has at Bloemfontein is the largest England has had since the Crimea, and it is hoped and thought there will be no difficulty in getting to Pretoria when once he moves, which, I believe, will be in the course of a week or two. The reason of the delay of his advance is, of course, getting his supplies and remounts to hand, but this has been progressing some time now; but in the meantime he has been harassed by the Boers threatening his lines of communication, and instead of getting the supplies through, the 8th Division has had to take precedence, thus delaying him. Remounts are arriving daily in hundreds and you can scarcely realise the difficulty in transporting them hundreds of miles over a single line, which is blocked day and night with such a tremendous amount of traffic; train after train arrives and is despatched, but of course the great difficulty is the single line and the sidings at various places, which are too short and quite inadequate for the traffic; however, there is a very able and efficient staff of railway employes, and its working, taking all things into consideration, is satisfactory. I was astonished to see the amount of rolling stock the Cape Government Railway have, they appear to be up-to-date with it and copy the Yankees. The military authorities, of course, work on a system—so many trains of supplies, troops, hospital trains, etc., run daily, and those who cannot travel by rail have to tramp it, in fact a great number have been sent from Naauwpoort and Norvals Pont to Bloemfontein, so great has been the strain. The working of the railway, needless to say, makes us very busy, for every 'detail' is telegraphed. Since my last letter, and after our exciting experiences at Rensburg and Arundel, we have had it rather quiet, for the Boers have all been driven out of the Colony, and after we were reinforced we re-occupied Rensburg. Our old Telegraph Office there bore evidence of their having been there, for the office, if I may term it such, was left in a filthy condition; the camp was strewn with offal and skins of cattle, and altogether the odour therefrom was very disagreeable. They had done no damage to the railway between Arundel and Rensburg, and the telegraph lines were intact, they had, however, found our earth lead which had been left buried and cut it, carefully covering it in again, but we soon found this out and made the connection again without any delay, they had also cut down an improvised terminal pole, but this was overcome by joining cable to the main line, the lines beyond had to be repaired, for which a special constructing party were sent forward. The Boers were chased out of Rensburg by the Inniskillings and Australians, and their laager bore evidence of their hasty retreat for they had to leave several things behind. The

KHAKI LETTERS—*continued.*

telegraphists of the Boers had not destroyed and taken everything away, as I had done when we evacuated Rensburg, for several telegrams were found, as was also a lot of their stationery, of which I enclose a few forms which I commandeered. I had the satisfaction of going to Colesberg immediately after their flight and the pleasure of visiting their positions, which seemed almost impregnable, and had it not been for the successes of Lord Roberts in the Orange Free State, they might have been there now. Our fourth contingent have arrived, some of whom have been sent to Norvals Pont and Bloemfontein, and I am having a change at Naauwpoort, which has turned out in the meantime a more important office, and we have had a lot of transmitting to do, being in communication with Bloemfontein, Norvals Pont, De Aar, Port Elizabeth, Bethulie, etc. The work will be falling off here shortly and I have no doubt the Colonial clerks will take it over, when I expect to move up again. It is not nearly so exciting here, and if it were not for the work we should find it very monotonous. We are fairly comfortable and do not have to bivouac on the veldt as most of the troops, but have our tents with the regulation two blankets and water-proof sheet. The heat is not so intense now during the day, but the nights are extremely cold, and I sleep in my clothes with my jersey and overcoat on, and find that none too warm. This is supposed to be one of the highest points in the Colony. I regret to say we have lost two of our comrades—Sappers Fairall (Mount Pleasant), and A. W. Hawkins (TSF), both of whom died from enteric, the former at Naauwpoort, No. 6, General Hospital here, and we knew nothing of it until after his interment, although constant enquiries were made at the Hospital. The enteric cases are kept isolated and no one allowed to visit, and I need scarcely say we were extremely sorry not to have buried the poor fellow, the 10th Co. R.E., furnished the burial party. Several of our men have been in Hospital, and some, I hear, are being invalided. I need scarcely say we shall be pleased to see Old England, for there's no place like home and its comforts. His Grace, the Duke, I hear, is due on the 17th. We heard of his resignation and his successor some days since."

No. 27,844, Sapper **John Fallon,** writing from Bloemfontein, April 14th, says:—

"MY DEAR COLOURS,—A few days after the despatch of my last epistle to you, five of us, then at Naauwpoort Junction, received orders to proceed to Bloemfontein, where we arrived on April 1st, at 6 a.m., having done about 250 miles in 18 hours (L.C.D.R. please note). We were all very anxious to reach the Orange Free State capital, and alighted from the saloon (!) at the station with feelings somewhat akin to pride. We at once proceeded to the G.P.O., where a few familiar faces greeted us, and the still more familiar Morse slip 'on the line' seemed to invite our particular attention. The 'click' of perforators, and 'whirr' of the transmitter, recalled *pleasant* memories of home, although it seemed strange not to see someone dashing about with an armful of blue slip trying to bribe people to write it up. Don't think we're quite up to date here yet. The staff is between 40 and 50 strong, and the 24th men are Lance-Cpls. Stevens and Hall (Jack, who has just got the stripe), Sappers Stimpson, Horton, J. Grant, Fallon, Hamer, Milton, Sainsbury, Samuel, Wyatt, Austen, Birch, Poole, R. Stevenson, W. C. Pickford, York, W. Wilson, and Evans. The office is worked in two reliefs, under Corporal Ruffell (TS), and Lance-Corporal

KHAKI LETTERS—*continued.*

Stevens assists the latter N.C.O. Sergeant Nelson is Acting Quarter-Master-Sergeant, and dishes out our pounds of bread and 'pegs' of rum worthy of a professional Most of the staff live in a house (formerly used as a store) adjacent to the office, but some preferred canvas walls to brick, and so a small minority occupy a couple of tents in the grounds of the above house. We have very little spare time, so can't say much as to the merits or otherwise of the surrounding country, but it appears to be far superior to the Colony. Bloemfontein itself is a fairly good sized town, and probably has been a large business centre—some decent shops and hotels, these latter being sacred to officers and civilians. Have not yet had No. 1 of KHAKI LETTERS, but have had a 'surreptuous' squint at a comrade's, and pronounced it 'good 'erbs." We all wish it every success. With best wishes."

✣ ✣ ✣ ✣

No. 4,313, Sapper **S. H. Townsend**, writing from Woodcote Farm, April 15th, says :—

"Just a line to let you know that all is well. Went through baptism of fire last Tuesday at Sundays River. The Boers started shelling camp from Biggarsberg Mountains about 6.30 (breakfast time), and so it continued till nightfall. The telegraph tent had a narrow escape, one shell pitching 40 yards in front of it. Officer in charge told us to take cover, which we promptly did. Didn't want telling twice. Quarter of an hour later had to strike tents. It was marvellous. About 12,000 troops under canvas here and in less than five minutes every tent was struck, except telegraph tent and a few officers' tents. The naval guns got into play and did splendid work. We left Sundays River about midnight, and marched to Elandslaagte. The stench from the dead horses at the last mentioned place was unbearable—as many as 40 on one kopje, and been lying there since last November. After leaving Elandslaagte we marched to Woodcote Farm, Sir Charles Warren's quarters for the present. Plenty of Boer prisoners in camp. Have not had our clothes off since leaving boat at Durban. Some nights have not had our overcoats, and had no covering whatever. It is very hot in day and at night very cold. Sleeping in khaki in open air is no conjure. Don't notice cold when you lay down as one is dead tired, and can drop down anywhere. Only had about 4 hours in Ladysmith. Most of houses and shops have shell marks. Have lot to say, but no more time. This is Easter Sunday—no church parade for us ; been out laying wire all day. . . . Give regards to Colour-Sergeant Kemp. Show him this—will drop him line when time. So long for present. Kind regards to all."

✣ ✣ ✣ ✣

No. 25,362, Sapper **G. W. Bannister** (of MR), stationed at Orange River, writing on Easter Monday, says :—

"DEAR COLOUR-SERGEANT KEMP,—Your letters, dated 2nd and 16th ultimo respectively. Many thanks for news they contained, and also for Nos. 1 and 2 of KHAKI LETTERS to hand. I must compliment you on the 'get up' of the latter. You certainly deserve every praise for your indefatigable efforts to keep our friends in the service posted in the doings of their comrades living in savage South Africa. By the way, that reminds me I saw a certain black lady at De Aar of immense proportions, in fact, worthy of our balloon section, whom the promoters of the Savage South Africa Show at Earl's Court, tried hard to secure for their show, but she could not

KHAKI LETTERS—*continued*.

be induced to leave her native heath for any monetary consideration. When I saw her she was stooping over a wash-tub, and I got a sort of back elevation view. Upon my word, I thought it was a balloon being inflated, and I remember inquiring what time it would go up. Now to matters serious. I expect Wilson gave you all particulars of poor Hawkins' death? It fairly cast a gloom over us. He was buried with full military honours, and we have had a nice cross erected to mark the spot where he is buried. . . . . I hope to be able to send you a photo of it if we stay here long enough. The stationmaster's wife has very kindly promised to photograph it in a day or two. Scarcely a fortnight had elapsed after the event just mentioned, when we lost Sapper W. R. Williams, of PY, after a very short illness. He was present at Hawkins' funeral. I can hardly describe how we all felt then. We buried him near his late comrade. The same chaplain officiated in each case, and I must say I never met a nicer clergyman. He is senior chaplain to the Australian forces. We are having another cross made exactly like the first one, and Woodrow has again undertaken to carve the inscription. I'm glad to say the rest of us keep fairly well. The doctors say the prevalence of so much enteric is due entirely to the water. We are very careful to see that all we consume is boiled now. There is very little doing at this place now, and yesterday two more were withdrawn from our staff for duty at Kimberley—Urquhart (IV), and Dellbridge 'Ponto' (TS). The men left here are Wilson (YH), Catling (EES), Williams (CF), and myself, with two guardsmen (a Scots Guardsman and a Coldstream) and one of the Buffs. There are also two R.E. linemen, Tovey and Edgeler. We work 8 hours duties. We have a black boy to do our cooking and washing. He is a Basuto, and rejoices in the name of 'Fire Basuto.' Yesterday some friends of mine in the 'C' pontoon troop, R.E., stationed at Zoutpans Drift, sent us a haunch of venison (spring-bok). I hear they have fine times at that place now. No Boers about there, so they go out shooting game occasionally—anyway, we had roast venison for dinner to-day. One of the guardsmen makes us lovely plumduffs nearly every day, so we fare very well indeed on the whole. I had a run up to Kimberley about a fortnight after the siege was raised. Found Jones, of Woolwich, there. Miller had retired to roost when I landed. Only had a few hours there. Saw some of the effects of the siege in the shape of houses ventilated by Boer shells. Eglington, of DY, was with me—I picked him up at Belmont. There were a few dead horses still lying about on the battlefield at Belmont, and the stench from them was enough to cause an epidemic. Small wonder fever is so rife among the troops. We saw three vultures gorging themselves on one carcase. From the railway, Magersfontein does not appear very formidable, but one can understand its impregnability after climbing a few kopjes. One of the kopjes at Belmont, which was taken by the Scots Guards, has been named 'Scots Ridge.' On our return journey our train passed through a swarm of locusts. They resembled a snow-storm as much as anything. We also saw several Secretary birds. These birds are getting scarce, and are now protected by law. They feed principally, if not solely, on snakes. The diamond mines at Kimberley resemble our English coal-pits on the surface, except that the deposits are blue. I got some specimens of the quartz. Eglington and I wandered through Kimberley at 1 a.m., in search of an old MR man. We found his address eventually. He gave us his experiences of the siege, which were very interesting. He also shewed us a bomb-proof shelter which had been excavated in the garden. The town guard challenged us several times during

KHAKI LETTERS—*continued.*

our rambles, but as we were in uniform we were allowed to pass on. 'Ponto' and I walked over to Hopetown last week. It is nine miles from here, and a sort of market town for the district. We followed the telegraph line and had rather an exciting time of it, getting over the boot tops in a quagmire at one part of the journey, and endeavouring to keep clear of some wild looking ostriches we saw. Tovey, one of the linemen here, was knocked down and severely assaulted by an ostrich a few weeks ago, as he was re-setting a pole about two miles out from here. They are very savage creatures sometimes, and can kick a good goal every time; they can only kick frontwards, so that it is advisable to take them in the rear when possible. Sambells is stationed at Hopetown, and he had a good dinner ready for us—no less than roast game being among the viands. We had a ride back in the civil doctor's 'rickshaw. I slept on a Dutch farm the other night—went over with a civil clerk from here who speaks Dutch. The people were most hospitable, and everything was spotlessly clean. I fairly enjoyed the luxury of a feather bed. Don't think there is any more news I can tell you at present. We have got some Boer prisoners here. They are continually singing psalms. My relief has just come, so will away to my tent. Again thanking you for your many kindnesses, and with best wishes."

No. 4,315, Sapper **A. H. Morse,** writing on the s.s. "Winifredian" at sea, April 19th, says:—

" .... Last night (18th) we had a fine organised concert in the stern. One fellow sang 'What do you think of the Irish, now?'... I was inoculated when two days out from Las Palmas. I found the officers were being done, so I thought better of it; seven of our fellows were done, including Macmurtrie. It does give you a tying up. I am quite well now. We have two sail baths rigged up, but we prefer to leave them to the other troops. We have the hose turned on us instead. I went to church parade on Good Friday and Easter Sunday. It is a shame the way our things evaporate. I have lost all my writing paper and towels; some have lost their boots and lots have lost money. I have only been sea-sick once, that was in the Bay. On the 11th, in the evening, we came abreast of a steamer about a mile off; we could see her lights plainly. She seemed to be waiting for us. She was on our starboard. All of a sudden she came to port and we went to starboard. She crossed our bows quite close to us and then stopped on our port and we 'stood by.' When I saw her against the sky-line she looked like a turret battleship. I have not heard what she was. Presently she showed a bright white light and then we burned three red lights in succession. That was all the signalling I could see. We both moved off after that. I sleep on deck regularly now. We only stopped at Las Palmas about an hour, as the captain received telegraphic instructions to proceed at once, as men and horses were wanted. It was very funny to watch the swarms of bumboats and the different official pinnaces. I bought 13 bananas for 6d. The hawkers threw up a rope with a basket at the end, which we hauled up. We placed our money in it and lowered it. We watched what they put in it. If we did not think it value we would not haul up. They could not stick to our money or we should have kept their rope, and probably pelted them with ginger-beer bottles. Some fellows bought boxes of cigars, 100 for 3s. The Grand Canary Islands look fine from the sea. We could see the Peak of Teneriffe a very long way off like a cloud. One or two horses die every day.

KHAKI LETTERS—*continued.*

Several have been operated upon for strangles. The vets. put a silver tube in a horse's throat when it has strangles, to assist its breathing. One operation was not successful. They shot the horse after a day or two. It took three revolver shots to completely kill the poor beast. A post-mortem is held on every horse that dies. We have got tired of watching them, now. We have dumb-bells, clubs and boxing gloves at our disposal. The stables are dreadfully hot and stuffy in this climate. I had to go there and grind corn the other day. I am glad I have been inoculated, I feel more confident. .... We tow a barrel or box at the stern for musketry practice. Gambling is about the only pastime on board; you would be amazed to see how much some of the men lose .... One of our men has been in hospital since we left Queenstown, another went in four days ago; several have been in for a day or two. Three weeks on this boat out of sight of the world is like three years at home. We live absolutely too well, now. On the 18th, in the morning, we sighted a steamer. She made for us, then stood off, then made for us again. We thought she was coming for us. She got pretty close then signalled us to send a boat, which, amid great excitement we did. She only wanted to give us some newspapers and news from Capetown. Very kind of her, but I don't think our C.O. appreciated it, as we were in a hurry. She was the 'Salamis' of Aberdeen, I believe she is a New Zealand mail boat. The passengers waved their handkerchiefs and we gave them three cheers; we were on parade at the time. A fountain pen and bottle of ink would be very useful to me. We had a thunder storm on Good Friday; there was some fine lightning. There are heaps of flying fish about; one came aboard and we caught it, it was about eight inches long. I was on 'sentry go' again on the 19th. April 21st.—It's a bit cold sleeping on deck now. We have to give in our letters this morning. I do not know why, because we are not in sight of land. There is a fine full-rigged sailing ship on our port bow just at present. It's a fortnight to-morrow that we left Las Palmas. Last night we did a lot of signalling to an unseen ship in the dark. We don't know where we are going to land. I am cook's mate to-day. My overcoat has evaporated. I shall have to pay for it if it does not turn up again."

❖ ❖ ❖ ❖

No. 4,363, Sapper **W. G. Carter,** on board the "Winifredian," writing on April 19th, says :—

"We are getting close to the end of this monotonous though fine voyage, and no doubt a few particulars of it will be interesting to yourself and a few of the 'L.' We left Southampton 1st April, Sunday, with a good send-off, and reached Queenstown April 3rd, and sailed again the same evening with another splendid send-off, almost every house in the place displaying a sheet, handkerchief, or something to wave, and a lot of bonfires and torches were lit, and as the place is built on the side of a hill we could see almost everything. The Munster Fusiliers came aboard at Queenstown, they being Section 'D' of the Reserve and Militia. They all came on board more or less drunk, as they had travelled from Limerick, so three of them went to the clink. They are very Irish, we can't properly read them. After leaving Queenstown we went across into the Bay of Biscay, and there we had a good roughing of it. Although this is a splendid ship, she rolled something awful, it was next to impossible to keep a footing, and when at meals, you had to hold everything to keep it from sliding away. It rolled so much that fellows slid down the forms of their mess. We reached Las Palmas Sunday,

KHAKI LETTERS—*continued.*

8th April, and we could see the mountains about an hour before reaching the coast. It was a grand sight, the town being one mass of low white buildings. Several large ships were in the bay, and a lot of native boats came out to sell fruit, but we could not get much as we did not stop as long as we expected. A British man-of-war sent out a cutter and evidently had important instructions, for we up anchor and away at once, and we expected to stop 24 hours. Since then we have had a lovely voyage, having nothing to do but one guard per week, of 24 hours each, other time was spent lying about the deck and playing cards. It was very hot in the tropics, and at the Equator we paraded with no shoes, or socks, or coats. When we first started the food, to us, was wicked, although the troops said it was fine. About the second or third day, when the officer came round we reported we could not eat the meat, he tried to cut it, and after trying hard managed it, and said 'Well, it is rather tough, but if you can't eat it you must bolt it.' Anyhow, after leaving Queenstown we paid 1s. per man per day, and went off the troop mess into a special mess by the chief steward, and after, we had steak, or ham and eggs for breakfast, three and sometimes four courses for dinner, and always meat or fish for tea, so that we live like fighting cocks. Several of ours were sea-sick, but I was not. Only 8 out of 46 of us were innoculated, including myself, and this partly laid us up for a couple of days. Plumridge has been in hospital four days from heat stroke, but is now all right again. I shall be pleased to get on land again and see some of the TS chaps and to hear the news. We passed a liner a couple of days ago, and both of us pulled up and we sent a boat out, and the passengers aboard her collected their newspapers and sent them to us, but the latest date of them was April 5th, and they said that the relief of Mafeking was expected every hour. We do not know whether we land at Capetown or elsewhere, but I hope it is Capetown. Must close, as letters are to be ready to-morrow, as we are going to stop and give them to the Cape mail if we pass her. Best wishes."

No. 4,333, Sapper **A. W. York,** sends the following from Bloemfontein, April 20th :—

"Dear Colour-Sergeant Kemp,—The great trek of Lord Roberts' column has not come off yet, consequently I am still in the town office here, where my section had orders to report on the 7th inst., the staff already here being very short-handed, while the delay was two or three days on military work, and more on private telegrams, a state of affairs which was soon changed, though even now there is far more delay than would be allowed at home. This is due to the fact that many wires are cut, and our only outlet is a well-guarded single wire to Kimberley, which is running slip day and night. We moved our tents to the garden of a commandeered house in order to be near the office, as the hours are very long, viz., midnight to 7 a.m., 2 p.m. to midnight one day and 7 a.m. to 2 p.m. next day. Our neighbours were Scotch people, who were very glad the British occupied the town, and their little children prattle merrily to us over the garden wall, often finding eggs for the tent. Greig is at Edenburg, Swan and A. J. Brooks at Springfontein, Arundel and Clark at Karee Siding, Campbell at Kaffir River. We have fine walks to the surrounding camps on our mornings off, and usually end by ascending a kopje, on many of which the R.E.'s may be seen at work building fortifications, while at the top there are artillery camps, and the heliograph is busy by day, giving place to the signal lamps at night.

KHAKI LETTERS—*continued*.

Hardly know what to make of the weather, one day is dull and cold, the next scorchingly hot, while frost is often seen in the early morning; and besides this, there are frequent thunderstorms, when all the dry spruits and watercourses become rushing torrents, the whole accompanied by vast sheets of lightning. The town is a little more bearable now that supplies have arrived, and it is possible to get jam, milk, and other little luxuries to add to the *simple* fare provided by the War Department, and another gratifying feature is that people are returning to their homes, quite a large assembly of townspeople mustering to hear the massed bands play on Easter Monday, this constituting the only relaxation Tommy had this Eastertide. I had a batch of letters on Good Friday, but nothing from you so far. At Communion in the little Cathedral on Sunday there was a very crowded assembly of soldiers of all ranks, including several generals and the Commander-in-Chief, who wore not a single decoration, and looked sad. The service was enjoyable, and the thought of all my friends at home doing exactly the same thing was very pleasant. No doubt you have read of the grand concert we had on the 17th, it was most enjoyable, and highly appreciated by the troops. I kept up the old custom on Easter Day by donning a new suit of khaki; later on, I parted with my moustache and a three week's beard, and as most of my hair left me at De Aar there are very few spots for the sand and dust to lodge in. Afraid you won't find this letter very exciting, but my imagination is not so vivid as some of the correspondents' to the home papers."

P.S.—Awfully pleased with KHAKI LETTERS just to hand. It is a splendid little book, please accept our gratitude. Pickford, Thomas (EH), Grant (AB), Evans (CF), Milton, Birch, Wilson, Fallon, Hall, Poole (IV), Horton (BM), Stimpson, Sainsbury, Quarmby (HF), Hamer, Wyatt (GY), and Sergeant Nelson, still here.

N.B.—A. W. York has been taken prisoner.

✧ ✧ ✧ ✧

No. 4,317, Sapper **G. H. Pickford,** 2nd Telegraph Division R.E., writing from Bloemfontein April 21st, says:—

"You will see by above that I've reached the Capital of the Free State. Hope soon to be in the Capital of the Transvaal, at least by the time this reaches you I shall doubtless be on the way. We are waiting anxiously now for the order to shift. Roberts is all ready, and it's rumoured the Column leaves next week, if so we go with it. We had a splendid journey out, stayed at Cape Town a few days (there saw my brother and Capon), then went to De Aar, and from there straight on here, the journey altogether taking four days by rail. The last two days we were in open goods trucks Am rather disappointed with South Africa, it's nothing to what I anticipated, instead of the lovely scenery you hear about, it's nothing but kopjes and barren ground. It's winter here now and the nights are intensely cold, although at mid-day the sun is scorching. It gets dark about 5.30 p.m. as soon as the sun sets, there's no twilight. Its a most infernal dear place here. Beer, 4s. a bottle, whisky, 17s. 6d., minerals, 9d., but owing to martial law being in force it's unobtainable by the troops. So you can guess what a sober and silent lot we are. Bread 1s. a loaf, no butter, jam, cheese, &c., obtainable at any price. Stores, however, are expected in a few days. Two train loads on the way at present time from Cape Town. Old Duke is here with me and looks fine in a beard. We are doing on average about 12 hours daily here, working Wheatstone to Kimberley, Ruffell is in charge. Ta, ta, kindest regards."

KHAKI LETTERS—*continued*.

No. 4,328, Sapper **W. V. Wheller**, Surprise Hill Camp, near Ladysmith, April 21st, writes as follows :—

"DEAR OLD KEMP,—Excuse the familiar form of address, but we usually think of you as 'dear old Kemp' in preference to the more formal 'Colour-Sergt.' The mounted linesman brought me out two K.L.'s from Headquarters this morning, so I feel l must just drop you a line. Charlie Minors wrote to you from the 'Cephalonia,' did he not? so I suppose he told you all about it. How we fared with our gallant militia friends. God help the Boers if they meet with the Queen's militia. Their language would play more havoc than Lyddite. To be brief, we anchored off Table Bay about a week overdue, to wit, March 21st, Wednesday. Personally, first impressions of Table Bay and Mountain were disappointing. It was in vain that those 'in the know' reminded me Table Mountain was such and such a level above the sea ; it didn't look half so imposing as I had dreamt it to be. We transferred to the 'Antillian' on Monday, March 26th (more delay), and arrived at Durban, Monday, April 2nd. Disembarked on Tuesday, April 3rd, and entrained for Ladysmith. We had a right royal send-off from Durban, the Colonials were most warm hearted. The country as far as Pietermaritzburg was glorious, deep green valleys and high and towering kopjes, and the windings in and out. Now the guard's van would seem parallel to the engine, and again we would appear to be going to exactly where we came from. Now and again the engine stopped for water, and we would be met by little knots of locals who would give us tea, fruit, etc., One place I must mention specially, I think the name was 'Gilletts.' A whole family met us here, and one lady took a photo of a group of the boys, and whilst she was doing it Mackness snapshotted her, amidst laughter. One little toddler, aged about six, gave me a bunch of flowers which I promised to send home with their love to Old England, but alas, I lost the flowers. At Pietermaritzburg we had tea and bread (butter was reported to be there, but scouts failed to locate him). This was about 7 p.m. From thence we started on our long weary and uneventful ride to Ladysmith. Carriages *à la* Chatham and no lights, save one or two candles surreptitiously procured. We passed Mooi River, Estcourt and Colenso, all in the dead o' night, and reached Ladysmith just at dawn. After a picnicky breakfast in the station yard, of bully beef and biscuits, we were marched to the Headquarter Camp on the hill by the Convent. Ladysmith is the third largest town in Natal (*vide* Colonial Guide), to an Englishman it looks suspiciously like a well-to-do village, with a fairly decent Town Hall and Market Square. On the authority of the said Guide, I may inform you that the town has a population of about 3,000 whites and 2,000 blacks. It is quite surrounded by hills, and the fact that White kept the enemy out, speaks volumes for his courage and persistence. Long Tom on Bulwana faces directly over the town, and well manipulated this gun could have put the place in flames under the hour. I am glad to say, however, that despite Mr. Kruger's prayer that God would direct the Boer shots, Ladysmith escaped with much less damage than was anticipated. The Town Hall had its dome knocked in. Wounded were being treated there at the time, and the Red Cross flag was flying, which was, to say the least, an ugly coincidence for the pious Uncle Paul. There are few nice shops in Ladysmith, about four or five real shops, and say a dozen or so small shoplets. The real shops seem to be chiefly in the possession of Hindoos, and of course the usual way of shopping is to offer half the prescribed figure. Everything is very dear there, small pots of jam a shilling, condensed milk 9d. and 1s., in fact if you take the English prices

KHAKI LETTERS—*continued.*

and double them, you will have a fair idea of what we are charged. Immediately on arrival we began to be split up for the various camps. Sinclair, Mackness, Townsend, Chubbock, Leaver, Collins, and several Provincials, left the same day for Sundays River, near Elandslaagte, and day by day little dribbles were sent out. I had a fortnight at Headquarters. The first week I was on general work, and you would have laughed to see me, perspiring profusely, trotting over the veldt with a sledge hammer, or holding on for grim death to an air line wagon, and trying to imagine I enjoyed it better than the E Group, with the gals we left behind us. The next week I was put in the Headquarter telegraph tent, and we had to work fairly hard at times, night duty and three or four hours a day as well I managed to get. On Wednesday last I was sent to this little camp. We have an ordinary bell tent with one buzzer. Have you seen a buzzer? Pardon the question. It's a kind of a technical mule, a cross between a telegraph and a telephone. We may be here only a few days or we may be here a couple of weeks. There are two clerks and two orderlies. The other clerk is a regular R.E., the two orderlies belong to the Devons. We were all grieved to hear of poor Hawkins' death. Poor old Tommy Atkins gets a rough time from dysentery and enteric. Each night at Headquarters we used to see the bullock waggon go by the camp with its little load of English dead, who were to help fill the nameless graves that abound here. All that was left to them of home, was the Union Jack that covered them. Now, dear old Kemp, I must conclude. Your printed envelopes are a grand idea. Kindest regards to the old Corps."

No. 4,321, Sapper **J. A. Brown,** writing from Star Hill Camp, Ladysmith, April 22nd, says :—

"DEAR COLOUR-SERGEANT KEMP,—I write to thank you very much for KHAKI LETTERS, received yesterday morning, and which I very much appreciate. No doubt you have had our journey out described by others of 'Cephalonia' party long before this, so I will leave that. Arrived at Ladysmith, I was told off with others for the front—Sundays River—but changed over with Jeffrey, so that he could go with his pal Leaver. Next morning I was sent up here, about four miles from Ladysmith, which is Headquarters. We have a sounder and a buzzer to Ladysmith, with Pounds Plateau an intermediate station, and are fairly busy. There are only two of us here, C. Barnes, of Exeter, being in charge. Was with Lord Dundonald's 3rd Mounted Brigade the first two days, but am now with General Burn-Murdoch, 1st Cavalry Brigade. Everything is quiet here. The only excitement we have had was about a week ago, when a private in 5th Lancers came into camp 10 o'clock at night, breathless, and said Boers had passed our pickets at Bester's Farm, nine miles away, taken his horse and carbine, and were coming on. He hid for two hours, and escaped under darkness. They made enquiries and found it was not right. There was a terrible thunderstorm that night, so I suppose it upset the poor chap. It also upset us, as our tent-pole (which was one taken from the Boers) snapped in the middle, and down came the tent—wires got entangled, and communication upset for hour and a half. It was pouring at the time, so we had it lively for a while. . . . Am all right myself up to the present, trusting you are all the same. Kind regards to all."

KHAKI LETTERS—*continued*.

The following welcome letter will be read with much satisfaction by the whole of the Service, especially by the C.T.O. members who have so anxiously awaited replies to two telegrams of enquiry :—

No. 23,610, Sergeant **R. C. Luttrell**, writing from No. 2 Stationary Hospital, East London (undated, received June 8th), says :—

"You will see by the above address that I have at last got to the Convalescent hospital at East London, I am sitting up in bed to write this, and the doctor actually says I may get up this afternoon and sit outside in the sun. Of course I can't walk—at least, shall be carried out. This is a much nicer hospital. It is like one of those large exhibition buildings, all made of galvanised iron, on wooden supports. It is divided by partitions into big rooms containing four rows of beds ; each row is called a ward. I'm in No. 6. We have nice beds, with mosquito nets hanging by a string from the rafters, which go all round you at night to keep off the little pests, which are very numerous here. I left Sterkstroon on Tuesday afternoon, at 5 p.m., just missing tea. I was the last but one to be carried out to the train, and got put on a hard horsehair shelf. Oh, how my poor bones did ache. No tea, too! The train started immediately we were aboard. I tried to sleep, but could not lie in any position, till I thought 'well, I will roll one of my blankets up and put under my hips. So I got the orderly to fold it for me, and found much relief. You see my hip bones and elbows are nearly through the flesh. I asked the sister before I left what I had suffered from. She says, 'Well, Luttrell, you have had a very bad attack of enteric fever, with malarial fever intermixed, and you are a lucky man to be where you are.' Well, the train sped on till we got to a place called Queenstown. Here some ladies came in with tea and bread and butter. They wouldn't let me have any, though. Just after, a fellow came along with an egg flip. He offered me one—it was lovely. A little while afterwards the lady came back with more egg flips. The doctor says, 'You may have one.' So I had it. After that settled down for the night, and slept till 3 a.m. We got here at 9 a.m., and into bed at 10.30, quite done up. A few minutes after they brought me a steaming basin of Bovril—soon brought me round. Only got milk that day—one tin of sterilized milk and two bottles of soda to last till morning. But at dinner time I saw them bring round hot fresh milk. I asked for some, and got my basin filled with rice and milk. Got another dose at 8 o'clock, when I drew the net and went to sleep till 1 a.m., then had some milk and soda and slept from 3 a.m. till 6 p.m. They served me out with 1 lb. bread to-day, so had bread and milk. This is the first solid food for five weeks and four days. But oh! I am looking forward to to-morrow, for I am going to have *chicken* and *potatoes* for dinner. 'Roll on to-morrow,' says I. On my board there is a huge **E**, which the orderly tells me means I shall be sent home as soon as I am fit to travel. Now, of course, I don't know if it's true. Your telegram only reached me on Monday afternoon. I can't tell when you sent it, but it had been all over the country to find me. If you only had put Sterkstroom it might have come direct. . . . I couldn't reply, because they take away your money and only give it back when you are discharged from hospital, so I haven't a halfpenny just now. Haven't had any letters lately, but expect them all in a heap presently. I will write a long account of what a hospital train is like when I get stronger, which I am doing every day."

✤ ✤ ✤ ✤

KHAKI LETTERS—*continued*.

No. 802, Sapper **A. Ray**, 1st T. B. R.E., undated, Naauwpoort writes :—

"DEAR COLOURS,—I've had so many letters from you, and written so few, I'm trying my fist once more. I dunno' if you've heard I've been sick. I succumbed to the salubrious smells of carcases round Colesberg, and caught typhoid fever (which doctors say is the same as enteric). Anyway I hung on for about a week, and at last when I felt a bit better went to the doctor to get something for my appetite. He promptly seized me after taking my temperature and told me I'd have to go to Naauwpoort hospital. This I refused to do, and as a compromise I agreed to go under him for a day or two and see how I got on. I went into the only hospital they had, a dirty room about twelve feet square, and after three days of dirt and mud, and of feeted orderlies' stamping and shouting, I was glad to get to NO. I was to go by the 1.30 train, which arrived at 6.30, and after shunting backwards and forwards at the station and nearly killing us, eventually left at 2 a.m. and arrived NO at 4.30 a.m. I was in the fever ward for five weeks. I don't remember much of the first week, but after a fortnight began to mend. Of the doctors and sisters one can't speak too highly. Their attention and kindness to every want were unremitting. I can tell you a month on milk took all the stuffing out of me. I'm now in the convalescent ward and am going to Capetown to-morrow almost for certain, and after about a week or so shall be invalided home. I've lost all the strength I had and can now, after being up near a week, only walk about 100 yards, and that tires me out for the day. I expect I shall be home almost as soon as you get this. Wright at NO office comes and sees me and brings letters every two or three days, and you can guess a visitor is very welcome. Don't think there's any more news, but if I was ill again I wouldn't wish to be looked after better than they have done here. Good-bye for present, and kind regards to any pals in I Co., and of course to yourself."

Quartermaster-Sergeant **A. E. Capon,** R.A.M.C. (of C.T.O.), writing from No. 5, General Hospital, Woodstock, South Africa, May 7th, says :—

"DEAR COLOUR-SERGEANT KEMP,—Have just finished reading No. 3 of your KHAKI LETTERS, which some kind friend has been good enough to send out to me from TS. Was very pleased to see it, and I think it a very good idea indeed, as I well know how interesting it is to receive news of office chums far away in South Africa. What also struck me as a good idea was that registered address 'Poniard, London,' perhaps I might be of some use this end, as Wynberg Hospital, Rondebosch Hospital and my own Hospital are within six miles of each other, and as they are the Base Hospitals of South Africa they receive all the serious cases, and no doubt it would be some consolation to any poor unfortunate 24th man's friends and relations to know there is someone handy on the spot to do anything that was possible to be done for him in hospital. A friend of mine at Wynberg has promised to let me know if any 24th men are admitted to hospital, and I should hear at once if any were admitted here, and you may depend on me doing anything that was possible for me to do to any unfortunate TS chum that was admitted to hospital. The Base Depôt of the R.E.'s is just the other side of our camp, and I have had the pleasure of seeing the last two parties of the 24th arrive and depart, Winkle, Pickford, George, Hudson were in the 1st; Pearce, Frew, Barber, Plumbridge, Jarvis, &c., were in the 2nd. Frew and Jarvis went to Kimberley, the rest went to Bloemfontein, I went round to have a look at them soon after they arrived. I found them all gay, but considering they were packed sixteen in a tent, two kit bags, water bottle, haversack, and valise each, you may be sure they were not very comfortable, so I invited four to sleep in my tent every night, they say they haven't been so comfortable since leaving England. Am looking out for the next batch I hear are coming. Well, ta, ta, Colours, kind regards to all TS chums. Have any amount of work here, 700 patients in this hospital, and we haven't even the satisfaction of knowing we are at the front."

Khaki Sidelights.

No. 24,816, Sapper **A. S. Rudd,** 1st Tel. Battn. R.E., writes April 17th, from Norvals Pont, O.F.S. :—

"We have been at this place since March 15th. It is the terminus—or rather, was—of the Cape Government Railway, and is just this side of the Orange River, the other side being the Orange Free State. There are about thirty houses occupied by the railway employees, but the station is the most important part of the place. We are fixed in the general waiting room and work to Bloemfontein, Springfontein and Bethany, on one circuit, and to Naauwpoort on the other. When we first arrived here, and in fact up to a week ago, we were continually blocked up with work, but now that nearly all the troops have passed through here into the State the work has fallen off wonderfully. Several of the fellows have gone on to BFN from here, but your humble, with Jim Creasey (News), and three other clerks still remain, presumably for the protection of Norvals Pont. To tell you the truth, chum, I am 'fed right up' with Africa. It's a lovely country—for Kaffirs and other heathens—but for civilised, intelligent, white, blue-blooded gentlemanly TS Telegraphists, it 'ain't *not* no class.' I don't think I will attempt even an outline of my 'goings on,' simply because I have been in no great battles or sieges, or hand-to-hand encounters. Once, it is true, I was surrounded by Boers, not ten yards away from me, and my waistcoat (beg pardon, ain't got one), I meant my *chest,* fills with pride, as I relate it (I am so modest), but there were no casualties as they were prisoners on the platform. We work to Metcalfe and Jimmy Brookes, who are at Springfontein, Govier is at De Aar, Orwin, I believe, has been sent to the Cape, Minors and Jeffreys I haven't seen, but hear they are in Natal. I am glad to say that I've been in grand health myself ever since I left home. Have seen several celebrities since we have been here, amongst them Lord Kitchener, General Gatacre, the Turkish Attaché (jewelled in forty places), Rudyard Kipling, Winston Churchill, Sir Ashmead Bartlett, Melton Prior, Bennett Burleigh, and the biggest gun of all I see every day—in the looking glass (mind the step!).

"Did a bit of mountaineering the other day, ascended to the summit of Norvals Kopje (the highest round here), but shan't try it again. The summit is 4000 feet above the level of the sea—(mind you, this place, Norval's Pont, stands very high itself). The next day I suffered excruciating pains all over, particularly in the calves and thighs. Was assured it would 'do me good,' but never no more. Thought of going to the Alps when I came home, but shall go fishing in the Grand Surrey Canal instead. The weather here now is getting comparatively cold. Day after day it is very dull and wet, and the nights are very chilly. I saw the loveliest sunset last night that it is possible to imagine ; in fact to those who have not been abroad, it is impossible to imagine anything so glorious. You must take my word for it, we stood enthralled, as no man could ever describe it. I saw one at sea, which was magnificent, but this beat it by streets, and yet we had scarcely seen the sun during the day. A notice has been put up by the Commandant that in case the Camp be attacked by the enemy, the whole of the troops (and civilians capable of bearing arms) are to assemble at a certain spot with arms and ammunition, in order to defend the Camp. Exactly—quite so. Noted. I am going to find the shortest route to the cellar under the Refreshment Bar. Good people are none too plentiful, and it wouldn't do to let the enemy get into the wine cellar, would it?

"We are living very well indeed out here now; the best day's menu we had last week was—kidneys for breakfast, roast leg of mutton and plum pudding for dinner, jam and marmalade for tea. Not so bad for active service, eh? (What do you mean, Micky Welch, '*and then you woke'?*) Our Cook made a duff yesterday of Boer Meal (Indian Corn ground), and covered it with jam and himself with glory. It was A 1. Kindest regards to all the boys. Thank everybody for their kindness to the 'absent-minded bounder,' and his dear ones at home.

"Roll on the big ship, and 'after eight.' Yours."

✤ ✤ ✤ ✤

"The Regiment" says :—

"The Signal Corps of the American Army have adopted electric automobiles in the Philippines. The waggons are of two sorts, one for carrying instruments and materials, the other for the *personnel.* The first is like a covered ambulance, with rubber-tyred wheels, and is driven by accumulators charged for 30 hours' work with a load of 1,500 lbs. Two motors, each of 3½ horse-power, drive the two rear wheels. The second waggon is a high cart, but in other respects like the first. Both have electric lamps inside and at the sides."

"Khaki Notes."

To all concerned.—I desire to heartily thank friends generally for the many kind letters of encouragement and congratulations I am constantly receiving. I suppose I could extract sufficient matter from them to fill more than a 20-page booklet. It has often struck me that I am a bit of a culprit when I leave them unanswered. I would gladly reply to all if I could, but owing to pressure such a thing is impossible, therefore I must tender my most sincere thanks by this means, in case any who have so expressed themselves should think their words of cheer have not been appreciated. There are others who back their appreciation by a bit of bright metal. They recognise the fact that every man at the front is receiving a copy of KHAKI LETTERS free, and that this and the postage runs away with over a sovereign per issue. Such help from "outsiders" (excuse the term) has not been sought, but should there be other friends similarly inclined—but afraid by timidity to offer it—they are welcome to relieve their feelings as much as they choose by sending to me their mites for the "Khaki Postage Fund." Why not? I should be sorry to say "Don't."—and I cannot, really I cannot, say "Do." I will acknowledge all such assistance in my Notes. NOTE—I will start now:—

Khaki Postage Fund.—Thanks are tendered to R. E. D., 5s.; A. J. B., 5s.; G. S. W., 2s. 6d.; J. B., 2s.; and several others for smaller sums.

According to promise.—After the C.T.O. had subscribed to the K.P.F., the Provincial and District men were notified that their turn would come. It is not necessary for me to repeat that all the men have copies sent them, and the *all* means Provincial and London men alike. Will readers—other than of the C.T.O.—therefore kindly see what they can do in this matter, and send in by July 13th.

A repeated request.—Will those friends who are supplying their chums at the front with KHAKI LETTERS kindly inform me. Duplicate copies need not be sent. They may retain the pleasure of sending, I will retain the copy.

Many Letters that arrive from the front are eagerly opened and read, but in so doing the envelopes are torn and thrown on one side or allowed to wear until mutilated. A use can be found for them.

Mr. G. G. Stroud, of the B Div., who is, I need hardly say, one of the best known Philatelists in TS, is willing to dispose of any stamps, postcards or envelopes that may reach our readers from the seat of war, and will hand all proceeds to me for the War Fund. Entire envelopes are much sought after, because of the interest afforded by the various Field Post Office Cancellations. Will our readers kindly communicate direct to him, please.

Our Officials at the seat of war have been so pestered from all parts of the world for the VRI stamps, that a stereotyped reply has been prepared declining to supply, saying they can only be procured in the ordinary way, namely, over the counter.

Correction.—Re design on Colonial Stamp the name should have been Mr. E. A. Sturman, an old 24ther (known as "Jack" Sturman), and not as previously stated.

Commandeering with a vengeance.—I have just received a letter from one of "Ours" at Bloemfontein, enclosed in a private envelope of my own. Undoubtedly annexed by the sender before leaving TS. Be sure your sins will find you out.

Copies of "Khaki Letters" have found their way from the front to friends in London, who in their turn have written notes of congratulation.

"The Sapper" is the organ of the Royal Engineers, and is published at 3d.—by post 4d.—from Brompton Barracks, Chatham. I have it, and can recommend it to all who wish to know more about our good friends the "Royals." *The Sapper* and KHAKI LETTERS side by side give all the news of the Telegraphists at the front.

The Loss of the "Mexican," I have every reason to believe, debarred us from receiving many letters from our boys.

The First British Flag hoisted in the Transvaal proved to be the well-known White and Blue—Telegraph Office—Flag of the Royal Engineers. This was at Cawood's Hope, and the lucky R.E.'s were Corpl. Arthur, Sapper Horn, and our own boy, Sapper W. C. Smith, of TS. Good!

It would be difficult to find a more suitable Volunteer for hospital duty than our friend, Quartermaster-Sergeant A. E. Capon, and we gladly look to him for news from time to time. His kind offer to one and all is highly appreciated.

Sapper Metcalfe.—Poor Met.'s relatives have written me asking for letters, belongings, etc., or any last wish that he may have expressed, to be sent them. They also want a photo of where he was buried, if it is possible. Can any of our boys assist?—for the sake of one we all admired.

"The Bloemfontein Friend" on May 1st assumed the title of "Bloemfontein Post." It is as interesting as ever. Its pages contain a much enlarged list of " parcels to be claimed."

Unintelligible.—On May 31st, " Poniard, London," received the following cablegram from Capetown, dated 30.5.00, 3.45 p.m., "Manning Hospital Woodstock dangerously ill Enteric fever." Every enquiry has been made for Manning, he is not known in the Telegraph Reserves or the A.P.O.C. Later: There are two Mannings in the R.E.'s, but neither are in the Telegraph Divisions. The telegram has evidently been mis-sent.

Sapper J. S. Tough, 24386, about whom so much mystery has been manifest, is I am pleased to say, reported to be improving.

Sapper H. Stormer, 211, arrived at Aldershot on June 10th, having been invalided home. Visitors report "he is looking well." Glad Bertie is better.

Sapper A. W. York, 4333 (of TS), together with Capt. O. T. O. K. Webber, and a 734 Sapper Hutchinson, was on May 22nd taken prisoner at Heilbron. Our men are thus going in for all kinds of disasters. We hope our comrade will simply "march past" Uncle Paul, with "eyes right," and a wink of recognition—just to say he has seen Oom, and then rejoin his Signalling Squad at the favourite call "C.I." (come in).

Roodeval Disaster, June 7th.—Amongst those wounded are two men of the A.P.O.C. and one Imperial telegraphist, names not given.

Pte. A. E. Prebble, 279, A.P.O.C., died at Newcastle, May 19th. Enteric.

Pte. E. F. Howes, 333, A.P.O.C., died at Bloemfontein, May 25th. Enteric.

At the moment of going to press we learn, with deep regret, the sad death of an old and greatly esteemed TS friend, Mr. H. W. Allaway, late Assistant Superintendent, who was pensioned in February, 1898. After bidding one of his sons good-bye last Friday, at Tilbury, he was taken ill, conveyed to the Infirmary, and expired the same evening, June 8th. Cause, heart disease.

Will friends who receive letters from the front kindly advise me of the movements of our colleagues, please!

Most of our Ex-R.E.'s have gone on home service for 12 months. Names and dates, please!

"Poniard, London."—For telegrams from the Cape regarding 24th Middlesex R. E. Reserves and others who may be known to us. All comrades should register their addresses with W. Payne, Esq., Moorgate Street Buildings, E.C. Don't fail to do this.

"Casualties, Capetown."—For telegrams to the Cape. Enquiries respecting the sick and wounded, etc.

COLOURS.

"KHAKI LETTERS," One Penny. By post, Three Halfpence.

All posted letters containing Remittances, Orders, MSS., &c., must be addressed to R. E. KEMP, 12, JERRARD STREET, LEWISHAM, S.E.

Postal Orders should be made payable at Loampit Vale, Lewisham, S.E.

Printed by E. G. BERRYMAN & SONS, *Blackheath Road, London, S.E.*

"Khaki Letters" from . . . .
"My Colleagues in South Africa."

CORRESPONDENCE FROM THE
POST OFFICE TELEGRAPHISTS
OF THE
24th MIDDLESEX (P.O.) RIFLE VOLUNTEERS
(Royal Engineer Reserves),
ON ACTIVE SERVICE.

THE BOND THAT BINDS US—FRIENDSHIP—COMRADESHIP.

Published fortnightly for the Postal Telegraph Service.
Conducted by COLOUR-SERGEANT R. E. KEMP, *Central Telegraph Office, London.*

Nos. 11 & 12.　　　JUNE 29TH, 1900.　　　PRICE TWOPENCE.

Central Telegraph Office,
London, E.C.

DEAR COMRADES, ONE AND ALL.

Greetings. With this issue of our little book, we find we have completed the first dozen numbers, and by your kind co-operation in the matter of correspondence, we hope to successfully continue to compile them. We are pleased to hear of your journeyings and experiences, and we encourage you to go on chronicling your adventures in the same happy fashion as heretofore. I thank you all for your many letters and kind expressions contained in them. I need not repeat that it is a pleasure to me to be of some service to you, and in this work a goodly number of friends are kept posted in the doings of Our Boys. I often wish I could do it much better, and more worthy of the company I am in communication with, but it is done with the best of motives and as a duty—a duty to fill in a gap that might have been overlooked.

Then there are my old friends " the Royals," as we have called them, I scarcely mention them in my booklet. They are old favourites of mine, and doubly so because they are chums of yours. Their doings are not detailed in this little book —" it seems hard."—They, however, read KHAKI LETTERS, I am told, and if they read this copy let me welcome them, and the more the merrier. I might tell them that I very closely watch their doings, and no one more appreciatively, perhaps, but you cannot get a quart of aerated water into a pint pot, and it's often more than I can do to deal with the 24thers. I read about them in their *Sapper, that* is their paper, while KHAKI LETTERS is ours. The sole (soul) object I have in view is to keep touch with our own, to attempt to do more would enlarge the field of labour to an unwieldy extent. You will, however, find one letter in " Sidelights " from a good old " Royal."

Well, comrades, you will notice there are many changes taking place. I compile these little notes for your special edification and interest as most of you know the actors personally. The little bit about the R.E.'s and their many units, I thought would amuse you. Although the writer seems to know all about it, he doesn't mention many specialities with which the Corps deal. For instance—photography, lithography, printing, &c.

Letters from Las Palmas, sent by the "Montrose" men, report they are going on well. You will find many fresh faces amongst them, with just a sprinkling of those whom you know.

We are getting near Camp time now, and all members are anxious to know how they are going on for their leave. The only note in orders up to now is a par. in the issue of June 23rd. It is as follows:—

All married Non-commissioned Officers and men proceeding to Camp must be prepared to supply dates of marriage and birth of children (if any). This information will be called for later.

A soft brown hat will be issued for wear in Camp with the Khaki Uniform, as a protection against the sun.

Hereafter there will be no thin red line, but a line of mud-colour. Khaki will be the real soldier's dress, scarlet, blue, and the time-honoured decorations will be his Sunday and holiday attire. "Khaki," says the *Daily Mail*, "is to be the hat of the future, and, moreover, it is to be of a type unknown in history. No more nor less than a khaki billycock hat is the War Office answer to the disaster at Aldershot. Tommy in a billycock hat will be a feature of the London streets as soon as Lord Roberts has put an end to the South African campaign. Also, the billycock is likely to carry with it a species of awning, carried on whalebone rafters and projecting from the novel helmet. That, of course, is only for field-days and days of exposure to the sun." Several regiments have already adopted the new head-dress, and they look remarkably smart. Another little matter that may interest you is appended:—

Re the Regimental Journals. *The Naval and Military Record* says:—"The war is responsible for the temporary suspension of many enterprising and well-conducted journals. Their editors, sub-editors, reporters, and contributors are away at the front, having had perforce to lay down the pen and take up the sword. The journals in question are the organs of the various regiments of the British Army. With their editors climbing up kopjes and their sub-editors digging trenches, it is hardly to be wondered at that the regimental journals have not 'come out.' The regimental journals of the army are, in very many instances, admirable examples of good editing, good writing, and good printing. Not every regiment, of course, indulges in the luxury of a journal; nevertheless, the regimental papers total up to a very good muster indeed. The 'Fighting Fifth' have for years issued an admirable paper in the *St. George's Gazette*, and the Royal Engineers publish *The Sapper*. Space, however, forbids the enumeration of all the papers published by British regiments. The regimental paper is usually edited by a commissioned officer, who draws his sub-editor from the non-commissioned ranks. The paper gives in terse, humourous fashion all the news and happenings in the battalion. There is, as a rule, an accredited reporter in each company, who contributes to each issue news pars and barrack-room facetiæ. Births, marriages, and deaths in the battalion are duly recorded, football and cricket results are given, regimental 'hops' and diversions are described with eloquence, and the regimental satirist lashes out at all and sundry. Commanding Officers are invariably good friends to the regimental journal. A line in print will shame a laggard company into the most heroic efforts of industry. It is notorious that in one gallant regiment a whole company 'went teetotal' on the strength of a sarcastic line in the regimental paper."

And the Semi-Official Journals. The *Tyro Trumpeter* in an inspired article says:—"The war is responsible for the existence of 'an enterprising and well conducted journal'—(so say the numerous subscribers whose weighty words would turn the scale at nothing less than 7 cwt.) the reporters and contributors of which are away at the front. They have not laid down the pen, as is evidenced by the correspondence on hand. Is not the pen mightier than the sword? It's Editor is not climbing Kops—he doesn't believe in 'Cops' of any kind, except perhaps, being as he is a staunch teetotaller he is rather partial to the ale that is sold under that name. The Sub-Editors may be digging trenches for all we know, they are not 'on duty' at present, and while it is hardly to be wondered at that some regimental journals cease to 'come out' we should be utterly surprised did K.L.'s fail to do so. As with the regimental journals, we have an admirable example of good—(hard word), good writing, and good printing, and altogether a luxury in which every officer can indulge, for while the R.E.'s publish *The Sapper*, the R.E. Kinsfolk publish the sappers' letters for the benefit of the homebirds. Space forbids the enumeration of all the interesting matter contained in the KHAKI LETTERS. Like the regimental paper, it is conducted by a non-commissioned officer, who draws attention to the fact that accredited reporters in each office, group or division, should contribute news pars., &c.—omitting the 'lashing out at all and sundry."

The last par. of our contemporary is sublime. If one *line* in print would shame a laggard company into the most heroic efforts of industry, what would one *par.* do? We imagine it would cause all non-subscribers to 'step over the line' and come out with a *pim pout*—or rather, a firm front for K.L.'s. We think the C.O. should be asked to write a par. Perhaps the editor is waiting for one from the Imperial Yeomanry?

It is with much regret we record the death of Lieut. E. J. Jelf, R.E., an Officer well-known to all the men of the T.Bs., not only in South Africa, but at home. He had been invalided home suffering from dysentery which had followed enteric fever. He embarked at Cape Town on board the Transport "Dilwara." All the way home he was in very low spirits and generally despondent. About seven o'clock in the evening of 2nd June, just before dinner time, he left his attendant and went right aft on the starboard side of the promenade deck. Without a moment's hesitation, he took out a revolver from his pocket, and before he could be prevented, placed it to his temple, and pulled the trigger. He fell to the deck uttering groans of agony, which were heard by those on the deck below. The Officer was almost unconscious when he was seen by Drs. D. C. Longden and Edwards. It was impossible to do anything to save him, and after lingering in the greatest agony for about fifty-five minutes, he died. He was buried at sea next morning.

Lieut. Jelf was the eldest son of Colonel R. H. Jelf, C.M.G., C.R.E., Eastern District, and was born in 1872. He was educated at Eton and the Royal Military Academy, Woolwich, and obtained his commission in the Royal Engineers in February, 1892. He was on leave from Gibraltar in October last when selected for service with the Telegraph Battalion in South Africa. After serving at De Aar and Modder River he was transferred to Sir R. Buller's command in Natal, and virtually acted as Director of Telegraphs to that Officer throughout all his operations up to and including the relief of Ladysmith. His health then broke down and he was invalided home. Only in September last he married Violet, daughter of Gen. Sir Richard Harrison, Inspector-General of Fortifications.

Now, Boys, I'll just give you another par before I close. You will say it is a grand one, and that I kept the best till the last. Dessert, you know. A little bird told me that our good old Commandant—Col. J. L. du Plat Taylor—who so reluctantly left us on the score of age limit, had been asking for KHAKI LETTERS, and in order to please him I sent him some. Hear what he says in reply:—

" Dear Sergt. Kemp,—I do not so soon forget old friends as you imagine, of course, I remember you very well. I am very much interested in your good work in bringing, as you say, Our Boys *at* the front *to* the front. . . . All honour to you for taking it up. I have, with much interest, watched the good work which the members of the dear old regiment are so efficiently carrying out in South Africa, and I have mourned with the regiment the deaths of those poor men who have lost their lives by disease in the service of their Queen and Country. I shall be glad if you will let the good fellows now serving know how much I am interested in them. My two sons serving in South Africa—one in the Horse Artillery the other in the Guards—often write to me about the Post Office Volunteers. I am sure the compilation of your little books and postage must lead you to much expense, so permit me to ask your acceptance of the enclosed small contribution."

Col. Taylor has often granted me the favour I have wished in days gone by. In turn, I have pleasure in " permitting " him to shew his practical sympathy with our little booklet. Apart from this kindness, I am sure you will feel, as I do, the intensity of his remarks to not only those who had the honour to serve under him, but to every man who can lay claim to an attachment to your well-known regiment, the 24th.

Don't forget to drop me a line as often as you can. Keep the pot a-boiling. Cheer up, you're doing splendidly, and may you all have health, strength, and good luck, and a safe return to your little back rooms is the earnest wish of

Yours most heartily,

R. E. KEMP,

Colour-Sergeant.

To the " L " Co. in South Africa,
Tuesday, June 26th, 1900.

After ——!

BEFORE, behind, the sombre Veldt lies still
While night's advance-guards fast in the pursuit
Of day come, swiftly, on: as shadows, mute
And chilling, they appear. The ragged hill
Had couched beneath the richest woof the sun
Could weave, with lengthening fingers, but the night
Has stolen it away, and now, the light,
With all its offspring, flees. The day is done.
Yet night is not supreme: the starlight falls
Calmly, around, revealing man and horse;
The dead; the dying, that with fevered brain
Review the battle through its hideous course;
The charge; the check; the shell; the burning pain;
The swollen tongue, which faint for water calls.
A fitting consummation of a day
To carnage given. The spectacle appals
All else but Death, the prowling shadow there,
Who comes, but not unbidden, from his lair.

TSF.   S. A. COASE.

Hoisting the Flag at Pretoria.

JUNE 5th, 1900.

THE hearts of the vanquished are aching,
    And broken in spirit they stand:
But the dawn of a new reign is breaking
    Resplendently over the land.
The embers of conflict are dying—
    The echoes of battle shall cease—
For the flag of the victors is flying:
    An emblem of prosperous peace!

Attackers, defenders, lie sleeping
    Where battles were lost and were won—
While the living who loved them are keeping
    The day of a history begun.
The sons of our Empire are meeting
    Where vain hopes and dreams shattered lie!
The sons of our Empire are greeting
    The flag floating bravely on high!

The heart of our Empire is throbbing,
    And its joy spans the seas that divide,—
At the great hour of triumph the sobbing
    Is lost in its jubilant pride!
May the victor who fitly rejoices
    Bless the nation that loses its name—
That the years as they pass make its voices
    Own proudly our flag and our fame!

Britannia! Earth rings with thy story
    Of kingship on land and on sea!
And thy flag hoisted high in its glory
    Tells the world of a nation made free.

C.T.O.   W. H. F. WEBB.

From time to time Our Boys favour us with photographs taken on service. Here is one. The reproduction represents the

Telegraph Staff at Kimberley.

Khaki Letters.

No. 4,314, Sapper **F. A. Mason** (of EDO), in a letter dated Ladysmith, 20th April, 1900, says :—

"Thanks for letters ; they had been accumulating, and, having arrived here before us, were kept at the Civil P.O. There is nothing I want except cash (mim). . . . . Things are so dear : 9d. tin of milk, 1s. a pint tin of treacle, and 6d. for a packet of cigarettes—latter is a bit off, and ran away with my 'oof.' I have a lot of tobacco, but don't care for it much. I called at the P.O. tent about mails. A fellow there stared at me, I at him. I couldn't call to mind his face, but at last he said 'Mason, of EDO'? 'Yes.' 'Well I'm Maccafery, of that office.' It was a surprise, I didn't recognise him, and he stared at me, of course, with my 'milingtary' moustache and short hair. . . . . Amongst my letters I had another surprise. Following is a copy of a telegram for me with them, handed in at Ladysmith, 16th March. 'To Sapper Mason, Tel. Div., De Aar, c/o Col.-Sergt. Tee. What Ho, 'Famos,' how's things? Sandy Ogilvie.' (Ogilvie formerly of Stratford B.O.) Well, the message only came to-day, and I have had no chance of going to P.O., but will soon, although, of course, he may be shifted, now that the country is more open. Fancy meeting him like that. A month's volunteer camp would be 'good 'erbs.' I shall take it on when I return, although, of course, I suppose they won't let me this year, besides, I shall have had enough for one twelve months. I hear Tim Kelly is coming out, but don't know anything definite. I don't suppose he will be here ; we are well supplied with R.E.'s and other army men of the Horse and Line who know the Morse. You should be glad you are not out here, old chap, for if you were at head-quarters (as I am) you would have to rough it. The others a few miles out get it better than we do. Of course, it's all your luck. We are at it all day, noses down to our pads, and as the offices are constantly being moved, we are frequently dis, and work accumulates—four or five hours delay. . . . . All military messages take precedence, and we get a lot of SM's from and to Chief of Staff. Buller is here, at the convent just behind us about 100 yards ; we get a good sight of him often and other big pots. The duties are : day duty, 7 a.m. to 1 p.m. (or after breakfast, about 7.20, to after dinner, about 1 p.m.) ; we are then off till after tea, 5 p.m., and stop till 10 p.m., that's 11 hours ; the next staff is 1 to 5 and 10 p.m. to 7 a.m.—13 hours, but a lot get away from 12 o'clock onwards ; others sleep in tent, although sometimes you are on all night, or till 4 or 5 a.m., getting clear. All transmitted work (Durban, Maritzburg, Mooi River, &c.,) goes down to P.O. by orderlies, but in a day or two we shall be DX to the P.O. It's a bit off climbing into your dark tent at 10 or 1 or 2 a.m. or having men climb over you. Lately we have had a light to put our bed down. We are called at 5.30. The linemen parade at 5.45 ; we don't, so stop in bed. Breakfast 6.30, and consists of coffee, no milk, and bread, sometimes tinned bacon,

KHAKI LETTERS—continued.

which the cook warms up, sometimes cheese, sometimes jam ; after that a wash and go on duty. Dinner,—we get the usual jipper always, and the meat is badly tough. At out stations they get good grub ; it's hard luck we fare worse. For tea—we get tea without milk, and bread, though often there is enough jam for every meal – three pots yesterday for ten men at breakfast, three pots to-day for tea. I think they must be presents. Letters are a treat. You cannot guess how eagerly we look for them and how jolly it is to read them. . . . . I went into 'dock' with a touch of the sun. I was well in two days and feel quite fit now. Bevan is out at Garrison Artillery Office, Woodcote Farm. with a lot more. That place is an important centre. I would not have missed this for worlds, and would go through it all again. Well, here's MQ. Kindest regards and best wishes to all."

No. 1449, Sapper **L. A. Bourlay** (of SY), writing from Riet Bridge, April 25th, says :—

"DEAR COLOURS,—Upon receipt of your circular announcing the impending departure of the 4th contingent of 24th men for the scene of the war, I was again reminded in a practical manner of the lively interest you take in the welfare of your comrades, and, tardily I must admit, decided that the least I could do to evince my appreciation of your thoughtfulness was to, in my turn, let you know, as far as possible, how things are going on here.

"So here goes. Of course you have heard the sad news of poor Hawkins' death, and also Fairall's and Williams', so I will not dwell on such painful subjects, but will try and give a brief sketch of what I have seen and heard. I moved up country from Capetown with the last batch about January 17th, and after spending two days at Dear, Dusty, Dry De Aar, was ordered with Messrs. Woolley, Williams (since dead), and a lineman to Rensburg, which was then Gen. French's Headquarters. Here we found Sergt.-Major Tee in charge, and Sappers Fallon, Samuels, Milton (24th), and Chapple and Bridge (2nd Division men), together with Capt. Fosset's section of the 1st Division. The pleasantest recollections we can treasure of Rensburg are the three weekly issues of rum which we there enjoyed and the successful culinary triumphs of 'Ben' Milton, whom, if he had not been a telegraphist, would certainly have had a brilliant career before him as a *chef*. I wasted my sweetness on the desert air of Rensburg until Gen. French withdrew most of his troops to the Modder, and then, deeming the staff adequate to deal with the work, Sergt.-Major Tee despatched Sapper Bridge (2nd Division) and myself to Modder River, which place we reached by the same train which bore Lord Roberts to his headquarters. We spent about four days at Modder, and then, in company with about seven others, we proceeded to Enslin, where we established a large and what proved to be a busy office, Sapper Pallet being in charge. We were not long there, however, for when Lord Roberts seized Jacobsdal the majority left for Modder River again, which office has always plenty of work. Immediately Kimberley was relieved the Railway Company R.E. set about repairing the line, and of course the T.B.'s commenced opening telegraphic communication with that town, and Messrs. Chapple, Cooke, Bridge and myself, together with Sergt. Miller in charge, were detailed to accompany the working party. Bridge and I were dropped at Merton Siding, which is close to the historic position of Magersfontein, so you may be sure we seized the first opportunity

KHAKI LETTERS—*continued*.

which presented itself of visiting it, and we found it well worth while. There were tons of ammunition, skins, biltong, tin trunks, flour, potatoes, and much ladies' underclothing; I am positive that forms no part of a gentleman's wardrobe! The presence of Amazons in the Boer trenches might largely account for the British repulse! Sergt. Miller also found a very interesting love letter, which might have been written, to judge from the plentiful allusions to 'Smiting 'em hip and thigh,' 'Amalekites,' 'Hittites,' &c., by a Puritan maid of 200 years ago. We passed a pleasant week at Merton Siding, and then returned to the inevitable Modder, where we found the third contingent (24th men and 2nd Division). Modder River office then having quite different clerks I, to my delight, was told off to a working party under Corpl. Bennett, of BS, and with them visited Rensburg, Colesberg, Joubert's Siding, back again to Naauwpoort, Rossmead, Steynsburg (which the inhabitants claim as Kruger's birthplace), Stormberg, Burghersdorp, Bethulie Bridge, and Bethulie, where Messrs. Usher and our genial Corporal were seized with fever and taken one to Sterkstroom and the other to Springfontein hospitals. We all wish them a speedy recovery. From Bethulie we proceeded to Bloemfontein, where I saw a good many old faces—Jack Fallon, Samuel, Birch, Austen, Bridge, &c., all looking in the best of health and as fat as butter. From Bloemfontein I was detailed to proceed to Riet River Bridge, where I was joined next day by Private Ridgewell, of the Buffs, who learnt telegraphy in India, and who was employed as a telegraphist at Dargai. The Riet River is here spanned by a bridge of four arches, and as Commandant Olivier, with from 7 to 10,000 men is somewhere round Reddersburg way, the bridge is guarded pretty strongly. There are two 4'7 quick-firers, a Vickers' Maxim, the remnants of the Suffolks (four Companies), about 30 Mounted Infantry of the 'Fighting Fifth,' and the 9th Battalion K.R.R. (Irish Militia). The latter are typical Irishmen—cheerful, light-hearted, and sturdy, and it would take a circular saw to get through their brogue. They hail from North Cork, and their only grievance is that up to now they've had no chance of having a go at the 'Dhirty Spalpeens,' as they call Mynheer.

"Well, Colours, until 'Bobs' makes another move, which may God speed, there is no more news to tell you, so with many thanks for your Xmas Cards and numerous cheery letters."

"P.S.—What price the 24th in Hyde Park next May? There can't be left more than Eight Companies!"

NOTE.—Had our comrade seen his old regiment at their Inspection he would have counted ten strong Companies, with over 200 recruits filling the gap made by the R.E. Reserves and A.P.O.C. Still there's more to follow.

No. 4,312, Sapper **W. M. Sinclair**, Jononos Kop, Elands Laagte, April 25th, writes :—

"DEAR SERGEANT KEMP,—Allow me to thank you for the KHAKI LETTERS received here last Sunday. They were indeed very welcome, and if you knew the pleasure they give us I am sure you wouldn't begrudge the time it must take to compile them. I suppose some of the other boys have given you very graphic accounts of our voyage and reception in Natal, so I will confine myself to one or two things which have happened since then. After an 18 hours' journey from Durban to Ladysmith, we started campaigning. Sammy Townsend and I got permission to go into the town to get a

KHAKI LETTERS—*continued*.

few necessaries, but, owing to the prices a very few had to suffice. We had a good look round the famous town, however, and tried to get into a pub for a drop of beer, but it was no go, a sentry being posted at each door. In the afternoon our little party was broken up, half remaining at Ladysmith and the others coming up to the front. With Mackness, Townsend, Minors, Leaver, Jeffries and half of the linemen, I was lucky in being included with the 'front' lot, and at 5 p.m. the same day we entrained for Elands Laagte. On arrival there we had a four mile march, and reached our camping ground at Sundays River in the dark, and all a bit done up. The next morning, however, we were all on parade at 6 a.m., fresh as daisies. We had about an hour's instruction before breakfast each morning, and fell in again at 8 for the day's work, which consisted in establishing communication between the different brigades by air line and cable. As a rule, we were dismissed at noon, and had only to fall in for roll call at 5 p.m. The afternoons were spent at the river, bathing and washing clothes, &c. This lasted about a week, when one morning, April 10th, just as we were having a second dip into the coffee tank, there was a boom, and were quickly aware that we were being shelled, receiving our baptism like soldiers of the Queen. The shells were dropping much too close to be comfortable, and our officer (Lieut. Hildebrand) ordered us to take shelter behind a kopje. Here we sat and had a smoke, watching the missiles alight. During a lull in the proceedings we rushed out and let our tents down, scampering back afterwards; but we were not in hiding long when a wire came through to put a cable down, and Sammy Townsend was the first operator to leave us. Five minutes afterwards another arrived to send a cable to Lord Dundonald, and Charlie Minors and your humble were the operators. Our route was past a large canteen, which the enemy were making a particular mark of; probably they had heard we were being charged a bob for a 1d. bottle of Kops, and wanted to put a stop to it. We put our cable down at the gallop, and reached our destination without mishap. All our boys were under fire more or less during the day, and enjoyed the experience. We struck camp that night, and, by the light of the moon, trekked—no one knew where. Our convoy was of great length, and it certainly looked a bit dangerous having a line several miles in length, 16 oxen and 8 or ten mules to a wagon, and not much of an escort. About 1 a.m. we went into laager, dossing anywhere and anyhow. We remained there for a couple of days, when we again went on the 'trek,' on account of the enemy being found too close to us. After a varied experience up and down country, doing the gipsy without his caravan, we eventually landed at Woodcote Farm (Head Quarters Staff). Sir Charles Warren took possession of Jononos Kop, and the following morning I was sent up (4,500 ft.) to establish communication. It was a bit rough at the start, as there was no track, and rations couldn't be got up, but a couple of hundred Kaffirs were put on to make a mule track, and now we have water, fresh meat, potatoes, bread, cheese, jam, &c., daily. George Pocock (CO) has been my companion, but he was withdrawn to Headquarters yesterday, and a private of the K.R.R., who knows something of dots and dashes, has taken his place. A lineman (Arthur Carter) completes our little party. We have to find our own fire, and cook our own food, but the life is very pleasant. We are in communication with the twelve-pounder battery naval guns and garrison artillery, and, by the aid of a very powerful telescope, can spot the Boer men twenty miles off. When they come near we instruct the artillery where to plant their shells, so you will understand from that that the position is of some importance. We have

KHAKI LETTERS—*continued*.

had one or two frights through reports that the enemy were going to dislodge us, and have had to change the position of our *tente d'abri* on several occasions, but they haven't done so yet. I haven't seen any of the other boys for a fortnight, but hear Charlie Minors has left with Lord Dundonald; Sammy Townsend is down below with the naval guns; Mackness and Pocock are at Woodcote Farm (HQ), and Bevan (Eastern Dist.) is with the garrison artillery. When last seen they were all in the best of health and spirits. We are all dying for a drop of stuff from the 'Blue Last.' We can't get to know what Bobs is doing since he took Bloemfontein, but hope he won't neglect to have us with him when he marches into Pretoria. With kind regards to all."

✣ ✣ ✣ ✣

No. 4,327, Sapper **A. J. Brooks**, 2nd T. D. R.E., Springfontein, April 26th, writes :—

"I expect you are kept pretty well informed as to our doings out here by that natty little penn'orth of Colour-Sergeant Kemp's. We all very much appreciate his energetic thoughtfulness, and the kindness of our chums in the office, who have arranged to let us have it free of charge. You can hardly imagine how interesting little bits of office news are out here. What a fix the office will be in this summer, with so many withdrawn. I guess you know how we got on up to the time we arrived in the promised land and went up to Bloemfontein. After four or five days of idleness in Bloemfontein, or rather just outside the town, Swan and I were sent down to Springfontein. We started from Bloemfontein early in the afternoon, and reached Springfontein at 9 o'clock next morning. The distance is 81 miles, so I think the Chatham and Dover can lift its head once more. However, we brought our rations away with us from Bloemfontein, a nice piece of beef, a loaf of bread, and tea and sugar. At Ferreira Siding, after assisting to rescue a mule which had fallen through the platform, we lit a small fire out on the veldt, fried our beef and boiled some tea ; these are the times when you feel that life is worth living. That evening we were treated to the most extraordinary lightning I have ever seen. The storm was preceded by a beautiful sunset, the western sky being absolutely cloudless, whilst the eastern sky was as black as ink ; the sun went down behind a low ridge, and tinged the edges of the clouds in a wonderful way. The rain fairly hissed down, and Swan and I crouched down in the corner of our open truck, whistling softly to ourselves, 'Why did I leave my little back room?' whilst the lightning played Old Harry all around. When we ultimately reached Springfontein, we saw Metcalfe strolling across to the office, and when we got into the station there was Macauley standing at the office door wondering when 'the bounders were going to relieve him for breakfast.' Macauley has now gone to Bethany ; it's as much as Swan and I can do to fill his place—in the eating line. At least, that's what the others say. We do live well here, the lineman (Sapper Stooke) is a first-rate cook, and for about a shilling a week each, we live like lords. For breakfast : Quaker Oats, cold roast beef, bread and coffee ; dinner : roast or boiled meat, bread and coffee, with some sort of duff three or four times a week ; tea : jugfulls of tea, bread, butter, marmalade and jam tart. You should have tried the pancakes we had on Good Friday ; we didn't envy you your mug of tea and two slices. We earn it all, though, for we have long hours and plenty of work here. The average is 14 hours per day, mostly owing to the fact that two of the chaps are sick down in the Naauwpoort Hospital. Metcalfe was

KHAKI LETTERS—*continued.*

a bit queer to-day, but seems better this evening. The fact is, the camp wants keeping a bit cleaner. I'm O.K. in health up to the present. We get plenty of scare rumours here. " Big Commando sighted by outposts just over those kopjes to-day," etc., etc., but nothing ever turns up. We have got a trench three yards (in front) from our tent door. It is one of the many which were planned by Lord Kitchener just before he left here the other day. We have a cosmopolitan lot of troops here at present, little detachments of English, Irish, Scotch, Welsh, Canadian Mounted Rifles, New South Wales Lancers, Ceylon Mounted Infantry, West Australian Infantry, etc., etc. There are also several hundred Native Indian Cavalry here, they look a treat when mounted, but are not here as combatants ; they are engaged in remount work, and are farriers, shoeing smiths, etc. We had a regular untamed lot of Basutos here the other day, they are going to work on the railway sidings. The niggers all get £4 10s. per month and their mealies. The way they work is very amusing. About 20 or 30 of them in a line with picks, all work in unison, lifting their picks as one man, and chanting away at some of their tribal songs. It is now close on 2 a.m., and as I am not on night duty, I must be getting off to bed. There is fighting going on between here and Bethulie to-day, and it is very probable that the Boers will attempt to cut the line of communication somewhere north of this junction. Wonder whether they will give us a call. Well, au revoir. Best wishes to all old pals. We very much appreciate the 'Balaclavas' which some of the ladies of the Met. were kind enough to give to 'Bunny' Ingram for distribution. I shouldn't like to lose mine now. The nights are getting very cold, and when lying on the ground, even under canvas, we can do with all we get. We have some unpleasant little bedfellows, big ants, blackbeetles, etc., etc. Ants I am getting used to, but I cannot reconcile myself to a big beetle nestling down between my eye and nose. There are scorpions about here too, but the only one I have seen as yet is one that Swan has got in a medicine bottle with a little paraffin oil. It is dropping to pieces though, so the paraffin is a failure. Sterling was here the other day with the C.I.V., he looks A1, and is enjoying himself immensely. They have since marched on to Bloemfontein. Bradshaw is here with the 22nd Field Hospital, expecting to move up every day. Wonder who else I shall meet out here. I half expect to see some of the TS girls on the hospital trains now."

No. 4,311, Sapper **C. J. Minors,** writing on April 27th from Natal, says :—

" Very many thanks for letter and Nos. 1 and 2 of KHAKI LETTERS, which came as a pleasant surprise to us all. What a task you have undertaken. I always did think you were a glutton for work on behalf of the members of ' I ' and ' L,' but I must confess this, your latest, beats all. Now I am going to give you some more in response to your invitation. . . . Our party arrived off Durban, Monday, April 2nd, landed next morning, and left by mid-day train for Ladysmith. Had a splendid reception all along the line. At several stations on the way up country the residents brought us tea, bread and butter, and fruit, *ad lib.*, which was very acceptable. At one of the stations some ladies took photographs of our party. We left an address with them to send on a copy. Arrived in Ladysmith station 4.30 a.m., Wednesday, and camp at 8.30 a.m. Our party was then split up. The following were for the front :—Bevan, Chubbock, Collins, J. C. Jeffrey, Leaver, Mackness, Minors, Pocock, Sinclair, Symonds and Townsend. The

KHAKI LETTERS—*continued*.

remainder to stay in Ladysmith. Those of us who came on here have had some fairly exciting times. We were served out with 50 rounds of ammunition at the railway station, and left at 4 p m. for Elands Laagte. From there we marched to Sundays River Camp, where we arrived at 7 p.m. The first night in camp we could hear the Boers sniping at our picquets. The enemy were only 3 or 4 miles in front. They did'nt trouble us much during the daytime We spent a very pleasant week, and were congratulating ourselves on our good luck in being able to have a swim in the river each day, when suddenly on Tuesday morning, April 10th, whilst we were at breakfast, they commenced shelling our camp. We had to pull down our tents and take shelter under the rocks, about 50 yards in front of the camp. We sat there for about an hour listening to the shells whistling over our heads and watching the effect as they dropped in the midst of the camps behind. Two parties were told off to go with cable carts, one to the Sundays River office, and the other to Elands Laagte to join General Clery's Brigade. Mackness was included in the first cart, and Sinclair and myself in the second. Both parties had to drive through the zone of shell fire. We had six mules to pull our cart across the veldt, one nigger holding the reins, the other a long whip, which he didn't forget to use. He made those mules skip across the open for all they were worth. We passed several regiments lying down, some in trenches waiting for the expected advance of the Boers. They, however, contented themselves with shelling us out of our camp. The whole division had to fall back several miles. Our party were out until 2 a.m. next morning laying cables, and slept out in the open until 5 o'clock without sheets or blankets ; all of us were dead tired, some —including your humble—having had nothing to eat since the morning before. Shelling again during afternoon and evening. Next day (Thursday), we shifted camp still further back to Woodcote Farm, about half south of Elands Laagte station (General Warren's Headquarters). We were kept hard at work (Bevan, Mackness and myself) at the instruments until 3 a.m., and so on till Sunday, when we had some assistance. Four nights sleeping in the open with plenty of work during the day and little food - ships biscuits and bully beef—made up a very rough week. Since then matters have been fairly quiet. Our party have been somewhat scattered. Sinclair and Pocock on the top of Jonones Kop, Bevan at Garrison Guns, Townsend at Naval Guns, Jeffrey at Elands Laagte, Collins and Chubbock at Modders Spruit, and Leaver at Buys Farm. Perhaps this is hardly worth mentioning as changes are made every few days.

" Last Sunday evening, April 22nd, orders were sent for large party to join Lord Dundonald's mounted brigade at Buys Farm. Immediately one cable and one air-line wagon were sent from our camp, and four or five from Ladysmith. About thirty linemen and four clerks, including Symonds and myself, and Peters from Ladysmith. This looked like business, but nothing happened. We had an easy week, and our party returned to Woodcote Farm this morning. You will be sorry to learn that Ingram is in hospital at Ladysmith, with dysentery. Mason was also in for a few days with sunstroke, and Cousal has also been in with dysentery, but is now better. Most of us have suffered more or less with diarrhœa, owing chiefly to bad water. I have enclosed an address for our party in Natal, which is perhaps the best, although some suggest ' Ladysmith, R.E. Head-quarters for Natal' ; anyhow, all our letters go there first and are sent on to us by our own orderlies. I have sent you a rough outline of the Natal party's movements, in case you have not heard from anyone else. They all send their best thanks for your note and KHAKI LETTERS. Kindest regards."

KHAKI LETTERS—*continued.*

No. 25,366, Sapper **C. Forth** (of LS), writes under date April 28th, from Bloemfontein :—

"No doubt you will have heard of my discharge from hospital, which took place on the 8th inst. About twenty of us were marched to what is called the convalescent camp, where one has to remain until fit to return to his regiment. All paraded next morning before the Major. I convinced him I was fit for duty and could report myself at the Naauwpoort office, to which he consented. Next day saw me performing a lovely split, 11 to 4, 5 to 6, and 8 to 10, although the rest of the staff were doing their twelve hours; but they thought eight hours enough for a chap just out of dock. An S.G. came for me to proceed to the Free State capital, which I cheerfully did by mounting an ammunition train at 11 a.m. on April 11th. It took twelve hours to reach Norvals Pont—a matter of fifty miles! Here I visited the Telegraph Office and had a good chat with a couple of ours, and then returned to my truck to sweet repose on boxes of lyddite shell. 6 a.m. April 12th, find we are anchored at Springfontein with little prospect of making any headway. Our engines (two) leave us for the sheds, the drivers thoroughly done up for want of sleep. About 2 p.m. notice a goods train preparing for off. Enquire, and find its destination is Bloemfontein, so transfer myself and baggage thereon. Every mile or so from here a dead horse, mule, or ox is seen on the roadside in all stages of decomposition. A snake over a yard long is seen on the railway track, and looks as though it was going to strike one of our wheels, but evidently changes its mind and glides away. Another interesting sight is a draft of about 200 sick horses being driven loose by Indian troopers. These I saw a few days later passing through the streets of Bloemfontein. At nearly every cross street several break away with a trooper in pursuit. Bloemfontein is reached about 8.30, but as we are shunted into a siding, and a mile and a half away from the office, I do not feel inclined to tramp that distance with all my war paint on, including accoutrements, ammunition, carbine, two blankets, and heavy kit bag, so under the tarpaulin I go, propping it up at my head with my carbine, which slips during the night. In the morning I wake early with little drops of water trickling on my face. This is caused by the moisture of my breathing, and want of ventilation, and no doubt accounts for a very bad throat. My tonsils are much swollen, and I feel far from well. When our train enters the station I place my stock in trade in a quiet corner, and have a jaunt round town. There is so much to interest me that it is dark ere I feel weary, and worn, and done up. Have had neither bite nor sup for 26 hours, and not inclined that way. But on returning to the station a Good Samaritan in the shape of an orderly on a hospital train asks me if I could do a drink of tea. This revives me somewhat and I set off at 8 p.m. for the office, but without my kit bag, which I cannot tackle. Next morning I visit the Mayor, who is a doctor and chemist, and pay him 5s. for a gargle which soon puts my throat right. As I did not appear fit for duty, they gave me a fresh air job—going with a team of mules and wagon to draw the daily rations, occupying about four hours, from 8 a.m. till noon, with sometimes a turn out in the afternoon; and this is all the *work* I have done for fourteen days. But I expect every day to be told off for duty in the office. The staff here is over sixty, and dozens more expected shortly. These are the duties at present —midnight to 7 a.m., same day 2 p m. to midnight, next day 7 a.m to 2 p.m., and then repeat midnight to 7 a.m., &c. This does not give much time for sleep and exercise, and there are always several on the sick list. Have not heard from Bert (Hayden of LS) for a month. Expected him up country again before this. Kindest regards to all."

KHAKI LETTERS—*continued*.

No. 4371, Sapper **L. Sorensen**, writes from Fort Knokke, May 1st, as under :—

"DEAR KEMP,—I don't know if any of the boys have written from here, so I thought you might like to know our whereabouts. The voyage out was uneventful and similar to many voyages you have already heard about. We arrived in Table Bay about 4 a.m. on Monday, 23rd, and were told to get ready to disembark at once. These orders were countermanded, and we were kept hanging about the Bay till Saturday morning, the 28th. This was on account of the enormous amount of troopers waiting to be landed; twelve transport waiting to be unloaded before us. On landing, we were refreshed by the A.M.B. ladies with lemonade and cakes, and marched off to Fort Knokke Camp, about three miles the other side of Capetown, reaching there pretty well fagged out after being without exercise for nearly a month. The Camp is pleasantly situated on the sea shore, just under Table Mountain, and bounded by the Hospital Camp and the railway. On the other side of the Hospital Camp are camped a lot of Boer wounded prisoners. We went over on Sunday evening and spoke with a few of them, One old chap, patriarchal-looking, white whiskered, with fine white teeth— a typical old farmer—told us in broken English that he did not want to fight the English. He had been commandeered, and had a large farm and five children, and said that all he wanted was to go home and settle in peace. He was captured in Cronje's laager, and spoke very gratefully of his treatment from our people, and gazed admiringly at Bill Pearce's shape, when he came up, remarking 'Have you any more rooi's like him'? Another prisoner was wounded in the head, a large scar on the side showing where the bullet entered. It still remains, and he feels no ill effects from it. They all spoke well of Lord Roberts and their captors. We have had a pretty easy time here. This morning we had a route march about halfway up Table Mountain ; starting out at 8 and returning at 11.30. It was a stiff climb, the ground being strewn with large boulders and stones over which we had to scramble. Many wild flowers, among others wild scented geraniums and arum lilies being in bloom, looking very pretty. Everyone enjoyed the walk and were looking forward to another to-morrow, but we had no sooner returned to Camp and dismissed when we fell in again, orders having come down that we were to move off to-night. Ten were told off for Kimberley, the TS men being W. Frew, D. Semple and E. J. Ash, under Lance-Corpl. Haycocks, of LV. The remaining 36 are to leave Saltwater Siding at 9 p.m. for Bloemfontein. The Kimberley men left here at 3.30, entraining at Capetown at 4.30, and we gave them a good send off. We have had a very pleasant time here, everything being so novel. There is quite a craze here for collecting badges, &c., of the different regiments, and many a man has been raised from want to affluence by parting with an old disused badge or regimental letters ; prizes are given for the best collection. Well, we are just packing up, and things are a bit mixed after sleeping 16 in a tent, and two kit bags for each man. Getting dark, and just going off, so farewell to all old chums."

✤ ✤ ✤ ✤

No. 4,327, Sapper **A. J. Brooks**, 2nd T.D. R.E., writes from Springfontein, O.F.S., May 3rd, as follows :—

"DEAR COL.-SERGT.— Did I tell you in my last letter that I saw Sterling here with the C.I.V.'s. He was looking as well as could be. Lieut. Garnett came in and shook hands all round. The Postal people have snaffled some

KHAKI LETTERS—*continued*.

of the other 24thers with the C.I.V. for postal work in Bloemfontein. The victims were very wroth about it, and if any inclination is shewn to keep them at postal duty, instead of letting them go with the C.I.V.'s, they are going to kick up a shindy about it. It will certainly be most unjust if they are compelled to leave the C.I.V.'s. About ten days ago Bethulie called me up, and lo and behold there was Bradshaw at the other end. He turned up in person next day, accompanied by the 22nd Field Hospital. The hospital is still here, but expects to go back and round up to Kimberley very shortly. They have established themselves in a little tin church here, quite a cosy little place, with varnished wooden walls, and transparencies depicting Bible scenes pasted on the windows. Poor old 'Met.' is occupying a little bed up on the rostrum. He is pretty comfortable now, but for the first three days he had to do as best he could on the floor. He has got a touch of dysentery, and when he is fit to be moved I expect he will go down to Naauwpoort. He is very cheerful, considering, and, as almost the whole of the hospital men are Lancashire lads,'Met.' gets on O.K. Bradshaw, too, is often in here. Last Saturday or Sunday afternoon, whilst sitting at our main circuit, I happened to overhear Norvals Pont telling Bloemfontein that Peter White wanted to speak to Jack Fallon. York, at Bloemfontein, replied that Fallon was not on duty, so I chipped in and Peter told me that he would soon be marching up our way, *en route* to Bloemfontein with the 35th Co., 11th Regt. Imperial Yeomanry. I hope to see him soon. A big party came through this morning—Stevenson, Bill Pearce, Bill Carter, Bell, Morse, Thrift (SW), Leitch, Kelly, Plumridge, and many others whom I did not see. I was only awakened just in time to see them before their train started off again. There is a big staff at Bloemfontein already, but as the Brandfort wire was opened to-day, I expect some of the Bloemfontein staff went on there. Anyway, I expect that still more will have to come out, as a good many offices between Bloemfontein and Pretoria will have to be fixed up. Ours is a busy little place now—new sidings being built, depôts established, &c. There are now only four clerks here; we, consequently, have a thick time. Our staff here is as follows : in charge, Troop-Sergt.-Maj. Foote, R.E. ; Sapper J.Read, R.E.; Pte. J. Longley, Derby Regt. ; Sappers Swan and Brooks, 24th ; Sapper Stooke,R.E. lineman; and a native 'boy.' This is not a very big staff for day and night working of two circuits. On one circuit we have Bloemfontein,Springfontein,Norvals Pont and Naauwpoort; on the other circuit we have Bethulie Station,Bethulie Bridge,and Queenstown. The counter and sending out require the sole attentions of one man, as in addition to our own work we deal at the counter with the railway work, and the railway wires do 300 daily. However, taken all round we have a good time; everyone does their best and so all goes well. Last night we had quite a treat. The Volunteer Cos. of the 1st Welsh Regt. and the S. Wales Borderers were waiting in this station for a few hours. It was after midnight, the night was very cold, and the men were perched up in most uncomfortable positions on the top of supply trucks; probably been there for two days, too. However, they were as lively as possible, and gave us a grand selection of Welsh hymns and songs. 'All Wales is a Sea of Song.' They certainly did their best to keep up its reputation. There are some fine fellows going through with the volunteer companies. The night before last the Suffolk Regt.'s Volunteer Co. went through ; half of them came from Cambridge University. That's patriotism if you like,—and they go up to the front on the top of supply trucks, coal trucks, or cattle trucks, in fact anywhere but in a carriage. We are having a tame time down here, now. Boer prisoners are occasionally brought in from the surrounding hills,

KHAKI LETTERS—*continued*.

but I think that Gen. Hart's brigade having occupied Smithfield and district, all cantankerous Boers will go north. . . . I hope that by the time you get this Mafeking will be free—they must be having an awful time. Thanks very much for KHAKI LETTERS, it's a 'fair pinch.' Hope you are keeping well in health. Best wishes to everybody."

Writing again on a postcard, May 16th, **Jim Brooks** says :—

"DEAR COLOUR-SERGEANT,—Herewith copy of *Bloemfontein Post*, containing account of a Smoker, in the getting up of which, some of the lads seem to have had a good share, I should like to have been there myself. Seems, from what the reporter says, that Percy Milton is not losing flesh (mim.) The M.O. in charge of the isolation tents here has asked us not to go there too frequently so have not seen Met. lately. Mr. Black and Mr. Howe of the Soldiers' Home here are very good to Met and Cooke (R.E. from Bethulie). They have gifts of all kinds, pyjamas from the Soldiers' Home, pillows from Canada, &c , &c. I hear to-day that both Met. and Cooke show decided improvement."

No. 28,201, Company-Sergeant-Major **W. G. Tee,** writes from Naauwpoort, on May 4th, as follows :—

"MY DEAR DICK,—Thirty-six of the contingent that sailed April 1st passed through Naauwpoort last night. They were detained six days in Table Bay before disembarking, and at once proceeded for Bloemfontein. Frew, Semple and eight others gone direction of Kimberley ; the former expressed a desire to join that column, in order, if possible, to meet his brother —Postmaster of Barkley West. The party, including 'Baby,' had an exciting adventure *en route* to De Aar; the engine driver of their train went raving mad, and they were called upon to render assistance. It took twelve of them to hold him down, the 'Baby' came off worse by slightly spraining his leg in the melee, he, however, settled the lunatic by jumping on his chest. The Civil clerks, of whom there are two or three Scotsmen here, gave their old confrères a good send-off, singing patriotic songs, finishing up with 'Auld Lang Syne,' and their train comprising stores and troops, steamed off up the incline to Bloemfontein, their ultimate destination not known. After a very busy three months we are now having a comparatively quiet time, most of my men have gone forward and the remainder of us expect to go shortly as I anticipate the civil people will take over the office. Life at Naauwpoor is very monotonous, the only recreation to be had is in the shape of a little hunting on the veldt, where buck and hares are plentiful, and. when opportunity offers, we go out with the Colonial clerks, who have very good dogs and firearms, and share with them in the sport. As far as Cape Colony is concerned. the war is practically over ; the ringleaders of the rebels are now on trial, those in this district are tried at Colesberg. I was informed by an Intelligence Officer that it would take at least three months to investigate the present cases. The Dutch appear to be very much subdued, and have learnt to respect ' Tommy,' and instead of treating him with contempt, treat him with respect ; on several occasions I have noticed them touch their hats on passing. We have not the slightest idea how long the campaign is likely to last, several conjectures—some three months, others twelve, but I fancy we shall be home in the autumn. Charlie Ray, who has been suffering from typhoid, is, I am pleased to say, convalescent, and left for Capetown

KHAKI LETTERS—*continued.*

last Tuesday, and it is thought he will be sent home. The lads here are very well and fairly comfortable, and wish to be remembered to all. With kindest regards to yourself and all."

Company-Sergeant-Major W. G. TEE again writes from Naauwpoort, May 21st, as follows :—

"MY DEAR DICK,—It is with sincere regret that I have to add another name to the death roll of 'L' Co. 23,603, Sapper J. Metcalfe, late of TS, after suffering from dysentery, expired yesterday, Sunday, May 20th, at 8 a.m., at Springfontein. The poor fellow must have been very bad, for it was reported he had not opened his letters for three weeks, and the unfortunate part he is a married man with a family. By the kindness and forethought of the Staff at Springfontein, a wire was sent to 'Poniard, London,' with a view of his wife receiving the sad intelligence through another source (doubtless through you) before receiving the usual stereotyped letter from the War Office. Arrangements are being made about his grave, and what can be done I am sure will be. I am sorry to hear Sergt. Nelson is in Hospital again at Bloemfontein, and Sergt. Luttrell was transferred to Sterkstroom Hospital some weeks since. I have been unable to get news from them, but I sincerely trust they are both progressing satisfactorily. In face of so much sickness, our boys are very cheerful, and am pleased to say the work of the Telegraph Battalion is proceeding very creditably considering the enormous army in the field, and the members of 'L' Co. are contributing their share in the work. All the Cape Colony offices are likely to be taken over in the course of a few days by the civil authorities, when our services will be utilised in the O.F.S. or Transvaal. Several of the O.F.S. clerks are already working in the offices, and they are offering inducements, such as a £50 rise, to the C.C. clerks to accept situations in the Free State. The reported Relief of Mafeking (which has now been officially confirmed) was received here on Saturday with much rejoicing. It was generally known the forces investing Mafeking had been reduced, and the siege likely to be raised any moment. Flags and bunting were displayed all over the Railway Camp, and trains arrived gaily decorated, the combined shrieking of the engine whistles and explosion of fog signals on the line all day in honour of the event was almost deafening, rendering work in the office almost impossible. At night a huge bonfire was lit on the hills, illuminating the camp for miles round. When the relief was known, a party of three rebels who were out on bail and waiting on the platform to proceed to their homes, and who did not appear to approve or join in the manifestations of rejoicing, were quickly spotted by some of the civil people and were rather roughly maltreated, but the intervention of the military police soon stopped it. To-day, Monday, is recognised as a general holiday in recognition of the Relief, not that it makes much difference to us, and there is nothing of excitement outside beyond a football match on the veldt. We are all pleased at the rapid advance and successes of Lord Roberts, and hope the end of hostilities is not far distant. We shall be in thought with you at the inspection of the old regiment this week, and only wish we could participate in it; but wait until next year, it will be worth coming to then. Kindest regards from all the lads to all the '24th' and friends at TS."

Khaki Letters continued on page 213.

Khaki Sidelights.

We are indebted to **Sapper John Read, R.E.**, for the following splendid letter. It proves again—if such proof is necessary—that harmony rules the relations of the Royals and "Our Own" Boys.

"Springfontein. O.F.S., Military Telegraph Office,

"Dear Kemp, "21st May, 1900.

"I am a total stranger to you, but the sad event which has taken place in our little circle here is certainly cause enough quite apart from your request in KHAKI LETTERS that events of interest should be forwarded to you; therefore, as I am certain that any details of such a sad event as the passing of our dear old comrade Metcalfe would be of mournful and pathetic interest, I am sure you and all his friends will be glad to hear my testimony as to his sterling worth, and grief at his loss. Poor old Metcalfe, on the 26th April, complained of feeling unwell, but, as he did not wish to increase the strain on any of our very limited staff, insisted on remaining on duty, till we at length, almost had to force him to rest. He, however, grew somewhat worse, and on the 29th, I myself took him over to the Field Hospital (a little iron church which was being used for that purpose). He was at once admitted, and everything was done for him that could possibly be done. We visited him as frequently as the hospital authorities would permit us, and he was placed in a cot adjoining Sapper C. H. Cooke, of the 2nd T.B., who had been admitted from Bethulie a few days before, suffering from the same disease. He was afterwards removed to the new General Hospital, No. 3, and the hospital authorities generously kept the two Telegraphists together all along, and I am sure that their company in the painful circumstances was of great solace to them both. Metcalfe had in his travels through the Stormberg district made great friends, and I must now ask you to particularly mention the great and very devoted consolation and sympathy afforded by the numerous visits (in fact, daily visits) paid him by Mr. Black, of the Soldiers' Home of the 3rd Division, and also to the cheerful and bright visits paid him by Mr. Oakley, of the same Home, who was acting as Chaplain ; and I would like to impress upon his friends that the attention paid to him by the two gentlemen named, was not merely that of Official Visitors or Chaplains, but was in the nature of friendly visits to a comrade and they spared no pains to endeavour to make his detention as free from discomfort as possible, and they even provided him with luxuries and invalid comforts to endeavour to make his recovery as rapid as possible. This was a great comfort to us at work, for we knew he had every possible attention, and that he had also specially careful nursing by the Red Cross Nurses. But unfortunately our hopes of soon seeing poor old Met. at work again were doomed to being frustrated, for, on the morning of the 20th, Swan went to the hospital, hoping to hear that he was still better, and you can imagine the shock he sustained when Sapper Cooke told him that poor Met. had passed away that morning. We could scarcely realize the fact, and I personally was so incredulous that I sent both Swan and Brooks back to verify the facts and to get particulars. Alas, the facts were too true, poor Metcalfe had passed away that morning at 8.30 a.m., and he was laid to rest on the following day at 3 p.m.

"It was at 2.30 p.m. to-day that a little group in Khaki assembled at Springfontein to pay their last respects to their departed comrade's memory. The group was composed of Sappers Read, Swan and Brooks, Rev. Mr. Oakley and Mr. Black (of the Soldiers' Home), Mr. Kays, Telegraphist (lately of Free States Telegraphs), and a detachment of Cavalry from the Remounts Depôt. Far across on the veldt the mournful cortège could be seen slowly wending its way towards the little space made sacred by its being the resting-place of some of our troops who have died here. The bright colour of our Union Jack, in which his body was enrolled, shone brilliantly against the dark background of the hills, and the impressive scene amid the intense stillness of the African scenery, as the guard of the 3rd Durham Regmt. filed into place and presented arms, while every hand was raised in salute. The Burial Service was read by his personal friend, Mr. Oakley, who was also seconded by Mr. Black ; and to the ordinary observer there was something solemnly pathetic as the bugle notes rung out the 'Last Post'; and as the last respects were being paid, the hymn 'For ever with the Lord,' pealed forth from the assembled troops, which, though few in number, were all of them personally acquainted with him, and when we had fulfilled the last sad duties, and covered him tenderly ourselves, not leaving the duty of filling in the grave to the fatigue party, we silently went back to Camp with the last phrase of the Service ringing in our ears, '"Till the Resurrection morn.'"

KHAKI SIDELIGHTS—*continued.*

"I have, my dear Kemp, attended many military funerals, but I have never attended one where so much personal feeling was shown by those who were but a few months ago total strangers to him, but who were as much affected at his loss as though they had lost a dear friend. We have put up a little wooden cross as a temporary measure, and inscribed upon it 'Sacred to the Memory of J. Lord Metcalfe, R.E., died 20th May, 1900, Aged 32 years,' and have had his grave neatly banked, and done as much as we would have liked his friends to have done for him themselves in the very limited circumstances at our disposal."

✧ ✧ ✧ ✧

An Officer, writing in the current number of the *United Service Magazine*, urges with some reason the reorganisation of the Royal Engineers. The corps is made up of a number of eccentric units, scarcely any two of which are similar. There is the "Bridging Battalion" and the "Telegraph Battalion," the former containing 2 "troops," the latter 2 "divisions." There is the "Field Depôt," containing 2 "Field Parks" and a "Training Depôt." There are 8 "Field Companies," half of which are on the "Higher Establishment." There is a "Mounted Detachment," which is really part of the Field Depôt. There is 1 "Balloon Section." There is a "Service Battalion," containing 22 companies, one of which is a "Railway Company," two are "Depôt," one is a "Submarine Mining Depôt." There are 4 "Survey" companies, employed on the Ordnance Survey of Great Britain. There are 2 "Railway" companies, one of which is included in the "Service" battalion. There are 12 "Submarine Mining" companies, one of which is included in the "Service" battalion. There is a "Training Battalion," containing 9 companies. There is a "West India Fortress Company." There are 2 "Local Companies Submarine Miners" for Hong Kong and Singapore. There is an "Indian Submarine Mining Company." There is a "Coast Battalion." There are 3 native corps of "Sappers and Miners," no two of which are similar in number or organisation, and none of which really form part of the corps of Royal Engineers. Of these various units, the "Survey" companies are mostly paper companies, and the officers and men attached to them are soldiers in name only. There is nothing whatever military in Ordnance Survey Work. The "Coast Battalion" is likewise more or less a paper battalion. It consists almost entirely of officers who have risen from the ranks, and of a few worthy fossils of non-commissioned officers. There are a very large number of surplus officers in the corps, employed on duties which cannot, by any stretch of language be termed "Sapper" work. Some are on the maintenance and repair of roads, and barracks, others on Survey, others under the Board of Trade, Home Office and Local Government Board, or as Mint masters, or repairers of drains.

The real duties devolving on the Royal Engineers in war—those specified in the Manuals of Military Engineering, Field Fortification, Permanent Fortification, &c., Field Exercises, Musketry Instruction, &c., are in peace time relegated to those rare occasions when a perfunctory "short course" is indulged in by companies at certain stations, such as Aldershot and Chatham. The only companies of Royal Engineers which constantly practice in peace time the duties expected of them in time of war, are the Submarine Mining Companies. It is submitted, and with much reason, that no man can faithfully, honestly, and truly serve two masters. He cannot be a fighting soldier and a peaceful civilian. He cannot be an efficient "Sapper" and a brilliant repairer of drains and constructor of barracks at one and the same time. He cannot take an interest in District Courts-Martial, Garrison Boards, Field Operations, Garrison Duty, Field Engineering, Musketry, Signalling, Telegraphy, Bridging, Well-Sinking, Ballooning, Fortification, &c. If he gains a taste for one class of work he is most likely to get a distaste for the other. If he becomes proficient as an architect and builder, he is certain to be wanting in military knowledge, discipline, and sapping and mining. Certainly to outsiders and the uninitiated the writer of the article seems to have made out a good case against the present organisation of the Royal Engineers.—*The Globe.*

Army Casualties. The following Circular from the War Office at the end of last month, will interest readers :—"In consequence of enquiries constantly made as to casualties to soldiers in the field, it is thought advisable to publish some statement as to the procedure adopted. All casualties, as soon as they are notified to the War Office, are checked, so far as may be possible, from pay lists, muster rolls, and other returns, and then published; and, in the absence of further publication, may be taken as a guarantee that no further information has been received.

KHAKI SIDELIGHTS—*continued.*

The information published contains all the particulars that have been received, and no further details as to nature of wounds, &c., are kept back from publication. It is to be observed that, while instructions are issued that every care should be taken in compiling the list of casualties on the spot, and, while there is every reason to believe that due care is taken, errors must, and do, constantly creep in, owing to the disadvantageous conditions under which the returns are compiled. Lists compiled as favourable opportunities occur during pauses in the operations are lost, owing to the individuals who compiled them themselves becoming non-effective later in the day, and the lists so lost have to be re-compiled under less favourable conditions, and from imperfect information. In cases in which the identity tickets of killed or wounded are recovered, there is comparatively little chance of mistakes occurring, but in many cases the tickets are never recovered, or are so obliterated as to become illegible. so that identification is very difficult. Many instances have occurred in which a soldier has been reported as killed, on the most circumstantial evidence of his comrades. and has subsequently been found to be only wounded, and doing well. When a soldier is not forthcoming, the officers on the spot have to exercise their discretion in weighing the evidence before them and, if he cannot be otherwise accounted for, he is returned as 'missing.' The term 'missing' means that a soldier's fate has not been definitely ascertained. It does not preclude the possibility of the man being killed or wounded, while it often means that he is a prisoner. In some cases soldiers, so reported, have found their way back to camp in a few days time. In other cases they have been found as the troops advanced. Moreover, discrepancies are often due to the almost impossible conditions under which the casualty lists are signalled or telegraphed, due to the isolation of troops, imperfect telegraph communication, and other causes.

Any names and numbers which cannot be identified are referred back, by wire, to South Africa for verification, as well as any discrepancies that may be specially brought to notice. It must, however, be borne in mind that answers to such queries are often delayed owing to the fact that the only persons capable of answering them are for the time beyond the reach of telegraphic communication. Reports of the condition of the sick and wounded in hospitals are constantly telegraphed, giving the names of all who are not doing well. If the name of a soldier reported wounded is not again mentioned in any return, it may be understood that he is doing well. Once a month regimental casualty reports are received by post, and the telegraphed reports are checked with them. Any casualties which then appear to have been omitted or incorrectly rendered are at once published, and the relatives informed. Instructions have been issued that constant enquiries are to be made as the troops advance as to the fate of the missing, and that any information relating to them is to be reported home at once. Casualties signalled from besieged towns are particularly liable to error, and are checked when the towns are relieved. Amended returns are then rendered.

The following terms when applied to wounds may be taken as conveying the signification stated against them :

'Slight.'—A wound likely to heal rapidly, not impairing the use of a limb or organ, and often not even entailing admission into hospital.

'Severe.'—A wound requiring careful treatment in hospital, but not necessarily dangerous, often involving fractures of bone, and sometimes even the permanent impairment of a limb.

'Dangerous.'—A wound such as might occur from the penetration of the head, chest, abdomen, or any vital organ.

In many cases, however, soldiers reported "dangerously wounded" have completely recovered, and the percentage of deaths from wounds of all sorts among those admitted to hospital has, during the present campaign, only reached 5 per cent. on the total wounded. It must be obvious that with the pressure and difficulties under which all ranks are working in South Africa, it is impossible to entirely avoid the occasional omission or mistaken announcement of casualties, but relatives of officers and soldiers may rest assured that all ranks out there are fully alive to the necessity of sending home accurate and speedy information, and that they are sparing no pains in their endeavours to surmount the difficulties of supplying it. There is a special office in South Africa dealing with casualties, in case relatives wish to telegraph or write direct. The telegraphic address is 'Casualty,' Cape Town.

KHAKI LETTERS—*continued*.

No. 2338, Sapper **Alfred W. Swan**, 1st T.D., R.E., writing from Springfontein on March 6th, says :—

"DEAR COLOUR-SERGEANT,—I hope you will pardon my delay in writing to you, my thanks for your many kind and thoughtful acts is late in coming, but it is none the less sincere. You will be sorry to hear that Metcalfe is laid up in hospital with dysentery. Poor old Met., he has been ill for a week now and he is still confined to bed, though, I am glad to say, he was slightly better yesterday when I called. A. J. Brooks and I are the only 24th men at this office. We live like fighting cocks, thanks to our comrade Sapper Stooke, who is a splendid cook. Chops for breakfast and tea, roast beef for dinner, and the puddings he treats us to ! It would make you TS chaps green with envy if you got a whiff of Stooke's 'duff.' Excuse hurried note, must run for post."

Writing again on May 20th, Swan says :—" I know that you and many others will be anxious to hear how Metcalfe is going on. I am glad to say he is improving, though very slowly ; the Medical Officer says he is to be invalided home when well enough to travel. Thanks for your 'Khaki booklet' with the photo of poor young Hawkins ; I am very glad to have it. I was shocked to hear of his death. I believe Metcalfe and Brooks have already given you a description of this place, there is nothing to add. There are very few troops passing up now, and in place of them we see our old enemies—the misguided Free Staters—coming back to their farms ; many are wounded, and all seem heartily glad that they are at last ' signed off.' Some very affecting scenes are witnessed at the meeting of friends who have been parted since the war began. I suppose by the time this arrives peace will be proclaimed, and so we shall be homeward bound. I'm afraid you will find all of us very rusty at drill, but I daresay Sergt. Jackman, with a little persuasive language, will make us buck up to our old form."

And again on the 23rd, Swan continues :—" I can well imagine how shocked you must have been to hear of poor Metcalfe's death ; it was a terrible surprise for all here, as he was reported to be improving up to Saturday, 17th, the day prior to his death. It is thought he had a collapse, brought on by a shock sustained by seeing another poor fellow pass away in the same marquee. In my last letter to you I reported that he was improving slowly ; that news was two days old. We were permitted to visit him only once a week, so I had to content myself with news of his progress from Mr. Black, of the Soldiers' Home. This gentleman and the Rev. Mr. Oakley (Soldiers' Home) were most kind and attentive to poor old Met. during his illness. Poor old chap, there's no mistake that in his death the Company lost 'one of the best.' He was the most good-natured and kind-hearted fellow I ever met. Just before going sick one of his last actions was to propose that a subscription should be raised for one whom he thought deserved it and to whom it would be acceptable. He was most loyal to his Corps ; even in chaff he would never allow it to be said that an ' L ' Company man played second fiddle to anyone. During his comparatively short term of duty at this office he made many friends, as was proved by the large number of soldiers who were present at the funeral. The interment took place on Monday, 21st, at 3 p.m. The body, covered with a Union Jack, was conveyed on a gun carriage to that part of the veldt reserved as a cemetery. A firing party provided by the 3rd Durham Light Infantry led the procession. The mourners were Sappers J. Read, A. J. Brooks, A. W. Swan, Mr. Black (Soldiers' Home), Mr. Dudley Kays (Civil Telegraphs), and detachments of the 3rd and the 15th Hussars. The Rev. Mr. Oakley

KHAKI LETTERS—*continued*.

(Soldiers' Home) read the Burial Service at the grave. As the body of our dear old comrade was consigned to its last resting place, the 'Last Post' rang out in solemn notes from the bugle, and the firing party paid the final honours to all that was mortal of that fine soldier. J. L. Metcalfe. The hymn, 'For Ever with the Lord,' was then sung, and Mr. Oakley concluded the service by pronouncing the Benediction. So ended one of the most touching scenes I have ever witnessed. A soldier's funeral is an impressive ceremony at home, it is ten times more so out here on the lonely veldt, and more especially so when the lost one is a good comrade and a close friend. We have erected a small cross pending a more fitting memorial. I trust you received the cable from Brooks and I in time to break the news to Mrs. Metcalfe before the official information reached. All at this office are well, hope it is ditto with you. Best regards to all."

"P.S.—I enclose the most recent photo of poor Met., which I thought you might like to have reproduced in KHAKI LETTERS; I have the loan of it from an Infantry Telegraphist, they were all given away when I arrived here. I also enclose a tribute from our Clerk-in-charge, Sapper J. Read. We all miss 'Met.'s' genial presence very much; his untimely death has cast a gloom over the place. Trusting you are very well."

NOTE.—The photo referred to was reproduced in KHAKI LETTERS, page 168. The wire to "Poniard, London," was also duly attended to.

No. 4612, Sapper **Frank Somerville** (EES), on board s.s. Montfort, May 10th, writes :—

"We are still going strong on board here, the favourable conditions still continuing, although, of course, as we neared the line we had some very tight weather indeed, so much so that everyone went about as near 'mit nodings on' as possible. We arrived at Las Palmas somewhere about 9 o'clock on Wednesday night. When we had anchored, everyone but officers, guard and police, were ordered below. Our little detachment have been appointed police, and were able to be on deck and see what little there was to be seen. I, however, being at the time one of the mess orderlies was not, of course, a policeman, still I rigged myself up like the other Johnnies, went up on deck, ordered people below with a commanding air and voice, passed muster all right, and was able to stay on deck as long as I liked. Soon after we got the decks clear a boat came alongside from the shore with a bluejacket and a flashlight apparatus. As no doubt you saw in the paper some time ago, the 'Sicilian' (which sailed shortly before the 'Montfort') went aground at Las Palmas. It was with regard to the 'Sicilian' that the flashlight was brought aboard to signal messages and orders to and from the shore. As the Morse code was used we were soon able to read what passed very easily, thereby astonishing the military officers on board not a little, one of them the Adjutant who was prowling around the deck heard us reading out the messages, pounced on one of our men and took him up near his own quarters to read him the messages as they came. He (the adjutant) was very anxious to know what our orders were, at least what the ship's captain's orders were, as there was some idea that we might be sent to Ashanti. However, there was nothing about Ashanti in the messages, the authorities only wanted to know how many men and horses we could take from the 'Sicilian.' Our reply was 24 men and 10 horses, after which we received the order 'proceed with coaling and await further orders.' Of

KHAKI LETTERS—*continued*.

course, we could not see our own flashlight, but were able to get near enough to read by sound the movement of the shutter. When I got on deck the following morning I was fairly astounded by the picture Las Palmas and the hills beyond presented. I never thought to see anything like it outside a picture book, the colours were absolutely beautiful for solid land, in fact I thought at first it was the effect of the sunrise on the clouds which made such a lovely picture. We were just finishing coaling as I arrived on deck, and soon after the native boats, stocked with almost anything from canaries to cigarettes, came swarming round us, their occupants offering their wares for sale in very broken and limited English, this being compensated for by their varied and excited gesticulations. So far as I could see there wasn't much of a capture in their things. Oranges were selling at 12 to 20 a 1s., bananas 1s. for 30, cigars (very green) from 2s. 6d. to 5s. per hundred, and tins of 50 of Wills' Capstan Cigarettes, 1s. White of TS, however, went shares in a very good bargain, succeeding in knocking a man down from £1 to 7s. 6d. for 100 'Henry Clays.' Being mess orderly I had very little opportunity of getting on deck and didn't trouble to get anything, thinking that I should have a good chance after breakfast, but whilst we were breakfasting away we steamed again with hardly any warning. I guess it would amuse you hugely to see me at the mess orderly business, so I'll give you an idea of the duties. Before every meal one of us has to parade at the Troop galley for the food, and in the case of breakfast and tea, the other orderly goes to the bakehouse and gets a small loaf for each man in his mess ; we are supposed to serve out every course into (in our case) 14 portions, so that every man gets the same amount. When all the animals are supplied we can have a cut ourselves. After breakfast, away one of us scoots to the galley for hot water for washing up, and think we're lucky if we get it once in six times. After washing up the crocks the table and forms must be scrubbed down, the deck swept and either scrubbed or mopped. As you may well imagine, the atmosphere in the Troop deck was very tight indeed as we got into the warm latitudes, and the perspiration would roll off us in great style when we came to the scrubbing and mopping, for of course we got over it as quickly as possible so as to get on deck in the air, our time being our own after the clearing up. When my turn of mess orderly came to an end I became one of the police on board, and went stalking about on deck with 'a nye like a nauk' for offenders, wearing a badge with R.M.P. on it on my arm. These badges were very home-made crude affairs, made of canvas begged from the bo'sun, and marked with the indelible pencil.

"Soon after leaving Las Palmas they started inoculating the troops ; a lot of the Sergeants were done first, and one or two of them had apparently a rather rough time, the worst part seeming to be the weakening after-effects. Young, Tozer, White, and Hargreaves, of T.S., went through it first of our lot, the first-named being rather bad for 2 or 3 days. I daresay the weather had something to do with it, we were nearing the line and it was stinking hot, so hot indeed that the doctor stopped inoculating until we had crossed the line. I considered well and weighed up the chances, and came to the conclusion that it was worth going through, as, after all, it was only a day or two of inconvenience, and I should feel very much safer and more satisfied in my own mind after being done. A lot of 'em cried off, simply, I think, because they funked the pain. Anyway I went for it, and feel very glad now that I did. You bare the side to start with, and have it rubbed over with carbolic acid. The doctor has a kind of syringe with a hollow needle at the end, and having drawn up sufficient serum, jams the needle into your side,

KHAKI LETTERS—*continued*.

and squirts in the typhoid serum. There is no pain in the above operation beyond the first pricking feeling, and you feel nothing for about half-an-hour. You have to go in the Hospital then and get into bed. I tried to get to sleep, so as to sleep through the worst part, but got no sleep at all that night. I found the pain, which seemed to me to be an exaggerated kind of stitch, gradually increase up to about the fourth or fifth hour, when it then very gradually began to get better. At its worst it was rather annoying, but I could always bear it so long as I kept still. This, however, was difficult to do, as I found it next to impossible to get a comfortable position in bed, and I can tell you was very glad when morning came.

"I have several times regretted that I didn't take advantage of G.'s offer of his camera. I have missed some jolly interesting and unique chances, notably one I had on the first Sunday after leaving Las Palmas; we had a canvas bath fixed up on deck, to be used from 4 a.m. to 8 a.m. I suppose the powers that be thought that the bath had not been taken full advantage of. Some of the men certainly appeared to belong to the great unwashed, so on the Sunday afternoon all hands except police and guards had to parade on deck, strip, and have the hose played on them. It was a sight for the gods, and caused no end of fun, the officers especially being immensely tickled, the men under the hose dancing about and yelling like so many fiends, their antics and noise reminding me strongly of those savages at the last Military Tournament. The Adjutant, on the occasion of his birthday some few days ago, offered several prizes for boxing competitions. Of course the scrapping went down in grand style, the exhibitions being very popular, although, with one or two exceptions, there was very little science displayed, 'bashing' being the order of the day in most cases. A grand concert was also organized, at which all the officers were present. I wasn't there myself, being in hospital through inoculation. For the last few days there has been a rather heavy swell on, and the boat has been rolling about in rare style in consequence, yet I don't think there has been a case of sea sickness. Up to crossing the line the weather conditions had been a lot in our favour, and we anticipated doing a record trip; since then we have had a strong head wind which has upset our calculations somewhat. I shall be pleased to get on dry land once more; its apt to grow monotonous on board, as we seem always to be in the same street when we look round. There's a rumour about that we (the R.E.'s) will go round to Durban, and possibly from there to Beira. I don't think it has much foundation however, I don't suppose anyone knows or will know our destination till we get to Cape Town.

"*May* 18*th*.—To-day we had a genuine bit of excitement and an item of news from the outer world, to afford food for discussion and congratulation for hours. We passed, at about 9 a.m., the S.S. 'Induna' (chartered by Elder, Dempster for cattle business) close enough to speak, and learnt from them that Mafeking had been relieved, and that Kroonstadt had been occupied by Lord Roberts. You bet we didn't forget to yell. I suppose there were grand doings in London when they heard the news. We're after a bottle of whisky to-night to celebrate the occasion; can't get much in that line, you know, and have to be very circumspect about getting it, and drinking it too."

Somerville continues his letter as follows:—

"Fort Knokke, Capetown, May 22nd.

"*Terra firma* at last! We arrived in Table Bay about 5 p.m., Saturday, the weather being rather dull. After hanging about all day Sunday, we eventually landed at Capetown on Monday afternoon by tug. As it happened,

KHAKI LETTERS—*continued*.

we landed at a very opportune moment, the day being observed as a public holiday on account of the Relief of Mafeking. The streets being crowded with sightseers and impromptu processions, which latter were received with great hilarity and deafening uproar. I've read, of course, scores of times about motley crowds, but I never fully realised what they were until I saw Capetown *en fête* last night. Upon my word, they were motley. Pretty well every nation under the sun being there, Asiatics predominating. It's no good trying to describe here what I saw, it seems as though I could go on for ever and then not be done. I shall really have to give it to you by instalments when I return. I had a rare surprise here on our arrival, yesterday. Who should I see but Catling, from EES, who is here recuperating, after having had two or three goes of dysentery. He looks in splendid health—much better than he was at home, as does Jenner, of TS, who is also here on the same wheeze. I had a fine time in Capetown last night (which, by the way, is like Aldershot for the number of soldiers about), being piloted round by Catling, who is going to take me on a visit to an old N.W district telegraphist who is Postmaster of Sea Point, near Capetown, and who, I understand, does the thing in rare style. So I suppose I shall be O.K."

No. 4373, Sapper **T. W. Stevenson,** writing from Kroonstadt, May 14th, describes the journey out on the " Winifredian " and the 67 hours' train ride from Capetown to Bloemfontein. His after experiences were not all honey. He says : – " Ruffell met us, and we took all our stuff (kit, working materials, &c.) into the office-yard. Sergt. Nelson found us quarters in an ex-butcher's shop, on the bare floor, full of fleas, &c., but we didn't care so long as we got a sleep. On 7 to 2 duty next morning ; Bill Pearce and I punching the whole time without stopping. Nosed round the town afterwards and bought a few luxuries—cheese, 2s. a lb. ; tea, 6d. a cup ; bread and butter, 3d. a slice, &c. Ben Walton and I were going to visit Bill Wilson, but were suddenly ordered to push on and catch headquarter column up (Tuesday, May 8th) Then our troubles commenced in earnest. We entrained at 8.30, but didn't start till 12.30. Travelled on open trucks all night to Vet River, arriving there 6 p.m. Got some tea, made with greasy water, kindly boiled for us in the Basutos' Camp. Then joined a trek-ox convoy. It took nineteen span to pull us through the river, as the Boers had made a nice mess of the bridge. Our party consisted of Ben Walton, Hamer, and self (of TS), Stevenson (BM), Poole (IV), and McQueen (GW). Slept that night on bags of bran, and trekked till 9 a.m. Laagered up and outspanned our 18 oxen, made tea with water from a stagnant pool as thick as soapsuds. Ugh ! Made shift with this, bully beef and hard biscuits. Slept till 3.30, when Ben went to a well a mile away for some drinkable water. Off again. 4.30 till 12, when we slept " 'neath the blue vault of heaven " till 6 a.m Then on to Zand River, where our rations gave out, and the convoy officer could not supply us with food or take us any further. We only got half a biscuit that day and then joined Lieut. Moir with an air-line convoy dragged by mules. They 'took' the Zand River in grand style, and then bivouacked for the night.

"Next morning off at 6, marching 12 miles on a pint of coffee and nothing to eat. Got my feet nicely blistered and finished the day's journey on the wagon. We had full rations served out again this night, and I mounted guard, 11 to 2. Found a fine pony straying and captured him, but didn't keep him myself. Off again, 7 a.m., and marched the whole 21 miles into

KHAKI LETTERS—*continued.*

Kroonstadt with only two hours' halt, nearly killing me, and making my left heel very bad indeed. Signed on here at 6 p.m. last night, and did 11 p.m. to 2 a.m. duty ; on again to-day, 2 p.m. to 10 p.m., and then eight hours off and eight hours on continuously. Hobbled round the town and got a note book at a shop filled with ' Swaddies,' half buying and half looting. Sentries at all 'pubs,' and no intoxicants procurable at any price. Can't spend any money at present, so am letting it accumulate. Am looking forward to a re-union loving cup with the pals, to whom give my kindest remembrances."

No. 4,381, Sapper **B. Walton**, writes a few lines in same letter, to say he's "all right, and likes the life immensely, 'tho it's rather rough." Sends remembrances to all friends.

No. 4,363, Sapper **W. G. Carter**, 1st T.D. R.E., writing from Bloemfontein, May 14th, says :—

"Dear Colours,—Several copies of KHAKI LETTERS arrived by the English Mail this morning, and those who did not receive them were very busy trying to borrow them from their more fortunate comrades, and they are very much appreciated. The 'Winifredian' arrived in Table Bay after a fine voyage, about 5 o'clock on Monday, April 23rd, and everybody was very excited and prepared to land. But instead of landing this Monday morning, the good ship 'Winifredian' laid in the bay till Friday evening ; so you can guess spirits were not of the highest, eating salt junk and bad potatoes in sight of land. We landed on Saturday morning, and the Refugee Ladies' Committee gave us buns and ginger beer, and then we marched to Fort Knokke. We pitched tents and got quickly into town to have our first glimpse of Cape Town and South Africa. We could get a second class return into town for 1½d., and the train would stop outside the camp, if asked. On the following Tuesday we had a route march round part of the base of Table Mountain, and got up as far as an old Dutch fort. When we got back to camp, orders had come for 10 of us to go to Kimberley, and 36 to Bloemfontein, amongst whom for Kimberley were Frew, Semple, Ash and Macmurtrie, from TS. We for Bloemfontein entrained at Salt Lake same night about 10 o'clock, and for about an hour sat up like sardines in a tin. After we had packed our kit bags, blankets and accoutrements, we managed to get five berths for eight men, but still, we got on pretty fair. We woke up at Worcester and had breakfast, and I might say here that Kelly, from Aldgate, is our cook, so you know we fare all right. We travelled three nights and three days, the second night the driver of our train went mad, and had to be taken care of. We passed Catling at Prince Alfred Road, and Ray as well, and Jenner at Victoria Road All of them going to Cape Town, either to Wynberg or home. The scenery soon begins to pall on one, as it is nothing but kopjes and scanty bush, with here and there a hut or a Kaffir kraal. We stopped at De Aar just long enough to get a few letters, and saw Govier and Quinn and Corpl. Whibley, all of whom were looking well. Same night we saw Sergt.-Major Lee, at Naauwpoort. At Norvals Pont Bridge they turned us out of our comfortable sleep at two o'clock in the morning, and had to proceed the rest of the journey on top of baggage waggons, and it was intensely cold in the night.   e saw Norvals Pont Bridge which the Boers blew up, and dozens of dead horses rotting all along the veldt. We travelled in the same way all the next day, and at Springfontein saw Jim Brooks, and Swan and Bradshaw, of the R.A M.C. (News). When we got a

KHAKI LETTERS—*continued*.

few miles from Bloemfontein the wagon next the front guard's van caught fire . . . . (Described elsewhere, R.E.K.). When we got into the town we saw Corpl. Ruffell, and soon got to our quarters. Ours is a nice house, one which has been deserted probably by some Dutch. There are a lot of houses full of furniture, but devoid of occupants. We work in three shifts, 7 a.m. to 2 p.m., 2 p.m. to 11 p.m., 11 p m. to 7 a.m., and there is always plenty of work ; but we do not mind that, considering the good news which keeps coming through. Tom Stevenson, Ben Walton, and McQueen have been moved up to Brantford, and several more expect to go to Kroonstadt very soon.

" Bloemfontein is a very dull place, and all civilians have to be in kip by 8 o'clock at night, unless allowed a pass. All the big colleges and the Raadzaal are used as hospitals, and all the troops are camped outside the town. The band of the 6th Division plays in the market square every other day, and what with the niggers standing round, and the Cape carts. drawn by 8 and 9 pair of oxen, and the white houses, puts one in mind of Savage South Africa at Earl's Court, only not nearly so savage.

" Great talk here that Roberts is trying to get into Pretoria by Queen's Birthday, and if he has no more opposition he may do it.

" I met Phillips, of the Electricals, here (of L Division), and they have done some good work, and now have been lighting up Bloemfontein station with electric light. Captain Palmer, of the A.P.O.C., is here.

" The Church of England Cathedral is pack full of khaki on Sunday evening, and a very enjoyable light service is held. Lord Kitchener was there last Sunday week. The Duke of Norfolk is here, being attached to General Kelly-Kenny's Staff.

" Surprised at the changes going to be made for Camp. How is the department going to spare the men, and what of the 150 men of the I Company. Good herbs !

" Best wishes to all friends and to yourself.

" Percy Milton has gone forward. Jack Fallon, Wright, C. Payne, Birch, Ruffell, Porter (Woolwich) are here."

No. 4,333, Sapper **A. W. York,** who was taken prisoner on May 22nd at Heilbron, writing the previous week, May 15th, from Kroonstadt, says :—

" No doubt you read in the papers about this date, of something under the heading of 'Roberts's Victorious March to Kroonstadt.' but as they did not mention your humble, here followeth a few notes by one of the marchers. I spent a month at Bloemfontein, most of the time being occupied by stiff work at the Head Telegraph Office. In the small amount of leisure we got we made friends with our neighbours over the wall, from whom we received some small comforts, but latterly lived in a house with a verandah and six or seven high-roofed rooms, but minus furniture. On the 8th, a small party of us left by train for Vet River, in charge of an affable Sergeant, but had the misfortune to lose our provisions, jam, milk, butter, &c., so were reduced to biscuits for a day. We slept on the veldt that night, and roamed about in search of transport next day, as the railways were blown up beyond, but only succeeded in getting a Scotch cart at 8 p.m., when we set off on a moonlight tramp of six miles to Smaldeel, where we found the Army resting At Smaldeel I joined my section with the air-line wagon, but as the route was along the railway, our work was principally repairs, which were necessary whenever we came to a destroyed bridge, and

KHAKI LETTERS—*continued*.

at several points where the enemy had shot off the insulators, presumably for want of targets. At night we rigged up a shelter with the wagon cover and some poles, which was rather better than sleeping in the open. We breakfasted on coffee and biscuits at 4.30 each morning, and averaged 16 miles per day, only halting for water or breaks, usually getting into Camp at 5 p.m., when we made a hasty cup of tea, and after clearing up, sat down to supper round the camp fire. This meal was by no means frugal, as we managed to loot poultry every day, and sometimes a sheep or hare ; mutton, hare and turkey soup is splendid. We halted at Welgelegen on the 9th, when I had my first wash for three days ; had it not been for the extra weight of dirt I should not have been tired at all. Next day there was a little scrap at Sands River, where the enemy had a splendid position, but a few shots from our naval guns drove them off, and the troops proceeded resistlessly on their way to Riet Spruit. Next day was our hardest for work, the line being totally destroyed for two miles, but we put up air lines and poles at the same rate as the convoy travelled. I was sent on in front and could not find the wagon for two hours when the camp was reached, so must own to being tired that night. Kroonstadt was reached at noon on the 12th, there being no fighting, to the surprise of every Tommy, although the Boers had a splendid position. The English were delighted to see us, and I had a good feed at one house, while cups of tea and coffee were pressed upon us at every turn. We had three hours' work repairing the line over a bridge, then went into the town and saw the march past, which was loudly cheered by the English residents. Am now attached to Headquarters in the Town Office, doing eight hours on duty and eight off. The place is smaller than Bloemfontein, but similar, about a dozen streets and houses along the railway. All shops are closed, but we get bread from friends.

"Please remember me to the Division, and let Colour-Sergeant Kemp see this. Pickford, Bourlay (SY), Poole (BS), and Grant (AB) accompanied me. First two left at Smaldeel, Grant at Brandfort. Poole (IV), Hamer, Walton, McQuinn (GW), Stevenson (TS), and Stevenson (BM.) arrived last night. Sainsbury also here. Hope you've seen my other letters."

No. 4,376, Sapper **W. W. Pearce**, writing on May 17th, from Bloemfontein, says : —

"DEAR OLD KEMP,—We arrived at Cape Town after 27 days on the water, five days being spent out in Simon's Bay. Taken all round, it was a good trip. Our quarters at Cape Town were Fort Knokke, but after being there three days, we were ordered up country,—36 to above, and 10 to Kimberley. Three days in the train, part of the journey being done on top of trucks loaded up with various stores. We met several TS men at various stations up country, and passed Jenner and Catling going down to the base, queer. The journey, although somewhat interesting at the start, developed into monotony with too much similarity of scene. It got interesting again when we entered the Free State, as, after crossing the Orange River at Norvals Pont, where a fine railway bridge had been blown into a cocked hat, we passed country where some stiff fighting had taken place. Horses, galore, were rotting, and for a long way you passed rudely made graves, with rough stones to mark them, where poor Tommy was peacefully at rest. From Worcester to De Aar, Ben Walton, Sorensen and myself, were told off to guard three Munster prisoners in the guard's brake. After passing Prince

KHAKI LETTERS—*continued*.

Albert Road, the engine driver went mad, and Sorensen and myself were sent up to tackle him. After a struggle in the dark, of about five minutes' duration, further assistance was procured, and eventually it took eight men to overpower him. I came out of the deal with a badly twisted knee, which has badly handicapped me since. Just before reaching Bloemfontein, while rushing down a decline, a truck caught fire, and before the train could be pulled up was well alight. There were seven or eight Tommies on top, and most of them took a flying leap before the train had stopped. The truck was packed with ammunition and blankets, and before they were thrown out were burnt through to their tin casings.

"We were met at Bloemfontein by Ruffell, and quickly marched off to our quarters by Nelson—who has been made Acting Quartermaster-Sergeant —to a broken-down house, evidently been used as a store by a misguided Free Stater. What a beautiful town this is, lying between two kopjes, and the surrounding country fairly level. The Post Office, situated in the Market Place, is a splendid structure, red bricked, with white edgings. The Market Place is at least 100 yards across, and three days a week the country people hold market there. All kinds of vegetables which we have in England are grown here, and very fine specimens too. The town is infested with Basutos, the Staters having to a great extent made their exodus. Lot of TS men here. Before our arrival, the Staff was working 15 and 16 hours a day, with about three days delay; but now we are cut up into three shifts,—7 a.m. to 2 p.m., 2 p.m. to 11 p.m., 11 p.m. to 7 a.m. Men are now being gradually shifted up to the front, including Stevenson and Walton, and shortly, I think, the majority will shift to Kroonstadt. We work Wheatstone to Kimberley, on a very rocky wire, and it is a matter of impossibilty to keep pace with the work. Enteric and dysentery have been a terrible scourge, and from morning to night a regular procession of funeral parties wend their way up Monument Hill to the Cemetery. They are quiet and unostentatious, the corpse on a stretcher, sewn in a military blanket, carried by soldiers.

"We shifted our quarters last week to a fort, strangely enough, formerly used as a School for Signalling and Telegraphy by the Free State Army. Numerous interesting relics were found, including diagrams of various instruments. I enclose one or two, showing the students to be no mugs at the game.

"The boys wish to be remembered to you, hoping you are well."

No. 4,351, Sapper **W. N. Kelly**, of EDO, writing on a postcard from Bloemfontein, O.F.S., May 18th, says :—

"DEAR COLOURS.—Pardon brevity. Hope you and all comrades are well. Will write when I get a moment. Don't find much spare time, as am on cooking. Thought card a novelty."

NOTE.—The card depicts Major-General Baden Powell leading a charge. It is a novelty, certainly, but on closer examination I find the card is published, not only in London, but within fifty yards of the 24th Mx. R.V. Orderly Room, to wit, Drapers' Gardens, E.C.

No. 220, Sergt. **J. W. Miller**, 1st T.D. R.E., Kimberley, May 21st, writes :—

"MY DEAR COLOURS,—The time no doubt will seem to you to be very long since you last heard from me, but it has passed very quickly here owing to the very heavy amount of work we have to get through daily. One would be surprised at the amount that passes through one wire (Wheatstone) to

KHAKI LETTERS—*continued.*

Bloemfontein in the course of the day, and I am sorry to say that, owing to faulty instruments at Bloemfontein, it causes delay and blocks both ends completely. Still, it usually vanishes, for nearly all the men do their best to see the line clear of slip and the pile of messages to be punched got rid of. I have had lately a staff af 53 all told, but owing to opening offices on the Mafeking line ('Content'), Warrenton, Warrenton Camp, Windsorton Road, Dronfield, Fourteen Streams and Boshof, and several men going sick, it has somewhat lessened the total. I am sorry to say that several have left for Capetown and some for home. Fenton, from Dundee, being the last to leave; others have gone since my last letter, Alliston, Jenner, Stormer, Maclaren; and those still in hospital are Greenfield (MR), Hurdle, Pallett (TS), Rice, and Usher (Ex-R.E. from TS). The weather has, I believe, a great deal to do with it, being hot during the day and starting to get cold directly the sun has vanished, when extra clothing is desirable.

"One soon gets tired of Kimberley, for there is practically nothing to see after six o'clock at night, for it is quite dark; scarcely a shop open, with the exception of Saturday nights, when the whole town turn out to do their shopping. Then it looks quite gay with the electric light burning in all the different roads. The only thing worth seeing in Kimberley are the Diamond Fields. I had the pleasure of paying a visit to De Beers mines one afternoon last week, and it was most interesting. Three of us—Sergt.-Major Aplin, Quartermaster-Sergt. Kilburn, R.E., and self—went through the works, where we saw the the pulverised earth being washed by machinery and divided to the large and small stones, going through the courses till they came to the shoot where they find the diamonds. They place grease on each layer as the stones come through, and the strange part about it is that stones will not remain on the layers by the force of the water, yet directly a diamond comes through it immediately sticks fast in the grease. When the attendant can see he has several sticking the machinery is stopped, all the grease and diamonds are scraped up and put in a very fine sieve when they are heated to allow the contents to be left clean. We then went to the sorting room and saw several at different tables, and the same stuff all had to go through different hands, under the supervision of a very old gentleman, who quietly watched each worker. From there we were asked to go to the Secretary's room, and were shown some thousands of diamonds, one would hardly realise the number found from the mine each day. Some were exquisite specimens. One being especially pointed out as being the largest that had been found for some time. A lovely pure white stone; stating in its rough state it was worth £160, of course it would be worth much more on its being cut. A visit was also paid to the top of the Conning Tower, which the Boers, during the siege, always used to be firing at, and being of a good height it did not say much for their supposed accurate shooting. A bugler used to blow his bugle when he saw the smoke leave the gun, and thus gave people time to rush to the trenches built in different parts of the town. A splendid view all round Kimberley can be had.

"I don't think this is very much like active service, having been here three months, but I'm glad I had a ripping time round Naauwpoort, Modder River, and a week's construction until I arrived here. Since then I've been a fixture, and it is my hard luck that I shall most probably have to finish up here till it is time to come home. Am pleased to say have had good health since I have been out, and very sorry to hear of our severe losses and the large amount of sickness. However, we are all doing our best each for the credit of the noble 24th and for the office to which he is attached All the

KHAKI LETTERS—*continued*.

lads here are especially pleased with KHAKI LETTERS, and I offer you my congratulations, good old Dick, and personally wish you every success. I hope Jacob is better and Sergt. Jackman quite recovered from his serious illness. Regards to all friends."

"P.S.—I hear to-day Hurdle is better. Had a big fire next to office, thought we were going to be burnt out on Thursday. Soldiers. Staff and Firemen all assisted and just saved office, which had begun to catch at the roof, 12 o'clock in the day. Plenty of hams commandeered Troops feeding well for breakfast. Staff bought a football to play a match against the Railway Staff also the Civil Office."

No. 4327, Sapper **A. J. Brooks,** writing from Springfontein on May 25th, says :—

"DEAR COLOUR-SERGEANT,—The letter you will receive from Swan *re* poor Met.'s death leaves little for me to add. We sent you a cable to 'Poniard' on the Sunday after, in the hope that it would reach you before the official announcement and perhaps enable his friends to break the sad news to his wife. The first ten days of his illness he spent in the hospital established in the little iron church here by the 22nd Field Hospital. Bradshaw (of News Division) was with this hospital, and Met. got every attention from all concerned, most of the hospital staff being from Met.'s own county. When No. 3 General Hospital arrived here the Field Hospital handed over their patients and went on. The General Hospital was a much more comfortable concern than the other, large airy marquees and everything necessary for the sick, and Met. seemed to improve considerably. We were asked not to go to the enteric marquees too often, so arranged to go every Sunday. Messrs. Black and Oakley, of the Soldiers' Home, were frequent visitors, and were exceedingly kind to both Met. and Sapper Cooke, who came up from Bethulie and lay in the next bed. They thought Met. had taken a turn for the better, it was therefore a great shock to us all when we heard the sad news on Sunday morning. Met. was generous and mindful of others right up to the very last, and his death has left a vacancy in our little circle that can never be filled. His funeral was simple and impressive, Mr. Oakley, of the Soldiers' Home, conducted the service, at the conclusion of which all present gathered around the grave and sang the hymn "For ever with the Lord." Mr. Dudley Kays of the Civil Tels. and Sergt. Kimber with a number of men of the 3rd and 15th Hussars very kindly came right across the veldt to pay this tribute of respect to our old friend. Met. made friends wherever he went, only last night some men of the 12th Coy. R.E., passing through this station invalided from the front, called in to see their old Stormberg chum. A small wooden cross made by a friend at the Soldiers' Home and lettered by a comrade of the Ordnance Corps has been placed at the head of the grave to mark his last resting place until something better can be done. I think Sergt.-Major Tee is seeing about the erection of some small memorial to our comrades who have fallen in S.A. If Met.'s friends in our old Division would like a little card or tablet placed on the grave, I will see that it receives proper attention. The rest of us here are in good health. Quinn and Whibley passed through for Bloemfontein last night with the 'Clearing House' all well. Things exceedingly quiet here at present, and practically nothing more to write about even if I felt like writing at such a time. Hope all goes well with you and all friends at home."

Sapper Frank Walter Robinson.

DERBY furnishes the fifth victim of the Telegraph Reserve Company to disease. Our comrade, No. 4335, Sapper F. W. Robinson, joined the 24th Middlesex R.V.C. as an "efficient," on February 6th, this year, and was transferred to the R.E. Reserves a few days later, sailing for South Africa on board the s.s. "Cephalonia," from Southampton, on Feb. 20th. He was born March 1st, 1874, entered the Service and appointed S.C. and T., at Derby, April 23rd, 1892, and succumbed to the scourge - dysentery— at Ladysmith, on May 23rd, aged 26 years. The first intimation of the death of our colleague was given in the dailies, but the initials were not those of our boy. Oh, how anxiously did we wait further intelligence, and hold tight to what we dared to think might possibly have been an error. Alas! for human frailty. "We regret to inform you." Ominous words those, and the many ears which were strained to catch any spark of hope were destined to know that it was forlorn. Possessed of vigourous health, a manly figure, good parents, and plenty of companions, how could a man be anything but content and happy in such circumstances. His cheery disposition won him innumerable friends, and the hearty grasp of hands with which we parted

company with him are true testimony to his genuineness as a fellow worker. Frank, during his service at Derby, had indeed endeared himself to all by his kind and pleasant disposition and friendliness. To say that he was respected by everyone in Derby, and that he will be greatly missed, seem very ordinary and common-place words when we apply them to him. The week previous to learning the dread news, a fellow-clerk received one of the most cheery letters it has been our pleasure to read. We mourn him. We sympathise with his parents and relatives. Ah, we weep with ye who weep.

No. 4,335, Sapper **F. W. Robinson** (of DY), writing 13th April, 1900, from Pound's Plateau, Ladysmith, says:—

"We are having quite a 'cushy' time of it. We got to Ladysmith on April 4th, after a railway journey through the most magnificent scenery. On the way, we saw the bridge at Colenso that was blown up by the Boers, and we saw some of their trenches by the side of the railway. But I am getting on too fast with my narrative. Will go back to Cape Town. We lay in Table Bay three days and then went into harbour for two days, but were not allowed on shore. We left by the 'Antillion,' a rather slow but wonderful clean and roomy boat. Major Glubb, R.E., was in command, and he is a clinking officer. We called at Port Elizabeth and East London. The former is a pretty place, but East London looks more like England, as we saw the first bit of green there since leaving the homeland. Port Elizabeth lies in a bay, but there is no harbour; whilst East London has a harbour for light ships, but there is no bay. We anchored in the open sea there.

"On the railway ride from Durban, the inhabitants treated us right royally. At every station we called there was tea, pine apples, bananas, oranges (green), and anything we liked to have. The vegetation of Natal is lovely. I have had a ride in a mule wagon, which is a treat. Ten mules going full gallop with a springless wagon over any mortal thing that happens to be in the track. Rock, dead horses—all alike, whilst the passengers hold on for dear life. One man drives and another whips.

"I was rather unfortunate at being left at Headquarters, as there has been some fighting up there. On Saturday, three of us helped to put up a wire to Field's Farm, about seven miles west of Ladysmith, and we took charge of the Second Cavalry Brigade office there. On Tuesday night the Camp was suddenly struck, and we retreated to Ladysmith in a heavy thunderstorm. We got lost on the Veldt, but managed to find ourselves on the banks of the Klip River, and after an hour's walk got safely to Headquarters. Next morning, we were rushed off to the Second Cavalry Brigade again, this time encamped at foot of Bulwana. Shall climb it to-morrow, as we have little to do just now besides cooking our meals and drawing our two pints of beer daily. We do all our cooking on an ant-heap, and I am getting a champion at mutton chops. The water we get is as thick as pudding, but we don't drink it until its been boiled, and made into tea or coffee. Standing with my back to Bulwana, Cæsar's Camp and Wagon Hill are on the left, Ladysmith is straight in front, and Surprise Hill just behind the town. Lombards Kop and Gun Hill are close to on the right, and Spion Kop looms in the distance. Ladysmith is a very small town. The food here is good, and, so far, I have no complaints or dissatisfaction with the life of a Tommy."

April 17th. "Since writing above, I have been up Bulwana, and stood in the sangar where Long Tom was fired. The floor is cement, boarded over, and the sandbags were a tremendous thickness. Yesterday we had some regimental sports here,—running, wrestling on horseback, &c. We have a game of cricket every morning. Nearly trod on a big snake this morning, when returning from my morning dip in the Klip River.

"Thanks for envelopes and paper, which were welcome, as my stock is nearly exhausted. Give my kind regards to everybody."

Requiescat in Pace.

Swift to the call of Britain's need
Her gallant sons unfaltering go,
O'er rolling Veldt, with dauntless speed,
To quell the rising of her foe.

And thou, our comrade, brother, friend,
Wast not behind the foremost there ;
Whate'er a patriot's soul could lend
Was gladly yielded as thy share.

Rest then in peace, thy fight well o'er,
Aye, rest within thy honoured grave !
Green will thy name be evermore
Thou worthy son of England's brave !

Postal Telegraphs, Derby.

—I. P,

"Khaki Notes."

The "Bloemfontein Post," May 14th, gives an account of the R.E. Concert. The following extracts are sufficient to shew that our boys are "all there":—

"A smoking concert, organised by the R.E.T.D., was held in the Wesleyan Schoolroom, last Friday evening. The little edifice was crammed, and the announcement in 'The Post' seemed to be taken advantage of, for the Tommies were there in full force. The Rev. Mr. Marklow kindly officiated as chairman, and opened the proceedings with a nice little speech. A few ladies who were present relieved the omnipresent monotony of khaki with their bright colours.

"Sapper Milton (of TS), the first 'turn,' sang with great gusto 'A Jovial Monk.' Indeed, he only required the long flowing robes of that jolly cleric to complete the picture of a jocose and stalwart monk. Next on the programme came Sapper Bannister (of MR), an able elocutionist, whose rendering of 'The Poet's Reverie' gained for him unstinted applause, and, when called upon for an *encore*, mounted the platform and said 'if he were not taking up too much time, he would try and give them 'Cronje's farewell to his troops,' which in effect amounted to a few dramatic motions and the words 'Troops, farewell!' This touch of humour again aroused Tommy Atkins, who let the humourist 'have it' for the second time.

"Mrs. Marthlow's appearance was hailed with enthusiastic acclamation, the delightfully appropriate song which this lady sang with intense feeling, and the gist of which was of home and relations, touched Atkins to the quick, and he yelled the house down on the completion of the song. Sapper Kelznack next obliged with a recitation, 'A Life of Love,' in excellent style, and the usual acclamatory furore naturally accrued. Mr. Feydish gave his hearers a decidly fine piece of violin music, and displayed no mean powers in manipulating the bow over the fairy strings, the outcome being exquisite melody. Sapper Cole's essay on 'The Mule,' composed by himself for the occasion, absolutely knocked 'em. There is no doubt the essay well deserved the applause it elicited.

"The Schmidt quartette sang very prettily, 'Away down upon the Swanee River,' the two boys' voices sounding remarkably clear and metallic against the more mature voices of the two older males. The next turn, erroneously designated by the reverend chairman as 'Trooper' Huson, treated his audience to a display of the comic element in singing 'Giving them all a Turn,' and received an ovation, acknowledging the same with a courtier-like bow. Driver Elphick, L.Y.H., next recited an equine yarn, wherein some young lady saves the honour of a certain young gentleman by riding his horse to win, but unfortunately, is thrown, and, as a natural sequence, dies. Elphick's elocutionary capacities are not of the milk-and-water type, but show the most casual observer that he has studied this difficult art, and his studies have not been in vain. 'A Great Big Shame,' by Sapper Little (of SW), was accorded great praise, as also the last 'turn,' Corporal Ruffell (of TS), who warbled sweetly, 'Love's Old Sweet Song.'

"After a vote of thanks to the chairman for his kind services, the National Anthem was sung, and the party dispersed, one and all unanimously declaring that the whole show went off with great *eclat*. Sapper Williams ably presided at the piano."

The A.P.O.C.—"A bombardier with the Natal Field Force at Sandspruit Camp is full of praise for the Army Post Office Corps. 'We ought to be glad we have such a grand corps (he writes); you should see them at work. There is one sergeant and three men to each field post office, and don't they work! They are at it from five in the morning till nine at night, and after that I have known them to go into the trenches.'"—*Evening News*.

The Mails. It has only just transpired that the Boers on the Zand River recently captured a train containing 2,000 mail bags conveying an accumulation of three weeks' letters for the troops with Lord Roberts. Two members of the Post Office Corps were killed and two wounded, whilst the rolling stock was as far as possible destroyed. There were £4,000 worth of stamps captured with the mail bags. These were English, and specially for the use of our troops, so that they will be useless to the Boers.—C.N. Telegram, Capetown, June 23rd. Where are our letters now?

Notification of the non-receipt of KHAKI LETTERS has reached me from several quarters. A copy has been posted to every man.

KHAKI NOTES—*continued*.

The Assistant Superintendents have taken over the old Senior dining room as their new cloak room, and moved in on the 25th inst., One unfortunight staff gentleman, off at 8 a.m., was occupied for 45 minutes in discovering the whereabouts of his locker. He found it in course of transit at an angle of many degrees out of the perpendicular, plus the contents of a tin of Nestlé's *out* and over his belongings. What joy! The old cloak room will be utilized as an additional lavatory. The "I" Division will also be extended, probably as far as the Controller's room.

Congratulations to the following on their promotions :—
Telegraphists—Messrs. J. D. Smith, E. Bird and Geo. Cowell to be Senior Telegraphists, dated June 9th, 1900. We would like to keep recording such pleasant news daily. Oh, what must it be to be there?

Also to the following gentlemen on their appointments :—
Messrs. G. A. Coates, of SG, and I. Co. (son of the much respected B. Div. Supt.) to Darlington, A. G. McNicol, B. Div., to Newport, Mon., H. J. Hunter, of TSF, to Middlesborough, W. J. Cockshott, also of TSF, to Newcastle-on-Tyne, and F. J. Allen, L. Div., to Mount Pleasant, all as Sub-Engineers.

Mr. Boyle, L. Div., has been transferred to the Surveyor's Office, Dublin.

Mr. Horwill was unfortunately plucked on medical grounds. We wish him better luck next time. A more promising young technical officer it would be hard to find.

Hearty Congrats. to our friend, Adam Gordon, on the eve of his marriage.

Mr. E. Kingston, of the B Division, has resigned, having accepted a Clerkship in Lloyds' Bank. He left TS on June 23rd.

At the attack on the construction train at Leeuwspruit, on June 14th, the Royal Engineers lost heavily, having one corporal killed, two officers and two men wounded (one of the latter since dead), and one officer and fifty-three men missing. These belong to the 7th, 10th (Railway), 20th, and 42nd Cos. R.E., and the Volunteer R.E.'s of the 1st Cheshire, 2nd Cheshire, Devon and Somerset and Electricals. A big loss when so much needed. 24th don't score this time.

Capt. O. T. O. K. Webber, R.E., was captured and taken prisoner at Heilbron, on May 22nd, and, according to Lord Roberts' wire, containing names of the released officers, we find that he recovered, on June 6th, Lieut. M. T. Webber, R.E. We have wondered whether this is one and the same officer. Although the rank and initials may differ, we venture to say they are both "O. K."

Pte. J. Goble, 572, A.P.O.C., and

Pte. F. Rutherford, 566, A.P.O.C., both of whom sailed on the "Montfort," 26/4/00, are reported by the General of Communications amongst the casualties near Rhenoster River, as wounded, June 7th. The Imperial Telegraphist also wounded there is, as anticipated, not one of our Royal Engineers.

Pte. G. Bill, 138, A.P.O.C., is reported dangerously ill at Kimberley, 25—6—00.

Lance-Corpl. E. J. Whibley, 24,387, of the Engineers' Office, has, I hear, suddenly appeared at Aldershot. This information came as a surprise to us, for we did not know he was ill. Enquirers are waiting reply.

Sapper W. V. Wheller, 4,328, I am sorry to learn, is in Ladysmith Hospital, suffering from enteric. "Poniard" is expecting a reply.

Sapper G. Bishop, 2,543, whilst walking up Table Mountain in canvas shoes, was stung by a cactus plant, which produced blood poisoning. Has been in Hospital at Winberg over a month, and underwent an operation to save his leg, and is now either home or very near it.

Sapper J. S. Tough, 24,386, was invalided home on May 31st, and should now be on our shores again, or very near it. We trust our old News Wires comrade will pick up, and regain full strength and vigour. Although AB colleagues claim him as theirs, TS does not forget his service at the C.T.O.

KHAKI NOTES—*continued.*

Sapper A. Ray, 802, has arrived, and is, or was very recently, in Herbert Hospital, Woolwich. He expects to be put on furlough shortly.

"'Poniard, London.' Gone home, thirteenth." Such was the telegram that came to hand on the evening of the 20th instant. It is believed to be a reply to our telegram *re* Bob Luttrell, who is, I hear, on the Princess of Wales' Hospital Ship, nearing Old England.

It is reported that the Duke of Norfolk will be invalided home as soon as he is well enough to travel. He is progressing favourably. Dislocation of the hip is a serious matter, but, fortunately, the Duke was able to receive immediate attention.

We much regret to hear that Mr. T. Mason, Supt. of the Racing Staff, had the misfortune to break two of his ribs on June 15th. This will incapacitate him from duty for some weeks. We trust he will have a speedy recovery.

We announce, with deep regret, the death of Mrs. May, wife of the Controller, who passed away somewhat suddenly on Friday, the 22nd inst. The Telegraph Companies tender their sincere condolences to their Chief in the hour of bereavement.

The sickle has again been busy amongst us. Comrades at the front will learn with regret, as did the C.T.O. staff a few days ago, of the deaths of Messrs.—

E. A. Haggerty, Asst. Supt., B. Div., from typhoid fever. Interred at Forest Hill Cemetery, June 19th.

Barrington Davies, of TSF, formerly of the old FG, from consumption. Interred at Hammersmith Cemetery, June 20th.

Tom Parker, of the News Div., also from consumption. Interred at Hastings Cemetery, June 19th. They passed away within a few hours of each other on Thursday, June 14th, 1900.

The B Division sent a beautiful floral tribute to Mr. Haggerty's funeral, on Tuesday, 19th June, as did also the Assistant Superintendents.

It will interest our T.S. confrères at the front to know that circuit diaries have been dispensed with, a weekly tablet being kept instead. The idea is good in one way, but experience proves the absolute necessity of records being kept of changes, reliefs, faults, and many etceteras, in order to meet a piece of "blue" a few weeks hence. Rumour has it that a popular Stationer was besieged with buyers of cheap pocket diaries lately, so strong is the feeling that a protective record must perforce be privately retained.

Holidays. Comrades are earnestly requested to arrange for their copies to be sent to them; or purchase of the Librarian on resuming duty.

Mr. G. G. Stroud, of the "B" Division, C.T.O., will willingly dispose of any stamps, postcards, or envelopes that our confrères care to send over. There is a great demand, not only in TS but throughout the Provinces. All profits to go to the War Fund, or any fund the sender may select.

Khaki Postage Fund.—Thanks are tendered to the following friends for their kindly help:—Col. du P. T. £2, J. H. (Jarrow) 2s. 6d., E. H. C., (FS) 1s. 6d., H.H. (SW) 10d., and a few smaller sums.

"Poniard, London," For telegrams from Our Boys to their relatives and friends at home, the addresses of whom should be sent us at once.

"Casualties, Capetown," for enquiries *re* sick and wounded.

"KHAKI LETTERS," One Penny. By post, Three Halfpence.

All posted letters containing Remittances, Orders, MSS., &c., must be addressed to R. E. KEMP, 12, JERRARD STREET, LEWISHAM, S.E.

Postal Orders should be made payable at Loampit Vale, Lewisham, S.E.

Printed by E. G. BERRYMAN & SONS, *Blackheath Road, London, S.E.*

"Khaki Letters" from....
"My Colleagues in South Africa."

CORRESPONDENCE FROM THE
POST OFFICE TELEGRAPHISTS
OF THE
24th MIDDLESEX (P.O.) RIFLE VOLUNTEERS
(Royal Engineer Reserves),
ON ACTIVE SERVICE.

THE BOND THAT BINDS US—FRIENDSHIP—COMRADESHIP.

Published fortnightly for the Postal Telegraph Service.
Conducted by COLOUR-SERGEANT R. E. KEMP, *Central Telegraph Office, London.*

No. 13.   JULY 13TH, 1900.   PRICE ONE PENNY.

Central Telegraph Office,
London, E.C.

DEAR COMRADES, ONE AND ALL.
Greetings! Probably my hektographed letter, posted a week ago, has reached you by now. It was a supplementary epistle to those that appear in our booklet. People generally talk a great deal about the weather in their communications, all I will say is, we are having extraordinary climatic varieties. June has gone, and good riddance, for taking it altogether, it was cold, wet and miserable. The last few days have been hot, excessively so. I notice one of your number says you get one and half inches of ice in the early morning and 100° in the sun during the day. That must be very trying to you. It's a pity it doesn't blend better. Continuing in my usual course, the idea of which is to keep you posted up in matters I believe you are most interested in, I will start with Camp. Up to the present time, as far as I can learn, nothing tangible is known. There is something on the board, and there it sticks; it hasn't come off yet. In an interview with the C.O. concerning our attendance at Minster—although the newspapers have repeated Salisbury as our manœuvring ground—he informed me that very few duties could be provided for. Indeed, few more than a score, and even this was uncertain. Another question was a postponement until September, by which time the removed G.P.O. staff would be in better working order, although as far as the Telegraphists were concerned no difference would be apparent. He has promised to acquaint me of the decision as soon as possible, up to now I have heard nothing, so all we can do is to keep our eyes open for sudden orders to clean up or—well, we will wait and see.

You will be glad to hear that our old comrade, Capt. Hodgson, now Sir Frederick Hodgson, Governor of the Gold Coast, has, with Lady Hodgson, escaped from Coomassie, and arrived at Accra yesterday, 10th inst., the remainder of the party being expected to-day. We are pleased to note this, for great fears were entertained for his safety, and the prospects of relief have been far from rosy.

The holidays are in full swing at the C.T.O.—as at all other offices—and, of course, the absence of so many men at the front during the usual summer pressure causes O.T. to be as plentiful as ever. This is what was expected, and daily the strain is getting more severe. You know all about it from your experience in times past. Well, this year it is just the same, only worse.

Your thoughts will, no doubt, have turned to Bisley, with its great N.R.A. Meeting, and perhaps one of the many things to interest you in connection with that event will be the composition of the Staff. The C.T.O. and 24th ("I" Co.) will be represented by the following in the Telegraph Office. Their marching orders are to report themselves as under :—

J. G. Hopgood and H. T. Richardson on Friday, July 6th, at 2 p.m.

W. M. Knight, R. W. Hill, A. E. Perry, B. W. S. Chambers, E. J. Dawe, and D. Davis, on Saturday, July 7th, at 9 a.m.

F. H. Halfpenny, H. H. Harris, L. D. Pither, F. S. Parker, W. Hill (Senr.), A. E. Clarke, and W. J. Kift, on Monday, July 9th, at 9 a.m.

H. Maidment, P. B. Thornton, E. R. Morton, and J. W. Baker, on Tuesday, July 10th, at 10 a.m.

A. Webster and H. G. Deal, on Wednesday, July 11th, at noon.

G. Balchin, A. Sudbury, W. F. Carrick, and J. Stone, Monday, July 16th, at 9 a.m.

Fifteen of above have not previously done duty there. These, with a few from the Provinces, will be, as usual, under the supervision of late Col.-Sergt. J. W. Parish, who did duty as a 24th man in the Egyptian Campaigns of '82 and '85.

Their neighbours, the great Statistical Department, who deal with the cards and are adepts at the game, are also selected from the 24th for service. One would almost take them for Yanks, so numerous are the Stars and Stripes they display. Here they are :—

Col.-Sergt. H. Fox (in charge), Col.-Sergt. W. Hamilton, Sergts. W. J. Hambling. J. Archer, A. Mason, J. F. Redish, E. H. Addiscott, and E. W. Canham, to report at Bisley, Sunday, July 8th, at 6 p.m.

Sergt.-Inst.-Mus. A. J. Bailey, Col.-Sergt. T. J. Bullwinkle, Corpls. S. Curry, V. J. Moody, and K. M. Kendall, the rear being brought up by Acting-Corpl. E. P. J. Lodge, who will report at Bisley, at 12 noon, Friday, July 13th.

If a 24ther wants to see his "number up" now's the time. A chance is given to Col.-Sergt. Fox, Sergt. Parsons, Corpl. Dibley, Ptes. C. Turner and A. H. Lawes, who will represent the Regiment for the Queen's and St. George's Competitions. There is a deal of discussion going on just now *re* Rifle Clubs and the like. One of the best military writers, commenting upon the Bisley Meet, pens the following lines. Listen to Elmaz :—" The nearer the approach of the Bisley Meeting, the less reassuring the prospect. It is not merely the deficiency of over 20 per cent. in the entries for the great Volunteer Competitions, the Queen's, St. George's, etc., which is to be deplored, but the still greater falling off in the entries for the Barlow and other competitions, especially advantageous to young shots, that is disquieting. The abstention of old rifle shots, so many of whom are in South Africa, was, of course, anticipated by the Council of the N.R.A. for this meeting at all events ; but the abstention of the tyros and the young men, in spite of so many special encouragements, could hardly have been foreseen." New conditions which prove to be not only unpalatable, but absolutely deterrent to many intending competitors, account largely for this. The decrease in the entries for the "Queen's" is 429, while those for the "St. George's" is no less than 454, or a falling off of from 1663 competitors in 1899 to 1234 this year, and from 1594 last year to 1140 this respectively. The match between the Regulars and Volunteers on Monday resulted in a win for the Citizen Soldiers, the figures being Regulars, 1073, Volunteers, 1143, a lead of 70 points. The usual wind and weather reports still flourish. You can hear talk of choppy, puffy, and fishtail winds galore, and as regards the temperature, it keeps up its record—"extraordinary." I have noticed that up to the present moment Bisley hasn't yet had its "most severe thunderstorm that has been experienced for many years." Doubtless they'll get it. The usual amount of grumbling goes on, everybody's ideas are *not* taken by the N.R.A. and until they are we must expect it, but for people who have the biggest tale of woe to tell,—the most unfortunate men on earth—give ear to the cry of the unsuccessful shooting man or the empty-basket-follower of Isaac Walton, and you've got it.

I have prepared a new card giving names of all the comrades in S.A. I am enclosing one in each booklet this time, which I trust you will accept with the very best wishes of

Yours most heartily,

To the " L " Co. in South Africa,
Wednesday, July 11th, 1900.

R. E. KEMP,
Colour-Sergeant.

COPYRIGHT.—"Khaki Letters" must not be used without permission.—R. E. KEMP.

Khaki Letters.

No. 2,548, Sapper **W. C. Smith**, writing from Warrenton, near Fourteen Streams, May 16th, says:—

"DEAR COLOUR-SERGEANT,—On Thursday, May 3rd, I started from Kimberley with air-line stores, loaded in two wagons, to proceed to Warrenton and join No. 6 Section, under Captain Wright. After trekking for three days, Warrenton was reached at 6 a.m., Sunday. The Section was preparing to move off, and as there were no clerks, I had to go with them without breaking my fast.

"I was soon informed that the balloon (which was taking observations), would be our destination, and after reaching it, an 'air-line' was run along the ground to the 4th Battery, R.F.A., which was near the river, about four miles N.E. of the balloon, or seven miles from Warrenton Camp. After fixing the instrument, I was told to remain with the Battery, and return to camp with them.   I had got comfortably seated on a drum of wire, when the Battery opened fire, which, however, brought no response from the Boers for some time. At noon the Boers commenced firing, and the first shell came whizzing over my head, and fell within ten yards of where I was kissing the earth.   It proved to be a shrapnel, and the pieces were divided amongst the men, keeping a piece myself as a memento of my 'baptism.' It was rather amusing to see with what gusto the Major in charge of the Battery 'potted' an ox wagon; when he had finished, there was only an ox standing, out of a span, and the wagon was smashed to smithereens. The Boer guns replied, but without doing any damage. In the evening I returned to Warrenton with the Battery.

"On Monday, I was sent out with the 66th Battery (Corporal Nurse). A few shells were fired, but without reply from the Boers, who had evidently retired during the night towards Christiana. During the morning General Hunter's helios. were seen away to the west, and later in the day his column reached Fourteen Streams (he had crossed the river at Klipdam).

"There is a drift near the railway at Fourteen Streams, but it is very rocky; it was quite exciting to ford the river (Vaal), and many a wagon became jammed in the rocks, and had to remain for several hours. One of the Telegraph wagons shared the same fate, and it took five hours to cross.

"The rest of the week was employed in putting up air-lines and repairing cable.

"*May 15th.*—Reveille at 5 a.m.   Breakfast 5.30 a.m.   Very busy packing up for an advance at 7. Directly the artillery began to move, we followed suit. The morning was rather cold, but as the day wore on it became exceedingly hot. The cable cart commenced laying the cable at 7.45 a.m. At 9 o'clock there was great excitement, as the height of our ambition had been realized,—'the Entry into the Transvaal.' This Column

KHAKI LETTERS—*continued.*

is the first to invade Boer Territory. After 15 miles had been traversed, a halt was made at a place called Cawood's Hope, about 15 miles from Fourteen Streams, and 10 from Christiana. At Cawood's Hope, the first British flag (Telegraph white and blue) was hoisted by Corporal Arthur, Sapper Horn, and myself. A correspondent noticed the flag flying, and made a note of it, and said it was an honour to the Detachment.

"The first Infantry Regiment to enter the 'Promised Land' were the Scots Fusiliers, who were also the last to leave in 1881. It is said they carry the old flag, which they intend to hoist at Potchefstroom. The Boers are supposed to be at Christiana, where we hope to have a good fight. The farms *en route* are all deserted, and the owners have joined the laager at Christiana or elsewhere.

"*May* 16*th* (Outside Christiana).—I arose at 5 a.m. this morning, and after having disposed of some porridge, I was ready for the advance which was to be made at 7 a.m., in the same order as Tuesday. A great deal of fun and amusement was caused at a deserted farm about five miles from Cawood's Hope; 'Tommy' spotted a lot of pigs, chickens, and sheep feeding in the vicinity, and quickly gave chase. When settling time came, it was found that our Detachment's 'find' was 14 fowls, one pig, and a ram. Had a fine 'Irish' Stew in the evening.

"At noon a halt was made about two miles outside Christiana. There was no need for a fight, as the Landdrost wished to give up the keys and surrender the town, thus were we grievously disappointed. The Boers had retreated to Klerksdorp. The General gave the order to return to Fourteen Streams at 8 p.m., and at 5 a.m. the following morning our old camp was reached."

"P.S.—When the river was crossed at Fourteen Streams, on Monday, Sapper C. J. Woode was detailed (with a body of Scouts to act as escort), to cut the Boer telegraph line, about 90 miles north."

No. 4,322, Sapper **T. H. Symonds**, writing from Newcastle, Natal, May 22nd, says:—

"My health, I am pleased to say, has been almost perfect up to the present, for which I am thankful, especially as there has been so much sickness out here. I think most of us are getting just a little homesick, and among the soldiers this feeling is universal, and the recent happenings—I speak of the relief of Mafeking and Buller's advance to Laings Nek—certainly bring such an event as the close of war within six weeks, not only into the bounds of possibility but even probability. Since my last letter till May 9th, when I joined the advancing column, nothing happened worth recording. On the 8th, however, I received orders to leave the office, I was then at Woodcote Farm, near Elandslaagte Station, and join on the morrow. I didn't tumble at first quite what a move it was to be. I thought at first it was a small flank movement by Dundonald's brigade, but as we went on moving day after day for ten days I began to see what it all meant, until now here I am at Newcastle, with General Buller and his staff here; 2nd Division at Ingogo with Dundonald, and our guns actually trained on Laings Nek, which they have already shelled. Ingogo, I might mention, is six miles further on and just this side of Laings Nek. In the advance I have come across many 24th men. Minors, who is at Ingogo; Jeffreys, Snow and Collins, here at Newcastle; Corkill, Peters, Sinclair, Leaver, Bevan, Mackness,

KHAKI LETTERS—*continued*.

Rowson and Townsend, who have been left at various offices on the way. The places we bivouacked at coming along are as follows : Sundays River, Waschbank, Vermaaks Kraal, Stonhill Farm, Dundee, Dannhauser and Newcastle. During the whole advance I acted as escort for wagons, and only came under fire once, and that only a short and feeble shelling as we were starting from Vermaaks Kraal on Sunday morning (13th inst), which a 4·7 soon silenced. As I expect you know, during the whole advance of 138 miles, only seven men were wounded, and therefore getting on all serene. The roads were very bad and sent you into a state of perpetual speculation (no Mazawattee dictionary here) as to whether the wagon would really go over this time. I remember when we came into Dundee, which is a very nice place, seeing General Penn Symons' grave with a Union Jack flying over it. It was a beautiful moonlight night, about 11 p.m., and I remember being much impressed and thinking how glad he would be could he but see this advance. I quite know the taste of the biscuit and bully beef by now, but as we supplement it by Quaker Oats, and potatoes, and things we - er— find, I am pleased to say we still live, in fact I'm getting quite a cook. We have no tents, and so I slept, same as all of us have to, in the open, which is no worse than sleeping in tents if you get your blankets and sheet, till I came to this Newcastle office last Saturday, May 19th. The office is rigged up in the parlour of a house which must have belonged to a fairly well-to-do Dutchman Fine big mahogany table, piano, marble clock, walls adorned with hunting trophies, etc., quite grand, I tell you . . . . [Mention is made of men who have been ill, but recovering] . . . . We were all much upset about poor Hawkins' death, which cast quite a gloom about us. Colour-Sergt. Kemp has been very thoughtful, and it is chiefly through him we are acquainted with doings of ours round the other side. Remember me to all the Bees. Hope you and all the chaps are well."

No. 4311, Sapper **Chas. J. Minors,** Telegraph Section, R.E., Mount Prospect Camp, writes on May 24th, as follows : —

"DEAR DICK,—What a banquet we are having to-day in celebration of Her Majesty's Birthday ! The authorities are giving the troops a treat in the way of extra rations—biscuits, cheese, bacon, and a tot of rum, in place of the usual biscuits and bully. I left Woodcote Farm, Elandslaagte, on Sunday, May 6th, to join Lord Dundonald's mounted brigade in readiness for Gen. Buller's advance. We are without tents, and well we know it. The nights are bitterly cold. Our rations consist of bully beef and biscuits, which is probably all we shall have to exist upon until we reach Pretoria. Doubtless you read in the papers of the magnificent marching of Genl. Buller's men ; 120 miles in 7 days including 2 days' fighting, over hilly and rough roads. It was pitiful to see some of the infantry in full marching order limping painfully miles behind their regiment. A broiling sun overhead and clouds of dust which hang like a thick yellow fog, do not tend to make marching pleasant. They shelled us at Vermaaks Kraal Farm on Sunday morning, May 13th, just as we were about to move off. I had been at work on the wire all night, which was fixed up in a bath room at the farm. The Boers directed their fire towards the house about five minutes after I had left. They fired on us again as we approached the Helpmaakar Road, but our artillery eventually shelled them out of their positions. We could see them scurrying across the Helpmaakar Road under our fire. We camped that night at Kemps Farm after a most trying day. Since Genl. Buller's

KHAKI LETTERS—*continued.*

advance commenced I have been at the front all through the march with the cable cart. As I write, the nearest 24th Middlesex Volunteers—Symonds, Collins, Snow, and several others, are with Genl. Buller and staff at Newcastle, about 20 miles behind. I had the honor of being the first telegraphist of the Royal Engineers to arrive in Dundee, Glencoe, Hatting Spruit, Dannhauser, Newcastle, Ingogo, &c., and sent the first wires off announcing British occupation, &c. We found the towns practically empty. Property looted, houses and buildings wrecked. I went into a number of houses and most everything in the way of furniture was smashed. Pianos, mirrors, bedsteads. paintings, &c., &c. They have done a lot of damage on the railway. All the immense water tanks at the different stations are blown up, and all bridges, culverts, &c. At Glencoe Junction we had our instruments in the refreshment bar. No drinks on hand. The platforms and offices were strewn with ammunition left behind by the Boers in their hurried flight. We had our instruments fixed and several messages through for Genl. Buller before he and his staff arrived. At Newcastle we put our instruments in what had been used as the drawing room of a well furnished house, but was now a bit of wreck. There was a fine range in the kitchen which we made use of to cook turkeys, fowls, and a sheep which we FOUND on the way. The inhabitants, chiefly women and children who have remained in towns during the war, say they have been fairly well treated by the enemy. I have done very little marching, having usually been perched on the tail of the cable cart, which gets along as quickly as the roads will permit. I was thrown off when travelling over some rough ground, but beyond a good shaking no damage was done. Next day the cart turned over completely whilst going down hill, and shortly after the air-line wagon followed suit, and lay on its back in a spruit. 'Twas a miracle no one was hurt. This occurred late in the evening of Saturday, May 19th. A corporal of the 18th Hussars and myself were then sent on with instruments and batteries to Ingogo station. Upon arrival we found the Captain and a dozen R.E.'s who had travelled along the railway on a trolley from Newcastle. Our party got the wagon out of the spruit and were on the way to the station when they were stopped by some natives who told them that the Boers were in force 500 yards east of the station. They promptly turned back and sent a mounted orderly to warn us of our danger. By this time it was dark, so there was no turning back for those of us who were at the station. Of course, we were then in communication with the troops by wire, and directly the chief of staff at Newcastle heard where we were he telegraphed to the Captain telling him he was in a very dangerous position, to keep a sharp look out during the night and if possible to get away at daybreak. We were out on outpost till 3 a.m. when all, bar myself and two others who were without arms or ammunition, having left it on the wagon, took up a position on a kopje overlooking the station and there waited and watched till daylight. We then got away O.K. leaving the instruments hidden in the long grass, joining our wagons and party later on. A patrol of five mounted Boers made their appearance shortly after we left but did not remain in sight long. Evidently they over-estimated our strength or surely we should have all been captured. Upon arrival in camp we were congratulated on our escape. A squadron of the South African Light Horse went down to the station later on and recovered the instruments. Whilst we can make use of the railway telegraphs we do so, as it saves us the trouble of putting up a line across country. I am now with the outposts at Prospect Hill under the shadow of Majuba Hill, three miles from Laings Nek, where the enemy are said to be

KHAKI LETTERS—*continued.*

in great strength. We are well within range of their guns but so far they have not disturbed us; shall probably stay here a few days. I cannot give you any information as to the whereabouts of the others of our party. They are scattered miles behind. Hope they are keeping you well informed as to their movements. Kindest regards to everybody."

No. 15,734, Lance-Corporal **V. E. Gray**, who left the I Company for the 79th Company Rough Riders, writing from the Imperial Yeomanry Camp, Maitland, near Cape Town, May 28th, says:—

"MY DEAR KEMP,—A few more lines concerning the Rough Riders may not be unwelcome for your interesting little publication. We had a good passage out in the 'Canada,' she doing the journey in 19 days. We only touched at Las Palmas, and that for a couple of hours. There were 1,500 aboard, including officers and men, all Yeomanry. We unfortunately lost one of our fellows by death on the way out. He was not feeling well when we embarked at Southampton, pneumonia developed, and after about a week out he succumbed to this dangerous complaint. The funeral was a very impressive scene. The ship was stopped, the battalion formed up round the deck, and as the "Last Post" rang out upon the bugles, the remains, wrapped in the Union Jack, were lowered into the angry deep. We arrived at Cape Town on May 3rd, disembarked and marched into Camp. Maitland Camp is a huge Yeomanry base, and after nearly a month here we are leaving to-morrow for Stellenbosch, *en route* to the front. We have had plenty to do since being here. Our horses were mostly unbroken ones, and we experienced great difficulty in getting them into shape for drill. I recognised several of the 24th boys at the review at Cape Town, where we were all taking part, on the Queen's Birthday. They had arrived a few days before, and were stationed at Cape Town, *pro tem.* You will be glad to know I have been made a Lance-Corporal in my Company. It means a bit extra responsibility on active service, but our non.-coms. generally are very good fellows, and I get on well with them. My kindest regards."

No. 1,450, Sapper **R. Campbell** (of EH), writing from Edenburg, Orange River Colony, May 29th, says:—

"Just a few words to let you know that the troops are going on all kiff. I've been somewhat lazy lately in acknowledging my correspondence. The varying temperature in this part of the country puts one off letter writing. It's a sort of see-saw between a grill and a freezing machine. We have very hard frost during the nights, and often a broiling sun during the day, so that the sudden variations of temperature make one wish for even a spell of EH ZM, with its proverbial east winds thrown in, it would be a welcome change. However, things are looking brighter now, and visions of home appear in the near future. Old "Bobs" is across the Vaal with rumours of his advance guard being in Johannesburg. All the other Divisions are closing in upon him in support, and Pretoria almost invites British protection. Edenburg, our 'appy 'ome, has assumed its usual peaceful garb, the inhabitants, Boer and British, pass each other on the streets with usual civilities and courtesies which lead to good fellowship. Shops and markets are opening up apace, prices are gradually being prefixed with the word 'Reduced.' Butter per lb. figures at 2s. 6d. instead of 4s.; eggs, without the

KHAKI LETTERS—*continued*.

prefix 'fresh,' reduced from 3s. 6d. to 2s. 6d. per doz. ; whiskey still at 17s. 6d. per bottle, consumption dying out ; 3d. boxes of cigarettes can be had at 1s. If you ask change for a tanner, a Boer merchant feels justified in charging you 3d. in lieu of coppers being scarce and so on (mim.). The Boers' 'moral and intellectual damages' have no ending here. The Band of the Garrison Militia Regiment plays in the Market Square every alternate afternoon. The *elite* of the town turn out *à la* Rooinek, to grace the proceedings. We are, in fact, becoming quite home-like. I am sending you a sketch of the belle of the town (mim.). On the Queen's Birthday the town was *en fete*, and it was very amusing to observe Union Jacks flying from some of fire-eating Boers of the past's houses. They've become Queen's loyal subjects all of a bound. It's very comic. In the afternoon we had grand sports on the town's commonage, obstacle races, egg and spoon races (although we had to substitute potatoes for the eggs owing to the high prices), horse races, and various other races. The proceedings terminated in the evening with a concert. The concert had rather a unique feature connected with it. The Court House stands outside the town on the veldt, where the concert was being held. The house was beautifully lit up with about three or four dozen candles, all the windows and doors being open. The glare of the light now and again shining across the veldt, revealed a sentry with glittering bayonet passing to and fro, or perhaps a mounted patrol. The contrast between the watchfulness of these armed gentlemen outside, and the crowd of Tommies inside, giving way for the moment to pleasure, vividly pictured how a soldier can adapt himself to whatever circumstances may come across his path, be it duty or pleasure. Concerts under armed protection are rather at a minimum at home (mim.). However, the concert passed off very pleasantly, the citizens wended their ways to their respective homes and the soldiers to their respective trenches and outposts. The other day the Commandant sent a paper round to be signed by every soldier in the garrison to the effect that owing to a large number of Boer houses in the town having been broken into and looted during the night, any soldier found guilty of taking part in these depredations *will be liable to be shot!* When I signed it I did feel a sort of cold shiver run down my back, not in any way that I felt guilty, but still it seemed so different from the usual 'please note, two hours extra duty' (mim.). I fear when I return I shall feel rather hardened to these lenient punishments. But then Militiamen take these things very philosophically, and if they could comfortably get away with it they'd think nothing of cornering a whole house and foundations and packing it away in their kit bags (mim.). They are the boys to take the freedom of a town without the usual formalities. They don't want the burgess ticket they want the town. Old Greig, of CE, and myself, went out on the veldt the other day prospecting. We heard of a diamond vein running along the veldt some distance from town, but its exact position could never be struck by the townspeople. That was enough for us, we felt the fever gradually creeping o'er us. We struck a bee line across, mentally calculating and arranging the best lines as to the flotation of a 'Limited Liability Company,' or a 'Greig-Campbell Diamond Prospecting Company.' We, however, came to the conclusion that it would be for the present, at least, better to equally share our day's diggings and afterwards sell our rights to the highest bidder. After an hour or two's laborious searching we returned with a few sparkling pebbles, which we were told were the first indications of diamonds being in the vicinity. We are bringing these home as mementos of our digging days (mim.). Yesterday I went out with the Postmaster and had a round of golf

KHAKI LETTERS—*continued.*

on the veldt. He happened to possess three clubs, but wasn't exactly sure what they were meant for. I took him out and tried to initiate him into the mysteries of the game, but I had great difficulty in explaining the exact meaning of bunkers, &c. He persisted in calling them dongas, spruits, valleys, &c., and when he tee'd the ball, he couldn't get past kopjeing it. Instead of keeping an eye open for ball-sneakers, the usual precautions were supplanted by that of keeping an eye open for Boers popping up on the ridges. The game proved very exciting, but the veldt is a poor substitute for the Braids. I shall now have to close up. By the way, I just left Kaffir River Station in the nick o' time. A few nights after I left a sentry was put on the station and was fired on during the night and seriously wounded. Just my luck! I often expected the same reception, especially at nights while I was there. It was a mad game leaving one man there. Old Dan Thomas is still at Bloemfontein having a hot time of it—plenty work. Whitten came up from De Aar with the Clearing House staff a few days ago. He has a very soft job of it. Bill Hendry is down with fever at Prieska, I hear, but improving. Jock Heigh has been in hospital with dysentery, but I think about recovered now. I think old Dan Whitten and myself are the three only fortunates who have escaped all these terrible diseases up till now. Don't hear anything about Aird, believe he is somewhere between KB and Mafeking, probably Fourteen Streams. Hear poor McLaren is on his way home. Hope he will get over it all right. Do write soon, if we are not on our way home before you have time to write. Expect to see you all in August."

✤ ✤ ✤ ✤

No. 447, Sapper **C. J. Jenner,** writes from Fort Knokke, Woodstock, Table Bay, May 30th, as under :—

"DEAR KEMP,—I have been unable to write you for some time as I was unfortunately stricken down with enteric fever at Kimberley about March 22nd. I was enjoying the very best of health up till then, in fact it was only remarked a few days before I went sick how very well and stout I was. Enteric is very prevalent at Kimberley, and four out of eight of those who occupied the tent in which I stayed were all taken ill with the same complaint, and two of them have been since invalided home—I will not mention names of those who are ill for fear of upsetting their relatives. I was very well treated in the hospital in which I was located, my dietary consisting of 4 ozs. of brandy per diem, together with as much milk, beef tea, and jelly as I wished for—no other remedy, except occasionally an ounce of castor oil and a cold sponge when my temperature was over 103, which was very frequently the case during the first three weeks; this was a treatment which I especially dreaded, as the Orderlies were rather cruel in the manner in which they blobbed one's burning body with the ice cold water; the nursing sisters were particularly kind to us all, and I owe them a great debt of gratitude. I was supposed to be a good patient and after five weeks I was on full diet although very weak, and then a few days afterwards I was sent to Wynberg, a charming place situated amongst the pine trees, about nine miles from Capetown, to recuperate. There I found Catling and Fenton, dysentery patients, both doing well. We are (Catling and I) now at Fort Knokke, situated by the sea, on light garrison duty, waiting to be passed by the P.M.O. for service at the front. I don't think we shall be sent up though as we are not for examination for another ten days, and then I expect the war will be at an end, such a turn have things taken for the better

KHAKI LETTERS—*continued*.

I don't know if this is news to you, but Tough has just been invalided home, and poor old Metcalfe died at Springfontein on the 20th inst. of dysentery. I am exceedingly grieved to hear the sad news. Catling and I are enjoying ourselves here immensely, we have every evening after 4 p.m. to ourselves and can get into the towns of Woodstock or Capetown in a very few minutes, and I am employed in the pay office and he gets the cushiest of jobs, so that we are, comparatively speaking, on a picnic. I am looking forward eagerly to meeting the old friends at home, and trust that there may be no more casualties among our fellows. The party in which was Stevenson, and that in which Lasham and H. A. J. Foster were among the number, have gone to Bloemfontein. I met the first party at Beaufort West whilst I was on the hospital train, and the other lot arrived at Fort Knokke last week and left a few days afterwards. Will now conclude with kindest regards to all enquiring friends, and remain yours very sincerely."

No. 4670, Sapper **W. E. Braybon,** writing June 16th, s.s. "Montrose," says :—

"Dear Kemp,—Have now been on board five days, and have not yet suffered with sickness. The first night was bitterly cold, and I must admit I had just a thought of an extra blanket. However, I dressed myself fully, and had a fairly comfortable 'down' after all. The weather has been very hazy indeed, and the boat rolls terribly. The horses are the chief sufferers ; the once fine chargers are now barely respectable four-wheeled cab horses, and several have gone under. I walk round and have a chat with them. They don't mind being stroked and petted now, but at first they snapped viciously. It seems a shame that animals should suffer for men's quarrels. We have some queer customers on board in the shape of Militia. They are of the pub.-lurcher class, and could do better with a pot of four-ale and a screw of shag than with a decent foe and a rifle. However, it is difficult to 'judge a sausage by its overcoat,' so will say nothing more derogatory of my comrades. The sea is still very wet, and not only are the crew very dry, but everybody else. We lined up to receive one pound of excellent tobacco yesterday, a gift from Messrs. Elder, Dempster. It was all the more appreciated as I had lost mine. Lost, I said? This boat rolls in a terrible manner, and several of the boys have been ill from the start. I have not yet started 'giving away.' The second day on board I was on 24 hours' guard, and was nearly starved to death. A young Bedford man took compassion on my careworn dial and administered two libations of hot coffee, one at bedtime, the other in the early morning. He saved my life. However, guard duty is better than ten hours in the 'rat pit' on Hastings, under the electric light all day. Up to now I have been fit and well, and feel twice as brave as usual. Perhaps there is some inkling in my mind that the Boers have no cruisers? We have excellent 'sing-songs' at night under the saloon, and the officers usually remain listening during their progression. We are terribly crowded here, and there is no room to move except on deck. We are carrying about 320 horses and 740 men. Of conveniences there are none. Still, we are happy. Kindest regards."

W. E. B. adds a command :—" P.S.—Thank the girls for gifts. I kissed them all." I do not know the girls, nor is it clear which friend B. kissed, the girls or the gifts.

Our Khaki "At Home."

O my Readers and All interested in the production of this little booklet, I extend the hearty welcome :—*Come*, come and have a little chat over the work of the past few months in connection with the efforts put forth to keep us all bound in the bond of unity while some of our number are on "Afric's Sunny Strand." It has often been told me, "No one knows the labour there is in putting forth this booklet," and I have been upbraided for not copying certain papers, magazines, etc., in the matter of printing a catchy Eulogy. Take any "Daily" and you will notice they all have their own trumpeters, they are not satisfied with reminding you now and then of the wonders they are working for your benefit; they constantly do so. I refuse to copy them. At the same time I have thought it would not be out of place to give you, in a sort of "report" form, some idea of the task I have tackled—with what result, you know. "Great minds run in the same channel," I have heard, and on the 3rd inst. I received a letter from a most popular Supt. which contained some very pretty things about me and the book, enclosing also a piece of poetry, with full instructions to "give it scissors," or, "without scruple, the W.P.B." The writer had forestalled me, unconsciously; the two great minds were on the same bent, and the result will be found in these four pages, which I am inserting in such a manner as to be easily detached from the rest of the book by those who may wish to do it. First, then, let us say the verses are intact, the writer "*intacta*," and the suppression of his name will ensure his remaining so.

A tiny barque, with "Khaki Notes" on sail,
Went boldly forth midst storm, and snow, and hail ;*
She was so slimly built, that hundreds feared
She could not live—but bravely on she steered.

Although her mast was bent with wind and storm,
Her course was bravely kept without a qualm ;
She reached our absent ones, and cheer'd their hearts
When working for their Queen in distant parts.

And give all praise to him who launched the boat,
When many thought her far too frail to float ;
Not only did he float her, but with art
Built her more taut than when she made the start.

So here's good luck to all our boys afar,
With sympathy for those who crossed the bar ;
Such always will be claimed for England's fame,
As stars in England's crown will shine their name.

C.T.O., *July 2nd*, 1900.

* "Hail, a salutation, to greet," says my dictionary. I think the poet must mean hail of this kind, for it was much too warm for the other. But there, let him alone. He is one of the very large number who appreciates effort, and who modestly remarks "it is merely a slight note of admiration of your pluck and perseverance in starting and keeping going the interesting little booklet." Add to this a Yorkshireman's testimony "I am going to have mine bound. Covers included ! The covers are worth preserving. . . . . as an interesting memento, both of the war, and of a work in which I took great interest, and of my first acquaintance with a grand fellow with a great big large heart, and unbounded energy, whose portrait I want to obtain, unmounted, to insert as a frontispiece to the book, and whose hand I hope to grasp some day."

Now, Readers, that is a sample of the testimonies I am constantly receiving. I ask all pardons for shewing it you, but the object is this—

Keep the Book Going.

Don't let one subscriber fall off, but put as many more on as you can. I *don't* want your praise, I *don't* want your money, but I want to keep the boys and their book to the front, and in saying that I say all.

There are a number of friends who have not had the opportunity of knowing how the book is run. A great number take it as a matter of course, just as they do most everyday things, and it never troubles them to think "How is this produced ?" Fewer still know its worth.

OUR KHAKI "AT HOME,"—*continued*.

Ever since the men started for South Africa, I have written them similar letters to those you are now familar with on the first pages of each issue. These were duplicated and sent out, some 20, 30 or 40 each Friday, as circular letters for every Telegraphist to read. In reply they sent me letters, which were copied into a book and sent round. So interesting did they become that I was often asked to print them, and as time went on—under strong recommendation—they appeared in the form of KHAKI LETTERS. The whole idea as to the get-up is mine, and all under my personal supervision. Even the printer was kind enough to submit various types, and from the material I saw I decided on the size, shape and style of the new venture. In a circular letter I had promised sixteen pages for one penny. Sixteen pages, you may not know, perhaps, represented about 10,500 words—without the cover—or, in other figures, 650 words per page. The bargain was struck with the printer, he was given orders to run No. 1, with the full knowledge that No. 2 might be doubtful, and No. 3 more so. No. 4 could hardly be thought of, and we dare not think of issues beyond. In a circular I had asked for 2,500 subscribers, and the result of my canvass was a little over half that number. But, thought I, No. 1 is ordered already, and out she must go. I could not play at speculation with subscribers' cash, and I had none of my own, so I printed what I considered would be the probable output. All my calculations were those of one "worse than the merest tyro," for no one was at hand to guide me, and I could not guide myself. However, out came No. 1, and with fear and trembling, I posted myself in a position to serve them out to my elected voluntary helpers. The piles of books soon diminished, and all were supplied, but I had not bargained aright. All my stock, including those over and above orders, quickly went. My distributors returned with smiling faces, "More, Sergeant!" "All gone," says I. "What shall we do?" says they. "Wait," says I, "I'll get some more printed at once." The orders were doubled there and then, the book was snapped up by those who had not the confidence to chance a little, and the first edition disappeared in less than two hours. More were quickly printed, and the second edition went in a few days. A third edition was prepared and put on one side in case more might be required, and now, as you all know, I am asking for No. 1 back again. Notice, too, that I had given four pages more than I had promised. This four pages is not supplied free. Someone has to pay, and it is a matter of £2 that is required to meet this extra expense. The reader has reaped the benefit, and I am afraid, from what I can learn, very, very few have even thought that it cost money to do this. I believe in giving full value. I have given full value all along. Every issue up to the present time has had four pages more than stipulated. Had I kept to the 16 pages my financial footing would have been firmer to-day. But I have always had the desire to please, if possible, the most exacting. I am not behind, however. I must not be. Did I get behind, everything else would get behind. I am glad to say my printer cannot grumble at me, nor can he give me an anxious glance, for his account is paid up to the very halfpenny. In fact, he deserves a word of praise, for he has been most considerate and obliging all the way through. And I may say *more* than obliging, for, sensible man that he is, he has thought fit to reduce the cost of production simply on account of my promptitude in paying him.

Another little item I must mention, it is a thing that can be easily overlooked. People are so accustomed now-a-days to getting up-to-date articles and they must be "just so." KHAKI LETTERS is "just so," and will continue to be "just so" if the support is given it that will allow it to be. I refer to the illustrations I have put in it. I never dreamt of illustrating the booklet when it commenced, but if you will permit me to say again, it was the desire to please that made me do so when the circumstances called for it. And in so doing I believe I have added to the beauty of the book, a sad necessity we must admit, but nevertheless, the readers have been brought into closer touch with the comrades who have borne the brunt of hardship, even in such a poor way as this. . . . In the course of conversations with fellow clerks it has always been a surprise, or an apparent surprise, to them to learn that these reproductions have cost money. Another instance of the expectant spirit with which we buy our everyday magazines; we are not interested in the trade nor its secrets; we never get further than passing our opinion upon the picture. We condemn, or congratulate, and we consider ourselves generous by our expressions. The little book called KHAKI LETTERS has had to stand this criticism, too, without the thought ever springing up in the minds of its many readers, "how is

OUR KHAKI "AT HOME," —*continued*.

it done?" Well, every block has cost money, and in addition to that there is the loss of type space. Take for instance the illustration in the last book. The cost of the block was nearly one sovereign and the loss of the page was as near as possible 10s., put that together and we find the reader has gained to the extent of 30s. It can be reckoned no other way. But while we can do this we will. The ultimate advance in the list of subscribers who recognise the efforts put forth will show a gain in the end. The photo blocks of our poor comrades are inserted—as far as the subscriber is concerned—free of charge. All to enhance the popularity of our little venture. The eight, nine, or ten shillings, however, that is paid for it, lessens the already small profits. I believe the idea is a good one and is just what it should be, the reader is asked most respectfully to remember this is another little item that is done for his benefit. Thus I bring to notice two very important points in my report. The extra four pages and the illustrations.

Now let me deal with something else. I won't call them hard names, but as you all know, there are so many people who can make alterations, and alterations are not always improvements. Suggestions are not always workable. Propositions are useless without personal effort. Fault-finding is absurd when remedies are not available. The task of pleasing everybody is a big one. I have tried it all along, and I find that a study of human nature, with a fair amount of perception of character, has been my best guide.

Now for a few answers to "things I have heard," told in a general way. To those who so fondly take K.L. in one hand and a popular penny weekly mag. in the other, and with giddy gesture presume to try the respective weight, I can only say there is fairness wanted by those who insinuate such a judgment. K.L. is not intended to compete with any known or unknown book or paper. It is entirely a brochure on its own and in its own sweet way. If K.L. is to be judged so ruthlessly as that—and such it has been—I can only say that if I had similar advts.—bringing in such vast sums—it would be given away instead of being sold. "Why don't you do so-and-so, and so-and-so, and——?" I have stopped them before they could say more, and shewing them my hands have replied. "I've got *two* hands. How many have you got?" And, believe me, they are very full. The correspondence in connection with this work is excessive. It is impossible to do all that I am aware should be done; but how is it to be overcome if only one person is on the staff? The distribution is also a very heavy item. In the C.T.O. there are willing workers, as also at other places. All my workers give their services free. I am most thankful to them, and for this reason readers should make their tasks as light as possible by helping them in it. The system of 3d. subscription is a good one, the 1d. a time is not so good. Some friends buy or refrain from buying—just as the maggot bites them. It is handicapping the booklet too much to put it on the same sale basis as a morning paper. It is also unreasonable to expect K.L. to be perfectly up-to-date with the letters. For is it not apparent to all that sometimes there is too much copy, and some must needs stand over? Besides this, many letters wait a fortnight owing to arriving while the book is in the press. Such things are uncontrollable. The very nature of the book, and the copy for it, is one of the most uncertain features of its life. It is not intended to be a newspaper, with letters written yesterday. All the letters claim a chance, and the experience I have gained tends to shew that whatever merit there may be in one, *none* is so interesting as that from a chum who left this or that section or office. It is looked upon as *that* section's letter, and all others are secondary to it. Thus you will see the cause of what some call "repetitions." It is unavoidable if you wish to please all. Some have remarked that provincial men's are not inserted. The answer is they have not come to hand. This is a case of want of co-operation. All letters submitted will—as ever—receive equal attention; the remedy is in your own hands. The variety is sought, and all my readers are again invited to assist by sending on copied portions of the correspondence from South Africa. In this way a dearth will be avoided, the interest will be more general, and, I have no doubt, a great improvement will be effected. Try it!

On the other hand, the danger lies in having too much. Pressure on space causes double numbers, and these appear irritable to some; I fail to see why. The advantage of a "double" is two-fold—more letters, less delay. The friends who object are of the lukewarm class; I would like to infuse a spirit of hearty enthusiasm into all. You get value for your penny, you get it for your twopence. The

OUR KHAKI "AT HOME,"—*continued.*

object of the book and its intended life is known to all; a special privilege should be accorded to it, and the copy—single or double—taken, knowing that you are benefiting your fellow workers, who look forward eagerly to every issue. I am glad to say that in nearly every case where one has seceded another has stepped in. Excuses such as "I don't know half the men," "I haven't finished reading the last one yet," "There are so many calls just now," and the like, are expressions that should be cast away and stifled before they mislead. All Telegraphists ought to be interested, and even if they don't read the booklet now, they may later on; if they don't think it worth reading, support it for those who do, for it *must* keep on. Experience has also shown that a fairly large number prefer borrowing to buying, and here we touch very delicate ground; but, as a fellow-worker, I ask—"If it is worth reading, is it not worth supporting?" We know the clubs and libraries exist to give facilities for extensive perusal of literature at a minimum cost, but is it the correct thing to treat K.L. in such a manner? I had hopes of the subscribers doubling in numbers. In readers they have trebled; if all readers became supporters what a grand work it would be. It is satisfactory to know there are hundreds who intend having their copies bound. This shows the interest they have in the poor venture—admittedly weak and imperfect. Another matter—I'm making money I have heard. Curiously, I did not know it. Fortunately, those who think so are very few. Increase the output, and you will increase the "accumulation of wealth," and I will then gain—What? Not one farthing—personally, but the profits will be more, and the sum to hand over will be greater; at present it is, as all reasonable persons must know, not a large one.

There are a great many other matters I might have mentioned, but I cannot enumerate all. The scheme up to now has gone grandly, the scope of its benefits reaching far beyond the ordinary imagination. Relations have been helped, as communications received from fathers and mothers about their sons shew. In short, in helping this you are helping you don't know who. Let us work harder for the cause of K.L. *Distributors* in some towns act as such for a period, taking it in turns. A good idea. All sections should have an assistant so that one or other are on duty, especially on Book day, for I have noticed that in sections where the "penny a time" system is in vogue, those who fail to receive their copies on Friday neglect to do so afterwards. Holidays, removals and promotions, have greatly interfered with our work.

I cannot say how long the book will run. Some friends have sent in their subs. for the next six months. Some for longer. But this I will say: all subs. in the excess of issues will be refunded; and it is because of the uncertainty of the length of time the booklet is required to run, that I have asked for payment for six issues instead of six months or a year.

From July 9th to August 6th I am on leave. I have tried unsuccessfully to obtain a substitute to carry on this work. The preparation and distribution of No. 13 will employ much of my time for the first week, the camp will probably claim two more—and I couldn't successfully cope with such a task while there—so that I think I can claim your indulgence and favour if I suggest, or rather, take French leave, and announce that No. 14 of K.L. will be issued four weeks hence, *i.e.*, on August 10th. Please note the date. Don't let your interest dampen, those who are backward with their reading will have "caught up" by then, and all of us will be ready to restart and work to the final issue with renewed energy and success. During my absence from the C.T.O., Mr. C. Belsten, Librarian, has kindly offered to represent me. Any one who requires lists of men at the front, back numbers, etc., can go to him and he will supply them. This arrangement is most convenient for those friends returning from leave.

Finally. Just another little tit-bit—one of three received by the same post on July 7th—from one of the best known men in the service, who led "The Cause" for years in days gone by, I refer to D.S. of MR:—"Dear Mr. Kemp,—Your effort is grand. KHAKI LETTERS to hand. Nos. 1 and 3 missing. Pray endeavour to get me them anyhow, ANY PRICE, from anybody." He thrice underlines any price. He says get them anyhow. I'm not going to *steal* them. Will some one oblige? This gentleman set you an example in times past, he sets another now. Do as he has done and order K.L.'s.

Yours in the Service for the Boys,

July 11th, 1900.   R. E. KEMP.

Khaki Letters—*continued.*

No. 4370, Sapper **E. P. Neate,** writes from Bloemfontein, undated :—

"Here I am right bang up the front, although now you would hardly call this the front, as Roberts has commenced his march northwards. The last time I wrote you I think was at Fort Knokke, Cape Town, wasn't it? Well, we were ordered up here Tuesday evening, and started by the 10 p.m. train. The journey up took three days, from Tuesday to Friday evenings. For the first 100 miles or so it was all up hill, and slow work, but after that it was one continuous open plain, or veldt, broken only by slight hills here and there. If you look out of the windows for a few miles you will have seen all the kinds of scenery there is on the journey. We were allowed tea sometimes if we stopped, but were served out with only four biscuits and bully beef. During the night our engine driver went mad, and had to be left at the next station. Bill Pearce got a nasty kick helping to hold him down, and has not got quite well yet. At De Aar we met some of our fellows, and got our letters. We passed several swarms of locusts. The second night we were woke up, and turned out of the train; after waiting some time, we were told to mount some loaded goods trucks, and that was how we entered the Free State. It was half past two in the morning, and very cold at Norval's Pont. We were carrying all our kit, and 130 rounds of ammunition for emergencies, six of us on one truck top. I made a little hollow in the goods, and actually finished my sleep. Woke up smothered with coal and cinders from the engine. All the next day we sat there in the blazing sun, without a drop of water. Kelly, of Aldgate, came on our truck from the next, as he couldn't keep hold there. . . . The bridge at Norval's Pont is a complete wreck, they evidently know how to use dynamite. . . . [describes burning ammunition truck, but adds 'three rounds in a rifle went off and shattered it.']. When we reached here, we were marched to the Post Office, then to a commandeered house, where we were quartered; of course, it is only the house without any furniture, but it is a rather large one. We lay our waterproof on the floor and then make up a bed with our two blankets. I found Laurie Birch here; he has been here some time, and was in hospital the day I came here. He came out next day, and was only run down with hard work. They have had to work very hard here, 17 hours one day, 7 the next, Sundays as well. I was on night duty last week, punching for Kimberley. We have about 10 circuits, with from two to four stations on each. The Kimberley wire goes *viâ* Naauwpoort and De Aar, a long way round perhaps, but the safest. We are working Wheatstone, but seldom Duplex Wheatstone, as some parts of the line are shaky. Bloemfontein is rather pretty, especially when comparing it with the places we have passed through on the way up. Am sending you the paper started by Rudyard Kipling for the troops. It was run by the War Correspondents until they left, and is now by a Cape Company. Living is rather dear for civilians out here, and Tommy, well, if he wants to *live*, it's dear for him. However, we are getting good food supplied now, although I haven't tasted vegetables for three weeks. We get half-a-loaf, 1-lb. of frozen meat with tea per day; every two days jam enough for one meal and also 1-oz. of cheese, rice occasionally. Rum is served out twice a week, but as I am T.T., that goes to the pals. When we came here first, we had to get acclimatised; by that I mean we, most of us, had slight dysentery for three or four days. It makes you feel queer, but the hospital physic soon brings you round again. It doesn't excuse you from office; no staying away and sending in a letter. They are very busy at present, have to work from the time you go on till you come off. A kettle of tea is brought up,

KHAKI LETTERS—*continued*.

that's all you can get. This week I'm on 2 to 11 p.m. duty, and am on punching and sending Wheatstone to Kroonstadt. Beside this we get all sorts of other work : Tuesday pulling a truck about with rations of meat, bread, tea, &c., all over the town until 1 o'clock or nearly 2, then sharp dinner, and at office till 11 p.m. Another day this week, I had to assist cook peeling pumpkins and cutting the frozen meat up for stew, then boil it, not bad practice though. I forgot to say we get pumpkins sometimes, but I can't stick them. We are getting very good food here, much better than one would expect on active service. Tommy Stevenson and Ben Walton were lucky enough to be sent up the front at once, hope I shall be soon. This week half of our party have been shifted to a fort at the East of the town. It was the barrack of Free State Artillery, and is full of old arms they left behind. Of course this town is under martial law, and that means everyone in-doors by 8.30 p.m., so there isn't anyone about except the police after that. I got pulled up twice going across the market square to home, a distance of about 100 yards, so that will give you an idea how the town is guarded. . . No one but military can ride a horse even in the streets. Have just heard Mafeking is relieved. Am so glad ; poor beggars, they could do with some of our spare meat here. Must close here, so sorry I can't stay to tell you more, but will write again shortly."

✣ ✣ ✣ ✣

No. 3,224, Sapper **C. P. O'Sullivan,** writes from Kimberley, June 3rd, as under :—

" MY DEAR COLOURS,—I was delighted to receive your long reply to my letter. . . . . You cannot expect anyone ' beleaguered ' here since the siege was raised to write you news fitting for KHAKI LETTERS. To tell you the truth we are not soldiers now, we have simply reverted to T.C.'s doing eight hours a day and sweating all the time. At first we were enamoured of Kimberley diamonds and thought of taking a few uncut home. But one might as well be in Shoreditch as on the diamond fields, so far as your chances of picking up cheap diamonds are concerned. We were all glad to get back to a little civilization, primitive though it is, and gloried in the idea of coming to Kimberley, never thinking we were to be caged in like this and remain here to the end of the war. I can assure you everyone here is thoroughly sick of Kimberley and wants to go ' up the line ' or go home. What's the good of it ? Up and down to the office, extra special T.S. dinners, bread and bread for breakfast, same for tea, and horribly hard up for clothing. So when we got the news of the occupation of Johannesburg and the rumour of the fall of Pretoria we all emphatically said ' good 'erbs,' and when we occupy Southampton the better for the lot of us. Not that we are ' fed up ' or anxious to get home, but we are tired of being stuck here at Kimberley."

✣ ✣ ✣ ✣

No. 4,602, Lance-Corpl. **R. D. S. Norman,** (of SS), on board s.s. " Montrose," June 16th, writes :—

" DEAR KEMP,—I hope you got report of farewell concert at Aldershot O.K. From all accounts it appears to have been the most successful of its kind ever attempted. Passes were not granted and this necessarily brought the proceedings to a close earlier than would have been the case otherwise. It is strange that although a heavy night was spent on Monday, there was not the slightest necessity for any persuasion to induce the men to rise on

KHAKI LETTERS—*continued*.

Tuesday, as they were all up before 'Reveille.' Breakfast was served in the recreation room at 6 a.m. This consisted of cold meat, bread, butter, tea and coffee. On the whole I think the men made a hearty meal. Kits were then packed on two G.S. wagons, and I and two men were detailed to look after the Lieutenant's personal luggage. By the time I was finished, the men had formed up and I feared I would be late. The old R.E.'s came to the rescue, however, and whilst one fitted my straps on another filled my water bottle with tea, and another started for the Square with my carbine, the result being that I got on parade O.K. except that I felt very hot. We were inspected by Major Friend, and then Captain Powell said a few words in which he complimented the Instructors on their work and the men on their smart soldierly appearance. Continuing, he said that he was not afraid to trust the honour of the R.E.'s to such men, whom he was sure would uphold it either working or fighting. We remained on the Square for forty minutes apparently waiting for a band which our Lieutenant had engaged, but as there was no signs of them coming we were given the order to move off. This order was thankfully received, for the heat, even in the early morn, was very intense. A good many of the Regulars turned out to see us off and gave us a right good hearty cheer. Several came down to the station carrying our carbines for us, and although we had no brass band it does not necessarily follow that we were without music. The Lieutenant was beating time, perhaps unconsciously, but none the less correctly, to the various tunes which were sang or whistled. We found the train waiting us on our arrival and immediately entrained, and within 15 minutes were ready to start. There were many cheers, but none more hearty than for our beloved Lieutenant, who by his kindness and generosity has endeared himself to all of us. We were treated to hearty cheers at every station, and especially at Brookwood, where we picked 100 of the Royal Irish up. We arrived at SO Docks about 11.30 and embarked on this Transport. I found on getting here that there were about 850 troops and 305 horses. Troops include T.B.'s and Balloon Section, Glo'sters, R.I., R.A., 16th Lancers and Bedfords. Our first meal consisted of soup or greasy hot water, followed by meat and unpeeled potatoes, five potatoes to every 20 men. Those not lucky enough to get the potatoes got boiled rice. Tea consisted of pasty bread and coffee, which was not much appreciated. The meals were no better on Wednesday, and knowing something would have to be done we agreed to pay 1s. per day per man to have a decent dinner. This has made a great improvement. I went sick on Wednesday morning and am still very shaky. This ship rocks without the slightest cause, and if one does manage to evade sea sickness whilst on deck you will go sick on going below, by which you pass the horse deck before reaching our black hole (mim.). The poor horses have suffered a good deal and we have lost two already. A good number of the men have also been down but all seem recovering now. We sleep in hammocks which in themselves are comfortable. This ceases, however, when you come to be packed like sardines. Everything seems to point to the fact that only half the troops should have been brought. Still we are making the best of matters, and if it does nothing more it will make us appreciate our home comforts more. The weather seems more settled now and the sun is much hotter, and I hope the voyage will terminate more pleasantly than it began (mim.). I am pleased to say that our Lieutenant is Acting Ship's Adjutant, and Sergt. Cooksey, of the Balloons, is Ship's Sergt.-Major. Yours truly being Orderly Clerk to the Adjutant, I was struggling through some copying whilst in the deadly throes of sea sickness (mim.), when the Adjutant told

KHAKI LETTERS—*continued*.

me to go up on deck and stay till I was better. This was on Wednesday and I am only now able to sit up and write. The Adjutant told the men that any who were sick and wished to write a letter could have the use of his cabin on sending a note requesting such. Also men short of money could be advanced sums although the same must come from his own pocket. It is these and like favours which have placed him in the highest pinnacle of the men's affection. Each night before retiring we have a nice sing-song, and the officers on the bridge above us appear to enjoy it as much as ourselves The gambling spirit is very much in evidence, some men not having time to be sick for playing cards (mim.). The Lieutenant has already dubbed us the best singers and worst gamblers on board (mim.). The Parson has got a choir party formed of the T.B.'s, and has had one rehearsal with which he was very pleased. We saw several dolphins on Wednesday and it was a grand sight to see them jumping about the water. They were soon scared away when the officers commenced shooting at bottles. It is a laughable sight to see about 800 men trying to wash in ten buckets all at one and the same time (mim.). The awning has been fixed over the decks and will keep the sun off us. The heat, however, has every appearance of lasting and increasing."

✤ ✤ ✤ ✤

No. 4672, Sapper **Arthur Revill,** nearing Las Palmas, on board the s.s. "Montrose," writes as follows:—

"June 16th, day after pay day.

"DEAR COLOUR-SERGT. KEMP,—We are all going splendidly, and met with a most enthusiastic reception on leaving Aldershot, and all along the line right away to Southampton, as the Khaki-clad train sped through the various wayside villages and stations. I had a most unique experience passing through the Bay of Biscay, viz., 24 hours' sentry-go on the bow of the boat, two hours on and four off right throughout the entire day. It was a bit lonely 'all on my little own' at midnight, and I had to exert my authority in a stentorian manner when two or three of the Irish Militia ventured on deck contrary to orders. Needless to say, they soon disappeared between the hatches when I belched forth 'Nobody allowed on deck.' There is a Major on board who is in charge of the horses, we all go about in very fear of him, because if we happen to pass along the line of horses and have not got a good excuse for being there, he will make us walk round and round with them (the horses) and also clean out their stables. We have managed to dodge him up to the present. We passed through a school of whales yesterday, who were blowing off like steam. Needless to say, we were greatly interested in them, and should have liked to havechanged places with them for a short while, as it is getting terribly hot, and the sun is nearly in a straight line overhead. The hammocks are O.K., but want a bit of negotiating; however, when once you are fairly landed it is all right. We have concerts on deck in the evening, and the R.E.'s supply fully 75 per cent. of the talent. I do not wish to disparage the other regiments, but I assure you that such is the case. *Au revoir*, with hearty good wishes to yourself and everybody in TS."

✤ ✤ ✤ ✤

No. 4644, Sapper **E. Sanderson** (of SU), on board the s.s. "Montrose," nearing Las Palmas, writes, June 17th, as under:—

"DEAR COLOUR-SERGEANT,—The inexpressible amount of pleasure with which I read KHAKI LETTERS whilst wielding dots and dashes at home in Old England, is now, I believe, exceeded by the delight I feel in contributing

KHAKI LETTERS—*continued.*

my little experiences to this worthy organ of Khaki boys at the front. Some considerable enthusiasm prevailed as we dropped down Southampton Water last Tuesday, where two American warships lay at anchor some little distance from each other. As we neared the first vessel our men (about 800 in all) bellowed forth three loud patriotic hurrahs. Then our American cousins responded with three cheers, and their band played 'God Save the Queen.' So the enthusiasm ran along our route until the blunted Needles raised their heads from their watery home; and then the troops settled down to their new quarters. The food supplied to us for the first three days was wretched, and altogether inadequate, but now, by paying a small consideration per man to the chief steward, we—the sixty T.B.'s—dine sumptuously every day, like the rich man in the parable. Owing to the large number of troops aboard, our accommodation is very limited all round, and we find it trying during the night time very much. There are 160 men in our mess room, in which all of us must sleep, either in hammocks or on the floor; and some idea of the discomfort to which we are subject may be understood when I say that the horses immediately above us are continually 'marking time' with their hoofs. That untractable animal—the hammock—caused all of us some trouble and anxiety the first couple of nights, nearly every one of us evincing a predilection to clamber in at one side and fall out at the other; or, when we were apparently correctly balanced in it, to topple over and find ourselves clinging tenaciously to a beam or rope. The only work which has fallen to us up to now is that of guard duty. This generally extends over a period of 24 hours, two hours on and four hours off during the whole time. For the two hours' duty we are generally sent to patrol the stables, where 300 horses need attending to. This is far from being pleasant during the night, for not only have we to provide them with water, but also look to their head gear, etc., and see that none are hurt by the rolling of the ship. When one of these ill-fated friends of man is taken sick no means are adopted to resuscitate him, but he is roughly hauled out of his stall and felled with a poleaxe. He is then thrown overboard. A couple of whales were seen spouting a short distance from us on Friday, probably they were on the alert for more carrion, as two horses were launched into the sea the same evening. The amount of vocal and musical talent displayed by this draft of T.B.'s is, to say the least, truly remarkable. Each night all of us muster on deck, and a first-class concert, consisting of patriotic and popular songs, is given, which is listened to with apparent pleasure by all the officers as well as the men on board. These scenes for the last night or two have been singularly striking : a few hundred khaki-clad figures listening intently to the singer, the bright uniforms of a group of officers on the bridge, the swish of the sea as the ship passed swiftly along, and the bright moon shedding its refulgent light over the surface of the dark waters, now like a dancing sea of silver—all combine in favourably impressing the spectator. To-day being Sunday a service was held on deck, attended by all the troops not on duty. Again the vocal talent of the telegraphists was prominent, the choir, including the organist, being composed of our men. We expect to reach Las Palmas to-night or early morning ; all of us are looking forward to some fruit. I may add, in concluding, that the owners of this vessel very kindly gave each soldier a pound of excellent tobacco and a writing-case replete with all the necessary materials. Needless to add, we all deeply appreciate such noble generosity. The sea is fairly smooth, but some of our men have been within the grasp of that sea monster, *mal de mer.* Kind regards to yourself and all old friends at home."

Khaki Sidelights and Notes.

Staff-Sergt. Leslie Cox, Regimental Staff, Kitchener's Horse (formerly of C.T.O., where he was well known as a prominent man in athletics, was Captain of the Rugby team of the E.A. Assn.; leaving London for the Cape Government service in August, '94, where he joined the Cape Town Highlanders, and rose to the rank of Sergt.), writes the following interesting letter:—

"Perhaps you are surprised to hear from me right from the seat of war. Well, when the Volunteers were called up, of course, we were the first in the field, but they didn't seem to employ us, except in dispatch riding in the Western Province, where the war was not. Then for a month I was in charge of the Cyclists on Buller's staff; went round to Natal, saw the fight at Colenso and the loss of the guns. Transferred back to Head-Quarters when Roberts arrived, and came round the coast. Met Captain Congreve, V.C.—he won that at Colenso, and although wounded, he was full of fight. He applied for my services from the Corps I was in, as he had been appointed Adjutant of Kitchener's Horse, then being raised. Luckily he got me away; and work—well, I've had some in my days, but that took the cake. I was appointed Staff-Sergeant, and worked on an average, 20 hours each day for 16 days. In that time we transferred 800 Cape Volunteers—Infantry—into Mounted Horse, and fully equipped them. As a matter of fact, 18 days after the Regiment was raised, it was in action with French's column at Klip Drift. As no doubt you have heard, I nearly got cut up in that convoy at Waterval Drift, having been with the regimental baggage, but managed to clear off just in time. Found the Colonel and Regiment at Jacobsdal, and joined in the Relief of Kimberley. I shan't forget that in a hurry, after a nice little scrap at Olivantsfontein, where the enemy caught it hot; we entered just at sunset, and were absolutely mobbed. Can't write about all the ridiculous things they did and said to us. Up again next morning, the whole column swung to the left, for news had come that Cronje had cleared down the Modder. Now commenced hell upon earth, for I've no recollection of that three days' fighting till we cornered him on the Sunday at Paardeberg Drift, except one, a nasty taste in the mouth, a blinding dust, no rations—an absolute fast for 50 hours—and men and horses going down right and left. We caught his rear guard up at Rondeval Drift, shelled him out, and captured 40 wagons. At Klip Drift the following morning he fought for four hours, and our corps lost heavily in men and horses. Cleared him out of that, and so on, the run one continuous fight. Gods! but it was something to live for, and I am glad that I have lived for it. You people at home, who see Tommy off, neat and clean in his uniform, would not have realized what the difference of active service under these conditions can mean. Every man was black as any Kaffir; Guardsmen, Coldstreams and Grenadiers, dirty, bearded, and cheerful in spite of everything, for we had fairly caught the old man on the hop, and everyone knew it. On the Sunday, however, we had left the Infantry behind, and had moved out to the right flank in order to head him off. We found him laagered up on the bed of the river, and his forces occupying all the surrounding kopjes, and we knew at once we were in for a thick time. Waited for rations, and up came McDonald's Brigade—Highlanders—and in we went. For twelve mortal hours on that day were we blazing away, and just at sunset managed to hustle him off the Kops into his main laager, from which he never again moved till he surrendered. We had lost our supplies, and two squadrons were sent foraging, and got somewhat cut up by a party of Boers in the attempt.

Altogether, in the Kimberley relief, till Cronje surrendered, we lost 19 killed, 68 wounded, and 42 missing. As you know, we Colonial Corps are always in the thick of it, and our casualty list is very, very heavy. Anyway I am glad to say that right through I haven't had a scratch. . . . . Well, Paardeberg was a frightful hole, rained the whole time and we slept in the mud and got used to it. Now don't think I'm exaggerating, every word here is simple truth. One item, we had an issue of rum on the 26th, and it was a godsend indeed, saved all our lives. Fancy, the old man surrendered on Majuba Day; the Canadians pushed up so close during the night that the old sinner had no option in the morning. From here we pushed on further, glad to get away from the death trap, for such it had proved to Kitchener's. On the morning of leaving Osfontein, where we were escort for the naval guns, and saw all the fun for very little loss, only having two men down. Reached Poplar Grove at night, and Kitchener's Horse were luckily quartered on a farmyard—sucking pigs, potatoes, fowls galore, which lasted us into Bloemfontein. Here we were joined by the C.I.V. Mounted Infantry who have been in our brigade ever since. Abrahams Kraal and Driefontein saw us fighting side by side. The

KHAKI SIDELIGHTS—*continued*.

latter place I was lying alongside Corporal Major Elliott, 2nd Life Guards, now Sergt.-Major of the C.I.V. That day, combined, we smoked about a ¼-lb. tobacco. Our losses comparatively slight here, and we pushed on rapidly into Bloemfontein, which we entered without opposition. Had ten days' rest there and were then sent on here to clear the enemy out. Left on 28th and came in touch on 29th. Chased 'em out of a chain of hills and drove them out on to the level plain on the morning of the 30th. Here we are now entrenched. The C.I.V.'s on our left and a battery of artillery on our right, the most northern of Roberts' outposts, and in touch with the enemy night and day. Had a football match in Bloemfontein with the C.I.V.'s, but I expect they will take care London hears of that, for they beat us by 1 goal and I try to 2 tries. This is just the position that suits us, for our men knowing the country steal all they can and slap at the enemy morning, noon and night. Old General Tucker is in command of us just now, and he tells our Colonel 'they're good men, Legge.' Legge's the Colonel's name, and he's real grit. I, who have to be with him, think he takes too many chances, and always look for a handy ditch. This is different work to the Mashonaland and the Bechuanaland rebellions, though I hope to pull through all right."

Lance-Corpl. A. E. Bradshaw (of C.T.O.), 22nd Field Hospital, R.A.M.C., writes from Kimberley, May 9th :—

"We arrived at East London on the 17th April, and hung about for 4 hours in the rain and darkness before proceeding on our first railway journey, which lasted four days and three nights. Well, we got on all right as far as Cathcart, where we were entertained by an English fellow, who cut me some lovely flowers, and invited two or three of us to tea. We also stopped at Queenstown, Burghersdorp, Bethulie, Stormberg, &c. At Bethulie, Stormberg and Olive we saw some of the dirty work of our brother Boers, who had neatly blown the bridges in two pieces. Our first Camp was Springfontein, where we had a Church for a hospital. I was awfully disappointed to learn when I arrived at Springfontein that the C.I.V.'s had just left for Bloemfontein, so didn't see Syd. Sterling. We stayed about a fortnight at Springfontein, when our orders to go on to Kimberley. By-the-bye, I met Jimmy Brooks and Swan at Springfontein, and am sorry to say Metcalfe has been in our hospital with dysentery ; we handed him over to the hospital that relieved us, so don't know how he is progressing. After hanging about for a time with nothing else to do but water cart fatigues and signalling, we suddenly packed up and started. The journey was really the most interesting we could possibly have had. We started for Kimberley at 7 a.m., and by mid-day next day reached the well-known battlefields of Graspan and Belmont. Both were marked with many a small tribute in the shape of a few piled stones or a simple piece of wood to mark the spot where brave fellows had lost their lives. We also saw Magersfontein, but only at a distance. We ran into Kimberley about six in the evening, and, of course, were ordered to remain in our carriages, but the temptation was too great. . . . . Now we are off to Fourteen Streams, and I can't write in the train. Remember me to all that enquire."

Writing again on May 29th, from Vryburg Camp, he says :—

"Just a line to let you know I am O.K., both in health and spirits. I have no idea where Syd. is, but have seen a rare lot of T.S. people, and have had many a meal with Webber, Waghorn, Semple & Co., who are all at Kimberley. It has been my job while at Warrenton to go down to Kimberley, a distance of nearly 50 miles, each day in charge of the sick. It is not pleasant work by any means, but it is a change. When you have some bad cases such as Pneumonia, Enteric, Rheumatic Fever, &c., and travelling all night without lamps, you don't know where you are. There is a splendid general hospital at Kimberley. It is equipped for two years, and a siding runs the sick right along to within about five yards of the wards, which are large marquees. All the marquees are lit by electric light and have wooden floors. It is really a splendid hospital, and I should say would hold fifteen hundred patients. We have not done very much hospital work ourselves as we move so very quickly. At Springfontein we only handled about one hundred patients, among them being Metcalfe, who has died since we transferred our sick to another hospital. At Warrenton we handled about a thousand patients. Most of our nursing is sick only. Of course there is a tremendous lot of dysentery, enteric and diarrhœa, but we only keep them as a rule 24 hours. We have treated a good many suffering from Natal or veldt sores, which, when they get into the system,

KHAKI SIDELIGHTS—*continued.*

take a long time to eradicate. The sick all come to the surgery at 9 a.m., where they are seen by the doctor, who either admits them to hospital or tells them to come to the hospital two or three times a day. When a man is admitted an inventory of his kit is taken. I can tell you some of these old soldiers are very hot. Without you are very careful when taking in their kit they will tell you half their kit has been stolen, or that they gave in a new coat and someone has changed it for an old one. We are all up to their little games by now, though. The patients get very well fed considering the difficulty in procuring stuff out here. The greatest drawback of all is the scarcity of fresh milk, so that we are compelled to use condensed milk, which, myself, I have no faith in. During the afternoon the doctor goes round the tents and sorts out those who are for Kimberley and those who are to resume duty. Some of the soldiers even ask the doctors to send them to Kimberley as they are ' fed up ' with the campaign. It is very amusing to hear them tell a deplorable tale in order to induce the doctor to send them to Kimberley, which is, of course, the first step towards getting invalided home. During my journeys down I have taken Sergt. Nurse who won the V.C. at Colenso. I also conducted a despatch rider, who was about the first man to leave Mafeking, and who was down with fever, but he insisted on going on, and had two trains stopped to wait for him, so important were his dispatches. Another of my patients was a baronet officer. I had the pleasure of being in Kimberley the day the relief of Mafeking was celebrated. It was really very fine; there was a cycle parade, and there were plenty of effigies of Oom Paul burnt that night. We are off on a nine days' march to Lichtenburg to-morrow, so you see we are in for a treat. Good-bye for present."

I have received the following communication from one who is wellknown, not only in the T.S., but in very many other offices. It is the first of its kind that has reached me, although from numerous provincial towns I have been informed that similar appeals have gone forth in like circumstances. Our friends, whom we term the Ex-R.E.'s, are Royal Engineers who have served their time with the Colours, and have been taken on the Staff of Postal Telegraph Offices, either as established Officers or as temporary men. The disadvantage lies with the latter, as regards pay, etc. I have learned that it is almost an unanimous practice throughout the Service to " make up " the pay of these good fellows, so that their wives at home should not be called upon to suffer more than needs be in their straightened circumstances. This is a case in point. The division to which poor Rudd was attached at the C.T.O. has (as is being done in other divisions) subscribed weekly for this object. All honour to them and to every man who can shew practical sympathy in this way. None of us have too much, more of us have too little; this case is among those of the latter band of workers :—

C.T.O., *July 9th*, 1900.

DEAR KEMP,—The news of the death of Sapper Rudd, at Bloemfontein, came as a painful shock to his colleagues of the " I." Division, rendered all the more sad that thereby a young and deserving wife with three little children—the youngest born only a fortnight prior to his departure for S. Africa, are left *totally unprovided for*. His very small wage on the temporary staff entirely precluded any scope for provision, and as an R.E. on the Reserve, one-half only of this wage was allowed during his absence. The " L " Division is unanimous in appealing to the whole of the Staff to raise a substantial sum to assist Mrs. Rudd and her children, and if any of the K.L. readers outside T.S. can help we shall be grateful to receive their contributions, however small. Alf. was devoted to his family. The knowledge that his Division would assist them during his absence, removed a great anguish from his mind. He told me that, whilst tears of gratitude welled up in his eyes. I am sure his last hours were comforted by faith in his fellow clerks doing their utmost for his widow and orphans. From a patriotic point of view he has a strong claim on us all. Let us do our part generously.

Yours, very sincerely,
D. W. JONES.

Rudd has been a most cheerful correspondent all through. We have seen a little of his correspondence in K.L. His decease was so unlooked for, and we sympathise with those who mourn his loss. If the promoters of the Subscription will communicate with me I will hand them the first sovereign expended from KHAKI LETTERS profit—a matter with which I feel no fault will be found. And from my own purse I will add another half most willingly.

KHAKI SIDELIGHTS—*continued.*

Coming Events cast their shadows before them, they say. Recently, I rushed to the bookstall at Cannon Street Station to purchase a paper, and as I grabbed the pink sheet and picked up my change a patriarchal person presented me with a pamphlet, which proved to be an advertisement for a popular song, "When the lads return." 'Twas in the Mall, the summer sun had lost its prostrating heat and the gentle zephyrs of autumn moved the leafy boughs of that historic park—St. James'. A large concourse of England's best had assembled, and every yard of space was occupied by the B.P. and B.W., all in Sunday attire and be-decked with favours and flags. Guns boomed as the Royalty arrived. Massed bands sent sweet strains over the shimmering scene, and martial music made men merrier and taller in stature than before. I looked and wondered. A distant murmur soon travelled nearer, increasing—as it came—to a hum; a shout—a continuous shout; a yell; a frantic, deafening full-voiced lusty hurrah, and the swerving masses made lane in their midst as Warriors, sunburnt and shrivelled, paced proudly on. One by one the favourite regiments were recognised as they passed by. Every person present appeared to know the Guards, the Highlanders, the Dublin Fusiliers. &c., but there was a hushed silence with the mob as a big battalion came in sight—a battalion the B.P. had never seen and hardly ever heard of. They knew they were British, but wondered what their territorial name could be. Quick as the lightning flash the word "Ubique" went forth, and the hurrah-checked throng recognised the R.E., the flower of the Army, and gave vent to redoubled cheering as they rushed into the ranks to bid them welcome. I saw the "Provincial Gallery" pour forth in its hundreds to press the hands of pals. I saw the "Met." ladies persistently pushing past gaping bystanders to pay their respects to confrères. I saw the friends intermingle with friends from far and wide, and the whole seething mass was jubilant in a glorious reunion. The scene was beyond description; it was bewildering, mystifying—sound, sight and sense seemed paralyzed, we greeted many a man; we spoke together for the first time for months that might have been centuries; we talked over the past and the future; the gaiety of the big throng gathered round the gorgeously decorated Hall lent lightness to every heart. 'Twas a dissolving view. The park was now a palace. Fragrant flowers filled the air with delicate perfume, while the fanning ferns lent beauty and grace! Lords and ladies were there; the Controlling Officers —military and civil—were there; the entire Staff of the C.T.O., in its most brilliant array; the District Office's talent; friends, relatives; ALL were there greeting and honouring the returned "I." Company. The "I" Company was there and I was there. We were in the seventh heaven of delight. Our ears were twitching to catch the eulogy of a robed and revered speaker. Silence reigned. The white-gloved hand of the conductor held the upraised baton—the artistes alert to begin, their eyes fixed on the magic wand of the leader, whose glance was in turn on the speaker. One, two—"three" had almost been given. The company rose, and the lads in khaki moved not; the bumpers were filled, arms stretched forth to lift the glass aloft simultaneously with the call for musical honours. The clarion note rang out from the Chair, the crash of music broke forth; voices vied lustily with each other. Instanter: feverishly; fearfully flushed, the——Proceedings were stopped by a voice, "You'll lose your train, Dad, if you don't look sharp." Dear me, I had been dozing while writing my Khaki Notes for the Boys. I scampered off to duty wishing all the way that something like the above may come to pass. No doubt that pamphlet—"When the lads return"—had laid its latent hand upon me. But it *may* come to pass!! Why not?

Notes. **The New List** of names of *all* the men who have gone to South Africa is on sale. Everyone who has seen it is pleased. It is a great improvement on the former editions. I would call attention to the fact that the third edition was a loss to me, as on the very day the list was published, sixty additional men were asked for, and all intending purchasers made the remark, "We'll wait until you put the new sixty on." Now the whole lot are on, and we want to see all copies go. They are worth the twopence, not only as checks on rumours, but as mementoes of those gone out. See that you get a copy of "My Colleagues in South Africa."

KHAKI NOTES—*continued.*

Montrose.—Our last detachment of 60 arrived at Cape Town per ss. Montrose, on Thursday, July 5th.

Sapper A. W. York, 4,333, who was taken prisoner on May 22nd, was, with several other R.E.'s, recovered at Pretoria on June 6th. It seems strange that we should not see this reported until July 7th. Rather a long time for a telegram to come from South Africa.

Sapper A. H. Morse, 4,315, one of "Ours," and Sapper Coil, 26,501, were taken prisoners at Fevredort, on June 7th. We did not know this until the casualty lists appeared on the 29th ult. They had then been captives for three weeks. It seems odd that these two men should have been taken together—yet not strange, for how could you have a *Morse* without a *coil* that would be useful for telegraphing?

Sapper J. Tough, 24,386, has arrived at Aberdeen. It is understood he is to report himself at Aldershot on 31st inst., and, if fit, may again go out.

Sergeant R. C. Luttrell, 23,610, has arrived at Southampton. Last Sunday our good old chum was visited by his better half, who reports he was quite convalescent and looking well. The first fortnight of the voyage he was lying down but pulled up wonderfully afterwards. We are indeed pleased to know this.

Under the heading of corrections the following par appears in the Casualty Lists of July 3rd :—Ptes. S. J. Carroll, 367, and H. F. Sales, 371, A.P.O.C., reported missing, Roodeval, June 7th. These men joined the "M" Co. on December 22nd, 1899.

Leeuwspruit.—The officers and men reported "missing," Leeuwspruit, June 14th, in the train affair, are prisoners of war. Casualty List, July 3rd.

Sergt. A. Chapman, 268, A.P.O.C., prisoner in the Boers' hands has escaped. Rhenoster, June 25th.

Pte. E. Harris, 391, A.P.O.C., died June 29th, Bloemfontein. Enteric.

Sergt. J. Dunscombe, 308, A.P.O.C., died, Ladysmith, July 5th. Enteric.

Sapper A. S. Rudd, 24,816, Ex-R.E., from T.S., died July 1st, Bloemfontein, enteric. See page 246.

Sapper W. F. Frew, 4,366, we regret to learn, is reported dead from Enteric Fever. Up to the time of writing this is unconfirmed, although we fear it will prove only too true.

Khaki Postage Fund.—Provincial Readers are respectfully reminded that their share for the K.P.F. has been asked for, and should be sent in early. See page 191. There are now about 230 men receiving free copies, postage paid. The C.T.O. would greatly assist if another collection of 1d. all round were made towards this big expense. I shall feel thankful if they will again take this matter up, appoint a Collector, and hand in to Mr. George Costello by August 15th. Thanks are tendered to the following friends for their timely help:—Newark, 2s. ; F.M.G., 6d.

Enquiries *re* Lance-Corpl. E. J. Whibley, 24,387, who was reported at Aldershot, have resulted in the return of my letters marked " not known."

"Poniard, London," For telegrams from Our Boys to their relatives and friends at home, the addresses of whom should be sent us at once.

"Casualties, Capetown," for enquiries *re* sick and wounded.

"Khaki Letters," One Penny. By post, Three Halfpence.

All posted letters containing Remittances, Orders, MSS., &c., must be addressed to R. E. KEMP, 12, JERRARD STREET, LEWISHAM, S.E.

Postal Orders should be made payable at Loampit Vale, Lewisham, S.E.

Printed by E. G. BERRYMAN & SONS, *Blackheath Road, London, S.E.*

"Khaki Letters" from ....
"My Colleagues in South Africa."

CORRESPONDENCE FROM THE
POST OFFICE TELEGRAPHISTS
OF THE
24th MIDDLESEX (P.O.) RIFLE VOLUNTEERS
(Royal Engineer Reserves),
ON ACTIVE SERVICE.

THE BOND THAT BINDS US—FRIENDSHIP—COMRADESHIP.

Published fortnightly for the Postal Telegraph Service.
Conducted by COLOUR-SERGEANT R. E. KEMP, *Central Telegraph Office, London.*

No. 14.   AUGUST 10TH, 1900.   PRICE ONE PENNY.

Central Telegraph Office,
London, E.C.

DEAR COMRADES, ONE AND ALL.

I am on duty once again. Four weeks have passed since writing you. Leave is over, and the pen and pencil are in my fist again—the former for my gallant boys and the latter for the great B.P. (B.P. Beg pardon! not Baden-Powell, but British Public—I thought you might think I was writing to the Major-General, don't-cher-know.) In case you are inquisitive and want to know all about my holidays, I'll just give you a brief idea. Whole of first week, squaring up KHAKI LETTERS; scouting and field days at various places—Hastings, Margate, Folkestone, Sandgate, Shorncliffe—at the latter place Tommy was hard at it in his greyback, crouching, crawling, and cracking with his L.M. pom-pom. He bobbed along the kopjes, took advantage of spruits and dongas, and rushed across the open veldt in ripping style. At each place I came across many invalided S.A. heroes, and although I tried to forget K.L.'s, I couldn't. A little skirmish, on my own, with the saw, plane and chisel, a little review order with the paint and varnish brushes, and just a wee bit of fatigue duty with the tar-pot created a new out-house in my garden, which friends have been pleased to name "Khaki Villa." It is now being christened, for there is a leak somewhere, and the rain is coming down at the "double"; yet people call it Bank *Holiday*. I could not go to Camp for the first fortnight owing to "urgent private affairs" as they say in the Army, but I was there in spirit; indeed, I am in S.A. *in spirit*, along with the Bhoys, for mine are not bottled, labelled, and kept in a cool place, as some are. Well, to hark back to Camp. The Orders contained the usual instructions as to the toilet of a soldier, attention being called that due regard should be paid to the position of the "D's" and the packing of the Valise; the stout lace boots, &c., &c., all so familiar to us that we could almost repeat the words by rote. The battalion paraded at Finsbury Circus at 2.15, Saturday, July 21st, entraining at Holborn Viaduct, en route for Minster, Isle of Sheppey, as part of the East London Brigade. Detraining at Sheerness and marching four miles found them on their camping ground at about 7.15 p.m. There were 26

Officers, 36 Sergeants, and 343 rank and file, or a total of 405 all told. This is a poor show against previous years, and one could hardly realise that it was really the 24th. The Battalion stood six Companies in Camp, made up as follows:—D, E, F and G, H and C, K, and remaining details and L.R.B. The A, B, and C Companies being detailed for the second fortnight. and the poor old I Company omitted from mention altogether. "The C.O." in orders, "much regrets that owing to the large number in Africa and other exigencies of the Post Office Service the numbers for Camp this year will not be so large as usual." We all regret that. Although I have been on leave, many notes of discord have reached me from my Company pointing out that they joined for service at the front and were disappointed; then they sought a sort of soothing syrup in the fortnight's Camp, but this, too, has been denied them; and some go so far as to vow vengeance by resignation. "It seems hard," indeed, it *is* hard, especially as the fortunates in Camp are drawing the luxurious pay of a soldier, plus separation allowance. The A, B and C Companies are experiencing much the same difficulty as the Telegraph Company. Neither can be spared from their official duties, and very few will be present for the second fortnight's Camp.

Their course under canvas commenced on Sunday by a Church Parade, at 9 o'clock, at Minster Church, which was less than 200 yards away. Thus they were sheltered from the burning rays of King Sol,—just a bit better than some parades we have seen in the open with the ambulance parties busy in rear with fainters, or feinters. They are also near a Workhouse, indeed they find relief there, their water supply being obtained from that building. The whole of the first week was devoted to musketry, the regiment finding its own markers. "Deliberate," "rapid," and "rapid independent" volleys at 300 yards; "deliberate" and "rapid" volleys at 500 yards, seven shots at each practice; also the "section attack" from 200 to 600 yards, 18 rounds. While this was going on the disengaged men did Squad and Company drill under their own Officers. The second week was noted for its "field training," under the Company Officers, and consisted of trench digging, pitching camp, advance and rear guards, and kindred subjects suggested by the experiences in the war in South Africa. They even went so far as to have an attack on outposts by Company Officers, the Field Officers acting as umpires. I have heard nothing about white flags or train disasters, but I have learned they enjoyed themselves immensely, and were spectators of a part of the Naval Manœuvres. Those of the first detachment who could not remain longer than 14 days returned to London, and the second portion went down to take their places by the 6.50 p.m. train from Holborn on Saturday, August 4th. More about these anon.

The pressure at home does not seem to diminish yet. Every available man is requisitioned for overtime service, and we hear of wonderful totals of hours done. Last Friday, according to the "oldest inhabitant," broke the record for breakdowns. 'Tis ever thus. A terrible experience is always worse than any that preceded it, as also does a pleasant and successful entertainment surpass anything ever before attempted; both, of course, when related by one who was there to one who was not. However, it was exceedingly severe, the storm did mighty havoc with the wires, and, indeed, with everything that came in its way. A long list of casualties report shipping disasters, wreckage of buildings, church towers, and even canvas camps. The 24th were in it, they had a merry time in rain and storm. In fact, one paper—reporting camp disasters—went so far as to record the curious incident that "tents were blown *bodily* down" (Introduce the gramophone, Mr. Printer, and let's have the laughing song). Bodily down! Could a tent fall otherwise? Do you remember the large marquee—the officers' mess—on Cove plateau, Aldershot, some twenty years ago? How it nearly fell *bodily* down in a perfect hurricane one night, how we were called up out of our trembling tents to hang on to the guide ropes, and somehow or other the report went round next morning that refreshments were lost that night? It's wonderful what a gale will do. But we hung on, it was a weird sight—and a very good job it was dark.

One little matter—a whisper in your ear—Don't run away with the idea that *you* need not write because others keep me informed. The more the merrier. We are glad and anxious to know your whereabouts, so don't forget.

Space gone. "Time's" called. MQ *must* be given. Sorry, extremely sorry. Best of wishes to every man.

Yours most heartily,

To the "I." Co. in South Africa,   R. E. KEMP,
   Tuesday, August 7th, 1900.   *Colour-Sergeant.*

COPYRIGHT.—"Khaki Letters" must not be used without permission.—R. E. KEMP.

Khaki Letters.

No. 4333, Sapper **A. W. York**, who has had some exciting experiences during his soldiering in South Africa, sends the following very interesting letter from the "Ex-Prisoners' Camp," Pretoria, June 10th, 1900.

"DEAR COLOUR-SERGEANT,—Sweet freedom once more smiling upon me, I am at liberty to resume the thread of my tale left off at Kroonstad. At the latter place we stayed ten days, spending our scanty leisure in bathing, fishing, and walks by the river, which was fairly well wooded for this country. I fell in with good Samaritans at the railway station, where the English residents were always pleased to see Tommy Atkins, and a cup of tea was ever ready for any soldier who chanced to call, while for those who were as fortunate as myself there were the elsewhere unobtainable luxuries of cigars, sweet bread, jam and vegetables. We of the Hd. Qr. Telegraphs left with the column on the 22nd May, and travelled in a buck waggon to Honning Spruit, where, after a repast of coffee and bully beef, went on duty till midnight, and half did 12 to 6 a.m. Next morning, Lieut. Webber, Sapper Hutchinson, Driver Mash, and myself, were sent to open an office at Heilbron. We took a light waggon, and thought we were in for a 'soft job'—an anticipation which turned out more true than we expected. About noon we fell in with a party of scouts, and assisted them to clear the arms and ammunition from a Boer farm. We camped in a pretty glade that evening with a couple of Ceylon M.I. who were rejoining Ian Hamilton's column, supposed to be in occupation of Heilbron. Next day we resumed at daybreak, having feasted off eggs and chicken, and reached Heilbron at 11 a.m., feeling somewhat uneasy at seeing no English troops about. I had got down from the waggon and was rambling easily along, when I was startled with the sensational cry of 'Hands up.' Turning round I observed a small party of armed Boers riding after us, but, somehow, did not seem to realise the situation and kept on. The officer, two Ceylons, and waggon were in front, and presently one of the Federals dismounted and pointed his Mauser at the foremost. We knew then what was the matter, and as the enemy was further reinforced, and our mules had no go in them, the Lieutenant reluctantly bade us return. They eased us of our carbines and equipment, and hundreds more galloping in, a small army escorted us to the Commandant (De Wet), who sent us outside the town with an escort. Here we waited till nightfall, chatting pleasantly with our guards who informed us they had driven Hamilton's column out (?) and told us that had we kept on we should have landed in their laager. Four of Marshall's Horse (Grahamstown) were brought in later, and after another examination by the Commandant we were driven off, together with a civilian, to the laager. They were full of questions, gave us plenty of good-humoured chaff, and sent us to Frankfort next morning. The little waggon was most

KHAKI LETTERS—*continued*.

uncomfortable and was certainly never constructed to carry thirteen men. We outspanned at a farm for bread and butter-milk and made some coffee, reaching Frankfort in the afternoon. Here we met with the most humane treatment, the Boers seeming somewhat simple and possessing a blind confidence in Steyn, who they said would soon be back in Bloemfontein. They fed us well, and lodged us in a billiard room with a young chap for sentry whom we had to instruct how to load his Mauser (mim). Our resting place next night was De Villiersdorp, where they seemed most suspicious and clapped us in the gaol, sending us over the Vaal next morning before breakfast. Our escort, however, were very decent chaps, and we outspanned three times that day for coffee, feeding on bread and sardines. At Graylingstad we entrained in a closed horse box and proceeded to Heidelberg, where we stayed a couple of hours, still being shut in. At Pretoria, which was reached early on the 28th, we had a wait of four hours in the Police Court yard and then were escorted to the Racecourse. Here we were greeted with 'Let 'em all come,' and sang 'God save the Queen' at night, to let them know we were not dispirited. Next night five British were brought in from near Johannesburg, bringing the welcome news that our troops were steadily nearing the capital, and that night the veldt was fired for miles around, in order that the advance of the men in khaki might be plainly seen over the blackened surface. Greatly to our chagrin they 'cleared the course' on the 31st, and ninety soldiers and fifty civilians were sent by train to Waterval, only the sick remaining behind. There was great excitement among the 4,000 troops there, and only the previous day British officers had been sent to cool them, but the presence of the latter only added to the uproar, as the poor fellows thought such an event presaged a speedy release. There was a row one night when we were having a concert, and the boys *would* sing 'God save the Queen,' to the annoyance of the sentries, whose Commandant said he 'Could not be answerable if his men fired on us'; so after going partly through the anthem three times the trouble subsided. We slept in sheds both here and at the racecourse, while the food was similar at both places, consisting of coffee, rice, mealie meal, and bread, with meat and potatoes as an occasional luxury. Firewood was seldom seen—at the racecourse we tore up portions of the grand stand, and when a load was seen at Waterval the troops burst through the gate and possessed themselves of logs, greatly alarming a very youthful sentry, to whom an old Boer was heard to remark 'That's how the Rooineks charge, there's no stopping them.' There were four long rows of sheds, named as follows: Church Street, Gloucester Road, Northumberland Avenue, and Electric Avenue. A portion of the latter was brilliantly lit by candles each night and called 'Monte Carlo'; games of chance being accordingly set forth on little tables. A triple barbed wire surrounded these, outside which sentries paced, while a little beyond was a shed containing a Maxim gun, the whole being illuminated by electric light. A field was also wired off for sports and bathing, but the energy displayed in the former did not seem characteristic of the British Army. The place was undoubtedly unhealthy, everyone was weak—over 200 in hospital—and the deaths were three or four daily whilst I was there. We were welcomed into the fold of the party of R.E.'s captured at Sanna's Post, and our neighbours were nine men of the Northampton M.I.—townies of mine—with whom we had several merry sing-songs. There was a church parade on Whit-Sunday under a British colonel, and a service at night conducted by a Colonial corporal. In the afternoon we got a couple of Boers to translate the *Volksstem* (Boer journal)

KHAKI LETTERS—*continued.*

to us, but did not believe much of it, and were amused by an item which stated 'The brave burghers' casualties were two slightly killed' (mim). Plenty of firing was heard on Whit-Monday and excitement ran high all next day ; huge bonfires being burnt to let the British know our whereabouts. Many destroyed their beds for this purpose. I am sorry to say they got two train loads of prisoners away on Monday (Gloucesters and Irish Fusiliers), and, doubtless, the intention was to move us all, but the British got the railway line—a fact of which we were made aware when the usual provision train failed to arrive and we consequently went short. But did we mind that ? Oh, no, not a bit ! Early next morning the roofs were crowded with eager prisoners, who were rewarded by seeing numerous small parties retiring to the distant kopjes at a mad gallop. About ten o'clock on the 6th June, a mighty burst of cheering arose as our cavalry scouts were seen advancing towards us, and on our sentries laying down their arms, we burst through the fences and rushed across the veldt to welcome our rescuers, who, I am afraid, came in for some rough embraces. We got back to the compound to wait for orders, feeling very jubilant, although some poor fellows were almost shedding tears, so great was the reaction. Doubtless you have read of the events which followed—the shelling of unarmed prisoners and the firing on the hospital. I saw a couple of shells drop near the water tanks and one quite close to the huts flying the red cross flag, while the little puffs of dust showed where the bullets were dropping in the recreation field. We caught up our blankets and scattered across the veldt, but were under fire for some time. Many of the sick left their beds and dragged themselves a few miles down the line, where they were left exhausted under a red cross flag till the train picked them up. We marched seven or eight miles, retiring under cover of our artillery, then got into the second train, which landed us here at 8.30 p.m., when we received a real British welcome, and told our tale as we feasted round the bivouac fires. There was an inspection by Lord Roberts next day, and we are now waiting the result of the court of enquiry, living on the fat of the land meanwhile, but not allowed in town. Kindest regards to all."

" Since learnt Hamilton's column made a detour of strategic importance. A driver was sent to recall us, but his horse dropped dead on the way."

A. W. York is not the only C.T.O. man who has been a guest of the Boers, as the following letter will shew :—

No. 4315, Sapper **A. H. Morse**, writing from Pretoria, June 10th, says :—

" . . . . Here at last. Since last Thursday week I have had a very exciting time. Been chased by Boers and in a railway smash. About every other night I have had to sleep on the veldt, every night without a tent and often with no blankets. At Vredefort Weg (Road), I dined at Field Cornet Le Roux's house. Lords Roberts and Kitchener slept in the verandah of the same house. Le Roux was detailed to look after the women and children in his district while the Burghers were fighting. I was the first to tell him the new name of the Colony. We took train from Bloemfontein to Railhead, which was just beyond Vredefort Weg. We had to wait there for a convoy. We waited nearly three days and slept about where we liked. I slept on a truck one night and in a half-blown-up out-house the next. On the 3rd day we got a convoy of about 150 ox wagons laden with stores and drawn by from 12 to 16 oxen each. Two days afterwards Vredefort Road was sur-

KHAKI LETTERS—*continued*.

rounded, and, I believe, taken by the Boers. The escort of the convoy consisted of half a Co. of K.R.R. and ourselves. We moved off at 6.30 p.m. (dark), and trekked as far as Railhead. We laagered up but we could not find the wagon with our blankets, so we dossed round the camp fire without them. It is all right dossing round a camp fire till you all go to sleep and the fire goes out. We get a sharp frost out here every night, so when sleeping out we have to cover our faces. I don't know what I should have done without a 'balaclava,' we wear them the wrong way round so as to cover our faces. Next morning we moved off at about five, and trekked to Steenpan where the K.R.R. escort left us, we went to Taibosch Spruit before we outspanned. Of course, the bridge was blown up here as well as everywhere else in the Free State. We had heard reports of Boers being about, but thought as our escort was so small that they must have moved off. I had a bathe and a wash in the spruit, I did enjoy it, but it was rather spoilt by the horrible stink from a dead horse some 20 yards to windward. It was no good being particular, as we had to make our coffee with the same water. At about five in the evening, when we were inspanning, an officer called our attention to a party of Boers on a kopje about half a mile away. He was very excited, and went half mad when he found that we (13) were the only escort. We were about six miles from a place where there was some Yeomanry, out of ten of them who went out scouting, nine were shot, the other came riding into our laager with a slight shot wound. We were ordered to retreat on Steenpan. Thirty wagons were already on the road forward, they were captured. The niggers yelled at the oxen, making an awful row. You never heard such a babel in your life, the bumping of the springless carts, bleating of the oxen, crack of whips, yelling of niggers, barking of dogs combined. It was quite dark now and the dust made it impossible to see all the oxen in one team at once. A lot of stores was thrown off the wagons, and to lighten them officers' luggage was slung off as well. When we got to Steenpan we found that it was now Railhead; we laagered up there. In the retreat the chain of our wagon broke, so we had to leave it. We spent another night in the open without blankets. In the morning we moved forward again at about five. We found our wagon. It was quite funny to see the escort we had this time. Infantry, Mounted Infantry and machine guns. At Taibosch we outspanned nearly on the same spot as before. We were unmolested this time. We inspanned at four and moved about quarter of a mile and outspanned again for the night in a more favourable spot in case of attack. Next morning we shifted off at daylight and trekked right to Vereeniging on the north of the Vaal without a rest. I saw the Vaal railway bridge. We forded the river in a shallow place. We passed two coal mines just south of the Vaal. We lost three oxen on this day, the poor things fall down from exhaustion. They are outspanned and left, sometimes they die and sometimes jump up and follow the convoy. At Vereeniging we took to the railway, travelled on loaded trucks as usual. We reached Elandsfontein just before daybreak next morning and had to change. We arrived at Johannesburg about 7 a.m. We found that only three were required in the Johannesburg office and we were sent on to Pretoria. We had to wait till about 6 p.m. for a train so we foraged round the town. I spent about 5s. on my lining. Johannesburg is a very big place and has some fine buildings. There is one bridge down between Johannesburg and Pretoria, at Irene. We left Johannesburg with the engine behind us. This time we had empty coal trucks. All went well till about midnight, when we were all asleep, we were awakened by an awful

KHAKI LETTERS—*continued.*

jerk and crash, we collided with two horses on the line. The first three trucks were overturned and thrown clear of the line, the next one was derailed, I (with a fellow from Frome, named Coles, in the Somerset Yeomanry) was in the next truck but one. There was a man of the S.W.B. Regiment in the first truck, his leg was shattered and had to be amputated. We got out at daylight and walked across Six Mile spruit (where the bridge was down) to Irene, where we waited till about 4.30 p.m. for a train. It was all down hill from there to Pretoria, and we travelled like lightning over the most wonderful bit of railway, through mountains all the way, the curves were wonderful. This place is not bad but it does not hold a candle to Johannesburg. We sleep in the Telegraph School and do eight hours on and eight off duty, which means twelve hours a day. Soldiers are not allowed in the town after 5 p.m. on account of the sniping which goes on from the bedroom windows, etc. A soldier was found suffocated three doors from here a few mornings ago. The Boers are surrendering by the dozen. They say that Kruger ordered three days prayer and during the time got all the money away in tin boxes. Mrs. Kruger is here and so is Lord Roberts."

Writing again to his parents, our comrade, now a prisoner, and not knowing " where 'e are," heads his letter " Boer Laager, Free State, June 18th, 1900."

" I hope you have not worried about me. I am all right. I was with the railway construction train at a place called Leeuwspruit, where the Boers had blown up a culvert on June 13th. We had cut in on one of the wires and were working with a buzzer with the stations on the line. At 1.50 a.m., on the 14th, I was on duty on the buzzer, and all the other fellows were asleep round the camp fires at the side of the line. I was sitting on the ground using the battery boxes as a table with a lighted candle in front of me. There was a party on the culvert working with a Wells' Light. We had no sentry. All of a sudden a hail of bullets screamed round us, I ran back to the camp fire to awaken our fellows. I loaded my carbine and laid down for orders, but all was confusion. The working party had no escort and their rifles were up in the train which had just gone away to fetch more sleepers, so except for our four carbines we were unarmed. Everybody was clearing off so I followed. Dozens of shots whizzed all round me, and one just pulled the flesh off the knuckles of my right hand, it is all right now. It was bitterly cold and I could not run any faster than an old woman. I wandered across the veldt for a few miles and caught the sound of wheels. It was still dark and I made towards the sound, thinking it might be an English convoy or artillery. When I got near I could distinguish some English soldiers, so I walked in. To my dismay I found it was a Boer convoy of British prisoners. That is how I came here. I don't know where I am or where I am going to. I did not receive the parcel. I think that mail was captured. Don't worry about me and don't try to send anything because it cannot reach me. I am grateful to be alive. Roll on Peace and Home Sweet Home. Good-bye all. *Don't* worry. Please write to Kemp."

" P.S.—I shall be free when Peace is declared. I don't expect to be able to write again."

NOTE.—We are pleased to hear that Sapper Morse was released unconditionally, and was reported to be at Ladysmith, July 18th.

KHAKI LETTERS—*continued.*

No. 4,322, Sapper **T. H. Symonds,** writing from Ingogo Station, near Majuba Hill, June 11th, says :—

"DEAR COLOUR-SERGT.,—I think you have been fairly well informed as to the doings of the Natal section, and I write this letter chiefly to thank you very much for the circular letters, and the KHAKI LETTERS with their invaluable information, which you have sent me, also to congratulate you on your ideas for the envelopes and wrappers, which are excellent. Our party of 23 has been singularly unfortunate, as you know by now, and I need hardly say that the news of the deaths of Milne and Robinson was a great blow to all of us. I can hardly realise it myself, as the last time I saw them was the day we landed. Ingram has been invalided home, and I am pleased to say the last report I heard of him was a favourable one. The short stay the column made at Newcastle caused quite a reunion among us, as most of the Ladysmith section came up. I accompanied the advance of Gen. Buller, along with most of our section, during which nothing exciting occurred till quite recently. The Boers shelled us at Vermaaks Kraal on Sunday, May 13th, but their shells didn't burst and no damage was done. At Dundee I noticed Gen. Symons' grave and Talana Hill. I reached Newcastle, Friday, May 18th, and was in the office for a short time with Jeffrey ('L' Div.) and some R.E.'s. It was a welcome respite, as while you are on the move you don't get much time to yourself. On Sunday, May 27th, had orders to join section going with the 4th Div., who were going to occupy Utrecht. Mackness, Sinclair, Pocock and Peters were also with this section. On the second day out we forded the Buffalo river and found ourselves in Transvaal territory at a place named Inchanga Drift. The night we spent there was the coldest I have yet experienced. It froze hard, and I found a thick layer of ice in my canteen the next morning. It is very hot in the day, so we can't complain of monotony as regards weather. The same morning we started back for Newcastle (as Utrecht had already been occupied), where we stopped till Tuesday, June 5th, when we again moved off, this time towards Majuba Hill and Laings Nek. Majuba is plainly in sight, and since we reached Ingogo, which we did on June 6th, constant firing can be seen and heard on Majuba and adjacent hills. This morning they shelled this station, but did no harm. Our forces are all round them now, and I think Majuba of '81 will soon be amply avenged. Have heard of the relief of Mafeking, and also the occupation of Pretoria, and it is probable that the war will soon be over. I give it another fortnight. Must close now, with kind regards to all."

No. 28,201, Co.-Sergt.-Major **W. G. Tee,** writing from Norvals Pont, June 18th, says :—

"MY DEAR DICK,—As I anticipated, Naauwpoort Military Telegraph Office has been closed and taken over by the Civil authorities, and this being our terminal office, I have been sent here. I was glad of the change, for life at Naauwpoort was very monotonous, and although it is equally quiet here, we have the benefit of the Orange River, and the scenery in the immediate vicinity of our camp is very picturesque, and in our spare moments a ramble along its banks and through the woods skirting its side relieves the wearied sight of veldt and kopjes. The river just now is very shallow and the water quite clear, quite a contrast to when it is in full flood and the rapid current sweeping everything before it. The bridge, three spans of which were blown up by the Boers and since repaired by the

KHAKI LETTERS—*continued.*

Railway Pioneer Regt., which regiment is largely composed of Johannesburg Mining Engineers, is a very fine structure measuring about 550 yards, and now carefully guarded by the men of the South Lancs., who are patrolling its sides night and day. The deviation which was constructed by the R.E.'s in the course of a few days, and which naturally assisted the rapid advance of the troops and supplies, is still in existence and runs parallel and a little to the left of the bridge, on old foundations which were discovered of an old bridge. When the river is high it is not safe for traffic, and recently on more than one occasion it had to be suspended, so in the event of the iron bridge being again damaged, the deviation and pontoon bridge—the latter a little to the north—could be resorted to again. We have little fear that the Boers will again attempt it, but in view of the fact that our line of communications has been attacked and still threatened, the garrison has been put in a state of defence and instructions issued for extreme vigilance to be maintained and everyone to be on the alert. The staff here are comfortably located, and when I arrived they were living in a private dwelling house, but since the tenant has returned, and we were politely informed by letter the house was wanted but that we might occupy another . . . . but being awarethere were vacant rooms in the Railway Barracks. approached the station master on the subject, and he kindly consented to allow us the use of a large room, where we are at present comfortably located, with a good cooking stove, so that we are as comfortable as in the Stanhope lines at Aldershot. We have had very fine weather the past few months, but the temperature varies very considerably during the 24 hours, at Naauwpoort and here I have found ice in the early morning 1½in. thick, but at mid-day the temperature has registered 100 in the sun. Extra clothing in the shape of woollen pants and khaki serge has been issued, and we have nothing to complain of in that respect, likewise the food is good, getting fresh meat and bread every day, so taking it all round we have much to be thankful for. Very little information from the boys in the Transvaal, but I hear a wire was sent you on their arrival at Pretoria. I trust they are going on well. I am pleased to say the staff here are quite well, and join me with kind remembrance and regards to yourself and all."

No. 4,670, Sapper **W. E. Braybon**, s.s. Montrose, "Just over the Line," June 25th, writes :—

" DEAR KEMP,—We were all very disappointed that we only just eased up at Las Palmas to take the despatches and hand over the mails to a man-o'-war's cutter. I was one of the first up to see if land could be sighted, but as the night departs and day breaks, and *vice versa*, all in one, you may guess land was nowhere to be seen. A light from a lighthouse, however, soon appeared, and then low down on the horizon could be discerned what appeared to be either the lights from a town (which would appear strange at so early an hour) or the serf breaking on the rock-bound coast. The former was the case. Slowly, very slowly, we approached the Grand Canaries, where more than one Transport has gone aground and where one even now remains. Presently ' Let Go ! ' rang out, and the anchor was dropped for about five minutes or thereabouts. Those who turned out were amply repaid for the denial of sleep. I wish I were a Byron to give a graphic description

KHAKI LETTERS—*continued.*

of the place. The first view of it reminded me of the words—

> " 'Tis midnight, on the mountain brown
> The cold round moon shines deeply down;
> Blue rolls the water, blue the sky,
> Spreads like an ocean hung on high,
> Bespangled with those isles of light.
> Whoever gazed upon them shining,
> Or turned to earth without repining,
> Or wished for wings to flee away
> And mix with their eternal ray."

You can picture to yourself a chain of six hills commencing with a large one and terminating with a small one, and instead of being verdure clad, they are a dull red and remind one of their volcanic origin. As the sun's power increased, so the mists arose from the valleys, and one could see clouds of it rising until it was either absorbed in the atmosphere or rising beyond view. Nestling at the foot of the mountains were beautifully clean looking villages all built of white stone, whilst in their immediate vicinity could be seen the bright green trees forming the orchards, and the fruit of which we had so longed to procure. Disappointment, however, was in store for us, as the picturesque long boats, with their equally interesting occupants and choice consignments of fruit, did not appear. They were not on at 6 a.m., so slept the sleep of the just and lost their 'overtime stakes.' We weighed anchor and were off again before many had a chance of seeing this great change of scene. I was pleased I rose early, and consoled myself that the fruit was probably sour! The weather has not been so very grand, and it rained incessantly for two days and one night. It was absolutely wretched on board. I got wet through once and those on guard were nearly drowned. You see we are all turned out of the lower deck, where we sleep and feed, to enable them to clean it, whilst the horses occupy the intermediate deck, and the rain deluged the upper deck. Of course, as horses are of more value than men, the hatches had to be left open so that the water poured into the lower deck all night and poured out again anywhere it could or splashed about, and was scooped up again in the morning. The Government do not know what a boon another £5 worth of wood for seats would have been. There is nothing to sit on except hatches, part of the machinery, or the hot iron decks. After sitting on the open hatches for half-an-hour, one would do for a human draught board. I am engaged as a 'swabber' now, that is I have to brush and clean the decks. This afternoon I shall be a policeman at the sports, and you bet I shall think of the enjoyable times at Winchmore Hill and elsewhere. The scene will, of course, lack the charm of the ever lovely gentler sex. . . . . Some of us have been through the inoculating process, and myself included. It is a simple process. The serum is injected under the skin by means of a syringe and a four-inch needle. The after effects are like a bayonet prod in the side, delirium of a mild nature and extreme weakness follow. I am thankful we have about ten days longer to go, as I am afraid I should be a sorry figure as a gentleman in khaki, carrying forty pounds on my back. You have seen that picture of the pirate decoying a merchantman? We look just such a motley crew. The khaki is black, except our serge suit. Of course, we have to wash the lighter one so it does not matter. Some wear a shirt and trousers only and all sorts of head gear. There are some real Irishmen on board, and one a bugler, about 43, is simply a card. The only difficulty is that his brogue is so pronounced, one has difficulty in reading him, and his wit is lost. We have some very youthful officers. There is, however, an old adage which says 'youth will be served,' and

KHAKI LETTERS—*continued.*

judging by the resistance of one of these young bloods when King Neptune came aboard yesterday he is a rough handful. I was a policeman on duty near the ducking tank and got a good share of water, being wet through for two hours. We consigned another lovely chestnut horse to the briny this morning. It is cruel to see how the poor animals suffer, whilst others have the sauce of the 'old un' himself. It is surprising how some of the more vicious ones will victimize the sick or gentler ones. I was watching them yesterday when the food was given out, a vicious animal started eating the gentler one's grub first, and biting his companion if he attempted to touch his own food. I had compassion and took a reef in his foe's off-side halter. Horses are very much like some human beings. . . . . We all watch the food like hawks, and now there is plenty. When we are real soldiers on terra firma I wonder what will happen? . . . . We have broken down four times up to the time of writing and the last was the worst; distress signals were flying from 1 a.m. to 4 a.m. this morning. We seem to be getting into the more temperate regions again as the continual perspiration has ceased, and a cool wind is now blowing. We have not seen a ship for three days. Last evening we had a glorious sunset. It sets very rapidly here and about 6 p.m. it is dark. It gets down quite as quickly as a man disappears for an extra pint into the dining room, and the sun's light goes down quite as quickly as the beer-biter's if he is caught. The sunset was one of those poor Benskin would have loved. There was the dark red glare, above which was a pale blue sky, and in this sky wonderfully tinted clouds and Venus shining brilliantly. A scene never to be forgotten. My old comrades who served in Egypt have seen these sunsets I expect. I am not going to repeat the approach to Table Bay as it has so often been given. I hope this will be interesting. Kind regards."

No, 4,353, Sapper **W. P. Walker** (of MR), sends the following from Kimberley, June 27th.

"DEAR COLOUR-SERGT.,—I have delayed writing you so long in the hope that I should be fortunate enough to be sent further up country, from where I might have had an opportunity of writing something interesting. This place is very uninteresting from an adventurer's point of view, as it is to an 'active service' man. Coming out here we looked for hardships and experiences, and what do we get? Twelve hours a day in an office, and located in a semi-town, for though the inhabitants call it 'town' it is but a pigmy place, and being so possesses few of the environments and accompaniments of such towns as we are accustomed to. Therefore we find when off duty there is little to engage our attention in the streets (the *only* theatre has been closed a long time—for want of a company, I think), and a good stretch over the veldt is our only pastime, with the exception of a game of football very occasionally. I was on night duty last week, so one morning Sapper Macmurtrie and myself mounted a truck bound for Modder, and there we spent a very enjoyable day in the brilliant sunshine. We took a loaf of bread and a tin of jam with us, and didn't we enjoy our breakfast *al fresco* on the banks! The travelling in the open truck gave us a fine opportunity of viewing the country, too. We returned with a good stock of bullets, &c., for which we searched and found embedded in the sand along the banks, and feeling the outing had been very beneficial. Now as regards the hardships, certainly we have not by any means the comforts of home,

KHAKI LETTERS—*continued*.

but we want for very little here. Good bread and jam, 'shackles,' potatoes, tea and coffee, then a good meal at 1s. 6d. is procurable at the restaurant, the 'Standard.' It is bitterly cold at night, but if one can keep warm under canvas, and so escape fever and other ailments, our hardships may be reckoned as few. Thus it is I write to you in a disappointed strain, knowing you will be disappointed when you open this letter, for you will expect some experiences and Kimberley affords none, therefore I have none to relate—this time. I feel it incumbent on me, however, to write you, if it be only to tender you my hearty thanks for your consideration and thought in troubling to send KHAKI LETTERS to me, which convey such warm fellow-feeling to all out here. It is a work which thanks alone do not repay, but such works have their reward. The latest is that we are to receive a bar for Mafeking's relief—all who were, at the time of the relief, west of the longitude line 26 and north of the Modder; we come well within this area. All the KB staff are well at present, but here one never knows their luck. One day you might be as hearty and strong as a Cumberland farmer and the next fairly 'gone in.' I am pleased to say that I personally have enjoyed good health here. Poor Greenfield, of MR, is to be invalided. Trusting I shall have the pleasure and opportunity of writing you in the near future from 'further up,' with kind regards."

✧ ✧ ✧ ✧

No. 4,644, Sapper **E. Sanderson** (of SU), writing from the s.s. "Montrose," June 28th, says :—

"DEAR COLOUR-SERGT.,—Since last I wrote to you a few hours before reaching the fair Canary Isles, we have progressed pleasantly and smoothly to within five days' sail of the famous Table Mountain and the town which nestles at its base. The weather has been comparatively cool, and, consequently, no one has found any inconvenience since we entered the Tropics. At 3 a.m. on the 18th, many of us were awakened by the vessel slowing down, and on arriving on deck were pleased to see the delightful town of Las Palmas, with its white houses and twinkling lights—for old Sol had not yet awoke from his slumbers—on our port bow. Visions of oranges, bananas and other luxuries loomed up before us in grand array; but judge our chagrin and dismay when the gunboat came alongside with telegrams and the ominous order for us to proceed with all speed. As our vessel steamed away along the shores of the island, with its rugged mountains now bathed in the golden light of the rising sun, and the scattered villas all in the Moorish style of architecture, our spirits rose in anticipation of the stirring scenes before us at the Cape. The sixty telegraphists aboard have a fair share of time on their hands, and manage to utilise it in reading, writing, smoking, and watching with interest the wonders contained in this deep azure sea around us. Instructive books, not necessarily of a spiritual character, are distributed by the chaplain, so there is no lack of good reading. Flying fish and sharks are constantly seen about the ship. The other night, as a group of us were standing near the rail, a flying fish fell on the deck, and was secured and placed in a large canvas bath. After watching its movements for a little time it was taken out, its gauze-like wings examined, and, after some debate as to whether it should form a part of our supper, it was liberated somewhat in the same way as a pigeon would be let loose. We don't, however, have such opportunities of examining our friends the sharks, although when a dead horse is launched they seldom fail to put in an appearance. Target practice is indulged in by

KHAKI LETTERS—*continued*.

the other companies daily, but we have done very little in this way lately, as we proved to be fairly efficient whilst at the Ash ranges down at Aldershot. The large canvas bath is a source of much enjoyment and pleasant pastime and few of us fail to indulge in this healthful exercise daily. Sunset in this quarter of the globe is a really gorgeous and inspiring sight. As King Sol sinks swiftly down into his western bed-chamber, the clouds and sea alike assume a golden tint far beyond the scope and genius of the painter to depict. Suddenly the orb of day disappears below the waters, then simultaneously myriads of stars appear—far more brilliant and in greater numbers than we see them in England. It is at this time that the phosphorescence is seen around the ship. This phenomena appears in the form of millions of sparkling atoms in the sea about the ship, caused, I believe, by the disturbance of certain salts as the vessel passes through the water. However, as these sparks near the stern of the boat they appear to expand into globes of a dull blue flame, thus rendering the sight a brilliant as well as a mysterious one. On the 25th inst. we passed over the equator, and the event was celebrated in the usual way. The canvas bath was requisitioned, together with one of the long tarpaulin air ventilators. Old Neptune, of course, was there in state, arrayed in robes becoming his high maritime rank, his head being surmounted by a golden crown hewn out of a margarine tin. By his side stood two masculine mermaids in brilliant dresses, their chief characteristic being their head gear, which consisted of long hempen curls in great profusion. Neptune's barber was there, too, with his brush and a pail filled with a mixture of tar, soft soap, and flour, which I found to be far from pleasant to the taste. I was one of the first to be placed on the throne with my back to the bath, and was about to reply to a question asked by the barber when a handful of soft soap was thrust into my mouth, and my face and head smeared with a large quantity of the mixture. Before I had time to recover from my surprise I was pitched backwards over into about four feet of water, my nose coming in contact with the bottom of the bath. Rude hands clutched me and pulled me out, but on regaining the surface another surprise was in store, for another of Neptune's adherents was there with a hose pipe, by which he washed my mouth out, nearly suffocating me during the operation. After being ducked again and again until I was apparently on the verge of another world, they lifted me a foot clear of the water, and, as a coup-de-grace, flung me head first down the long narrow ventilator, the gentleman with the hose pipe again being assiduous this time in accelerating my progress from behind with a strong jet of water. It was indeed a relief to reach the deck once more and to release the soft soap, &c., from my khaki and my carcase, during which thoughts of revenge arose in me against Neptune, but finally terminating in the happy conclusion that I had never enjoyed myself so much since pa died. Although we have been stopped through some defect in the machinery no less than four times, we are now rapidly passing along and hope to sight Table Mountain in a few days. Some of our men have been inoculated, but this operation is in disfavour with the majority of us. We are all in first-class condition, and ready for any amount of hard work. So allow me to conclude with kind regards to yourself and all my old pals in the 'cauld north.'"

※ ※ ※ ※

No. 4373. Sapper **T. W. Stevenson,** writing on June 30th, from Elandsfontein, says:—

"DEAR KEMP,—It is about time I dropped you a few lines to let you know how it feels to be a real soldier, and how I have progressed up to now.

KHAKI LETTERS—*continued*.

The voyage was void of any startling incidents. We did our full share of duties, and found some of them a bit onerous. Corn crushing for three hours was an unpleasant novelty, and sentry-go over 125 horses for two hours, having to keep their mangers filled, and keep the sleepy ones awake was ditto. We had 500 of them on board, and I think they were responsible for the terrible rolling we experienced when broadside on to the waves. The heads of the 250 on one side would come out, and the tails of the 250 on the other would go back, *vice versa*, making one gigantic swing of the old tub. The food was a disgrace to the Leyland Co., and I maintain that a small loaf of bread and a mug of vile unmilked tea is totally inadequate to last a man from four o'clock one afternoon till seven o'clock the next morning. By a special arrangement and payment of 1s. a day, we lived like fighting cocks after the first few days, and all went well. We arrived in Table Bay on the 23rd and were anchored in the roads till Friday night. This got a bit monotonous, and we used to while away the time by signalling to the different transports, and watching the Boer prisoners on the Bavarian. We marched off at two o'clock on Saturday afternoon to Fort Knokke, and stayed there three days having a look round the town and sampling some of the export and tickie beer. Found 15 men with two kit bags per man a bit of a crowd to sleep in one tent, and we had to fit in like puzzle maps. Had a route march, or rather scramble, for three hours on Tuesday morning up towards Table Mountain, and on returning found orders for ten to proceed to Kimberley at four, and the remaining 36 to Bloemfontein at 9.30. Bill Pearce and I walked to the station and saw Dick Frew, Davie Semple and Teddy Ash off, they being the only TS men for KB. We entrained at Salt River after waiting from 9 till 11.30 for the special. It was a regular go-as-you-please journey, they pulled up when they liked, and crawled along best part of the time. Met Catling and Jenner going down, and they both looked very queer. Arrived at De Aar at 3.30 on Thursday. Saw Govier, " Hooligan" and Whibley, looking well and smiling. Spent an hour at Naauwpoort Junction with Tee, who looked quite happy and contented with his beard and slouch hat on. An hour before reaching Norval's Pont we were ordered to get all our things together, and they turned us out of the passenger train, and made us get on to loaded open trucks. Skipper Crecy brought some officers' candles and lightened our darkness a bit. When we moved off it was bitterly cold, and I had to hang on for dear life, putting my rifle, kits, and accoutrements on one side of the ridge to balance and keep myself up on the other. It was a wretched phase in the journey, and I was glad to get to Springfontein, and change trains, getting a flat-topped loaded truck this time. Saw Jimmy Brooks and Young Bradshaw (News), and was sorry to hear poor old Met. was down with enteric. Just before we reached Bloemfontein a truck caught fire, and it was a bit exciting saving the ammunition, blankets etc., from the flames. I valued my skin before a mere box of ammunition, and kept a respectful distance away. Anchored at the town station at 6.30 Friday evening, having occupied 67 hours over the journey. (The scenery was very uninteresting, being all veldt and ant-hills, the redeeming features were chats to different detachments at camps on the way, and throwing pennies and biscuits to the yelling, half-naked nigger boys who ran after the trains.) Ruffell appeared on the scene, and we staggered up to the office with our kits and stores. *Sergeant* Nelson marched us to our diggings, an ex-butcher's shop, full of fleas and rats, and although fagged out we were told to keep in our fours and make a show. Found a drop of cold tea that had been left over, and we soon kipped down, and

KHAKI LETTERS—*continued*.

enjoyed a comfortable though hard sleep. On at 7 the next morning doing 7 to 2 duty. Lots to do. Bill Pearce and I punching hard the whole time, and then leaving 200 waiting. Attended service at the Cathedral, on Sunday evening, and was never at a more earnest and enjoyable one. Read the order at 11.45 on Tuesday night to join HQ the next day, and fall in at 6.45, in light marching order. There were six of us, Poole (IV), Stevenson (BM), McQueen (GW), Hamer, Walton and myself (TS). We took a Wheatstone receiver and some slips, and they kept us diddling about on the station from 8.20 till 12.30. Open trucks to Vet River, and then four days' trekking on ox and mule convoy, catching HQ at Kroonstad. Nice, quiet, pretty town, nearly surrounded by the River Valsch. Absolutely nothing to be bought, bar an occasional loaf at 2s. a time. The column pushed off on Tuesday, March 22nd, and, fortunately, myself with them, and I have had a glorious time since. We have averaged 15 miles a day since, joining up each afternoon, and staying till about 6 the next morning. Following the railway mostly, we could see the mess the Boers had made of the bridges, culverts, and line generally. Reached Elandsfontein as the enemy were being driven out the opposite end, and were given tea, coffee, and bread by several ladies. Saw all the captured wagons and rolling-stock, and were disappointed when Lieut. Crookshank rode up and told us we had to go back two miles to Germiston. Slipped into the P.O., and replenished my kit with knife, fork, spoons, and just missed the flag, which some one picked up in front of me. Stayed a day and a-half and then moved into Johannesburg. A regular triumphal march through, and our chaps were given all sorts of things. We pushed on 2½ miles north and out-spanned at Orange Grove, a pretty little place. Up in the trees striking matches, and found lots of oranges, which were a luxurious novelty. Had a blow-out-tea and supper on biscuits, bread, sago, tea, condensed milk, jam. cheese, and anchovy paste. I am feeling splendid, and this open-air life agrees with me. We move on Pretoria to-morrow. Sorry to hear of poor Metcalfe's death. Was pleased to hear on the wire Billy Wilson was picking up, and trust he will soon be well enough to go home. I am afraid you won't find this letter of much interest, I could entertain you better with my experiences verbally. Letter-writing is not my forte. Glad to see the 'LETTERS' are going strong, and the corps is in such a flourishing condition. I have been exceptionally lucky getting right through, and am afraid it will cause a bit of jealousy. Remember me to old friends, please. I'll close this now, as I'm going to have forty winks. Kindest regards to yourself, trusting yourself and family are well. Crossed the Vaal River at 10.2 on the 27th March alongside the 'Long Toms.'"

✤ ✤ ✤ ✤

No. 2554, Sapper **E. C. GOVIER,** sends the following from Prieska, dated July 7th :—

"DEAR COLOUR-SERGEANT KEMP,—Our interest in KHAKI LETTERS is well rewarded by the manner in which it brings us all in touch. A good many of us have not the slightest chance of seeing each other until we are in London again, unless, of course, we return *en bloc*. We in the Western District have just been requested by the D.A.T., Pretoria, to furnish a complete statement of the date of embarkation and employment since in South Africa. What does this portend ? Once again I find myself in the North-Western Province, which, though capable of great agricultural development, is sparsely dotted with squalid groups of buildings, the fronts of which are

KHAKI LETTERS—*continued*.

of Dutch clock pattern, and the roofs corrugated iron. These groups are called towns, and each group, however small, contains the inevitable Dutch (Reformed!) Church, this being one of the qualifications to send a Representative to the House of Assembly, and many churches, many members; thus the Dutch scheme in a nutshell. Prieska, however; is prettily situate on the banks of the grand Orange River, is partly surrounded by ranges of kopjes, and in the distance can be seen the Griqualand Mountain Ranges, the river banks are prettily wooded, among which exist monkeys, baboons, and other animals which require watching after 'lights out.' I almost forgot to mention the fact that this paradise was reached by me from De Aar by convoy, the whole journey, 130 miles, occupying ten days. This operation is called 'trekking', now trekking is an art, and more adapted to the habits of the Boer than Briton. In the first place, one requires a spirit of resignation, then you need not wind your watch up before starting, you put your calendar in your kit bag, and reckon the days as suns, one sun, two suns, and so on, and it is wisest to reckon one sun as one hour, or the exhilarating rate of 1 to 1½ miles an hour becomes unbearable to all except the oxen and five prisoners, who we were taking to Prieska under escort for trial. It is very fortunate for England that the rebel movement was promptly grappled with. Originally started by some 200 Transvaalers from over the border, the movement grew in strength (in some districts by intimidation, and in others by desire) with the intention of setting the whole of the Cape Dutch from Griqualand and Gordonia, down to even Cape Town itself, aflame in the rear of our now advanced forces. Thanks to Lord Kitchener and Col. Adye—the latter officer carrying out in great detail the plan designed and executed by Lord Kitchener in the rough - the attempt was a failure, and the jails are now overcrowded with prisoners awaiting trial, while numbers are on parole. They are now classified as follows :—Class I.—Those who, once cautioned, have again taken up arms. Class II.— First offenders. Class III.—Awaiting evidence. Personally, I think Class I. embodies the pervading spirit of the whole. It is generally supposed that Class I. will lose their lives. Martial law reigns supreme in the North-West Province. It is not a mere blowing of bugles, at dawn and dusk, but a thorough spring cleaning, inside and out, even the Postmaster here being obliged to vacate his own house in favour of the military, and find accommodation where he can (I sleep on the office counter); while periodical sales under the Military Power are held, thousands of confiscated cattle being disposed of. That such action is justified can be proved by the fact that these extreme measures are only just adequate to cope with the determination of our enemy. There is not much doubt that the whole Boer plan was fairly well conceived, and that their failure is chiefly due to their weakness in leading or repelling attack. After these rebel trials I have to proceed to Kimberley Headquarters of the Western Section, where I might, perhaps, hear something about our proposed trip to England and Home, Sweet Home. Trusting you are in good health, and receiving good news from all of 'ours.'"

" P.S.—Universal regret at poor Metcalfe's death, and sympathy with his wife and family expressed amongst us. He performed a Trojan's duty with that singularly unlucky column of Gatacre's, and which bad luck has even enveloped his telegraphists."

Sapper Walter Francis Frew.

THE C.T.O. has, we are sorry to announce, sustained a sad loss by the death of our beloved colleague, W. F.—more familiarly known as "Dick"—Frew, and the 24th Middlesex men have missed a comrade whom they had learned to value and esteem. Walter was born April 23rd, 1866, appointed Telegraphist at the C.T.O. August 14th, 1880, and promoted to the Old First Class June 28th, 1890. He joined the Post Office Rifles early in 1883, and enlisted in the R.E. Reserves May 23rd, 1884. He obtained his discharge Nov. 27th, 1893. When the present war was on he volunteered for service, with many others, and was re-enrolled March 15th last, and sailed for South Africa April 1st, per the s.s. "Winifredian."

Letters from the party on board that boat refer to him thus: "Dick Frew is the father & handyman of the party, all consult him on anything serious or anything difficult to tackle. He is, as of yore, a "typical soldier" (page 120 'K L.'). A testimony which many of us can emphatically uphold We have soldiered with Dick at many camps, both at Aldershot in the trying heat, and at Bisley in the bustle of business, and none could wish for a more genial confrère, or a more ready and capable helper. His last station was Kimberley, where all went well until Death's dread agent—enteric—claimed him on July 7th, and a fine, upright, symmetrical form ; a sterling friend ; a devoted Volunteer was cut off in his prime, at the age of 34. He leaves a sorrowing wife and one child, and our condolences go tenderly out to them.

Sapper W. F. Frew, 4 366, was photographed with the "Winifredian" party, and the reproduction is enlarged from the group taken at Aldershot prior to embarkation. The following extracts are from letters sent by him to his brother.

Writing from Kimberley, May 20th, Walter says :—

". . . . Still in good health, although getting a bit black. On May 12th, I got three days' leave, so drove out Barkley West and saw Harry. . . . about 26 miles . . . . Barkley is a nice sized place—should not mind living there myself, as the Vaal river runs alongside the place. I hear it was a 'record' to obtain three days' leave while on active service, so I shall retain the pass as a curio . . . . Expect I shall soon be shifted, although by all appearances the war will soon be over and we shall soon be on our way home again; the sooner the better. . . . . Still use those printed envelopes."

And again on June 27th, he continues :—

. . . . " Still well and fit. Harry has returned my visit, he came and stayed Saturday to Monday. It was perishing during nights so I expect he was glad to get back to his show. . . . . We had a very pleasant time together. Re suggestion about the bike, am sorry I have not taken it on, although the roads out here are a bit loose, ... but there! we are working twelve hours a day now, so have no time. . . . . I see by Lord Roberts' telegram I get the Mafeking bar, what price that? The fellows who went round to Bloemfontein only getting a bare one, and we were reckoned the outcasts when we volunteered for Kimberley. Hope well and jolly."

✤ ✤ ✤ ✤

No. 4,36c, Sapper **E. J. Ash**, writes from Kimberley, July 8th, as follows : —

" MY DEAR COLOURS,—You will no doubt be surprised to hear from me after so long a farewell, but I have seen that your valuable and much appreciated booklet is invariably crowded out with much more interesting matter than I could write—hence my silence. To-night I feel I must write you, having lost a very dear friend in poor Frew—a friend of 16 years standing. You can imagine how deeply grieved I, indeed every man who has served with him, felt on hearing of his death. I visited him at the Hospital early after his admission. He was always cheerful, and died like a true-born soldier. My dear Colours, in Frew we have lost a real good comrade, one who was always ready and eager to help a less experienced soldier. His death cast a heavy cloud over our camp, for he was universally liked and looked up to. Personally, I have lost my dearest friend in this campaign, and shall feel his loss very deeply. My dear Kemp, there is no more to say, only that we shall be glad when this war is finished, and get back to dear old England, for TS is a Paradise to Kimberley, with 12 hours a day and the ground to lie on. With best regards to you and all the boys."

✤ ✤ ✤ ✤

No. 4374, Sapper **D. Semple**, Kimberley, July 8th, writes :—

" DEAR KEMP,—The sad news of poor Frew's death has cast a great gloom here. He was *beloved* by everyone. Little did we think when I brought him to hospital last Sunday, that on the following Saturday he would have joined the big majority. Personally I feel it as acutely as if I had lost a brother. We never parted since leaving England 'till now.' My *deepest sympathy* to all his relatives in their sad, sad trouble."

" P.S.—Thank you very much indeed for KHAKI LETTERS."

⊣ Khaki Notes. ⊢

The Rudd Subscription List. Sincere thanks to the following K.L. readers for their kind help :—Col. du Plat Taylor, £1 ; Miss Hodges, 2s. 6d. We are glad to hear the " L " Division have subscribed over £10 for this worthy object.

Photographs of the graves of Sappers Williams and Hawkins have been received by me for friends, and duly despatched to them. They were taken by my old brother-photographer, Sergt. Brook, of Huddersfield, who says, " I had to borrow a camera, and have done the best I could under the circs." Another kind act by a comrade which will not pass unnoticed I'm sure. Brook wrote on June 30th, from Kimberley, saying, " I am first-class up to the present. Kind remembrance to all."

KHAKI NOTES—continued.

A telegram was received by Poniard, dated Cape Town, July 21st, saying, "Out of hospital.—Frank." To whom it refers I know not. Nevertheless we are glad of the good news, whoever Frank may be.

A.P.O.C.—Intelligence from the front seems to be somewhat belated at times. We are startled by hearing that men have been unconditionally released, of whose capture we had not been informed. For instance, the War Office, on July 12th, issued the following:—Information has been received from General Sir Redvers Buller that 659 unconditionally released prisoners have recently arrived at Ladysmith, among whom are 433 men of the 4th Bn Derby Regt., 59 men of the Royal Engineers, 50 men of the Cape Pioneer Railway Regt., 33 men of the Imperial Yeomanry, 26 Mounted Infantry details, 17 men of the Post Office Corps, and other details. On July 13th the names were published. They are as follows:—Post Office officials captured at Roodeval—269, Sergt. Julyan. Ptes.: 534, E. J. Blunt; 344, J. Fowler; 551, C. H. Ison; 514, W. T. Noyes; 552, W. C. Strother; 579, Sergt. W. James. Ptes.: 367, S. J. Carroll; 548, J. Hughes; 540, J. E. Jones; 553, C. A. Pearson; 523, A. S. Williams; 429, W. J. Tuohy. The whole of these non-commissioned officers and men have been released, and are now at Ladysmith. Then a little later on the C.N. reporter captures them and sends home a "story of privations" under the heading—"Captured Postal Corps." Here is the cablegram: "Standerton, July 20th.—Several members of the Postal Corps captured at Roodeval, and lately sent to Natal, arrived here to-day. They report that they suffered great privations while in captivity, and were practically half-starved during the whole time. On one occasion they had only half a biscuit provided as rations for three days. The Boers were very short of provisions, and, in fact, had only mealies and a small supply of meat. The corps encountered bitterly cold weather, but all the prisoners survived their very trying experiences." It is a pleasure to know our comrades are on the right side again, but what experiences! I refer to my notes and find many only joined the A.P.O.C. on April 23rd, and sailed in the "Montfort," April 26th, from the Royal Albert Docks, with 14 of Our Own Boys. They must have run up country rather smartly, for they were taken prisoners at Roodeval, south again to Ladysmith, and back northwards to Standerton, all in so short a time; and yet people complain and say: "Where's the Post Office? What are they doing?" etc. Now it is partly explained.

On Tuesday, July 24th, Messrs. R. Weeks, A Div., W. Ives, K Div., F. C. Green, of SG, and R. E. Gamlin, F. Div. Senior Telegraphists, were technically examined for the appointment of 2nd Cl. Asst. Supts. (Seniority in the order named). I learn they were all successful, for which we can heartily congratulate them.

C. S. Covington, Esq., Asst. Supt. Telephones, late of SG, has been appointed Postmaster of Truro.

R. H. Broadway, formerly of the B Div., SG and News, but lately attached to the Telegraph School, Moorgate Street Buildings, and a leading light in the C.T.O. Temperance cause, died on July 23rd, 11.20 p.m., of cancer, after a few weeks illness. He was buried at Finchley on Saturday, July 28th. Wreaths were sent by the News and P.O.T.A.S.

R. M. Catherall, of the "D" has been "invalided" from the service—July 21st. Those of us who have known "Bob" for many years, will know also how to sympathise with him.

W. T. Ball, of the night staff, formerly of F Div., was pensioned a fortnight ago owing to ill-health.

Jack Davies, ex-postmaster, Alford, Lincs., is with us again, having resumed duty in his old division—the News—on Monday, July 30th.

W. Robson, Esq., Asst. Supt., Night Staff, resumed duty on the Day Staff, Bank Holiday, August 6th, after a prolonged absence on sick leave.

Peter White, of the Special Staff, is home again, having had a very trying time with the Imperial Yeomanry. He don't complain much of the fighting, of which he had plenty, but he does the feeding, which was not plentiful. He was wounded in the knee, but I am glad to add is O.K. again.

Sapper D. McLaren, 2,340, was seen in Edinboro' recently, and my informant reports "he is looking very fit, gave him K.L. and a list—for which he was very glad. Going to Chatham and probably S. Africa again shortly."

Sappers 447 C. J. Jenner, and 23764 C. T. Catling, having passed the doctor as being again fit for the front, rejoined their units at Bloemfontein, June 24th, after convalescence at the Cape. Postcard BFN 28.6.00. Good!

KHAKI NOTES—*continued.*

"**Dear Colours,** no 'K.L.'s' have arrived since No. 13," etc. Quite a number of friends have written to me thus. I must respectfully refer them to page 238 D). It is gratifying to know so very many have missed them, and have sought them by a gentle reminder. It bears convincing proof that they are appreciated by a big number; in fact, one correspondent goes so far as to *implore* 'Dear Colours' not to cease issuing them until the Boys are home again As if he ever thought such a thing! There's air! Yes, and plenty of it. It only wants the breeze to be kept up, and the sails filled, to carry the craft along. Do *your* part, I'll do mine, right gladly.

I have received a copy of the "Potchefstroom Budget," issued under military authority. It is a four-page paper, about the size of our "evening ha'porths." No. I. was issued Saturday, June 23rd. Page 1 gives V.R.I. Proclamations in English and Dutch. Page 2. partly advertisements and leaderettes. Page 3, news and humorous, and page 4, advertisements. The type is large and well spread out; price not given. I cull the following par from page 3 :—" At thirty a man suspects himself a fool; knows it at forty, and reforms his plan. At fifty, chides his infamous delay. Resolves, and re-resolves—and dies the same." I have passed the "suspecting" age, and arrived at the full knowledge of the fact, not on my own estimation exactly, but because I am told so, and I *always* believe what I'm told. Then, of course, there are reasons for one's friends' plain speaking and kindly information. Here it is—" You're a fool for not charging 2d. for 'K.L.'s.' they'd appreciate them all the more, and I'm sure they're worth it." But I always *did* make mistakes, you know, so when I'm fifty I'll begin to chide. Thank you, C. J. W., for the paper.

Another new newspaper comes to hand. This time the "Pretoria Friend." No. I. made its appearance on Tuesday, June 26th. It gives notice that the "Bloemfontein Friend" was started soon after the occupation of that place, and hopes to provide news for the troops in Pretoria at the rate of 3d. daily. Profits to charities. But where will Tommy get his threepence from? It is a four pager, printed in first-class style, on very stout paper. Pages 1 and 4 are Proclamations, as also is half of page 3. The remainder is devoted to news. In size it is about 15 by 10 inches. One official notice, dated Pretoria, June 7th, orders :—" All civilians are required to remain in their houses between the hours of 7 p.m. and 6.30 a.m., unless provided with a pass. No civilian is allowed to ride or drive, or ride a bicycle within the town. Liquor stores, bars, and Kaffir eating houses are closed until further orders." Thank you, J.F., for the interesting paper.

Khaki Postage Fund.—On page 191 (No. 10. K.L.) it was intimated that Provincial and District men should subscribe and send in by July 13th their share towards the K.P.F. I am sorry to say this has not been done, or it has been overlooked—few have responded. I do not complain, however, as nearly all offices are now defraying cost of postage of their own K.L.'s, a small burden unknown to my C.T.O. colleagues. I must therefore ask TS to help me again. Will all C.T.O. readers kindly give one penny to the K.P.F. and appoint a collector to receive it, handing it over to Mr. George Costello by August 15th, or as soon after as possible. 230 copies are sent out each issue, the cost of which is, roughly, 30s. every time. The previous C.T.O. subscription amounted to £4 1s. 11d. (see page 171), but then *all* did not assist, owing to a misunderstanding. Let's *all* assist this time, for it is a big burden to bear by the very slender profits of K.L. Thanks are heartily tendered to the following for their subs. :—" S," 5s. ; Miss H., 6d. ; Miss S., 6d. ; J. W. W., 6d. ; Mr. P. (Stamford), 6d., and a few others for odd pence.

"**Poniard, London,**" For telegrams from Our Boys to their relatives and friends at home, the addresses of whom should be sent us at once.

"**Casualties, Capetown,**" for enquiries *re* sick and wounded.

Another.—2556, Sapper E. H. Wyatt, died Aug. 3rd, meningitis, Vereeniging.—" Poniard."

"KHAKI LETTERS," One Penny. By post, Three Halfpence.

All posted letters containing Remittances, Orders, MSS., &c., must be addressed to R. E. KEMP, 12, JERRARD STREET, LEWISHAM, S.E.

Postal Orders should be made payable at Loampit Vale, Lewisham, S.E.

Printed by E. G. BERRYMAN & SONS, *Blackheath Road, London, S.E.*

"Khaki Letters" from ....
"My Colleagues in South Africa."

CORRESPONDENCE FROM THE
POST OFFICE TELEGRAPHISTS
OF THE
24th MIDDLESEX (P.O.) RIFLE VOLUNTEERS
(Royal Engineer Reserves),
ON ACTIVE SERVICE.

THE BOND THAT BINDS US—FRIENDSHIP—COMRADESHIP.

Published fortnightly for the Postal Telegraph Service.
Conducted by COLOUR-SERGEANT R. E. KEMP, *Central Telegraph Office, London.*

No. 15.   AUGUST 24TH, 1900.   PRICE ONE PENNY.

Central Telegraph Office.
London, E.C.

DEAR COMRADES, ONE AND ALL.

Greetings! Since writing you last, few incidents of note have transpired. The House is up and that makes us a bit quieter. The Holiday work, plus War news—more or less stirring—keeps us plodding along. When we tire of South Africa we talk of China, and when we get slack on China we go back to Africa. We get worked up to a high tension as to the safety of various garrisons; we scan the freshly-exhibited placards with their knotty questions "Is De Wet caught?" or another with excitingly large letters "Within striking distance," "Are the Legations safe?" &c. Then, howling down the thoroughfare, rushes the breathless, boisterous boy, unfolded papers across his left shoulder and contents bill in hand—mad, utterly mad. We're mad, too; mad with eagerness to see "Ministers safe" or "Peace proclaimed,"—but what do we read? As the urchin nears us we catch sight of "Brilliant"—and we instantly portray a big military achievement,—the flapping paper falls flat and displays its entirety, and a shock comes over us as we discover "Brilliant batting by So-and-so." Neddy ironically chimes in with "This afternoon I saw some little boys playing cricket, and further on some men with whiskers were doing the same!" The light side of things, however, keeps us from despondency. Let's get on.

The Camp is now over and the troops are back to Civil life once again. They have enjoyed themselves immensely, indeed, as we always expect to do, and at the same time experience has been gained, lessons learnt, and every man knows more about soldiering than he did prior to his stay in the "Emergency" Camp. Not being able to go down at all this year, I am, therefore, not in a position to lucidly relate the wondrous works and daring deeds that were doubtless achieved by the seekers of notoriety. As far as I can gather, no V.C. has been recommended to any of them, although the V.H.C. has been freely bestowed upon sundry. In order to keep two sets of warriors together—the one in the Isle of Sheppy and the other in South Africa—I have received reports from my *Very Extra Special Correspondents,* the pith of which will suffice. In my last letter I gave you a brief summary of the doings of the first fortnight's contingent. The latter lot went through much the same programme.

On Saturday morning, August 4th, about 230 of the 24th, with other detachments of the East London Brigade, returned to London, and only about 170 (24th) went down, leaving for the second fortnight a little over 300. The camp was pitched on a magnificent piece of turf on the top and the side (nearest Sheerness) of a gradually sloped hill. A splendid eminence, far and away better than anything the 24th had ever before experienced. A beautiful country E. W. and S. and the sea on the N.— simply grand in fine weather. The tents were discernable from Rainham, L.C. & D.R., quite 15 miles away. On the Friday before the Bank Holiday a storm arose, and the Sergeants' Mess (a marquee 60ft. by 18ft.) was carried away, most of the canvas torn to ribbons, and crockery-ware galore smashed. Saturday was tolerably fine but rather a strong wind. The second detachment of the corps arrived late on Saturday, and from that time until 2.30 a.m. Sunday, detachments of other corps kept coming in. Sunday—Church Parade (Minster Abbey Church), ZM fair, evening very cold, great coats worn. Monday opened fine, but, as there was an oily sun, it was plain that the weather was unsettled, and at 12.30 down came the rain, which lasted until evening when it held up, but the wind was blowing a gale. At 9 p.m. away went one third of the General Canteen, the remaining two thirds was held up by the guy lines until the piano and other things were removed, and then the order to let go was given and down it went amid cheers. During the evening other marquees were seen to be in a critical condition, and the Permanent Staff were called upon to throw extra guy lines over the tops and make them fast to new pegs. A great deal of fun was got out of the competition of throwing the lines. Sergt.-Instructors Jackman, Graham and Slee being particularly "handy men" at this work, under the able guidance of Colour-Sergt. March, who told them exactly how it should be done. The whole business in camp is now entirely different to what we have experienced for so many years in Aldershot. The Isle of Sheppy was in a state of war, and everybody had to be on the alert. There were no special parades, no inspections to see if you had a button off or a shoe lace missing (Church Parade excepted), simply so many parades at stated times for out-post duty, carrying with them their great-coats and blankets. This went on at different hours, day and night. The Camp itself was a curious sight—badly pitched compared to the canvas towns we have been accustomed to—near the Church, 3rd Middlesex Artillery. 24th next, then the 2nd Tower Hamlets, the T.H. Gun Detachment, and 500 Royal Engineers' Recruits—all mixed up. It was difficult to see the divisions between the various corps, where one began and the other ended. The men spoke highly of the food—splendid fresh meat and locally baked bread. The field ovens, under the charge of Sergt.-Cook Savage, your old "L" Company man, but of later years a member of "I" Company, were a great success; the water too was a great deal better than the Aldershot coloured liquid.

The Commander-in-Chief, Generals Sir E. Wood, Harrison and Fraser visited the camp and outposts on Monday, the 24th formed a guard of honour when the H.Q. Staff arrived because they happened to enter the camp close to our lines. All the Corps were formed up and saluted. Lord Wolseley and Staff afterwards left to see the night operations at Sheerness, the search-lights, five or six of them could be seen from the camp, and were a very fine sight.

The Quartermaster and his assistants have had a busy time. Rations had to be provided at any time a new detachment went out.

Another War Correspondent says :—"We got to Minster on Saturday, Aug. 4th, about 11 p.m., thanks to the L.C. & D. R. The Companies that had the most men down there were formed into four, and all that were left of us made one known as the 'Details Company.' Sunday we had Church Parade in Minster Abbey, and at five o'clock in the evening, half the Battalion were ordered to parade with over-coats (worn) and waterproof sheet (rolled) for a turn of out-post duty. We marched off wondering where we should be posted, and found that our station was at a point on the edge of the cliff known as Busby's Hole. There were five of us (including three L.R.B. men) and a corporal. We had to watch the beach, it was a cold job, pouring with rain, and the only shelter was the furze bushes. Sleep was out of the question, but we had to stop there until two o'clock on Monday afternoon, when we were relieved by the other half of the Battalion. In the evening we were all in the canteen having a concert; Mike Murray was about to commence a song, when there was a snap of the pole, a tearing sound and a general rush to get clear,' and the canteen was no more. On Tuesday afternoon we paraded at 2 p.m. to relieve the others, this time taking a blanket with us in addition. We were rather more fortunate, as our post was in the corner of a meadow and the weather was fine, although the night was exceedingly cold, and our blankets were soon wet through with the heavy dew. The people at the farm were very good to us; cooking us hot tea and breakfast, new laid eggs *ad lib.* but we were not sorry when 2 p.m. came, and we were again relieved. This finished our term of outpost duty, and the rest of the week was given up to musketry, the naval ranges being close handy. The last week we had a lot of Company and Battalion Drills, and also an Inspection by General Fraser, who spoke in complimentary terms about the regiment; two field days to finish up. It is a very nice place in fine weather, plenty of sea bathing, &c. On Thursday last the inmates of the Sheppy Union were given a treat, £18 odd having been collected by Ours and the Tower Hamlets; sports in the afternoon for the youngsters, and a concert in the evening for the old people, who thoroughly enjoyed themselves. I missed the T.S. boys very much, but hope to see them next year."

By the time you have digested these glowing accounts, I think you will have a fair idea of the good old regiments' camping out. The "I" Company are, as you may guess, very disappointed, and many there are who, procrastinating as they are, begin to wonder how and when they may become efficient.

By the local African papers you so kindly forward to me I see you are kept well informed of the big events, so it is stale news for me to say Coomassie is relieved, and Sir Frederick Hodgson—an old 24ther—is relieved, as also is Pekin.

I hope you have been able to sing to each other that rattling song I was enabled to send to some of you? If you can't read the music, you will not mind me remarking that the tune is the well known "When Johnny comes marching home again,—Hurrah!" Yes, *Hurrah* right royally when the "L" Co. come marching home again. How delighted we shall be. At present they are arriving in ones and twos, and I shall be glad to hear from, or of all who may thus return.

Now, boys, I'll again give way, for more precious items. I daresay you have heard the latest catch phrase, if not, allow me to introduce it to you—" You'll have to go through it." One of our poets curiously enough wrote some verses with a somewhat similar title, and I cannot do better than give them a space on this page.

Cheer up, my good comrades, may success always attend your labours, may health and strength continue, and a speedy and safe return is the earnest wish of

Yours most heartily,

To the "L" Co. in South Africa,   R. E. KEMP,
    Tuesday, August 21st, 1900.   *Colour-Sergeant.*

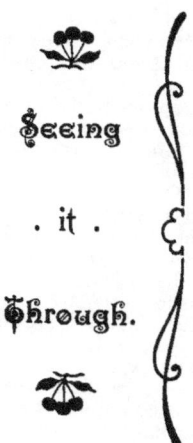

Seeing . it . Through.

I've heard of the "Dublin Fusiliers,"
   And the kilted Gordons' "Cock o' the North,"
But to-day I drink, with mighty cheers,
   To the gallant men of the Twenty-fourth.
If the line be good, or the line be bad,
   I've learned one thing, and I swear it's true—
Despatches, casualties, press reports,
   The Telegraph Corps will see it through.

The Mauser bullet, the bursting shell,
   Don't fall where the lightning-grinders are;
But to dot and dash in a living hell
   Of fever and dysentery's worse by far.
If the line be good, the water's bad,
   And it's endless work, on a poorish screw;
But life and death hang on the wires,
   And the Telegraph Corps must see it through.

When the war is over, and honours fall—
   Crosses, and swords, and glory's crown,
The Telegraph Corps return to work,
   And they'll grind away in the same old town.
The work was hard, and the line was bad,
   But I've learned one thing, and I swear it's true,
The tales of the heroes would all have missed,
   If the Telegraph Corps hadn't seen it through.

C.T.O.   F. PERCIVAL.

COPYRIGHT.—"Khaki Letters" must not be used without permission.—R. E. KEMP.

Khaki Letters.

No. 198, Sapper **F. H. Woodrow** (of SO), sends extracts from his diary on June 10th and 26th from Ventersdorp. (Note, the delay on the letter is explained.)

"I have not written you lately owing to the fact that the Post Office has not yet rejoined the Division, to take over our letters. I have had a splendid time since leaving Vryburg, although there was plenty of hard work to be done, and very little rest to be had. There is one thing I am very thankful for, and that is the Balaclava cap and gloves, which have proved invaluable whilst bivouacing. I will run over a few notes I took on the march, which will give you a little idea how we have been doing with Genl. Hunter's Division. The Staff Officers show us every possible consideration, which makes things much easier when there is work to be done, and if we require anything, we have only to ask them for it.

"*May* 28*th*.—Entrained for Doornbult, slept in the open; bitterly cold and thick white frost. This was about the coldest night I have known.—— *May* 29*th*.—Marched 12 miles without halting, owing to scarcity of water, then put up 2½ miles of wire to Marigobo Pan. We then had to work the wire till midnight, and open again at 5 a.m. We managed to make our office in a cowshed here, and very pleased we were to get even that.—— *May* 30*th*.—Dismantled office at 7 a.m., told off for working party to erect line. We did this in two sections—1st started from Camp, 2nd took a certain point 7 miles out, to work from, and between us we got up 15 miles of wire to a place called Geizdorp. Here we had to again open office, and work nearly all night—this time without even a cowshed.——*May* 31*st*.— Erecting line same as before—doing altogether 18½ miles in the day. Everywhere farmhouses deserted by men, leaving in some cases women and children, with the white flag flying from roof. On the whole the people seemed pleased to see the British advance, and it was amusing to see the different flags exhibited—supposed to represent the Union Jack. This brought us to Barbers Pan, where Boers had previously a permanent telegraph office. We made this our headquarters for the night. I came across a revolver which I promptly annexed as a curio.——*June* 1*st*.— Boer line intact so had no work to get on with. Marched to De Klip Drift (17 miles) where we made office. Was here asked if I would undertake to ride ahead to catch up General Hunter, as he had sent back for a clerk, and, owing to our having to put up line as we went along, we were two days' march behind. I agreed to do this and was supplied with a moke (fit for the knacker yard) which had a most awkward jog, which I little appreciated, and it made me wish I had said 'No.' However, I

KHAKI LETTERS—*continued.*

managed to get used to him and by the constant use of the whip I caught the General about noon at Beijesvlei, joined up instrument and disposed of about 100 messages for him, with little delay. Whilst doing this he went ahead, and after having some food, I started again to catch him. This I did about 5 p.m. at their encampment Krooikraal. Reported myself to the General, who thanked me. He personally saw about getting me food, &c., and came several times during evenings to see how I was getting on. Managed to get off large amount of work, but he insisted on closing the office (in a Bullock waggon) at 10.——*June 3rd.*—General sent me his trap in which to proceed, as he said he had a lot of work for me on arrival at Lichtenburg, and he wanted me as fresh as possible. Reached there, in advance of column, and took over Telegraph Office from Lieut. of Signallers. Splendid office with every comfort. Extremely pretty place, with small rivulets running along the streets. Boers came in by the dozen; handing in arms and ammunition. They all seemed glad that they had finished with it, and now that they see how they have been 'let in,' they are doing their utmost to help us carry everything off successfully. Boer magazine found here, containing two obsolete guns, and thousands of rounds of cartridges. Whilst here, lived a treat—our orderlies making good cooks. Saw Baden Powell, who had ridden over from Mafeking. ——*June 4th.*— Received official wire of capturing Pretoria. Great rejoicing; extra issue of rum.——*June 5th and 6th.*—Nothing out of the ordinary, with exception of breaking up all arms handed in.——*June 7th.*—Very wet. Started on march once more. Rigged up eighteen miles. Proceeded in advance of column. Boers in neighbourhood.——*June 8th.*—We put up 24 miles wire. Reached Ventersdorp, a place similar to Litchenburg in appearance. Took over Office, and worked through successfully. Boers arriving here to hand over arms—all conditions, sizes and ages, thrown in. Boys of fourteen have lately been issued with rifles, &c., to fight us, but they looked greatly relieved when they had to hand them over.——*June 9th.*—General Mahon's Cavalry Brigade arrived here.——*June 10th.*—The whole Brigade left here at 3.45, leaving only about 50 men to guard town.——*June 11th.*—Forty-nine of this 50 left town in morning (myself being the one), but General Hunter and staff arrived about 10. Work very brisk.——*June 12th.*— Kept going at instrument all day—no help whatever.——*June 13th.*—General Hunter and staff left for Potchefstroon. Managed to get wire through to Pretoria who had had communication cut off for past week owing to Boers blowing up railway and telegraph lines at Kroonstad. Had to take all Lord Roberts' work on hand, and then send to Kimberley—kept this up to 1.30 a.m., when I turned in. ——*June 14th.*—Started work at 6.30 a.m., and transmitted again. Towards evening the Colonel of Telegraphs at Pretoria asked for my name, and thanked me on behalf of Lord Roberts for way I had stuck to my post.*
. . . Had good clerks the other end of wire, so was able to show a good record, but beyond this I did nothing. Worked incessantly till 12.30 a.m. ——*June 15th.*—Started work at seven. Cleared Lord Roberts' work from Pretoria. Ditto, from Kimberley. I then experimented, joining them

---

* I have seen a copy of the highly complimentary communication received by our comrade, thanking him, urging rest and to avoid overtaxing himself, but deem it prudent to withhold publication. It is gratifying to know health, strength, and opportunities have assisted him in his work, and while not minimising in the least our colleague's experiences and zeal, it seems only fair to say others would, in all probability, have done the same.—R.E.K.

KHAKI LETTERS—*continued*.

right through successfully, and that left me with very little to do. Another clerk arrived late in the evening.——*June* 16*th*.—An old English family here, asked if they could do anything for us. Cooked all our meals, making pies, &c.——*June* 17*th*.—Resumed working, but unable to gain Pretoria.—— This little diary will give you some idea how things are going with me. Ventersdorp is a pretty little place, as is also the surrounding country, the English people are doing every possible thing to make us comfortable. I have made a mattress with two mail bags and straw, so now I am quite contented. Have not received any letters from home for about four weeks now, so that I am quite cut off as regards news. Hope soon to be with you all, as things seem very nearly over."

Writing later (and delivered same day, July 21st,) from same place, Ventersdorp, *June* 26*th*—

"Am now enjoying temporary rest after the big spell. It's impossible to send letters regularly, or more than one at a time, we have to make use of any troops riding through, or we should never be able to get one through. There are only two clerks and one man to keep line in repair. All other troops have now left the village. People in neighbourhood are very subdued and send in vegetables now and again."

✠ ✠ ✠ ✠

No. 4.336, Sapper **J. H. Mackness**, writes from Paarde Kop Station, June 23rd :—

" . . . . We have been on the tramp again from Newcastle. We joined Buller near Mount Prospect, where we had our big guns, and, for the first day there, lazily watched them banging away at a Long Tom on Pugwanie and another gun on Majuba. The former is a similar mountain to the latter, about three miles apart. The next day I was sent to Ingogo Station, and had a very decent time of it, although they tried to make things hot for us one day from Pugwanie, but all the shells fell short. . . . . After six days at Ingogo we packed up and joined our section at Charlestown, which, like most towns north of Ladysmith, chiefly consists of a few corrugated iron houses or wooden ones. The following day we were off to Wakkerstroom, a two days' journey, where several Boers came in to give up their arms, leaving, after a day's rest, for this show, where they have dropped two of us, the rest pushing off with Buller for Standerton, where I expect we shall join them. Expect to leave at any moment, as the railway is all right up to a few miles this side of Standerton, where the enemy have blown up a bridge. And this brings my doings up to date. The weather has been very severe, lately—bitterly cold. I never thought they had such thick winters. Several times on waking in the morning I have found the water, left in my canteen to clean it out for breakfast, frozen quite half an inch thick—and a white frost all round and on the top blanket. I haven't noticed the cold so much myself, getting used to outdoor life. The only drawback to me is having to pack up blankets wet, with no chance to air them, as sometimes we are on the go before daylight and not in camp again until dark, and the clammy feeling of wrapping up in damp blankets is a bit off at first, but it is all right when they get warm. The country looks very bare and played out just now —all brown and black patches (as much black as brown) where the grass has been fired, and I guess you would have some difficulty in recognising us after a two or three days' march without a wash, what with the dust and the soot. However, we are all keeping very fit; our appetites are enormous, and it requires a little 'manœuvring' at times to satisfy them with the

KHAKI LETTERS—*continued.*

rations we get on the march, being unable to supplement them out of own pockets. Nevertheless, the life we are living will do us a world of good, and I bet you will find a great change for the better in most of us when we return, mentally and physically, especially the youngsters."

✣ ✣ ✣ ✣

No. 4602, Lance-Corporal **R. D. S. Norman** (of SS), on board the "Montrose," writes as follows. (The letter is dated June 24th to July 3rd. Much interesting matter has been deleted) :—

"DEAR KEMP,—As we are now nearing the Cape, I will endeavour to give you all the items of interest since writing from Las Palmas. On Sunday, the 17th, the Adjutant, Lieut. Elkington, informed the troops of a mail being prepared and handed over at the Canaries to be taken homeward by the first mail boat. I was detailed to collect for, and despatch this bag . . . the bag contained over 1,300 articles. I never expected to make a bag up for SO from here when I 'listed, but the duties of a soldier are many and varied. We 'lay to' off the town at 3.30 a.m. on the 18th, and plainly discernable were the lights of the town, and just off our port bow was the transport " Denton Grange," which had some mishap whilst conveying troops some time ago. . . . We passed some lovely villages on our way, which, in a background of brown rocks, towering high in the air, shone like shells on some fairy beach. We could not get a glimpse of the peak, as an island was between us. . . . We had a very nice service on Sunday, and expect one each Sunday we are aboard. The food is very much better now, as the men are beginning to know which part of the ship the cafés are situated in. A grand concert took place on the night of the 18th, both officers and men helping. This was held on the fore deck, and the bridge was lit up with electric lights, and all through it passed off very well. One on a smaller scale is held each night, and the R.E.'s furnish the choir for the services on Sundays. . . . We have a nice sail bath of salt water fixed up, and I can assure you that swimming is out of the question. . . . The officers requiring the bath one morning ordered that no one should bathe between 6 and 8 a.m., so that they would have the bath clean. Tommy, however, found no necessity for disobeying orders, but desiring a bath at the same time, came before 6 a.m., and enjoyed it (mim). Next order was, no one to bathe before 8 a.m., so Tommy had to forgo his bath in early morning. . . . Dolphins have been passed in great numbers, and have acted as a moving target to many ambitious sportsmen. . . . We have been provided with boxing gloves and dumbells, etc., just to keep us warm. Weather getting very warm. Rain commenced to fall very heavily on the 22nd, and continued until night of 23rd. The men took advantage of this to wash all their togs, and I am afraid they hardly looked quite as they look at home. However, from their expressions they seemed happy, and that is the main thing. There are many curious tricks played here, and I will relate one I have now in mind. When the shooting commenced there were various men who fancied themselves better shots than anyone else, and two of these getting together, resolved to prove it by a wager of 5s. The money was handed over to a certain man to keep until the match came off, and one condition agreed to was, that if through any reason the match could not be proceeded with, the money was to provide refreshments for the others interested. It is sad to relate that the night before the match was to be decided, some villian severed the rope of the target, the consequence being that the match was off, and the money went to the canteen. The weather since the rain ceased is much

KHAKI LETTERS—*continued*.

cooler and better for us and the poor horses, which, being near the engines, are often in danger of being suffocated. . . . On crossing the 'line' on the 25th, some fun and excitement relieved the monotony of the voyage. King Neptune, his wife, child, and retinue of bears came on board, and, proceeding to the after deck, they read out the penalty for daring to enter his domains. They then said that those who had not before crossed the line must be initiated. The form of ceremony was as follows. The person called, approached the throne whereon His Majesty was pleased to rest. This consisted of a couple of beer boxes. He was handed over to the doctor, who examined him, and prescribed for any imaginary disease which could be cured by a pill. This pill was of a mixture of tar, cayenne pepper, mustard, and vinegar. The victim was then placed on a high seat, to the rear of which was a bath of salt water. He was then operated upon by the King's barber, who lathered him with a mixture of tar, flour, lamp oil, soft soap, and other ingredients too numerous to mention. The lathering brush was an old whitewashing brush. Whilst this was in process, the doctor asked the age of the victim, and when he opened his mouth to answer, the brush invariably went in (by accident). The shaving was carried out with an immense wooden razor, 4 feet long, after which the bath received, and for a time retained, the victim, who, in the clutches of the bears, had not much chance until he was pitched into the wind shoot and helped through with the hose. The officers and men were served alike, and several who did not desire to go through it were handed up by the *posse* of Police who were detailed for the work. I am sorry to say that one young man fell from the bridge upon his head, and is now seriously ill, suffering from concussion of the brain, besides a broken arm. The weather is now much cooler. . . . The ship's sports had to commence on the 29th, and programme was drawn up on 27th. There were eight events, but the most interesting was the last event, viz., tug-of-war. The R.E.'s entered a team, and the R.A.'s who also entered, expressed a wish that they might be drawn against the Penwipers. Strange to say their wish was gratified, and the R.A.'s were looking for a dirty part of the deck, so that they could sweep it with the Penwipers. From some strange cause the R.E.'s pulled the R.A.'s over, and, from the same cause, pulled their semi-final on the 30th, and were in the final against the Glosters. Here the R.E.'s were more than matched, and after pulling five times, and two men disabled, the R.E.'s were beaten, and got second place. Our Lieut. is very proud of his clerk athletes. R.E. team consisted of Corpls. Morris and Norman, Sappers McBurney, Tait, Lane, Barron, Robinson and Gibson, also Corporal Eastwood and Sapper Stanton of the Balloon Section. Our team had a good pick from GW to Jersey We hope to reach the Cape on Thursday morning, and will most likely stay there for a few days. Last church service was held on 1st, and the minister spoke very well. . . . We have no idea where we are going to yet. . . . Been a marching order inspection to-day (3rd), and kits been straightened considerably. Just few articles missing now. The Royal Irish commenced to playfully smash each other's heads last night (2nd) with broken bottles ; the consequence being bandaged heads. Fined 7s. 6d., and 24 hours' cell for two of them. We expect to reach Capetown late to-morrow night, and I will therefore close this to-night, as there is sure to be a lot of work to be done before we disembark.

"P.S.—Going to Port Elizabeth, thence Bloemfontein."

KHAKI LETTERS—*continued*.

No. 4,318, Sapper **T. H. Corkill** (TSF), writes from Standerton, June 24th, as follows :—

"I've been waiting for an opportunity to write for weeks. You will, no doubt, notice the paucity of correspondence from the Natal section, and no wonder, we've been on the move almost continuously since May the 12th, when Buller advanced from Ladysmith. I was sent away from that fever-stricken spot with seven others on an ox wagon to overtake the advance section, which we did after five days, at Dundee, which the Boers had just evacuated. The journey was a terribly rough one—nothing but young mountains day after day, and anything over fifteen miles a day is considered hard work for the oxen over such country. By-the-bye, I saw Charley Peters at Waschbank, where he was stationed. Dundee was in a horrible state, all the houses being looted by the enemy before their hurried departure. It's not a bad little town, apparently about the size of Ladysmith but much more English looking with its neat little villas here and there. The grave of Penn Symons is in a square in front of what, I suppose, is the Town Hall, and had a Union Jack waving over it. We bivouaced that night near the hill where he was killed. At Dundee the whole of the Natal telegraphists were together for the first time since landing, but the following morning we were split up again, and I was packed off to Glencoe Junction with three others. I spent a fortnight there, living like a lord on the good things Sammy Townsend managed to obtain from the supply people. Glencoe is nothing of a town, but is an important junction for Dundee and Ladysmith. When we arrived there the platform was strewn with thousands of rounds of Boer ammunition, most of them tipped with verdegris, as the Boers say to accelerate the flight of the bullet, but I think it also served another purpose. I picked up several rounds, but, unfortunately, the poison is wearing off. Prisoners of war and rebels are daily brought into the station *en route* to Dundee jail. When the railway was completed to Newcastle, the civilians took over the telegraphs at Glencoe, and we left on a railway wagon for Newcastle. There were five trains in quick succession, and as the first ran off the line, owing to the flimsy repairs, we took eight hours to do the forty odd miles. It was a cold job, too, as the air was very keen up there. The bridges and water tanks were, I think, without exception, blown up everywhere, and the tricky way our people overcame the difficulties was worth noticing. We spent a week in Newcastle doing general labouring, loading and unloading wagons, but we had tents at night, which was decidely comfortable, as sleeping in the open at this time of the year is chronic. Many a night we had severe frosts, and I've seen my blankets more like wood than anything else on rising in the morning. After leaving Newcastle we began to experience more serious conditions of life. We bivouaced every night for three weeks (with the exception of three nights when we had tents) and, my goodness, it *was* 'parky.' It's just like the English December here, frost every night without exception and a cutting wind nearly every day. I don't know where we got to after Newcastle, as I was lost entirely ; we seemed to do nothing but march round and round great hills. We evidently tried to get through Laing's Nek, and were marched off one morning at 5 a.m. six miles to Ingogo, but as our troops were engaging the enemy there we turned back, and covered twelve miles for nothing. We saw a little shelling going on at Ingogo, and from what I could make of it, our guns were on three hills shelling the Boers on a fourth one, and they were splashing the hill hot and strong for hours. We were quite close to Majuba, and it took us just a week to get round it *via* Botha's

KHAKI LETTERS—*continued*.

Pass. At one spot we covered half a mile in two hours, the road being blocked by hundreds of transport wagons; and such a road, too! The day we negotiated the pass I shall never forget. After getting through we spent a couple of days in the Free State, and then passed through a portion of the Transvaal *viâ* Volksrust to Charleston, where we stayed a week near Laing's Nek and Majuba. We spent a very comfortable time here, nothing to do all day, and there was generally a concert every evening at one of the many regiments camping around. Some of them were very decent affairs—out in the open, of course—but there was always a commandeered piano and a roaring fire to make things more home-like. The greatest success in this line was a concert given by the 18th Hussars and B.M.I. combined, at which General Brocklehurst was present. I forgot to mention that during these wanderings I saw my first real bit of warfare, at Almonds Nek. We lay all day behind a large hill in perfect safety, what ho! listening to the guns thundering away, and watching stray Boer shells falling about a quarter of a mile away. I saw one or two drop over this hill, but a horse shot through the neck and a mule through the leg were the only casualties near the Telegraph Battalion. While we were having the usual bully and buscuits one of the Dorsets was brought in on a stretcher, having been killed by a shell. A more horrible sight one could hardly imagine; the half of his head, a hand and a foot being blown off, and his knees completely shattered. They sewed him up in his blankets to await the arrival of the chaplain for burial, which took place on the spot. Our loss on that day was, I think, about 15 killed and 100 wounded. I was on duty that night in a tent where the 'scrap' had taken place, and in the morning the stretcher bearers were busy bringing in the dead and wounded, mostly Boers, I think. We saw four dead Boers next morning on the veldt, and, I daresay, could have seen more had we been anxious. The enemy must have suffered severely that day (but you will know more about that than I do), as it cleared the way completely to the Transvaal. From Charleston we trekked *viâ* Volksrust, Sanspruit, Paardekop and Platraan to here. At Sanspruit a mule 'scoffed' my braces and carbine sling, and had serious designs on my ammunition pouch, when I discovered the tragedy. The bounders will eat anything—bits of wooden poles are common diet, and my equipment was, apparently, an exceptional dainty. I don't know how long we shall stay here or what we shall do next, but, as we rigged up tents last night, we will likely stay here some time. You will notice that we have lost two men, Milne and Robinson. We have been a most unlucky party, as out of 35 who came out, two are dead, four gone back to England, and, I think, no fewer than ten have been in hospital. That horrible Ladysmith has accounted for most of this, and we are lucky to be out of it; the place abounds in fever, arising, no doubt, from the scores of dead cattle lying all around. It's very healthy up here, and one can drink water with impunity. I am as fit as a dog with two tails, but I've had my 'dicky' moments, especially about a month ago, but now there is no curbing my appetite, and I can stick this with good health for months yet. The war seems to hang on in a peculiar manner (to us at any rate, with no reliable news), but it surely can't continue much longer in this desultory manner. All our chaps are expecting to come home by September, but I think Christmas will be nearer the mark. Best respects to all. Hoping to receive some more letters."

KHAKI LETTERS—*continued.*

No. 24,305, Sapper, **F. T. Stimpson,** writing from Taaibosch, O.R.C., June 25th, says :—

" Have not had any letters for the past six weeks, so we know very little of what is going on at home. Can't get anything to read, and grub is a minus quantity, but still we are alive for all that and hope to keep our end up for the old country. We were originally on the Railhead party, but, fortunately, we dropped in for this job by Lord Kitchener. When Vredefort road was surrounded our party was split up, two going to Kromellenbaag Spruit, and Milton and myself coming on here. Our lineman went with the corporal to see what was going on south, and they had not left us about a quarter of an hour at Wolvehoek when they came back full gallop, Boers after them, and our train was ordered to start immediately and we just managed to dodge them. We hadn't got the wind up (not half), so we gradually left them with carbines in hand. We had two chaps captured at Vredefort road, where they were only thirty strong and were given twenty minutes to surrender; that lot was all captured, and we had another captured at Roodewal. They must be having a rough time, as they are being carted about by the Boers from pillar to post. The Boers made a complete wreck of Roodewal station, and burnt a truck with a lot of ammunition, 2,000 pairs of boots and a lot of clothing, and about three hundred 240-lb. shells for the 9·45 guns. This capture is just what we expected, as no troops at all were left on the line of communication. We just missed being attacked on the construction train, being told for Taaibosch. They were attacked about 1 a.m., and had ten casualties, two men being killed, so my luck was in. This Taaibosch Spruit is about one of the most God-forsaken holes I have been in. We are perched on top of a kopje, with the 9th K.R.R.'s—a very decent lot of chaps for Militia battalion, from County Cork—and we get a bit of living and other presents for a bit of news ; of course, we are never short of that, you bet. It is horribly cold at night—the ground is covered with frost every morning—and the day is as warm as you are getting at the present time, I daresay. The Derbyshire Militia got completely cut up close to Roodewal a few days ago. They were encamped at the foot of a kopje and the Boers swept down on them at daybreak, killed about 40, wounded 107, and took 600 prisoners. The ground and camp looked horrible—blood-stained helmets and towels—most of the men were killed and wounded in their tents. De Wet is still roaming about here, and we have to sleep with our clothes on and carbine by side ; in fact it seems as though we are starting again in the Orange River Colony. Have not been to Johannesburg or Pretoria, and shall be sorry if I miss it, as we are only about 60 miles from Johannesburg. . . . . Remember me to all the lads I know. Roll on, England."

✤ ✤ ✤ ✤

No. 4672, Sapper **A. R. Revill,** s.s. Montrose, July 2nd, writes :—
" DEAR COLOUR SERGEANT KEMP, ... (Describes Las Palmas and the disappointment of not calling there) . . . . Last Friday something went wrong with the engines and we had to stand still in mid ocean while they were being repaired. While in this state a great liner swooped down on us to see if we were in need of assistance, and on our replying that it was only a slight mishap she steamed away amidst great cheering on both vessels and the deafening sound of sirens ; three hours later we were again steaming full speed for Table Bay. I have just come off another 24 hours sentry duty, this time it was on the officers' deck, and as they (the officers) paid us two

KHAKI LETTERS—*continued*.

surprise visits during the day and night, it behoved us all to keep well on the alert for defaulters, &c., &c. Father Neptune came aboard with all his officers and attendants, dressed in the most grotesque costumes, the other day, and took up their positions near the great sail bath and lathered their victims with the most vile stuff imaginable, and then toppled them over head-first into the water, from which the victims emerged more like drowned rats than anything else, they tried to snaffle me, but I am pleased to say that I managed to completely outwit them, they managed to collar about 30 of our men and they operated upon them with all their clothes on, poor beggars, I did so feel for them. We have not passed a ship of any kind for eight days neither have we seen land for fourteen days, but we hope to arrive at Capetown next Wednesday or Thursday where I shall post this. We are all going very strong and feel all right after recovering from inoculation, which was a most terrible time for two days. I think I had better close now, with love to all."

No. 1,275, Sapper **C. J. Woode**, Lichtenburg, on July 8th, writes :—
"DEAR COLOURS,—It is quite a long time since I wrote you. I have not had a KHAKI LETTER for ages, but I saw an o'd one at Ventersdorp whilst on a visit. I looked at the letters, and they interested me greatly, for since leaving Kimberley, two months ago, I have hardly seen a 24th man. The names of the writers of the letters in the book seemed all new to me. I am afraid that we who have been out through the campaign are tired of writing letters, though I cheerfully answer every one I get. They many times go astray. Parcels, they must all get lost, for I have had various parcels on the way for ages. They never turn up. After having had a long stay at De Aar, and then a month at Kimberley, I managed to join General Hunter's column, at Fourteen Streams, the day of the Boers' evacuation. The trenches there, and stores that were left behind were curious, and in fording the river my boot got jammed between two stones, and I could not free it, but managed at last—but it spoilt my boot. At Fourteen Streams had a job to cut the Boers' telegraph wire. That was the first 'iron' pole that I had ever climbed. Then we went to Christiania, back to Fourteen Streams, thence by train to Vryburg, where we had the Mafeking rush of work. Vryburg to Maribogo to Maribogopan, Geysdorp to Barberspan, where I stayed for a few days till the 10th Division had all passed through. The lady (Dutch) in whose house my office was, wanted me to pay the rent, and threatened to evict me. We had many squabbles, but eventually she became fairly good friends. From Barberspan (where Prince Teck spent an evening inside, he inquiring to what Volunteer corps I belonged, and I helped him smoke his tobacco—I had little) to Lichtenberg, where I still remain, with W. Proudfoot, of Carlisle (brother to Proudfoot in 24th), assisting me. Last Sunday orders came for me to report at Potchefstroom at once, on horseback, 80 miles distance, on the Monday morning. I started, journeyed to Putfontein, a farmhouse, 20 miles distant, and at that farmhouse I enjoyed a luxury for the first time since leaving England, of sleeping on a 'real bed.' It was delightful, I can assure you. Next day I continued my journey, and when about six miles out it commenced raining, and hail-storm, lightning and thunder all mixed. I got off my pony to take my coat off the saddle, and that confounded pony ran away and left me and my coat on the veldt. He ran back to the farm, and I trudged after him. 'Still, it taught me a lesson.' I continued my journey to Ventersdorp. On my arrival

KHAKI LETTERS—*continued*.

there, I found that, owing to Lichtenberg being under control of another Captain, I had to return. So I had just over 80 miles long, lonesome, and solitary ride. Talking about riding: the other day, when out for an afternoon's ride and shooting, I had a nice experience. My horse, when fording a drift, simply lay down in the water and had a good roll, much to my discomfort, for the banks of that drift were awfully muddy. Still, I could not help but laugh. I was uninjured. I am awfully sorry to hear of so many of our fellows succumbing to fever. To-day I hear of Frew. On the column, several days since, two R.E.'s were playing with a revolver, one shot the other, and Corporal Arthur died the following day from the effect of the wound. They are now making enquiries as to those of us who wish to stay in the country. So I have started making inquiries as to when we may probably start for home. I am thankful to say that I have kept in the best of health throughout the campaign. I present a curious spectacle. Have not had a single article of clothing since leaving Aldershot. With best wishes to you and those in TS."

No. 1546, Sapper **R. Eglinton** (of Derby), sends the following from Thabanchu, O.R.C., July 9th:—

"DEAR COLOURS,—It is many moons since I wrote you last from Belmont, and since then there have been great happenings. Bloemfontein has been occupied, Ladysmith and Mafeking have been relieved, the Free State annexed, Pretoria taken, and the end is not yet. It may be of some interest to you to learn by what steps I arrived here since leaving Belmont, although there is nothing startling or blood-curdling to chronicle. I left Belmont at the beginning of March with Collins, of SY, under orders for Colesberg, which we were never destined to reach. A short and sharp thunderstorm chased us out of the open truck we occupied, and after stoppages at Orange River and De Aar, where we spotted some old familiar faces, we reached Naauwport in the early morning. We waited orders here, and were directed to move on to a place whose obscure name I don't think you will find on the map, viz., Thebus. The railway was being repaired from here to Bloemfontein, and we always seemed to keep the railhead party well in front of us. They made such good progress that we were able to proceed on to Steynsburg next day, a fine little town, whose inhabitants were so pleased to see British troops, that they could not do enough for them. Here I left Collins in the lap of luxury, and went on that day by rail to the Railhead which was at a place called Henning, also unknown to fame, but where the Boers had busted a bridge. This repaired in miraculous time by the Railway Pioneers, we went on to the next place of Boer destruction, patched it up, and won our way into Stormberg, whose name all who run or ride may read, as it is written in huge white letters on the mountain side. Here I met Tough, and poor ill-fated Metcalfe. I had only time to exchange a few words with them as they left next day for Bethulie, and I was left in sole charge for a day or two. Then Monty Andrews took over, and I went on with Fowler's party, amongst whom was Bourlay, of SY, and Stevenson of BM, to Bethulie Bridge. Here I found Tough, and Collins came up next day. After two days here, Stevenson and I crossed by the road bridge, saved by the bravery of an officer of the Derbyshires, from the fate of the railway bridge. After a few days hard graft at Bethulie station, I pushed on for Edenburg, via Springfontein, still accompanied by Stevenson. There we joined Henrici's construction party, and leaving the railway, started off by

KHAKI LETTERS—*continued.*

buck-waggon for Jagersfontein and Fauresmith, putting up the line as we went, and bivouacking at night. Stevenson took over the Jagersfontein office, and I was left at Fauresmith, where were already two R.E. telegraphists. Fauresmith is a thriving little place where we were made extremely comfortable, having our meals in state at the hotel. It was over all too soon however. The Boer success at Reddersburg encouraged their brethren up our way, and we had to make a hasty exit by spring cart at two hour's notice. Passing Jagersfontein's diamond mines, Stevenson had already left, we reached Edenburg half frozen at 11 p.m. Greig, of Carlisle, was here. Early next morning the rail took us to Bethany, and with Mackworth's party, including McAuley and Lemaitre, we marched next day into Reddersburg. Here I spent a miserable wet and cold Easter in the office, and then again at two hour's notice, marched to overtake Moir's party, which, after two days march, we came up with at Wakkerstroom, and found the Boers in front of us. Here I first listened to the music of the pom-pom, the shells humming right over our bivouac, but we were sheltered by the kopje from damage. De Wet cleared off, slipping through Genl. Rundle's fingers, most unfortunately as future events have proved, and the road was open for the 8th Division to Dewetsdorp and Thabanchu, into which latter place I accompanied it April 27th. I took over the office on the 29th, and have been in charge ever since. McAuley, of TS, was left with me. After the pressure of work due to the passing through the place of the various divisions, the 8th, 3rd, and Brabants, things settled down, and there is no cause to complain of overwork. The Winburg circuit was discontinued, leaving us only the line to Bloemfontein, and we had to fill up our spare time with concerts, cricket matches, and athletic sports. Thabanchu is a struggling township situated at the foot of the mountain of that name, and is situated in one of the best pastoral districts of the new Colony. The land is recovering from the scarcity left by the passage of troops, and food is plentiful, if not cheap. Eggs are 1s. 6d. per dozen, Butter, 2s. per lb., and so on. Being close to the borders of Basutoland, of which it formed part only a few years back, before being annexed by the Free State, the native population is in large proportion to the white. The Barralong tribe is located here, and it is a picturesque sight to watch the crowds of Basutos clad toga wise in their gorgeously hued blankets passing to and fro for employment on the railway at Bloemfontein, which is 42 miles west of here. They seem to consider it necessary to stop every few yards on their way, to watch one or more of their number execute some fantastic contortions, to the sound of a deep chested bass chorus, one long drawn out note, a sight and sound to be remembered. They are a friendly and polite race, and manage to conceal under a child-like and bland demeanour a good deal of the subtlety necessary to get on in this world. They have a charming facility in making promises, which they seem to find as difficult to keep as their more cultured white brethren. And their morals do not seem to have much benefited by the large native mission which is established here. De Wet still continues to cause trouble in the district, making sudden descents on the Railway, and creating Hades. But I believe he is now if not already demolished, at least bottled up safe for future consumption. But news is so scarce and unreliable that I know little of what is passing. We have had the usual scares of approaching Boer commandoes, and our small garrison of 250 or so Worcesters have been held in readiness, but nothing has come of it, although on two occasions we have distinctly heard the distant roar of big guns, apparently from the Ficksburg direction. McAuley and the two

KHAKI LETTERS—*continued.*

R.E. linemen were ordered in to Bloemfontein last week, and I am now here solus, with the exception of two assistants from the ranks. Being 5000 feet above the sea here, the weather is very cold at times, the ground being white with hoar frost every morning, but the climate is very healthy and bracing, and we have some lovely, bright days. Your KHAKI LETTERS are simply invaluable to me. Without them I should know little or nothing of the movements and well being of my comrades, although I have got to know that my Belmont confrere Harry Porter is at Bloemfontein. It was with deep regret that I read of the death of Frank Robinson, of DY, at Ladysmith. It took me quite by surprise, as I had just had a letter from him brimful of spirits, and saying how much he was enjoying the experience. Three weeks afterwards he was dead. I hope the rumour that Luttrell is also one of the fallen is untrue. I am waiting anxiously for the next issue of the K.L.'s to dispel all my doubts and difficulties, it keeps me in touch with my widely scattered comrades out here, and the doings of the Regiment at home. May it and its originator go on and prosper, is the heartfelt wish of yours truly."

✣ ✣ ✣ ✣

No. 4,328, Sapper **W. V. Wheller,** writing from Ward 4, Cavalry Hospital, Pietermaritzburg, July 13th, says:—

"I was sent down to this hospital in the "sick train" the day before last. I had a lying-down bunk, and made a triumphal entry through the streets of Pietermaritzburg on a stretcher. I am allowed to get up now, and can manage to toddle about the ward, and the doctor has put me on some stewed chicken to-day for the first time. I had six weeks in bed."

✣ ✣ ✣ ✣

No. 2,544, Sapper **J. W. Creasey** (the gallant skipper), writing from Norvals Pont, July 23rd, says:—

"DEAR COLOURS,—I feel I must just drop you a few lines to thank you kindly for KHAKI LETTERS, which are very interesting. Am pleased that it is such a success, and hope it may continue. I am sorry to say there is nothing here of interest that I can write about, for I think other people have given you a pretty good description of Norvals Pont. I and my dear old friend Alf. Rudd, who has just left us all, I am very grieved to say, arrived here March 15th last, and, as we were the Railhead staff, naturally thought we should have kept on with the Railhead up country. But here I am sticking, and likely to do, until the end of the campaign. I have seen nearly all TS pass up country, as this is the main line from Capetown, and I think a great many that have passed up will not forget the treatment they received from us as they passed up. There has been a great many changes in the staff since being stationed here, and now there are only two of us. It is a bit monotonous, our daily average 20 messages per day. We live in fine style, we keep very chummy . . . . and, of course, come off trumps. We have never been under canvas since arriving here. I have sent you by this same mail a photo of our staff, taken three weeks ago. . . . . Am pleased to say have been in the best of health since being out in this country, but have just about had enough of it. The civies say, 'Why, you haven't seen the country yet.' 'Well,' I tell them, 'I have been out here since February, and seen nothing else but country, veldt, and kopjes.' It is bitter cold here to-day, and blowing a gale—suppose it is just as hot at home. Well, I must hurry up, as the P.O. are keeping the bag open for this. So please excuse paper. Hoping you are quite well, kind regards to self and all TS. Should like to know how poor old Bob is. Good bye for present, and roll on the big ship.

Sapper Ernest Henry Wyatt.

GRIMSBY mourns the loss of a colleague, and the 24th Mx. R.V.C. of a comrade, by the decease of another of "Ours," No. 2,556, Sapper E. H. Wyatt. Poor Wyatt was born August 22nd, 1873, and first tasted P.O. service as a messenger, at Banbury, 1888-90; then as an unpaid learner at the same town, 1890-91. He was Acting-Assistant at Winchester, 1891-92; ditto at Marlborough, 1892-93; and again at Winchester during 1893, until his appointment at Southampton as Telegraphist, on December 22nd of that year. He was transferred to Grimsby on September 1st, 1895, where he remained until his departure for the seat of war. He joined the P.O. Rifles as an "efficient" in November, 1898, and after a short stay in "I" Co., enlisted in the R.E. Reserves, February 7th, 1899, and was one of the first to volunteer for active service. He was accepted for the second draft, and left Grimsby on November 25th, 1899 for Aldershot, amidst much enthusiasm, both on the part of his office chums and the general public, and sailed from Liverpool in the s.s 'Canada,' Dec. 1st, last year. He was a good correspondent to those at home, his letters appearing in the local press, and as there was no indication whatever of any ailment affecting him, the news of his death came as a tremendous shock to all. He passed away at Vereeniging, on Friday, August 3rd, 1900, in his 27th year, the cause of his death being meningitis, and leaves a widow and two young children. To them we tender our deep sympathy and condolence in this dark hour of trial. Our comrade was much liked, and the Grimsby staff are doing their best to shew practical sympathy by making up the weekly wage. All honour to them. May the Father of all Mercies incline the hearts of many others to help the heroines who have given their bread-winners—their all—for their Country's cause.

The last letter to his Grimsby comrades was despatched from Heilbron, July 18th. The following extracts are from it :—

" I was ordered to Ventersburg with Poole (BS), to open an office. We started at 5 a.m. with one lineman, two natives, and a single current set for fixing. We didn't go far before halting for breakfast, which we made from muddy river water. After travelling about 20 miles, we came to a tin hut. We decided to halt. It was bitterly cold, so we spent nearly half the night in ripping up the floor, and made a fire and cooked part of a sheep (you ought to have seen me killing him with a dinner knife). We had just got comfortably asleep, when the lineman whispered in my ear that he could see Boers coming towards us. I threw my blanket off me to load my rifle in the cold frosty air, and although only half awake, I could plainly see the enemy—about a dozen strong—in the moonlight making towards us. . . . . We soon learned their errand—they were not after us, but their horses, which had strayed away and got to us. Four days later we had orders to march to Heilbron with the Highland Brigade; the sight of the brigade with their new clothing and their pipes screaming put new life into me, and I resolved to go through everything with them. We soon heard shots, and our advanced guard was engaged. The Boers made a very poor stand that day. The next day was most eventful of that week's march. We had only gone three miles, when the scouts came in with news that the enemy had occupied a strong position right in front of us. They were told to go back and draw their fire; in consequence, four of the poor fellows were shot dead. One of their horses halted close to me, and suddenly there was a terrible rifle fire from a kopje close to us on our left. The bullets were dropping ten yards from us. This was something quite new to me, but the old soldiers, who were laying down, disapproved of my excitement, with the remark of ' Get down, you fool.' I saw six buried that day. I shall never forget that sickening sight—couldn't sleep at all that night. There was fighting again for the next three days, and we were very thankful to get to Heilbron safe. The two naval guns which were with us did splendid work with each shot, amid much cheering. We had to walk to Lindley one night, a distance of three miles from camp. It was ten p.m. when we started (after marching 18 miles) and our only guide an old stable lantern. We found our way there alright, and we were warned to keep our 'daylights' open, as the place was full of Boers, and on our way back we hopelessly lost ourselves. We wandered about for nearly four hours, and got into camp just in time to catch the column.

"When we arrived at Heilbron we found ourselves in a pitiful plight. Every wire was cut, and wires go into all directions from here. We walked about two miles out with instruments and tried the Kroonstad line, and got through, but the enemy didn't let us rest long. After a night on the veldt working hard, the line was cut. We then tried the Johannesburg line and got through there, but only for about two hours, but we got some very important messages through. Next day a man of the Seaforths, who had had a little experience as lineman, was sent out to find the break on the Kroonstad line. He was chased back by the Boers, Next morning he went out again with an escort of six men. Half an hour later we heard heavy firing, and one of the escort returned breathless and told me one man was shot dead, four horses shot dead, one man wounded, and two taken prisoners with our invaluable lineman. We did not get communication for over three weeks, and here we were on one biscuit and a quarter, with a little fresh meat. A telegraph section has now arrived and are repairing all wires. The colonel in charge of the section said we did well to get through at all, and complimented us. I will never grumble at anything when I get back to dear old Grimsby (not even counter work). Am very much afraid we shan't be home before Christmas. Should like to write to all of the dear old boys, but they know I havn't time. I am afraid we don't get half our letters. Hope I shall soon get some new clothing. My toes are out of my boots, and am wearing a pair of Boer trousers and shirt."

Khaki Sidelights and Notes.

Our Comrades of the A.P.O.C. have, as most of us are aware, been well under fire. The following extract from a letter dated Bloemfontein, July 3rd, from "An Officer," will prove interesting to members of the 24th and others:—

".... You probably have had news of the hole we got into at Roodewal. Twenty-three men and myself were waiting there with about 1,500 bags of mails for Bobs' column, to be forwarded by rail when open, ox transport having been exhausted. There was also at the station warm clothing for three divisions and a vast stock of gun ammunition. The station was a mere spot in the wilderness of the veldt, open on all sides. For four days we enjoyed ourselves. On the Monday news came of raiding bands about threatening us. So we erected barricades of mails and clothing bales, and wired for reinforcements. None came till Tuesday night. When the 4th Derbys came in, nothing happened, so they hurried on 2½ miles to a river and camped happily under a kopje. Next morning, friend De Wet, with four guns and about 1,500 men, attacked us and the Derby's simultaneously. After three hours they gave in, and the Boers turned all guns on to us. We were 143 all told, and had stood one gun and heavy rifle fire from 6 to 9 happily. But four guns pumping shell in from three sides was no catch, and as 90 per cent. of shell burst in our laager, which only measured 50ft. by 100yds., we gave in at 12.30 p.m.—8 killed, 23 badly wounded. Tuffen, P.O.C., was shattered by one of the last shells. Gobel had his shoulder badly smashed by one of the first shells. Two of our fellows, Carroll and Spollen, did ambulance work in splendid form, and behaved magnificently. All the men behaved well. We could only put in long range volleys, as the Boers did not come within 1000 yards. For a baptism of fire, it was as hot a corner as one could wish for. The Boers behaved well when they came in, except that they would not spare the mails, and by accident or design destroyed all my kit. After two nights in their laager I caught a violent chill, and was sent to a hospital then in their lines. The following day Methuen came along and drove the Boers off, and I was sent down to Kronstad, where I remained for 10 days with jaundice. The other poor chaps, except Sergeant Chapman, who was also sick, and Minter and Rutherford, slightly wounded, are still prisoners. I am fairly fit again, and very busy."

The "Natal Witness" for July 13th, gives an account of the experiences of the 750 prisoners who were recently released, under the heading of "How the Guests fared." One of the "guests" favoured me with the copy from which the following extracts are taken:—"A representative of the *Natal Witness* on Wednesday paid a visit to Ladysmith, to have a chat with the men who were, on the previous Thursday put over the Berg by the Boers, and who are now camped at Tintown. At Leeuwspruit a surprise was in store for the prisoners, who found themselves in the midst of a fight between the enemy and a body of 'sappers.' The latter were soon overwhelmed and were added to the squad of prisoners, who were ordered to continue marching. At 6 a.m. they reached De Wet's laager, and were allowed a few hours' rest, and had a biscuit a man served out as food. The approach of a British force on the north cut short the opportunity for rest, and the men were soon again under way. None of the men had more than one blanket, and many were not even so well off. Some of them were compelled to walk about most of the night owing to the cold, their only 'refreshment' being the contents of a water bottle, frozen into a solid lump of ice. The Fieldcornets and Commandants lived on the fat of the land, but the rank and file of the burghers, though they had their coffee, were subsisting on a diet very similar to that of the prisoners. One Field-cornet showed his authority in a most repugnant manner. A halt was called at a spot where there were two pools, in one of which some of the Boers washed their feet and stirred up the mud. From the other they got their drinking water. The prisoners were ordered to obtain their supply from the dirty pool, and they indignantly reported the matter to the Fieldcornet. He, however, insisted on the order, remarking "anything is good enough for rooineks!" Luckily his reign was of short duration. The rank and file of the Boers were civil enough, and, in some instances, went so far as to sympathise with their prisoners. The men were ordered to climb down the mountain side. This was in many cases the last straw to their endurance—to be compelled to make the descent of the Berg in the darkness, after their continued marching had rendered all footsore and weary, and many bootless. But the order was imperative. The road was not to be used. The poor dilapidated wrecks of manhood were ordered to march all night, and if they were within gunshot in the morning they would be fired on ! The prisoners cared

KHAKI SIDELIGHTS—*continued.*

nothing for this brutal threat so long as they were free, and shortly to come in contact with British again. On Friday morning, the 6th, two men got to Acton Homes, and reported '800 starving prisoners are roaming about on the veld.' On Saturday and Sunday some of the men walked in in detachments, while others were brought in by wagons. De Wet, who is a very big man of about 45 years of age, and who wears a beard, has a staff composed almost entirely of Frenchmen and Germans, who so it is said, dodged behind Lord Roberts when he advanced on Johannesburg."

✧ ✧ ✧ ✧

Notes. **Proler** has been deciphered. In K.L. No. 10, I notified that four men had arrived in Pretoria. The cablegram included the mysterious gentleman named Proler. This I thought was a mutilation of Porter, whereas it was intended for Pooler (Poole, R.). So the saving of 2s. cost the honour due to Poole to be given to Porter. Fullest apologies to my Inverness Colleague, no doubt the Woolwich Infant would have been glad had he gained the distinction. Lance-Corpl. Poole, I hear, says, "It's a good job the operator who created the error isn't on his staff; he'd stand a chance of doing office work all day, guards all night, besides losing his badges if he cribbed.—KK. Loud laughter. KK.

There is a little matter I must settle. In one letter these words occurred:—" A fountain pen and a bottle of ink would be very useful to me." The writer says, " it looks as if that suggestion was made to the whole world, a very blunt hint thrown out on chance, whereas it was meant solely for the recipient of the letter."—Of course it was. We all knew that. I've been asked over and over again " What can I send out? What do you think would be useful?" And what could be more useful than a Swan ; I always use one, so does B.P. Suppose the whole world had sent my friend a fountain pen, the whole world would have misunderstood his request. Suppose several had done so, and our friend finding that one was sufficient, gave the remainder to needy chums, the several would have erred. Oh no, he did not throw out any hint for himself, but he unknowingly gave a splendid bit of advice, and if he only saw some of the letters that are written in hard pencil, he would be pleased to learn that he gave a remedy that would save many a tedious task of deciphering partly erased words. My friend is acquitted, without a stain on his character. So am I, I hope.

A Friend writes me from Newhaven explaining a little curiosity. He has received a letter from Sapper W. H. P. Woolley, and an extra sheet—page 10—of another letter enclosed in it. This he has kindly forwarded to me. We are glad to hear the testimony of our comrade :—" I am thankful from the very bottom of my heart to the Matron, Nurses, and Orderlies, for the way I have been cared for during my bad time. I am glad to say that I am up now and gaining my strength rapidly, and hope to be home amongst you all in a very short time. I was in bed from 27th of May till 4th July." This portion of the letter was received by last mail. Were there not ten pages? "Where are the nine?" Thank you, E.J.W.

In No. 10 K.L., I asked for information *re* poor Met., adding, "his friends would like a photo. of where he was buried, if possible." Several of Our Own have replied, as also has that Stranger—no, no, that kind colleague of ours, Sapper John Read, R.E., who journeyed with a photographer to the last resting place, obtained the picture, sent it home, and now the relatives desire him to know how fully they appreciate his kindly action, and thank him and the others sincerely. If the little book can only do such service as this, for the comfort of bereaved ones, or for the satisfaction of saddened homes, my labour will be amply repaid.

Another request is made by the relatives of our late comrade, E. H. Wyatt. They desire to be furnished with similar particulars. If any of the Boys can send home the last wishes of their dear one, don't fail to do so. It shall be sent on to the proper quarter. Such acts of kindness are valued beyond measure.

The Rudd Fund now amounts to over £70, and is still open to those who would like to mark their sympathy. Thanks are heartily tendered to Mrs. G.W.B. 5s., Miss J.O. 2s. 6d. and Miss N.K. 2s., which sums have been duly handed over to the promoters of the general subscription.

KHAKI NOTES—*continued.*

Glad to hear so many enquiries after "Dear Bob," and the many requests for something authentic. Here you are: Sergt. Luttrell, writing from Margate, August 19th, says he was recommended to go there. Thinks it's doing him a bit of good, am more of a male nurse than a holiday seeker. No instructions yet, and he adds I don't know how the "1" Co. will go on for camp yarns this year as they have'nt been away. Why, Bob, we'll read K.L. and give up our own chatter to listen to that of the "L."

Sergt. Nelson biked round to the Editorial Office of K.L. on Saturday, August 18th, and reported that he, together with our friend

Sapper W. Wilson, arrived at the R.A. Docks, per the s.s. Lake Erie, on the previous Monday. He looks well and he also is awaiting instructions.

Sapper J. S. Tough (of AB.), has extension of leave till the end of August. He is still suffering from muscular rheumatism and ague. His office colleagues, Sappers Grant and Eaton, are in the Zeerust district, and "going strong," although their waist measurements are considerably reduced.

Special. I should be extremely glad to hear from men "invalided," either that they are under orders for, or have arrived, home. I need not send K.L.'s to S.A. then. Also their orders, if any, *re* future movements. We *do* like to know.

The Official List of Casualties, issued August 20th, gives the names of a number of Prisoners captured at Klerksdorp by the Boers on July 25th. Telegrapists Coles and Davies are amongst them. We have a D. G. Davies, a 24th man from Cardiff. Is it him?

Pte. H. G. Sanders, 272 A.P.O.C., died at Newcastle, of Enteric Fever. The Official casualty list gives date of death as July 30th, another journal (*The Post*), gives it as June 1st, and a Colour-Sergt. read a letter from a P.O. man at the front during the Bisley Meeting (middle fortnight in July) which reported Sanders was dead.

Sergt. C. Hicks, of K. Co., was walking with a T.H. Sergt. on August 9th, at Minster Camp, when he accidentally fell and the heavy T.H. man tripped on to him, with the result that our old friend sustained a broken leg. We hope Charlie will make speedy progress and be himself again.

See Page 280.—July 25th. Just received 6, 7, 8, 9 and 10, K.L. and, in fact, I had a sack full of letters dating back from April. Woode *must* be happy now.

The Khaki Postage Fund. Every Division, Group and Section are respectfully asked to appoint a Collector—if not already done—to collect pennies for the K.P.F. This fund will lighten the expenses of K.L, and shew the "correct" feeling exists between colleagues at home toward those in South Africa. Mr. George Costello will be pleased to receive the sums thus contributed. I would like to publish some of the very pretty letters I receive, but cannot. The following amounts have been received and are cordially acknowledged with many thanks:—D.S., 1s., Mrs. G.W.B., 4s., "Three pensioners," 5s., N.H. and A.J.D. (Chicago) 2 dollars (8s.), J.H.N., 2s., C.L.S., 3s. 6d., Prov. Check, 2s. 7d., Received Check (per A.L.W.) 4s. 7d., Glasgow, 2s., and a few odd pennies. Later.—Just before returning proof to printer, I received a note saying "I have great pleasure in forwarding you herewith the sum of 14s., being a donation from the Leeds staff towards the K.L. Postage Fund." I can assure the Leeds friends that I have equally great pleasure in thanking them. Also Stratford B.O., 2s., and the Special Staff, 3s. 2d. TKU.

"Poniard, London," for telegrams from Our Boys to their relatives and friends at home, the addresses of whom should be sent us at once.

"Casualties, Capetown," for enquiries *re* sick and wounded.

BQ's. J. F.—Yes, Mafeking postcard duly received. Could not publish. R.D.S.N.—Photos only just arrived. J.W.C.—Thank you, much appreciated. "To be a farmer's boy." EX-GUEST—Next time.

"KHAKI LETTERS," One Penny. By post, Three Halfpence.

All posted letters containing Remittances, Orders, MSS., &c., must be addressed to R. E. KEMP, 12, JERRARD STREET, LEWISHAM, S.E.
Postal Orders should be made payable at Loampit Vale, Lewisham, S.E.

Printed by E. G. BERRYMAN & SONS, *Blackheath Road, London, S.E.*

"Khaki Letters" from ....
"My Colleagues in South Africa."

CORRESPONDENCE FROM THE
POST OFFICE TELEGRAPHISTS
OF THE
24th MIDDLESEX (P.O.) RIFLE VOLUNTEERS
(Royal Engineer Reserves),
ON ACTIVE SERVICE.

THE BOND THAT BINDS US—FRIENDSHIP—COMRADESHIP.

Published fortnightly for the Postal Telegraph Service.
Conducted by COLOUR-SERGEANT R. E. KEMP, *Central Telegraph Office, London.*

No. 16.   SEPTEMBER 7TH, 1900.   PRICE ONE PENNY.

Central Telegraph Office,
London, E.C.

DEAR COMRADES, ONE AND ALL.

Greetings! Here we are in September—just twelve months' since we began to wonder whether war would be declared or averted, and if, unfortunately, strife was unavoidable, whether the Reserves of the Royal Engineers would be called upon. By the time you get this, some of you will have been with the Colours for one solid year. *Tempus fugit!* And, sad to relate, the band is still playing and "your 'umble" is still handing round the programmes. There have been many additions to your ranks and several distressing removals. Some have returned to us, others are on their way. These are they who have fallen from the ranks, faint and undone. We look listfully and longingly for the day when *all* may come back to the dear Old Homeland and lay down their arms, for the duty is done, the war wageth no longer, and peace reigns supreme. May God speed that day.

Just a little more music! Cricket is played out. The willow-weilders have batted well, some have played for "centuries." Their lives have been charmed, they've lived and lived, and the curtain drops on the die-hards—still in their race for supremacy. Two of them seem to have existed through no less than eleven centuries, and, as far as I can make out, are trying for more. How greedy of them. Football entered the field on the 1st inst., and everybody appears to be filling up coupons—those funny pieces of paper, full of squares, for which a postal order is the only pressure that proves sufficient for its perusal by the papers that publish them. It may not be a relief to us, but it will be a change. We shall forget the exciting sarcasm and taunts—the glaring eyes and the feverishly impatient follower who, for the three days occupied in the bat and ball conflict, persistently asked "What about Surrey now?" And he, too, who, as the expected centurion was dismissed with a duck, slyly winks and says, "Hur nur?" (Englishized—How now?) There are a number of you at the front whom I personally know would enjoy a good game, others whose delight is to watch one. "Same as you."

I made a remark in my last letter to you *re* V.C. and V.H.C. No one has asked me what V.C. was (suppose they have all got one), but several have been inquisitive enough to enquire "What is V.H.C.?" I think it very rude of them to read the letters

I write to you and I cannot Very Highly Commend them for it, but they *will* do it, you know. Yes, several have had the V.H.C. The organ swells, and in Regimental Orders dated August 29th, *vox celeste* is prominent as it sweetly renders: "The Commanding Officer desires to express his entire satisfaction with the conduct and appearance of the Battalion while in Camp at Minster. The duties were promptly and well performed, and the Camp was very orderly and clean. The Commanding Officer hopes that all ranks derived benefit from the instruction in Musketry and in Company training, and also in point of health from the good air and sea bathing." For which we are all glad. But our ecstacy is not yet. A moment later *tremelo* is abruptly closed and the sweet *vox humana* opened trills out—mezzo-piano—" Colonel Thompson has been granted one year's extension of command, from the 2nd of September, 1900." The 2nd of September being a Sunday lends pathos to the piece and the *grand organ* is drawn, the pedals applied, and—fortissimo—" Many happy returns of the day" is rendered in full chorus. This is not all. We are accustomed to sweet silvery tones from the Press—when work goes to their satisfaction, when it doesn't, you can reckon *their* organ wants cleaning—and again it pays a high compliment to the Bisley Staff, but this year a little innovation has been introduced. The *echo* is always "taking;" we have been enchanted with it many a time, it is always captivating, but in this instance intensely so. It comes from away across the sea—distant Toronto, Canada, and in clear accents gives the voice of the "Evening Telegram," as follows:—

"Mr. J. W. Parish, the officer in charge of the Telegraph Department is a first-class General in handling his staff. What he does not know about the business of his department could all be written on a three-cent piece. I must not forget those under him, a more obliging, willing, and civil lot of men never touched key, and it is not all lavender with them in their work either."

Isn't *that* music? But wait! There is more. *Diminuendo*, yet decisively:—

"The Commanding Officer has pleasure in publishing the following letter from the Statistical Officer, Bisley Camp :—

"The Non-commissioned Officers of the 24th Middlesex Volunteer Rifle Corps, on statistical duty, have at all times afforded me the most willing and cheerful assistance, and the success of the meeting has been in no small measure due to the way they have done their duty."

Yet more music. I referred to the Workhouse Sports at Minster during camp-time. We'll draw the couplers for both bands—2nd T. H. and 24th turned out to make the old folk young again and the lambkins skip and be merry, for Thursday, August 16th, was a festival not to be forgotten. There were races for the children, ditto for the old 'uns, while the sick and infirm looked on, forgetful of their impotency. Then came the tug of war, after which our sergeants took their piano from the mess to the 'House, presented each old chap with a decent briar pipe and an ounce of Players' Navy Cut. The old ladies, curtseying, received ½ lb. of tea, 2 lbs. sugar, and 1 oz. of snuff each—how very shocking—while the little lads and lasses took a packet of innocent chocolate. In such exuberance they all sat down to a high-class tea, given by the two Volunteer regiments. After tea, a grand concert was given in the large dormitory, which was suitably decorated by the inmates, including even the homely word "Welcome." (Not yet, dear friends; we may be welcome, but pray postpone it, it may come all too soon). This *affaire* having passed off, a sandwich supper, with minerals *ad lib*, brought the Union to a close, and, as I can readily believe, the old people were greatly affected by the kindness shewn. It's wonderful what a subscription of £18 will do, isn't it? This was the amount the Post Office Regiment and the 2nd Tower Hamlets raised for the occasion. Chorus—*crescendo*: "Well done!"

To-day the harmony continues. Seraphic sounds are dimly heard from beyond the rolling seas, e'en from "Afric's sunny strand." They are signs of sweet peace heralded in by the proclamation of that Great Soldier — Lord Roberts. The Transvaal is annexed! The Transvaal, however, is not yet the tranquil State we hope to see it. Discords are still in existence, there are little wind instrumentalists in that band who require a course at Kneller Hall. May the big bass drum recognise the little side-drums, the leading clarionet smile upon the simple tinkling cymbals, and the famous First Cornet beam upon the Field Cornets, until not a jar is heard, as they all, with heart and voice in one accord, render that grand old Anthem : "God Save the Queen!"

Roll on that day, that happy day. Meanwhile, may good luck go with you.

Yours most heartily,

To the "L" Co. in South Africa,   R. E. KEMP,
    Tuesday, September 4th, 1900.   *Colour-Sergeant.*

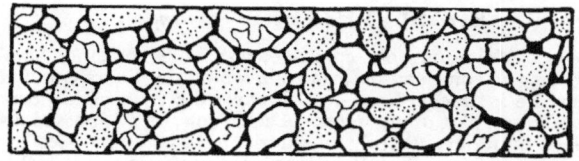

COPYRIGHT.—"Khaki Letters" must not be used without permission.—R. E. KEMP.

Khaki Letters.

No. 4,316, Sapper **J. Macmurtrie**, Kimberley, writing July 11th, says:—

"MY DEAR KEMP,—As camp life (especially on active service) affords little facility for letter writing, perhaps you can see your way to excuse me not writing you long ere this. Well, since May 3rd I have being doing battle here at head office, under charge of Sergt. J. Miller, of TS. Our duties up to latter end of June left nothing to be desired—only doing 8 hours per day, but orders were received from head-quarters to the effect that the office was to be worked on two duties, so that we are now performing a 12 hours' duty. I have been enjoying excellent health here, only been off duty with sickness twice. We now work quad to Bloemfontein, to which station we are very busy. Working Wheatstone to Pretoria (PR), which, of course, is our busiest circuit. Kimberley is a wealthy little place; rather pretty when viewed from some of its surrounding parts; is lit by electricity; boasts of a Town Hall (the only decent building in the town), a market, and steam cars, which run to Kenilworth and Beaconsfield, two surrounding villages. Articles, other than food, are very expensive. I have invested in a book of 21 tickets, costing £1 4s. 6d., averaging 1s. 2d. per dinner, so I dine in Standard Hotel every evening. Several of us do this and find it great good 'erbs. What O! I have enclosed you a menu card, so you can see for yourself how well we fare at the front. Being on night duty, and having all day to ourselves, my pal and I have had some pleasant outings. We went to Modder River one day, and were all over the scene of battle there—breakfasted in Boer trenches. In the village we bought carrots from the schoolmaster, who was a burgher, and later we had some excellent sport—making Kaffirs run races for remainder of the vegetables. Fell in with some war relics. Saw where Gen. Wauchope was first buried (afterwards removed to Matjesfontein), and also visited the graves of forty of the Black Watch on the bank of the river. We could view Magersfontein splendidly from here, and have booked it for a future outing. One day I went to Dronfield, ten miles north of Kimberley in Mafeking direction, to visit a chum there in office. Went over the ground there where French engaged the Boers. Searched the evacuated laagar, and found several war relics, including part of a Boer shirt of many colours (mim). Parts of Boer bodies were protruding through their graves, and the smell, Oh '—when he opened the lid (mim). My chum came over from office on horseback, so I got on it and did a bit of scouting on my own across the open veldt. It was all kif. My chief pastime here is billiards, engaging occasionally in a game of football

KHAKI LETTERS—*continued.*

with the boys. Morse, my old comrade, was taken prisoner at Vredefort while proceeding to some station in a train which the Boers captured, but as far as I know he is free again. . . . . I envy the half of his experiences. Now comes the sad part of my letter. Dick Frew, of TS, passed away from amongst us on Saturday, 7th July, of enteric. He had only been in hospital for a week, but had been ailing for a long time previous to going there. The burial was most touching, and took place yesterday, Monday, 9th, 35 of us attending. His decease has cast quite a gloom over our little camp. How much we all miss him. He was a thorough soldier, and had a kind word for all who came in contact with him. We extend our heartfelt sympathy to those of his who are left to mourn the loss. We are erecting a headstone in memoriam. I am greatly indebted to you for KHAKI LETTERS, which I thoroughly appreciate. She is living, undoubtedly. Best regards to all the boys of the 'F' and to yourself."

No. 4,332, Sapper **T. H. Symonds,** in a letter from Zandfontein, dated July 11th, says :—

" . . . . Your letter only took seven weeks to reach me. After an effort like that I think the A.P.O.C. are resting as I have not yet received some papers and parcels that had a prior code. Let the boys know how I'm getting on. I would write to each of them individually, if possible, but I am afraid that is out of the question, they will understand, however, that because I don't write to them, it's no reason why they shouldn't write to me. You might break this idea gently to them when they're in a good humour. . . . . must be seeing something to write such long letters. Bit different this side, as although I have been practically—to use Milton's (the sapper, not the poet) words—" right bang up the front," all the time there has not been very serious fighting. Indeed I have not been under fire more than four or five times. C—— grew an awful ginger beard, and when I met him for the first time after, I passed him twice and didn't know him. After some days of advice and opinion gratis, which we all gave him very freely and constantly, he secretly made himself presentable again, and peace reigned once more in camp.

I have spent a very pleasant fortnight at Standerton. I was in the office 8 hours on and 24 off, so you see I had plenty of time on hand. Football matches were arranged. I played outside right for the Engineers. The Devons beat us 4—0. In the return match we beat them 2—0, and we drew with Head-quarter Staff one goal each. On Thursday last, July 5th, I was on the wire to advanced troops at Vlakfontein, when it came through to Johannesburg and Pretoria, so I had the satisfaction of being the second man this side to be through to the other. The first one of course was the Vlakfor clerk. Well they've sent me here with a lineman. I have got the office rigged up in a little one-roomed platelayers' hut by the side of the railway line, about six miles S. from Platrand. It is an awfully lonely crib, and the outlook is typical of S. Africa, as in whatever direction you look, you can only see the rolling veldt, with a kopje or two showing very dimly a long way off. It is, I am afraid, rather a weak spot in our line of communications. Just before I got here, or a week ago, 40 Boers rode across the line and left 22 dynamite cartridges, and also cut the cross-country wires. Three nights ago (I was here then) a picket which stops a hundred yards from here at night, was fired on. Next night Boers appeared about a mile to the west, and an outpost had to retire, so altogether I shouldn't be

KHAKI LETTERS—*continued.*

surprised if there's lively times one of these evenings. Not much assistance near either, a half battalion just over a mile away. Well, if they come I'd like to pop one of them, if it is only just to say I've done it. Rather vain of me, I know, still I'm no worse than a lot of others.

Well, I think the war will soon finish, and though I am not anxious to resume duty, yet how glad I shall be to see you all again. What a time it will be to be sure to see the troops when they return! I should like to see them all get a similar reception to what the sailors had. They deserve it, especially the Ladysmith troops, and the relief column. I have conceived a deep respect for the fighting men since coming out. Remember me to all friends."

No. 220, Sergt. **J. W. Miller,** Kimberley (undated — probably July 12th), says :—

"DEAR COLOURS,—It is sometime since I wrote to you, but being so extremely busy I have not had much chance to let you know how we are going on. I regret I have very sad news to send you. Poor Dick Frew, I am sorry to say, died in hospital after a week's enteric. His brother Harry came in to see him on Saturday, July 7th. He arrived about 6.30 and came to the office and we chatted about poor Dick; he had not left 5 minutes before we all heard that Dick had expired at 6.20 p.m. Everybody was amazed and the deepest sympathy was expressed by everyone who knew him. Those who did know him, knew him to be "one of the best in the world," a *man* who has done his work like a man. Never did he ever shirk from work, one of the best-hearted one could come in contact with, and one who was also a most excellent and experienced telegraphist. His loss will be felt very much indeed among his numerous friends in T.S. His funeral took place on Monday, July 9th. He was buried about three miles out of Kimberley. A company of 27 R.E.'s, composed of R.E. Telegraphists, two linemen, and members of his old regiment, the 24th, with myself in charge, followed him to his resting place. We intend erecting a stone to his memory. . . . I must tell you now of a narrow escape I had outside my tent on Monday, 25th of June. Standing watching some black boys cleaning our plates, &c., all of a sudden a bang was heard of a shell being fired. 'Look out!' and in less time than can be imagined, a great piece of shell struck a stone just a yard away from where I was standing. As it struck it sounded like a bell. I picked up the piece which could hardly be held, being so hot. Everyone in camp ran to see what it was and wondered where it came from. Some thought from the Boers, others from a private house; but it was discovered a young fellow in the yard of a silversmith's shop was trying to open a shell between his legs with a crowbar. He, of course, was blown to pieces, and the piece of shell that came so near me must have travelled about a mile. I consider myself very lucky. So I can't say that I have not been under fire. I have not had much chance to do that often, considering the long time I have been in charge of Kimberley office, one of the busiest, if not the busiest of the campaign. We have been working to three big stations, viz., Bloemfontein, Pretoria, and Mafeking, and we never do much less than 1,800 a day, sometimes over 2,000. The staff have been working extremely hard lately, 12 hours a day, but we are in hope of being augmented by another ten men of the last batch that has arrived at Capetown, which will give our men an eight-hour duty. Corpl. Winkle is taking charge with Lce.-Corpl. Haycocks from LV, and all of us

KHAKI LETTERS—*continued.*

find plenty to do. We have quad to Bloemfontein, Wheatstone to Pretoria, and S.C. to Mafeking, besides another wire to Warrenton, Fourteen Streams, Christiana, Bloemhof, and Wolmaranstad. We are getting our stores away rapidly to Bloemfontein by order of the D.A.T., to be in readiness when peace is proclaimed, which gives us some hope that it will not be long before we hear that this terrible war is over."

A postcard dated Mafeking, July 14th, says :—" Thought I'd drop you a line from B.P.'s old show. Glad to say I'm in best of health and wish you good luck with K.L.'s, and may I soon come home."

No. 4,670, Sapper **W. E. Braybon,** writes (apparently from Bloemfontein, about July 15th—letter undated and postmark unreadable) :—

" DEAR KEMP—We had four breakdowns on the good ship ' Montrose' before we reached Capetown. We, of course, had the usual excitement generally experienced on such a journey—to wit, sharks—both on board and where they ought to be, whales, &c., &c. King Neptune came aboard with much unnecessary roughness, and, consequently, some dozen or more suffered with concussion, sprains, and wrenched toes. A sailor likes a joke at the expense of a soldier, and *vice-versâ*. I did not find the voyage at all monotonous. I thought, well, this will prepare us for what is to come. I hope it has. I unfortunately gave myself a bad wrench on board in giving our tug-of-war team practice, otherwise am O.K. as are most here, except Jack Hargreaves, who is in hospital seriously ill. I visited him the first day of my arrival and was sorry to see my " pup " so ill. I was only allowed about three minutes, as he was rather delirious. He is receiving the very best attention. Thank God for sending us these gentle sisters to nurse the sick and also for the gentle-hearted men who perform like duties.

Reverting, we were on board nearly a month, and were greatly disappointed at not being allowed to land at Capetown. Several, however, went ashore disguised as stokers. You have had sufficient descriptions of Table Bay, &c. Well, off we steamed for Port " Lizzie," and Great Scotland Yard, what a change ! the glorious sunshine we had basked in for about two days at Capetown (where, by the way, I ought to mention, we landed shoals of mackerel, and a lovely dish full I had prepared was stolen from the cook-house after they were cooked), was given place to by a most dense fog, in which we were reported to have been in too pleasant proximity to a ship during the night; this fog lasted two days and a night, the fog horn (not our affable pal in the K) going every half minute for the whole of the time. The most noticeable thing about the experience was the terribly anxious face of the Captain of the ' Montrose,' who, I believe, never left his post but to change his fog-soaked clothes. It is a remarkable thing that for eight days we did not pass a vessel, and then we have a narrow squeak of ' hugging.' Well, Port ' Lizzie' was arrived at in overdue course, and the tug had waited since three in the morning, and we arrived about 5 p.m. (?) We were off early next morning and had a good welcome from this pro-Boer town. All along the route we were welcomed most heartily, and I must not forget to mention we had two captured corridor compartments and I was lucky to be esconced in one. We were told to bring Kruger back in them both by natives and Colonials. The carriages were all of iron except the windows. Any remarks ? We had occasional stoppages along the line where large fires were in readiness with boiling water. I was thankful from the depth of my heart for the first day's canteen tin of tea. I

KHAKI LETTERS—*continued*.

had just said I would give a "quid" (that is a sovereign, ladies) for a cup of tea, and up pulled the train and out we were told to 'hobble,' for we were as stiff as nails, and lo, and behold, there was the necessary 'Oopackoolong.' It was the best tea I have ever tasted (apologies to mother). Here we saw and conversed with English, beg pardon, British ladies. I do not know how it is, but the latter seem no part of our existence. We also saw some native ladies, their short frocks of various tints, their neat bodices and artistic white cotton head-dresses made them quite attractive. Their glorious teeth were the admiration of all, and their 'eye' play is quite equal to that of our belles. If ever you hear of derogatory remarks respecting our gallant officers and men who have failed in some instances, look with compassion, I beseech you, upon the idiots from whom they emanate. I have apologised over and over again. Nobody but those who have seen have the slightest conception of the hundreds of miles of kopjes we passed. Those who have been up Scawfell have a very very slight idea of them. Do not imagine they are grassy slopes like Primrose Hill. You have seen a cart shoot the granite blocks in a road? Magnify these from ten to a thousand or ten thousand times, and you have the surface of these hills. If they are not stones, they are covered with jungle, gigantic cactus, and another tree shrub which looks like so many regiments of men with a red plume sticking from their heads. . . . . It must abound in undeveloped mineral wealth, judging by the strata. Of course we passed lots of filthy looking native villages, and the villagers cheered lustily. The Colonists say the soldiers are spoiling the blacks by their freedom. I doubt it. A soldier allows no liberties. The work is very heavy and the lengthy cypher messages are rather trying. The town is very quiet and war prices are still in the ascendancy. We are fortunate to have fresh meat and a potato almost every day, and the bread is excellent. It is amusing to see 20 bullocks drawing a van, the load on which a Midland Railway cart horse would paddle away with. I was greatly disappointed with Bloemfontein, and, as a capital, it is excessively poor, and so far as I can judge, we have crushed a not over ambitious race, so far at least as finish and sanitation goes. Most English towns possess a large open space as a market place, and in this respect Bloemfontein excels, for there is a large open square of buildings and shops in the town. The shops are mostly poor, or diminutive, like those one sees at railway stations along Liverpool Street, but on a smaller scale, whilst the sanitation is just typical of the Dutch. You see boulder strewn open places here and there and general untidiness. You would expect to see a park or pleasure grounds, there is nothing but the sun-scorched, blinding, dust-covered veldt. There are, of course, some picturesque villas and handsome edifices. The Dutch want an infusion of Saxon blood. You would be surprised to see the sheet of ice on the water every morning and the white frost-bound ground. When the sun gains power the cold icy winds are mollified, but, without it, one is nipped up. I was on duty at seven this morning. I never felt so cold in my life. Just think of the poor fellows who have fallen for their country, the pioneers of the war, who have made things just tolerable for we late comers. Here we are in a room ; truly some of the windows are out and we are sleeping on a grimy floor, but we have two blankets and a ground sheet, and we have now commandeered a mattress. The gallant fellows who have placed England in the position she holds have been from 600 to 700 feet nearer the skies than us and protected by what they stood up in, wet through with dew and frozen at night. Help the widows and orphans of these noble men who have perished for their country. With kindest regards.

P.S.—Hargreaves a little better to-day, I am pleased to say.

KHAKI LETTERS—*continued*.

No. 27,844, Sapper **John Fallon**, Pretoria, July 16th, writes :—

"Dear Dick,—I've been rather neglectful of you lately . . . . but as we've had some new blood introduced to our ranks, who were willing to render you an account of our doings, it would be selfish on the part of some of us older campaigners (!) to try and monopolize your valuable space (correct phrase for a correspondent, eh?) to their exclusion. Tom Stevenson told me he was writing you an account of our 'trek' north, including our occupation of Johannesburg and Pretoria, and he having the reputation for 'laying it on thick,' all the remaining 24th men considered that his efforts would meet with your approval as well as theirs. I've heard that you received our telegram despatched from here on 6th June—day after occupation, and wondered if you 'tumbled' to the name of 'Pooler' in the name from. This was intended for Poole, R. (of IV.), and was written Pooler to save 2s. During our first fortnight here very little telegraph business was transacted, owing to the presence of the enemy on our line of communication. About a week after our arrival we were reinforced by fresh operators from Bloemfontein, in the persons of little Willie Pearce, Sorenson, and others. They had rather a rough passage, part of the convoy to which they were attached having been captured by the Boers before reaching the Vaal River, where they were delayed several days. Then, when about 20 miles from Pretoria, their train ran into a horse, who was having his 'first down' on the permanent way, and shook them all up a bit; but, notwithstanding these little inconveniences, Willie and his gallant band reached their destination in safety, very little if anything the worse for their tossing about. Willie now takes nourishment fairly, and, all things considered, I think we shall rear him. I believe an advance further north is contemplated some time this week, and if it comes off, most of the present military staff here have received orders to move also. Fine life trekking. I'm sure you've had it described to you so often that it would be impossible for me to introduce anything new, and as to how we 'tap in' and 'open office,' that has been so ably dealt with by *real* R.E.'s that it would be presumptious on the part of a 24th man to even attempt to describe it. It's wonderful! no 'kid'!! Well, Dick, isn't it sad that, hardly a month goes by that we don't have to record the death of a comrade. This time it's that genuine and stalwart soldier poor Dick Frew, who has joined the great majority. Accustomed as we have been of late to hear of a comrade's death, poor Dick's came upon all of us as a terrible shock. We can hardly realise yet that we have lost him, and can only imagine how those who were nearest to him can bear their affliction. To these we tender our sincerest and heartfelt sympathy. . . . . Rudd (2nd Div. Reserve) has also gone to 'that bourne whence no traveller returns,' and all from that dreaded scourge—enteric. All our men, as well as R.E.'s, are, I am pleased to say, in robust health, and anxiously looking forward to the proclamation of peace, and our subsequent home-going, though very few of us expect to see England in 1900. 'K.L.' arrives regularly, to be as regularly 'gobbled up' by the staff. Regards to all 24th men. Hoping you're all 'kiff' yourself, as we say in the Harmy."

No. 1,457, Sapper **H. J. Hayden** (of LS), 1st Tel. Div. R.E., writing from Honingspruit, 18th July, says :—

"I arrived at Bloemfontein on Whit Sunday, at 3 p.m., after my convalescence at the Cape, the railway journey covering exactly three days and

KHAKI LETTERS—*continued.*

three nights. I commenced duty there the next day, taking up my quarters in the Free State Artillery Fort, which commanded the north of the town. Several deaths from enteric occurred here daily, each Regiment having its own plot of ground for burying. Left Bloemfontein on the 22nd June for Kroonstad, about 120 miles further north; travelled first-class on a truckload of coals, taking with us batteries and Buzzer. Our stay at Kroonstad, however, was only for a night, and the next morning left for Honingspruit Camp (about 22 miles north of Kroonstad), to open an office. The troops here consist of Gloucesters, King's Royal Rifles, Wiltshires, Lancs. Fusiliers, South Lancs., Northumberland Fusiliers, and one or two other units, with two 15-lb. guns. With the exception of the Artillery, all the men are ex-prisoners of war, taken at Dundee, Colenso, Rensburg, and Spion Kop, and they tell some most bloodthirsty yarns, &c. The Telegraph Detachment consists of another 24th man (Picker, of MR), myself, and an R.E. lineman (Moses, of Southampton). We are strongly entrenched, all the men having to sleep in the trenches, and stand to arms every morning at 4.30, until everything is reported clear. We, ourselves, are fortunate in having a bell tent. The troops here also patrol the railway and telegraph lines each side for a distance of twelve miles. De Wet and his Commando are the source of all the trouble around here. We had been here only two days, and just getting nicely settled, when the alarm was given that the Boers were in our vicinity, and an attack was expected at daybreak. Any signs of firing being heard, we had orders to drop the tent and take up positions in the trenches. Fortunately for us, however, nothing came of it beyond getting the breeze up. Our living is very good indeed, considering we are away from any supply depôt. The only drawback is, we are unable to obtain bread. We draw good supplies of tea, coffee, sugar, chocolate, fresh meat, jam, and biscuits; also get rum, bacon, and cheese every other day. Butter and eggs we are able to purchase from Dutch farmers in the neighbourhood.

"The other day I bought a chicken for 1s. 6d, and a duck for 2s., which our nigger boy cooked splendidly. Water is very scarce and of poor quality, and we congratulate ourselves if we get a wash every other day. There is a Store about two miles away from here, but things are very dear, Sunlight Soap being 3s. a box, and Condensed Milk 1s. 9d. per tin; these articles, I believe, cost about 4½d. in England. Lord Methuen's Convoy (about 200 wagons, with 16 oxen in each) left here the other day with supplies for his Division. This made us fairly busy. Lord Kitchener is knocking about round this way, and I think some big move is on for surrounding De Wet. Hope by the time this reaches you he will be captured. I am pleased to say we are all "Sir Garnet," and in the best of health. Got weighed to-day, 12 stone 2½ lbs.; not bad, you know. Kind regards to everybody, trusting all are well.

"P.S.—Was working to Foster (late of Leeds) on the Bloemfontein-Kimberley wire. He sends his regards to all. He told me Shillitoe was round Ladysmith way."

✤ ✤ ✤ ✤

No. 199, Sapper **F. J. Sainsbury,** writing from Rietvlei (Headqrs. 1st Tel. Div.), July 19th, gives the following *resumé* of the march on Pretoria:—

"DEAR COLOURS,—Being the first man of the 24th to leave Bloemfontein with Headquarter-Staff, *en route* for Pretoria, I feel I ought to give you a brief summary of our adventures on the road up from that time. Our

KHAKI LETTERS—*continued.*

first halt was Karree Siding, where we had a taste of purely *al fresco* working for three hours, before pushing on to Brandfort. Here we took over the P.O., which meant plain sailing ; *not* so at our next stopping place—a ganger's hut, in a terrible mess, where the late occupants had evidently left in a hurry. They had left their fowls behind ; needless to say poultry was on the menu card that night for supper. 'Twas here, whilst I was drawing some water from the well, Lord Roberts had compassion on a broken down mule, and requested me to give the 'poor old mule' a drink. Still advancing, we reached Smaldeel, May 6th, where the column halted a day or two for supplies. Here our staff was reinforced : we had had a stiffish time of it already, being very shorthanded.

"When we got on the move again, Kroonstad was soon reached. Here we had tons of work ; quite an army had converged on the town,—'twas where resistance was confidently expected. We were at Kroonstad about a week, and was glad to get on the move again, for it was painfully dull, and the town had been drained out of all provisions after the first day.

"We now began to see visions of Pretoria and Johannesburg looming in the distance, many went as far as to predict some approximate date of our return. This journey was the worst of the lot. We got very little sleep, duty every alternate night ; always required our overcoats, so cold and frosty were the nights. Always turned out before daybreak, in order to pack up everything and have a biscuit and cup of coffee before starting trekking at six. We tramped all bad roads, and 'shoved up behind' when necessary, riding occasionally in a six mule buck-wagon, which at times nearly shook our insides out. Officers were rigged up in all manner of shanties, usually in a barn, stable, or a tent. Many suitable snapshots for the Kodak were passed *en route*. Very funny to see the cavalry chasing stray chickens with a lance or some other outrageous weapon, and lost infantrymen, donkeys to carry their kits on the road. At Klip River, one wheel of the big Naval gun went through the bridge ; nearly a regiment of Tommies and Jacks were engaged in the efforts to pull her out. Before the troops entered the Transvaal, the railway was lined on either side by a barbed wire fencing. Now the barbed wire remains, but the posts have all disappeared, having been required as fuel for our camp fires. The Boers made pitiful sights of the railway and its bridges ; there was no half-and-half about it, they were complete wrecks. We saw several skirmishes, chiefly at Vet and Zand Rivers, and, above all, the excellent shelling just outside Pretoria. We watched our men popping the shells into the enemy's fort, and also the Boers, when they retaliated. Fortunately, the latter's shells are of very little use, so practically no damage was done. Suddenly we heard a shell whizz over our heads, and found they were having a shot at our balloon, which was then just about to ascend. When we reached Johannesburg, we were all in good spirits. Johannesburg is a fine town, with lovely surroundings. We didn't reach our camp till dark, by the way ; it was on the side of a road. We soon discovered ourselves alongside a plantation, and felt justified, after what we had been through, in helping ourselves to oranges, much to the wrath and indignation of the owner, who made a strong protest, personally, next morning to 'Bobs.' We entered Pretoria, as of course you know, on the 5th. Lord Roberts halted at the station prior to his official entry at 2 p.m. ; we came on and took possession of the office. Two of us were then despatched back to the station to fix up a wire, to meet the requirements of 'Bobs' for the time being, and I had the luck in dealing with his lordship's first despatches on the wire announcing the welcome news. You will have read from the papers

KHAKI LETTERS—*continued.*

the news in connection with the march past, &c. The people struck me as being afraid of each other ; the cheering was only half-hearted, and not by any means enthusiastic. The troops marched past in fine form, appeared in fine fettle, and looking much more cheerful than they had done hitherto. Perhaps they considered the war was over, but, alas ! it would appear we have yet a long way to go. I was at PR nearly a month before being sent out here—Rietvlei—where at first we were dealing with work for Mahon, Hutton, and latterly French, now they have moved forward, and at last we have a little time on our hands, which we appreciate, expecting every moment to get orders to shift. We distinctly hear the booming of the cannon in the distance, and only hope that our troops are meeting with success to put a speedy termination to this terrible campaign, and enable us soon to return to our native land. In conclusion, let me congratulate you on the success of your excellent little book. With best wishes to all.

No. 4,602, Lance-Corpl. **R. D. S. Norman,** (SS.) writing from Bloemfontein, July 22nd, as under :—

"DEAR KEMP,—We have now got fairly settled down in our new place, and from all accounts, I think the boys are quite satisfied with this, in the absence of something better. It is certainly not near so rough as some of us had expected. Our food, as regards quantity and quality, is very good, although the cooking leaves something to be desired. This, however, is one of the drawbacks of which we had expected many. We relieved the last boys of the ' Montfort ' party, Tozer, White, Allen, Robson, Bramwell, &c., and, besides providing the staff for this office, we have sent the following—Crafter, Deeble, Forster, Garland. Hughes, Jones, Johnson, McBurney, Perkins and Watkins, to Kimberley ; Gibson, Clift. and Harding to Kroonstad ; Butt and Dodds to Winburg ; and Lowe and Rendle to Brandfort. Nearly all the boys have suffered from cold, toothache, neuralgia, and other minor complaints, although none are seriously ill. I understand we are likely to be here for some time. and as the fighting is coming our way again we have nothing to grumble at. Several of our more bloodthirsty colleagues wish to go to China to quell that disturbance, but I am afraid if the truth were known it may be the sea voyage which is causing their patriotism to boil over. We are quartered in the fort which was the headquarters of the late F.S. Artillery, and many rifles, &c., are still in the armoury here which have never been used. On the roof of our room is a crest of swords and bayonets said to have been taken from the British at Majuba, whether or not this is so, we are unable to say, as they are beyond our reach ; of course we would only examine them and put them back. I am pleased to say our Lieutenant is still here with us, and we sincerely hope he will stay and take us home again ; his kind ways have made him esteemed and respected by the boys. The welfare of his men seem to take his first thoughts and he is ever ready to do his best to rectify any reasonable grievance we may have. He is at present acting as D.A.T. here. The work here is very heavy at present, through so many of our lines getting cut, &c. Still we are making some impression on it, and it may not be long before we are NN all round. The boys were all pleased with their K.L.'s and are looking forward to some more. The place here is nothing much to look at, but we are now seeing it at its worst."

KHAKI LETTERS—*continued.*

No. 4,315, Sapper **A. H. Morse**, writing from Fort Napier, Pietermaritzburg, on July 22nd, gives an account of his capture in the following letter:—

"DEAR COLOUR-SERGT. KEMP.—If you received the paper I sent you by the last mail, you will not be surprised at the above address. Don't you think I am in luck, knocking round the country like this? I am writing this letter in E. N. Watts' diggings (I mean Watts late of C and E Divns. and 24th, and now in Natal Telegraphs). . . . . I see that in the *Daily Mail* of June 20th, my name is omitted from the list of missing in the Leeuwspruit affair. When did the news reach you? If you did not know, I suppose my people would not know either. The Boers let us 'write' letters on two occasions, but, of course, they would not accept them unless we said how kind they were to us, &c. They said they would send them into our lines under a flag of truce, but I don't believe they did; in fact, don't think they tried. How are Neate, Marshall and Payne? I am anxious to know how they got on. At Leeuwspruit we had 'cut in' and were working a buzzer to Vereeniging and Vredefort Weg on the north, and Kroonstad and Kopje on the south. The 'office' consisted of three battery boxes for a desk. We were working in two-hour shifts through the night. At 12 I relieved Neate. The moon had not risen, and I was working by candle-light. It was very cold sitting out on the veldt without a tent, so I put a blanket over my shoulders. At about 1 a.m. I found I could not get any station on either side. I suppose the Boers had cut the wires. At 10 mins. to 2 I shouted back to wake the chap who was to relieve me, and asked him to keep the fire up. I was tired and very cold, so was eagerly anticipating a comfortable sleep near the fire, but it was not to be. At 5 minutes to 2 the bullets came pinging in almost as regularly as the tick of a clock. They did not frighten me, simply because I did not know what they were. I thought some one was throwing stones at the wires. The noise was just like that made by hitting a telegraph wire with a stone. I looked up at the wires to the right and left of me, and then I looked behind me and could see the shots striking fire against the iron goods truck of the construction train. Then I realised what was up, and that I was sitting behind a burning candle. People can say I am slow, but they did not see me at about 2 a.m. on the 14th of June. I did not think to put the candle out, and I even left my pencil behind. I bobbed down behind the battery boxes and crawled back to the line to awaken the rest of our fellows. I must say I completely lost my equanimity when on rousing them they would sit up and unconcernedly drawl 'What's up.' One fellow actually stood up and rubbed his eyes, but he came down all of a sudden. I thought, poor chap, he was shot, but he wasn't—he had only suddenly realised ' what *was* up.' I loaded my carbine and laid down in the orthodox manner, and waited to see what 'our side' would do. All their rifles were on a train which had moved off about 10 minutes before, so, of course, we were completely at the mercy of the enemy. It would have been like signing my death warrant to have fired under the circs., so I followed the popular example and sought to put the train and as much distance as possible between myself and the Boers. I picked up my equipment, haversack and carbine, and threw them under the train and crawled through myself. The fire was getting hotter every minute, so I was unwavering in my purpose to hurry (mim). The Boers were firing through the gaps between the trucks at the retreating figures. Once I found myself in line with one of these gaps, and the bullets were whizzing round me by the dozen, and one just grazed my right hand. I immediately inclined to the

KHAKI LETTERS—*continued*.

left. I struck off eastward for about two miles and then south-west, intending to keep in that course until I met Kitchener's force, which was about ten miles down the line. I was taking my direction by the Milky Way and Southern Cross. I had not gone far in the S.W. direction when another unfortunate joined me. He had no rifle, it having gone away on the train. He insisted that I was going in the wrong direction, but I would not change my course. Suddenly we heard a lot of rifle shots about a mile in front of us, so we laid down for a bit. The full moon was now up, and we could be easily seen from a good distance by our dark shadows on the light veldt. I felt sure we were on the right course, but my new acquaintance, an old soldier, prevailed on me to go N.E., which was right in the opposite direction. I had to give in, because he said he had been ten weeks in the vicinity, and so ought to know where he was going. We 'toed' on till nearly daybreak, when we heard the rattle of a lot of wheels, like a great convoy. There was a great black hill in front of us, and the sound seemed to come from the other side of it. We made for this hill, intending to hide and see if the convoy was British or Boer, but suddenly we distinguished it quite plainly winding round our side of the hill. We walked along with it, but gradually closing in. When we got within about 400 yards we saw the khaki uniforms and helmets of British troops. We stepped forward very light-heartedly, until we saw some ungainly fellows with white and multi-coloured blankets over themselves and horses. They saw us almost as soon as we saw them. About five of them reined up and faced us, one calmly loading his rifle which he kept at the 'ready.' Our first idea was to make tracks or else lay down, but before we had made up our minds they had seen us. Neither party spoke. They stared at us walking like two spectres towards them. I still had my carbine loaded, which I kept at the 'trail.' When we got within hail, I shouted 'Are you Boers?' One of them said 'Yes,' so I replied, in a very melancholy tone, 'Well, I'm afraid it's all up, I suppose we are your prisoners?' We walked in and were questioned a bit, disarmed, &c., and told to wait for the Commandant. We hung about a bit and then mixed up with a lot more prisoners and mooched off. I had my pockets chuck full of Mauser cartridges and clips which I had been collecting. I dropped them as I went, as I expected to be searched. You know the rest from the paper I sent you. We expect to go round to Capetown this week. Jim Brown and Sam Wheller are here in hospital, and their hospital records are both marked 'Transport, England.' In the C.T.O. of this town are E. N. Watts and Pipe (late of TS), Neate (late of CF), Williams (of CF), Bagley (of BM), and Titherley (of EX). I think the war must be nearly over, but no symptom seems to be reliable. Do you think any of us will be for China? I have only received three letters since I have been out here. I saw the dam on the Tugela, and also Lord Roberts' son's grave. I am longing to get my letters. There ought to be enough to fill a pantechnicon, waiting for me somewhere. I like reading KHAKI LETTERS very much. . . . Hoping you are well. Kindest regards to yourself and all old friends. P.S.—What an awfully long letter!"

In another letter Morse gives more experiences :—

" . . . . We were put over the Drakensburg mountains one night, with a 'sailor's good-bye.' We were all pretty well starved. Several times we had a couple of handsful of raw Kaffir corn per man for a day's ration. It used to take me about two hours to grind my portion into meal between two stones and make porridge of it, which we called 'Burgoo.' We used to get

KHAKI LETTERS—*continued.*

a lump of mutton or beef (old trek oxen) almost every day. For some days the only way I could cook my meat was by laying it on the embers of a fire, but things improved when I managed to knock up a frying pan out of a discarded biscuit box. There is absolutely no wood in the Free State. Our fires were made of dry horse and cow-dung, which we used to collect in our blankets on the march. It was as cold at night as it is in England during an ordinary winter. We only had one blanket apiece, and that was like a piece of frosted cardboard in the morning. I saw one of our officers one morning balancing his shirt on his finger by the sleeve. We used to march all through the night sometimes, when dodging the British. The Boer sentries would often fire close to us to frighten and warn us if we strayed away too far in collecting 'fuel'; a very efficacious method too, you bet! The other night, ahem! Watts fetched me down to his place in a rickshaw to dine!! Hindoo waiter! nigger waiter! menus! I tell you I felt a bit awkward in my dirty khaki and hobnailed boots. When I got to Ladysmith, my hair was about three inches long.

July 28th. Writing again, "Ex-Guest" says:—

"Dear Colours.—This is just a P.S. to my growl of Sunday last. I don't think I told you about our concert in the Boer laager. One night we got the Commandant's permission to have a sing-song. One of the Boer officers gave us a few logs for a fire (firewood is jewellery in the Orange River Colony). I regret not being able to give you a list of the songs. Among them were 'Stand up,' 'Them chickens do roost too high,' 'Queen of the Earth,' 'A Jovial Monk,' 'Drinking,' 'Simon the Cellarer,' 'For old time's sake,' &c., a lot being comic songs. I must not omit to mention the 'duet' which two of our Boer guard favoured us with. They sang, rifles in hand, in a very high tone and jerky manner, like little shy boys. Of course the song was doubly Dutch to us, but it was to the old familiar tune of 'Oh where and oh where has my wee doggie gone.' We all roared. The song only lasted about three minutes. In 'For old time's sake' (is that the correct title?) you know the chorus runs something like this '. . . . Don't let your enmity live, Shake hands and let us be friends, for old time's sake.' Whenever the singer came to that part, he took the hand of an old Boer who was sitting down within the ring, and shook it. At first the old farmer looked pained or indignant, but later he seemed to grasp it, and every time when the singer came to that part in the chorus, the old chap put his hand up and smiled, and nodded his grimy old head, and made it evident that he comprehended. When the concert was over, one of our officers stood up and said 'Now, my lads, 'God save the Queen.' Let 'em have it.' And we did. It was on the side of one of the most rugged hills I have seen in the country, and I can tell you it did sound. I was surprised that we were not interrupted. We are being made use of here. I was first made a boilermaker's labourer, but yesterday I was sent to assist the Electrical Engineer Volunteers. Once our Sergeant caught me reading a copy of KHAKI LETTERS. I was sitting down behind an old cistern. He let me off very lightly. It is a fact that the Boers once, when there were two large pools of water, one dirty and one clean, made us drink the dirty water. I did not know anything about the order, and went down to one pool with my old peach can to get a drink, and finding the water bad I threw it away and made for the other pool, but was stopped by a sentry. He motioned me back and I attempted to discuss the point, but he raised the butt of his rifle and would have given me one across the shoulder, I believe, if I had not

KHAKI LETTERS—continued.

waived the point and retired. I did want to sling my old tin at him, all the same. At that time we were under a very ill-disposed Field Cornet. A red, camel-faced, tall man (a 'go-a-long-time-without-water' kind of a face he had). One Field Cornet was very nice. He was an Australian, and refused to take up arms against the British, so he was placed in charge of convoys of prisoners. He never carried arms. When he left us we gave him three cheers. We were several times transferred from one commando to another. The Harrismith commando put us over the border. De Wet is a nice man. A Boer insulted one of our officers, and De Wet heard of it; he asked the officer to point out the man and he would have him shot. The officer declined. De Wet also issued an order that if any Boer took any private property from a prisoner he would be shot. But, nevertheless, several fellows had wrist watches, &c., taken from them. One of the prisoners was a Yeomanry Scout, named Deason; he came from St. Helena, and owns a farm there on which a lot of the British prisoners of war are kept. . . . Just now I am on an electric lighting job. My part of the work consists of sitting on a bag of coal, and watching the fire in the brazier. Two other chaps are on the roof, playing 'noughts and crosses.' I believe there are three more up in the canteen, at least they went that way. At Johannesburg and Pretoria I made a fine collection of Boer money, but I had to spend it all while with the Boers, to buy food. We get more reliable and fresher news from a London paper than from the local press. The war is getting awfully monotonous. We have been served out with entire new kits and slouch hats. I pay Jim Brown and Sam Wheller a visit every day. They are both extremely convalescent, and live like lords, though Sammy does not look *quite* well yet. Oh, I forgot to tell you that there were several 24th men of the A.P.O.C. among the prisoners. I forget their names. . . . I have never received a copy of KHAKI LETTERS myself, but still I like reading them when I get a chance. I shall get all mine together, I expect. Good luck to your enterprise."

No. 1,275, Sapper **C. J. Woode**, Lichtenberg, July 25th, says :—

DEAR COLOURS,—At Lichtenberg we are all expectation. Delarey lives here and he is expected to return. We have a garrison of about 200, so shall have a warm time when he does come. We have dug wells behind the two churches and the court house, and I have erected telephone to the camp. But they were due here yesterday, but no signs of them yet. I am keeping well. I might say that Corpl. Arthur was accidently shot by a comrade and died the following day from the effect of his wounds at Potchefstroom. Two days previous he gave me a new pipe he had had sent him, he being a non-smoker. He was Corporal in charge of the cable cart, and was well esteemed by all of us. For present I will say *au revoir*.

No. 4,367, Sapper **H. J. Harrison**, Johannesburg. July 31st, writes :—
"DEAR COLOURS,—I feel it my duty to write a few lines to KHAKI LETTERS, although having arrived in this country too late to have much experience in trekking, &c. I'm afraid I cannot contribute much of interest. No doubt others of the s.s. 'Winifredian' have supplied you with details of the journey on the sea, and also the train ride through the Colony and the (then) Orange Free State, to Bloemfontein. Sergt. Flanagan and 35 of us arrived at the latter place on May 4th, and were destined to remain there until

KHAKI LETTERS—*continued*.

July 15th, when the next 60 from England relieved us. I was among the fortunate ones to proceed to Pretoria, but only remained there one day and was sent back here. However, it gave me sufficient time to visit a brother of mine in hospital there who has been through the campaign from the beginning. It was while visiting the hospital that I received my orders to leave the town, the corporal in charge sending one of the sappers to warn me. The train that brought us from Bloemfontein it appears was the first one north for ten days, owing to small parties of Boers knocking about. Fortunately we got through all right, but as you no doubt have read in the papers a train shortly after was captured and burnt up, and 100 Highlanders taken prisoners. Our accommodation was, as usual, on loaded trucks, and the first night of our journey had nothing but our top coats to keep us warm, our blankets being stored away in another truck. The cold was almost unbearable. Several of us were perched on a box and had to sit it out for a couple of nights, not daring to sleep for fear of falling off. We passed an armoured train between Kroonstad and Elandsfontein, and at night saw plenty of veldt fires which looked grand in the darkness. Trenches and sandbag redoubts were round all the camps as we got further north. We saw Bob Lasham at Virginia near the Zand River and exchanged greetings. He said he was afraid we should never see Pretoria, meaning I suppose that we should be seized by the Boers. However we arrived there at 7 p.m. on the 17th. There were 33 of us all told, and out of those, two corporals and nine sappers returned here. We left there at 5.30 p.m. on the 18th, and had to change at Elandsfontein. Did not arrive at latter place till 10 p.m. distance (36 miles); a record, eh? Owing to there being no train for Johannesburg that night we bivouaced on the platform, and went by the 10.20 a.m. next morning. Everyone was anxious to have a look at the mines, or rather the exterior of them. This place is simply grand and everything up to date. Electric light in every house and telephones everywhere. The office is a splendid building, especially the interior. The instrument room is very spacious, in fact is said to be the biggest, best, and busiest in South Africa. However the latter phrase is not correct at the present time, as there is not sufficient work for half of us here. Our quarters are in a nice house in the main street, where we have a cook from 26 Coy. R.E., who not only gives us a dinner that would beat a TS one, but actually waits on us and washes up our utensils (with the help of a Kaffir), which is a treat after the usual way of going on in a campaign. To sum it up we are having a gentleman's life. Much to their regret, two of our party (Sapper Mcpherson and Fox) have been sent to Heidelberg and Klip River. Everyone hopes that he won't be the next. The only TS men here besides myself are Woodrow (TS, now SO), F. Clark and J. Davis. Armed sentries patrol the streets here, and are very particular at night. Everyone must carry a pass or take the alternative. We get scarcely any news here, and at time of writing, not received letters for three weeks. The Boers are still busy blowing up the line south, and so preventing things coming up. Thanks for KHAKI LETTERS sent me. Wish you every success. Afraid we shan't be with you this year, but hope some time next."

✣ ✣ ✣

No. 4,321, Sapper **J. A. Brown,** writes, August 31st :—

"DEAR KEMP,—Just a line to let you know that I am back home again having been invalided after enteric. Came home on the 'Orotava,' arriving at Southampton August 27th. Have got two months furlough.

⊷❰ Khaki Sidelights ❱⊶

A Soldier's Grave.—*Sapper John Read, R.E.,* Clerk-in Charge, Springfontein, M.T.O., O.R.C., writes July 12th, 1900:—

"Dear Kemp,—As a wish has been expressed by some of Met.'s friends through you in K.I., No. 10, for a photo of his grave, I am glad to be able to be of service, and beg to enclose you herewith two unmounted photos. One copy you may forward with my kind regards and sympathy to his relatives. You may wish to know the names of the figures. The centre figure is Mr. J. N. Oakley, an Assistant Chaplain, one of Met.'s very firm friends, and who tended him kindly throughout his illness, and performed the funeral service when he was laid to his last, long sleep. Met. mentioned him in his Stormberg letters to you, in very high terms. To the right of Mr. Oakley is seen Mr. Harold J. Blevin, Secretary to the Soldiers' Home Organisation in South Africa; on the other hand is your humble servant.

"I am so sorry I can give no personal details about Met.'s death beyond what I have already written you. All letters, &c., are, I believe, with the Authorities.

"You will pardon this hurried scrawl, but I hope the photo will be some consolation to Met.'s relations, and the many friends he may have had among your Company."

It is with pleasure also that I learn Sapper Read was enabled to supply the photograph through the kindness of Mr. F. J. Wild, of the O.R.C. Railway, Springfontein, who so willingly accompanied Read with his camera, and has effected such an excellent result. Our hearty thanks to both of them.

Corpl. J. H. Winkle, R.E., our old T.S. friend who could not see the Bhoys leaving for the front without throwing in his lot with them, writes from Kimberley, July 13th, as follows:—

"My dear Kemp,—Jimmy Miller has left an unfinished letter addressed to yourself. He has gone to Mafeking on pleasure bent for a day or two, so am sending it on so as to catch the mail. 'Ere you receive this you will have heard of the death of poor Frew. I saw him the day previously in hospital, and he seemed

KHAKI SIDELIGHTS—*continued.*

much better than he had been, and shook hands with me, remarking, "very pleased to see you, Wink." Such news always travels rapidly, and it was a very great shock to us all; he had endeared himself to everybody in the Camp by his general affability, and as regards the office, we always found him 'there' when wanted. His loss is deplored by everyone that knew him. We propose erecting a suitable stone to his memory. Mr. Harry Frew (Dick's brother) happened to be in Kimberley, and needless to say was very greatly affected.

"Everybody is getting tired of the country, and are anxiously waiting for the 'Ship I love.' I venture to say that September will find us on the 'waters blue.' The fighting is practically over, and peace may be declared at any moment now. I have been at Kimberley the whole time, and have done my best to make things as merry as possible: got up several Smoking Concerts, and they have been a great success. We had one last night, almost the whole of the staff being present, also men belonging to the A.P.O.C. and other arms of the Service. Sapper Kelly (CF) presided at the piano, and manipulated in a style worthy of a Tito Mattei; Curnew (TS) is in grand 'song,' and amused us with 'More work for the Undertaker,' and 'Poor Pa Paid'; Sapper Ash (TS) did good service to 'Where did you get that Hat?' Sapper Treacy (CK), 'My Old Dutch'; Sapper Williams (DN), 'We've been touching 'em up a bit'; Sergt. Newman, A.P.O.C., 'Father O'Flynn'; Corpl. Robbotham (North Lancs.), 'Genevieve'; Sapper Jimmy Jones (CF), 'Topical Song,' which gave the roof a fearful shaking; Corpl. Winkle, 'Thy Face I never see'; Sapper Nash (CF) 'It was beautiful,' and it was! Sapper Perkins, 'Etcetera'; Corpl. Montgomery (R.S. Fus.), 'He didn't get a wink all night'; Pte. Doughty (R.S. Fus.), 'As your hair grows whiter'; and the evening wound up with a good-fellowship feeling all round, your 'umble in the Chair, assisted by Sapper Treacy.

Writing again, "Wink" says:—"A lot of our men, No. 8 Section Telegraph Cable Cart, have been captured, including two of our Officers; you will remember this is the Section I came out with; very hard lines to drop into these people's hands, as they treat them very badly in comparison to the manner in which we treat their prisoners. When Kruger said, things out here would stagger humanity, he was very near the mark. The deaths from Enteric have been extraordinarily large; personally, I am pleased to tell you that I am in splendid fettle, and as fit as a fiddle, and it is a singularly strange thing that the number of deaths of those I have personally known, has been greater amongst those with an inclination to lead a quiet life, than *vice versa*. Anent the correspondence going on just now in England about the Hospitals, my own personal opinion is that everything that could be done, has been done. I have myself visited several hospitals, and found them scrupulously clean, and the men have told me they were treated well. Naturally enough, individual cases arise where it would appear that proper treatment had not been meted out, but it is obvious that in a country like this the greatest difficulties have to be contended with. It is nothing short of a miracle to me how well we have done, especially so when we consider that most of our Transports are with convoys (bullock wagons), and they have to trek over most shocking country. Then again, some cases are treated differently than they should be, owing to a wrong diagnosis, no doubt this frequently happens at home, and, of course, there are cases here peculiar to the country, which it is most difficult to diagnose properly. I am perfectly certain that Lord Roberts has done his very utmost to alleviate the sufferings of the men; of course, I have opportunities of knowing how things are going, being where I am.

"The Telegraph Lines are not infrequently cut for long distances, and this increases the difficulties. It seems a favourite game of the Boers, as soon as we get through to Stations north of here, and begin to work OK, down they go. To liven things up a bit, I have been getting up a few Smokers, and they have proved a great success, inasmuch as they have drawn the men into line a bit more. We had a slashing attendance, and the talent was excellent—that is if I am any judge. A Dutchman was playing with a large shell here the other day, and the thing went off and knocked him into Kingdom come; a large piece of it struck our camp, and, I am pleased to say, missed a Sergeant of ours by a 'short head.'

"Nothing startling, but ere you receive this a lot of the Troops will be 'Homeward Bound,' and right glad they will be. The Brigade of Guards, I guess, will be the first to embark, probably with the Reservists. You will be glad to know that my medal will not be a bare one after all, as all troops north of the Modder are to get the 'Mafeking'—anyhow, it has been recommended by 'Bobs,' and I guess that's good enough."

KHAKI SIDELIGHTS—continued.

One of our boys at the front sends a suggestion—or, as he says, *merely* a suggestion. Suggestions are never nerve-breakers, for you can always "take it or leave it alone," and it's your own fault if you get hurt. You would like to know what it is? Here you are then: "As you are unfortunately aware poor Met. is not the only one of our Corps who will never return to the Old Country. Another greatly esteemed friend—Sapper Frew—was buried at Kimberley last Sunday, after a very short illness. Both were married, as also was poor Milne, of Aberdeen. Now what I would propose is this:—On our return, there will doubtless, be the 'usual dinner' to celebrate the event. Could we not instead, organize a gigantic Conversazione and Dance at (say) the Holborn Town Hall, obtain the patronage of . . . . ., and devote the whole of the proceeds to the Widows and Orphans? I feel confident that being a welcome home to the 24th. and having the other deserving object in view, a very large attendance would be assured. I simply make this suggestion, so that in the event of short notice of our return, preliminary arrangements might be made. I would do my little towards assisting you, and you would have the co-operation of many other 24th men here." Now that Lord Roberts has proclaimed the Annexation of the Transvaal, many people give the war little longer life. No one knows, but steps towards the formation of a Provisional Committee might be well. C.T.O. Ladies and Gentlemen please bear this in mind, even if it is too premature.

Our Casualties up to date. Weeks and months pass quickly by, and in the bustle of business we lose count of events. The following are the losses the 24th has sustained during the South African Campaign as far as can be ascertained.

No.	Reg. No.	Rank and Name.	Died. 1900.		At	Cause.
		Royal Engineers.				
1	458	Sapper Hawkins, A. W.	Mar.	13	Orange River	Enteric
2	28865	,, Fairall, C. A. G.	April	6	Naauwpoort	,,
3	4306	,, Milne, A.	May	21	Ladysmith	Dysentery
4	23653	,, Metcalfe, J. L.	,,	22	Springfontein	,,
5	4335	,, Robinson, F. W.	,,	23	Ladysmith	,,
6	4366	,, Frew, W. F.	July	7	Kimberley	Enteric
7	2556	,, Wyatt, E. H.	Aug.	3	Vereeniging	Meningitis
		Army P. O. Corps.				
1	142	Corpl. Bruns, F. W.	Jan.	1	Pietermaritzburg	Enteric
2	241	Sergt. Watson, S.	Mar.	17	Modder River	,,
3	283	,, Minards, C. E.	,,	24	Pietermaritzburg	,,
4	238	,, Caney, P.	April	4	,,	,,
5	299	Pte. Rush, F. W.	,,	15	,,	,,
6	360	,, Taylor, T.	,,	21	Ladysmith	,,
7	453	,, Baker, B.	,,	29	,,	,,
8	279	,, Prebble, A. E.	May	19	Newcastle	,,
9	333	,, Howes, E. F.	,,	25	Bloemfontein	,,
10	272	,, Sanders, H. G.	June	1	Newcastle	,,
11	439	,, Tuffin, A.	,,	7	Roodewal	Killed in action
12	572	,, Gobel, J.	,,	9	,,	Died of wounds
13	391	,, Harris, E.	,,	29	Bloemfontein	Enteric
14	308	Sergt. Duncombe, J. T.	July	5	Ladysmith	,,

Royal Engineers, 7.   Army P.O. Corps, 14.   Total 21.

Also 24816, Sapper A. S. Rudd of C.T.O., Ex-R.E., July 1st, Bloemfontein, Enteric.

Grimsby writes :—"I am glad to inform you that we have managed to provide for Mrs. Wyatt's present necessities in the following way :—Subscribed by Telegraph Staff, £1 10s.; from "Daily Telegraph" Fund, £3 ; "Patriotic" Fund, £7 ; "Office Fine" Fund—Postal and Telegraph Staffs, £5 ; Local "Mayor's" Fund, £1 10s. Total £18. You will understand that the whole of the poor woman's income ceased with her husband's death."—We are glad to know that so much has been done for the widow and her two fatherless bairns. At such times, and for such cases, we cannot refrain from wishing we were millionaires, so that more might be done for the desolate and distressed.

⇥ Khaki Notes. ⇤

All for Tommy.—Reference has been made in K.L.'s to the sumptuous eighteenpenny dinners enjoyed by the Kimberley Staff. I have been favoured with the printed Bill of Fare, which will, perhaps, interest and enlighten some of our readers. "The Standard Restaurant. *Soup*: Giblet. *Entrees*: Crumb Fillet Beef and Italian Sauce. Mutton Pie. Roast Stuffed Fowl. Roast Pork and Apple Sauce. Roast Lamb and Mint Sauce. Roast Sirloin Beef. Roast Leg Mutton. Boiled Corned Beef. Boiled Ox Tongue. Boiled Bacon and Cabbage. *Vegetables*: Potatoes. Cauliflower. *Pastry*: Red Currant Tart." What more do you expect when on active service?

Congratulations to the following on their appointments:—
Senior Telest: R. Weeks to be 2nd Cl. Asst. Supt.
Telegraphists: H. Eden, W. Ferneyhough, J. Twyford and H. G. de B. Reed to be Senior Telests. All promotions are dated August 24th, 1900.

Likewise to the undermentioned who, as Sub-Engineers commenced their new duties on the 3rd inst.—At Mount Pleasant: Messrs. H. C. Stone (I. Div.), G. Harrison (SG), M. A. Beetlestone (F Div.), P. A. Roberts (News), A. E. Roberts (C Div.), and H. Eager (TSF). At Holloway: Mr. J. Markwick (News). E. in C's Office: Messrs. W. J. Cockshott (TSF) and Hatfield (Spl. Staff). Appointments dated June 1st, 1900.

Corpl. Arthur, R.E., who, we regret to learn, was accidentally shot by a comrade, was the non.-con. who, with Sappers Horn and W. C. Smith, hoisted the first British flag in the Transvaal. (See page 192 K.L.)

Khaki Postage Fund.—The following amounts are thankfully acknowledged:—Mrs. M., 3s. 6d.; Mrs. W., 2s. 6d.; E.H.C., 2s.; Miss L.E.C., 1s.; J.G.H., 1s.; Miss F.M.G., 6d.; Miss S., 6d.; H.N., 6d.; W.E.J., 6d.

A K.L. sent to one of ours at the front has just been returned to me marked "dead." I am glad to know that is not correct. On the other hand K.L.'s addressed to poor fellows whom we know will never return to their loved ones here, have never been sent back. Strange!

Owing to inability to attend camp, many "I" Company men are at present non-efficient. The next musketry day for recruits is September 12th, and for trained men September 19th.

The Rudd Fund.—Miss E. H. (Epsom), 5s. Thank you. This Fund is closing. A full statement will be given in next issue of K.L.

Special. I should be extremely glad to hear from men "invalided," either that they are under orders for, or have arrived, home. I need not send K.L.'s to S.A. then. Also their orders, if any, re future movements. We *do* like to know. Numerous enquiries reach me respecting men who have not lately been heard of. Can anyone give the whereabouts, or other particulars, of Sappers C. S. Ingram and F. J. Hurdle?—Sappers A. Ray, W. S. Roberts, and D. McLaren are at Aldershot.

A Cablegram received as "K.L." went to press last issue reads as follows:—"Capetown, 17/8/00, 3.25 p.m.—Poniard, London—Frederickstad, well, Davies."

B.Q.'s.—Where are the nine? Several friends have kindly found them and sent them on. Thank you.—The reproduction in this issue is reduced from a half-plate photo.—Mafeking: "Cadey" safely to hand. Think I know who will value it most.—A.T.P.: Previous letter not received.

"Poniard, London," for telegrams from Our Boys to their relatives and friends at home, the addresses of whom should be sent us at once.

"Casualties, Capetown," for enquiries re sick and wounded.

"KHAKI LETTERS," One Penny. By post, Three Halfpence.

All posted letters containing Remittances, Orders, MSS., &c., must be addressed to R. E. KEMP, 12, JERRARD STREET, LEWISHAM, S.E.
Postal Orders should be made payable at Loampit Vale, Lewisham, S.E.

Printed by E. G. BERRYMAN & SONS, *Blackheath Road, London, S.E.*

"Khaki Letters" from ....
"My Colleagues in South Africa."

CORRESPONDENCE FROM THE
POST OFFICE TELEGRAPHISTS
OF THE
24th MIDDLESEX (P.O.) RIFLE VOLUNTEERS
(Royal Engineer Reserves),
ON ACTIVE SERVICE.

THE BOND THAT BINDS US—FRIENDSHIP—COMRADESHIP.

Published fortnightly for the Postal Telegraph Service.
Conducted by COLOUR-SERGEANT R. E. KEMP, *Central Telegraph Office, London.*

No. 17.   SEPTEMBER 21st, 1900.   PRICE ONE PENNY.

Central Telegraph Office,
London, E.C.

DEAR COMRADES, ONE AND ALL,

Greetings! If there is anything that makes us feel happy in connection with this long-lingering war, it is the fact that the newspapers contain very much shorter lists of sick, wounded, and deaths during the last few months. I am constantly on the look out for casualties—or, rather, the absence of them—amongst Our Boys, and I am not alone in the big burst of joy when I fail to find a name that is known to us. The lists which so many of us have, together with the K.L.'s themselves, have done wonders in the C.T.O. The staff is as cool as possible. They know all about you. If Smith, Jones, Brown, or Robinson is reported sick or wounded, out comes the list, and the Regimental number and initials are compared and, presto ! "Not *our* Smith, not *our* Brown, &c.," runs round and chokes any rumour-microbes that may lurk in the minds of the mischief-makers—however unintentional their mission may be. And so we go on, glad to hear, glad to know, and glad to congratulate our gallant Boys away across the mighty main. But although TS is so peaceful, and although the weather is so pleasant, at the present moment the colleagues at home are in a most excited state. They have had their photos taken. They are eager to know how they have come out. At the present time only those in the dark room know. Some negatives have got as far as the printer's hands, who, to his discredit, plays upon the eagerness of the sitters by passing obscure observations from his point of view on the expected result of the picture he is dealing with. Other negatives are as yet unseen, the retoucher is making his mystic signs and wonders upon them—spotting out little flaws, subduing the highlights, enlivening the shadows, and using his experience—meagre or much it may possibly be—to present something pretty to the expectant sitters. Oh! what a state we are in. We would —if such a thing is compulsory—have put our penny in the slot, squinted into the bell-receiver-looking lens, and even have gone so far as to double the expense by providing a gilt frame (total 2d.) so as to get the result "while we wait." But no.

A tripod—I should say trio, perhaps—was placed in our office some two or more months ago, rigid and firm, brass-bound and beautiful to look upon. Each part mature, seasoned and well selected, terminating into a head—a trinity known as a Commission. This was the Camera. It took views here, views there; first with the single lens, then the double, the narrow angle and the wide angle, the view lens, and with apparently no effort, even adapted itself for stereo work. So marvellous were its means of making mysterious matters microscopically easy, it ignored the stand and took to "hand work." Snap-shots were taken everywhere, notes of exposures, stop used, light, time, &c., were all jotted down. Films and plates were replenished, and when "enough" had been called, the apparatus was re-rigged up as a cinematograph, and living pictures will become the order of the day. Anyone can "take the cap off," but the artistic beauty of a sun picture lies in the knowledge—gained mostly by practice and experience—of where to place your Camera, taking full calculations as to light falling on, and shade given, by the object. The object under notice is the Economy of Staff, proficiency in practice, &c., &c. Was the Camera level? Was the —— But wait. We are not taking the picture, we will be content to look at it when done. We must not criticise.

Every operator has his fancy developer. Doubtless, these latent images have been subjected to good old pyrogallic, and hydroquinone, amidol, metol, and all the other ols—variety is charming, you know. The thing is, is it a good bold crisp workable neg.? Soon we shall know. Then the papers will compete. All the P.O.P.'s will be tried, all the platinas will take turn—the carbons, the bromides, and possibly, too, dear old albumenized will stand a chance, for nothing much be lost to render perfect the picture. Toning in chloride of gold, lead, uranium, and risky concoctions with hyposulphite may be introduced—but what of the result? Will it ever get on the mount? Or, if on the mount, burnished or enamelled? It may be. Yes, and this is as far as most photographs get. There's a step beyond, a stage that marks approval and pride, in so far that a difficult work that was attempted is now a *fait accompli*—that state is the framed photo displayed on the wall, to be seen and admired by the many. Will *our* picture get there? Notable negs. are used to amuse and instruct on the screen by the dissolving limelight lantern. We will take the series in rapid succession. The abolition of the permanent Night Staff, some of whom have put in as many as 35 years. The old Night Staff arriving on day duties at times commencing at 6 a.m., and terminating at any hour up to midnight. The Staff on night duty, 11 p.m. to 6 a.m., rotating fortnightly. The 3—11's coming on at 3.45 on Saturday, and remaining until 11 p.m.; the 4 to 11.45's doing 4.15 to 12 on Saturdays, &c., &c., in endless array. We may also anticipate the humorous biograph portraying the "loss of the last train and the walk on the wet night," "the sleepless single-man lodger awaiting 4 a.m.," or "the married man's mate devotedly watching the sweet repose of her lord and master," prepared to call him when his time is in—He to get up, she to go down in happy remembrance of "dividing time" in bygone days. Even a scene from Cloth Fair may depict the auction of night rugs or the exchange of same for an alarm clock.

One of the London Morning Haporth's of to-day contains half a column of "Telegraphists and their hours." The operator's case is a complaint poorly put and incorrect; the "Official's Views," which is intended to explain "Why it is done," is also—as many a negative—chemically fogged, for it says, "Changes of hours are contemplated." As a matter of fact, the men have received definite instruction to commence on September 23rd, 24th. The Night Staff, according to our newspaper, will be a night "Shift," a term more associated with iron foundries, coal mines, cement works, &c. We prefer the old term, "Duty," while its reference to the working hours of pressmen goes to prove they have taken two pictures on one plate—and you know what that means.

So endeth the first lesson. On Monday next, all the Instrument Staff go on day duty. The Supts. expect to follow in a few weeks. While the Check Staff, with all its multitudinous duties, is left untouched until the isochromatics can be brought to bear upon its members. But as I previously said, we know not all—only a part. We will see things clearer when the ruby medium is removed and we encounter the welcome rays of King Sol, even the experience of the new duties.

Talking of King Sol reminds me of the *Sun*, which this evening launches out with the following Kodakized par. Someone has touched the button, and *they* have done the rest. Here it is:—"P.M.G. determined. It is not generally known that the newspaper offices in Fleet Street have for many years monopolised the services of the most skilled of the telegraph operators employed at St. Martin's-le-Grand. No sooner has a man made himself thoroughly competent to perform his duties than he seeks and obtains a position on what is known as the "private wire" staff. The Postmaster-General has now, we understand, decided that the public are no longer to be deprived of this skilled service, and in future newspaper proprietors will be required to provide their own telegraphists." There are very big changes on, we know, but time will prove.

Hoping you are all well, and ready soon to return, I remain, as ever,
                                      Yours most heartily,

To the "L" Co. in South Africa,   R. E. KEMP,
    Tuesday, September 18th, 1900.   *Colour-Sergeant.*

COPYRIGHT.—"Khaki Letters" must not be used without permission.—R. E. KEMP.

Khaki Letters.

No. 4,327, Sapper **A. J. Brooks,** writing from Vredefort Weg., O.R.C., July 9th, says :—

". . . . I left Springfontein about five weeks ago for Bloemfontein, as having lost our Queenstown circuit at SFN., Swan and I were no longer required. At Bloemfontein we took up our quarters in the old Queen's Fort, situated on a small hill to the South of the town, and from which a very pretty view was obtainable, especially in the early morning. The Fort was a decent little place, well planted with a sort of Christmas tree and blue gums. About a dozen of us, amongst whom were Swan and Jack Little (SW), slept in the room formerly used by the Free State Artillerymen as a Telegraph School. The instruments, etc., had been removed, and the only interesting things left were a number of school books and exercise papers recording their progress in the art of telegraphy. All entries in the school's books ceased on September 5th. I expect they began to get their guns ready about that time. In another room of the Fort were a large number of rifles, from ancient sniders right up to the very latest Brum-made Lee-Metford's, most of the older weapons had been taken from us in previous Boer wars. We got on very well altogether in Bloemfontein. The Kimberley wire was the busiest wire in Bloemfontein whilst I was there, the wire to Pretoria being down at the time. After about ten days in Bloemfontein, four of us were sent up to Kroonstad, Swan had already left for Pretoria. Our little party—Picker, Hayden, Mulligan (a Colonial telegraphist), and yours truly—paraded at 8.30 a.m. one morning with the intention of going off by the 9.20 train, which train ultimately got off at 3.30 p.m. Saw Capt. Palmer, A.P.O.C., at the station very busy with mails, but didn't happen to catch his eye to speak to him. The only 'carriage' available was a heavily loaded coal truck upon which a dozen Guardsmen had already perched themselves. We made ourselves as comfortable as possible by hollowing out little 'nests' for seats. The scenery was pretty much the same as that through which we had already passed right away up from Capetown ; veldt and kopjes, with here and there a very small tree. At Glen, where we crossed the Modder River, the usual amount of bridge destruction had been done, and we crossed the river by a temporary bridge of wood. At Karee the Boers made a bit of a stand against Roberts, the result of which is seen in the little group of graves by the side of the railway, with their pathetic little wooden crosses. When we got to Brandfort it was quite dark, so that

KHAKI LETTERS—*continued*.

we didn't see much of the place, but as we were getting awfully cold we got so ne hot water in our canteens from the engine and had an *al fresco* supper, coffee, hard biscuit, corned beef and treacle. It was a very queer meal, we had a bit of candle stuck in an inverted helmet and all crouched around it, d gging our heels well into the coal to keep ourselves safe with the train going at about 14 miles an hour across the veldt. The night was bitterly cold and we were glad to get out at every stopping place for a run up and down. All along the line were the little camp fires of the piquets and guards, who implored us to 'chuck us out a bit o' coal, chummie.' Of course we entered into the thing with spirit and must have got rid of nearly half a ton of coal between us. Whenever we got off our truck for a run we had to be very careful where we rushed to, as the whole of the men who guard the line sleep in trenches along the line, fully armed. Morning found us at Virginia siding, where we had to wait eight hours, the engine having run short of water. All around, as far as the eye could see, were biscuit tins dazzling like silver in the sun; the track of the army could easily be traced by the bully and b scuit tins. The train passed through Boschrand (Bush Hills), where the Boers had constructed such elaborate entrenchments, and then across the Valsch (False) River, by the usual deviation and temporary bridge, into Kroonstad. Kro nstad is not much of a place, very slipshod and very dusty; as usual we noticed that most of the business was in the hands of people bearing British names. We were all very pleased to find that we were booked for small places up the line, starting off next morning with two trucks of telegraph material, some of which belonged to us, the rest being in charge of so ne linemen who were repairing the line. Our train consisted of an engine, tender, and our two trucks, the guard sitting on the back of the rear truck. There were about nine of us altogether under a Lieutenant, and we were quite enjoying the spin, when suddenly a horsemen came galloping towards the train, calling upon us to stop. It turned out to be Captain Ridout, R E., in charge of a convoy; he reported that his scouts had seen large numbers of Boers on some kopjes just ahead and about 1,500 yards off the railway line. On we went again, having, by the Lieutenant's orders, put our belts, etc. on, and got our carbines and ammunition ready. He ordered the driver to go slowly and kept good look out through a pair of glasses. As we came in line with the kopjes we could distinctly see the Boers moving about in small parties, the Lieutenant estimating their strength at 400 men. We longed for a little snipe on our own, but as they didn't fire at us we had to refrain. Just a little way ahead was America siding or Katbosch, held by about 100 ex-prisoners sent down from Pretoria, and armed with old Martini rifles. At Honing Spruit, a little higher up the line, were about 300 men, also ex-prisoners, armed with obsolete guns. These two places, Katbosch and Honing Spruit, were surrounded by Boers the day before we turned up, Ho ing Spruit suffering badly. losing eight killed and 17 wounded, our men being unable to reply to the Boers who were shelling them with three big guns. The men said that when the Boers noticed the short range of the rifles, they came out into the open and simply laughed at the Martinis. At Katbosch they lost about four killed and a dozen wounded, and but for a small party of Canadian Mounted Rifles who happened to be with them, they would have lost more heavily. When the Boers came round the little camp, the Canadians, numbering about 20, moved out to get round the enemy. They were not successful in doing this, but they prevented the camp from being surrounded. Four of the Canadians got on a small kopje and determined to stick there, sending one of their number into camp with

KHAKI LETTERS—continued.

all the horses and a message to say that 'they were going to stop and make a fight of it.' The man who brought the horses in was wounded in three places whilst returning, but he got his own back on two Boers, one of whom was up a pole cutting the telegraph lines, the other being busily engaged in destroying a cable which had been laid out on the veldt. One man got a bullet clean in the centre of his forehead and the other was shot through the temple. Of the three Canadians left on the kopjes, one was severely wounded, the other two, Corporal Mellin and Private Kerr, were killed. Everyone out here praises the Canadians, they certainly have got some real grit. The men at Katbosch were surprised to see our train, they said they thought the line had been destroyed again, they didn't look very bad, although some of them were captured by the Boers last November and December. Not many of them complained about their treatment whilst prisoners, except that they got fed up with the mealie pap. Of course they are quite out of condition now and couldn't do much marching. When we got to Honing Spruit we came across Frank Owens, he looked A1., and we were very pleased to meet. He was down at Katbosch when they were shelled and told us all about it. We stayed the night at Honing Spruit, and leaving Picker there, and Hayden at Katbosch, Mulligan and I went on with the railway construction train, with orders to get out at Serfontein Camp and open up communication from there. At Serfontein siding we saw nothing of a camp, so decided to stick on the train and go on to Roodeval, but on the way we passed a solitary gun and about a dozen artillerymen half-hidden in a trench on the veldt. This was evidently the camp intended, although the infantry, who were sure to come to protect the gun, had not yet arrived. However, we were unable to jump off the train as we had so much gear with us, batteries, recorders, etc., for other offices, so were compelled to go on to Roodeval. There was once a station, etc.. at Roodeval, but nothing is left of it now, for hundreds of yards around the veldt is strewn with great stones, burnt clothing and torn letters. Great shells, most of them weighing 280 pounds, are scattered all over the place, torn about like cardboard. On the line there stands a sort of skeleton train, it being merely the ironwork of a train that was standing in the station when the Boers paid their surprise visit. They gave the place a terrible shelling and then burnt everything to the ground, destroying all the mails and dynamiting an enormous stock of big shells. Some lives were lost here, about half-a-dozen of the Railway Pioneer Regiment and some of the A.P.O.C. being killed. Some of the graves are just alongside the line, the R.P.R. having erected large wooden crosses over each. I only noticed one of the A.P.O.C. It was inscribed ' Pte. Timmins, A.P.O.C., killed in action.' Mulligan and I shifted all our stuff on to a water tank attached to an engine going back, and after waiting a few hours we started off, getting down at Serfontein camp late in the afternoon, when we had to buck up. A Company of the East Lancs. Regt. had just arrived and we all had to set to and entrench ourselves before dark, the C.O. ordering us to dig ourselves a trench to work in before we did anything else. This done, I had to shin up the nearest pole and 'tee' (nearly tie it on) a line to the 'Top East' wire. We then fixed up a buzzer at the foot of the pole and got to work. We found that we were in communication with Rhenoster River (Kopjes), Vredefort Road, Viljoen's Drift and Vereeniging on the North, and with Honing Spruit, Katbasch and Kroonstad on the South, not to speak of about a dozen railway telephones, and the induction from the Bloemfontein-Pretoria line. We made our presence known, and having disposed of a few messages, we lit a fire and

KHAKI LETTERS—*continued.*

boiled some mealies for our tea ; these are very nice when well-boiled, with a little sugar or salt. After tea, having no candle or light to work by, we curled ourselves up in our blankets—taking the 'receiver' of the buzzer into 'bed' with us so that we could hear a call—and went off to sleep under the starry sky, whilst all around were long lines of veldt on fire, and in the distance great piles of flame from burning farmhouses. We slept like the proverbial top and woke up at dawn to find the whole place as white as snow with hoar frost, with a number of little whitey-brown mounds marking the camp. These were the troops rolled in their blankets which were covered with frost ; we have very heavy dews and bitterly cold nights here. About noon the Lieutenant rode up, and with him came a small Cape cart in which I rode up to Rhenoster River (Kopjes Camp), distant about 13 or 14 miles. It would have been a pleasant ride but for the awful stench from the numerous oxen and horses who had died along the wayside. At Rhenoster the railway bridge had been twice destroyed and the railway line both North and South, had been blown up in a fearful manner. Every few yards the two rails lifted themselves up like gigantic snakes into the air, the trains running on a temporary road alongside. We crossed the river by a drift, our two scraggy little ponies keeping their feet grandly. The water at the drift was only about a foot deep, but the banks sloped down to a great depth ; of course we descended and ascended obliquely. About a mile North of the river were some rough kopjes, where Methuen and Kitchener recently routed the Boers. The camp was situated on the flat tops and was entirely invisible until we got on top of the kopjes. Marshall was working away at the buzzer when I got there, he had put up a few sticks and some old wagon covers for a shelter and office which was just about 3 ft. square and 4 ft. high. He has had an exciting time since he has been out here ; he went straight up to Pretoria and was then sent down with some others, including Neale (G Group) and Morse (F. Divn.). At Leeuw Spruit the Boers had torn up the line and heavily shelled the train in the darkness. There was a lot of confused firing, but the attack was so unexpected that half of them could not find their rifles, and, in fact, Marshall couldn't even find his boots which he had taken off. Finding that they could do nothing, he and a few others cut across country for about six miles, and fortunately came across Kopjes Camp. From all I can hear, I think poor old Morse is missing still. The afternoon after I arrived at Kopjes, the little camp at Serfontein that I had just left was surrounded by Boers, small parties of whom we had seen all around just before I left. The Commandant at Kopjes sent out reinforcements, but they were not needed as the enemy scooted off on their approach. We saw a large body out on the plain about four miles from our position, and our infantry went down to the foot of the kopjes waiting for them to come on, but as they were not inclined to do so, our five-inch gun presented them with four beautiful shells, nicely polished and ornamented with brass bands, which burst grandly. We saw several fall, but it was marvellous to note how quickly they all buzzed off, leaving a few dead horses behind. Next day I had to shift off to Vredefort Road, as that place was rather busy owing to the movements of Hunter, Methuen and Macdonald. I took my bundles—an old sack containing grub, etc., and my blankets rolled up, and went down to the railway line to jump on the next train, but I got fed up with waiting there, so tramped up the line for a bit— 'With me bundle on me shoulder, faith, there's no man could be bowlder.' I did look like a Boer, though, with my old slouch hat, bundles and carbine slung across my back, and no wonder I startled a man of the Lincoln Regt.

KHAKI LETTERS—*continued.*

who was picking up chips of firewood from the wrecked sleepers. He said he made sure I was a Boer, more especially as a farm, which was well in sight, was known to be occupied by a small commando of about 70 men, under Bruytenbach. A little further up the line I got into Kopje's station, deserted and partly wrecked, now occupied by a small piquet of K.O.S.B.'s. Here I waited for a train and just managed to scramble up on top of a truck, the only adventure on the way being the falling off a truck of a Coldstream Guardsman, who had been trying to get a little snooze. At Vredefort Road I met Pickford; we get on A1. here. We work a bit here— 7 a.m. till midnight, and all work done on the buzzer, too. We sleep—that is when the friends of Keating's will allow us to sleep—in what used to be the booking office. I don't know how I am going to post this, I expect I shall have to give it to a guard. We are quite out of the world here, so expect that by the time you get it, August Bank Holiday will have come and gone. I hope you will have a good time in camp. I wish I could get hold of half the stuff now that I used to take down to Aldershot. I have got nothing but what I stand up in and my blankets, having had to leave my kit-bag at Bloemfontein. I even lost my soap and had to go five days without a wash, not that I missed the soap much, for anyway, I couldn't get water. You would hardly believe your eyes if you saw us sometimes, as we were at Roodeval for instance, crawling under the engine to catch a few drops of hot water, and not clean water either. The engine drivers are obliged to refuse us water because very often they are stranded themselves through giving a drop away. I have borrowed a piece of soap now, but should like to devise ways and means of getting a change of clothes. I think I must wash 'em late at night, dry them in front of the fire, and get up in the morning a new man. When one hasn't got a bed to lie on, one can't very well go on the old dodge, and lie in bed whilst your clothes are in the wash; moreover, we do our own. We tried a suet pudding the other day, but the chief difficulty was what it was to be boiled in. White handkerchiefs were suggested, but they were not nearly large enough; then we seriously considered the claims of a clean shirt, but could'nt tie it up very well, so ultimately fell back on a big red handkerchief of Pickford's. When we got the pudding out of the old kettle at dinner time, we thought the cook had prepared a surprise for us in the shape of a jam rolypoly, but unfortunately it turned out to be the dye from the handkerchief. We made the best of it and picked out the white pieces. We shall all be quite unfit for civilised life after this job. I know that when I get home, I shall want to make my bed down out in the back yard, with a bag of coal for a pillow. Although I cannot say that I am 'right bang up the front,' I think I may reckon that I am along the side. I am thankful to say I'm keeping in good health. Perhaps you will hardly believe that we have no earthly idea of the day of the week. A few weeks ago four of us had a 6d. sweepstake on the day of the week; I plumped for Saturday, but on reference to a calendar which we had dug up, and which suggested the sweep, we found that it was Wednesday. Since then, however, we have lost count again, and I don't know now whether it is Thursday or Sunday, or any other day of the week. Sunday makes no difference here, no Church parades or anything of that sort. Let the Colour-Sergeant have this."

This letter has been unavoidably delayed.

KHAKI LETTERS—*continued*.

No 220, Sergt. J. W. Miller, writes from Kimberley, July 24th, as under :—

"DEAR OLD COLOURS,—Once more I will add a few lines, and I sincerely hope it will be the last from Kimberley. It is now over four months since my arrival, so I think it is a good stay in one place. We have had a very busy and hard time of it, but I must give the highest credit to the staff who have worked in this office and those working at the present time, which numbers 48. One thing I should like to mention is that I have been fortunate in having a good lot of skilled telegraphists. There are a few from TS amongst us—Sappers George, Mcmurtrie, Semple, Ash. Adams, Humm, Curnew, Waghorn, Webber and Corpl. Winkle, and F. Usher (R. E. Reserves). Pleased to inform you all in good health at the present time and nobody in the hospitals. When we are likely to get home again seems to be a mystery. We all thought the latest would be at the end of this month, but the present state of things seem to point out that it's more likely to last till Christmas, owing to the troublous times the army are having in the Orange River Colony. When I wrote my last khaki letter to you I had to get Corpl. Winkle to finish it, to catch a mail, as I had to take a few stores and letters and deliver them to the various stations on the line up to Mafeking. Left Kimberley on Saturday 14th, at 8.30 a.m., and had as a companion, an old soldier, who told me a few excellent tales all the way, till we got to Fourteen Streams. I was hardly allowed to speak in answer to his supposed actions. We first made a stop at Warrenton, where Brooks, of S.W.D.O., is in charge of the office. Was invited to dinner, but unfortunately the train went off too soon. Fourteen Streams passed and proceeding to Taungs, we had to go over a deviation made by the R.E.'s over the Vaal River. I got to Vryburg at night about seven o'clock, and was met by two of the R.E.'s from the office, who had kindly got me a nice dinner, for which I was very thankful; as a train was proceeding at 9 p.m. I thought I would chance the guards' van, as there were no carriages put on for Mafeking. After the start I thought I would get down between my blankets. But talk about sleep, out of the question, how it did jolt ! Got to Mafeking at last at 6.10 a.m. on Sunday morning, and on asking for the Military Telegraph Office, I was directed by a clerk 'right over there where those tents are.' Over I went about three-quarters of a mile ; couldn't see anything of an office, so spotted a line running through the camp and followed that. On getting to the terminal I found I had followed a telephone wire to the Protectorate's Office ; so back I went and saw someone who showed me where our Colours were flying—the blue and white flag. I entered the office, all the office staff fast asleep. But when they heard there was some letters they were soon up, and not long after, all having a good breakfast together ; a nice hot pot, full of 'Burgee' and eggs. After breakfast, Roby, of MR, Cleeve, RE, of LV, and 'self went for a splendid stroll all round and saw the old gun they found, made fixed up on a stand, also another gun made at Mafeking by Major Panzera. We then listened to the 'Bedfords' band after they had been to Church, and also saw the long stream of Tommies at the canteen, walking slow march in twos ; was amazing. Dinner time came and it was most enjoyable. They all were very kind indeed at MF, Gwilliam of TS being there, and Brewster, from MR. In the evening had another walk round the town, and it ought to be seen to credit it, to look at the holes the shells have made in almost every house round the market square; in fact hardly a house was untouched. They must have had a shocking rough time. Came back Monday morning at 9 a.m. The train went frightfully slow ; talk

KHAKI LETTERS—*continued*

about the London and Chatham and the South Eastern, they are Expresses to these ! We could only go fast going down small kopjes, then they would almost come to a standstill. At Maritzana there were some of the Somersets walking up and down, having a chat to other Tommies in the carriages, trying to learn the latest. One came and had a chat and he asked me if I would like some eggs. 'Yes rather,' 'all right, we can get them 1s. a dozen ;' so off he went to a black girl and offered the 1s. She wanted 2s., but his pal that was with him sung out 'play the policeman's game, Bill,' so off came his helmet and the 12 eggs were paid for, and the Kaffir went off smiling. He said, give me another 6d. and I'll get you another 8 eggs ; off he went and commandeered the lot ; so I came away with 20, which were a luxury, considering I have paid so much as 9d. for 2 at Kimberley. I was very kindly entertained by Sapper Aird (EH), at Taungs about 1 in the morning, and reached Kimberley 6.10 Tuesday morning. Then had my breakfast of eggs, and off to the office on duty at 8 a.m. after a very interesting journey. Am very glad I saw Mafeking, and where the great B.P. resided. Well Dick, old chap, I don't think I ought to have written such a lot, it won't give others a chance. I hope Sergt. Luttrell has arrived home safely ; shall be glad to know definite news in our KHAKI LETTERS. I hope the most interesting phamplet will meet the success it deserves. Kindest regards to all."

P.S.—I do hope I don't have to write any more Khaki's, I want my six weeks' furlough badly.

In another letter, dated Kimberley, August 6th, Miller says :—

"DEAR DICK,—I have written you again as I'm still a fixture, and glad still O.K. We can't say when we are likely to start for home, it looks as if we shall have a twelvemonths' stay, but hope we get home in time to be able to sit round the Christmas-table rather than having our 'shackles' out of a canteen. Sorry to say W. C. Smith has had to come down from Kraipan to go into Kimberley Hospital with dysentery, hope he will soon get better. He has had rather a rough time of trekking about all over the veldt for miles. There is not much fresh *re* the war, so there is no news to write, and I expect you get a few letters from some of our lads here. Every success with KHAKI LETTERS. We all appreciate it very much indeed, and by it being addressed direct to Kimberley I get it every fortnight. My very kind regards to all and yourself."

No. 29,477, Sapper **C. H. Payne,** writing from Wolvehoek, O.R.C., August 1st, says :—

"We were going to be done-in last Wednesday. Early in the afternoon some dots appeared on the skyline. They turned out to be Boers, and as they got nearer, they sent in a man with a white flag, who kindly asked us to surrender, or be blown to smithereens. On our declining with thanks, he said we should have 15 minutes to get the women and children (stationmaster's family) into a place of safety. This was done, they were put into a railway truck with a red cross flag flying, and shunted up the line. All the men then took their places in the trenches, and I was kept as busy as a bee on the instrument. Well, they came a bit nearer, and a few shots were exchanged, but no harm was done, at least on our side. They eventually cleared off, with their tails between their legs, so to speak, and the affair was put down as a piece of bluff."

KHAKI LETTERS—*continued.*

No. 25,322, Sapper **F. D. Horton** (of BM), writing from Viljoen's Drift, August 5th, says :—

De Wet is still at large although considered to be surrounded, and we tightened our Cordon round him yesterday by six miles. Prinsloo has surrendered with 3,500 men, and 750 gave in yesterday. Botha, it is thought, will give in when De Wet is done for..... Went to Vereeniging yesterday to bury a 24th man, he comes fiom Grimsby. We had no minister, so Corporal read the service, and we filled in the grave. He was simply sewn up in a blanket. It is very sad and does not tend to raise one's spirits..... The way the Boers are fighting is not worthy the name of war. You speak to a man one day as a friend, and the next he is serving with a Commando, and firing at you from behind a rock or farmhouse, over which is probably flying a white flag.

August 7th.—Perhaps you would like to know how I spent Bank Holiday here. It was not very exciting, and there were no excursions to the seaside (describes minutely his duty, &c.) . . . . After dinner, two of us visited the stores and inspected some photos. I also bought some thread. It was interesting to see the Kaffir women making their purchases—their babies hanging at their backs. By the way, one seldom hears the black babies crying, they lie about in the sun without any protection. Generally they are very dirty, with eyes and ears filled with dirt, &c. At four o'clock a New Zealander and myself went to Vereeniging on horseback. At 8 p.m. several men who came out on the 'Gascon' with me passed through Station for Pretoria, they have been at Kimberley since that place was relieved. Eight of them came to my place to tea, and they said I had got the most comfortable place they had yet seen. Am going down a coal mine this afternoon (8th); went down one last Friday, it is very interesting. (9th), the line is blown up again this morning in four places. De Wet has escaped again."

✦ ✦ ✦ ✦

No. 1,456, Sapper **A. T. Poole** (of BS), Pretoria, August 6th, writes :—

"DEAR COLOURS,—I hope you don't think me ungrateful, or forgetful of the grand work you are doing on our behalf. I have written to you once before this, but having seen no reproduction of my *letter in KHAKI LETTERS, I fear that letter cannot have reached you. I am sorry I cannot give sufficient time now to give you anything like a full account of my manœuvrings of the first few months, suffice it to say. that they have been very rough and varied : quite beyond all my expectations of campaigning, I assure you. Of course you know now of the death of our dear old Comrade Wyatt ; my chief object in writing this letter is to tell you something of his doings the last three months of his life. I was with him the last three months, leaving Bloemfontein together in May, we proceeded to Ventersburg to open office : at that time, he was in grand health. After a stop of a week at Ventersburg, we trekked for seven days with General Colville's column, to Heilbron ; during those seven days' march we were doing more than twenty miles a day, and the work and exposure at night was very great ; but in spite of all this my dear old chum was weathering it all in fine style, not showing the slightest sign of ill health. On our arrival at Heilbron, we found all telegraph lines cut to pieces, and, having no linemen with us, we commenced to repair some dozens of breakages ourselves. Climbing poles, making joints, and extending

* Letter mentioned was not received by R.E.K.

KHAKI LETTERS—*continued.*

all lines to Heilbron Station, kept us busy for the next few days. Fortunately, we succeeded in getting through to Johannesburg, Kroonstad, Vredefort, and Vereeniging, at critical moments. All this time we were living on the starvation quarter and half rations, but all this seemed to have no ill effect whatever on my dear old friend. After this, Lord Methuen came in with troops and provisions, and then we lived well—for soldiers on the warpath. We remained at Heilbron for two months, and the Officers of the 9th Division, before leaving for Pretoria, came and personally complimented us both for the work we had done, wishing us, at the same time, ' Goodbye, and a safe return to our homes.' It was only in the last fortnight of our stay at Heilbron that my dear old chum complained of feeling unwell and suffering from a great thirst, but the next day he would feel better and laugh it off; I can safely say that neither he or myself thought that anything serious was the matter. At Vereeniging he got worse, and complained all the time of feeling a great thirst. We were able to get eggs for him, and all the time he was ill, I made beef tea and bovril for him (stuff I had a few weeks previously commandeered). When I left Vereeniging for Pretoria, I was unable to go to Hospital to wish him goodbye, but, whilst waiting for train at station, I wrote him letter wishing him ' Goodbye : Good Luck, and hoping he would soon be all right again,' so you can guess what a sudden and great blow it was to me to hear of his death two days afterwards. It is very, very hard indeed to be snatched away from this life after having done nine months of the hardest work of the campaign. May God console and comfort his wife and family is my earnest wish. We were all very anxious to come out, but now we are still more anxious to get back with our families and old associations. August Bank Holiday has come and gone, but still we see no early prospect of embarking on the ship for dear Old England. Our password now is : ' Roll on, roll on, the good old ship.' Since leaving the Old Country, I have been enjoying the best of good health, thank God. Now I will conclude with my very best wishes for the continued success of KHAKI LETTERS, and with kindest regards to you, dear Colours, and other friends.

No 25,362, Sapper **G. W. Bannister** (of MR), Mil. Tels., Vereeniging, writes on August 7th, as follows :—

" DEAR COLOURS,—When last I wrote you from Orange River Station concerning the deaths of two comrades at that place, I little thought the painful duty would again devolve upon me. We cabled you on Saturday last, ' Poniard, London,' notifying the death of No 2,556, Sapper E. H. Wyatt, of Grimsby, which occurred in the Station Hospital, Vereeniging, at 9 p.m., on August 3rd. The cause of death was Bright's disease. Poor old ' Wee Gee,' as he was popularly nick-named, came to us about a fortnight ago from Heilbron, when that place was evacuated by our troops. He had been unwell for some little time before leaving Heilbron, and his comrades had endeavoured to induce him to go into hospital. He would not, however, give in, and held out until he was scarcely able to walk about. They admitted him to hospital here on Wednesday last, and the doctor was unable to diagnose his case for a couple of days. For the satisfaction and comfort of his friends at home, I may say that everything possible was done for him, but he rapidly sank, and on Saturday morning he scarcely knew me when I called to see him. He did not suffer much pain until the last day or so. We buried him on Saturday afternoon, on the Orange River Colony side of

KHAKI LETTERS—*continued*.

the Vaal River, not far from the famous Vaal Bridge. His body was drawn from the hospital in a wagon pulled by 12 mules. Eleven of us attended the funeral, and marched with arms reversed. Horton, of Birmingham, who is stationed at Viljoens Drift, was present, as were also Corporal Thomas (EH), Sapper Dalton (LV), and several men from different units who were with Wyatt at Heilbron. There is no clergyman here, and, beyond the grave being dug for us, all the other arrangements fell upon our shoulders. Corporal Thomas read the funeral service, and we all helped afterwards to fill in the grave. Everything was carried out as reverently as possible. I am trying to have a cross made, after the style of those we got at Orange River, to mark the spot where our comrade lies. I understand that poor Wyatt leaves a wife and several little ones, and that he was uninsured. I trust something may be done for his bereaved family. And now to reply to your welcome circular letter, dated 6th July. Many thanks for the new list, which is more evidence of your indefatigable labours on our behalf. Yes, thanks, I think we all get our KHAKI LETTERS as regularly as the erratic posts permit on this side. De Wet appears to have disorganised postal arrangements lately. Your letter is the quickest I've had since I've been in the Transvaal—nearly three months now. . . . I sent you a paper from Bloemfontein containing an account of a 'smoker' the R.E.'s got up during my stay there. Did you get it? When Orange River office was closed we were packed off in an open truck to Bloemfontein, at which place I was stationed for a fortnight. Then a party of us were sent to join the headquarters staff at the front. We travelled from Bloemfontein to 20 miles north of Kroonstad by rail, again in an open truck, piled up with telegraph stores. We found Milton and Stimpson at railhead, where we transferred our stores to mule wagons, and commenced trekking after Roberts, who was about two days ahead of us. We crossed the Vaal at 5 p.m. on May 27th, a few hours after the troops, and eventually came up with headquarters at Klip River, a day's march south of Johannesburg. Our trekking occupied four days, and we slept on the open veldt each night. Rations were not too plentiful, and 'seemed hard.' We stayed at Klip river one night, and then, just as the march to Pretoria seemed well nigh accomplished, Grant, of AB, and myself—much to our disgust—were sent back here, and have remained here ever since. We hope to have a run up to JH and PR when things quieten down. This is a decent little place, close to the Vaal River. We get plenty of eggs, milk, etc., and altogether matters are very comfortable. Stimpson and Milton are now at Taaibosch Spruit, seven or eight miles south of here. 'Stimmie' came to see us yesterday, and is looking very fit. Expect Percy Milton up to-day. Horton, at Viljoens Drift is also looking very well. Bourlay (Bottom*) of SY is with him. We have a nice office here. Three main lines meet at this place, and are all led in here and terminated on a test box of the umschalter switch type. We get a fair amount of plugging through, and testing to do. The most important line (Pretoria to Bloemfontein) has been interrupted a few times by De Wet and his crew. The wire is known as 'Top East,' and it has occasioned more trouble than any other wire I know of. Some of our fellows are so fed up with it that they will be in danger of sending telegrams when they get home saying, 'Dis Top East,' 'Earth Top East,' 'Top East now right,' etc. (mim.). I don't think there is much more to tell you, except that we got up a scratch team from this office on Sunday, and played a cricket match with the Vereeniging Estates people. Harry Barber and Grant made three each (highest scores), Dan Thomas and

* 'Bourley Bottom,' an old 24th Camping Ground at Aldershot.

KHAKI LETTERS—*continued*.

myself just broke our duck. It was very enjoyable though. We were entertained to lunch in the pavilion. Some of us are still feeling jolly stiff. I suppose you will all be in camp now. Hope you have a good time. The following 24th men are here :—T. R. Stevens, (GW), J. Grant, (AB), and self ; also from Heilbron — Dan Thomas, (EH), H. Barber, (TS), and W. H. Baxter, (CF), are with us until Heilbron is reoccupied. Very many thanks for your kind thoughtfulness, trusting to have more cheerful news for you next time."

No. 4,315, Sapper **A. H. Morse**, writes from Fort Knokke, Aug. 8th :—
"DEAR COLOUR SERGT. KEMP,—I have made another move. We left Maritzburg at 3 a.m. on the 1st for here, *via* Durban ; came round on the ' City of Vienna.' There were only the 62 of us on board in the way of troops. We brought four Boer prisoners from Durban to E. London. We laid off E. London a day and a half, waiting for an opportunity to land them, the weather was so rough. One night the stairs to our troop deck fell in during a storm, and everything movable was hurled across the deck. The troops fairly ' got the wind up ' (I hope that is not out of your depth). We arrived here early on the 7th, and landed in the afternoon. It would be impossible to find a more amiable set of officers than there were on that ship. The crew were Lascars. I called on Capt. Price yesterday, he was with Lieut.-Col. Treble (I think that is the correct rank). He said he was glad I had called, and he very kindly wired to Bloemfontein for my letters. I shall be glad to join our fellows again. The fellows here take a kit-bag, and go along the shore gathering mussles ; they boil them and eat them for tea. It is too cold to bathe and enjoy it. We have been given three new blankets and a ground sheet, but we have not yet been re-equipped with arms, &c."

No. 2,333, Sapper **W. Brewster** (of MR), writing from Mafeking, August 10th, says :—
" DEAR COLOURS,— Herewith please find the ' cadey ' worn by Sapper W. C. Smith, in conjunction with a set of whiskers. He came in from Barberspan the other day, and looked such a howler that no one knew whether he was Boer or Briton. Being somewhat better off in the way of headgear, we supplied him with another and sent him on his way (to Kraaipan) rejoicing. Thought possibly this might fetch something for the War Fund if put up by auction in TS. Am doing A1 myself. Hope ' K.L.' will still flourish."

See "Khaki Notes," page 327.

No. 1,275, Sapper **C. J. Woode**, writing from Mafeking, August 10th, says :—
" DEAR COLOURS,—Just a short note to you hoping that all is going well. I had to move from Lichtenberg to Ottoshoop, as Delarey, with a large force, was expected to pay us a visit shortly. We trekked to Ottoshoop. I stayed there waiting with my instruments to go back to Lichtenberg, the column, Lord Erroll and Carrington, meanwhile going on to Zeerust. There the force was too strong for us, and Zeerust retired on Ottoshoop, and from Ottoshoop we all retired to Mafeking. Mafeking at present date is in a state of huge excitement, large numbers of troops being in here. Telephones erected to the forts once again, and suspects

KHAKI LETTERS—*continued.*

being shifted from the town. They have just at present more R.E. T.Cs. here than they know what to do with, and actually wanted to attach the spare ones to the infantry camp. . . . To-night we are sleeping in the garden at rear of post office. Gwilliam and Brewster are also here. Smith retired from Barberspan to Lichtenberg, and has now gone on to Kimberley."

✧ ✧ ✧ ✧

No. 4,363, Sapper **W. G. Carter**, 1st T.B., writing from Heidelberg, August 11th, says :—

"I was three weeks in Pretoria, arriving there four days after Lord Roberts, but we were awfully delayed on the road, through the Boers, &c., and during those three weeks at PR. Tom Stevenson and I had four days out with Gen. Hutton's column, to meet Baden Powell. Soon got fed up with PR, plenty of work, and doing 8 hours on and 8 hours off, so not getting proper rest and was rather glad to get a shift here, George Willis (SE) and I. It is a fine place, very small of course, and supposed to be a country resort. Nice office, plenty of good grub, and no night work, except anything special. A big fight outside the town last Saturday week ; we woke up to the sound of rifle firing, and 200 Dublins kept over 1000 Boers with two big guns at bay till the camp turned out, and then Gen. Hart went out, and then, the usual, the bounders ran. Now they are back again and supposed strong laager just over the kopje. Three nights ago we had an alarm, and all the troops sent out, but appears their object was to rifle two farms to replenish their stock. We had a concert in the Town Hall this week, excuse the term Town Hall. We have a man here, McConnel of the R.E.'s, who went through the siege of Ladysmith ; he plays the mandoline, and so we often have a 'musical' on our own. Awfully grieved to hear about Alf. Rudd ; I left Bloemfontein the day after he came there."

No. 4,670. Sapper **W. E. Braybon** sends the following from Bloemfontein, dated August 11th :—

"DEAR KEMP,—We are still at the old shop, and the days are rolling rapidly past. Work and sleep are of course the chief things by which the 24 hours are aided in their flight. We have occasionally time for recreation, and Messrs. Tee, Ruffell, Stevens and Co. do what is possible in the direction of time off. These kindnesses are much appreciated, as on certain duties it is impossible to get out in the daylight, owing to the shortness of the days. A favourite walk and climb is to the summit of Naval Hill, from which altitude a distance of 70 miles can be seen. In the near distance is Spitz Kop, where there are late Boer trenches, and an outpost, whilst nearer are the kopjes of Thabanchu, and yet nearer those at the Waterworks. The Royal Engineers have had a big task as regards the water supply, as mains have been laid to the principal camps around the town. It is gratifying to belong to so useful a force in all its branches, and to be of so much service assisting in the carrying out of the prodigious organisation of the brain-working upper section, even as a 'lightning grinder.' I am not going to say that I think the strain placed upon the telegraph section is considered. I do not believe it is. A lot of condensing could be done with most messages, and I fail to see why a great many more official ones could not be sent by train—such as weekly returns of how many onions and potatoes are in store. But there, 'Ours not to reason why.' We are having a 'dust gale.' I feel sorry for

KHAKI LETTERS—*continued.*

those in hospital, and generally for everybody under canvas, or worse—under heaven. Under canvas you only get a small proportion, under heaven you get the full blessing, which not only falls on you, but stops there. I got a good idea from a Kaffir, who had a brewer's cap—our sea-kit cap—pulled down over his head, and he had his vision through the meshes of it. An odd sight in the distance, as he looked as though walking backwards. And speaking of odd sights, there are a few to be seen as regards dress. A nigger in a Norfolk jacket and breeches, bare fore legs, and brown boots, with a bowler hat, looked all right. It is surprising to see them in full khaki rig-out; discreditable displays, which I should like prohibited. The washerwoman's agent, who claims descent from native Royal blood, brought a baby with her the other day; it was a bright, intelligent-looking little bundle, and being a family man, I naturally noticed it, and made a few observations to it. I firmly believe it took me for its father, and thought I had whitewashed my face for its amusement. It is a common thing here to see 'piccanninies' round the refuse heaps finding jam tins, and to see them sitting dipping a finger in for the coveted luxury. Some of the prospectors will find plenty of tin mines here, unfortunately, battered and used ones, but close to the surface. I went down to see the Boer prisoners; some are fine, handsome men, but the majority are of the inanimate order. Stolid, stupid-looking, they seemed to me to even lack low cunning. It may be due to their position, and to their worn-out weariness. Three Dutch women stood close to me, and conversed and gesticulated freely in their native tongue of, or to the Boers, when presently one turned and said, 'What a treat it is to see the dear Burghers again.' This was in English. These dirty-looking, unshaven, unkempt scoundrels to be welcomed, was intended as a slur thrown at the English. I could have slapped her. I could not help retorting, 'Yes, we are pleased to see them come from behind the rocks.' Wretched curs, cornered, they plead for mercy in thousands, not hundreds. Their mode of warfare does not look like a 'driving into the sea policy,' even from their initial attempts. There should be a splendid field here for tradespeople and persons with trades. Carpenters earn 25s. a day, and a man here for eight years generally owns a house or two in that time. Telegraphy here is as played out as it is at home, and those who are at it reckon themselves jays for ever having taken it on. It is a thing which, if known, you never need starve, that is, if you are good at it. You can always get a job out here, I am told. Salaries range from £180 to £280. It costs you £7 a month for board, &c., here. Niggers get £4 10s. a month for sitting round a fire to keep it from blowing away. I have only seen one man really working, and he went for it for all he was worth. He was digging graves for our noble men who lie buried in the pretty graveyard here. It is a terribly impressive sight to see the fever-eaten bodies, wrapped in a blanket, lowered to their last resting place. It is a morbid subject upon which to dwell, yet it always strikes me that death is worse for the mourners than the departed. There are nearly 2,000 graves here, and the pretty pepper trees are in blossom, and the drooping foliage seems bent in grief for those who rest beneath their shade. The graves are well made, and many tokens of grief and respect mark the spot where comrades sleep. Have been appointed to relieve the Boers at Heilbron, Reading, and Frankfort, and open up the offices. Hulatt and Sim (lineman) go with me. Am very pleased to get a move, although sorry to leave many esteemed comrades and friends. Yet up to now it has been a very inglorious career, and one might almost persuade one's self that it was a

KHAKI LETTERS—*continued.*

special event, with the exception that we are never clear, and that it is a one-horse race, and there is no chance of making a bit, as it is a hundred to one on H.M. the Queen's 'John Bull,' by 'Empire,' out of 'England' Was on duty at 7 a.m. yesterday, and had marching orders at 10.30 a.m., waited until 1.15 a.m. the next morning, and then was told ' No trucks going up to-night, so go to the Soldier's Home.' The R.S.O. who spoke to us and directed us in so kindly a manner, was a gentleman whom one could love and serve through anything, it raised my tired spirits in a marvellous degree; it had the effect some inspiring tune will have on drooping spirits. He was beset by belated 'swaddies,' yet there was no *hauteur*. He kindly and carefully instructed all. This is the man to win men's hearts to valorous actions."

✦ ✦ ✦ ✦

No. 4,376, Sapper **W. W. Pearce,** sends the following from Pan Station, August 13th :—

"DEAR OLD KEMP,—No doubt you will think I have neglected you, but as several have written to you describing our party's trek up to Pretoria, I reserved my effort till later. After a stay in Pretoria of about six weeks, we moved off again to meet Lords Roberts, Kitchener, and Staff at Mark's Farm, near Erstfabricken. Included in our party are the following TS men :—Tom Stevenson, Jack Fallon, Dave Hamer, Arundell, and York (Duke), with Corporal Taylor (BS), and Lance Corporals Bob Poole (AB) and Freddie Cooke (BR) in charge. After a stay of three days, we moved on to Bronkhorstspruit, where we met Lord Roberts, who came on by train from Pretoria. We moved off early following morning after Botha, but there was no sign of the gentleman, and after a long day's trek arrived in Balmoral late in the afternoon, just in time to get out of a fearful storm, the pitiless rain falling all night. Fortunately, we secured the telegraph office at station, so we kept dry. The following morning Lord Roberts and Staff hurriedly returned to Pretoria, and we went on in charge of General Pole-Carew. We found Botha had made a headlong flight early the previous day. Another long trek, and we arrived at Brugspruit in the afternoon. On the way it was amusing to see Tommy Atkins chasing poultry and porkers, the latter with fixed bayonets. The following morning Bob Poole and myself were under orders to proceed to Witbank, where an engine was supposed to be waiting for us, to try and get into Middleburg, as French had entered it the previous day by another route, and was without telegraph communication. On arrival there, found engine had broken down. After waiting some time. Captain Crookshank, acting D.A.T., and Bob started on a trolly, I being left to follow with stores directly engine was repaired. It eventually turned up, and a broken down thing it was, belonging to the Transvaal Colliery Company, and in absence of an engine-driver, the general manager, a burly Englishman, volunteered to drive it. Captain Wright, Reuter's correspondent, was also on the engine. After proceeding five or six miles at a painful speed, our amateur driver discovered he had the steam brake half on. Relieved of that, she somewhat improved her rate of progression, but her old joints were certainly rheumaticy, as they squeaked and clanked in an alarming manner. We arrived at Groot Oliphants River Station without incident, and watered the engine. A mile further on I was stopped by an officer, who inquired where I was going; upon telling him, he said that Groot Oliphants Bridge had been charged with dynamite, and could not say if it had been extracted, and added that his troop of M.I. had been ordered back into Middleburg, the line was unprotected, and that I proceeded at

KHAKI LETTERS—*continued.*

my own risk, and asked me to report *re* the dynamite to General French when I got in. It was with mixed feelings that I crossed that bridge, a very lofty and narrow one, and devoid of parapets. A mile further on came up with the Captain and party, including Mr. Gwynne (*Daily Mail* correspondent). I now found that the dynamite had been extracted during the morning, but to make sure, Bob Poole divested himself of his clothing and swam round the parapets, the blacks refusing to be lowered down from the top of the bridge. An incident occurred to show the way the wily Boer leaves his family. A woman with half a dozen young children came out of a cottage while we were testing line to Brugspruit, and stated she and her children were hungry, and without means to procure any food. Captain asked her where her husband was, she replied that he had left her a few days ago and could not say where he was. Captain promised to bring her case before General French. After rewatering with improvised biscuit tins at Uitjyk (or something like it), our old crock brought us within 200 yards of Middleburg Station, where she refused to budge another inch. We soon established communication with Pretoria, the telegraph line being intact the whole way. Clear about 12, and up at 5 a.m., and was on duty till 3.30 next morning. The rest of the party trekked up, and our office was shifted from station to the telegraph office in the town. This is rather a pretty place, about half the size of Bloemfontein. Numbers of Boers handed in their rifles at the Landdrost office, and it was amusing to see some of the cunning ones march in with an antiquated sporting gun. The number of women and children in deep mourning gives the lie to the oft-repeated Boer slight losses of 1 killed, 2 wounded. Sainsbury and Swan came up from Bronkhorst Spruit, where they had been with the railway construction party. Arundell was sent to Wonderfontein, one of the outposts; Swan is with a cable cart at Strathrae, whilst Jack Fallon and myself are at Pan, which is well entrenched, and about 13 miles N.E. of Middleburg. Several train loads of Boer women and children have passed through here *en route* for Belfast. A motley lot they looked, and put you very much in mind of a school treat given to the poorer class of children in London. Transvaal flags were strongly in evidence, and all wore the national colours of red, white, blue and green. One could not help feeling for the youngsters, as a journey at night in open trucks at this time of year is as much as a strong man can stand. But still, no one can blame Lord Roberts, as he had no other conveyances to send them in. One young Dutch woman, speaking very good English, and addressing an interested group of Tommies, said, 'They told you soldiers at home that we were blacks, now you can see for yourself we are white, with red blood like yourselves.' Tommy Atkins quietly bantered back, and the young damsel lost her temper and heaped abuse on the British Army in general, and wildly waving a Transvaal flag, said, 'This shall float over Pretoria yet' Expect we shall be on the move again shortly, when our party will get together again, and it's the hearty wish of every one of us that this campaign will soon be over. Jack Fallon and myself send kind regards to all old chums, hoping you are OK, and not quite worried to death with your interesting book, which one and all eagerly read directly it arrives. I cannot conclude this letter without alluding to poor Frew and Metcalfe's deaths. Two better jovial and good-hearted comrades I never had, and was dumbfounded when I heard the bad news. 'Dick' was the father of our party on the 'Winifredian,' and endeared himself to all, and it was with great regret that we took different roads up country. Death and sickness has been meted out to the 24th men with unsparing hand, but I sincerely hope a turn in the tide has taken place.

KHAKI LETTERS—*continued.*

No. 802, **Sapper A. Ray,** writing from Aldershot, Aug. 30th, says:—
" DEAR COLOURS,—Very many thanks for " KHAKI LETTERS " received. I'm down here soldiering you see, and it's very nice. Roberts (TS) and Maclaren (EH) are here also, the former in the Pay Office, and latter at Hdqrs. Tel. Office. I'm out in the open air working, I'm glad to say; out on air line and also permanent wires. I'm very sorry to see Wyatt is gone. I remember how when we retreated from Rensburg I got some tea made for our chaps, and he came in about 4 o'clock p.m., and was very queer. He was so glad to get tea and a lay down. I went over to a farmer I knew, and managed to extract his last new-laid egg. I can see now how eagerly he sucked it, and was so grateful he made me take a knobkerry he had. I little thought that was the last I should see of him. He was a nice chap, and I'm glad I was able to make a drop of tea even for him, now he's gone. We've lost heavily over this business, and some of the best too."

✣ ✣ ✣ ✣

ONE OF THE SECTIONS OF THE DRAFT THAT

Sailed per S.S. "Montrose," June 12th.

Jackson, T. W. (Oxford). Robson, J. P. (Newcastle). Brown, F. P. (Oxford). Names, unfortunately, not supplied by Sender.
Rendle, J. (Exeter). Bordeaux, C. E. (Birmingham). Perkins, C. W. (Manchester). Norman, R. D. S. (South Shields). Cliff, H. (Exeter). Butt, H. (Dorchester). Armstrong, D. (Edinburgh).

⇥ Khaki Sidelights. ⇤

The **"Bloemfontein Post,"** August 15th, publishes the following:— "BOER BARBARITY.—Mr. Alex. Thompson, J.P., of Chavonne, Hay district, Griqualand West, writes to the *Cape Times*, giving an account of the way the Boer commandoes behaved in his district. It will be remembered that the Boers, alarmed by the British advance, vacated Hay, only to return very shortly. Mr. Thompson had been elected Magistrate by the Loyalists when the Boers left. On the Boers' return all British subjects were arrested and put in prison. Some were taken out of bed at two o'clock in the morning. Mr. Thompson says: Before sunrise General Liebenberg (the Boer leader) came into the yard and asked one of his men if we had all the ——rubbish together. Good; he would give them ——. At sunrise we were taken out (14 of us) and tied with ropes and placed on the public streets to be insulted and loaded with indignity, and to witness one of the most inhuman acts ever perpetrated in this country. One of the loyalists was a slightly coloured man. This man, a respectable tradesman and a proprietor of town and farm property, was accused of the terrible offence of hustling against one of the burghers, which was without foundation. At any rate no pleading or explaining would help, and he was taken by six men, stretched and held fast over a cart-pole, and the General, with his own hands, administered 25 lashes with the harness pole strap, an instrument any man would hesitate to beat an ox with. At every stroke the human tiger would scornfully repeat 'God Save the Queen.' Three of the strokes cut the man's face open, loosening some of his teeth so much that for days he could not partake of solid food. He was then tied to the cart-wheel, his lacerated back to the sun, that the blood might dry, thereby increasing the physical anguish of the unfortunate sufferer. His wife and two children were then permitted to wash his wounds and remove his gory clothes. The General (the devil incarnate Mr. De Pass called him to his face) is a man fervent in prayer. To hear him in the laager, especially on Sundays, one would imagine the Rev. Mr. Spurgeon had reappeared from the dead, so grand is he at preaching.

Rudd Fund.—Messrs. Driscoll and Welch report the following subscriptions have been received by them for the wife and children of the late Mr. A. Rudd, of the "L" Division, up to Sept. 17th:—

Groups "A," £1 12s. 6d.; "B," £1 10s. 3d.; "C," £1 7s. 6d.; "D," 15s.; "E," £1 2s.; "F," £1 3s. 6d.; "G," £1 10s.; "H," £2 12s.; "I," £2 19s.; "K," 10s.; "L," 15s. 3d.; "M," £1 3s. 3d.; total, £17 0s. 3d.

Divisions "A," £1 1s. 6d.; "B," * * * ; "C," £2 9s. 11d.; "D," £5 2s.; "E," £3 18s.; "F," £2 11s.; "G," £3 8s. 6d.; "H," £1 2s.; "I," £2 16s. 6d.; "K," £3 9s.; "L," £13 6s. 6d; total, £39 4s. 11d.

Other Sections—Night Staff, £1 11s.; News Staff, £4 0s. 6d.; Special Staff, £5 13s.; Stock Ex., * * * ; T.S.F., £4 3s. 6d.; Check, £1 15s. 6d.; Counter and Dely, * * * ; total, £17 3s. 6d.

KHAKI LETTERS, £1: Subscribers to KHAKI LETTERS, per R. E. Kemp, Col. Taylor, £1; R. E. Kemp, 10s.; Mrs. G. W. B., 5s.; Misses E. H., 5s,; J. O., 2s. 6.; A. H., 2s. 6d.; E. B., 2s. 6d.; M. K., 2s.; total, £3 9s. 6d.

From the Front—C. Rodway, 5s.; B. Walton (2s. 6d. worth of stamps sold for) 3s. 9d.; W. G. Carter, 10s.; total, 18s. 9d. Grand total (up to date), £77 16s. 11d.

* * * Accounts not yet sent in.

⇥ Khaki Notes. ⇤

The Telegraph Companies will be sorry to learn that our well-known and much-esteemed Segt. Instructor, Wm. Graham, from the R.E.'s, has sustained a great loss by the death of his wife. Leaving her last Thursday (Sept. 13th), he had been at the Orderly Room less than half-an-hour, when a telegram called him home. The "I" and "L" being all telegraphists, always had a honoured place in Billy's book, and we now assure him that he has the best sympathy comrades can offer in his severe trial.

Casualty Lists are shorter in length than they were a few months ago, for which we are all most thankful, but it gives pain to many of us to reread in them the names of comrades whose deaths were published long ago. Last week several deaths were given that occurred as far back as March.

Sir Fredk. Hodgson arrived at Plymouth on Sunday evening, Sept. 16th. He had a tight corner in Coomassie, and his old 24th comrades are exceptionally pleased to know he is safe and sound in the Old Country again.

KHAKI NOTES—*continued*.

The Cadey referred to by Sapper Brewster was not put up for auction in TS, although it was on view for several days, and caused much amusement, especially in the group from whence its last owner sallied forth to war. Many colleagues expressed a wish to become the happy possessor of it, but there was one whom I know who would value it even more than they Here you are :— " Deal, Sept. 10th, Very many thanks indeed for the kind parcel containing my son's ' Boer Hat,' you may guess how we appreciate it, &c." I transmit those thanks to friend Brewster, who will, I am sure, feel satisfied that we can peg another hole in our scoring board of " Little deeds of kindness."

Note of hand.—It is the practice in most sections of the C.T.O. to provide small pieces of paper—about 3½ by 3 inches—for use by those who sign as substitutes for the duties of fellow-clerks, or volunteer for overtime during pressure. The wording in all cases is proverbially stereotyped. One of these " little bits of blue " was sent to a man at the front, with the hint " Perhaps this may be useful to you." Our comrade saw the joke, and it has duly reached us filled in as follows :—" I volunteer to come home from South Africa as soon as possible, as am fed right up." It is duly signed, we won't say by whom, but such a little gem has caused great amusement amongst those who have seen it.

" For Sale."—A set of slightly soiled rugs, pillow, and bag, complete ; little used of late ; suitable for a ' parcel ' in the coming winter ; or would exchange for a reliable alarum. T.S. 6 to 2.—P.S. There is no night (staff) there." Such Ads. may appear in the Dailies, you never know.

Delays.—If Baden Powell's postcart, with all his letters of thanks, etc., can be lost, and Buller's important despatches captured, wonder not that a common Colour-Sergt.'s little lot may also suffer loss and delay. Have I not experienced it ? Why, certainly.

Medals for Volunteer long service have been awarded to Private J. G. Hopgood, " I " Company, and Lance-Corpl. Dan Thomas, " L " Company. The latter, who is now in South Africa, conducted the funeral service in the case of poor Wyatt.

Returned.—A note from Huddersfield says Sapper E. H. Quarmby arrived Southampton, Sept. 10th, per s.s. " Assaye," invalided.—Sapper " Bunnie " Ingram writes from New Malden saying, " I am quite safe and well in Old England, invalided from Natal after dysentery.—Sapper Rodk. Campbell, of EH., writes from Netley Hospital, saying he is " invalided home from the seat of war after a rather bad time with enteric fever, but I am thankful to say I am progressing very favourably. Accept best thanks for your kindly interest in those exiled. How much they appreciate your self-denials you cannot adequately realize. Expect to go on furlough at end of month, and will sojourn at Edinburgh."—Sapper Alliston writes from Forest Gate, " I'm still in the land of the living ; have got two months' extension of furlough. Received a call from Tommy Pallet, who looks much improved."—Sergt. Luttrell has a month's extension of furlough.—Sapper Woolley writes that he is invalided, and will be with us again in a week or so. He is now on his way home.

Khaki Postage Fund.—The following amounts have come to hand, and are heartily acknowledged herewith. Thank you. Sheffield, 5s 6d. ; " Comradeship," 5s. ; " I " Group, 4s. 10d. ; Recd. Check (per A. L. M.), 3s. 6d. ; " C " Group, 2s. 8d. ; Anon. (NT.), 2s. 6d. ; H. S. J. (MA.), 1s. 7d. ; and H. F. (CV.), 1s. 6d.

B.Q.'s.—W. M. S.—Your letter, Heidelburg, June 27th, to hand September 11th. Sorry it was not seen sooner. Jack Hargreaves.—Thanks for photos. Glad you are in charge of Capon and getting on well again.

" Poniard, London," for telegrams from Our Boys to their relatives and friends at home, the addresses of whom should be sent us at once.

" Casualties, Capetown," for enquiries *re* sick and wounded.

" KHAKI LETTERS," One Penny. By post, Three Halfpence.

All posted letters containing Remittances, Orders, MSS., &c., must be addressed to R. E. KEMP, 12, JERRARD STREET, LEWISHAM, S.E.

Postal Orders should be made payable at Loampit Vale, Lewisham, S.E.

Printed by E. G. BERRYMAN & SONS, *Blackheath Road, London, S.E.*

"Khaki Letters" from ....
"My Colleagues in South Africa."

CORRESPONDENCE FROM THE
POST OFFICE TELEGRAPHISTS
OF THE
24th MIDDLESEX (P.O.) RIFLE VOLUNTEERS
(Royal Engineer Reserves),
ON ACTIVE SERVICE.

THE BOND THAT BINDS US—FRIENDSHIP—COMRADESHIP.

Published fortnightly for the Postal Telegraph Service.
Conducted by COLOUR-SERGEANT R. E. KEMP, *Central Telegraph Office, London.*

No. 18.   OCTOBER 5TH, 1900.   PRICE ONE PENNY.

Central Telegraph Office,
London, E.C.

DEAR COMRADES, ONE AND ALL.

Greetings! During the past fortnight very few events of a military nature have transpired, indeed, we could write them all on our thumbnails. The gallant corps proceeded to Bisley on Sept. 19th, to perform the usual class-firing, and the new volley-firing. This was mostly for men who were deprived of the pleasures of Minster Camp, with its sea-bathing, &c., and the drones who invariably leave things until the eleventh hour. Big efforts had been made to get every man down on that occasion, and some dissatisfaction was naturally caused when it became known that the P.O. men had been given a day off in order to facilitate their appearing before the targets, while the Telegraph Company experienced the usual difficulty of providing subs., or exchanges of duty, at their own expense. As a result, the "last" day must doom their prospects of efficiency for 1900 unless there is another "last" day during this month, for all non-efficients did not manage to show up. There are also many men who want drills in order to pull them through, and, unfortunately, all military exercises are suspended until Oct. 8th, owing to the General Election. So what with one thing and another the poor "I" Co. are not having a very rosy time of it this year.

The General Election, as you can well imagine, is making us very busy, and just when the Telegraph Service should be preparing for emergencies, the Manchester Office was burnt out. This was on Wednesday afternoon, Sept. 19th. MR was isolated, the whole of the instrument room suffering, while great damage was also done to the floors below. The fire raged furiously and lasted but a short time—thanks to the efficiency of the Fire Brigade. Of the Staff, of which nearly 500 were on duty at the time, no one was hurt. Although the conflagration spread with such rapidity, fortunately every person managed to effect their escape—and all without panic. Liverpool largely assisted by train to keep up communication for Manchester, and the big provincial offices sent aid in the shape of Engineers,

Linemen, apparatus, &c. For such a big office the task of supplying spare sets was a very difficult one, and TS presented a peculiar appearance in the evening time, by so many instruments having been removed from their customary places. Great credit is due to all concerned for the excellent manner in which the difficulty was met and the remarkably expeditious way in which MR was again joined up to the principal offices. Although there must necessarily be great inconvenience still experienced in the Cottonopolis office, very few days elapsed before it was officially announced that the public notice of delay to MR could be cancelled.

There are some promotions out for the officers of the A.P.O.C., and we are pleased to notice that in the issue dated September 11th, Captain (Local Major) G. W. Treble, is to be graded Deputy Asst. Adjutant-General whilst Army postmaster in South Africa. The other officers of the 24th who are assisting him, are to be graded Staff-Captains. All to date from June 1st.

Returning to the most important of all themes, the talk o' th' day, we find we have seen the new duties and tasted some of them. There is a big cry out about them on all sides, and some of the newspapers are telling the public all about it. There have been meetings and interviews by press reporters, and during the course of the articles appearing in the papers, we are assured that we are contented. When you are in such an excited state, and don't know what you are or where you are, it is just as well that someone should tell you. We are told we are contented, so of course we *are* contented; but the night staff who have been put on day duty so suddenly, are anything but pleased. They have always done their bit well, and have been accustomed to the one regular hour of duty. They are not taken up with the idea of going all round the clock. Indeed, to very many of them it comes as a tremendous strain, for we are not used to going to bed at 9 p.m. to get up at 4.30 or thereabouts. One paragraph was most interesting to those of us who have been on the regular night staff. Here it is. In an interview by a "Daily Mail" representative, our Controller is reported to have said: "The change in our staff has been a long time in contemplation, and has been made under medical advice. We found that continual night work was injuring the health of the men, and so we arranged that they should take their turn at day work." This is most considerate of them, but as one of the staff concerned I must confess I am surprised, for I am thankful to say that during nineteen years' night work. I have never had one hour off through illness on my part. Some other men of the regular staff can show similar records. But there, it is not my intention to criticise. A soldier is forbidden to criticise his officers, and is held responsible for communications to his relatives and friends, and especially those that find their way to the press. I have always borne this fact in mind when dealing with your epistles for Our Booklet, and I bear it in mind also as regards myself, for discipline must be upheld. Talking of discipline, a superior officer made a curious remark to me a week or two ago. I had related to him a small discrepancy on the part of a soldier, and informed him that the punishment meted out was so many days C.B., when he innocently remarked "Good gracious, they are getting as strict in the Army as we are here." Knowing a little of the Army discipline, I should be sorry if the P.O. Service was really more severe, but of course he didn't quite know. As an instance of the contentedness of the Staff, I am sorry to say that a very old friend of mine, a water-colour artist of no mean merit, and whose pictures have received the coveted "hanging," resigned during the first week of day duty.

Photography is all the rage in telegraphic circles just now, and although my last letter to you bristled with terms pertaining to the fascinating art, I hear that there was very little difficulty experienced in understanding it. What one did not know he easily learned from a dabbler in Sun pictures. I will not inflict more obtuse terms upon you further than to say that an analysis of the solution used at the change of development was as near as possible made up as follows:—45 6 to 2's, 79 7-3s, 75 11-9's, 150 3-11's, and 52 4-11.45's. Total, 401 parts. Something like 50 11-7's—this is the new night duty—were also on. During the week some modifications were introduced, the Special Staff was increased by about 30, and it is evident that we are not very settled just yet. The *Evening News* of October 1st, says:—"After much discussion and an assurance from the Controller that the telegraph operators had no grievances, the secretary of the Post Office has written the Controller instructing him to ask the secretary of the Postal Telegraph Clerks' Association to prepare a full and detailed statement of the men's grievances."

Now I will close. Wishing you every success, and hoping to hear from you as regularly as in the past, and especially of those returning,

Yours most heartily,

To the "L" Co. in South Africa,   R. E. KEMP,
Tuesday, October 2nd, 1900.   *Colour-Sergeant.*

COPYRIGHT.—"Khaki Letters" must not be used without permission.—R. E. KEMP.

Khaki Letters.

No. 32,764, Sapper **C. T. Catling,** writing from Pretoria, July 20th, says :—

" Pleased to say I am in the best of health at present, and hope to keep so. Jenner and I were both passed as fit some six weeks ago at Fort Knokke, and about 10 days later were suddenly warned to proceed to Bloemfontein, where he—Jenner—is now doing duty as clerk to Captain Fowler; I stayed there three weeks, and was then ordered here. We were three days and two nights in a third-class carriage, packed like herrings, to Bloemfontein, . . . but the worst journey was from Bloemfontein to here. We entrained on the top of stores in an open truck at 6.30 p.m., and were shunted about till 9.30, when we moved off. I suppose this was to see if we could hang on. We were nearly frozen to death each night, it was so cold, and we were unable to get a wash the whole of the journey. The road all the way up here was strewn with dead oxen and horses. I also noticed the veldt was on fire in three separate places. I guessed the Boers were knocking about on account of this, and was quite right in my conjecture, as the road was destroyed soon after we had passed. I am doing night duty here at present, and it is much easier than daytime, although when the Boers cut the wires we are much pressed on any outlet we may have for our work; last night I had over 300 messages to key, and they averaged 60 words each. Tim Kelly is still at the waterworks outside Bloemfontein; I had several chats with him; he was OK then."

No. 4,379, Sapper **G. E. Plumridge,** writes from Rhenoster Camp, July 24th :—

" Have just come in from seeing a grand fight, about ten miles west of us. We could see the shells bursting a treat—pom-poms and rifles giving the Boers 'what oh !' They are still at it—can hear big guns going off quite plainly from our tent. Since I wrote you last week, we have had an exciting time here. On Friday night we had report that the notorious De Wet was about here with 3,000 men, and General Broadwood was chasing him. On Saturday, about midnight, our wires south to Kroonstad were cut, and De Wet crossed the railway line, pulling down several poles and cutting up the line about nine miles south. He also captured a train, taking prisoner the escort, after a severe fight; he then captured all the supplies and burnt the train, and got clear away. On Sunday, Broadwood came here with two cavalry brigades and infantry. It was a grand sight watching his force cross the veldt, we could see them for miles. . . . We had a shocking storm Sunday night. We managed to keep our tent up by all holding on to the

KHAKI LETTERS—*continued.*

pole. The poor fellows outside who had no tents (and they were in thousands) were soaked, and what with the wind howling, and the oxen, mules and horses bellowing and crying, we had a lively time of it. About midnight the wind dropped, and we got down between our blankets and soon asleep . . . You wouldn't know me, I'm sure. I go about in a Boer slouch hat (a curio I shall try to bring home). . . . H. Barber is still at Heilbron, and all right ; I had a long chat to him yesterday."

In another letter, Plumridge relates some more experiences, Aug. 15th :—
On Saturday we had a most fearful experience, in the shape of a sand storm. As per usual, it commenced early in the morning. and by nine o'clock was at its height ; tin boxes and huge pieces of rock were hurled about like pieces of straw, and at times it was impossible to see a yard in front of us. We had two tents, one for work, and the other for ordinary use—the former is now ' no more.' The wind soon began to tear round the sides, and while some of us endeavoured to hold it up, the others succeeded in moving the instruments and batteries into our remaining tent. A pile of messages went flying down the kopje, Marshall, Bramwell, and myself in full cry. We chased these messages a distance of about two miles over the veldt to the Rhenoster River, where, between us, we recovered about fifty ; a good many were blown to pieces. We were simply covered from head to foot with sand. I am indebted to Captain Webber for the note-paper am now using, also a shirt and two handkerchiefs, which, as you may imagine, were indeed very acceptable. Am feeling O.K. in spite of the sandstorm. With kind regards to all."

✣ ✣ ✣ ✣

No. 1,274, Sapper **W. F. Adams**, writing from Kimberley, August 13th, says :—
"Still jogging along in a very slow sort of way, plenty of work, not much else to do . . . . We have just entered the annual period of dust-winds, which may last for two months. It's dust everywhere. The wind is very cold at nights, too. Froze hard last night, but it's very warm to-day."

No. 25,322, Sapper **F. D. Horton** (of BM), writing from Viljoen's Drift, August 14th and 16th, says :—
"Things are very quiet, and there is little to record. Many trains filled with Hollanders going South pass here daily. You will probably have seen from papers that the Hollanders and suspected persons are being placed over the border—that is, at some place south of the Orange River. Hundreds of women and children have passed here in open trucks, which they have to sleep in during the cold nights, but the Imperial Railway are very short of passenger coaches, so that the bad accommodation cannot be avoided. There is thought to be a considerable amount of treachery going on here, some of the principal inhabitants are suspected of communicating with the enemy. One woman has a brother in the English army and one in the Boer forces, and she has been in the habit of riding out to the Boers on the plea that she is endeavouring to get them to give up their arms and come in, but she has been stopped at that game. . . . She used to be very bitter when the British prisoners were brought through, but she is very attentive to the English soldiers now, for her husband has warned her as to her behaviour. Am afraid I cannot give you much news of an encouraging nature ; the war still drags on, with no appearance of an early termination.

KHAKI LETTERS—*continued*.

Even should the war end, it would scarcely be safe to leave the country without a very considerable force remaining behind, the Boers are playing such a treacherous game. No doubt you have read of the Pretoria plot to murder the English officers and take Lord Roberts prisoner. The troops are very bitter at this, and, given their way, I am confident the majority would like to start in the south of the Colony and shoot every Dutchman they came across, right away up to Pretoria. . . . Some of the higher class Boers, male and female . . . acknowledge a bitter hatred of everything English. One lady was especially bitter, and whilst admitting that Lord Roberts was a kind man, said she would, without compunction, kill Kitchener, Chamberlain, and Rhodes, if she had an opportunity. I hear Lord Roberts is going home in September. . . . Of course, England, as the centre of civilisation, must be careful how she acts, and it would not have been to our ultimate good to have treated the enemy as perhaps any other European power would have acted. No doubt the time has, however, come, when different treatment must be meted out to the Boer. The darkest hour is that before the dawn, and may-be, things will assume a brighter aspect shortly, possibly before this reaches you."

No. 29,095, Sapper **A. Gwilliam**, writes from Maribogo Siding, August 16th, in the following lighthearted strain :—

"DEAR PEOPLE,—The man who invented the saying 'One knever knoes,' was a philosopher of the deepest dye; it is particularly applicable to me under the present circumstances, for here am I, who, up till late last Saturday night, was expecting to spend the remainder of my active service in Mafeking, instead of which, I now find myself engaged in watching the railway line some 45 miles south of that place. The order came about 11 p.m. Saturday evening, 'Sapper Gwilliam to proceed to Maribogo.' Sapper Gwilliam proceeded, and on the Sunday morn you may have beheld him with buzzer and separator duly tapped in and joined up on to the MF KB No. 2 wire. I am beginning to love the buzzer, it is like unto a dear friend, it is a small voice from a distance, it talks to me in lonely moments, and when I am not able to fraternise with the lads from Zoomersetshire (the lads referred to are the boys composing the half company of Somersetshire Light Infantry which is posted here); these, and a few Cape Police, along with some details from other regiments, bring the effective strength of our little force up to just over a hundred men, our business being that of guarding the lines of communication at this point. This place is composed of a hotel, a farmhouse, a railway telegraph office, and a store, in which I have fixed my instrument; north, south, east, and west, the endless veldt rolls away into distance, unrelieved by any sign of habitation, and the nearest places worth mentioning are Mafeking and Vryburg, respectively 45 and 50 miles up and down the line. In my advance up the line, following the relief column, I was the first clerk to enter the railway telegraph office here after its occupation by the enemy, and well do I remember wading through blue slip up to my knees in order to reach the instruments, and little did I think then that the Boers would again threaten this part, and as a result, cause me to be brought back here for duty; but, as I observed before, 'one knever knows.' Carrington's retirement into Mafeking has, however, left the country practically open, and we rather anticipate that the Boers will prove a bit frisky, and try to take a rise out of us; but, should they come, I don't think we shall be caught napping. Just opposite this store,

KHAKI LETTERS—*continued*.

and on the other side of the metals, a splendid little fort, constructed of stones and earth, is nearly complete, whilst upon this side of the line my office is flanked by barricades of old railway lines, big bales of wood, wire entanglements, and what not, and in addition to all this, we are surrounding this little spot with an elaborate system of entrenchments, so that I think you'll agree with me that we ought to pull through smiling should anything happen, providing that heavy artillery is not pitted against us, for we are at present deficient thereof—seems hard. But, 'tis a poor heart that never rejoices, and so I am gathering comfort from the facts that I have escaped from the region of the 'Dust Devil,' and that I can now procure eggs at a shilling per dozen. The 'Dust Devil' must be seen ere it can be realised; in favourable country it appears with every wind, and when it rages, one feels inclined to say naughty things. There is no escape, it permeates everywhere and anything. You eat it, and sleep in it: you go to bed with it, and get up with it; it fills your eyes, mouth, nose, and ears, and gets down your back, and generally makes you wish you'd never been born, or longingly think of the Parish Vestry system of good Old London, with its local watercarts. Such is the 'Dust Devil,' of which I experienced a beautiful sample during my last day in Mafeking. Bye-the-bye, talking about eggs, I have just left in Mafeking a past master in the art of purchasing them. His name is 'Paddy,' his object—rigid economy. He would sort out the coolie shopkeepers, of which Mafeking seems full, and striding up to the counter, would demand a dozen of *black hen's* eggs. Great Scot! I often felt like exploding when watching those niggers' faces. Of course, they had to declare their inability to distinguish *black hen's* eggs from any other hen's eggs, which just suited Mr. Pat, for he would then coolly select the biggest, explaining all the while that those were exactly what he wanted. Go thou, my female friends, and do likewise, for it is profitable; only after a time or two those niggers' faces generally betokened that they knew a thing or so. However, I suppose that they put it all down to the war, just as we do if anything startling happens. But, should you wish to see something unique in the way of shopping, I would recommend you to pay us a visit, and watch how we barter with the Barralong maidens for milk, etc. I wish I was skilled in the art of talking nicely to a girl upon my fingers, but then I'm not, and so it comes rather awkward, for we have to largely depend upon pantomimic action, and should the price offered not come up to their expectations, woe betide us! for they simply pulverise us with a look which is calculated to make a mere man squirm. 'Twas ever so with the sex. Well, I suppose I must bring my chat to a close, and retire up on my corned beef boxes, *i.e.* get up on to my perch, for the bugle is just sounding the 'last post,' and as we have to stand to arms from 5 a.m. till sunrise, it is wise to bear in mind the old maxim, 'Early to bed,' etc. I wonder when I shall be on at 12 noon again?—ah, I wonder!—roll on a long time. Meanwhile, we live in hope, but when I do return, may I find your eyes brighter, and your handshake stronger than ever in the days of yore—if that be possible.

✤ ✤ ✤ ✤

No. 24,305, Sapper **F. T. Stimpson,** writes from Taaibosch Kopje, O.R.C., August 16th, as follows:—

"Just a few lines to let you know I am still keeping my end up, and pleased to say I am in excellent health, and I suppose a lot better in health and pocket than if I were in an office; it is a fine healthy spot, with plenty

KHAKI LETTERS—*continued.*

of water, not of the best, unfortunately. We are on top of the kopje and command a big stretch of country. We have a Regiment of K.R.R.'s, and two guns of 74th Battery, and a Squadron of Lock's Horse. We live fairly well and are able to buy condensed milk and a few eggs now we have some splosh, but I am properly fed up with the scoff and also the campaign, and as things are at present, there does not seem much prospect of bringing it to a termination before Christmas. but I sincerely hope I shall be home by then. I am sorry to say poor old Bob Luttrell has been invalided home, it was reported that he had died, but I saw in KHAKI LETTERS that he was sailing in the 'Princess of Wales' boat. It is also reported that poor old Dickie Frew has died of enteric at Kimberley, which, if true, I am very sorry to hear. KB seems to be a deadly place, and I am pleased I joined Roberts' Column instead of shifting up there. Four out of my tent party at Modder are now invalided home, and I don't think there are many of the first party of clerks left out here. I hope when this post is closed that we shall shift up to Pretoria. They are getting a lot of civvies at PR and JH, and drafting our chaps out to the district offices. It is rumoured that they are offering our chaps £250 as a minimum wage to stop out, and I should think that a good number of the younger branch will stop. I don't like the idea of going back to TS after this healthy life for 12 months. I think there will be a few of our chaps with three bars up, and a good many with two. What price the next Inspection? My time is up next January, but I think I shall be tempted to take on again if it is only to be with the old chums that have rejoined. There has been a lot of fighting round about us since Bobs arrived at Pretoria. Olivier is reported this morning with about 2000, and six guns about Heilbron, Genl. Hunter chasing him. This place is only eight miles from the Vaal or Vereeniging. I paid them a visit last week, and Bannister is coming over with a friend to-morrow (Friday) to see me. Sorry to say we buried another of ours, Wyatt from Grimsby, at Vereeniging, last week. Well, I must farewell, kind regards, hoping to be in Old England ere long."

✣ ✣ ✣ ✣

No. 4,607, Sapper **W. H. Butt** (of DO), writing from Winburg, O.R.C., August 17th, says:—

"DEAR COLOUR-SERGT. KEMP,—Although it is a few months since I last wrote to you, and that in the Old Country, you will doubtless have no objection to again hearing from me. I must acknowledge first of all, with many thanks, the receipt of 'K.L's.' which have arrived regularly, and especially No. 13, with the list of 'Ours' enclosed. What a lot of trouble you must take, and time give up, in our interests. I can assure you the book is eagerly looked forward to by one and all, and am able to speak from experience upon that point, for whilst at Bloemfontein I heard several enquiries from some of the old hands for No. 9, which reached us just before leaving Aldershot, and had not been received at BFN. I handed mine over and received a grateful 'thanks.' This trip out will have been, no doubt, fully described, and in print long before this reaches you, so I will say nothing about it beyond that I enjoyed it immensely. About the only chief item of interest to you will be the arrival here of the Boer prisoners, captured by Generals Hunter and Rundle, and that alone was a sight worth coming out here to see. Talk about your Lord Mayor's Show, Jubilee Processions, etc., I don't reckon they are in it compared with these. The prisoners arrived in two batches, the first lot numbering between 2,000 and 3,000. They took over three hours to arrive, and the length of the mob was

KHAKI LETTERS—*continued*.

estimated at nine miles, the dismounted Boers were riding on ox wagons and some in Cape carts. Close upon 2,000 were on horseback, riding four abreast. On each side marched our troops, a few paces interval, with fixed bayonets, and outside these was a line of mounted men. The prisoners consisted of local commandos, Winburg, Senekal, Ladybrand, Brandfort, etc., etc., and there were plenty of spectators to witness their arrival, the civilians mustering in strong force. They naturally recognised and were recognised by many; one old dame in particular coming in for a good share. I saw quite a dozen get off their horses and give her a double-barrelled kind of a hug and a good kissing, after which she would have a good cry. I thought perhaps they hurt her, the way they went at it. This first lot were in charge of General Paget and escorted by his brigade, the 20th. They laagered on the outskirts of the town until train accommodation could be procured to take them to the seaside for their summer holidays. They arrived on a Wednesday, and by Sunday morning were all away. On the Sunday afternoon another batch arrived, escorted by the 21st Brigade and in charge of General Bruce Hamilton. There were not quite so many in this lot, but none the less interesting, one thing in particular being the arrival of two guns belonging to 'U' Battery, R.H.A., that had been recaptured. The Camerons were escorting them in, and many appeared to be in a sorry plight, all more or less 'fed up,' and no wonder, for they had been after the enemy for three months, and on three-quarter rations the whole time. The uselessness of the kilts was very evident with respect to fighting in a hot climate, all the bare skin visible being nearly black. It is all right at home, but a failure out here. They were all glad enough to taste bread again and made the most of their opportunity whilst here. The influx naturally gave us plenty to do, but by sticking to it we managed to clear up every night. This is a very nice little town; was formerly, I hear, capital of the Free States, suppose prior to the railway being built. It is a branch line here from Smaldeel and is at present a terminus, but the line is marked out and begun to connect this with Harrismith. In conclusion I again thank you for the great trouble you are taking."

No. 4,363, Sapper **W. G. Carter,** writes from Heidelberg, August 18th, as follows :—

"DEAR COLOURS,—Many thanks for your circular letter, we are receiving KHAKI LETTERS all right here, and they are read and appreciated by a good many 'outsiders.' On the 30th, 12 of ours and myself were ordered to leave Bloemfontein for the front, and forthwith railed as far as Vredefort Weg, where we had to wait two days for a convoy. The day after we left, Vredefort was surrounded by Free Staters, and the Commandant called on to surrender. We left Vredefort at 6 o'clock one evening and marched till about 10 p.m., then we outspanned till daybreak and then on the march again till 10 a.m., and then outspan till 4 o'clock. When we were at Taaibosch Spruit, we had been outspanned all the day, and were just inspanned ready to start off, when we saw two parties of Boers ride into a copse close to a farmhouse, barely a mile away. There were only thirteen of us, telegraphists, to guard the convoy of about 200 wagons, and it looked at first as if the 24th were going to be called on to defend this big convoy. However, we retreated, and in the muddle lost our wagon and blankets for one night. We reached Vereeniging safely and took train to Johannesburg, taking 15 hours to do about 50 miles. We spent one day in Johannesburg

KHAKI LETTERS—*continued.*

but were sent on to Pretoria; the train which took us came to grief about 2 a.m., the engine left the line and several trucks overturned, and one soldier got his leg shattered, and died next day. We reached Pretoria on Saturday, June 9th, 4 days after Lord Roberts' entry, and were soon enstalled in the Telegraph School. Whilst there Tom Stevenson and myself were sent off to join Gen. Hutton's column, şent out to meet Baden-Powell, between Pretoria and Rustenburg. We had rather a rough wet time, and we couldn't get through on the buzzer, although Baden-Powell gave us a message. I have now been here two months. When we first came the Boers came in in dozens to surrender, but now very few indeed come in. Gen. Hart had an engagement with Hans Botha's commando about twelve miles out last Saturday fortnight, and Gen. Hart spoke well of the fighting qualities of the R.E.'s; 110 R.E.'s belonging to the construction train being engaged. When we first came we had to sleep in our clothes, with our carbines and ammunition close handy, but the neighbourhood is pretty clear now, although we had a night alarm last week. This is a very nice little village and considered healthy. My only complaint at present is that we have had no letters for some weeks. Have met some very nice fellows amongst our colleagues, the regular R.E.'s since I've been out here. Was very sorry to hear of poor old Dick Frew."

No. 1,546, **R. W. Eglington** (of DY), writing from Thabanchu, August 20th, sends the following interesting letter :—

"I am quite isolated here, and know little of what is happening to the members of our corps except through the invaluable KHAKI LETTERS, and by information from Bloemfontein. It is lonelier than ever here now. Two companies of the Worcester Regiment have been moved on to Ladybrand, and have taken our only football with them The garrison is now only one company of Worcesters, about 30 of the Wilts Yeomanry, and a few Australians, who act as police. The latter are all six-footers, and splendidly made. I have to be my own linesman just now, as the nigger I had was a duffer. Had to show him how to refresh the batteries the other day, although it's a job I never tackled before. My bit of technical knowledge helped me through, however, and the Serjeant's boot helped the nigger through. I got sick of the office yesterday, . . . so I shook the dust of Thabanchu off my shapely beetle-crushers, and footed it 18 miles out, through the Nek, with a telegram for Quin's Farm, at Lovedale. I got bogged once, but arrived there safely at 1.30 p.m. . . . Quin laughed and said it was a record to have a telegram delivered 18 miles. He gave me a fine dinner. I started back at 3 p.m., and I got home at 7.15 p.m., walking latter part of way under an African moon. It gets dark at 5.30 p.m. now; sun rises at 5.30 a.m., I think, but I am not quite sure of that. I don't rise from my two blankets on the office flure till 7.30 a.m., when Bloemfontein calling up is my *réveille.* Thanks for the bit of hawthorn. I showed it to a Dutchman, and he was enraptured—at least, as much as it is possible for a Dutchman to be. The prettiest thing I've seen out here is the golden wattle; I enclose a sprig. It grows on the farms here, and when in bloom it is a picture; then it has a delicate perfume, and reminds me of the pleasant walks about Derby. There are a few signs of coming summer here, green grass beginning to show in places, peach trees a mass of blossom. In spite of the cold weather and night frosts the oranges have been ripening through the winter, and now we can occasionally buy them at 10 a shilling,

KHAKI LETTERS—*continued*.

and they are very grateful and comforting. This is the only fruit we can buy, and spuds are the only vegetable; coffee and tea are the only liquid refreshments, and khaki the only wear. You even see niggers strutting about rigged out in brand new suits of khaki, field service caps and all, and yet the sick men passing through here by convoy, from the unfortunate 8th Division, to Bloemfontein and home, are in rags, and nearly bootless. I took one lot some papers and cigarettes, and they were glad to get them. As they were on hard biscuit and bully beef, we offered them some grub, only to have it indignantly refused, as implying that they were unable to take care of themselves. As they said, ' Do you think as we are are in a country like this that we don't know how to work it?' and discovered to us a pot-full of a savoury stew of a miscellaneous description. I amuse myself now making crayon portraits of the soldiers to send to their sweethearts, and have had flattering enconiums passed on them by the Commandant and others. I think I shall open an art studio here, and put your photographic efforts in the shade (mim.). I have made several sketches of the scenery (what there is of scenery). . . . I have received a commission, on the strength of my supposed artistic powers, to execute the printing of some notice boards for a local carpenter. . . . I enclose a few lines that I wrote as a small tribute to Frank Robinson's memory. I only wish I could be on the spot where he died, that I might see that everything was done that should be done; but suppose his comrades would well attend to that I have turned a pair of iron wagon pins into passable dumb-bells, and often have a go at them; they weigh about 8 lbs. It keeps me in trim. The weather here is getttng warm again now, . . . and having got down to the weather, I have reached the end of my tether, and in mercy to you I conclude."

NOTE.—Our comrade refers to some lines he has written to the memory of his late office-colleague, F. W. Robinson; these will be found on another page.

No. 28,866, Sapper **W. H. P. Woolley,** writing from No. 11, General Hospital, Kimberley, August 23rd, says:—

"DEAR COLOURS,—No doubt you have heard from one of the others that I have been down with enteric. I have to-day passed the Major Doctor for England, and shall probably leave here on Monday or Tuesday for Capetown, and about a week later I expect I shall be on my way home. Am feeling quite myself again. Thanks for K.L.'s and patriotic programme. Kind regards."

✤ ✤ ✤ ✤

No. 1,275, Sapper **C. J. Woode,** writes from Ottoshoop, August 23rd:—

MY DEAR KEMP,—I have now left Mafeking and we started for Ottoshoop again, the column left the day previous. We were unable to procure necessary transport that day. Our Corporal commandeered the mail coach, a coach that puts you in mind of the pictures one sees of old coaching days in England. It is admired by all troops as a relic of bye-gone days. We left Mafeking about seven in the morning, caught the column up some distance out. As we neared Mafeking we encountered the enemy— some sharp firing occupied our attention for some time. Since that day we have now been occupied with the enemy more or less for the past week. I regret to say we have lost many of our brave men: men from Australia and New Zealand who had been longing for a fight have now had their fill, and

KHAKI LETTERS—*continued.*

their comrades have gone. We came out here with a convoy of foodstuffs, the original idea being to supply Kitchener and Methuen, who were chasing De Wet. These two columns being dependent on us for their food supply, we have been unable at present to reach them, so they are still hungry, as far as we know. Eaton, of Aberdeen, is also with our party, which is in charge of Corpl. Casement, R.E. After the column left I shifted my office to a little farmhouse just under our guns' position. Our Column had to retire from the Zeerust Road, and now are all here and we encounter the enemy on all sides. Lichtenberg, my old place of abode, is now a Boer stronghold, and I think that our next journey will be in that direction. Two days since a party of the enemy cut our lines to Mafeking, and after we were unable to get them for some time, a civilian telegraphist and myself went out to find the breakdown. Our escort caught us up on the road after three quarters of an hours' gallop. We found the break, which I mended under rather peculiar circumstances, for on a ridge a decent distance off was six men. It was dusk, we could not positively say who they were, nor they us. They laid down and watched us, while my escort did the same, each side refraining from giving the first shot. We found out eventually that this party were some of our scouts. I put one wire through, and our party went out and made permanent repair the next day. This part of the Transvaal seems still very unsettled, and I doubt not that unless we give some decisive blow, will linger on for some considerable time yet. I will now close with kind regards to yourself and all old friends. I am well in health and spirits, though shall be quite content to resume even three to eleven, and the comfort of a roof."

✤ ✤ ✤ ✤

No. 2,548, Sapper **W. C. Smith**, writing from 11th General Hospital, Dynamite Sidings, Kimberley, August 25th, says:—

"I am now convalescent, and am getting on first-rate. I have been in here just over three weeks, and needless to say, feel much better for the rest. Am allowed up all day, and as there is a good reading-room in the hospital, and plenty of games as well, time soon passes. . . . On the 27th July, received wire at 10 p.m. to evacuate Barberspan and retire on Lichtenburg, 53 miles away. I was not well at the time, and had been sick for two or three days. As I was the only telegraphist at Barberspan, and only eight other men, there was naturally no doctor there, so had to shift for myself. Well, at midnight we were ready to cut camp and run, as the saying is, I in the meantime having detached my instrument, and climbed the pole and joined the Schweizer-Reneke line to the Lichtenburg line, so that communication would still continue between those offices. Saturday afternoon we reached Biess's Vlei (which is halfway between Barberspan and Lichtenburg), and camped there for the night. We should have started again at midnight, but it was nine o'clock before we shifted, and Sunday night, just after dark, Lichtenburg was reached. We were astonished to see the Boer population turn out to meet us, and it was not until the officer in charge of the hospital enlightened us, that we could fathom it. He told us that the British troops had evacuated Lichtenburg thirty hours before, and they were expecting the Boers in every moment, hence the people turning out to see us come in. They evidently took us for Boers—and we were not unlike them, as we all had slouch hats. Lichtenburg, as you can imagine, was no place for us, so we had to clear out within two hours and retire on Ottoshoop, which we reached the following day, just before dusk. Here we found the troops, and

KHAKI LETTERS—*continued.*

our anxiety was at an end. I lost my blankets and waterpoof on this trip, so have none The Captain had wired several times during the day as to my whereabouts. I was instructed to hire a cart and come into Mafeking, but only stayed at Mafeking a few hours. Was then sent to Kraaipan, as the Boers were threatening the Kaffirs at Kunana, and the telegraph office had to be fitted up. When I was at Lichtenburg the doctor there asked me if I would like to go into hospital, but I said no. So you see I tried to shake it off, but it was no go. . . ."

✢ ✢ ✢ ✢

No. 4,320, Sapper **C. A. Peters** (TSF), writes from Volksrust, August 28th, as under :—

"DEAR COLOURS,—I'm almost ashamed to start writing to you after having been out here so long without doing so. However, it's about time I let you know that your efforts on our behalf are heartily appreciated by all, and by no one more so than myself. I am sending by the same mail two photographs, which I thought would be of interest to you. They were taken by Mr. H. B. Turnbull, an ex-R.E., who has thrown up telegraphy for photography, and I believe he does not regret it, either for financial or other reasons. He was kind enough to suggest that a copy should be sent to you, and presented me with one to forward. I enclose a slip giving the names of those in the Volksrust photo. Of these, Lance-Corporal Laing, and Sappers Peake and Weller went through the siege of Ladysmith, and many are the tales they tell of the hardships they endured whilst there. As for myself, I cannot say that I have seen much 'war,' but have done my share of hard marching, etc., that comes to everybody when on active service. I think you have had Buller's journey up from Ladysmith pretty well described by others who actually saw more than I did. I have been very unfortunate in being left behind all through the piece. Going from Ladysmith to Dundee, after participating in the work during perhaps the hardest and roughest part of the journey, I was drooped at Waschbank, and remained there until the dismantling party returned, and then assisted in pulling down the lines to Elands Laagte. Hard work this, doing long journeys each day in a hot sun. From Elands Laagte the march was resumed to Newcastle, and that occupied some few days. We only stayed there one day, and then were ordered on a column proceeding towards Utrecht, but we did not reach that town, as, after we had crossed the Buffalo, the Natal-Transvaal border, we were ordered to return. I was left at Newcastle when Buller made his final move which compelled the Boers to evacuate Natal, and so missed the heavy fighting which occurred on the border. I remained at that office until the telegraphs were entirely taken over by the Colonial Government in Natal, and then was sent up to Volksrust. The journey up was made in an open truck by rail, and the ride was none too comfortable. To start with we were compelled to crowd into a truck which already was fairly full of niggers and coolies, and anyone who is acquainted with the peculiar odour which comes off their bodies, can appreciate how objectionable it is to be herded with such a crowd. The journey occupied 16 hours, and as night approached it became bitterly cold. We slept on the station platform, and the dew was so heavy our blankets were completely soaked by the morning. There was a sharp frost too, but we are all fairly used now to sleeping in the open, and one gets to know how to take full advantage of the blankets. After a few days at Volksrust, we were sent up to Standerton, but I was again sent back to Volksrust, where I think I am likely to remain until the

KHAKI LETTERS—continued.

end of the war, and to all appearances, some considerable time after. Since I have been here it has been found that the Boers have not entirely left the district, and they are constantly blowing up the railway line, and cutting the telegraph wires, causing great delay and inconvenience. One day last week 200 of them appeared on a low hill only two miles from the town, and could be plainly seen from the windows of this office. They retired, however, without doing any damage, and as they were also making their appearance at short intervals along the railway to the south, it was conjectured that they were looking for a weak spot to interfere with our communications. Sure enough they found one, not far from Newcastle, and they blew up the line in two places. Since then fighting has been going on daily round about this district. They generally come up in parties ranging from 200 to 800 men, and usually attack two or more places simultaneously. . . . This place itself is strongly held, as it is the supply depôt for Buller's force, and indeed, to a large extent, of Roberts'. . . . The 5th Division Ammunition Column met with a serious mishap last Saturday week. A grass fire in the vicinity was the means of one of the tents catching fire, and a high wind blowing at the time, it was not long before everything near was on fire. We heard the shells bursting, the fire not being more than 300 yards away from the office, and the tale quickly spread that the town was being attacked. Owing to the dust, we could not see exactly what had happened, and, of course, gave credence to the yarn, and I thought that at last there would be some fighting. However, we were quickly undeceived, and the wind behaving itself for a little while, we were enabled to watch the shells bursting. It is just possible there may be some fighting close handy in a day or so, as they (the Boers) are hanging round pretty closely. Well, Colours, I must close this yarn now, and get down to a batch from Newcastle. . . . Accept my best thanks for your kindness since we have been out here."

No. 4,671, Sapper **G. Hulatt,** writes from Ventersburg, August 29th, as follows :—

"At Bloemfontein I was having a rattling good time, living like a lord. Towards the latter part of my stay there we had two infantry men to do our cooking. They were married men, and old stagers, and did not require the aid of a cookery book. With their good catering we were served with rice and curry, plum and jam tarts ; oh, lor ! heaps of other trifles, in fact I got so fat I had to let my belt out three holes, now I wish almost I was back again, for I have had to tighten four holes, and am as thin as the dead horses on the plains, only a goodly amount of spirit is still within me. Getting a bit fed up with staying in Bloemfontein, I volunteered to go up country. After a time I heard that the enemy were at Heilbron, and that two clerks were wanted for that place, so I and Billy Braybon were sent up. Our orders were to go to Heilbron, then march with the fighting column on to Frankfort and Reading, and open up those places. We went from Bloemfontein in the middle of the night, on the top of a truck load of telegraph stores. It was very cold, and it was very difficult to make one's self comfortable, but I sat on the edge of the truck with the long legs of mine hanging over the sides, frozen, and wishing I was in a Chatham and Dover third-class, thinking of the little ones at home. Though it was cold I slept like a top till the jerk of the train nearly threw me overboard. At each station we

KHAKI LETTERS—*continued.*

stopped at I saw telegraphists I knew, and at Virginia, Bob Lasham came up smiling and looking very well, with a charming beard. Owing to the enemy being in the vicinity of the railway the authorities would not let us travel north of Kroonstad during the night, so we stayed at Kroonstad for a few hours, then on again, passing through the most desolate country to Wolvehock. Here we were told we had to change for Heilbron, and that as the Boers were down that way, we would have to wait a couple of days for an armoured train. Walking into the telegraph office, to my great surprise, who should I see but Sapper E. P. Neate, looking well and hearty, also Sapper Payne, late of the H. Group; so you see I was landed. Neate and I went for a walk on the Sunday morning. After two days up came the armoured train and escorted us to Heilbron, at which place we saw the Highlanders in their war paint, clothes torn and tattered, faces thin for the want of good food and rest, and black for the want of soap, but on the whole they looked very fit. They had just driven the Boers out of the town and had taken possession. Having reported ourselves to the officer commanding the telegraph section, and handing him the stores, he told us to make ourselves at home in the linesman's camp, which consisted of a cable cart and some other wagons. Looking round for tents was unnecessary, for there were none, so we had a dinner of bully, and settled down to a rough and ready life. Didn't I think of the good things at Bloemfontein! Having nothing to do after tea, we threw down our blankets and slept on the veldt, like only soldiers can. At 5 we were called up to breakfast with the others and sat round the camp fire, shivering and listening to the yarns of how we captured this and stormed that, till the sergeant shouted out for us to get about our business. There was nothing for Billy and I to do, so the sergeant put us to twist wire stays for the poles, and screw on insulators until we were fed up, then we went and had a bath in some muddy water about a mile out. Getting back a good feed of shackles awaited us, but they did not go down well, owing to a heavy dust storm choking everything up. Just as we finished, an order came that we were to pack up and march in fifteen minutes with the Column to Kroonstad. Now this was contrary to the original orders given us at Bloemfontein, so we asked what we should do, and to our surprise, Bill was told to stay and work at Heilbron, and I was to march with the forces. It was hard luck leaving Bill, but as I wanted to have a real military experience I did not weep over it. Starting away at 4, we marched till dark, then camped for the night. Up at 3.30 and off at 4.30, we marched twenty miles. On the way a large number of oxen and mules fell out, and a lot of the men would have done the same, only they did not like to be left behind. Marching with full equipment twenty miles is no joke, and I arrived in camp rather tired and very hungry. The water we had to drink was vile tack, muddy with dead mules in it, but we had to drink it. After tea I was sent with cable cart and tapped the wire. Next day was just the same, though instead of the heat we had a beautiful downfall of rain, as if it had come to wash away the sins of the Boers, and we marched into Kroonstad wet through to the skin. At Kroonstad I was put into the office to work. There were several TS men there and they are comfortable. I spent three days there, then I was ordered to prepare to join Hunter's Column which was going to relieve Col. Ridley, at Ventersburg, who was surrounded by 1,000 Boers. I was the only telegraphist, and as the relief column was entirely a mounted one, I was given a Cape cart and two horses, so I was all kiff, especially there being a chance of seeing fighting. Drawing provisions for the day and packing the cart with

KHAKI LETTERS—continued.

stationery and instruments occupied a short time. I joined the Column, and like a rolling stone was away once more. A Cape cart is a very nice affair on a smooth road, but the roads of S.A. are not made to order, and we bumped and jerked over large stones, down gullies, and through muddy streams, over hills and down dales, stopping at farms to search them, until we camped for the day at Riet Spruit. Whilst the Billy was boiled, I amused myself grooming the horses. After tea I reported myself to the Commandant and he gave me some despatches. The wire being three miles from camp, and outside the outposts, I was escorted by three armed men, who had to act as guards and messengers. Arriving at the wire in the dark, I soon got my machine to work. It was no cop, sending and receiving out on the veldt, with the wind blowing strong and the night bitterly cold. At 2 a.m. I cleared the line and spread out my blankets and went to sleep by the instruments till I got up at 4. Seeing a farmhouse about 300 yards off, I went up and asked if I could get some water and boil it. They didn't mind, so I made a fire in their kitchen, and bought a dozen eggs for 2s., and a pound of butter for 5s., and fairly enjoyed my little self. Disconnecting my instrument at 5.30, I joined the column again, and we marched into Ventersburg. Just my luck; once more we were too late to see some fighting, Bruce Hamilton was there before us. Now I have taken possession of the post office and have joined up. To-night I will sleep under a roof for the first time for a month, but what sleep I will get I don't know, for I am the only clerk, and it is now the giddy hour of midnight, and I am writing this whilst the Col. deliberates. The Boers having trekked south, I expect we will leave this place again to-morrow morning. Now I will get to bed. I am in grand health and am enjoying this life."

No. 4,613, Sapper **W. J. Hargreaves,** writing from No. 5, General Hospital, Woodstock, Capetown, August 29th, says :—

" DEAR COLOUR-SERGEANT,—You will be surprised to have a few lines from me, at the above address, where I arrived last Sunday morning, about 1 a.m., by the Boer ambulance train from Bloemfontein. I shall probably be here for a few weeks yet as a 'convalescent.' Don't know whether they will invalid me home. I don't fancy London fogs in November, when we have the summer coming on. It is just grand now. We are right opposite the sea. I am getting on very nicely, having found two good friends in Staff-Sergeant Capon ('C' Div.), who is acting Sergeant-Major, and Corporal Pickford (brother to our comrade of 'D' Div.). I have got a nice hospital rig-out, and Capon is going to have a snap-shot this afternoon. Kind regards to all. Bill Braybon and the great Arthur were going strong when I left Bloemfontein.

✣ ✣ ✣ ✣

No. 2,555, Sapper **W. J. Sambells,** writing from Vredefort Weg, says :—

" August 7th.—It gets very monotonous here now—no news of how things are going on out here or in China. A Colonial paper is an unknown luxury here, and all the news we get is from home papers. The Station here consists of one stone building (which we occupy), a goods shed opposite, two or three tin huts, and about 600 troops. It's flat country all around us. August 15th.—We are having rather a lively time of it here at present.

KHAKI LETTERS—*continued.*

Small raiding parties of about 200 are continually breaking up the line, but they are getting very much fed up, or, rather, down, with it, as they can get no provisions, and their horses are nearly skeletons. All the farms between here and Kroonstad have been burned to the ground, because they were found to be in league with De Wet and his marauders. I've been for a lovely gallop this morning across the Veldt, on a young Argentine horse. I gave some riding lessons to Bert Pickford on Sunday. He gets on all right, only says it shakes him up like a jelly. We have commandeered a cooking range, which we have built up in the garden, wherein we cook sundry tarts, rice puddings, &c. I shall be quite an adept in the culinary art by the time I reach home, and be able to relieve mother in making pasties. Bert says he is almost worried to death by the 'game' that runs over his carcase. August 29th.—De Wet has come back to the Free State again, and I hope will soon get caught. Then we shall be able to reckon on our return home, or to China, whichever the case may be. Bert and I are running a race as to which weighs the heavier. I beat him at present by three pounds. I go exactly twelve stone, so that is not bad for a thin 'un, eh! We go out riding together nearly every day on our cobs. We still live in first-class style here. Wonder where I shall spend Christmas this year?

Khaki Sidelights and Notes.

Friends have often written expressing a wish that as much as possible might be done for those of our colleagues who have been cut off from amongst us, while on the other hand, our good comrades at the front have frequently mentioned in their letters their willingness and perseverance, amidst the hurry and bustle of their roving lives, to tend, with loving hands, the spot where their fallen fellow-workers are taking their last, long sleep. Several photographs have reached me, and it will perhaps, be consoling to some, and sadly interesting to many, to have, in even this small token, a proof that the lost ones have received considerable attention. Attention all the more remarkable when we consider the circumstances and difficulties which surround them. It is more than lies in the power of my poor pen to describe my feelings when I look upon the original photograph of such handiwork as this, speaking as it does, of such loving kindness and esteem for the departed. I must leave my readers to find their own words of expression. The grave is that of Sapper A. W. Hawkins.

KHAKI SIDELIGHTS—*continued.*

The following poem has arrived from the Front.—Written by ONE OF OURS.

TO FRANK ROBINSON,
Died at Ladysmith, May 23rd, 1900.

NOT in the churchyard where his fathers sleep
    Beneath the cool, green, daisy-spangled mounds,
Where the sad yew's dark shadows o'er them creep,
    And the merle's evensong their requiem sounds;
Soothed in his slumber by no rippling stream,
    His couch unperfumed by the rose's breath;
And yet he sleeps—a sleep that knows no dreams—
    His lips sealed by the icy kiss of Death.

Upon that once warm heart the cold stones rest,
    Grey, rugged boulders, jealous of their prey,
Amongst whose crevices the lizards nest
    Like the quick thoughts that animate the clay.
And the cicada's loud, shrill monotone
    Sounds like the heart-throb with deep anguish wrung;
And yon dark shade that falls and then is gone,
    Is from the Aasvogel's unclean pinion flung.

Yet mourn not thou for his untimely end,
    And deem not his is a dishonoured grave;
The axe will on the goodliest tree descend,
    And sacred is the soil that tombs the brave.
And if to suffer and be strong is well,
    And if 'tis noble to do thine essay;
We should be glad the tree bore fruit and fell,
    And lingered not in barren-souled decay.

And yet the strain of joy will not arise.
    While stilled for ever is that generous heart;
And griefs outpourings spend themselves in sighs,
    Quelled by the thought—he bore a hero's part.
But gladness and regret go mingling by,
    The river sweet, the ocean's bitter flow;
And from their conflict there ascends a cry,
    Half a triumph song and half a chant of woe.

Adieu! dear comrade, fain would friendship save
    Thy memory from Time's constant tidal bore;
Fame's setting glory crimsons Life's dull wave,
    Ere it is dashed upon the eternal shore.
Still there's remembrance in the silent deep,
    Naught is forgotten in its secret hoard;
And I must leave thy soul to it to keep.
    Until its hidden treasures be restored.

THABANCHU, 1900.
                                      R. W. EGLINTON (of Derby).
                                                  24th Mx. R.V.C.

KHAKI SIDELIGHTS—*continued.*

W. * O. * HYETT.

THE Central Telegraph Office has many representatives at the front besides those belonging to the R.E. Reserve of the 24th Middlesex R.V.C. There are some who, as ex-R.E.'s. have joined their units, Reservists with their regiments, enthusiasts with the Imperial Yeomanry, City Imperial Volunteers, R.A.M.C., Electrical Engineers, etc., and we are glad to record the fact that the casualties have been comparatively few.

T. S. F. has lost another member of its staff at the front, in W. O. Hyett, the eldest son of our respected Assistant Superintendent. Although the death occurred as far back as June 12th, no information could be obtained until Sept. 11th, when a reply to a telegram of enquiry was received from Capetown, confirming a rumour which had kept his parents in the greatest suspense for weeks past. The entire staff sympathise with them, and mourn the loss of a good colleague.

William Osmund Hyett was born Sept. 17th, 1881, entered TS from the Telegraph School, on the 12th March, 1898, being attached to the "B" Division. From the "B" he was transferred to the "E," where he remained until Dec. 11th, 1899, when he was removed to TSF, and became a member of the Cable Room Staff. He was a Lance-Corporal in the 1st Vol. Battn. Essex Regt. (Romford Company), and when the call for Volunteers was made, he was one of the first to respond, being enrolled in the Volunteer Service Company of the 1st Essex Regt. He left TSF for Warley Barracks on January 18th, 1900, and sailed for South Africa in the "Nineveh," from Tilbury Docks, on March 1st. He went to the front immediately with his regiment, and was with Lord Roberts in the historical march to Pretoria, but was taken ill and went into hospital at Johannesburg, where he succumbed to the fell disease—dysentery—on June 12th.

His last letter to his parents, written from Kroonstad, on May 21st, gave no indication of anything being amiss. It ran as follows :—

"DEAR MOTHER AND FATHER.—You can see we are now well on our way to Pretoria. We reached here last night, having done a forced march with a convoy from Virginia, on the Zand River. It took us a day-and-a-half to get here, a distance of about 40 odd miles. We stood it well, and had only one case of falling out, but the fellow is now alright. The regiment is here, and I got some more letters, also a tin of tobacco from you, for which I am very glad, as it is a change from the hard tobacco. The regiment is expected to leave here on their way to Pretoria, so you

KHAKI SIDELIGHTS—*continued.*

must not expect another letter for some time. I am in fine health and spirits, and feel O.K. The advance on Pretoria was delayed till now, because of the scarcity of food, but this is now being rectified, as convoys are arriving, and the railway is being rapidly repaired. The railway, as we came along, was a pretty sight—bridges blown up, rails torn up and bent all shapes. At the Zand River bridge, where the railway at present ends, men are working day and night, and when we started at night it looked a pretty sight, as they work by electric lights, which show up grandly. I don't think the war will last much longer; this place where they expected a great battle was taken without opposition. The other night, when we got out of the train, I went to have a warm by a fire. and sat amongst some Boer prisoners; they were fine strong men, and no wonder we had a strong resistance. I see some more Volunteers are coming out, but I do not think they will be wanted. Your accounts of grub makes my mouth water, but I will show you how to eat when I come home. I am glad to hear you are all well at home."

✠ IN MEMORIAM. ✠

When the Empire was ringing with war's alarms—
   When the national honour and power were at stake—
You sprang with the sons of the Empire to arms,
   To live or to die for England's sake!
With comrades who met from the ends of the world,
   As true to their blood as our heroes of old,
In defence of the flag that shall never be furled,
   Your name—which you sealed with your life—you enrolled.

And England, so long as her history runs,
   Shall forget not the deeds of her fallen sons:
And the grief of their kin shall be tempered with pride.
May the living, whose tears for your dear sake are shed,
   As you sleep with the bravest and best of our dead,
Find a solace in this—that for England you died!

C.T.O.   W. H. F. WEBB.

Rudd Fund.—We are now able to fill in the omissions in our last issue, and, happily, add more subs., as follows:—"B" Div., £3 12s.: Stock Ex., £2 1s. 6d.; Dely and Ctr., 10s. 6d.; Profits from sale of photo., 13s. 6d.; Mrs. Brooks, 3s.; Sapper A. J. Brooks (at the front). 10s.; J.H.N., per Khaki Letters, 3s. Total, £7 13s. 6d. This, with the amount mentioned on page 327—£77 16s. 11d., making a grand total of £85 10s. 5d. We thank all concerned for their generous gifts; such practical sympathy speaks louder than words. There is an old saying, "Pity without relief is like mustard without beef." Here we have the two sweetly blended, and although the fund is now closed, any further subs. will not be refused, nor will they be less heartily appreciated.

⇥ Khaki Notes. ⇤

Khaki Postage Fund.—I beg to acknowledge with many thanks, the receipt of the following sums:—News Div., 7s.; G Div., 3s. 6d.; W. G., 2s.; Mrs. J. B., 2s.; Miss A. S., 3d. There are many divisions, groups, and sections who have promised assistance in this matter, but I am as yet unable to record their contribs., owing to the non-receipt of their subs. As we are now MQ for four weeks, I hope to see all the missing links come in during the interval.

A Friend at St. Austell (Cornwall) informs me that some photographic negatives have been received. She cannot, however, say who sent them, but believes it is the same person who so kindly redirected my Christmas card to her some months back. In reply to further inquiries she says, "I gave the photographer a small sealed tin, he developed them so far, and charged 2s. 6d.; he still holds the negatives. I should be very glad indeed to find the person to whom they really belong." I have the untoned prints—nine in number—they are useless

KHAKI NOTES—*continued.*

in their present state, as exposure to light has greatly affected them. A scrap of paper headed, Lt. Legard, 17th Lancers, gives the title of the pictures, and amongst them is "10th Hussars at Frankfort," "R.H.A. in action," "My Horse," and "Me." If any K.L. reader can inform me who "Me" is, and who the Kodak negs. are intended for, my Cornish correspondent will be pleased to put the photos. in the possession of the rightful recipient.—KQ.

P.S.A.—Pleasant Sunday afternoons are passed in various ways. A C.T.O. gentleman and his wife were sitting on a seat on a suburban common just recently. Two young ladies appeared and shared the same shaded spot; one opened a novel and commenced reading, and to the C.T.O.G.'s surprise, the other dived into K.L.s for an hour. But why "surprise?" Do we not hear from all sides that it is most interesting? Another C.T.O. gent., unconsciously exhibiting his current number of K.L. at the house of a friend, was greeted with a startled question, "Oh! do *you* take that in?" "Yes, do you?" "No, but in a packet of magazines purchased from a second-hand bookseller I found several numbers, and enjoyed them very much." Who is the person that makes money by selling K.L.s? Not "Colours," certainly.

Re Photo. on page 326. My Liverpool correspondent writes:—"Reading from right to left, please note names are W. H. Turnbull and F. Robinson, both of Liverpool. Perhaps you will like to know this."—Certainly, and it is "noted" with thanks and a reciprocation of your good wishes.

Comrades at the front, as well as those at home, will be pleased to hear that the efforts made on behalf of the widow of our late Sergeant, Jummy Lankstead, have this week been rewarded by the appearance of a little bit of blue in the leadened sky. We hope she may bask in the silver lining ere long, thanks to those influential gentlemen who have so readily lent their aid.

The following telegram is worthy of note:—"Johannesburg, Sept. 21st. The last issue of the "Potchefstroom Budget" contains details of the relief of the town by Lord Methuen on July 30th. The paper says that the Boer commandant sent an emissary with a flag of truce to Gen. Smith-Dorrien demanding instant surrender. Under cover of the white flag the Boers pushed their attacking line to within 200 yards. The British outposts commenced a heavy fire before the emissary had time to explain his mission. The "Budget" also reports that two British telegraphists who were sent out to repair the wire though unarmed, and making no resistance, were shot in cold blood at such close range that the clothing of one was singed, and in the second case the coat seams were blown out. "Who were the telegraphists?"

We are very grieved to notice that it has been necessary to solicit assistance for our old colleague, Bob Catherall, who is described as "without employment and practically destitute." The petition to the P.M.G. on his behalf has failed, but it is hoped the Staff will respond in their usual generous manner.

Cricket at the front. Standerton, 50 and 56—106. R.E.'s, 6 and 40 (for 5 wkts.) 46. Townsend, 0; Sinclair, 2; did not bat in 2nd innings.

B.Q.'s.—W.G.T. (Bloemfontein). The splendid photograph of the BFN staff has just come to hand and will be much valued. Thank you. Sorry letter too late for present issue.—F.R.W. (Kroonstad). Your photograph to hand same time as W.G.T.'s, Oct. 1st. Kindly thank the Staff for me.—H.G. (Edinboro'). Thank you. Most interesting. Regret too late for this number. Book made up before it arrived.—C.J.M. Thanks for paper.

"Poniard, London," for telegrams from Our Boys to their relatives and friends at home, the addresses of whom should be sent us at once.

"Casualties, Capetown," for enquiries *re* sick and wounded.

COLOURS.

"KHAKI LETTERS," One Penny. By post, Three Halfpence.

All posted letters containing Remittances, Orders, MSS., &c., must be addressed to R. E. KEMP, 12, JERRARD STREET, LEWISHAM, S.E.
Postal Orders should be made payable at Loampit Vale, Lewisham, S.E.

Printed by E. G. BERRYMAN & SONS, *Blackheath Road, London, S.E.*

"Khaki Letters" from ....
"My Colleagues in South Africa."

CORRESPONDENCE FROM THE
POST OFFICE TELEGRAPHISTS
OF THE
24th MIDDLESEX (P.O.) RIFLE VOLUNTEERS
(Royal Engineer Reserves),
ON ACTIVE SERVICE.

THE BOND THAT BINDS US—FRIENDSHIP—COMRADESHIP.

Published monthly (formerly fortnightly) for the Postal Telegraph Service.
Conducted by COLOUR-SERGEANT R. E. KEMP, *Central Telegraph Office, London.*

No. 19.   NOVEMBER 2ND, 1900.   PRICE ONE PENNY.

Central Telegraph Office,
London, E.C.

DEAR COMRADES, ONE AND ALL.

Greetings! Here we are at the end of the Volunteer Year and by the time this is in print we shall have embarked on another. I can look back upon twenty-two years of quiet, consistent service in the Old Corps, and can say, I have tried to uphold its name, but I cannot claim to having assisted in winning for it honours—great honours—such as you who are serving in South Africa have done, a fact and a feature of which one may well be proud, we of you, and you of ourselves. We have, unfortunately, a few non-efficients, who by their neglect tend to cool others, however enthusiastic and zealous they may be.

The new duties are still on, although counted very much "off" by the big majority. The fortnightly night duty is much disliked by most of those who have tasted it, although there are a few who profess to like it. It's the new broom with them, the novelty has not yet gone. The 6 a.m. to 2 p.m. is a terror to all but a very small number, while the 12 midnight Saturday turn breaks the heart of all. These are the verdicts of men who have performed them. The Night Staff supts. and the Night Staff check continue on their old fashion duties and——But let me tell you something else. Doubtless every one of you will get hold of newspapers by hook or by crook, and read the columns upon columns descriptive of the C.I.V.'s Home-coming, their welcome, etc., but you may not see a word in them concerning your own Corps or its doings. I will attempt to supply it. Let us head it "Personal Narrative." On Saturday, October 27th, I was up very early in order to don my war paint, and arrived on duty at 8 a.m., when I learned that the "Aurania" had not yet been sighted, and the first degree of depression was registered on the "Spiritometer." Conflicting rumours came round until news arrived that she had passed Prawle Point, and rumours stood aside and calculations took their place. Knots, nautical miles, h.p., tonnage, canvas, steam, varied with imperfect geographical knowledge (and a call for maps), timing speed, pilots, &c., &c., were discussed. Eventually we were set at rest, the official information arrived postponing the procession until Monday. The 24th assembled on the Embankment near Blackfriars Bridge at 12.45 p.m. and were soon afterwards dismissed. Monday, October 29th. Up at 4.30 a.m., on duty at 7, and off just in time to parade at 12.45 as before. The crowds had already put in an appearance, and journeying down

Newgate Street, Old Bailey, I found Ludgate Hill well kept. The police stood in the gutters, and no person was off the sidewalks. But wait. This was at 12.40. At 12.45 we fell in, some 350 strong, and remained at the brigade rendezvous until 1.45 p.m. No one knew where we were to be stationed. We marched along Queen Victoria Street, and into Queen Street. Here we had many stoppages and enliveners in the way of ticklers, trumpets and flattering (?) remarks. Turning into Cheapside we found the L.R.B. and police severely pressed, and at their invitation "Come on, Post Office" we gave them and the mob a friendly push, widening the "lane" an inch or two, so densely were the people packed. Along Cheapside in fairly good order until we arrived at the G.P.O. end, where eight of H.M.'s Life Guards stood. They were very restive; while one reared high in the air and endeavoured to bless us by the laying on of hoofs, another backed into us and let out with his left rear, and formation was no more. Re-assembling in St. Paul's Churchyard, we moved into Ludgate Hill where we were from the first helplessly blocked and at the mercy of the crowd. Whether we were ordered to "halt" or not, I cannot say. All I know is, we couldn't move. We opened out and tried to help one or two police whom we found there. The crowd was swelling from every side street. This was the street that two hours previous was so well kept, and orderly. Had we been brought over then, things would have been different. Our united efforts were of no avail. Placing our rifles butt to butt on the ground with our comrades opposite, pushing against each other we forced the people back a little. The immense crowd easily overcame us when they tried, and we were, as it were, kissing the rank opposite, crushed into utter helplessness. The rifles were now apparent as a nuisance and a danger, for they got entangled in our legs, while our great coats, rolled and strapped to our backs, formed a lever for pressing us down. The faces of the men were stern, serious and determined; those of the women tearful, beseeching and sad. I heard many imploring voices, many cries of dispair, and not a few pleaded for God's sake to be allowed to get out. There seemed no cessation of the pressure. To extricate oneself seemed an impossibility. A lady near was ill and looked terror-stricken too. She asked a constable to help her to get to a hospital. He tried and failed to move, your humble assisted, and by coaxing, persuading and loudly giving a reason for our retirement, I, with her, arrived at an outlet, having taken about twenty-five minutes from Wild's Hotel to Straker's corner—a distance of 40 or 50 yards. The idea of returning was futile, and had to be abandoned. So after parading twice, going to a lot of trouble, getting a good hustling and a Turkish bath in the bargain, I saw not the returning C.I.V.'s. The consolation I have is that I did one person a good turn. and on arrival home immediately sent my belt to the saddler's to be repaired, for the crowd had wrenched the braces and buckles asunder. I hear to-day that three of our men were injured about the feet, but cannot say to what extent. All the newspapers cry out to-day about the "Confusion" and "Muddle" and some call for an investigation. The Queen's Jubilee crowd was nothing to it, nor was there ever such a big one before. The C.I.V.'s had to fight their way through by one's and two's and were three hours late at the banquet.

Referring to the casualties, the *Globe* this evening (October 30th), says :—" The great event of the day was, unfortunately, not free from those accidents incidental to the assemblage of dense masses of people in limited areas. An alarming incident happened at Ludgate Circus about an hour before the procession passed. A mail van, upon the roof of which a dozen men had mounted, was overthrown by the pressure of the crowd, and in the panic, men, women, and children were knocked down and trampled upon, and no fewer than 61 surgical and medical cases were treated at St. Bartholomews Hospital. St. Mary's, Charing Cross and King's College Hospitals, also treated cases of accident during the procession. Sad to relate, two fatal cases have to be recorded among the day's casualties. At about half-past three two men were brought to St. Bartholomew's Hospital dead. They had fallen from a scaffolding at Salisbury house, Finsbury Circus. The St. John Ambulance Association were kept busy all along the route, and their record (professedly an imperfect one) shows over 1,600 cases treated at the 28 stations. At the three stations in the Strand 197 cases were treated; at Bouverie Street and Ludgate Circus over 100 cases, seven of which were very serious; at the Marble Arch, 40; at Trafalgar Square, 36; at Hyde Park Corner, 41; at Wood Street, 86; and at Lothbury, 115. The total number treated is considered to be probably nearer 3,000.

Hoping this number will prove interesting and that all are thoroughly well,
Yours most heartily,

To the "L" Co. in South Africa,   R. E. KEMP,
Tuesday, October 30th, 1900.   *Colour-Sergeant.*

COPYRIGHT.—" Khaki Letters" must not be used without permission.—R. E. KEMP.

Khaki Letters.

No. 4,333, Sapper **A. W. York** (2nd Tel. Div., R.E.'s), writing from Waterval Onder Station, September 1st, says:—

" DEAR KEMP,—We had nearly a month at Middleburg, which was a decent sort of place, and lived in a tent amongst the trees—park, I suppose, they called it—at the back of the P.O.; the only luxuries we could buy being sausages and rice. The latter is easily cooked, and goes down very well with bully and biscuits, fresh meat not being so plentiful this journey. We passed our time in bathing and bicycling (the inhabitants were ordered to give them in temporarily), and enjoyed listening to the band every evening, a treat supplied by the Guards. There was a tiny English church, too, where we had the pleasure of hearing Canon Knox Little, who gets on splendidly with the soldiers. Welcome orders to trek came on August 24th, and we did the first part by rail, getting out at Wonderfontein and marching into Belfast with the Guards, preceded by French. I had the luck to get on the cable cart again, and have been with that section since. We were first at the station, and started work on the buzzer at 1.30, the shelling continuing briskly meanwhile, and lasting the afternoon and all next day. The main body of Boers, under Botha, were making a stand on the Sunday, and we ran the cable out about four miles for General Pole-Carew. French was on the north and Buller south, so they had to fight, and a hot day it was, too, artillery and rifle firing lasting all day. We watched it from the hollow at the back of the Monument (the highest point in the Transvaal), and only one shell came our way, bursting with a terriffic roar, though several spent bullets buried themselves angrily close by. The enemy had a Long Tom, which our two 5-inch siege guns could not silence, and we expected a peppering when we moved off on the 27th, but found they had cleared off in great haste during the night. There was a notable group at Belfast on the morning before the fight at Monument Hill--Roberts, Buller, French, and Pole-Carew having a confab, but the Commander-in-Chief was not present during action. We rigged up a telephone for General Pole-Carew to confer with Lord Roberts on the 27th, and the former was very affable in my 'Tent d'Aubri.' The wind was very bleak in these high altitudes, and blew the dust about unpleasantly, making the troops soon assume a grimy hue. We meant to get to Waterval Onder on the 29th, but got stuck in a drift, and opened office, after running 10 miles of cable at Middlepunt. Up at 3.30 next morning, and had another block at a mountain top, the Boers having blown up the road, and turned a stream into it ; so we had to descend a preci-

KHAKI LETTERS—*continued*.

pice by a very rough road, strewn with boulders, over some of which the cable cart had narrow escapes from capsizing. The result was we camped at Helvetia, Buller being a few miles ahead, and French on the right. Most of Pole-Carew's troops did not turn up till next morning, so we did not get to Waterval Onder till noon, and halted on top of the mountain, overlooking the town. I should have said our cable was for the 11th Division, Buller having an air-line party with him, and French another cable section. There was a conference with the Commander-in-Chief at Waterval Bover this morning, and we (11th Division) are to keep with Buller; but the cavalry is to go to Barberton, and will be replaced later on by Hamilton's column, which will escort our convoy while we push on to Lydenburg. The country here is frightfully mountainous, not merely kopjes, and Roberts compares it with Afghanistan. The Captain walked into the town this afternoon, and I followed with an instrument, teeing on to the railway line, and am now comfortably ensconced in the station office. We got some stores close by, and there was plenty of butter, milk, and tinned-stuff to be found; so am in the lap of luxury just at present. The cable cart comes on to-morrow, and we expect to be here a few days more. Kind regards to all."

No. 4,670, Sapper **W. E. Braybon,** writing from Gottenberg Halt September 3rd, says :—

"DEAR KEMP,—You will see by the above I have had a big forward move. I was ordered to proceed, in company with G. Hulatt and Tim (a lineman), with a truck-load of batteries, drums of field cable and air-lines, poles, &c., and sufficient stamps to open up three offices. We were bound for General Hunter's force. I was on duty at 7 a.m., and released at 10 a.m., and we had to be on the truck in Bloemfontein siding at 12 midnight—extra duty without pay ! Well, we were there, and waited until 1.30 a.m., when the R.S.O. informed us no trucks allowed to-night. We were in bed (?) at 2.30 a.m. The next night we were on the truck at midnight, and started at 3.30 a.m. It was a frosty night, and the lumps in bed (?) were very hard; so we were glad when day dawned and the sun thawed us. By cadging a drop of hot water from the waste-pipe of an engine, we managed to get coffee and tea once or twice, and at Kroonstad we bivouacked by the side of the truck and line. We stayed here, as no trains were allowed to travel at night further north. As we got further on, all were on the *qui vive* for Boers, and the helio was used between stations. We passed the remains of three trains. The engines, tenders, and carriages were complete skeletons, nothing but the wheels and iron framework remaining. The Boers had done their work of destruction very thoroughly. Roodeval, the scene of the 4th Derbys' disaster, was very impressive. Imagine a sandy plain, and in the distance a small elevated piece of ground, which could not be called a kopje, as it is too insignificant for that. The pitch where the Derbys were was a nice one for Volunteers out camping; now it is a cross between a dustyard and an old iron and rag yard; the earth torn up by shells—two of which we had brought in took two Kaffirs to lift—a mercy they did not explode. Here, still, were blood-stained tunics, fragments of shells, cartridge cases, &c. I picked a piece of shell from one blood-stained tunic which told its own tale. At Wolvehoek we were stuck for two days, and went on to Heilbron with the armoured train, near which place the Highland Brigade dealt with Mr. Olivier, and 40 wounded were brought in. We were attached to No. 7 Company of the R.E.'s, and very nice comrades we found them.

KHAKI LETTERS—*continued.*

Here we parted, Hulatt and Tim going with the H.L.I. and Black Watch, and I was kept at Heilbron with the Seaforths. The field work was more interesting than office work. We were engaged cutting poles, fixing insulators, and making double and single stays, &c. My next move was to the above place, which consists of three farms and a few kraals. I had to fix a buzzer and open up communication between Wolvehoek and Heilbron. Our only excitement is, perhaps, a train a day and the Boers sniping. Last Sunday, 60 of them rode clean between the camps (450 men all told), and as they were in full khaki they got clean away. (A small ejaculation here, please !) The Boers are all round Heilbron again. My pal (one of the Seaforths) and myself are 1½ miles from camp, close to the railway, in a small Kaffir hut. The instruments are on a sleeper, across two sacks of mealies, and another sleeper ditto does for a seat. In the cottage there is joy(?) We have a decent supply of bully-beef and biscuits, coffee and tea. What more does one require? Bread, butter, and fresh meat are luxuries. Do not try and persuade yourself the war is over, and ' Tommy ' is now having a picnic. Such ideas are an absolute frost. Well, thanks, Sir, I am dry."

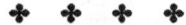

No. 4,327, Sapper **A. J. Brooks,** writing from Kromellenboog Spruit, O.R.C., September 5th, says :—

" The *People* is borrowed all over the camp. I get 'em pretty regularly now, thanks. The guards bring them up from Vredefort Road, and pitch them out here. The 'fags,' when they turn up, must be very carefully kept out of reach of the other fellows in camp, or I shall certainly lose the lot. The infantrymen here are often reduced to Boer tobacco, made into cigarettes with newspaper. Every day I am asked, ''Ave I got an old bit of " *Lide's* " to spare to make a fag with?' That's what my *Lloyd's* and *People* come to. They are usually returned minus the margins and odd bits of the advertisement pages. You won't find this place marked on any map, but it's nine miles south of Wolvehoek (Heilbron Road), and six miles north of Vredefort Weg. Kromellenboog Spruit is its name, and it combines the spruit business with a bog branch. Now the wet (De Wet) season is coming on, the bog (boog) part is becoming unpleasant. The trenches are flooded, and, without exaggeration, in some parts (where, a few weeks ago, men were bivouacking) one can now swim comfortably. Fortunately, tents were sent up from Kroonstad last week, so that we are all ' kiff.' In the evening the men sit round their little fires and talk about De Wet, and going home, and spin fearful yarns about one thing and another. Then, about 7.30, they retire, and get between the blankets, and sing all the choruses they can think of—not over loud, because, of course, there'd be a bother if a noise is made. They usually start off with ' Sweet Rosy O'Grady.' After each chorus they always chant

Tra-la-la-lum (doh-me-soh-lah),

and, what with the choruses of ' Rosy O'Grady,' ' Strolling Round the Town, ' Jerusalem,' ' Beer, Glorious Beer,' ' The Holy City,' ' Break the News to Mother,' and about half Sankey and Moody following each other in quick succession, with only that ' Tra-la-la-lum ' in between, a very funny effect is produced. When they at last fall off to sleep, the chorus is taken up by the bull-frogs, who are here in their thousands since we have had a bit of rain. At one time our spruit was merely a succession of water-holes—drinking water, washing pool, and a pool wherein nearly a dozen oxen have met their

KHAKI SIDELIGHTS—*continued*.

fate, and now lay half buried in the mud, were all quite separate. Now, however, the spruit is one and indivisible, the 'beef extract' pool has amalgamated with the drinking-water pool, and, although the result is much better from a landscapic point of view, it doesn't improve the flavour. One thing, we in the telegraph tent do our own cooking, &c. We are not treated to frog broth, like the other fellows. The water is so muddy and thick that any number of giddy young frogs get bailed up in the camp kettles, and every dinner and tea time there's always the same old complaint, 'Hi! I'm going to see him (the poor cook) about this. *Two* frogs this time; I thought *one* was bad enough at dinner-time, but two in one pint of tea is a trifle thick. We are getting rations fairly regularly now, but until recently we were living very badly, owing to our supplies getting overcarried. No one seemed to know the place at all, but the men had their own name for it— 'Hot-water Camp.' This was because a certain captain, when complaint was made that two-and-a-half biscuits a day, helped down with muddy water, was not enough for a man to live on, replied, 'Well, whadderyermean—you get your water boiled, don't you?' A man (an Irishman, of course) yesterday complained to the commandant that 'the quantity of *tea* served out for the whole trench was not enough to make *coffee* for half-a-dozen men!' Such a lot of our supplies have to be set aside for the benefit of the Boers in the neighbourhood. Besides the widows and orphans, there are a lot of farmers, who, having returned to their farms and taken the oath, find everything gone, and starvation staring them in the face. These people, of course, have to be rationed. De Wet is still knocking about in this neighbourhood. We see either his or Theron's patrols every day, and frequently we are prevented from fetching water until the coast is a bit clear. However, everyone here wishes that the Boers would pay us a visit. Although only about 250 strong, we are so well entrenched, and the surrounding country is so bare and flat, that no commando, however strong, would venture near enough for a bit of fun, so we hope in vain. The nearest kopje (coppee-jee, Tommy calls it) is some miles away—too far away for effective artillery fire. In order to do something to lessen the marvellous mobility of De Wet's force, all the Cape carts, horses, mules, and dogs within twelve miles of each side of the line are being brought into camp by the mounted infantry. The camp will soon be like the Dogs' Home at this rate. The South African dog is a coughdrop. You've only got to whistle to him, and round his tail goes like 40 Indian clubs—pleased isn't the word for his state of feelings. All the dogs are alike. No matter what breed they may be, they are as chummy as can be. The dogs are being brought in because it is found that whenever our mounted men go to surround a farm where it is known that a Boer patrol is visiting, the dogs give timely warning, and enable the enemy to skip off. The Cape carts are taken because otherwise they would be commandeered by De Wet, who finds them very useful. The mules and horses, of course, are brought in owing to De Wet's habit of changing 'old lamps for new.' Apart from this, the mules have a bad habit of straying about, and making themselves a general nuisance. On a dark night, a mule suddenly looms up in front of a sentry, who, after challenging and getting no response, fires. The camp is alarmed, and everybody turned out whilst investigations are made. Oh, the language! The last sentry who shot a mule was fined ¾d. (three farthings) for wasting a round of ammunition. I've learnt a thing or two about grumbling since I've been out here, but I think I shall make a rush for a civilised dinner (even a TS one) when I get back. We get served out with bread (local manufacture) so

KHAKI LETTERS—*continued.*

'sad' and heavy that it is a wonder it doesn't die with a broken heart. The meat is plentiful, and (for trek ox) fairly good, but not a solitary scrap of fat can be found. This lack of fat, considering that we cook our own dinner, is a bit of a difficulty, as we have nothing wherein we could boil it or bake it, and only an old frying-pan for frying purposes ; so it's fried meat and bread every day, and not cooked according to Mrs. Beeton. Bread and jam for breakfast and tea is also feeding up week after week. The other week our 'office' was blown right away. I was sitting at the instrument, when down the pole came, knocking instrument and biscuit-box table all over the place. The tent itself soon tore loose from the guy ropes, and went sailing away in shreds. We rigged up a blanket shelter, and wired for a fresh 'office,' which came up from Kroonstad next day. The 'new' tent is as leaky as a Turkish man-o'-war, and as it *rains* when it rains out here, we have a moist time. I had a letter from Bert the other week. He was at Warrenton, and going on OK. My other brother, Arthur, was last heard of with his regiment when they were near the Rhenoster, under Kitchener, about a month ago. It's very sad losing poor old Alf. Rudd; he was such a genial chap. Pickford and Sambells are at Vredefort Weg, Plumridge and Marshall at Rhenoster (kopjes), Payne (H. Gp.) and Neate at Wolvehoek, Harry Barber at Heilbron (evacuated again now, though, I think), and Braybon at Gottenburg Holt, midway between Wolvehoek and Heilbron. That's a list (not quite complete) of residents in our neighbourhood. Last night we got information that a Boer advance party would cross the railway from west to east, just south of us, as soon as they could. At 11 p.m., therefore (a few minutes after we got our news), a party of 24 men and 2 officers, in very light order—nothing but rifles and ammunition— 'sallied forth' to see what they could do. They went two miles down the line, and then laid in wait in a spruit. A similar party was sent out from Vredefort Weg, and they also came two miles down the line, so that the distance between here and Vredefort Weg being only six miles, it looked a close thing if the Boers should attempt to cross. They waited there until dawn and then returned, having seen nothing, but reported seven heavy explosions, which we in camp had also heard, and which were caused by the blowing up of the railway line by the Boers just below Rhenoster. We were congratulating ourselves upon having frustrated Mr. Boer in his intention to go east, when natives came in with a report—which was afterwards verified—that 65 Boers, with several mule wagons, crossed the line 15 minutes before our party arrived on the scene. This morning, a Boer from Theron's laager stopped at a Kaffir's hut near here, and asked for a drink of water. The Kaffir went to get it, but first asked the Boer to dismount, as he was afraid the English patrols would see him. The Boer accordingly got off his horse, and was immediately seized from behind by two other Kaffirs, who disarmed him, and drove him into Wolvehoek Camp. Very smart dodge for the Kaffirs. I don't know whether I told you about the Gilbert and Sullivanesque 'attack' on Wolvehoek some weeks ago. A commando suddenly appeared, and, surrounding the camp, sent a man in under the white flag, demanding instant surrender. The bearer of the message shook hands with the sentry, and asked to see the 'officier.' A major of the Royal Irish Rifles was commanding, and the Boer, on being introduced, addressed him as 'Your Royal Highness.' He handed the Major a note signed 'Viljoen,' demanding surrender and allowing ten minutes in which to get the non-combatants away. The 'non-combatants,' however, refused to go, she preferred to stop in the station with her husband who was station-

KHAKI LETTERS—*continued.*

master. The Boer went back with the sad news that the garrison would not surrender. The valorous commando fired a few shots, the garrison did likewise, and the siege terminated. Wolvehoek reported that the enemy retired in our direction, but beyond an exchange of rifle shots between their scouts and our Mounted Infantry, we heard nothing of them. When we return, I'm afraid we shall be an uncouth lot of savages though. We shall regard you as the Chinese do, as a race of very peculiar people ' who have to wash themselves frequently.' Have just received a letter from Bill Carter who is at Heidelberg, he tells me that Samuels is at Standerton. Local newspapers and postage stamps are *non est*, relics of an effete civilization.

✢ ✢ ✢ ✢

No. 24,305, Sapper **F. T. Stimpson,** writing on September 5th, from Taaibosch Kopje, says :—

"I am in excellent health but fairly fed up with it, but I don't like the idea of returning to TS after this fresh air. Sorry I was not able to get back about the middle of August, so as to have a good summer furlough, and I sadly wanted to see the Paris Exhibition, but my only wish now is that I may get back by Christmas, which I really think will come off. They are going at it hammer and tongs in the Lydenburg district, and I think it is Bob's idea to finish it off as quickly as possible, as the rainy season is with us next month, and malarial fever will be very prevalent in that district. Lasham is at Smaldeel, and the only Ben at Kroonstad—have not seen him since I left Bloemfontein."

✢ ✢ ✢ ✢

No. 4,312, Sapper **W. M. Sinclair,** writing from Pretoria, September 9th, says :—

"Four of us came up here from Standerton about a fortnight ago—one 18th Hussars, one Irish Fusilier, Samuels and self. Sammy and Minors are still at Standerton. I was very lucky in capturing a few hundred cigarettes and a dozen or so boxes of tobacco, which had been accumulating for me at Bloemfontein and which Whibley had brought on here with him. We found him here in addition to O'Hooligan Quinn, both on staff billets in Clearing House, but Samuels and I are the only 24th men doing duty at PR, with the exception of Jack Hall, who takes charge conjointly with the civilians. I found several old pals amongst the civilian staff here, amongst whom were Jim Carr from NT, Shearman TS, and Harrison and Johnston DN. They are all very smart at dots and dashes. They have been given a start under us at £250. I also found an old MR man here named Jack Griffiths. Pretoria is a very pretty town, something after the style of Buxton, and of course there is no lack of interesting places round about. We had a very pleasant journey up in an open truck—leaving Standerton at 2 p.m. and arriving here at 8 a.m.—slept like a top from about 9 till 6, tucked up with my 18th Hussars Corporal pal. The latter was very sorry to leave PR, as he was smarting under a crushing defeat at billiards administered to him by yours truly. I forgot to mention that Hann, an old newsite, is also amongst the civilians employed here. I initiated Samuels into the mysteries of golf the other morning at the Cricket Grounds, and we have a game at cricket opposite our bungalow occasionally. Although the work is heavy it is done in a very free and easy style, smoking being allowed at all hours with occasional bursts of harmony. One of the civilian bosses led off the other night with 'Why did I leave my little back room,' and was well supported. Haven't heard anything of Mack

KHAKI LETTERS—*continued*.

for a long time. He started with Buller from Paardekop, trekking towards Ermelo and Carolina, but don't know whether he has been dropped on the way or gone on to Lydenberg. I met Jimmy Daly on the platform at the railway station the other day. He has had some marvellous experiences on trucks on the way up, but looks none the worse for the outing. He is employed on the Imperial Military Railway as a telegraphist. Our little Natal army is now so much scattered that it is impossible to say where the men really are. Jeffries passed through the other day on his way to Machadodorp. He has been in hospital, but is now O.K. and looks in the pink of condition.

✤ ✤ ✤ ✤

No. 4,374, Sapper **D. Semple,** writing from Kimberley, September 14th, speaks in praise of the hospital treatment in the following words :—

"DEAR KEMP,—I am not aware that any of our men in South Africa have written you what life is as a patient in a military hospital on active service. If not, perhaps a few lines on the subject may not be uninteresting to many of your readers. Suffering from S.C.F. (slow continued fever), I was admitted into hospital on the 16th of last month, and, after being examined, was ordered immediately to bed. My food for the first four days was plain milk (six pints daily) ; afterwards a pint of beef tea and two eggs were added. When I was allowed up, my food was changed to chicken diet and 'extras,' consisting of porridge, tea, bread and butter for breakfast, half-roast chicken and potatoes for dinner, rice pudding and a pint of milk at 4 p.m., then tea, bread and butter at 5 p.m. During the last fortnight of my stay a pint of stout was added daily. A nursing sister comes night and morning and takes your temperature. The doctor afterwards comes round (twice daily) to prescribe medicine and diet, and if any complaints. I am only giving you my *personal* experience, as I have been told often while in hospital that up to a month or so ago the hospital was not near so good as now. How far this is true I do not know, nor can I say whether the improvements (if any) are due to the army or civilian doctors ; but I can honestly say that the treatment meted out to me could not possibly be better. The hospital, which is named No. 11 General Hospital, is situated about two miles from Kimberley, adjacent to the De Beers' mine, and consists of 114 marquees, each containing from 7 to 10 iron beds, and lighted by electricity. The bedding consists of mattress, bolster, and feather pillow, 2 sheets and 3 blankets, and counterpane, spotlessly clean. Every Monday, the bedding, and also your underclothing is changed. There are four sections—A, B, C (sick and wounded), and D (convalescents). About 24 doctors (majority civilian) and same number of sisters professionally attend the patients, numbering at present time about 1,000, suffering from 'all sorts and conditions of disease.' In the very serious marquees, an orderly, sister, and doctor are practically always in attendance, day and night. A reading room and library is provided—the library of about 400 good novels, presented by Mrs. Dick Chamberlain, and conferring a great boon on the patients, who otherwise would find the time hang rather heavy. Cards, dominoes, and other games are also provided ; two ounces tobacco per man served out every Friday, gratis. A good many of the patients have had the arduous task of relieving Ladysmith and Mafeking. They seem cheerful and happy enough, but, like myself, wondering shall we spend Christmas in South Africa or at home ? I must not trespass too far on your limited space, but my excuse is the kind treatment I received during my five weeks' stay in hospital. Kind regards to the 'News.' Thanking you for 'K.L.'s.'"

KHAKI LETTERS—*continued.*

No. 28,201, Company Sergeant-Major **W. G. Tee**, writes from Bloemfontein, September 15th, as follows :—

"MY DEAR DICK,—Your latest complete list of Telegraph Reservists duly received ; also copies of KHAKI LETTERS, for which we all feel very grateful. Since writing last from Norvalspont, I have been to Bethulie, but, after short stay, was instructed to proceed to Bloemfontein, where I arrived in July. Passing through Springfontein, I had an opportunity of visiting poor Metcalfe's grave, which, through the kindness of the staff there, I am pleased to say has received every attention, and compares very favourably with any grave in the country, of which I should say there are at least 300. Bethulie was a quiet little place and I felt reluctant to leave it, and the short time there, the few English, of whom there are about a dozen families, treated me very well. It is, however, a notorious Boer centre, and although they appear to be very much subdued, I have no doubt if a commando came through, several who are on pass would willingly join. There is no likelihood of that, unless the enemy get south again. Business and farming is going on as usual, and everything quiet. Beyond the District Commissioner, with his staff of provisional mounted police visiting the various districts and farms, rendering a census and reporting all burghers absent, one would imagine there was no war. The provisional police are chiefly composed of mounted Colonials or Imperial Yeomanry, and have taken on the job for a certain period, and get 7s. to 10s. a day, out of which they have to provide their own forage. They are, as a rule, a fine body of men, and a good percentage are likely to remain in the Colony. Bloemfontein is fairly lively, and I like it better than any other place I have visited up country. Business is carried on as usual, and most of the people who had cleared out have returned, and objectionable characters removed over the border. There is a very good theatrical company here, who are waiting to get to Johannesburg, and have nightly performances at the Town Hall, with a varied programme every week. Things had been very quiet until recently, but the Boers have been moving south again ; consequently, the garrison had to be reinforced, and a strong flying column despatched to Thabanchu and Ladybrand, which has checked this southern movement, and I hope to hear that they are surrounded again, as they were at Ficksburg and Fouriesburg, when Prinsloo's lot surrendered with his little mob. Last Sunday it was known the Boers were not very far away, and had not heard from them for some time ; but whilst on one of the kopjes outside the town, could hear our patrols engaged quite distinctly, and the pom-pom quickly blazing away. Our troops were taking up positions on the hill for the night. The reinforcements and the columns that had been sent out soon checked them, and everything appears normal again, with the exception of the loyal farmers, who are coming in for protection, and the doubtful characters, who are brought in under escort and will be guarded here. We are having a busy time at the office, and find plenty to do to occupy our minds. We have two quads, one working to KB and the other to PR, DX to PE and Kroonstad, and several other wires to stations in the Colony. The telegraphs in the O.R.C. are entirely under and worked by the Engineers, the civil authorities —with the exception of a few clerks engaged as operators—having no control whatever ; so you may guess the R.E.'s have plenty to do, and a few hundred men are soon accounted for. We have a fairly big staff here, and the work is progressing satisfactorily—average hours about 10 a day, with a 5-hour duty Sunday. The Boers are constantly cutting our lines and blowing up the railway, but we find other outlets for our work, so that it is of not

KHAKI LETTERS—*continued.*

much consequence, although somewhat irksome. We are comfortably located ; most of the men are in the barracks that was used by the O.F.S. Artillery, and others are in a house at the rear of the old fort. Rations are very good, and prices of provisions coming down— butter, 2s. 6d. per pound ; eggs, 2s. 6d. dozen ; ale, 2s. 6d. pint bottle ; whisky, 8s., &c. I am sending by this post a photograph of our staff, taken outside of Telegraph Office. I also enclose a key to it, which I hope you will understand. With kind regards and thanks for your untiring energy for our interests."

✢ ✢ ✢ ✢

No. 4,363, Sapper **W. G. Carter,** writes from Greylingstad, September 15th :—

"You see I have had another shift. I left Heidelberg a week ago, and was sent here to take charge, and General Clery is going to make this his headquarters. The office is a small house by the railway, under a big hill, where there is a 5-incher on top, which sometimes speaks for itself. The windows are blocked with sandbags, and sandbags all round—s'pose that's to stop the bullets. There are only four houses here all told, so, you see, it's not very lively ; but the work is, though—keeps us going pretty well all day, and not 'tanner' ones ; 100, 200, and 400 words quite common. Buller is doing good work up above, and I saw Jim Jeffrey a few days ago for a few minutes. He was going through to join Buller's force at Machadodorp. Kruger, as you know, has gone on six months' leave. There are small parties all round here, but they won't fight, only damage the line. We had a big prisoner brought in to-day for shipment down country—De Villiers. I was surprised about 24th Camp—only 300—what awful disappointment there must have been, especially among the recruits ; still, I expect some of the 'moppers' have had a good innings this year. Am sending you a couple of photos of the Heidelberg staff. You might show some of the pals, if you like, and notice 'Oom Paul' in the photo. I've got infantrymen here with me, not R.E.'s, and very decent chaps they are, too. Kindest remembrances to all friends. Hope to be able to soon send V's on the B side of Grimsby or Peterboro'."

✢ ✢ ✢ ✢

No. 4,610, Sapper **A. E. Stevens,** writes from Bloemfontein, 20th September. . . . .

"Things with us are getting a bit more regimental. Up to now we have been doing pretty well as we like. Some were going it very strong, wearing 'riding breeks' and fancy caps of other corps, that really one didn't know what they belonged to. The captain has issued an order against wearing these fancy 'rigs out,' also that more attention is to be paid to washing of 'khaki.' and no excuse for not shaving ; but the worst of all is that we must be in barracks by 8 p.m., barring those on duty, for at that time the roll-call is performed and lights out at 9. Before, we could stay out pretty well as long as we liked and burn a light same period, but now these privileges are knocked on the head. . . . . The 'Scotch Brigade' and the North Country-men generally are a warm lot. It doesn't matter where a Scotsman is or under what conditions he is living, they contrive to have their 'porridge,' and they will, by hook or crook. One can see 'em making it for breakfast, dinner and supper, and when on night-duty also. We have also a couple of chaps from far-off Cornwall—'the country which is attached to England for rations.' They say it is noted for 'handsome women and stalwart men.' I

KHAKI LETTERS—*continued*.

twit 'em about their countrymen all rushing to England when anything goes wrong out here, they try to excuse themselves by saying they only come home for the pilcherd fishing; it must indeed be a profitable occupation to bring them away from the mines of Johannesburg. Last week we had a couple of linemen come in our room, who had the pleasure of being in De Wet's company for a month, and by all accounts they had a particularly lively time of it; what with trekking from 30 to 40 miles a day, sleeping out on the open veldt with a blanket and half-starved. They say that each man with De Wet has three or four horses, and they commandeer most of their food from various farm houses and stores as they move about. The real Boers are heartily sick and tired of the war, and his force are a mixture of all races, harum-scarum vagabonds, cut-throats, outcasts, etc. There are several families trekking with them, and the women and children used to come round and grin and jeer at the prisoners, who were about 150 strong. When captured they were told to hold up while they went through their pockets, being covered with rifles all the time; some of the old burghers used to treat them with respect and talked about the war. They used to hand over about a dozen sheep and some mealies to the prisoners, and they had to cook and divide it the best way possible; our two chaps had a bully-beef tin to eat, drink and cook out of. The best feed they had whilst with them was one night when De Wet captured a supply train going to Pretoria. On one occasion whilst on the trek they passed a store kept by a Jew; the Boers went through it first then told our prisoners they could go in and buy what they liked. Don't forget they had taken all money from them beforehand, so I suppose this is 'Boer humour.' Well, at-any-rate, they went in and through the place, the same as the Boers had previously done. It was very funny to see our chaps climbing over counters, up on shelves, and into every hole and corner of the place, whilst the poor old Jew was standing by with his eyes staring out of his head, but of course simply powerless, and the Boers laughing heartily at our 'Tommie's' antics. Kids at the age of 16 and old men of 60 make up his force, and some of the kids can't hold a rifle up to shoot, unless lying down. Well, all our chaps could lay hands on was a galvanized pail to cook their grub in, and what they thought was a great capture, was a full Huntley and Palmer's biscuit tin, and they were looking forward to a banquet when laagered up, but fate decreed otherwise, for lo and behold, the tin contained 'currants'! Well, after a week or so with De Wet, the Britishers began to get in touch, and then things began to hum a bit, and if the prisoners happened to drag a bit, they were urged onwards with the whip or sjambok. The papers have published accounts where the English prisoners have been treated as kindly as possible, so I only think it fair to quote an instance where they have not. Well, things were going on like this till Methuen and Broadwood were close on his heels, and they mention an instance when the 4th Battery of Artillery opened fire, the first shot smashed a wagon completely, and the next laid out five oxen, in fact, the first five shots each copped a wagon and signed it off at once; one shell fell right in the centre of the prisoners; it was a common shell and providentially didn't burst. This is the time to see the Boers, they jump and dance about, spur and whip their cattle terribly, especially the poor oxen, whom they lash to death. It was here that their opportunity came, so 80 of them turned and ran towards our artillery, but upon the Boers seeing this they also turned on them and called out for them to stop, and would you believe it, 20 of them turned back, but the others caring not for the Boers' rifle fire at them, as they ran like grim death across the veldt, kept on, and the only casualty was one

KHAKI LETTERS—*continued*.

shot through the hat. But their troubles were not ended yet, for they came in sight of some Yeomanry first, who, upon seeing this motley crew advancing, immediately dismounted and were just about to give 'em a volley, when they noticed their frantic gesticulating and throwing up hats, which saved them. Our two chaps were a picture to behold, their trousers being slit up both legs, sand shoes, a civvies' coat, and a straw hat they pinched out of the store alluded to previously. They got to know the parties' name that used the lash on them, and vow vengeance when he returns to his peaceful farm again, and as they are both candidates for staying out here, they will have an opportunity of getting a bit of their own back, and if they get half-a-chance I firmly believe they will, if it falls to their lot to get round the Kroonstad district, for that is the district where they hang out, these Godfearing, peace-loving farmers! After knocking about with Methuen's party they were sent on to Mafeking, thence to Kimberley and on here. It has now been confirmed that Theron has been killed; his band of marauders were a cut-throat lot, splendidly mounted. all foreigners, and employed chiefly to tear up the line. He has met with his just reward. I hear the C.I.V.'s are mobilizing at Pretoria. This, no doubt, is preparatory to their home-going. We have some employed as our orderlies, also the military P.O. have some. It's rather amusing to see them, perhaps bank clerks or solicitors, struggling through the street with a mail bag on his back. I wonder how they would like that occupation, struggling through the crowds in the City at home. 'Roll on, pig's life and civvie tack.'

No. 4,373, Sapper **T. W. Stevenson**, in a letter from Nelspruit, dated September 20th, says :—

"Have been hanging on to get the mail of the 17th August, to see if the fags would turn up ; but, as usual when troops are moving, everything but munitions of war and supplies are blocked, and I expect the letters are moulting on some obscure platform, and might be a long time reaching us. On the 15th July, I walked out to Rietvlei, five miles off, and dined with John Sainsbury, who was in charge of a testing station (where air-line finished and cable commenced) on the buzzer line, between Irene and General Hutton's column. We made a good fry in General Erasmus's house close by, using an old wash-stand for firewood. I went into Pretoria to go east with headquarters, and on July 20th, fourteen of us started with three wagons. We reached Mark's Farm, fourteen miles out, and spent four days there with just a buzzer for SGs. Used to stroll over and see Sorensen of a day, and play a game of 'nap' of an evening. I was dropped for a week at Brugspruit, and joined again at Middelburg, where we stayed three weeks. Reached Belfast on August 26th, and the first three days there were very exciting. On the Sunday morning, at breakfast time, a shell burst 200 yards from us, and in the afternoon we could see our troops clearing away from the pom-pom shells, which the Boers were placing beautiful all round Dingaan's monument. On Monday, I was in a small tent on the platform with two buzzer sets to Generals French, Buller, and Pole-Carew, and could hear Buller hotly engaged on our left front at Bergendal. All of a sudden, Long-Tom shells commenced to drop about 100 yards off, and got the wind up a bit. They stopped at three, though, and our field guns got them set and pounded them all the afternoon. Lord Bobs came in about four, all smiles, and told any troops he passed Buller had had a splendid time. We found BF very cold, and had a pokey little office, so were glad to move on Macha-

KHAKI LETTERS—*continued.*

dodorp on the 10th. We had two fine airy rooms for office, and our sleeping tent was on a plateau. We could get a swim in a spruit about 500 feet below. Left there on 18th September, and the country and railway was grand. From Waterval Boven to Waterval Onder it is a three-quarter-mile slide with all brakes on. The line runs on the side of a hill for about a mile—a sheer drop of several hundred feet on one side, and a solid wall of overhanging rock on the other. Waterval Onder is a lovely little spot, right in the midst of the mountains. Met Mackness there, and he and his fellow clerk have rigged up quite a civilized office. We passed through Nooitjedacht, and saw where the prisoners had been cooped up. At Godwaan we caught sight of our wagons outspanned, and I was off the truck sharp and cadged some biscuits, and went for some fat that steaks had been cooked in. If the corporal in charge of the wagons had not given us some meat, biscuits, tea, and coffee, we should have had fresh air to eat. Arrived here at four o'clock, and officed up in two thatched Kaffir huts. Had just got the tent fixed up outside, when a real tropical storm burst—awful lightning and thunder, and sheets of rain swamping everything. There are no supplies here at present, and this morning I was given a rasher of bacon and fourteen ounces of flour. I wetted the said iron, and made some chuppatees, cooking them on a bit of galvanised iron, and it's 'What ho! she bumps!' at present with me. Had a lovely swim in the Crocodile River this afternoon, and then sat on the bank *ad naturalibis*, and had a grand *battué* of Tommy's pals, finding any amount, gleaned from the Kaffir huts. To go back, you would have smiled at Middelburg to see me playing Sainsbury at crib on the banks of the Little Olifant's River, dressed in a white felt hat, while my only clothes were drying. We get some very sultry infantry clerks attached to us, and the slip writing is fearful and wonderful. Bill Pearce is at Godwaan River Station, and Dave Hamer is only other TS man here. Arundel pushed on to Kap Muiden on a trolley this afternoon, with instructions to be careful and not be captured. I'm horribly 'fed up' with this greasy life, and shall be glad to get back to civilization once more. Lord Bobs moved back to PR to-day, and I hope we shall soon return, too. Dead-off on job here at *any* price. Young Bert Eldridge was here yesterday, and Major Poore told him he must consider himself prisoner of war at present."

✣ ✣ ✣ ✣

No. 2,342, Lance-Corpl. **S. G. Davis** (of LV), writing from Welverdiend Station, September 21st, says:—

"DEAR COLOURS,—I have not given you a few lines for such a long time, but now that I am sitting on my roll of blankets, a single current baseboard a table, and apparel loose, for just now, 11 a.m., temperature is about 101 in the shade, and canvas does draw the heat, doesn't it? I will start with the troubles that surrounded us at Potchefstroom. Things in this historical town went very smoothly for about six weeks, although during those six weeks we had the main Transvaal wires (which pass through Potchefstroom as a testing office) were twice cut north or PR side. Here again the 'bulldog breed' came forward, and twice wires were repaired under the enemy's very noses, which organ is generally covered by scrub—I cannot insult hair by associating unwashed, uncombed, unbrushed matted stuff one sees on the majority of prisoners brought in. Now after six weeks' occupation our garrison was deemed expensive for a 'quiet' town, hence very few officers, N.C.O.'s and men, were left to guard the headquarters of the district which extends to Lichtenburg, Ventersdorp, Krugersdorp, Venterskroon, Harte-

KHAKI LETTERS—*continued.*

beestfontein (that's good enough for a place, ain't it?) half way to Wolmaranstad and Vereeinging. This latter place is pronounced Fe-ren-e-con; these pronounciations make one ponder and query within themselves if they have not the fever or dreaming they are in a place they only know how to spell, and that, by-the-bye, requires a very good memory. No sooner were we left with this small garrison then we had a succession of sniping on our outposts, our wires north were again cut, leaving us with eight wires south standing. Our next trouble was with a native of Potchefstroom, in whose grand house, arms, etc., were found; consequently, property confiscated and his family had to take up quarters in a small three-roomed house, who, when he heard of this, surrounded town and cut us off from *everywhere* up to this time, although Klerksdorp had fallen into the hands of Boers either from ignorance or design, left us through to KB., Bloemhof and Lichtenburg. The prison was made our stronghold. Two guns and about 300 R. W. Fusiliers were sent to relieve us. Orders received to entrench strongly for about eight days, seven days on short rations, two men existing on a loaf, about the same size as a twopenny cake and colour, that was, well, more like chocolate, and were it not for the possibility of procuring a bit of bread from townspeople, I should nearly have eaten my peck of dirt in those seven days! Sugar, too, was an unknown luxury for ten days Ordinary 2d. per packet safety matches, a few dozen at 5s. per dozen. Milk and tea quite out of the question. Then came Lord Methuen with mails 10 weeks late arrived, stayed three days, proceeded S.W.—very good for another few days. Lord Methuen sent in empty convoy with about 50 men who were considered 'bootless,' these were fired on. Convoy loaded and then came the surprise —all officers and men in Potchefstroom were to accompany the convoy out. Now, Colours, this meant evacuating the town. The staunch Englishmen who had formed themselves into a town guard were to come or stay, as they pleased, leaving their homes and families to the mercy of Boers and Boer women, who are like tigeresses. We were seven days before we caught up the force, nearly touching De Wet once or twice near Frederikstaa. At this place we were instructed to build a line 14 miles cross country to Ventersdorp, but time was too short and nine miles of wire had to be abandoned. It was a scratch team that built that line, there were one Sergt.-Major, one Sergeant, two Corporals, one Sapper and two Infantry clerks, myself included. We had orders to proceed, some to Johannesburg, Pretoria and Krugersdorp, myself to JH. entrained after considerable hurry necessitating less speed and more breakages. Our wagons, easily off-loaded by electric crane, but as they had to be run up on a rude platform and lifted into a coal truck by already tired hands, it was no joke. About 11 p.m. we lay down and slept, myself not waking till reaching Welverdund, despite the shunting which I hear was also done in a hurry! Arrived at JH, found Sergt. Walker, Sappers Birch, Clark, Fox, Harrison, Hunter, Roberts, Woodrow. Now, Dear Colours, you will, I doubt not, have received a description of Johannesburg by men who *can* wield the quill. However, struggle, strife and dishonesty suggested itself to me almost everywhere when town in full swing, of course now it shows a very bankrupt front. Tariff, well, here's an example: cup of tea, 6d.; tarts, 3d.; steak and bread, 3s.; eggs, 7s. per dozen. I could not make myself at home in *that* town anyhow, and I understand £400 a year is not as good as £120 at home, so roll on and lets have an excursion to Eastham or New Brighton on what one would pay for a cab fare to office in JH. The office at JH. is one of the very best, very elaborate, as in fact all the Government offices are in the Transvaal.

KHAKI LETTERS—*continued*.

On the 27th we started back for Potchefstroom near Welverdiend, Sappers Birch, Woodrow and self, remain for the present. General Hart has been down to Potchefstroom, captured about 40 prisoners all of whom has taken oath, killed and wounded a number, evacuated the town again, bringing families on here where they were sent to JH. . . . they have to leave their hearths and homes to the tender mercy of Boer women. Well, Dear Colours, I think by the time you and a few more get this I shall be back in Potchefstroom, when I hope to soon send you 'Peace' and its effects out here already. We play quoits, hockey, rounders and *cards*. I cannot thank you enough for your great thoughts for our welfare and news imparted to us which we would never otherwise learn minus 'K.L.' Christmas—Oh! shall I see you by then?"

P.S.—When Sapper W. C. Smith hoisted the first flag in the Transvaal, he omitted the names of the other 24th men with General Hunter's staff who were on the spot and waiting to open Christiana office if such had taken place; those names are Sappers C. J. Woode, F. H. Woodrow and self. September 22nd, Sapper Frampton had a very narrow shave the other day when out repairing the line. A very plucky try, whilst working the buzzer, shots came thick and fast—mount and off was the order, but a shot fell very near his horse causing the beast to shy, dislodging Frampton and getting loose, but the old "bulldog breed" was once more visible in Driver Day, who pluckily caught his runaway horse and helped Frampton to mount although under short range volleys, but when about 100 yards further along Frampton became giddy and fell again; again Drs. Day and Gregory came to rescue, picked him up badly injured and brought him along, supporting him on either side.

✣ ✣ ✣ ✣

No. 3,224, Sapper **C. P. O'Sullivan** (TSF), writing from Christiana, Transvaal, September 22nd, says:—

"Since writing from Wolmaranstand, we have had to evacuate that place owing to the approach of the enemy. Klerksdorp was taken by the Boers two days before we left, and as the garrison consisted of only ten men, we thought it the wisest course to do a moonlight flit. However, we were taken by surprise and had to move off about 5 p.m., as the enemy were beginning to put in an appearance. We were informed we would also be cut off, so this added more speed to our flight. Three Scots Greys, one Enniskilling Dragoon, one 7th Dragoon Guardsman, the Assistant Commissioner (a Lieutenant from Lumsden's Horse), three telegraphists—Ponto (Dellbridge), Raven (2nd Division), and myself—made up the fleeing details of Lord Roberts' Army. We were all mounted and reached the next post—Bloemhof—40 miles off, by midnight. When we arrived there, the "breeze" was at its highest, and we had to prepare for another shift, finally falling back on Christiana, where we have been since August 1st. I kidded myself somewhat, riding along with the crack cavalrymen lately left behind from one of General French's marvellous moves on account of their horses dying, or rather, being killed by the over-exertion imposed by the 'new riding measter.' Since arriving here the alarm has sounded on several occasions. So far, the Boers have not attacked, though they are hovering about at distances of above five miles. The garrison here is between four and five hundred strong, and we are wonderfully well fortified—so well, indeed, that I am of opinion the Boers could never muster enough courage to make an attack. We have also got a Pom-pom and a 3in. Nordenfelt quick-firer. That's all I can rake up to tell you this time. Best regards to all.

Khaki Sidelights.

Rudd Fund. One cannot help feeling proud when reflecting upon the generous assistance rendered by the C.T.O. staff and others towards this praiseworthy object. The list has been formally closed, but I am happy to say we do not refuse help even now. The following extracts will interest K.L. readers :—Sapper Fred Brewin, R.E., writing from Mafeking on September 21st, says :—"My dear Kemp.—Personally you are a stranger to me, but by name and repute a well-known personage. I have often wanted to drop you a line to thank you for your many kind words for the Royal Engineers out here, which I am one of some 16 years, but strange to say, I have always found myself either busy or too bashful to commence a correspondence with a total stranger as you will doubtless understand me, and the slight embarrassment that would exist under such circumstances, so I kept putting it off and off, till now, when I feel sorry to say, a sad duty calls upon me to finally make up my mind to communicate with you. I refer to poor old Alfy Rudd's sad end. I see by your book that T.S. has nobly started a subscription for Mrs. Rudd, and that you were very willing to offer your services to help the fund by receiving subscriptions for it. I enclose you a letter for her, if you will please post or hand to her. I have left it open for you to see each signature who has joined me in subscribing to the fund. We only number seven here, five 24th and two of ours. I, knowing him exceedingly well, old man, felt bound to help to my very utmost, knowing how he was situated and how sad a trial it is for his poor wife to bear. If I live long enough, I should like to tender her my sympathy in person, but as the chances of seeing her are so very remote, please ask you to do it for me, hoping you will not deem it any extra trouble on the top of your heavy shoulders, as they must be with so many undertakings, irrespective of your usual daily work. I am very much impressed with your book. I would very much like to have them bound, to read in years to come of the many pals I have made in the 24th. I tried very hard once to join but found the number allotted to MR (my office) was full, and joined Section "D" instead. I am in charge here. I have Roby and Brewster here from MR, which makes it pleasanter than otherwise, being able to tell one another of home. Waghorn and Govier of TS, and Kelly of CF, all jolly good fellows. I hear we shall be coming home this year. If so, it will be very nice to spend Xmas at home with our wives and families. This is a very nice little place and quite historic. It shows very good marksmanship of the Boers, as there is not a sound house in the town. We had a fearful heavy cyclone breaking over the town a fortnight ago, doing more damage in 5 minutes than the whole 7 months' seige, so terrific was the hail, wind and thunder and lightning. We are now very slack in comparison to what we were a few weeks ago, when Lord Methuen brought his force into Mafeking, after having had two months on the go all the time. In anticipation of your kind favour, dear Kemp, I thank you very much, and tender you my very best wishes."

Enclosed in the above was £2 10s., and in a second—try-to-catch-up-the-first-letter—another 10/-. Needless to say, the message to which our comrade refers, has been sent to the widow, who will appreciate the kindness of those seven stars of Mafeking.

Another R.E., Sapper, **R. E. Eve,** writes from Kimberley, Sept. 16th :—

DEAR KEMP,—Happening to come in contact with one of your 'Khaki Letters' a few days ago, I was glad to see that a fund had been inaugurated on behalf of the wife of our late comrade, Sapper (Alf.) Rudd, I immediately started a list here, and the response I met with in such short time speaks for itself. The few subscribers who came out on the 'St. Andrew' with him, or knew him at T.S., have very kind recollections of his good qualities. He was a genial companion, and some of his good jokes can be recollected to this day. I can assure you, dear Kemp, that it was a great shock to us when we heard of his death, and if you will kindly convey to his wife our very heartfelt sympathy, you will be doing us a very great favour."—This letter contained Postal Orders for £1 12s. 6d.

Both these men speak in very high terms of poor Rudd, but space will not permit of their letters being given in extenso. The "great favour" was cheerfully rendered for our Kimberley colleagues, and we heartily appreciate their kindly thoughtfulness.

A most modest R. E. at the front who does not wish the wide, wide world to know his name, also sends 10s. Major Ogilvie added 10s. and an old L.R.B. man another 2s. 6d. This sum of £5 5s. added to that previously acknowledged (i.e. £85 10s. 5d.) brings the amount up to date to £90 15s 5d. Well done, everybody, you'll never miss it.

KHAKI SIDELIGHTS—*continued.*

Blobswitch!! Ever heard of him? No? He's the War Correspondent to the *Sapper*. Have often enjoyed his contributions. He has favoured us with a bit of his light-heartedness. We'll let him say and think as he likes.

> Hail! little Khaki-covered booklet, hail!
> The Sapper greets thee, from far Afric's shore
> Thy spicy little anecdotes regale
> And help cement comradeship 'tween both corps.

DEAR COLOURS,—Am I too late in offering you my congratulations on the production of your ubiquitous booklet, yclept KHAKI LETTERS? It is a novel idea, and one which I observe seems to "catch on" with the "24th," although my innate sense of modesty seems to tell me that some of the letters it contains go a trifle beyond the pale of truthfulness,* or shall I put it down to an elastic imagination produced by an over-long sojourn in this kopje-bound country? The dry air has a wonderful effect upon one's imaginative powers, *e.g.*, Kruger imagined he was going to drive us into the sea, whilst we in turn imagined the war would be over in three months! We have also indulged in the fond hope that that peripatetic tyrant, but none the less admired, De Wet, would very soon be brought to earth, but, alas! our "contact" with him has been of brief duration, and he has "cleared," to turn up again in a spot where he is most unlooked for. Very kind of him. Even our own "K. of K." with his splendid technical knowledge is unable at present to bring his slippery-heeled adversary to bay. Just on eleven months ago, I think it is, since your humble left the shores of merry England, and many a sorry sight have I witnessed since my stay in Africa. Many a good fellow has, alas! bitten the dust, and who shall say but many more have this fate in store for them. The dread diseases, enteric and dysentry, have carried away hundreds of those whom we knew, and for them we had more than a passing comradeship.

> "The grim, hoary angel has spread out his wings,
> "Destruction and death in his walk he aye brings."

We are camped beside the river, or rather we were, but the District Commissioner, together with the Sanitary Committee, had an idea that we were polluting the river, so promptly had us moved, and we are now pitched beside a church, enjoying the spiritual benefits which that sacred building radiates. Happy thought to bring us within the very doors of a church, for now we are not likely to suffer "moral and intellectual damages," like a certain South African magnate did, whose present palatial residence is a railway car at Pilgrim's Rest. Appropriate name, indeed. The bigoted, hypocritical old President posing as a pilgrim in a railway saloon! The position is worthy of a Gilbert and Sullivan opera.

> "Chased o'er the veldt by 'Rooineks' with great zest,
> "Poor Uncle Paul has found a Pilgrim's Rest."

Anent our shifting camp, I have a few verses :—

A detachment of T.D.R.E.	But the detachment of T.D.R.E.
Weren't allowed in one spot long to be,	Weren't destined very long *here* to be,
For the District Commissioner	For the parson objected—
Found a sanitary petitioner,	Said his flock were subjected
Who said polluting the river we'd be.	To sights which moral folk shouldn't see.
So he chased the T.D.R.E.	So away went the T.D.R.E.,
From the place where in peace they could be,	Like a storm-tossed old derelict at sea,
And with holy intent	Chased from river to church,
Near a church pitched their tent,	They are still on the lurch,
Far away from earth's revelree.	And for some time are likely to be.

It rained here for three days in succession last week. None of your puny midsummer showers—a real sky-juicy downpour. I was on night duty, and hereby hangs a narrative. Myself and comrade, at 10 p.m., started forth for the office, a matter of five minutes' walk from the camp (under ordinary circs.). The night was dark and stormy (this is an original phrase, I believe), and as we gingerly

---

* "Beyond the pale of truthfulness" indeed! Who so insinuates? Bobs, or Blohs? Which?? Did the suspicion ever arise, the delinquent would be called upon to answer a "blue," instanter. No, no, it cannot be, we leave such things for others.

KHAKI SIDELIGHTS—*continued.*

stepped from out our tent, we religiously (being in such close proximity to a church) stepped into a pool of water. Knowing the topography of "our" street, we made for the middle of the road, which we knew as being so many miles above the sea level, but, alas! the spirit of mischief was dogging our footsteps that night, for instead of walking on the high-level system, we found ourselves in the gulley, which, by then, had assumed the proportions of a well-nourished spruit. Not knowing but what we might disappear down a yawning abyss any moment, we continued paddling along the gully, when a lantern hove in sight. The effect of light suddenly appearing from out of the stygian darkness, and then disappearing like a will-o'-the-wisp, is, to say the least of it, stupefying, when one's path is infested with miniature spruits and duck ponds. Still pursuing our aquatic way, we made enquiries at an officer's quarters as to the whereabouts of the Post Office. Adhering strictly to details supplied, we sallied forth again on our nocturnal quest, finally reaching the office at 10.45 p.m. Needless to say, we were both wet footed. Having the good luck to discover a pair of clean socks in my overcoat pockets these were immediately brought into requisition. We then improvised sandals out of the backs of pads, with the addition of a little red tape (Yes, we've got it even out here). I observed next morning that a house at the top of "our" street rejoiced in the possession of three boats. Now, had we been aware of this the previous night, we might have rowed ourselves to the office; as it was, we paddled there instead.

There is a remarkable wire out here which runs from Pretoria to Bloemfontein, which is geographically known as "Top East," and on whose qualities I have expatiated in verse, as follows:—

> Now, doubtless you've heard of that marvellous wire,
> Which is known far and wide as "Top East;"
> If you haven't, I'm sure you will never desire
> It's acquaintance too long on to feast.
>
> Chorus of telegraphic spooks—
> It's "Top East" that, and "Top East" this,
> And "Top East" all the day;
> It's either "earth," or else it's "dis,"
> Or something out of the way.
>
> Should this marvellous wire, for one solitary day,
> Only happen (by chance) to be straight,
> Then the powers that be will immediately say,
> "On this curious cause we'll debate."
>
> Chorus of terror-stricken telegraphists—
> It's "Top East" that, and "Top East" this,
> They've "Top East" on the brain;
> And when it's neither "earth" nor "dis,"
> They can't let it remain.
>
> They test it at night, and they test it by day—
> They test it to see if it's there;
> They all test together, in a different way—
> A *real* fault on "Top East" is quite rare.
>
> Chorus of demented operators—
> It's "Top East" that, and "Top East" this,
> It's "Top East" here and there;
> If it isn't "earth," they'll make it "dis,"
> Or a "contact" find somewhere.
>
> Now, this warning I give to all T.C.'s out here,
> Let "Top East" religiously alone,
> If you wish to keep sane, then you must e'en steer clear
> Of "Top East." It'll work on it's own.
>
> Chorus of staff *avec gusto*—
> It's "Top East" that, and "Top East" this,
> And "Top East" is their song;
> And if it's neither "earth" nor "dis,"
> It won't remain so long.

KHAKI SIDELIGHTS—*continued.*

These nocturnal devastations on our lines of communication (whew! that's a mouthful) are rather amusing if they were not so aggravating, and the big ship and white helmet seem even more and more remote. It is universally acknowledged that the Boer never washes. Now, Sir, this is a base slander, for I, with my dual optics, did see, yea verily, and forsooth, gadzooks, etc., one of these our enemy (a prisoner) washing himself one very cold morning in about half-a-pint of cold water. But do not mistake me, the said individual was performing his matutinal (or possibly perennial) ablutions in his overcoat. "Moral and intellectual damages," did you say? The gentleman (?) who averred he would not wash until all the Rooineks had been driven into the sea, must be in an extremely bad way by now.

How delightful it would be if *we* drove the Boers into the sea. What a gathering there would be of the great "unwashed!" 'Twould indeed be "staggering humanity" to see these revellers in uncleanliness actually enveloped in a seething mass of water. This benighted town is similar to most towns in South Africa. The houses, with their galvanised iron roofs, look as if they were chucked into the place, and remained where they had been precipitated. There are some rather embarassing walks in the town. You go up the main street and turn down another to find you are in the main street again. Funny, isn't it? But then you can walk through the town in 15 minutes.

At the present moment I fail to see what use this vast expanse of veldt can be put to except for the purpose of drying clothes. It's a splendid country for that, on account of the rarified air. Then, again, there is no need for clothes lines, as the high cactus plants and long white thorn bushes make an excellent substitute for that domestic commodity, and anyone will tell you who has had the misfortune to get hung up in one of these plants, that they would hold a span of mules. There is an excellent opening in this country for washerwomen and sanitary inspectors. The manufacturers of so and so's notorious insect powder would, I venture to think, reap in unlimited shekels.

I *have* been told that there's a war in S. Africa, but surely my informer is erring! *I* don't believe it. Do you?

But doubtless I am encroaching upon your space by this time, in fact I feel it incumbent upon me to "quit chin music-ing," so with these few words of explanation I will conclude, wishing you further success in your work.

Believe me, yours sincerely,
"BLOBSWITCH."

Kroonstad, O.R.C., September 6th, 1900.

[Thank you, Blobs, for your interesting contribution. Yes, *I* think there's a war, and sufferers by tens of thousands, worse luck.]

The "Buzzer."

(N.B.—Royal Engineers must not read this par.) We have heard so much about the "buzzer" in the letters from Our Boys, that every week —Ah! every day, almost—I get a confidential enquiry, "What's a buzzer?" In order to give you something of a technical description of it I have commandeered an old R.E. who puts it in this form: "The buzzer was invented by Major Cardew, R.E., as a means of working through very faulty lines when the currents are much too feeble to move an ordinary relay. It is a combination of morse, telephone and induction coil. The signals are sent through the primary coil in the usual way by key, but their continuity is broken by the rapid vibrations of the armature of the induction coil resulting in a buzzing or singing of dots and dashes. The secondary coil is connected to line, and through Adey's hand telephone receiver to earth, which is made by means of a perforated iron pipe driven into the ground. The signals can easily be read, even when the wire is lying on the ground—as in the Nile Expedition—for some distance. The telephone itself may be used for speaking on short sets, as it was by our old comrade, Sapper Richardson, in the Soudan Campaign, when watching for Rail breakers on the Handoub lines." Another R.E., who served in South Africa, adds: "In 1884, in Sir Charles Warren's Expedition to Bechuanaland, the buzzer was used with much success on the Vyrburg-Mafeking line (for the intermediate small stations, who came in circuit twice daily). Many old R.E.'s will remember Corporal Evans's cornet selections, and Bugler (now Sergeant) Ancell's ocarina solos on this useful instrument, This was done by the Ader receiver being placed in the bell of the cornet, and the delighted Staff used to receive 'The Lost Chord,' YQ., over ninety miles of wire when the day's work was done." I may add, the buzzer is a combination of a telegraphic and telephonic instrument, and when in use much resembles the hum of a bee.

Sapper Thomas Hamilton.

GLASGOW is now called upon to bear the loss of a bright comrade at the front—not by shot or shell, nor by disease—but by some untoward circumstance. It was with deep regret the Telegraph Staff at that city received the news of the untimely death of their young and popular colleague, Sapper Thomas Hamilton, No. 4,386, at Kroonstad, on the 22nd ult., the result of an accident, the nature of which has not yet transpired.

The Casualty List reported him as "accidentally dangerously injured at Kroonstad, October 21st," and on the following day further reported his death. This sad event brings the loss sustained by the P.O. Telegraphists up to eight.

'Tommy' was a young, unassuming fellow of 22 years. He entered the Post Office as a messenger, and had about five years appointed service as a telegraphist. He was a member of the Signalling Corps of the Volunteer Battalion Glasgow Highlanders, and responded to the call for volunteers for S. Africa, and was taken on the strength of the 24th Middlesex R.V., together with seven other Glasgow telegraphists — on March 13th, and transferred from the "I" Company to the R.E. Reserve two days later (the 15th). The men assembled at Aldershot, and numbered 46, forming the sixth detachment of the Post Office Rifles for duty with the Royal Engineers, sailing from Southampton, per s.s. "Winifredian," on April 1st.

The staff extend their heartfelt sympathy to his parents and friends in their sad and sudden bereavement, and if any comfort is derived from the knowledge that he was held in esteem by his colleagues, we would assure them this war will never be recalled but with kind thoughts and pleasant memories of Sapper Thomas Hamilton.

Glasgow has responded well to the call for Volunteers, no less than eleven men having gone to the front. Attention is called to "A Grand Idea," page 370.

Khaki Sidelights and Notes.

SERGEANT C. JONES.

IT is with regret that we have to record the death of another Cable Room Volunteer, Sergt. C. Jones, of the 1st City of London Volunteer Artillery, who fell a victim to consumption at the early age of 25. He had a bad attack of pleurisy about twelve months ago, when so many of his comrades were volunteering for active service. Already his name was accepted, and it was a bitter disappointment when it was found he was too ill to serve. It is feared he resumed his duties too early, for he never recovered his former health and spirits. He performed duty for the last time on June 10th, and died in Brompton Hospital on 14th October. He was buried with military honours, Friday, 19th ult. The cortege was an imposing one, the firing party of 20 men of his regiment leading, were followed by the full brass band with muffled drums, then a gun carriage and limber drawn by six horses, with men of the Royal Horse Artillery bearing the coffin, covered by the Union Jack, on which rested deceased's busby and sword. On each side of the coffin walked four sergeants as bearers, among whom were Sergt. Jackson, L.R.B., Sergt. Barrett, 1st City of London Artillery, and Sergt. Pritchard, 24th Middlesex, all from the Cable Room. Next came the officers of his Company, followed by the mourning coaches conveying the relatives and the numerous wreaths. The procession started from Clapham Junction about 2.30, and reached Putney Vale Cemetery about 4 p.m. The ceremony was touching and impressive. After the three volleys had been fired over the grave the band rendered the hymn, "For ever with the Lord," and the last earthly honours had been paid to the memory of a good citizen soldier. A number of colleagues from the C.T.O. were present.

TSF is very loyal in supporting patriotic funds, etc. It is also to their credit to record the fact that the Clerks of the Cable Room subscribed £5 for a bed for poor Jones at the Brompton Hospital.

A Grand Idea. The following suggestion has been handed me by a TS. colleague:—" In connection with the part the C.T.O. and other offices have taken in the South African Campaign, I should like to make a suggestion that a memorial plate be subscribed for locally in each office interested in commemoration

AS A CORPORAL.

KHAKI SIDELIGHTS—*continued*.

of the Campaign, and more particularly in memory of those of our number who have lost their lives in it. The plates should be erected in suitable sites on the local P.O. walls, either inside or out, as preferred. I am sure the Postmaster-General would assent to the idea, and assist, in so far as he is concerned, in affording facilities."—As regards the C.T.O., its huge staff, and its constant flow of public visitors, what would be nicer than to record the loyalty of telegraphists than an " In Memoriam " brass affixed to the wall of the instrument room, bearing the names of our TS and TSF comrades who have given their lives for their Queen and country. Such an idea could be carried out neatly and well, and would never interfere with the official work in any way, while it would keep the names of those we have loved fresh in our memories.

A retired Volr. who has put in twenty years with the L.R.B., writes for the entire series of "that excellent publication, which contains more information of interest than anything I have read respecting the Boer War. . . . for both my family and friends wish to read them. 1/10/00." "KHAKI LETTERS to hand, for your kindness in supplying me, please accept my best thanks. I have by me some seven or eight volumes *Graphic* and *Daily Graphic*, which would amuse our friend Tommy and help to keep him out of the canteen and garrison pub. If you know of any Soldiers' Institute or Convalescent Home, I should feel only too happy to forward two volumes, carriage paid.—5 10 00." Now the L.R.B. and the 24th have always been the best of friends at Aldershot under canvas, and at H.Q., Bunhill Row. At the same time the 24th is securely linked to the Royal Engineers, so the blend stands L.R.B. 24th R.E., therefore I suggested that the books might go to Aldershot for the R.E.'s, as at the present moment a goodly number of our own men who have been invalided are stationed there as well. This friend writes again saying the volumes shall be sent to Sergt. Luttrell as suggested, and "if the books are approved he may be pleased to suggest a destination for the remainder." 2s. 6d. is also enclosed for the Rudd Fund. This is another kind action, and my colleagues will join me in thanking our unknown L.R.B. man.

Notes. The *Evening News*, October 30th, gives an interview with the Chief Clerk of the City Police force, who is reported to have said: "You take a city of six million people, and get a day when about a quarter of them decide to spend several hours on the pavement in a limited area of the town. Add to that the output of all the excursion trains every railway into London can find room for, and what is the result? Why, there they are, twelve or fourteen deep on the pavement and thirty or forty deep at places like Ludgate Circus."

Under the heading "Death of a Convict," the *Daily Mail* of October 29th reports that a Coroner's inquiry was held at Dartmoor on Saturday respecting the death of a convict named Henry Ives, clerk. He was sentenced to five years penal servitude at the Central Criminal Court in May last year for forging a telegram. One day last week he complained of feeling unwell and was sent to the hospital, but he died in the evening from heart disease.

Hooliganism.—Mr. A. W. Ward, Asst. Supt. of TS, had a visit from burglars in the early hours of Saturday morning, October 20th, who managed to capture articles to the value of about £10. Amongst the things taken were a number of Kruger and other coins, and also unused stamps which had been sent home by his son, Trooper A. B. Ward, of the Imperial Yeomanry, who had succeeded in collecting same from captured Boers whilst operating in the Orange River Colony and Transvaal. Our respected Supt. valued these coins very much and would have lost almost anything rather than these. The thieves were evidently determined to secure anything connected with the war, as they took the trouble to remove all the stamps from his son's letters besides those already mentioned, leaving the envelopes and enclosures scattered about the room.

I can't understand how it is K.L.'s manage to get into Suburban shop windows. Only this week a well-known Supt. informed me that a small parcel of them, bearing a very flattering and catchy notice, was lying in all its beauty awaiting an admirer and a purchaser. By-the-bye, the admirers always outdo the purchasers. I wish they could run a dead heat.

KHAKI NOTES—*continued*.

Sergt. G. E. May, 24th Mx., N.W.D.O. postman, received a gift of Dum-dum bullets, with one of which, we regret to learn, he took his own life. Overwork seems to have played a part in the tragedy. On Tuesday, October 9th, he said: "I am going to have a little rest; they won't grudge me that." He was afterwards found lying on the bed with his rifle between his legs. The shot had carried away the whole o˙ the upper part of his head, and only his lower jaw remained. The jury returned a verdict of "suicide while of unsound mind," although one juror said that he was not satisfied that there was evidence of insanity. He was buried on Tuesday, October 16th, a military funeral being accorded him, and a number of his friends and comrades were present.

Postmastership.—There was much hand shaking and expressions of goodwill, as our old friend Horace Parker, of the "F" bade us farewell on Friday last. We congratulate him on his appointment as P-M. of Erith, which post he takes up on November 1st.

Reg. Office.—Messrs. C. F. Hilton and J. W. P. Gribble, are appointed to the Registry Office, Secy's Office. We wish them luck.

Quite an army of young operators who are accepting appts. in South Africa, will make their exodus shortly. TS alone loses some 40 or 50. Besides this it is whispered that 40 P-M-ships are offered to men of not less than twenty years' service.

Congrats to the following gentlemen on their promotions :—
Senior—Wm. Ives to be 2nd Cl. Asst. Supt. Dated September 27th, 1900. Telegraphists—E. L. Witteridge and J. H. Field, also dated September 27th, and F. Benson, dated October 25th, to be Seniors.

Returned.—The following "L" Co. men have re-assembled at Aldershot:—Sergts. R. C. Luttrell and J. H. Nelson; Sappers W. Nixon, W. S. Roberts, T. W. Pallet, F. J. Hurdle. D. McLaren, E. S. Williams, A. Ray, H. Stormer, C. S. Ingram, W. J. Greenfield, J. S. Tough, G. Bishop and H. Alliston. W. J. Hargreaves arrived October 18th, and is on furlough, at Barrow-in-Furness, until 18th inst. W. H. P. Woolley arrived per s.s. "Trojan" October 15th, and is at Newhaven on sick furlough. Wm. Wilson also writes saying he is on leave.

Sick List.—The following officers of the C.T.O. are on the sick list, unlikely to resume duty and probably pending pensions :—W. Robson (Asst. Supt.), J. Baker, TSF., J. J. Fielden, TSF. (Seniors); G. S. Betteridge and A. S. Woodrow (Telsts.).

Pte. A. R. Skegg, No. 418, A.P.O.C., died at Capetown of Enteric, October 2nd, 1900, while quickly following, another member, *i.e.* :—

Pte. G. Platt, No. 544, A.P.O.C., was reported dangerously ill of enteric at Pretoria, on October 3rd, and on October 6th, his death occurred.

Pte. A. S. Layzell, 568, A.P.O.C., drowned whilst bathing, Capetown, October 27th. This brings their loss by death up to 17.

A Cablegram, from Capetown, October 14th, 12.30 p.m., "Poniard, London—Home, Kemp, well, Rustenberg, Woode," received here October 15th has been dealt with.

Khaki Postage Fund.—The following sums have been received and are duly acknowledged here with hearty thanks :—Liverpool, 5s., D. Div., 4s., Recd. Check (per A.L.M.), third sub., 4s., Miss J. H. (second sub.), 3s., King's Cross, 2s. 6d., Miss. G. (Met.), 2s., F. W., 2s., Miss S., 6d., Miss N. K., 6d.

Attention is called to page 2 of cover. It will interest you.

"Poniard, London," for telegrams from Our Boys to their relatives and friends at home, the addresses of whom should be sent us at once.

"Casualties, Capetown," for enquiries *re* sick and wounded.

COLOURS.

"KHAKI LETTERS," One Penny. By post, Three Halfpence.

All posted letters containing Remittances, Orders, MSS., &c., must be addressed to R. E. KEMP, 12, JERRARD STREET, LEWISHAM, S.E.
Postal Orders should be made payable at Loampit Vale, Lewisham, S.E.

Printed by E. G. BERRYMAN & SONS, *Blackheath Road, London, S.E.*

"Khaki Letters" from ....
"My Colleagues in South Africa."

CORRESPONDENCE FROM THE
POST OFFICE TELEGRAPHISTS
OF THE
24th MIDDLESEX (P.O.) RIFLE VOLUNTEERS
(Royal Engineer Reserves),
ON ACTIVE SERVICE.

THE BOND THAT BINDS US—FRIENDSHIP—COMRADESHIP.

Published monthly (formerly fortnightly) for the Postal Telegraph Service.
Conducted by COLOUR-SERGEANT R. E. KEMP, *Central Telegraph Office, London.*

No. 20.   NOVEMBER 30TH, 1900.   PRICE ONE PENNY.

Central Telegraph Office,
London, E.C.

DEAR COMRADES, ONE AND ALL.

Greetings! "Here we are again coming up smiling for another round. Let me see, the last exploit," etc. That is the way one of your worthy chums commences his epistle to me. Following his lines, and having "seen," I find I was trying to tell you about the return of the C.I.V.'s. Well, well! That is forgotten, as also is the suggestion that for such services, then rendered, I should get the V.C. But the C.I.V.'s are not forgotten. Whether they have all been fêted by now, or not, I am unable to say, but I am constantly reading of the men being regaled by their respective regiments, who vie with each other for making the biggest and best possible "reception." One runs down the list of names of those who illuminated the gatherings by their presence, until the eye is dazed. Eh? Oh, it is impossible for me to name them—suffice it to say that they are among the élite of the land, military and otherwise. As far as I know, nothing has been done for our little lot; we only sent a few—indeed they could rightly say, "We are seven," and as seven is the perfect number I presume we shall hear something soon. Speaking of our C.I.V. detachment, it will be a matter of interest for you to know that our officer, who has returned with them all safe and sound, has left us for the army. The *London Gazette* of the 9th inst. contains the following information:—"The Royal Welsh Fusiliers—Lieutenant Walter Brookshank Garnett, from the City of London Imperial Volunteers and 24th Mx.V.R.C., to be Second-Lieutenant. Dated 5th May, 1900, but not to carry pay or allowances prior to 10th November, 1900."—"It seems hard."

That the C.I.V.'s have been thoroughly well boomed and received no one will doubt, and it has been a matter of wonderment to many of them to read of the glorious deeds they have done. It is far from my intention to minimise in the slightest manner their enthusiasm, zeal or gallantry, or to begrudge one iota of praise that has been lavished upon them; but what about the citizen soldiers who went out as Volunteer Service Companies, attached to the "Liners," and who shared and fared with them the real drudgery of an ordinary soldier? I am right glad to know that now many such Companies are ordered home, their respective towns are preparing for them in no less hearty a manner—that they will receive a welcome from their admiring townsfolk and regimental friends. They may not have the freedom of a city bestowed upon them, nor may they be thought so much of as to have a letter inserted on their behalf in a London daily suggesting that every man should have a substantial pension on reaching the age of forty; but they are every whit as entitled to the thanks and approbation of the British public as those who have already received it. More, every soldier at the front has performed his task, be it great or small; every man is worthy of our best recognition. "England expects," and she has seen, that every man has done his duty.

A change is anticipated in the training of the army—a great change. It is said that by the system now in vogue Tommy Atkins gets but a shadow of a military training. The *Daily Mail*, after outlining a soldier's work in the field and his multitudinous duties in the barracks, on fatigues, etc., which does not prove of great educational value, says:—

"All this is to be changed. The day-labouring work, hitherto performed by the private soldier, it is proposed to get done by employing time-expired men, who will form a corps somewhat similar to the present barrack wardens and barrack labourers. The British soldier is to have ten months' thorough military training every year, instead of a mere routine six weeks. This period is to be divided as follows:—Four months are to be devoted to company training under company officers. In these four months the soldier is to be taught how to scout, how to build trenches, bridge streams, construct redoubts, and to take shelter. We are, in short, to have an army skilled in field engineering, instead of simply one corps of Engineers for the whole of our military forces. From this it does not follow that the Royal Engineers will be placed on any different basis, though the men in the other regiments will be taught much that has in the past been considered Royal Engineers' work only. Four months are to be devoted to battalion manœuvres, during which the men will be exercised in attacking and defending positions, battalion field firing, and other important work. Two months of the year are to be given up to grand manœuvres, carried out under strictly service conditions; that is, as nearly as possible under the same conditions that would obtain in actual warfare. The remaining two months will be taken up by the furlough period, etc."

The musketry is to receive special attention, and the inspired *D.M.* continues:— "To this end it is proposed to largely increase the allowance of ammunition. At present this stands at 200 rounds per man per year, all of which have to be blazed off in a stated period and without any special attention being given to the hits made. But under the new system marksmanship is to be made the first consideration. Regiments are not to be sent to the butts to loose off a certain number of cartridges per man and then go back to barracks again. Targets are to be stuck up all over big areas to represent an enemy, and the men are to be taught to fire at these with the intention of hitting them, to take cover, and deport themselves generally while firing as though the targets were real live enemies with rifles in their hands. Officers as well as men have got to learn to scout and shoot straight, for even a second-lieutenant will have to gain the extra certificate in musketry before he gets promotion. This condition is to apply to officers of the Militia, Yeomanry, and Volunteers, as well as to those in the Regulars."

I cannot do better than call your attention to the "Sidelights" and "Notes" in this issue, which I think will bring you almost up to date as regards the way the world wags Londonwards.

It appears the convalescent invalids who have been resting on their oars for some time, and about whom so much correspondence has taken place, have at last received orders to rejoin—not the drafts for the Cape, but their respective offices. I hear they made their presence known at the 'Shot yesterday, when they said good-bye to their chums down there, and they are down for duty in TS and other offices to-morrow. It is to be hoped that you will all be relieved soon, and there seems to be some reason for such hope being fulfilled, for we hear from all quarters that So-and-so has sailed or is soon to start for the Cape. When all this new blood gets out there (and I believe they will number some 250) there seems a good chance of your places being taken by them.

It has been a source of pleasure for me to know this little booklet has proved interesting to you; but why some get it and others miss it I cannot explain. This one should reach you in time to catch you talking of Christmas and the old folks at home, and I think the next issue, which I must issue at the year end, will be the MM of KHAKI LETTERS, for by the time that is in print very little more will, I trust, remain to be said.

Trusting you are all first-class, in good health, and grand spirits, I am, as ever,
Yours most heartily,

To the "L" Co. in South Africa,   R. E. KEMP,
Tuesday, November 27th, 1900.   *Colour-Sergeant.*

KHAKI LETTERS.

To the Boys Yonder.

Heartiest Season's Greetings.

May your Christmas be made a merry one by receiving orders for Old England, and the New Year dawn when you are on your way to Home, Sweet Home.

Home to the Motherland.

THE heart of the Empire is throbbing with pride
    And the earth rings again with her jubilant song:
For a love the deep waters can never divide
    Is voicing the triumph of right over wrong.
Home! Home at last from the red fields of war—
    Their ears tingling still with the thunder of guns;
And dearer by far now than ever before—
    The Motherland welcomes her battle-tried sons!

Chorus.
    Soldiers of Empire! You answered the call,
        And gloriously have you fulfilled the command!
    The love of your kindred—the pride of us all—
        Welcome again to our dear Motherland!

Heroes of highland, of lowland and plain—
    Heroes of backwood, of bush and of town—
Heroes patrolling the wide, breezy main—
    Full well have you fought for the flag and the crown!
The challenge that fired you, that rang round the world,
    Was flung to the race that has yielded to none!
And back from the conflict with red banners furled,
    You bear the bright laurels so valiantly won.

Chorus.
Soldiers of Empire, &c.

But homes have been shattered—vain prayers have been prayed
    For the many who battled and fell where they sleep;
The great price of victory they fearlessly paid
    That Britons their heritage proudly might keep.
God rest them where heedless of honour they lie!
    To the comrades who fought with them render our debt—
For the story they made for us never shall die,
    And the foemen that met them shall never forget!

Chorus.
Soldiers of Empire, &c.

C.T.O.

W. H. F. WEBB.

COPYRIGHT.—" Khaki Letters " must not be used without permission.—R. E. KEMP.

Khaki Letters.

No. 4,375, Sapper **C. H. Jones** (TSF), in a belated letter from Harrismith, O.R.C., August 25th, says :—

"After staying at Senekal about a fortnight we left for Bethlehem, which is a pretty place, there also being seven churches in the town, but they only had morning services, as there was no oil in the town, so evening services were out of the question. I have made it a point of going to a church at each place I have been, after stopping at Bethlehem (Holy City, 7 churches) I came on here. Dadswell of the D. Division, Wright of the News and myself have been together since Winburg, and a very fine trio we have been, have got on absolutely A1 together; we go share and share with everything, and needless to say a friendship has sprung up between us which will want some breaking. Just after leaving Senekal we had, I may say, the second best sight I have had since my arrival here, viz., the prisoners who surrendered under General Prinsloo, at Retiefs Nek. Saw them on the veldt as we were trekking to Bethlehem—there must have been quite 4,000 of them, with I believe 2 pompoms, and several 9 and 15 pounders. I tell you it does you good, a sight like that. We walked and walked and fancied we were treading on air, after we were treated to that sight. The Boers were all mounted, and the majority were leading a spare horse, others were riding in Cape and Scotch carts, several of which had wounded folk in them—they know how to do it. There were a great many of our troops engaged as escort, mostly Munsters, and a battery of the C.I.V.'s—gallant C.I.V.'s! We generally when possible travel on our own, as we have a wagon to ourselves, and if we happen to see a farm in close vicinity to the road Dadswell and myself invariably make a bee-line to it, and ask for a cup of coffee. One farm I remember quite distinctly where we decided to outspan and give the oxen a rest, we could not find any water, so Dadswell and I volunteered to take 'dicksey' to a farmhouse about three-quarters of a mile away to get some water. We went, the others went collecting our usual fuel out here on the veldt, viz., cow-dung, which makes capital burning stuff, and to get the fire all ready for us. When we got near the farmhouse, the children who were playing near the place ran indoors, and one little chap especially cried as if his heart would break. We opened the door and enquired if they could oblige with some water. The old lady could not understand English, so I took the water from a tub and tried to ask for it afterwards, when a girl of about 17 years came to our rescue; she acted interpreter—best looking girl I've seen in this country. I started talking to her, and naturally asked whether they were short of coffee; she said they were getting short, but would we wait whilst she made us some

KHAKI LETTERS—*continued.*

(mim.)—what ho !—whilst waiting for the coffee I was questioning a boy who could also speak English, where his father was, as I did not want to be sitting down and become the object of a hidden Boer's rifle. I was satisfied that there were not any Boers there, so had the cup of coffee and some bread, chatting meanwhile, and had a second cup, not giving our other chaps a thought, who were anxiously waiting our return. Before leaving I made chums with the little chap, who cried ; but when we returned to the other fellows, didn't we get it !"

✧ ✧ ✧ ✧

No. 4,602, Lance-Corpl. **R. D. S. Norman** (of SS.), writing from Ladybrand, September 8th, says :—

" DEAR COMRADES,—As you will observe from the above, I have at last made a move, for how long I am at present unable to say. I was on duty at BFN. when the rumour that Ladybrand had surrendered was received, and the Inspector detailed a party consisting of a lineman, driver and I, to proceed to Ladybrand and open communication with Maseru and Winburg if possible. We left on Monday, the 3rd, armed with revolvers and carbines. We arrived at Waterworks 4 p.m., and had to take instruments down to (Modder) river bed so as to protect them as much as possible from shell fire, for the Boers were only five miles off and making for there to attempt to cut off the water supply for BFN. Of course we were there to prevent that (mim.). This must have been the reason for their non-appearance. We were working till about 9 p.m. and then settled down to try and get a few hours' sleep. Every man, almost, was in the trenches, as the place had to be defended at any cost. The Boers did not come as expected, and we were thus deprived of getting rid of some of our ammunition. Next morning hardly a man could be seen, all having proceeded to Thabanchu. We saddled up and got on the way also, and reached Thabanchu at 4.30 p.m. on Tuesday the 4th. Just before we arrived we heard the police had been fired on and three wounded. We could not leave there until we got an escort, as the Boers were known to be just outside. We could not move until Saturday morning, when 25 police moved out to try to reach this place. We attached ourselves and were thus able to get on the road. All went well until we were about eight miles out, when a native boy (they are all boys, regardless of age) approached and said the Boers had looted a store in a kraal about two miles to our left. The police all formed up and charged magazines and set off, telling us to stick to the road and be ready for anything. They extended in skirmishing order, and on arriving found the Boer laager about four miles ahead and two spies endeavouring to reach it. They were quickly headed off and taken prisoners, then the party retired. We pushed on as hard as we could, for we had 40 miles to go and no chance of changing horses. We halted for dinner about one, and then observed a great number of troops approaching. They turned out to be Hamilton's force returning after relief of Ladybrand. We pushed on then very quickly, as the road was reported clear of enemy, and nothing further happened until we reached a spruit about 10 miles from here, when one of the police horses dropped dead. A mile further on we turned two adrift, done up, and a mile or two from here another two were treated similarly. Our ponies were really fagged out, and one looked like dying through it. We walked good part of the road to ease them. The roads are something awful, and it is really surprising how these horses can climb them—nothing but drifts and kopjes all through. This place is a lovely place, and something like a

KHAKI LETTERS—*continued.*

minature Switzerland, surrounded by immense hills with narrow neks and great fissures in the face of them, which makes it suicidal to approach them at dark. The town itself is the prettiest place I have seen, and indeed is said to be the best in the Colony. We arrived about 8 p.m. Saturday night, and as you will see, from the first, we have been just too late for any fighting. I had a walk to the Fort on Sunday where the brave little garrison were entrenched, and the fact of 150 holding 3,500 and guns at bay, shews what our poor Tommies have had to contend with in shifting them from similar positions. For three days' bombarding and over 320 shells, they accounted for three men wounded. The rocks are smashed and chipped everywhere with shells and bullets, and the oxen and mules were all shot. The sight and stench was horrible ; every one was shot as they were inspanned, and lay all in a line. The shelling was very accurate, which is attributed to the information supplied by a prisoner who escaped from here and gave the range of every place to a yard. Directly our men came in sight the Boers hopped it lively, and disappeared as quickly as they had appeared. When we arrived they were reported approaching, and the Major gave orders to prepare the Church for a siege, as he was going to defend it with six men, and hoped to hold out until force arrived. Directly the relief column were sighted the officer climbed up a telegraph pole and fixed a Union Jack, whilst bullets were flying around him like rain. I expect he will get a D.S.O. for his work. The relief column have gone from here, and it is said the reason for leaving this place without troops is to entice the Boers in again, when the force will relieve from the opposite direction, which will force the Boers to fight or surrender, as there are only two ways of getting into this place. We went out on Monday and repaired the line to Maseru, and are now working O.K. We have joined a vibrator and separator to the Winburg line, by which means it is sometimes possible to work through a break, but up to the present we have not been successful. I don't know where we will go to now, but hope to go to Winburg, as there is fighting around there ; it is about 70 miles from here, so we will have to commandeer our grub and sleep on a blade of grass (mim.). It is really astonishing how nice bully beef and biscuits taste when they are the only things procurable, and how soft a wooden floor is to what one would expect (mim.). We find water is the best thing to drink ; tea and coffee, etc., not being procurable, are not at all appreciated. We very nearly had a change for our dinner whilst out mending the line, for it happened that some geese got very near to our Kaffir dog ; the wings frightened the poor dog or I am afraid he would have got one, and then we would not have known what to do with it (mim.). Am going out now for spare instrument and stores left at a farm whilst the siege was on ; got a 25 mile ride between dinner and tea, so will have to examine farms *en route* for Boers (and food). We occasionally impose the duty of police on ourselves when it is likely to be profitable to us. The roads here are very well marked and not easily lost, for every mile there is a dead mule, ox, or horse. It is a grand climate, and with the grand grub and numerous comforts, I am really gaining in weight. I am not sure whether it is that or the responsibility on my shoulders (mim.). Think about NN for present again. So will conclude. Best respects to all."

✢ ✢ ✢ ✢

No. 25322, Sapper **Frank Horton** (of BM) in a letter from Viljoens Drift, dated September 12-13th, says :—

"The affair looks like lasting some time yet. This district is more unsettled and dangerous than it was in June. Numerous skirmishes have

KHAKI LETTERS—*continued.*

taken place here lately. Two of our mounted police went out yesterday and returned minus horses and arms, having been attacked by Boers (said to be lads aged 16 to 18) a mile or two from here. Early this morning a mounted Orderly left here along the Railway for a post only two miles away. Nothing has been heard of him since. I often take walks, but rely on my glasses to give me warning of undesirables. Two of our men were trallying towards Frederikstad from Potchefstroom after a fault when they received a volley from a party of Boers; the Corporal was killed instantly, the other man held up his arms in token of surrender, but he was shot; not content with this, the Boers stood over them and blew the Corporal's head nearly off and then stamped in his face; the private had seven shots in the region of the heart. We have had a series of train wrecking in this district lately, three being burned in one week; the line is invariably cut each night. Railway traffic after 6 p.m. is suspended. Hostilities are now on in the Thabanchu District, which we thought we had finished with last May. Half a mo.; just going to send a Railway message to a Stationmaster at Wolvehoek, nearly all figs. I hope I'll finish it (the message) before mail leaves to-morrow night. He's given me 'tic' while he shunts a train. 13th Sept.—Managed to get through it in 25 minutes. The Government Railway are offering billets as telegraphists to soldier signallers at £10 and £15 per month and allowances; if employed in Transvaal, from 33¼ to 50 per cent. on salaries. Government will also bring out wives and families free. An old TS friend is employed at this office, Alf. Lewis late of 'C' Division. Lewis left telegraphy some years ago and took up Secretaryship of Brewery in J.H., the Brewery closed during the war, Lewis was expelled from Transvaal, went to England, got temporary employment in TS, returned to S.A. and has taken up telegraphy until war is over, when he hopes to get something better. Just had a letter from Billy Stevenson; he's at Balmoral, and OK., Watkins at PR, Abbott at KB.

No. 1,546, Sapper **R. W. Eglinton** (of DY), in a letter from Thabanchu, dated September 20th, says:—

"At last the excitement has cooled down, the pressure of telegraph work has ceased, and I've got a few minutes to tell you all about it, or some of it, anyway. It was on the evening of Sunday, August 26th, that the Town Commandant warned us to look out in the night for important telegrams. About 7 a.m. the news came over the wires that the irrepressible De Wet had attacked Winburg about 6 a.m., been beaten back and was on his way to Thabanchu.

> "Then rose from sea to sky the loud farewell,
> Then shrieked the timid and stood still the brave."

I didn't shriek and I didn't stand still; on the contrary, I prepared to fold up my tents and gather up my valuables, including the office cash-box, and silently steal away. Lord Roberts sent Major Gibbs, commanding the detachment of 200 Worcesters here, orders to retire either on Ladybrand or the Waterworks. It was hard lines on Major Gibbs, who is a fighting man, and would have dearly liked to have shown his quality, but the position for defence is bad here, being commanded by hills on every side and water being scarce, so the poor old chap had to obey orders and retired on the Waterworks. The Assistant District Commissioner decided to stop and see it out, so of course I was only too glad to stop too and see some fun. I had everything packed on a cart we had commandeered, bar the instruments, which I

KHAKI LETTERS—*continued*.

could not disconnect till the very last minute. All that long day we waited and waited, but we never saw a Boer. The troops had left a heap of stores of all descriptions behind them, and—well, we didn't starve. It was sinful to see the waste, as bags of flour and other stuff were destroyed to prevent it falling into the hands of the Boers; but we saw that all of it wasn't wasted. Some of the bolder townspeople took out arms to deal with the enemy, and when I went to see the Commissioner on some business after nightfall, he was pleased to stand me a tot of rum and to say: 'You stand by me and I'll stand by you.' I felt like a Baden-Powell all at once. The night passed off quietly. The morning came fine and warm and the sun shone upon the peaceful scene. The place looked deserted, most of the inhabitants having chosen the better part of valour. There was little office work to do and I enjoyed the excitement of suspense all by myself. My two assistants, as the enemy wouldn't come to them, had saddled their nags and gone to seek the enemy, but they returned in evening and had seen nothing. Wednesday morning broke in awful fashion, high wind, heavy rain, thunder and lightning. Bland went out scouting with an English native of the place named Percy Hanger. A few Yeomanry (about 20) came to reinforce us, although Boer commandoes were reported all round us within 13 miles, and our garrison was then about 40 all told. Thursday morning the Commissioner seemed to think it was time to be going, and gave me orders to be ready to start, but as he had given orders for my commandeered cart to be returned to its owner I was left without conveyance. Lieut. Saunders, the only other officer, a fine fellow who commanded the police, was much annoyed at Commissioner's action, and, I believe, gave him a chewing-up. But there I was, with my retreat cut off and the Boers hourly expected. I burnt all my papers and got ready to smash the instruments up as a last resource. Bland and Hanger had not turned up the night before, and we were thinking the Boers had got them when they arrived with 13 prisoners—disloyal farmers who had been trafficking with the Boers and whom our two men dragged off from their farms. A necessary measure, as night of first alarm a plot had been discovered just in time, to co-operate with Boer commandoes, by surprising Thabanchu, taking the stores, and then advancing on the Waterworks, Bloemfontein, and so into Cape Colony. Bland and Hanger got highly commended for their action. Bland had spread report amongst the farms that we had 5,000 troops here, and the next we heard was that the Boers had moved to attack Ladybrand which is about 40 miles to the East of here. The next day, Friday, matters were getting decidedly warm. We heard that reinforcements were on the way from Bloemfontein for us, but on the other hand the Boers were within 15 miles, and it was a toss up which would get here first. Bland and Percy Hanger came in and reported that they, with a trooper named Donkin, had been fired on by the Boers 15 miles out at a range of 200 yards. Donkin's horse was shot, so they all dismounted and returned the fire. Seeing that the Boer horses were all loose together, the Boers having dismounted to fire, they directed the fire at the horses, thus stampeding them. Then they mounted again and galloped off, and as stampeded horses follow each other the Boer horses followed theirs. Then when they got near enough they stopped, caught one of the advancing steeds, remounted Donkin, galloped to a safe distance and returned the enemy's fire, and eventually got home in safety with a poor opinion of Boer marksmanship. That night was an anxious one. Horses neighed and cocks crowed all night. We saw distant fires on the kopjes in the enemy's direction, which might be veldt fires or watch fires. But morning came and

KHAKI SIDELIGHTS—*continued*.

no shell tearing through the roof woke us, but our eyes were gladdened by the sight of a detachment of Worcesters and three field pieces camped in the Market Place, and the worst was over as far as we were concerned. But my woes had started ; officers poured in with telegrams and inquiries, and to crown all, the wire worked badly, the chronic contact on the line becoming very bad. Cypher messages, 500 words long on a bad wire, make you sit up ! Bruce Hamilton's force marched in on Monday morning, the Cameron's with their pipes playing and the Bedfords with their band in full blast, all splendid troops. This is the first band I have heard in the country, and it fairly warmed the cockles of my heart. Hunter's force came in later in week—foot, horse and guns, and I was again up to my eyes in work. Hunter came in office after a telegram. He looks very young for a General. Goddem and I have been working night and day for some time. Bland is out scouting most of the time. The fault on the wire was still apparent. I sent the linesman out, changed the batteries, cleaned the contacts and did everything, but it was cruel. However, by dint of hard pegging we worried through, and the ducks at Bloemfontein discovered the fault and set it right after all the work was over. I have managed to get a fresh clerk from Sussex regiment and things have improved. Bland goes to Bloemfontein to-day as Police Sergt.-Major. The weather here is now very warm and pleasant, like an English June, and the apricot and peach trees are a mass of bloom. Remember me to all."

✤ ✤ ✤ ✤

No. 4,314, Sapper **F. A. Mason** (of E. District), writes from Laing's Nek, September 22nd :—

"After being with General Coke a little while an office was wanted at Laing's Nek. So over I came on an ox wagon with the instruments and the lineman to this place just as the Boers had commenced an attack upon Ingogo, and the railway. I assure you we were none too happy having no escort, but we got here safely (on August 18th) and I've been here since under the most comfortable circumstances it is possible to conceive. The Dublin Fusiliers are here, and a nicer set of fellows and officers you could not wish to meet. Active service ? Humph ! Life is a picnic. On Friday last was my birthday. I approached the Adjutant for half a case of whisky. I got it, Johnny Dewar at 2s. 6d. a bottle, and at 10.30 the Quartermaster dropped in, took the chair, and sang us a couple of songs. Next morning some cases of presents for the Dubs. were opened, and I got 2 pipes, 2 lbs. of light plug tobacco, 2 lbs. soft tobacco, 3 pairs socks, 2 pairs woollen drawers, and three Irish poplin handkerchiefs, a pair of porpoise hide laces (much needed), and five tins of Eiffel Tower lemonade. What is more, as my clobber is rather in the worse state for wear, I've had given me a pair of civilian khaki trousers, a regimental jacket, and a pair of serge trousers, and I'm also down for a new suit, putties and boots—this latter issue I shall try and save for ceremony visits at home. When the sun got hot the Quartermaster gave us a double tent in place of a single, and now the sun doesn't penetrate. The lineman sleeps on an iron bedstead ; I have a Boer camp bedstead; both of us have sacks stuffed with hay and straw as mattresses, so you see we are very comfortable. As regards food--well, it's just jolly. We have built a cookhouse out of corrugated iron ; we use it also for stores. We have heaps of everything, get a lot given us ; a ham the other day, a chicken, sometimes sausages, sometimes tins of saveloys, and we also have had half a sack of flour—result : cakes, jam tarts, and suet dumplings in the stew —

KHAKI LETTERS—*continued.*

thickening with liver and bacon, and melted butter with cauliflowers, which sometimes we get at a tanner a time. Oh! I shall make a fine cook when I return. Carrots, turnips, and greens we get at 6d. a bunch. We use Eno's fruit salts to soften the greens as we have no soda, and it answers the purpose beautifully. Rice custard is a common dish with us. Eggs we get at 2s. 6d. a dozen. By Jove, we do live! I dread to think what I shall suffer if I go home on a Government Transport and put up with salt junk again. Of course every day isn't a day of feeding; about once in three is the average. Steak, mashed potatoes, onions, rice and jam, with a cup of tea or coffee (for we don't dine till 8), is the generality of dinners. A nigger comes to us and washes up for a shilling or two a week, he also does our clothes on payment. He won't scrub the instrument table (a large box); I have to do that myself, for once he got a shock. He says now 'alive fire.'"

Writing again on October 12th, Mason says :—

" I'm still with the Dubs. I don't know where our own men are. At Volksrust there's Charlie Peters (TSF). and Symonds (TS), Sapper Laing in charge, also Peake, both of BS and 2nd Division. All Volunteer Companies are being disbanded. I wonder what they will do with us. Can we be spared, I wonder? Somehow I think I shall be here another six months, and sometimes I hope to be back by Christmas. Got nothing to complain about whatever, only general stagnation and the absence of knowledge when we go home. Kindest regards to all the boys."

✣ ✣ ✣ ✣

No. 29,095, Sapper **A. Gwilliam,** Maribogo Siding, September 28th, writes :—

" DEAR COLOURS,—It is about time that I gave you a short note of thanks for your kindness in sending KHAKI LETTERS so regularly. It is very interesting and useful to us all ; more especially do we find it so when, as is often the case, we find ourselves isolated, and stranded in a hole composed of about three houses upon the boundless veldt. Such is my experience at present. We are all beginning to turn our eyes homeward again, for all signs point to an early termination of the war. Roll on, England ! With kind regards and best wishes."

✣ ✣ ✣ ✣

No. 4,376, Sapper **W. W. Pearce,** writing from Godwan River station, September 30th, 1900, says :—

"Our party which left Pretoria last July are now all split up, and I don't know where they are. I was sent here in advance of Headquarters with Jack Fallon, John Sainsbury and two others, to open this as a transmitting station for Generals French, Pole-Carew, Hutton, Mahon and others, and for a few days we had a hot time with a huge pile of work which had accumulated at Machadodorp. When H.Q. went on to Nelspruit things became quiet, and now John Fallon and myself only remain. To-morrow, I hear, we are going to be transmitting station again. We are in the valley between the mountains, which runs from Waterval Onder to Komarti Poort, and is known as the Valley of Death during the rainy season, which is nearly on us. The heat and consequent depression is very bad here, and our only relaxation from the monotony is the trains bringing back the Guards and Colonials, *en route*, I believe, for home. The Krokodile river flows through here and we get good bathing. We exist on bully, but we get bacon, rice, and other things, which are luxuries to us. A lot of Boer prisoners have been sent to

KHAKI SIDELIGHTS—*continued*.

Pretoria during the last few days, one train to-day alone carrying 130 of them ; the majority looking well fed, clothed and happy. Well, I believe our boys are sick of this campaign and life, and look forward to meeting our friends in the near future."

No. 4,327, Sapper **A. J. Brooks,** writes from Kromellenboog Spruit, October 4th, as follows :—

" I'm afraid I miss a lot of mail matter. I've had no ' K.L.'s ' for some time now, and certainly didn't get the one you refer to in your letter, so was pleased to hear where so many of the chapses were. Those cigs., too, I have given up as having 'foundered' on the way. Don't send any parcels out here, O.M., they pass through so many hands other than P.O. men, that it's ' 10 to 1 against.' Lord only knows how my letters get here at all ; they are handed to me by all sorts of people, and sometimes they come up the line and sometimes down, and sometimes, as I have said, they founder on the way. We had De Lisle's Mounted Infantry Bde. and the Colonial Divn. under Dalgetty, here yesterday. They have just come across from Heilbron and Frankfort districts, and almost succeeded in nabbing De Wet at Elands Kop. De Wet himself acknowledged that he was never so near being Kopt as at Eland's Kop. However, on the night of the 1st, or rather at daybreak on the 2nd, we were awakened by terrific explosions and big gun fire. Of course we found our wire 'full earth' to the North, and with good reason, for De Wet was just then five miles to our North with 2,000 men and some big guns, and had dynamited half-a-dozen poles, besides destroying the railway line. His scouts, disguised as Loch's Horse, had surprised the outlying picket and took them prisoners without a shot being fired. De Wet's scouts are all dressed in khaki and have adopted the well-known badges of Loch's Horse—brown leather leggings, slouch hat with feather, and a broad band of crape (in memory of the late Lord Loch) worn on their left arm. This villainy will, in future, be put down with a very heavy hand ; it's quite impossible to be merciful to an enemy who stoop to such underhand practices. De Wet has promised the Boers, some of whom escaped into our camp, that he will end the war by October 13th. He says he can see the light of the 'coming dawn,' and that if only the Burghers keep fighting a little longer their independence is assured. He has vowed to take a camp along this section of the line, in order to obtain ammn. and food, even if he loses 500 men. Perhaps the brave Burghers might object to being one of the 500. Anyway, by the latest report, De Wet has only a few hundred with him now, but there's no telling when they may all come together again. I forgot to mention that the armoured train had a slap at them the other morning, but it was rather too late to do much damage. If only the picket had fired a few shots before surrendering things might have been different. Three of the genuine Loch's Horse from Wolvehoek were mortally wounded, all by explosive bullets. It is to be hoped that De Lisle and Dalgetty will get De Wet within the next fortnight. The men of De Lisle's and the Colonial Divn. had evidently had a rough time around Heilbron way. I can tell you that I never expected to see 10s. paid for a loaf of bread when I came out here ; yet yesterday a trooper of Kitchener's Horse paid 10s. for a small loaf of doughy bread that would not have fetched three-halfpence in London: in fact, no baker would have dared to sell it. There were plenty of others eager to buy at the same rate. Some one in camp had three boxes of ' Three Castles ' cigarettes (10 cigs. in each box); these sold at 7s. 6d. each,

KHAKI SIDELIGHTS—*continued.*

and were snapped up as hungry sharks snap up scraps. A man of the Kaffrarian Rifles paid a guinea for an old wooden pipe (value 9d.), a cake of hard tobacco (value 4d.), and a packet of cigarettes (value 4½d.) This lot was put up for auction owing to the great number of prospective purchasers, and, as I say, it fetched a guinea. A tin of common jam, worth about 5d., changed hands at 6s. Yes, our troops do live, especially those poor beggars on the flying columns. I must say, however, that we in these camps have nothing to complain of except, of course, the monotony of the food. We get plenty of bread and meat. My brother Arthur went up on a train the other day, but unfortunately I wasn't lucky enough to see him. I expect Bert has had a shift from Warrenton now, as I don't think there are now any military telegraphists in the Colony. Are any of the invalided homers back at the office yet? I haven't seen any 24thers lately, in fact I'm here out of the way altogether. I saw the C.I.V.'s go down on their way Home. Lucky beggars! There's many a swattie out here who would give quids to be Home by Christmas. Well, to save your patience, and also because the thousands of moths have practically put the candle out, I will now 'dry up' and get between the blankets, with one ear open for calls."

✧ ✧ ✧ ✧

No. 1,275, Sapper **C. J. Woode**, sends the following diary from Oliphant's Nek, near Rustenburg, dated October 5th :—

"On the 7th September I joined General Douglas's column at Mafeking. He was to work in conjunction with Lord Methuen, and our orders were to scour the neighbouring country, taking stray Boers, removing food supplies, and collecting horses. Herewith a somewhat rough account of my doings or rather the doings of the column. I may mention that instead of going on the General's staff, I was attached to the 11th Co. R.E.'s who do field works, having about 10 mounted men with whom I travel. There has been absolutely no telegraph work for me to do, but I generally hold the horses for the men whilst they repair drifts, roads, bridges, or fix the pumps for the water supply. Our usual mode of life is to rise between the early hours of one to three a.m., moving off with the cold gnawing at your loins and small of your back. Our breakfast being coffee which, with all my hardships and rough food, I am still unable to drink, and a biscuit; trekking on then till 11 or 12 noon; dinner about four, tea at six, bed soon after. The scenery being various, flat country for the former part of our journey, now in the mountains with their rough and rugged passes, which cause great destruction to the wheels of the wagons and hard work for the transport animals, many dropping dead by the roadside. On the 7th I journeyed to Mafeking, joining the column. As soon as I got there we started back, camping at Louw's Farm.—8th : Ottoshoop was reached.—9th : On the Lichtenberg road, fighting started as soon as we left our camping ground, continuing all day, we shelled them out of several kopjes, camping at Foster's Mills, where a good stream ran, we obtaining good supplies of forage for our horses from the farm there.—10th : We trekked after the Boers, camping near a large range of hills; no fighting.—11th : As our outposts were coming in to camp at 3 a.m. they were fired on, some wounded, so we were delayed, having to fight our way out of our camp, fighting continuing for some time ; we camping on the veldt, our water supply being from a huge hollow, which was very pretty, being of tremendous size and very rocky, also studded with trees, the water at bottom being of great depth. The sides of hollow being the home of various birds.—12th : We camped at a

KHAKI LETTERS—*continued*.

farm called Kunana, where we captured large stock of cattle, several wagons and many prisoners, some took refuge in the fields of forage, but unfortunately one man turned evidence for the English and told their hiding place. Sentries were placed at various parts and the forage burned, eventually bringing forth the hiders.—13th and 14th: We had a short march into Lichtenberg. Here we stayed, taking all provisions, forage, cattle and several prisoners. I saw several men here who had not been fighting for many months, many of them being obliged to again take up arms, and some with the Boer ambulance, owing to the English evacuating this place after occupying it, caused great distress and much trouble to the inhabitants. In Lichtenberg I managed to secure two air pillows, which I can tell you cause it to be a great deal more comfortable, for the ground is often very rocky to sleep on.—15th: Leaving Lichtenberg we went due south, camping at an Englishman's farm—Pool's Farm; his house was not in any way destroyed neither his stock.—16th: We camped at another farm near a vlei (a marsh with a little stream running through).—17th: We went to Bessiesvlei, these several places being where I came some months since with General Hunter.—18th: Went back to Barberspan, where I stayed for ten days in May. I had piece of luck, the storekeeper giving me a chicken and cup of coffee.—19th: Went to Commdt. Lessler's Farm at Leuwpan. It was an ideal farm, being well laid out with furrows (ditches), kraals (cattle enclosures), and the farm contained three beautiful irrigation pumps, on the dredger bucket system, the supply of water being quite adequate for all our needs and that of the oxen.—19th to 25th: Here we rested at the above place, though we had to put up with awful storms of dust. We had sports one afternoon, which relieved the monotony a little.—26th: Had long march cross country, and were rewarded with very bad water which one hardly cared to wash in, much less drink.—27th: Camped just outside Lichtenberg. —28th: Went through Lichtenberg and camped at Kunana again.—29th: We camped Dulkfontein, the scenery of mountains ahead being somewhat pretty.—30th: We camped at foot of mountain, one of Witwatersrand.

October 1st: Enemy in sight at Reitpan, several shots being exchanged. —2nd: Kleinfontein, camped, scenery still pretty, though water extremely scarce.—3rd: Bivouacked at farm house, pretty sight.—4th: We reached Oliphant's Nek, here we came to a pass between two ranges of mountains.—5th: Still here, where we remain for a few days waiting for our convoy to return from Rustenberg with fresh food supplies. To-day and yesterday I have had to patrol river bank for a mile or more to prevent its pollution at parts used for drinking purposes; our convoy of troops for the last couple of days all having to proceed in single file as the road was made through the mountains, as it were. To-night we have had a decent storm; have to post our letters to-morrow, so farewell for present. Kind regards to all."

No. 4,670, Sapper **W. E. Braybon**, writing from Heilbron, Oct. 9th, says:—

"DEAR KEMP.—I think when I wrote you last I was at Gottenberg Halt—through on a buzzer—at which place the 2nd Bedfords were lying a mile and a half from me. It was here that sixty Boers in full khaki rode between the two camps and killed our outpost, and were off like a shot midst a shower of shrapnel. We found seven wounded Boers at a farm, so got our own back. Heilbron was evacuated for the third time, and I was picked up *en route* by the last train to leave. It was a little excitement to see

KHAKI LETTERS—*continued.*

the trains steaming past, loaded with soldiers' stores, civilians, Kaffirs, horses, &c., &c. A friendly ganger stopped the train or I should have had to trek it with the 'Beds.' We were exiles at Wolvehoek, being located in a room adjoining the guard room, and we had a lively time of it. Many farms have been burnt round here. One night alone we killed seven rats in our room, so what with change of guard every two hours, and rats, we had little peace, and during the day there were thousands of flies in the place. We averaged the number on one matchboard and the total came out at 6,500 in one room. Talk about no flies on me! I was a mass of them! We had to turn out one night, as the Boers attempted to cross the line and fired on the picket, and do not forget it, the latter were not slow in responding, and the Boers cleared. The next night, De Wet and 2,000 men with 14 guns surrounded the picket, whom they captured without a shot being fired, and De Wet crossed the line: the very thing we had been trying to prevent, so once again we were outwitted. It was a clever ruse. The Boers personated the local mounted infantry, Loch's Horse, and came up and said 'We are Loch's Horse team,' and then 'Hands up.' The armoured train came up accidently and got at the rear-guard, and were the means of capturing two wagons with the big ammunition in them. The next day I had a trip in the armoured train, and we again shelled somebody and turned out the 3rd Buffs on the line. Proceeding on our journey we found a bridge partly destroyed, so I was busy on the buzzer, sitting on a rock on a kopje. We were joined by the Colonial forces, who are a red hot lot of dare-devils. We had a lot of work to get off. The place was called Leeuwpoort; rather a pretty little place, consisting of one farm, some trees—a rarity—and a river from which we had a fish breakfast, which was a treat. My piscatorial efforts read: one hour, one herring. Overtime pays better. I was not built for an Isaac Walton. Can't stand worms. Had them once. They've had me more often. The next day, as the armoured train was leaving Leeuwpoort, she was fired on, so we saw a very lively 'dust-up' for half an hour, but, as usual, the Boers hooked it. De Wet is playing the gang of thieves style: they come together, make a grab, and when *the* 'Bobbie' comes they scatter. We sent off thirteen prisoners from here this morning, the result of a combined action of Le Gallais' and Charles Knox's forces. The participators in the move cursed their luck, as the Boers got wind of their movement, and so they again missed a good bag. Things will be pretty hot here for a time yet, and the police and regulars who will remain will have plenty to do. What a marvellous change there will be in the O.R.C. in a quarter of a century! At least there should be. There is ample scope for improvement and development. I met Sambells the other day; he came from Vredefort in the armoured train. Aubrey Richards called here to-day, looking remarkably fit. Nothing exciting to report."

No. 1,274, Sapper **W. F. Adams,** writing from Kimberley, October 14th, says:—

"This week has been fairly eventful. On Wednesday evening last, I, with a few more of ours, went to the usual soldiers' concert. In the middle of one of the items, and by the way, just before the refreshments were to be served, an orderly rushed up to the platform and said that every military man was to at once proceed to his camp and await orders. The ladies who dispense the cakes and coffee, and provide the entertainment, naturally got very alarmed. They asked us to stay a few minutes to have some coffee and

KHAKI LETTERS—*continued.*

cake, and it was while so engaged that I struck oil, or in other words, another musical friend, he was down for a banjo solo. He wanted an accompanist so I immediately volunteered to do what I could for him so long as I remained in Kimberley. He was very pleased and asked me to come and have a little practice with him and his banjo quartette. I went, and a more enjoyable afternoon I haven't spent out here. We played together for about 1½ hours, when I had to leave to go on duty. The next appointment was for a quiet practice Sunday morning which came off to-day, and was very successful. We seem about as near getting away from here as we were a long time back, but under the altered circumstances I shan't mind staying a bit longer. One of the civil Supts. and a clerk left KB. yesterday for a holiday trip to England for Christmas. The clerk's name is Freddie Foote (late of 'C' group), and he will probably be looking round TS. Well, *tempus* is *fugit*-ing, so must now close, with kindest regards to all."

No. 4,614 Sapper **F. R. White**, writing from Kroonstad, October 23rd, says:—

"DEAR KEMP,—It is with a sad and heavy heart that I forward you particulars of the loss of another of our colleagues, by the death, under painfully distressing circumstances, of Sapper T. Hamilton, late of Glasgow, who, it will be remembered, sailed on April 1st from Southampton on board the 'Winifredian.' On Sunday morning last, October 21st, he, together with McQueen, also of Glasgow, and myself, went for a walk, in the course of which we rested for some time against a big stone not a hundred yards from the military cemetery. Little did we think as we sat there that in less than 36 hours we should pass that spot again—the one, sleeping his last long sleep, borne on the shoulders of one companion, the other companion following in silent grief. Returning to camp about noon, 'Tam,' seeking refuge from the sun and heat, stretched himself beneath a Cape-cart in which were seated two of the fellows (perhaps I ought to explain that a Cape-cart is a vehicle very similar to an ordinary trap, but has a hood and a centre pole in place of two shafts). He had been there but a few minutes when a strong and sudden gust of wind caught the cart and caused it to tilt backwards upon poor Tam's head. As quickly as possible we righted and moved the cart, and were horrified to find one of the nuts of the spring beneath it had entered his left temple, inflicting a terrible wound. All that we could possibly do was done for him, being assisted by two nurses from the Scotch Hospital, who were in church close by, and gently and as quickly as we could, we conveyed him on a stretcher to the Scotch Hospital, a mile or more away. He never regained consciousness, and passed away at 8.15 next morning, death being due to 'fracture of vault of cranium and laceration of brain substance.' About five the same evening he was laid to rest in the military cemetery which stands out on the veldt to the north of Kroonstad, being borne to the grave on the shoulders of four of his colleagues. Full military honours were accorded him, the attendance including an officer and nearly 40 men of the R.E.'s. Tam was held in the highest esteem by all, and to say the occurrence cast a gloom over the staff but feebly conveys our feeling. Just entering manhood, it seemed cruel for him to be cut off with such awful suddenness, yet, sudden as was the call, it did not find him unprepared. Though he did not parade his religion, Tam was a firm Christian, and true to his faith, even in camp life; this knowledge must afford some solace to his sorrowing friends. Second to none with regard to ability and always ready

KHAKI LETTERS—*continued.*

to do their best, Scotland in general, and Glagow in particular, has reason to feel proud of the telegraphists she has sent to South Africa. In Tam she has lost one of the bravest, best and noblest of her sons, and the heartfelt sympathies of those who knew him go forth to his stricken relatives in this their hour of sorrow."

✤ ✤ ✤ ✤

No. 4,610, Sapper **A. E. Stevens** writes from Bloemfontein, 28th October :—

"What do you think of the state of affairs round about us here? Now Boers seem to be all round us, and even our outposts have been sniped at, and at a place called Dewets Dorp, a small town the garrison of which had been withdrawn, the Boers entered very early one morning, knocking at the room where the chaps were sleeping (in the office); they only shouted out, 'Go away, you old fool; the office isn't open till 7,' but they knocked a bit louder and eventually 'twas opened, and judge of our fellows' surprise at being covered with several Mausers! They commandeered the stamps, cash, etc., and took the T.C.'s over to the hotel, gave 'em a good feed of the best, paid for it in paper money, then told them to push off. Later they were met by a column coming to their rescue. It looks as if the war in the O.R.C. is just commencing, and they will have to bring a lot of cavalry down to clear them out, and go right through the Colony. Armed picquets patrol this place at night, and after 8, soldiers are challenged. Civilians are allowed out till 9, and after that time if they have not the countersign or a pass they are detained for the night in quod. Civilians are not allowed to congregate round the market square from 5.30 p.m. to 5 a.m., or else they get a night's cheap lodging. Weather very hot now and an occasional sand storm by way of a change. Am still going strong and well."

✤ ✤ ✤ ✤

No. 4,338, Sapper **D. G. Davies** (of CF), writing from Nelspruit, October 23rd, says :—

"DEAR KEMP,—I thank you very much for having taken so much trouble in my behalf with regard to my supposed capture and escape from the Boers at Frederickstad. I do not know who the Sapper Davies referred to could have been, but as he has fortunately escaped from his captors, it will matter little now. One thing is certain, I am not the person referred to. July the 25th, the date of Davies's capture, I was with a party of telegraphists *en route* from Heilbron to Vereeniging, the former place being evacuated by our troops at the time. Poor Wyatt, of Grimsby, whose death was recorded in 'K.L.,' accompanied us. He was unwell at the time, but did not think anything serious was the matter. I left Vereeniging with Poole (of BS) for Pretoria on the day of his admission to Hospital, and was astounded when I heard, four days afterwards, the sad news of his death. This place lies in the Crocodile Valley, and situated about 220 miles East of Pretoria. The scenery in this valley is the prettiest I have come across since my arrival in the country, but being a bushy as well as a low-lying country, it is considered very unhealthy during the rainy season which has just commenced. I don't think we shall be here very long, as there is too much risk of the malarial fever breaking out among the troops. I cannot wind up without thanking you for the bright little 'K.L.' which arrives at this out-of-the-way spot with such punctuality. Trusting to have the pleasure of meeting you on my return. With kind regards."

KHAKI LETTERS—*continued.*

No. 4,672, Sapper **Arthur Revill**, writes from Bloemfontein, November 4th, as under:—

"DEAR COLOURS,—It is some time since I wrote you, but so many of my comrades have covered the same ground that I should have done, so thought I would give it a rest for a bit. I must tell you that three others and myself met the great 'B.P.' here a short while ago; he was coming down the main street. We gave him a smart salute, and needless to add we felt very proud on his returning the same. We afterwards saw him upon the railway station platform, and were particularly struck with his entirely unassuming and very manly bearing, and yet the Hero of Mafeking was most natural in his general address. Things have been very lively around Bloemfontein of late, the Boers buzzing around like so many swarms of wasps, and it appears to me that not many of our South African heroes will be on the way Home this side of Christmas at all events. We have heard the reports of the guns on several occasions during the past few weeks. The Military Authorities are very vigilant in Bloemfontein. Thanking you for 'K.L.'s,' and wishing yourself and all a very Merry Christmas, nothing more now remains for me to add."

✣ ✣ ✣ ✣

IN MEMORIAM.

✠

Sergeant Charlie Jones, 1st City of London V.A.

Died at Brompton Hospital 14th Oct., 1900, in his 25th year.

✠

> FAREWELL—the long farewell! The days are past
> When suffering watched your pulse's every beat,
> While cruel Fate drew near with laggard feet—
> Full certain of his victim—claimed at last!
>
> Who can but view, with spirit overcast,
> The young, strong life thus ended—incomplete?
> Yet who would say relief were less than sweet,
> Though love bereaved stand sorrowing aghast?
>
> Rough, rugged heart—yet true to inmost core—
> It's kindly impulse stayed for evermore!
> Though sullen earth our loss may never tell,
> The thoughts of those who loved, who knew you best,
> Go sighing to the spot that gives you rest:
> And grieving, breathe our saddest word—"Farewell!"

T.S.F.
W. H. F. WEBB.

Khaki Sidelights and Notes.

The Victoria Cross.—For many years now the Post Office Rifle Volunteers have been connected with the Corps of Royal Engineers, and the Staff generally has taken an interest in the connection that has linked so many of their colleagues to that Royal Corps. It is well known that the duties of this body are many-sided, as has been recorded in previous pages of "K.L.," and although our attention has been directed almost entirely to the doings of the Telegraph Section to which our own men are attached, we, nevertheless, are not unmindful that that branch is but one of the component parts of the regiment to which they have the honour to belong. We feel that we should be neglectful of our duty in these pages if we did not record the valiant deeds of a member of another section, for the benefit of those members of the Reserve for whom this booklet has been compiled; and this we do with as much pride as were it one of our own. We will take the Regimental paper — *The Sapper* — for November, and let that trusty journal be our mouthpiece.

TROOP SERGT.-MAJOR F. H. KIRBY, R.E.

"Hearty congratulations to No. 26810, Corporal Frank Howard Kirby, R.E., Field Park! (And so say all of us.—"K.L." readers.)

"It was with no small amount of pride that we heard on the 6th of last month that Her Majesty had conferred the Victoria Cross on one of ours.'

"Previous to the event which led to the award of this decoration, Kirby had distinguished himself in many a hard-fought engagement in the South African campaign, and had been reported on in despatches in the highest terms.

"Only a few days prior to the grant of the V.C., the *London Gazette* notified that the Queen had been pleased to approve of the award of the medal for distinguished conduct in the field to Corporal Kirby, in recognition of his gallant conduct in the present campaign. Kirby was corporal at this time, but since the award of the V.C. he has been promoted Troop Sergt.-Major. He has only $8\frac{8}{12}$ years' service.

"We think we are correct in saying that Troop Sergt.-Major Kirby is the only one of the rank and file who is in the unique, not to say proud, position of being the possessor of both the Victoria Cross and the Distinguished Conduct Medal.

"The official announcement of the award of the Victoria Cross reads as follows:—

"'The Queen has been graciously pleased to signify Her intention to confer the decoration of the Victoria Cross on the undermentioned non-commissioned officer, whose claim has been submitted for Her Majesty's approval, for his conspicuous bravery in South Africa, 1900, as stated against his name.

"'*Corporal F. Kirby, Royal Engineers.*—On the morning of the 2nd June a party sent to try to cut the Delagoa Bay Railway were retiring, hotly pressed by very superior numbers. During one of the successive retirements of the rearguard a man whose horse had been shot was seen running after his comrades. He was a long way behind the rest of his troop and was under a brisk fire. From among the retiring troop Corporal Kirby turned and rode back to the man's assistance. Although by the time he reached him they were under a heavy fire at close range, Corporal Kirby managed to get the dismounted man up behind him and to take him clear off over the next rise held by our rearguard. This is the third occasion on which Corporal Kirby has displayed gallantry in the face of the enemy.'"

KHAKI SIDELIGHTS—*continued.*

Rudd Fund. I find that a slight error has crept in on page 365. The gentleman who did not wish his name to be known sent 10s., and although this was intended to be added in, it somehow eluded my eye, thus causing the total up to the last issue to be given as £90 15s. 5d. instead of £91 5s. 5d. Since that date, G.S.W. adds 5s. and Sergt. Phillips sends 5s., making the amount handed over to Mrs. Rudd £91 15s. 5d. Appended is a copy of the receipt given by the widow to the two gentlemen of the "L" Division who have had the matter in hand.

"Received of Messrs. Driscoll & Welch the sum of **Ninety-one pounds, fifteen shillings and fivepence,** the same being the whole of the subscriptions to the above fund." "(Signed)   LOUISE RUDD.
"*14th November,* 1900."

Subsequently some stamps were received from E.J.A. (at the front), to be sold for the fund, and another 4s. is, therefore. to be added.

"The Sapper" in its November issue contains the following notice which will be read with interest by "K.L." subscribers who have so nobly helped in this good work :—" It has been a source of pleasure to us to notice how the little booklet KHAKI LETTERS, conducted by Colour-Sergt. R. E. Kemp, has been putting before its readers the case of one of 'ours,' viz., Sapper A. S. Rudd, who died of enteric fever at Bloemfontein on July 1st last. Rudd formerly belonged to the Central Telegraph Office, but left to help his father. After his father's death he joined the Royal Engineers, served his time, was transferred to the reserve, and, after procuring a situation elsewhere, finally found himself back again, on May 18th, 1897, with his old colleagues at the Central Telegraph Office, London. He was recalled to the colours January 3rd, 1900, and sailed for South Africa a few days later, together with a number of N.C.O's. and men of the 24th Middlesex (Post Office) Rifle Volunteers. who. as is known, form the Telegraph Reserve of the corps, and in whose interest KHAKI LETTERS is published. During the whole of the time Rudd was on active service his old division clerks subscribed amongst themselves sufficient to give his wife the usual weekly wage, and this they carried on right into the month of October. When his death was announced they felt they had lost a genuine friend. A thought of the widow and her three little ones at once prompted an appeal to the Telegraph Staff generally, and KHAKI LETTERS opened its pages to proclaim it. The result has been watched by us. The divisions. groups, and sections, into which the chief office is divided, have heartily and liberally responded. Comrades in South Africa, Post Office Rifles, R.E., and others, have also assisted to swell the funds, which now stand at just over £90, and still the subscriptions are rolling in. We tender our very best thanks to all concerned in this good work, but especially to the Editor of KHAKI LETTERS and the Division clerks who made up the late Sapper Rudd's usual pay to his wife, while he was on active service. Such practical sympathy speaks louder than words."

Hospitals at the front.—We have seen in the papers recently so much criticism on the hospital arrangements in South Africa, that we are glad to be able to again bear testimony in regard to "one of ours." I extract the following portion of a letter it was my pleasure to receive from Staff-Sergt. F. OLDHAM, St. J. A. B., Kimberley. dated Oct. 15th :—

"Dear Kemp,—To-day I had the pleasure of perusing No. 16 of your 'K.L..,' and as it concerned employees of the Postal and Telegraph Service, it interested me very much, I being in the Crewe office (when not interviewing Kruger and his mob). I notice in two letters which appear in No. 16 of your issue, that reference is made to the late 4366, Sapr. Frew, of the 1st Tel. Batn. R.E. In June and July I was in charge of a section of this hospital, 300 odd patients, and on July 1st, I well remember poor Frew being admitted into my section. On admission to hospital all particulars are taken, and when I found that he belonged to T.S. I had several short chats with him about the 24th V.R.E's. On the 5th July he was taken much worse, and he was placed in a 'special' marquee, and received every attention from the Orderly (Palmer). On the 6th he seemed to ramble. and gradually get lower. Sister Lawrence gave him the best attention, as did also Dr. O'Reilly. On Saturday, the 7th July, he was much worse, and through the day spoke of his brother. We tried to understand where his brother was, but he only muttered which we could not decipher. About 6 o'clock the Orderly called my attention to him, and I noticed a great change, so sent an Orderly to ask the Sister and Doctor to come to see him. Everything possible was done for him, but he failed to rally, and passed to his long rest about 6.20 p.m. After tea I thought I would go down to the P.O. Telegraphs, and

KHAKI SIDELIGHTS—*continued.*

see if anyone knew him. It is 2½ miles from the hospital. When I reached the Post Office, one of his comrades told me his brother had just left the office. I told them poor Frew had left the sorrows of this world, so they tried to find his brother. On Sunday his brother came to the hospital and spoke with me. The Doctor, Sister, and myself stood by as Frew passed quietly away. I must tell you in fair justice that the best attention was given to him. We are shocked with many hospital scandals just at present, but in this case, as in all others I have seen in this hospital, he was well cared for."

Poor Dick Frew was so well known in the C.T.O. and so highly esteemed by all, that we feel much indebted to Staff-Sergt. Oldham for his kind and thoughtful letter.

Doubtless the numerous K.L. readers will be as much amused at the following communication as I was:—"My dear Colours,—I heartily congratulate you on your recent acquisition of a row of houses out of K.L., and I am sure you will no less cordially wish me joy in the use of 'A Champion Swan Fountain Pen,' which you have been so good as to present to me in recognition of valuable services rendered. I wish you could see me in the Khaki Cycling Costume in which (it is alleged) I have been madly careering round the district distributing K.L.'s; which costume, be it known on the QT., I have purchased out of the fabulous sum which I collected ostensibly in aid of the K.P.F., but which, if the truth were permitted to leak out, was in reality a 'Local Secretary's Levy'! Oh, we are a grand pair, you and I! We *do* know how to pat each other on the back and say nice things to each other! And shan't we have some good laughs together when I tell you how I 'diddled 'em' out of their pennies; how I pinched their K.L.'s and sold 'em over again! &c., &c., &c., for I have accepted the very kind invitation you have sent me (for which I most sincerely and gratefully thank you) to spend my holiday with you and bring the wife and nipper! It is most kind of you to offer to pay our return fares to London, and to promise us such a royal time! Truly, as you remark, K.L. have done good in more ways than one! How on earth did you manage to obtain from Paardeberg the ox-hide and khaki serge uniform in which you are going to have bound an edition de luxe of K.L. printed on hand-made paper, with your autograph photo. as frontispiece, for presentation to H.M. The Queen, Lord Roberts and Kitchener, and Khaki Ent? Eh, Dick lad, tha'art an enterprising chap! I am negociating with the tenant of a large shop in the main street in Leeds for the use of his best window for a week, to display my copy to the admiring and envious gaze of the public of Yorkshire! I hope you don't blame *me* for 'letting on' about your houses or my fountain pen, old man! I have never breathed a word! I only hope my misappropriation of the K.P.F. won't reach *your* ears! Never mind about the information of the Presentation Copies coming round to me,—I'll be as surprised when I receive mine, as tho' I had never heard of it!"

Just one, from a large number of similar letters, for our comrades at the front will be pleased to see the name as well as read the expressions of our Second in Command:— "Godalming, Nov. 9th, 1900.

"Dear Colour-Sergeant Kemp,—I enclose a further subscription for my KHAKI LETTERS. I am sure I have more than my money's worth of interest, and I hope they will continue for some time yet, though I should like to think they would cease only from the fact of all our brave comrades being once more safe at home. Though all of us in the regiment know the stuff that our men are made of, your publication of their letters shows very plainly how cheerfully they take their hardships, and their letters will bring home to many the fact that war is not all beating of drums and waving of swords, but that besides this, men are patiently and cheerfully doing their share of the work in lonely spots, exposed to danger and disease, with little chance of getting any notice such as the fighting soldier gets. I wonder how many of the thousands who crowded the streets at the return of the C.I.V.'s thought of this? But our welcome home to our own heroes, though it may not be so magnificent, will be none the less hearty, and I trust we may soon see them safe home. I can only wish that the A.P.O.C. had found a Col.-Sergt. Kemp to organise and edit their letters as you have done for the R.E.'s. Thanking you for the pleasure your little Magazine has given me, I am, yours truly,

(Signed) E. MATTHEW HALE, Lt.-Col., Post Office Rifles."

Dear me! What curious ideas some people have—so curious, indeed, that they do not like to own them, putting them on paper and sending them through the post under a *nom de plume.* This is what he says:—"DEAR COL.-SERGT. I think your 'K.L.' splendid, and cannot find words to express my appreciation of

KHAKI SIDELIGHTS—*continued*.

them and also to thank you for the time and trouble they must cost you. 'Not satisfied' is the cry at TS, so perhaps you will excuse a suggestion. When your book ceases to be published. I, as many others probably, will have them bound, and I do not think it will be complete without a frontispiece, and my suggestion is that our *dear, devoted* and *respected* Colour-Sergeant's portrait should be there, as I'm sure all would be pleased to show such a comrade to their chums. I know the expense of these pictures as you have described in 'K.L.,' but we are willing to go without somebody's portrait to have yours. Hoping you will see your way clear to comply, I am, dear Colour-Sergeant, yours very truly, 'One of the "I" Compy.'"

[I cannot say who the writer is, but should imagine he is good at writing love-letters. See how nicely he puts it. Could it be nicer? Whether he has contaminated other poor mortals with his outrageous suggestion or no, I cannot say, but I know that many others have approached me on the same subject, and have been so persistent in their appeals, that I have had to send them away with the semi-satisfactory answer, "I'll see."]

The Buzzer "R. Q."—The writer of the short description in our last number regrets that his memory was not technically accurate. The buzzer or vibrator is wound in the ordinary manner, not as induction coil, though the currents are broken in the same manner as in the induction coil. The buzzer is joined in circuit as a shunt, and has the effect of producing the rapid variations so desirable for reading by telephone. The instrument is not generally used when ordinary apparatus will answer the purpose, but when lines are bad it maintains communication much longer, and has worked through 16 miles of bare wire lying on the ground.

Run on the P.O. The *Evening News* of Nov. 22nd is responsible for the following:—"HOW A SHEFFIELD MERCHANT HAD REVENGE ON THE AUTHORITIES.—An extraordinary scene has been witnessed at the General Post Office, Sheffield, as the result of a dispute between the postal authorities and Mr. J. G. Graves, with reference to the postage of parcels. Mr. Graves is desirous of posting in bulk numerous parcels, often amounting to several hundreds, which he despatches nightly, but is not allowed to do so, therefore he has adopted the expedient of sending some three hundred of his employees, each bearing a parcel, which was singly handed across the counter to the despatching clerk. Such an influx occasioned the total disorganization of ordinary work of the office, and the general public for some time were entirely unable to even approach the outer door. Mr. Graves intends to persist in the same course of action until his difference with the Post Office has been amicably adjusted." The *Daily Mail* adds, "The Lord Mayor of Sheffield, it is said, will intervene between the Post Office and Mr. Graves with a view of adjusting the points in dispute."—An armistice is on.

The "Civil Service Times" came into existence on November 17th, 1900, and "to afford a birdseye view of service doings, a meeting ground for all classes of Civil Servants, a forum for the discussion of all service questions." The first number contains a cablegram from Lord Roberts as under :—

"Government House, Johannesburg, 14th November. Editor, *Civil Service Times*. Postal Corps have done good work under exceptionally difficult circumstances.—ROBERTS."

In conspicuous type the following appeal appears :—"The time is approaching when our Comrades, the Army Post Office Corps, now 'doing their country's work' in Africa, will be home once more, and we have the honour to propose that a proper organization should be called into existence to secure them the hearty welcome they deserve. Such a welcome must be one representative of all who are proud of them and of their work, without distinction of any sort. 'Duke's son and cook's son' connected with the great department of the State on which they have shed such lustre and distinction by their magnificent work must stand shoulder to shoulder to cheer them, and sit side by side to drink their health. The great commercial world, too, have a right to share in the privilege of helping to make their reception a magnificent one, for, in a way, the members of the A.P.O.C. are 'sons of the City.' We who have lived and worked with them knew that they would do their duty well when we wished them 'God-speed' as they left us, and now every comrade, friend and well-wisher—aye, and every member of the general public too —will be glad to have it on the highest authority—that of the Commander-in-Chief—that they did do their duty well, and have been a credit to the department to which they belong and to their country." Without talking much about lustre, etc., we have already intimated in "K.L." that something similar must be done for the R.E. Reserves, a fact that must not be lost sight of.

Notes.

A letter from the front depicts a native runner, in whose hand is an envelope, with my address upon it; under it are these words:—
"I'm only a nigger, Boss, but safely dodged the Boers,
And brought this little letter to England's white-cliffed shores."

Khaki Postage Fund.—I have much pleasure in acknowledging the following amounts that have been received up to time of going to press:—Divisions:—"C" 14s. 2d., "D" 6s. 4d., "E" 4s. 8d., "G" 3s.,* "I" 10s.,* "K" 9s. "L" 13s. 7d.; News, 8s. 6d.; Special Staff, 6s. 3d. Groups:—"A" 4s. 6d., "B" 3s. 9d., "C" 3s. 3d., "D" 3s. 4d., "G" 4s. 6d., "H" 5s. 6d., "I" 8s. 8d., "I," 3s. 9d., "M" 6s. 11d.; Glasgow, 1s.; W.S.R and T.W.P. (Aldershot), 5s. And by post on Monday last I received a letter from Our Boys at Bloemfontein, in which the writer, L. Corpl. A. Stevens, says:—"I thought it would be a pleasure to many of us, if we could, in a small way, add to your funds, appreciating as we do the disposal, for charitable objects, of any surplus. The ready response I obtained shewed that I was quite right in regard to the wishes of my comrades, and I have the pleasure of forwarding you the sum of £2, to devote to Khaki Postage Fund, or whatever fund you deem fit." I did not ask our comrades at the front to do this, but isn't it grand! They can rest assured that their £2 will not be used for the postage of books to them, but will be held over until I can add a bit more to it for "charitable objects." In our next number, I hope to see other Sections' subscriptions recorded, as it will be the last chance they will have.

*These are not yet finished.

Official acknowledgment.—I desire to draw my friends' attention to the receipt handed me on Monday afternoon, a copy of which is reproduced here:—

The "Daily Telegraph" Shilling Fund, for our Soldiers' Widows and Orphans.

"Daily Telegraph" Offices, Fleet St., E.C.
November 26th, 1900.
Received, with thanks, from Mr. R. E. Kemp, "Khaki Letters" Booklet, the sum of £10 (200 Shillings).
Stamped and Signed by the Cashier.

It is well known that the D.T. Shilling Fund is dropping off of late, and that its list does not now appear daily, as heretofore. So I have asked that the above contribution may be inserted in the first list next week. Look out for it. Personally, I am very glad to give notice that I have been able to hand even this small sub. over to such a worthy object. But cancel the big personal pronoun, friends—that ever-recurring "I," and let me thank *you* for enabling me to do so, which I sincerely do. "Colours" has been accused—perhaps only playfully—of "hysteria" when he returns thanks in these pages, but let me say there is no such element in the real earnestness with which I always endeavour to acknowledge a deed that is so kindly done. (Aside: I wish it had been £100, don't you?)

Efficiency.—It will interest our comrades at the front, as well as those at home, to know how the old regiment stands as regards its efficiency at the end of the Volunteer year, i.e., October 31st. (The figures represent efficients, non-efficients, and strength of Company respectively). "A" 74, 6 = 80.—"B" 104, 16 = 120.—"C" 107, 12 = 119.—"D" 91, 0 = 91.—"E" 97, 1 = 98.—"F" 84, 0 = 84.—"G" 64, 2 = 66.—"H" 94, 2 = 96.—"I" 86, 8 = 94.—"K" 82, 0 = 82. Staff, 22, 0 = 22. Giving a total of 905 efficients, 47 non-efficients—3 of whom joined too late to qualify—altogether 952. To this must be added "L" Co., 196, all serving with the Royal Engineers, and "M" Co., 318, 1 = 319. These are the Army Post Office Corps men. A grand total of 1,467 all told. It will, however, be remembered that 249 men were sent out with the R.E.'s, but of this number many were merely attached to the 24th and are apparently not included in the above return. Of the non-efficients no less than 42 belong to the Headquarter Companies ("A" "B" "C" and "I"), who were not able to attend the Camp of Exercise at Minster, where so many rely on wiping off all their odd drills and rendering themselves efficient.

Prizes.—Some people are always on the look-out for prizes, and on the 15th inst. they had a chance. It was a day devoted to shooting by the 24th, and was doubtless very wet on that account. The ZM clerk seems to know the P.O.

KHAKI NOTES—continued.

Rifles. Well, in the afternoon a little group of Sergeants, wet through, but elated, were discussing their successes and were wondering if anybody would arrive to upset them. At 3.30 the sky cleared and a general brightening up took place. Mr. Topscorer remarked: Well, I don't think anyone else will come down now, but I wish I had waited; the weather is now grand, good light, no rain. Suddenly a growler hove in sight; the musketry merchants had misgivings. Really it is coming towards—No, can't be—Yes, by Jove it is; it's here! and out stepped Sergt. Parsons, who, failing to catch the connecting train at Woking, had cabbed it from thence to Bisley. Lying down, all high and dry, the new arrival fired away and "wiped 'em all up," and to add to the dismay of the last prizewinner, he dropped 5s. from his share, or just the amount paid to the cabby. " The last shall be first"—in this case.

The " K " Div. recognises that they have nine colleagues at the front, and in order to remind them that they are not forgotten, have sent out by last mail a pipe and a quarter-pound of tobacco for each man.

The " D " Div. will mark the return to duty of our esteemed C.I.V. comrade. Pte. S. E. Sterling, by a little token of regard in the way of a very suitable present.

Christmas Pressure.—During this month there have been large withdrawals of juniors of under six years' service from the C.T.O. in order to assist on the P.O. side. Some 170 commenced their new duties at the Circulation Office on November 5th, and later on another 25 took post at the Parcel Circulation Office. Early in December a further batch of between 45 and 50 (including about a dozen females) go to render service in the Returned Letter Office ; of these latter they resume duty at the C.T.O. at various dates, during January and February, and most of the withdrawals give us a look up on Christmas Eve to help us over our little influx of Season's Greetings. Although this is so thoughtfully arranged, we hear some of the youths find it distasteful to them, and elect to tender their resignations, some five or six having already done so.

The P.M.G. has appointed T. Mason, Esq. (Supt. Telegraph business, race meetings, &c.), and E. Trenan, Esq. (Chief Supt. for Telegraphs for Manchester), to be Telegraph Traffic Managers. They will be attached to the Secretary's office.

B. Phillips, Esq., 1st Cl. Asst. Supt., of the " A " Division, has been promoted to the Postmastership of Maidenhead. Our hearty good wishes go with him.

Congrats. to the following gentlemen on their promotion :—2nd Cl. Asst. Supt. M. Hanifin to be 1st Cl. Asst. Supt., Senior Telest.; F. C. Green to be 2nd Cl. Asst. Supt., and Telest.; F. F. Green to be Senior Telest. All dated November 14th, 1900.

Technical Exam.—The following seniors were called upon to face the music on Friday, 16th inst. :—Messrs. C. H. Mitchell (Special Staff), W. H. Butler (Test.), H. Phillips (Test.), and H. D. Gill (" G " Div.), and from what I can learn, we shall soon hear of their promotion to the rank of 2nd Cl. Asst. Supts., they having satisfied the Examiner, for which feat we congratulate them.

Appointments.—The following Telests. proved successful in the recent competitive Exam. for the post of Examiner of Stores :—Messrs. Wright, Bragg, A. Hudson and Phayre (all TSF). Parsons (B), Byne (L), and Smallwood (News). Their duty terminated at TS on the 3rd inst., and they entered their new element on the 5th.

C. Rollo, Senior Telest., died on Nov. 11th, and was buried at the City of London Cemetery, Ilford, on Saturday, 17th inst. Our old colleague had been ill for a very long time, but returned to duty for a short season ; his last attendance at the office being C.I.V. Day.

" Poniard " will continue, though the book ceases. Any cablegrams from the front will be dealt with as usual. Friends have always been invited to send in their names. No fee is charged.

KHAKI NOTES—*continued*.

Appeals.—We in England have been reminded over and over again in the Press of the soldiers returning from the front, and the welcome they receive. The Temperance organs have not let the matter go unnoticed; indeed, the opportunity has presented itself, and they have gobbled it up. We cannot all see eye to eye with every whim they propound, even though we may be T.T.'s ourselves. So I am not going to quote any of their views, or enter into any controversy, but simply record in this little book the fact that both Lord Wolseley and Lord Roberts have made eloquent and strong appeals against the habit that obtains nowadays—*i.e.*, the treating system as regards the Welcome Home of the Soldiers of the Queen. First, then, Lord Wolseley, in his circular letter, concludes with these words :—" I trust that our greeting to the brave soldiers returning from this war may be something better than simply an incitement to excessive drinking, and that all will remember that whoever encourages them in this, far from being their friend, is really their worst enemy." While "Bobs" says it is a subject he has very much at heart, and in a very strong appeal these words occur :—" I am very proud that I am able to record, with the most absolute truth, that the conduct of this Army from first to last has been exemplary. Not one single case of serious crime has been brought to my notice—indeed, nothing that deserves the name of crime. . . . . The men bore themselves like heroes on the battlefield, and like gentlemen on all other occasions." Injudicious friends chose unhappy ways of speeding the parting soldier. " I fervently hope there may be no such scenes to mar the brightness of the welcome home," is Lord Roberts' final sentence.

A Volunteer Officer writes to the *Daily Telegraph* complaining of the War Office in dealing with his regiment. It appears that on returning from their camp of instruction they very gallantly obliged the railway company by starting at a time suitable to the latter. The W.O. people made the discovery that 300 men had not performed a fortnight's duty as they should have done in order to gain the grant. They had done all the time except *four minutes*, and the Volunteer Officer declares he would have delayed that train four minutes had he known it. The men have been paid their money by the Corps, and now the Corps cannot "get their own back" from the War Office. What price that? The par. winds up with the words, "Comment would be a superfluity."

T. Sayers, Esq., Asst. Supt. TSF, has been pensioned.

Important.—The next number will be the final issue of " K.L." In it I propose giving as fully as I can some account of the " business side " of the book. In order that I may do so, I must ask that every account be closed by the middle of December. It will be impossible to weigh *every* penny, and account for it in the last number, because the last number will not tell its tale until it is sold and settled for. But as nearly as it is possible to do so, all figures shall be given, and I hope to be able to add a bit more to a charitable fund. Will distributors kindly note this, please? There are not two lasts this time. The next (No. 21) is final.

B.Q.'s.—Two Victims.—Had already had it, thanks. PHOTO.—As it is apparently the desire of many readers to see a reproduction of " Colours " in the book he has placed before them, he will endeavour to satisfy them by giving a special sitting during the dark days of December to a good photographer. Khaki, patrol, or private? Don't matter which. All right.

24 pages again! It's just as well to count them for you. But how is it done?

Seven resumed duty to-day—November 28th.

" Casualties, Capetown," for enquiries *re* sick and wounded.

COLOURS.

" KHAKI LETTERS," One Penny. By post, Three Halfpence.

All posted letters containing Remittances, Orders, MSS., &c., must be addressed to R. E. KEMP, 12, JERRARD STREET, LEWISHAM, S.E.
Postal Orders should be made payable at Loampit Vale, Lewisham, S.E.

Printed by E. G. BERRYMAN & SONS, *Blackheath Road, London, S.E.*

"Khaki Letters" from ....
"My Colleagues in South Africa."

CORRESPONDENCE FROM THE
POST OFFICE TELEGRAPHISTS
OF THE
24th MIDDLESEX (P.O.) RIFLE VOLUNTEERS
(Royal Engineer Reserves),
ON ACTIVE SERVICE.

THE BOND THAT BINDS US—FRIENDSHIP—COMRADESHIP.

Published monthly (formerly fortnightly) for the Postal Telegraph Service.
Conducted by COLOUR-SERGEANT R. E. KEMP, *Central Telegraph Office, London.*

No. 21.   JANUARY 11TH, 1901.   PRICE ONE PENNY.

Central Telegraph Office,
London, E.C.

DEAR COMRADES, ONE AND ALL.

Greetings! Right Happy New Year's Greetings. And this for the last time in the printed pages of KHAKI LETTERS. It has never been my thought to alter the "regimental prefix" to this, my letter to you, although some of my office chums have found a little amusement in whispering either "part one" or "part two" of it *en passant.* The thermometer of comradeship stood high at the start—it stands high at the finish, and has been high all the way through—*semper idem.* The work has been a very pleasant one to me, although a very difficult one, and, at times, a very perplexing one. Two heads are better than one, even if they are only sheep's heads—you get better broth; and many's the time when I've longed for a first mate to give a hand when difficulties have loomed in our course. The guiding star has been goodwill, the buoyancy of the craft has been duty, and the cruise has been continued in the confidence that all hands would stand by her and bring her safely to port again. Such is so. We're neither wrecked nor damaged. She's sprung no leak, her timbers are still sound: all is taut and tight; she takes in her pennant and is out of commission—she's paid off. Why? Because her skipper is tired? No, not by any means. There is no need for her now. She was chartered for a special object—that object has ceased to need such special facilities: the correspondence from Our Boys is less and less. Many are home, and it is believed many are expecting to leave shortly; be that as it may, their communications do not warrant the further service provided solely for them.

Numerous rumours are afloat *re* the R.E s' new draft for South Africa. One newspaper says it is 50 more are wanted, another says it is 50 linemen and telegraphists—lately they have got up to 100 are wanted. A few have gone. There was quite a flutter in the "I" Co. a fortnight ago; a number of the Boys wanted to go there and then, just because they had "heard something." It didn't come off. Some of our Reservists got as far as Aldershot, were rigged out with khaki, and then didn't start. I received a letter yesterday from a certain party, who is on the spot and ought to know, but don't know, so I will confess I cannot tell you.

A special Wheatstone Staff of fifteen telegraphists have gone to the Cape.

A curious item in the casualty list has just come to my notice. If you turn to the list of names in this issue you will be surprised to find the pairs that are there. We have unfortunately lost nine men, and although I allude to their names in this manner, I do so with reverence. Perhaps it may help us to remember them better. There are two F's, two H's, two M's, two W's, and one R.

I am told the war is over. Can I believe it? I am tired of reading about it. Tired in this way. Something occurs, and the troops move, and every other telegram from the front winds up with these words: "in hot pursuit." It's so trying, you know. No wonder people say the war is monotonous and lose interest in it. Turn to the China column, and the telegrams from there are all in hot pursuit. Li Hung is ill, Chang is well, Chang is ill—well—ill—Well, each follow in hot pursuit of the other, and we are sure of only one thing, that's this: they have examined his credentials and found them "All correct." Quite Armyism.

I have seen in your letters descriptions of thunderstorms, sandstorms, and all kinds of "weather," but you don't appear to have enjoyed any fogs. We have had several nice ones lately, but on New Year's Day we had a beautiful lemon-coloured one. The S.E.R. marked time, and when it put us down at Cannon Street, I was inclined to ask the traffic policeman to direct me to the C.T.O. The pavement was in a state of stiff batter, so easy to slip, so hard to step, put me in mind of the drill that was introduced some few years ago (but soon condemned) of turning on the ball of your foot instead of the heel.

The photographs that you have herewith were taken in that splendid atmosphere that makes one always wish for the fireside. My amateur co-workers with the camera will be pleased to know the particulars of those pictures. Time of day 2.30 p.m., Stop f11, Empress plate, 15 seconds exposure. The one portraying the den, was taken a little later in the afternoon, as you can see, and required Your Humble to sit perfectly still for two solid minutes. The cap was removed by one of the inmates of this work-house (it *is* a work house, or a house of work) and, of course, I did the rest. I didn't wish to flatter myself, it is entirely untouched in any way, so you see him as he is at the close of his "Khaki" career.

There are many "Generals" on the unemployed list. We are always more or less at their mercy. They know what the officers in S.A. ought to do and how they should do it. I was pleased to read the following lines by Mr. H. C. MacDowall, in the *Spectator* :—

Through bitter nights and burning days
He watched the veldt stretch bare and grim;
At home beside the cheerful blaze
We wrote our views of him.
We mourned his curious lack of brain ;
We judged him stupid, judged him slow ;
How much of what he knew was vain,—
How much he did not know !
Too well he loved each foolish game.
" Is War a game ?" we sternly cried.
And while we talked of England's name,
For England's sake he died.

The C.T.O. is very quiet just now; during Christmas time we were pretty busy. I had my first turn of the new night duty—" night " duty is right. It is most pleasant to leave at 6 a.m., get home at seven, have breakfast and go to bed just before daylight. It is also somewhat startling to find they are just lighting the gas when you awake, and you get up to your tea—or a combination of dinner and tea—still in the dark. In order to get a little bit of daylight, I divided my sleep into A and B portions, rising at dinner time (or lunch, if you like ; it's immaterial)—this was " A " part—remaining up and about until tea-time, and then going " down " again for the " B " part. It's " all night " every night, and every day is night. If you want to see the sun, should he be up, you must get up too.

Prior to our invalided comrades leaving Aldershot to resume duty at their respective offices, a Shooting Match with the R.E.'s was arranged, but owing to the weather, was abandoned. The "Steak and Onion Supper," however, did not fall through ; they were all " all there." I received a glowing account from " Our Bob," and regret I cannot reproduce it here. Suffice it to say that Sergt.-Major Stead, R.E., occupied the Chair. Toasts were exchanged, harmony enjoyed, and the best of friendship expressed and sealed. Certainly, we have always been close friends.

In this issue you will read all about the book. I will only add that everything is paid up ; as the cash came in it went to the printer by tens and twenties of golden goblins. I have always known where I was, *i.e.*, in front--he in " hot pursuit."

I have had intense pleasure in thus working for you. I can honestly say I have been able to help several of your friends by answering enquiries. Poniard will still go on. Some of you, I hear, are on the way ; others will be relieved shortly, so we give up the book but not the bond—the friendship we have always had towards each other. Another thing, my time must be devoted to a certain course that spells D.I. You know what I refer to ! So with my kindest regards and best of all wishes, " May God bless you and keep you," and bring you safely home to your loved ones in perfect health and strength, I conclude, remaining as ever,

Yours most heartily,

To the " L " Co. in South Africa,
Tuesday, January 8th, 1901.

R. E. KEMP,
Colour-Sergeant.

COPYRIGHT.—" Khaki Letters " must not be used without permission.—R. E. KEMP.

Khaki Letters.

No. 23,764 Sapper **C. T. Catling** (EES), writing from Belfast (Transvaal), Oct. 25th, says :—

"I thought I had told you I had been ill and in dock, and I think I've had my share of it. Jenner and I came down country one day after each other ; I was in the marquee at Wynburg Hospital, when I thought I recognised somebody crawling along, and it turned out to be Jenner. We were both at Fort Knokke together and enjoyed ourselves A1, and soon got quite well again, and when we presented ourselves for medical examination, neither of us could do all the buttons of our Khaki up ; I weighed 12 stone and Jenner over 11, consequently the doctor had no sympathy for us and marked us as 'fit,' and very soon after this we were on our way to Bloemfontein, where I left Jenner, he having been commandeered by Capt. Fowler for his clerk. I only stayed at Bloemfontein three weeks, and then left for Pretoria, stayed there a month and then on to Bragspruit, and then to Middelburg, and now I am at Belfast, where I hope they will let me rest till they order me home ; in fact, I have made up my mind I may perch here till I do get such orders, and have made myself a bedstead from some timber I pulled down ; it is much better than sleeping on the floor, my hips don't get so sore. Well, my opinion of active service is that it is very rough, and that disease is a bigger enemy than Boers or bullets. I have stuck to it and done my little bit same as the rest, to the best of my ability, and I hope every satisfaction has been given. I am not exactly fed-up with it, but of course shall be glad to get home once again. De Wet doesn't seem to have had enough yet himself, but the Boers almost to a man have, and they will be glad when it is all over. It is not surprising that there should be some friction between the Russians and Japs, considering the former did the latter out of her spoils of war. I am sorry the regiment has lost so many men, and I sincerely hope we shan't lose any more. Everybody was surprised and deeply grieved to hear about poor Dick Frew. He was a general favourite, and he will be greatly missed by all who knew him. Glad to hear Bob Luttrell arrived home safe, and is now well again. I was chatting to Rowson the other night on the Machadodorp wire. He is keeping well, but will be glad when it is all over. He has been having some rough times, trekking and long hours. I only get a few of the many papers that are sent me. The Boers will be forced to the conclusion that it is best to accept the inevitable with a good grace, and the sooner the better I shall like it."

✣ ✣ ✣ ✣

No. 4,670, Sapper **W. E. Braybon**, writing from Heilbron, Oct. 28th, says :—

"Dear Mr. Editor,—Here we are again—coming up smiling for another round. Let me see : the last exploit was the armoured train at Leeuwpoort Bridge (?), where our quiet piscatorial recreation was rudely

KHAKI LETTERS—*continued*.

interrupted by the Boer attack on the armoured train, where, as usual, we gave them plenty of change. You see we are once again in possession of Heilbron, but practically prisoners, owing to the snipers about us. Of course, KHAKI LETTERS is a private paper, and subscribed to privately, so I trust a few innocent remarks by a volunteer will not be a breach of discipline. Our wires to Frankfort, Vrede, Vereeniging, and Kroonstad are cut, and our only outlets are by way of Wolvehoek, 30 miles from the main line, and garrisoned *en route*, and Vredefort Weg (Road). Lieut. Elkington is here, the A.D.A.T., and Asst.-Insp. Glue and staff, anxious to re-establish telegraphic communication. It is safe to go two miles out of the town, and that is all. Drastic precautions have been taken as to the exit and entry of strangers, and anybody out after 9 p.m. is promptly shot, no challenge being given. We had the addition to the family circle of a useful toy—a 5-inch gun. I expect it will give the Boers a change of diet for breakfast to-morrow. I am anxious to hear its remarks. They say it has a deep voice, and its breath is obnoxious, and its behaviour very unceremonious, for it sends forth a nasty unpleasant something like a thunderbolt, with this difference—one comes from the heavens, this sends you nearer to that place than you would most probably otherwise get. There is not the least shadow of doubt that we have been too humane in the conduct of the war. An intelligent foe would have appreciated their conqueror's leniency, but the Boers are now punishing wives and families and compelling us to destroy property. Loyal Boers say they are not their countrymen who are now fighting, or only a very few. A great number are marauding thieves, robbing and plundering in lieu of wages, and adopting a similar sort of warfare which existed very near home not long ago, and which augurs badly for success at the eleventh hour of adoption of similar tactics here. All efforts to shut De Wet in have up to the present proved abortive. Generals Barton and Charles Knox (our boss) have each knocked corners off him, and Le Gallais and the Colonials—who should be christened "Hell's Own"—are continually on his collar. The latter had him at their mercy months ago, but a certain "humane" general, who refused to strike at the opportune moment, and instead of a glorious victory, saw frozen animals and benumbed men in the morning. . . . Well, talk about blunders! No, do not. . . . Be merciful. These kopjes are not Hurlinghams nor Sandown Parks, and the surroundings are so different to Cairo, and, hang it all! the Boers don't come out and fight. It was very different in Egypt. Why, those black devils came out and fought us, and we simply slaughtered them! When some of the infantry tell people at home the number of miles they have marched, it will astound people. Hunter's men must have "plodded the weary hoof" thousands of miles. Most of them will have had sufficient walking till the end of their days. Things are now getting exceedingly lively and interesting—at least, from a naturalist's point of view. The whole of the plagues beset us, and a few more which perhaps did not count at the time the chosen few were bestowed upon the disobedient one on the north of this continent centuries ago. The flies are just like the British house fly, but the African one is more of a cannibal, and makes desperate efforts to eat portions of you in penny numbers. He is most uncivilised, and attacks desperately; you chase him off your nose, he nips your forehead, and then, benefiting by his military observations, he executes a flanking movement on to your tender, sun-scorched neck. As one sits writing during a hot, humid evening, a surprisingly large and varied number of beetles come, with a buzz and a smack, up against the shade of the lamp, or against

KHAKI LETTERS—*continued*.

you, or cremate themselves in the flame of a double-wicked candle, or, like many soldiers, get maimed for life. We have hundreds of lizards of various colours about, and a few scorpions and centipedes and snakes have already appeared. When the height of summer arrives we shall be busy killing. There are scores of interesting and yet loathsome things about, but we are not so pestered as are some owing to the lack of cover, rocks being few and woods very distant. No reasonable man would ever covet this country for its beauty. But, like many other rough surfaces, there is something good beneath, and no doubt the greater proportion undeveloped. Of course, one can get used to anything, but personally I would sooner have 10 years at home than 20 out here with treble the salary. Talk about John the Baptist in the Wilderness of Judea ! He would have had a splendid chance here, snakes and all ; and he would have had to cry mighty hard for an audience. There is very little entertainment in these small towns, and I suppose, as in England, the women scandalise and the men smoke and drink and watch the Kaffirs do some work. In this town there is a fair sprinkling of British, and I saw ladies indulging in the old English pastime of croquet, assisted by the parson. Of course, in a country like this, where the grass is here to-day and gone to-morrow, a substitute has to be found in a well-rolled brown-substanced pitch. How it must detract from the pleasures of the game ! Cape Colony and Natal are Gardens of Eden compared to the O.R.C. and the 'Vaal. Natal, I am told, easily bears away the palm. The rainy season appears to have started, and with that comes sickness. There are hundreds of cattle buried round the places where men encamp, and in this respect the authorities have been lax. It would not take much brain power to devise and convert a wagon into a conveyance for carting the carcases a mile or two outside the camps. This has, to a considerable extent, been done lately, but the big mounds all around containing the rotting bodies washed by heavy rains, it only stands to reason a proportion of the offensive decay must reach the water supply, to say nothing of the objectionable stenches arising therefrom. In haste for mail."

No. 4,371, Sapper **L. Sorensen,** writing from Eerstfabricken (Transvaal), Nov. 6th, says :—

" Everything in the garden's lovely. As I sit at the window wide open, and look out on the verandah, across the carriage drive, shrubbery, orchards, &c., &c., at the passing trains, I can't help contrasting the present life with the TS sloggery. I am not at all anxious to return to the 'factory,' but all the same, I am fed-up here. It is getting a trifle too monotonous—the same thing day after day. Wish they'd settle matters one way or the other. The climate certainly is grand, though very hot, but even a good climate and fresh air feeds one up in time, and I am waiting anxiously for the end of the campaign. People at home who prophesied that the war would be over before we reached the Cape were sadly mistaken. ' It's just a yachting trip to Capetown and back.' Time has proved it very different ; we seem as far off from returning now as when we landed. The latest yarn is that we must leave the country by last day of year in order to get home, and furlough over by 1st of March, to start duty when summer pressure begins. Not much faith in it myself—don't much mind if it's right—anything to end present state of affairs. It's unsafe to go a mile out unless you want to draw your 'Northampton.' Went out for a ride on trolley the other day—caught in storm—drenched in about two seconds—took refuge in hut, and stripped

KHAKI LETTERS—*continued.*

to dry the clothes. Patrol came up searching for Boers and mistook pal and myself for them—were going to run us in just as we were. Explanations ensued—officer laughed—gave us nip to keep damp out, and we got back O.K."

✢ ✢ ✢ ✢

No. 1,275, Sapper **C. J. Woode**, writing from Kimberley, Nov. 7th, says :—

"MY DEAR KEMP,—Seeing that it is now two months since I wrote you, I make another attempt. In notes of your last issue you query who the two telsts. are who were 'murdered' near Potchefstroom. They were 'Corpl. Cummings,' of the 1st T.D.R.E., who had, prior to coming to S.A., only just returned from Egypt. Private Croucher, of the Royal Welsh Fusrs., who was a telst. in India, on return to civil life applied for duty in P.O., but owing to smallness of wage, he accepted a position as porter in the P.O. He was a well-educated and technical telst. He was with me at Lichtenberg for some time, and looked forward to his return to England, with the hopes of settling down. On the 7th Septr., I became attached to 11th Field Co. R.E., for duty as telst., accompanying the mounted sappers. We had two months of a tour in the Rustenburg, Marico, and Lichtenberg Dists. Unfortunately, the last few weeks I suffered from dysentery, so when arriving at Zeerust, Harry Waghorn relieved me, and took over my pony, and he is now on the trek with Genl. Douglas, in my stead. I came down to Kimberley, and I can assure you quite enjoy being down here after six months' roving. I saw W. C. Smith at Mafeking; he has recovered from his illness, but did not look up to form yet. Some of the men at Kimberley, I am sorry to say, have that worn office look, just the same as we see at home ; the work here seems to have been one continuous strain, and those men who have been here six months or more have had no easy time. On our trek round we visited several places of note—Oliphant's Nek, Margato Pass, Rustenberg, and Elands River. The scenery was indeed grand. I could not but help feeling sorry for the infantry men, marching all day long ; yet they looked a picture ! Not a spare ounce of flesh on one of them ; all grit they seemed. The Boers would snipe every day, and only on one or two occasions did we get a fair stand-to for an hour or so. The women-folk seemed most treacherous—oftentimes finding ammunition concealed on farms where only women were. The object of the column was to denude the country of supplies. This we did most earnestly, burning crops, and now the starvation of the Dutch people is extreme. It was necessary, as the Boers kept getting their supplies from various farms, their only means of existence being now (mealies) maize. Though I came in sick, I am now in best of health. Will now close, with kind regards to friends and self."

[It is rather curious that Charlie Woode makes no reference to his telegram of October 14th to "Poniard, London."—See page 372, K.L.]

✢ ✢ ✢ ✢

No. 4,314, Sapper **F. A. Mason** (PEI), in a letter from Laing's Nek dated Nov. 8th, says :—

" I must plead the paucity of news. Really, I should not know what to say now were it not for the fact that there have been some changes in the disposition of troops about here. . . . I'm O.K., thanks, and getting on splendidly. No work, as per usual, and living in grand form. There was some talk of a shift to Pretoria a month ago, but it has been decided that

KHAKI LETTERS—continued.

Laing's Nek, although only requiring a few troops to defend it, is far too important a post to leave unprovided with an office—for a time, at least. I'm rather glad; it's a healthy, bracing spot—indeed, I should say the best in South Africa. One thing: the water is magnificent, which is a great boon. I got fed-up a little while ago with it. We did our own cooking, and we got too lazy; we practically lived on nothing after a jolly time, but now, with the advent of the Dorsets, we are 'all kiff,' as you will learn. You will remember the Dublins were here, and that we had a fine time of it. The officers were very good to us. One used to come in—a second lieutenant—of an afternoon regularly and sleep on my bed. His tent was a single one, ours a double, and always cool. He brought me books and light cut tobacco. He had a 'Kodak,' and took my photo. in several ways, but is sending to the Kodak Company to get printed, so I shan't see them. . . . The Adjt. did likewise, and has promised me copies, together with others he has taken. Last Wednesday they all left for two or three miles from Volksrust. The Colonel and several others came to say good-bye, and assured us they would do their best to get an office and us with them. I hoped so, but I fear not; there are no clerks to spare; we could only leave when this office closes, and that won't be. Before they left they gave us a case of whisky. 'What ho!'. . . Well, the Dorsets came (two coys.) in their place, under a Major. . . . As I said, we were sick of cooking and other graft, so I applied for an orderly; we got him—he is a section "D" man—'ground-man' for Portsmouth Football Club. They don't make his wife any allowance, so he is rather glad to come to us and get every night in bed instead of every other, and milk, eggs, pickles, butter, etc., for nothing. He is a splendid cook—makes us grand meals—duffs (we buy flour). He has found a bed of mushrooms, and now it's mushrooms with everything. He is glad to be with us. Well, what do you say? Every swaddy doesn't get cabbage for dinner, as we do, fruit all day, celery for tea, etc. . . . About 9.30 the last message comes. I always deliver that myself, and get NN from the officers. Night before last—'Won't you sit down,' said the Major. 'What ho!' The Dubs had put in a good word for me. I sat. 'Oh, take that easy chair,' said he. 'Will you have a whiskey and sodah?' said the Captain. Well, I stayed an hour, to cut a long story short, had two whiskeys and 'sodahs,' and came away. Last night the same occurred again, with cigars this time, and we talked as if I were same like officer (mim). The subject ranged through Marconi, sound, light and heat, stars, 'Boahs' and organ-pipe making, which was a favourite recreation of the Captain's. They were most anxious to know if we were comfortable, and got a good cook. Said he would look in, and he did, and I gave him egg, whiskey and milk. 'This fine, ah! don't yer know,' he said. 'Bai jove!'. . . It doesn't look by being home Christmas now, does it? There is a strong rumour we demobilise in March—should say that was about right. Roll on. They are going strong on the Mounted Infantry and Police, and guess when the establishment is complete they will break up the foot troops and we shall go. I believe they are taking on a lot of Civvys. Hope everyone is all gay at home. Give my kindest regards to all."

No. 24,305, Sapper **F. T. Stimpson** writes from Taaibosch Kopje, Nov. 8th, as follows :—

"Pleased to say I am keeping very well under the circs., but the grub is far from being good—the meat for dinner I never touch ; we get a ration of

KHAKI LETTERS—*continued.*

bacon for breakfast in lieu of a qr. of meat; for dinner, if it wasn't for a few eggs and Quaker oats, we should fare very badly. The place being on top of a kopje, is very healthy; we have a spruit just at foot of kopje and get the luxury of a swim, which is much appreciated. Wolvehoek—about ten miles south of us—are rationed for water, and we sometimes get the chaps over for a good wash in our stream. It was very sad indeed the death of Dick Frew; it seems that the majority that go under are the strongest looking chaps, or chaps with a good deal of flesh on them. We have lost about eight or nine now, I think. You can guess that I am fairly fed up with it after having a full twelve months out here, as it will be November 12th, and no earthly prospect of being home for Christmas. There are rumours of a lot of Civvys being down at C.T. waiting to come up, but I think they would bring them up if they had them, as the Civvys they have got at Johannesburg and Pretoria are doing O.T. I had a trip to Johannesburg, it is about 40 miles from here; the town was very quiet, all the shops were closed and barricaded, the firms being mostly English. The post office is a splendid building with all the latest improvements—the instrument room in particular. It is very lofty, only one instrument on a table, with two electric lights and an armchair for seat, which it would be a pleasure to do a duty of ten hours in. There are only about ten R.E.'s working in the office, the remainder being civilians, but there is very little work doing. There are some very good buildings in the town, notably the Exploration Buildings, now Government offices, formerly connected with the mines, South African Bank, and various other business premises. The roads are in a shocking condition, not having been touched since the commencement of the war. There are trams all over the town, but not running. I shall probably run up again to get some stores if we are booked here for Christmas. There is a decent little park, and the band plays twice a week, reminding me of good old Hyde Park. We have had DeWet not many miles from here at Parijs Drift. He had a rough time for about a week with Generals Barton and Knox, as you have read, I expect; in fact, you get more news of the war than we. Well, good-bye; hoping to be in old England soon."

No. 4,304, Sapper **W. Brook** (of HF), writing from Kimberley, Nov. 19th, says :—

"Dear Kemp,—I have to-day forwarded a packet of photos. of poor Dick Frew's grave : half-a-dozen for his widow, one to Col. Thompson, and one for yourself. I have sent them all together to prevent being damaged in transit. Would you kindly send to Mrs. Frew? It was a sad blow to us here. Sorry for the delay, but having no proper tackle or convenience—only the tent—you will understand my difficulties. I have nothing but a bucket and a dinner soup-plate to develop plates, tone, and fix photos., so that they can hardly be expected to equal my home work. The weather, too, has somewhat delayed me—wet, though not of long duration, but all there while it's on—everything flooded in a few minutes, and the sandstorms are a terror, which are long and often, when photography is out of the question. . . . I have nothing to communicate except that the Boers have blown up the railway between Modder and Orange, and to the north of us, near Taungs; this you have probably heard from your numerous correspondents. We seem doomed to spend Christmas here. We certainly expected to be home for Christmas some couple of months ago, but it is now off. Kind remembrance."

KHAKI LETTERS—*continued*.

No. 4,612, Sapper **F. Somerville** (EES), writing from Springs, Transvaal, Nov. 13th, says:—

"My life, since I last wrote, has been a very uneventful one. The armoured train left Klip River somewhere about Sept. 23rd, and came up to this place, which it had been decided to re-garrison, and I had to open an office here, and here I've been stuck since. I took possession of the old Boer Post and Telegraph Office (Post en Telegraaf Kantoor, as they have it). To do so we had to practise a bit of amateur 'Bill Sykes,' and eventually effected an entry through one of the windows, all the doors being barricaded up, and the windows, with the exception of the one we got through, being screwed on the inside. By Jove! the place was in a state. The floor a foot or so deep in old slip, forms, broken bottles—in fact, *débris* of every description, the whole covered with several inches of dust, and seeming to me to be a very good example of what chaos might be. However, there wasn't anything there worth commandeering—someone had been there before us; so we lost no time in making things a bit more comfortable, and settling down. We had some very decent times here at first. There were four of us: a corporal, two linemen and myself; and there being very little work, we often beguiled the time away by impromptu cricket. Very much impromptu: the bat, a home-made affair of string and khaki; still, it served its purpose; we enjoyed ourselves, got very hot and thirsty, and very stiff, so what matter? However, these times were not allowed to last. First the two linemen were shifted, and then the corporal, and so now I'm entirely on my lonesome, with an orderly to deliver messages. Under these circumstances you can understand that it's liable to get monotonous at times, especially as I'm pretty well tied down to the office all day. Of course, I have hours laid down, which are: 6 a.m. to 8 a.m., 10 a.m. to noon, and 2 p.m. to 9 p.m.; but I must also take messages, if urgent, between these hours, so that it isn't safe to leave the office for any time. Still, 'it's a poor heart that never rejoices,' and I find solace at the washtub (it's a pail, by the way), as my own washerwoman. Of course, there are Boers hanging round here, or we shouldn't be here. They're just about five or six miles out. Our patrols see them every day, frequently exchanging shots with 'em, and they often get saucy and try to get in here. They've made three attempts to take this place during the last few days—two night attacks and one at midday—but they haven't half enough 'go' in them; might just as well try to take the moon. We look upon their presence just outside as quite a matter of course, and it doesn't seem to worry anyone here except the stationmaster, who is a Hollander, and gets the 'wind up' shockingly if an attack is expected. I slept right through one of the recent night attacks, quite oblivious of it all, although the pom-pom and other machine guns were being fired for all they were worth not very far from this office, and nobody troubled about waking me. I am hoping to be recalled to Kroonstad shortly, where there's rather more life. I expect I shall be out here for Christmas, and am not anxious to spend it here. . . . . I'll wish you and all the other boys the compliments of that festive season. Kind regards. 'Have you got that £10 note?'"

→✳ End of Khaki Letters. ✳←

MM—SOUTH AFRICA.

Sapper Bullamore Walton.

AGAIN the Central Telegraph Office is thrown into mourning through the untoward decease of another of its members—a man of good physique, soldierly, and much esteemed—to wit, Sapper Bullamore Walton, No. 4,381, R.E., better known as "Ben." He was born September 28th, 1868, and entered the Post Office Service at Grantham in February, 1882. He was of a military turn of mind, and while at that office joined the 2nd V.B. Lincolnshire Regiment. Leaving Grantham in August, 1889, he came to the C.T.O., and was not long in making many friends by his bright and genial manner. Soon afterwards, his transfer from the provincial corps to the 24th Middlesex R.V. took place. The Corps of Army Signallers was formed in 1891, and Ben was then to be found among the first entrants to that useful branch. This new institution was on much the same lines as the R.E. Reserve, but the little Corps was short-lived and was disbanded in the latter part of '92, whereon

Ben, with most of the other members, returned to his former Company—the "I"—on April 15th, 1893 and remained with us until the close of that year, when he took his discharge He, however, was always full of enthusiasm, following his old Corps on many occasions in town and camp, and on the call for volunteers for the front, could no longer resist rejoining, which he did on March 12th, 1900, was transferred to the R.E. Reserve on the 15th (same day as Frew), sailed for South Africa per ss. "Winifredian" on April 1st with both him and Hamilton—a trio of the "true and tried" whom we shall see no more amongst us. On Thursday, December 27th, we received the news of poor Ben's death, he being another victim to the dreadful enteric at Kroonstad, on Sunday, December 23rd. How unprepared we were for such news may be seen by the last letters to hand from him:— SERFONTEIN, O.R.C., *October 25th*, 1900.

"Pleased to hear that all going well; am going on O.K. myself, and keeping well. You will see by the address I have had a move since last writing you. After a spell of seventeen weeks in Kroonstad, was sent up here. It is a fresh office opened on the line of communication, about thirty miles north of Kroonstad. We are camped on the side of a kopje, and it is a rough place—nothing to see but veldt for miles. Militiamen stationed here, about as bright a lot as you could find, too. The other man here is a signaller from the 16th Lancers. Next to nothing to do, but would rather be back in Kroonstad. Can get nothing in this show : in fact, it is hard to get a letter posted. Best wishes to all friends. Hope well. Let's know how things going."

Again from Serfontein, *November 15th*, 1900 :—

"Just a few more lines to say I am still going strong. Still stuck in this show. It is now 15th November, but goodness knows when or how I shall get this posted, as it has to go to Kroonstad. By the time this reaches you it will be close on Christmas, so will take this opportunity of wishing you a Merry Christmas, etc., etc. The same to all friends Hope all well."

The 24th Middlesex Royal Engineer Reserves.
A New Year's Greeting.

CHRISTMAS gone! and still at the front,
    Many a comrade "Out o' the hunt,"
Oh! for the puddings they mean to "shunt,"
    When will the boys come back?
As staunch as the day when they sped their way
Athwart the ocean to Table Bay,
Sudden the call! but ready were they,
    True to the Union Jack.

Christmas gone! and the toast has been
"The Khaki Boys" and "Our Empress Queen"!
Yet here and there just a tear was seen,
    For one who might ne'er come home.
Parents, sweethearts who bravely bear,
And noble wives who ne'er despair,
Sighing for one who is still "out there,"
    Under the starlit dome.

Christmas gone! How the year has run!
Grief and gladness! shadow and sun!
Pluck, devotion, and victories won!
    Deeds that will live for aye!
Some true comrade will e'er be missed,
Whose brow the Angel of Death has kissed,
With eager eyes we have scanned the list
    Anxiously day by day.

Christmas gone! and the New Year here!
Bright with holly and Yuletide cheer,
What is the message to comrades dear
    As our festival lanterns burn?
"Health and Happiness"! May they feel
Our thoughts are theirs for the Empire's weal,
Duty the watch-word! True to their steel!
    "Good Luck, and a Safe Return!"

Jan. 7th, 1901.   J. H. W.

⤙ Khaki Sidelights. ⤚

"My Colleagues in South Africa."—The publication from time to time of a suitable card, convenient for the pocket, and intended to minimise errors, subdue rumours, and give authentic information as to who are Our Boys when names have appeared in the numerous casualty lists, has had a good effect in Service circles. If by misfortune a T.B. man has been injured, or has gone to that last long sleep in South Africa, the above-quoted list, giving as it does all particulars of the men, has been consulted, and the identification at once known. Now that the last number of K.L. is on hand, it is thought most fitting to reproduce a portion of the little volume, so that the names of all the 24th Mx. men may figure in its pages, and thus make our book the more complete.

ENTIRE LIST OF 24th MIDDLESEX (P.O.) RIFLE VOLUNTEERS who have proceeded to South Africa for active service with the Royal Engineers, alphabetically arranged, together with the Offices from whence drawn :—

4 Abbott, W. .. BM	7 Davis, J. .. TS	9 Hughes, H. E... BE
3 Adams, W. F... TS	1 Davis, S. G. .. LV	9 Hulatt, G. .. TS
1 Aird, H. .. EH	9 Deeble, S. A. .. SX	3 Humm, H. E... ,,
8 Allen, E. J. .. TS	3 Dellbridge, W. A. TS	7 Hunter, E. A. .. PR
1 Alliston, H. R... ,,	9 Dickinson, A. .. BK	3 Hurdle, F. J. .. HH
3 Andrew, J. H... NN	9 Dodd, R. .. GW	5 Ingram, C. S. .. TS
9 Armstrong, D... EH	9 Dodds, G. E. .. NT	7 Jackson, H. J. .. ,,
1 Arundell, J. H. TS	6 Eaton, G. J. .. AB	9 Jackson, T. W... OF
7 Ash, E. J. .. ,,	3 Eglington, R.W.L. DY	7 Jarvis, F. J. .. CN
3 Austen, H. .. ,,	4 Evans, A. .. CF	5 Jeffrey, S. J. .. TS
3 Bannister, G. W. MR	4*Fairall, C. A. G. MTP	1 Jenner, C. J. .. ,,
7 Barber, H .. TS	3 Fallon, J. .. TS	9 Johnston, E. .. LV
9 Barron, G. .. BS	3 Fenton, E. J. .. DE	4 Jones, Charles.. WOL
7 Bateman, C. N. NG	3 Fergusson, H.H.A. LV	7 Jones, C. H. .. TSF
7 Baxter, W. H... CF	1 Flanagan, J. P. MC	9 Jones, D. W. .. CF
9 Bell, J. H. .. AB	9 Forster, J. D. .. BS	3 Jones, Jas. .. ,,
7 Bell, W. R. .. TS	4 Forth, C. .. LS	4 Kelly, F. P. T... ,,
9 Bellwood, E. E. YO	8 Foster, H. A. J. TS	7 Kelly, W. N. .. ACN
9 Bennett, A. D... SX	7 Foster, W. .. CV	7 Kyle, W. .. GW
5 Bevan, W. L. .. ACN	7 Fox, J. Y. .. GW	9 Lane, J. .. NT
3 Birch, L. G. .. TS	4 Frampton, H.W. ND	1 Lang, T. .. EH
3 Bishop, G. .. ,,	7*Frew, W. F. .. TS	8 Lasham, R.W. E. TS
9 Bordeaux, E. .. BM	9 Garland, W.H.G. DN	5 Leaver, A. W... ,,
3 Bourlay, L. A... SY	6 George, T. B. .. TS	7 Leitch, D. .. ,,
8 Bramwell, J. J... NT	7 Gibson, A. E. .. GW	8 Lincoln, J. W... NT
9 Braybon, W. E. TS	9 Gibson, C. .. EX	4 Little, J. A. .. SW
4 Brewster, W. .. MR	7 Gilchrist, J. .. GW	3 Loosemore, E.G. CF
6 Brook, W. .. HF	7 Gilmour, W. .. ,,	9 Lord, J. S. .. HF
3 Brooks, A. A. .. SW	4 Govier, E. C. .. TS	9 Lowe, W. F. .. EX
3 Brooks, A. J. .. TS	6 Grant, J. .. AB	4 Luttrell, R. C... TS
9 Brown, F. P. .. OF	1 Greenfield, W. J. MR	5 Mackness, J. H. ,,
5 Brown, J. A. .. TS	3 Greig, J. .. CE	7 Marshall, W.H.S. ,,
9 Burden, W. E... SO	6 Gwilliam, A. .. TS	5 Mason, F. A. .. PEI
9 Butt, W. H. .. DO	1 Hall, J. J. .. ,,	4 McAuley, A. .. TSF
1 Campbell, R. .. EH	1 Hamer, D. J. .. ,,	9 McBurney, H. C. BE
7 Carter, W. G. .. TS	7*Hamilton, T. .. GW	1 McLaren, D. .. EH
3 Catling, C. T. .. EES	9 Harding, F. .. SW	7 McMurtrie, J. .. TS
5 Chubbock, J. M. TS	8 Hargreaves, W.J. TS	7 McPherson, J. F. GW
1 Clark, F. .. ,,	7 Harrison, H. J. ,,	7 McQueen, J. .. ,,
9 Clift, H. .. EX	5 Harvey, H. .. LV	8 McSweeney, J. J. MR
5 Collins, J. C. .. TS	3*Hawkins, A. W. TSF	2*Metcalfe, J. L... TS
3 Collins, W. G... SA	7 Haycocks, S. H. LV	3 Miller, J. W. .. ,,
5 Corkill, T. H. TSF	4 Hayden, H. J... LS	5*Milne, A. .. AB
5 Cousal, A. .. TS	7 Heigh, J. .. EH	3 Milton, P. A. .. TS
9 Crafter, E. W... CF	1 Hendry, W. .. ,,	5 Minors, C. J. .. ,,
4 Creasey, J. W... TS	9 Hewitt, J. R. .. HF	6 Morris, F. J. .. CF
1 Curnew, P. J. .. ,,	1 Horton, F. D. .. BM	9 Morris, T. M. .. NU
7 Dadswell, W. .. ,,	9 Houghton, J. .. LA	7 Morse, A. H. .. TS
3 Daniels, F. B. .. NC	9 Howell, B. R. .. SF	6 Nash, F. J. .. CF
7 Davies, D. G. .. CF	6 Hudson, W. .. TS	7 Neate, E. P. .. TS

KHAKI SIDELIGHTS—continued.

1	Nelson, J. H.	TS	5	Rowson, C.W.	EES	9	Turner, H. W.	BK
4	Nixon, W.	BM	1	Sainsbury, F. J.	TS	1	Urquhart, A. J.	IV
9	Norman, R D. S.	SS	1	Sambells, W. J.	,,	4	Waghorn, H. C.	TS
4	Orwin, L.	TS	3	Samuel, E. J.	,,	8	Walker, J. H. E.	LV
1	O'Sullivan, C. P.	TSF	9	Sanderson, E.	SU	7	Walker, W. P.	MR
7	Page, L. D.	,,	9	Saunders, W. H.	ST	9	Walkley, A.	BS
1	Pallet, T. W.	TS	7	Semple, D.	TS	7*	Walton, B.	TS
4	Payne, C. H.	,,	5	Sinclair, W. M.	,,	9	Waters, A. J.	SX
7	Pearce, W. W.	,,	3	Smith, W. C.	,,	9	Watkins, R.	CF
9	Pearson, W. A.	YO	5	Snow, H. J.	,,	9	Watling, A. G.	NC
9	Perkins, C. W.	MR	8	Somerville, F.	EES	7	Warburton, B. F.	NG
5	Peters, C. A.	TSF	7	Sorensen, L.	TS	4	Webber, A. J. S.	TS
8	Picker, H. F.	LV	9	Staines, C. F. G.	YO	9	Webber, S.	BS
6	Pickford, G. H.	TS	4	Stevens, A.	MR	1	Weir, J.	EH
9	Pilley, O. G.	SF	8	Stevens, A. E.	TS	9	Wheatcroft, T.W.	SU
7	Plumridge, G.E.	TS	7	Stevens, T. R.	GW	9	Whelan, W. J.	DN
5	Pocock, G. A. W.	CO	7	Stevenson, T.W.	TS	5	Wheller, W. V.	TS
3	Poole, A. T.	BS	4	Stevenson, W. C.	BM	1	Whibley, E. J.	E.-O.
1	Poole, R.	IV	1	Stimpson, F. T.	TS	8	White, F. R.	TS
3	Porter, H. S.	WOL	3	Stormer, H.	,,	7	White, H. J.	LV
1	Proudfoot, J. G.	CE	1	Swan, A. W.	,,	1	Whitten, J. A.	EH
1	Quarmby, E. H.	HF	5	Symonds, T. H.	,,	9	Whitworth, E.	SF
1	Quinn, C. H.	TS	9	Tait, G.	GW	3	Williams, E. S.	CF
3	Ray, A.	,,	3	Tee, W. G.	TS	1	Willis, G. H.	SE
9	Rendle, J.	EX	1	Thomas, D.	EH	3	Wilson, C. M. E.	YH
9	Revill, A. R.	TS	7	Thomas, W. S.	EC	1	Wilson, W.	TS
7	Roberts, H. T.	LV	9	Thompson, J. T.	NT	1	Woode, C. J.	,,
1	Roberts, W. S.	TS	7	Thrift, E. A.	SW	1	Woodrow, F. H.	SO
9	Robinson, F.	LV	2	Tough, J. S.	AB	3	Woolley, W.H.P.	TS
5*	Robinson, F. W.	DY	5	Townsend, S. H.	TS	4	Wright, T. H.	,,
9	Robson, J. P.	NT	8	Tozer, W. W.	,,	3*	Wyatt, E. H.	GY
8	Robson, R.	,,	9	Turnbull, W. H.	LV	6	York, A. W.	TS
1	Roby, W. P.	MR	9	Turner, E. A.	SF	9	Young, J. J.	SU

* Died on Active Service.

The figures before a man's name in the foregoing list refer to the Ship by which he sailed for South Africa. By arranging the names under their respective figures it will at once be seen of whom the party was composed.

No.	Ship.	Sailed from	Date.	Our Boys.
1	"Gascon"	Southampton	Oct. 21st, 1899	37
2	"Bavarian"	Liverpool	Nov. 8th, ,,	2
3	"Canada"	,,	Dec. 1st, ,,	35
4	"St. Andrew"	Royal Albert Docks, London..	Jan. 21st, 1900	22
5	"Cephalonia"	Southampton	Feb. 20th, ,,	23
6	"Oriental"	Royal Albert Docks, London..	,, 28th, ,,	10
7	"Winifredian"	Southampton	April 1st, ,,	46
8	"Montfort"	Royal Albert Docks, London..	,, 26th, ,,	14
9	"Montrose"	Southampton	June 12th, ,,	60
	The 24th Mx. R.V. Reserves sent out up to end of 1900			249

Up to the date of going to press between 30 and 40 of the men have returned, invalided home, and others have fallen as is already known. It should be noted that only 24th men have been included in the notifications for more than one reason. (a) Because they are known to be P.O. men; (b) Because every victim that has Tel. Battn. after his name in the Casualty Lists is *not* a telegraphist, and it has been utterly impossible to discriminate other than 24th men; (c) Because the publication of every T.B. man's decease would tend to thoughtlessly create a scare in home circles, and make our Service's loss appear greater than it is.

KHAKI SIDELIGHTS—*continued*.

War Funds.—C.T.O. Giving.—It would not be well to close the pages of KHAKI LETTERS without in some measure referring to the splendid spirit of giving that has pervaded the whole of the Telegraph Service. During the short time I have had the privilege of corresponding with various provincial centres, I have learned that the generous character is general, and many offices have not only helped local funds, newspaper funds, and patriotic subscriptions, but have kept the wives and families of comrades who have been called to the front jogging along with the weekly wage. In some cases the whole amount has been made up, in others the difference (or stoppages) has been provided. TS has done its share. Calls for practical sympathy have been made and nobly responded to, and, be it to their credit said, magnificently sustained over a prolonged period—a period none of us ever dreamt would extend to such a length of time. With a view of giving some idea of what has been done in this matter, I thought I would take the C.T.O., knowing full well that to attempt a larger area would be beyond my power, and in order to arrive at an approximate result, I prepared a form and handed it round to my good staff of distributors. As the call for cash has covered considerably over twelve months, I was not surprised to get some replies saying the items were either forgotten or the amounts were now unknown. Some who had not personally taken an active part in the specified object, could not give figures at all, nor could they obtain them from colleagues, but pertinently remarked, "Had you asked for particulars of the number of wedding and other presents, fresh air funds, and various other objects we had subscribed for, we might have been able to have told you." Yes. In dealing with the matter now under notice, we are fully aware that the War is not responsible for all the bright bobs that are so willingly withdrawn from our pockets to help some straitened stranger or fortunate friend about to enter a new sphere of life; hence our figures will only represent a portion of the freewill gifts that the C.T.O. Staff have bestowed during the year that has just closed.

It is unnecessary for me to repeat the amounts collected section by section for the Rudd Fund; every division and group responded to the call, as will be seen in previous pages (327-347) of our booklet. Perhaps the Khaki Postage Fund may also be excluded, as all sections have figured in that too, but we may note that it amounts to about £19 7s. 6½d., and does credit to all concerned. Taking the C.T.O. then, by divisions and groups alphabetically, we find the Provincial galleries work out as follows:—

"A."—Lady Buller's Fund, £2 13s. and private subs.
"B."—Presents, etc., Lady Buller's Fund, £8 15s. 6d.
"C."—*Daily Telegraph*, £3 12s.; Lady Buller's Fund, £10 10s.; for a reservist, £1, by penny subs. weekly; and presents of tobacco and cigarettes.
"D."—This division claims the promotion of the Absent Minded Beggar Concert, which realised no less a sum than £100 (see page 135). It should be noted that TS generally responded for the Concert. It also sent £8 2s. to Lady Buller's Fund, and recently presented a diamond ring to a returning hero (see present number).
"E."—*Daily Telegraph*, £2 5s.; *Daily Mail* A.M.B., £2; Lady Buller's Fund, £6.
"F."—Various monthly subs. to *Daily Telegraph*, amounts now unknown. Lady Buller's Fund, £3 13s. 6d.
"G."—This division did splendidly through the medium of Mr. Mead, whose energies were repaid by gaining the ideal he had set before them of giving to the *Daily Telegraph* Fund 1,000 shillings. Their record stands: *Daily Telegraph*, £50; *Daily Mail*, A.M.B., £5 16s.; £26 weekly sub. for a reservist (and still going on); £2 for another reservist, and 14s. for tobacco, etc. Lady Buller's Fund, £3 2s. 6d.
"H."—This division has also done magnificently. *Daily Telegraph*, £1 13s.; *Daily Mail*, A.M.B., £37 0s. 3d.; Transvaal Refugee Fund £5, and 20 Balaclava helmets, papers and stamps.
"I."—*Daily Telegraph*, £4; and a large number have contributed privately; also £9 6s. to Lady Buller's Fund.
"K."—*Daily Mail*, A.M.B., £10 3s.; £13 6s. 6d. reservist's wife; Lady Buller's Fund, £4 4s.; £1 5s. for pipes and tobacco, &c., own men, and £1 6s. presents for troops generally; also £1 1s. collected at concert for Lady Buller's Fund.
"L."—*Daily Telegraph*, £2 5s.; weekly subs. for a reservist's wife, £117 17s. 6d. This was the division that so nobly assisted poor Rudd while he was serving in South Africa, and from this division, also, the Rudd Fund originated. Lady Buller's Fund, £6 2s.

KHAKI SIDELIGHTS—continued.

"News."—*Daily Telegraph*, £9 6s. 3d.; Lady Buller's Fund, £10; £2 2s. presents for our men, and smoking outfits.

"Special Staff."—*Daily Telegraph*, £18; Lady Buller's Fund, £13 16s. 9d; and several parcels for our own men.

"Stock Ex."—Mansion House Fund. by weekly subs., the splendid total of £52 7s. 6d. has been handed over; Reservists, 15s.; presents of cigarettes, &c.

"Central Hall."—*Daily Telegraph*, £3 10s.; flowers for wounded soldiers in Herbert Hospital, Woolwich, 7s. 6d.

"Provl. Check."—*Daily Telegraph*, £2 10s.; Mansion House Fund, £1 10s.; *Daily Mail* A.M.B., two parcels containing about 100 gifts, also magazines.

"Night Staff."—Lady Buller's Fund, £2 10s. For the same Fund, "Test," £1 6s.; "Fleet St. Staff," £1; "Delivery," 15s.; "Schools," 14s.; "C.L.S.," 13s. "Glass House," 11s. 6d.

"TSF"—Last, but not least. By periodical collections the sum handed over to the *Daily Telegraph* Fund amounts to £150. First *Daily Telegraph* Concert, £10 10s.; Second *Daily Telegraph* Concert, £20; A.M.B., £2 7s. 6d.; for presents, £2 6s.

The Metropolitan groups contributed £17 17s. for Lady Curzon's Mafeking Relief Fund, Lady Buller's Fund, £7 3s. 3d., and individually as under:—

"A."—*Daily Mail* A.M.B., £5 5s.

"B."—*Daily Mail* A.M.B., £2 5s.; £4 for shirts, socks, handkerchiefs, caps, papers, tobacco, &c.; and Lady Buller's Fund, £2 2s.

"C." *Daily Telegraph*, £2 2s.; £2 5s. for presents for our own men, socks, handkerchiefs, sleeping caps, tobacco, &c.

"D."—Mansion House Fund, £2 10s.; for presents, £12; and private parcels, 10s.

"G."—*Daily Telegraph*, £10; *Daily Mail* A.M.B., £1 10s.; for presents, £1 10s.

"H."—A series of subscriptions to the *Daily Telegraph* Fund, amounting to £28 15s., per Mr. Land. Also to the Mafeking Women's Fund.

"L."—Balaclava caps, comforters, socks, underclothing, &c., for our own men.

KHAKI LETTERS brings up the rear with its profits, and after placing £1 on the Rudd Fund, contributes £10 to the *Daily Telegraph* Shilling Fund in November and another £10 January 7th; making a total of £21, or on the average, £1 per number.

We see, then, that the Central Telegraph Office has helped the *Daily Telegraph* Fund by some £340; had a hand in the *Daily Mail* Absent Minded Beggar Fund to the tune of between £150 and £160, assisted Lady Buller's Fund by giving over £100 and had a share in the Mansion House Fund to the extent of about £55 or £60, and had a finger in Lady Curzon's Mafeking Relief Fund, the Transvaal Refugee and various other T.S. subscriptions amounting to another £150 odd.

Thus it will be seen the C.T.O. have been up and doing. Although the amounts given (including the Rudd Fund) go considerably over £800, it must be borne in mind the above list is very much below the mark, for many groups and divisions have lost count of what has been done, thus rendering the list very imperfect. It may also be remarked that the Sections vary considerably in point of numbers comprising their respective Staffs, as also do they vary in the numbers who don't believe in this, or that, or anything else, but prefer to act upon a most peculiar "principle"—a principle that costs little to uphold in aught else but wordism.

Sections that are omitted have either failed to reply or are unable to render an account, but all have done well in this noble work, and I for one would heartily congratulate the many colleagues who have in any way assisted to bring about this result. We, however, have not yet done with it. As long as the necessity is there, WE MUST BE THERE TOO, remembering that we are helping, or trying to help, those who have suffered much more keenly than the vast majority of us. If it is a strain on our pockets, let it be a strain cheerfully met, for as true Britishers we must give with a British heart and hand to appease the sufferings—in some measure—of those who so sadly need it.

The New Century has begun, and already some new local subscriptions have begun, for from more than one section of our Office Reservists have been again called up for service at the Front.

Mystified.—Fleet Street Sub-Editor to new Special Wire Relieving Clerk; —"Has he answered my query yet?" Raw Recruit:—"No, sir; your SG has gone, he gives MQ, and says he'll KQ with a BQ in a tick." The Sub. subsides.

KHAKI SIDELIGHTS—continued.

The Queen and Her Soldiers. The subjoined was issued from the War Office on Dec. 18th :—" Her Majesty the Queen commands the Adjutant-General to convey to the Militia, Yeomanry, Volunteers, and Colonial troops who have served during the past year in South Africa, the Mediterranean, and elsewhere, her grateful appreciation of their signal services. Her Majesty has been glad to observe the testimony borne by general officers to the admirable spirit by which all ranks have been animated, as well as to the zeal and discipline which they have displayed. The Queen deeply regrets the sickness and loss of life which have occurred, and highly values the sacrifices made by soldiers of all ranks in these branches of the Service in the cause of the Empire, despite personal inconvenience and pecuniary loss. Her Majesty relies on those still employed abroad to continue to use their best efforts in aid of her Regular Army, and trusts that the day may not be far distant when she may welcome their return home.

"War Office, Dec. 18th, 1900."   "EVELYN WOOD, *Adjutant-General.*"

Throughout the life of our booklet many letters have been received from friends,—relatives of comrades at the front, and some have been pleased to use it as a medium for expressing their gratitude for favours shewn.

C.T.O., *December* 11*th*, 1900.

"MY DEAR KEMP,

"Will you allow me, through the medium of your valuable and interesting booklet, to thank those friends who have expressed their sympathy with us in our bereavement. They are so numerous that it is impossible to communicate with all,

so we shall be glad if friends will accept this as an acknowledgement. I have, however, asked my brother (the Postmaster of Barkly-West) to personally wait upon 'Dick's' late colleagues at Kimberley to thank them for their very great kindness in erecting a memorial to his memory—a photograph of which they have been good enough to send me. His death has been a terrible blow to his wife and relatives. 'Dick' was a real man—to know him was to love him. A sweeter disposition it would be hard to find. But the severity of the blow has been softened by the sympathy extended to us by his hosts of friends, for which we are truly grateful.

"Believe me, Sincerely yours,

A. A. FREW."

In a Letter to me dated Dartmouth, December 14th, Mrs. Frew acknowledges the receipt of half-a-dozen cabinet photos of poor "Dick's" grave—similar to that reproduced here—and expresses sincere thanks for the same, adding, "Will you kindly thank your friend Mr. Brook for his most thoughtful kindness, and for the trouble he has taken for me, and I should also like all Wal's comrades at the front to know, if you will tell them, that I am truly thankful for all their kindness to him." Yet another little deed of kindness, amply repaid by the satisfaction one has in knowing that one's efforts have been appreciated. Keep it up, boys! It's worth more than silver and gold.

KHAKI SIDELIGHTS—*continued*.

Presentation Smoker.—On Thursday, December 20th, 1900, a Smoking Concert was held at the "Blue Last," Ludgate Hill, E.C., in order to welcome home our young friend, Private Syd. Sterling, who has served with the City Imperial Volunteers in South Africa. It will be remembered that when the war fever was at its height in the latter part of '99 and the early months of 1900, recruiting was very brisk, and the members of "I" Company were not behind in offering their services for the front with the Royal Engineers. It was, however, discouraging to many a man that his hopes were doomed to disappointment, for the supply exceeded the demand, and many were "crowded out," amongst whom was our comrade S.E.S. He had only joined the 24th in December, '97, and during his recruit's course took the premier prize for drill and shooting (combined) with 154 points to his credit. The R.E. Reserves filled up, but he was not to be denied. As soon as the chance of service in that direction appeared to be closed against him, he volunteered for the C.I.V.'s, and was accepted. How he fared will be found in the pages of KHAKI LETTERS (page 27), and many of his wanderings are recorded in our book. He did not return with his regiment, owing to an attack of enteric, but was not far behind them when they arrived in old England once again. He resumed duty at the C.T.O. in his old division a few weeks ago, and although he has had many private welcomes from his fellow-clerks, the occasion under notice was their Official or Formal Welcome Home to one whom they esteem and admire.

At 8 p.m. the company began to gather, and at 8.15, the time for commencement, more put in an appearance, but owing to the fact that the concert was free, and everybody thinking that all the other everybodies would be there and room would be wanting, the numbers were not so large as one would have wished; the uninviting, wet, slushy night had also its part to play, and it certainly helped to keep many away. At 8.30 a start was made, the proceedings being opened with a pianoforte overture by Mr. Blunden. The toast of "The Queen" was given by the Chairman, and received in the usual loyal manner. We were then treated to some excellent harmony, Mr. C. A. Kindon leading off with "The Longshoreman," in fine style, closely followed by Tommy Sadler with "Obedient to the Call," with much feeling. Mr. Aldred caused much amusement with "The Cork Leg," a song apparently as long as a Lee-Metford, although he (as he told us) omitted 40 verses. A C.I.V. chum, Mr. Andy Lloyd, sang "'Ackney, with the 'Ouses Took Away," in 1900 Cockney style, evoking much applause; after which Mr. Flood brought down the house with a clever mandoline solo. Sergt. W. M. Knight charmed us with "A Soldier's Song." Mr. P. Y. Mercer gave a good recitation, "The Billiard Marker"; Mr. Dalby accompanied himself with "Star of Bethlehem," and Mr. G. Willcox caused much amusement with his song "When Father laid the Carpet on the Stairs." After which the Chairman, Mr. Charlie Bent, one of the boys of the Old Brigade and a right royal R.E., tapped the table with his hammer and jumper—I should say his hammer, and jumped up to do the duty of the evening. Looking towards the Gentleman in Khaki, whose shoulder-straps bore (in red) C.I.V., and glancing around, attention was found. Then, in soldiery accents, said he "Gentlemen, we are gathered together this evening to extend a cordial and hearty welcome to our friend and colleague, Private S. E. Sterling, C.I.V., on his return from South Africa. You will all remember the dark days of last December, when the reverses to the British troops at Stormberg, Magersfontein, and Colenso revealed to us that we were not engaged in fighting a gentle pastoral farmer, as our pro-Boer friends had led us to believe, but with a nation armed to the teeth with all the latest improvements in modern ordnance. It was at that time when we knew what stern and terrible work was before us, that our colleague responded to the call of the Lord Mayor, proving that he was not alone Sterling by name, but Sterling in patriotism and Sterling in courage. (Cheers.) Gentlemen, we in the C.T.O. have reason to be proud of the part our colleagues of the 24th Middlesex of the R.E. Reserve have taken in the War. Though not there as fighting units, they have had to pursue their technical calling under all sorts of difficulties and dangers, sometimes under shot and shell fire, and on other occasions they have taken part in the defence. (Applause.) We have to mourn the loss of Frew, Metcalfe, Hawkins, Rudd, and Williams, who have died in their country's service. Others have been prisoners of war, amongst them our Divisional colleague, A. W. York, who was the first of the C.T.O. men to enter Pretoria, owing to Boer hospitality. Likewise our comrade, A. H. Morse, has also seen captivity. But, Gentlemen, Mr. Sterling has a stronger claim on us than the R.E. Reserve ;" they are receiving full

KHAKI SIDELIGHTS—*continued*.

pay at home and working pay at the front, both in addition to the ordinary pay of the soldier, which latter remuneration our friend Sterling was content with. It was therefore an easy task for our Old Veteran, Secretary Harry Richardson, to collect for a Souvenir to mark our esteem and admiration of Mr. Sterling's services. Gentlemen, I need not tell you how many miles he marched, or how many engagements he took part in; it is sufficient that he did his duty, and that in the words of Lord Roberts, ' He was a hero in the fight, and a gentleman always.' (Loud cheers.) Gentlemen, the City has conferred the Freedom on our friend, they have entertained his regiment at a gorgeous banquet, the people of London have given them a record welcome ; this, however, our friend did not participate in, but I am sure he will feel that the welcome from his fellow-clerks is not the least of the honours conferred upon him." (Prolonged cheers.)

The Chairman then handed to Private Sterling a handsome diamond ring, amidst applause and many kind expressions, followed by the usual musical honours. The elements having again become somewhat normal, Mr. Charles Wolff gave "Soldiers of the Queen," with stirring effect; Mr. H. Rider recited in telling fashion "King Henry of Navarre"; Colour-Sergt. Kemp sang his Volunteer song, "The Banner of Britain" (page 78 K.L.), which went down with as much gusto as in a more military audience.

Mr. Sterling rose to reply, and in a few modest words thanked his comrades for the manner in which they had welcomed him, and for the splendid present they had made him, and sat down amid a ringing cheer. After which Mr. Flood again delighted us with another mandoline solo. A. Buffin pleased the company with his "Little Bit off the Top." Q.M.S. Pusey sang "Smoke, Smoke, Smoke." Sergt. Billy Knight again rendered in fine style, "Thy Sentinel am I." Mr. Blunden brought up the rear with "The Last Rose of Summer," and "Auld Lang Syne" terminated one of the most enjoyable and pleasant Smoking Concerts one would wish for.

About 70 members of the C.T.O. were present during the evening, and much praise is due to the worthy Chairman, Messrs. L. Dalby and Blunden who manipulated the ivories, Mr. Geo. Willcox who acted as Musical Director, and to Harry Richardson, who so ably did the work of Hon. Secretary. The "D" Div. have done well in recognising in so practical a way the services of one who has returned to them safe and sound, and the "I" Company can again claim Private S. E. Sterling as on its roll, and proud enough they are of it.

Here is a testimony to the valuable services rendered by our Army Post Office Corps, as recorded in a Johannesburg newspaper:—

"15th Brigade F.P.O.—A presentation by the officers of the 15th Brigade to the sergeant and subordinates of their Field Post Office took place on Monday at the officers' mess of the 2nd North Staffordshire Regiment. There was a representative attendance of officers. Colonel Bradley, O.C. troops in garrison, presided. Addressing the company, he said : ' Sergt. Davison, Ptes. Williams and Saunders.— I have very much pleasure in making this presentation. You have well earned these tokens of our respect. You have at all times been respectful and obliging. One can hardly realise the immense amount of work involved in a Field Post Office. I think we have been fortunate in our F.P.O., for I very much question if any of our correspondence has gone astray, so well has it been looked after. Letters are looked forward to on active service, and the advent of an English mail was always associated with the name of Sergt. Davison.' Colonel Bradley then called upon Sergt. Davison to accept a silver tea-set. Sergt. Davison, in returning thanks to the officers for their handsome present, said he had never expected such a present; in fact, never expected a present at all. The extremely kind manner in which he, with his subordinates, had been treated by everybody of the 15th Brigade, from the General downwards, had been sufficient thanks for what they had done. Unfortunately, correspondence had been lost, but the bulk of the loss was due to General de Wet. Still, in proportion to the immense amount of matter dealt with, what was lost was infinitesimal, bearing in mind that they were on active service and in a hostile country. Privates G. E. Saunders and J. F. Williams were then each presented with a very handsome tea-set, Colonel Bradley accompanying each presentation with very complimentary remarks, concluding with an exhortation to the two privates to try marriage—if they were not already married—and to use the handsome and useful presents."

[The above par. is the cutting referred to by Col. Thompson in his letter.—QV.]

⊰ Khaki Notes. ⊱

Cut this out!—Friends of the late Sergt. Lankstead (24th Middlesex) will be glad to hear that his widow has taken over the "Farriers' Arms," Mersham, near Ashford, Kent, as a living for herself and three children. The house is situated in one of the prettiest districts of Kent, being four miles from Ashford and two miles from Smeeth Station. The locality is an ideal one for cycling, from whence easy runs may be made to Folkestone, Dover, Canterbury, Maidstone, Hastings and other interesting places. Any of our readers who may be in the vicinity, could materially assist her by their patronage, either *en passant*, or by making the house their head-quarters.

Our Comrades at the front and colleagues at home will be interested to learn that a "record," suitably inscribed and beautifully framed, was placed upon the walls of the Manor Park and Little Ilford Constitutional Club, a week or so before Christmas, to the memory of poor "Dick" Frew, he being a member of that Institution. Herewith is a copy of the same :—"ROLL OF HONOUR. The name of the following member of the Manor Park and Little Ilford Constitutional Club is entered on this Roll of Honour as a record of his patriotism in having fought for his Queen and Empire in the South African Campaign of 1899-1900 :—Sapper W. F. Frew, Regtl. No. 4,366, Royal Engineers (Telegraph Reserve), enlisted for service in South Africa on 15th March, 1900; died of Enteric Fever at Kimberley, on July 7th, 1900." This is very gratifying to us all, but we hope there will be no necessity for any more such records. Had we our wish we would be most pleased to see all our friends' names on the Rolls of Honour that hang on the office walls, giving the duties they are "down for" week by week, and that for many years to come.

Nota Bene.—The following par has been sent me :—"At a Town's Meeting held in the Reading Room, Ilford, it was unanimously resolved that *all* Volunteers or Army Reservists *domiciled in Ilford*, and who went to the front in the South African War, should be presented with a suitable souvenir. A Public Dinner will be held in the Volunteer Drill Hall, Ilford, on Tuesday evening, the 15th January, 1901 (Councillor W. P. Griggs presiding), at which all the Ilford Volunteers and Reservists who have returned home from the War will be entertained at dinner, and each presented with a Silver Lever Watch suitably engraved, with name of recipient, &c. Those men not returned from the front by the 15th January will have their watches forwarded to them in South Africa. It is anticipated that nearly 50 (fifty) Volunteers or Reservists of Ilford will receive this public recognition of their gallant services to their country." It should be noticed that the above resolution includes *all* Volunteers domiciled in Ilford. My informant gives me to understand that the original proposition was to recognise the services of the local C.I.V.'s and Volunteers, until an influential reader of K.L. pointed out that there were Ilford men amongst "our little lot," and very generously the resolution was extended to them also. Just another little bit of work by K.L., that's all.

Volunteers' War Service.—The War Office has notified that the Volunteers who enlisted for South Africa are, on discharge from their engagement, to be shown in the record of attendance at drill of their Volunteer corps, with the date of their original enrolment and that of their rejoining from the Regular forces, the period during which they served with the Regulars being stated in the "Remarks" column.

The C.T.O. Library has just completed another successful year's business. The number of volumes now in stock is close on 4,000. Several well-known and frequently-quoted books dealing with the present campaign in South Africa, and the events which preceded it, have recently been added, the best known probably being Fitzpatrick's "Transvaal from Within," and Prof. Bryce's "Impressions of South Africa." Dr. Conan Doyle's "History of the Great Boer War" is also in great demand. Fiction, however, is the branch of literature in most request; and in this line the Library keeps well up to date, the novels of all the most popular and best known authors being placed in circulation as soon as published. During the year 1900, over 20,000 exchanges of books have been made. The new quarter of the Library commenced on January 1st, 1901.

Khaki Postage Fund.—The following amounts are acknowledged with many thanks :—"A" Div. 3s. 4d., "I" Div. (to complete) 1s. 6¼d., "K" Group 4s. 10d., Provincial Check 2s. 8d., "Stock Ex." 5s. 5d., a Lieut. 8s.; thus, with odd pence, making a Grand Total of £19 7s. 6½d.

KHAKI NOTES—*continued.*

B. Phillips, Esq., 1st Class Assistant Superintendent, who was appointed to the Postmastership of Maidenhead, declined it for domestic reasons.

Mr. A. Levett, Senior Telegraphist, who for many years has been on the Racing Staff, has accepted the Postmastership of Newport, Salop. He left TS on December 31st, and our best wishes go with him.

H. Toothill, Esq., is appointed Supt. of Racing Staff *vice* T. Mason, Esq., 5.1.01.

Mr. Halcrow, of the Controller's Office, has been awarded a testimonial by the R.H.S. for saving the life of a drowning boy at Worthing last August.

About 320 vacancies are announced for the next examination for TS.

Miss Greer, the Matron (well known to us all), left on December 31st, 1900.

Mr. W. O. Williams, late of the "L" Co. and TS, who recently left the service on a bonus, has taken up an appointment in the Cape Government service, and is at present at King William's Town. We hope he will renew his strength and meet with success in his new home.

T. Pain, universally known as "Tom Pain," I regret to say, died on December 15th, and was laid to rest at Forest Hill Cemetery on Saturday, the 22nd ulto. We have often felt sympathy for our old friend who has for so many years been "marking time" at the top of his class, and have—as it has been our pleasure to know him—lost a good member of the Old School.

Wm. Walklin, popularly known as "Joe," passed away on December 18th, after many months' absence on sick leave. Buried at Plumstead Cemetery December 22nd. He leaves a widow and four children, to whom our sincere sympathies are tendered.

Pte. R. Mills, No. 353, A.P.O.C., died December 13th, at Middelburg, enteric.

Among the officers who have returned from the front, per the "Canada," which brought Lord Roberts and his staff home, we are pleased to notice the names of two of the 24th Mx. R.V., Captains A. Palmer and F. A. Labouchere.

Numerous enquiries have been made by TS friends *re* our comrade Sapper L. Orwin. I am pleased to be able to answer them now. Writing on January 2nd, he says :—"I have been invalided from R.E. and have been granted sick furlough pending discharge until February 26th ; on that date I report again at Aldershot for final settling up and discharge." Till recently he was in the Cambridge Hospital, Aldershot ; he is at present near Maidstone.

Another Official Acknowledgment.—I again desire to draw the attention of K.L. readers to the following receipt, handed me on Monday afternoon, a copy of which is reproduced here :—

The "Daily Telegraph" Widows' and Orphans' Fund.
"Daily Telegraph" Offices,
135 and 141, Fleet Street, E.C.
Received, with thanks, from Colour-Sergeant R. E. Kemp, "Khaki Letters" Booklet, a Second subscription of £10 (200 Shillings).
Stamped and Signed by the Cashier.

I have arranged that it shall be published in their first list that appears on or after Monday, January 14th, so that you may all look out for it.

Poniard. On Dec. 15th, a letter was received by some provincial friends informing them that one of our number had been taken to hospital at Bloemfontein very seriously ill. They immediately wired through Poniard, and on New Year's Day we were enabled to forward them the following cablegram :—"Cape Town. Jan. 1st, 10.40 a.m. Poniard, London. Thirtieth progressing favourably."

BQ's.—Hearty thanks to C.S.M. Tee for splendid R.E. Christmas Card, on which is a photograph of the G.P.O., Bloemfontein. To Sappers J. Davies and F. Clark (Germiston) for "The Transvaal through a Camera," being a series of grand photos of Pretoria, Johannesburg, Krugersdorp, Gold Mines, &c., &c. To Sappers Dadswell, C. H. Jones and others, for photo of their Harrismith Office, showing themselves at work in front of their instruments and KHAKI LETTERS at rest in rear of their apps. Also to many others who have sent cards and tokens with the Season's Greetings.

"Casualties, Capetown," for enquiries *re* sick and wounded.

COLOURS.

KHAKI OFFICE WORK.

A Glance at "Khaki Letters."

According to promise, I give some account of the "business" side of KHAKI LETTERS, and it is well that it should be so. I started my Book when I was as green as grass in matter of book production, and I am just as verdant now; but one thing I have kept to myself—for more reasons than one—and that is the answer to the ever-repeating questions: "How many copies do you have printed?" "How many copies do you get rid of?" "What's the circulation now?" A fair queston—admitted—when innocently put, but in every business there are secrets, trade secrets, and in mine there was one, to wit—the number of copies produced and sold. I have always politely refused this information, deeming it prudent to keep at least one item quiet, for so many are given to mathematics that they are apt to work themselves in a big hole if they began to weigh up the production, the cost, the circulation, and the receipts. The refusal to satisfy the questioners has invariably been graciously received when it has been pointed out to them that it is "my only secret," except, in one or two instances, where I have received a sharp "Well, I can easily find out if I like." If he "liked," why didn't the friend find out instead of bothering me? especially, as it was easy. The fact is, our little booklet started wrong—very wrong, in some people's idea—and its progress has surprised them. Many converts have come in—as all broad-minded men would—when they saw the sole aim of the venture was for the sake of Comradeship; there are others, however, who can never think good of it, as facts in my knowledge have abundantly proved. There has never been War in my mind—I repeat it, emphatically. If friends are inclined to continue to think so, this last issue will bring "peace with honour" to all concerned, I hope.

I give you, as a start, a picture of the den in which the deed was done. You will observe it is very dark—as dens mostly are. You will notice the occupant is there—evidently concocting some scheme or other calculated to ruffle the

KHAKI OFFICE WORK—*continued*.

temperaments of all and sundry. Before him are many letters. If he can't get at the bottom of their meaning, he "weighs them up" on the scales in front of him. Dimly descernable are the post-boxes, the regimental orders, the nest of drawers he devised for his work, shelves encumbered with many things he thought might help in his work, a calendar and a clock to keep him regular in his habits; and this is the work he did :—

In the circular issued notifying the proposal to issue KHAKI LETTERS in pamphlet form it was pointed out that 2,500 subscribers would be necessary. A big item, a large number to expect to take on with a project they had never seen in tangible form—a list it was impossible for the most sanguine to hope for. Result, 3,000 K.L's. came out and evaporated immediately. A second edition of 1,000 was ordered the same day and were disposed of as soon as received, and a 3rd edition was ordered. A 2nd edition was also necessary for No. 2, and in that manner the pulse of the purchasers was felt. No. 3, naturally, was produced on the experience gained from 1 and 2, and subsequent issues on their predecessors, and "so they ran," all through the piece.

Expenses. It must be clearly understood that as the book is not finished with until the present issue is quite cleared off, that it is impossible to give the exact amount expended, *to the penny*, as I would wish, but it will be found herein as near as it is possible in every respect.

Sub-editing. All copy has been prepared by me. This entailed very careful reading and constant thought. Not that I feared anything distasteful from any quarter, but I have kept my weather-eye open for the deletion of any expressions that might mar the work or the writer. The search for typographical discrepancies was quite a new work for me, and, as will be understood, that although an E (or other letter) may be inserted upside down, if he passes as "fit" he is upside down for ever, and you hear of it from many quarters later on. But, thanks to a most experienced man at the printers', that difficulty has not been great. It has, however, all been re-read and the book built by Your Humble each issue.

Photo. Blocks. When I launched KHAKI LETTERS I had no idea of illustrating the book at all, but owing to the splendid response, I endeavoured to give full value for money, and make it as tasteful as possible. It is to be regretted that most of the reproductions are such as will remind us of many very dear friends, but that our little book has been the means of bringing their memories more vividly to the mind is gratifying, and in that measure I have been pleased to present them. Some 20 or so blocks have been put into the pages, and the cost of same has amounted to £12 3s. 4d.

Number of Copies produced. The number of each issue has not exceeded 5,000, nor has it been so low as 4,000. There have been 21 numbers, and as three were double numbers (*i.e.* 4-5, 8-9, 11-12) we find 18 issues. The "doubles" count as two singles, and we have the average number of copies per issue as just over 4,700, or a grand total of **99,120.**

Free copies have been sent to our comrades at the front. A glance at the table given in another page will shew how many men there were at various periods. As time went on the numbers increased until 249 copies were sent each issue. From March, 1900, 125 copies were sent ; April, 179; May, 189; June and on, 249. These, however, have been gradually reduced as men have returned, or have unfortunately been called home. It will thus be seen that, after making a reduction for men who have returned, some 4,400 copies have left for Our Comrades in South Africa, each of which cost one half-penny to send, which brings their postage account, alone, to the respectable figure of £9 odd. Free copies have also been sent to various other persons, institutions, etc.

Distribution. To distribute this vast number was a work in itself. TS volunteers came forward at the call, every man of his own free will—not one has ever been asked to do the duty—and this is most creditable to them. The provinces elected their own men in the same manner, and all has gone well and in a free and easy way. The C.T.O. has always taken a good half, and on the day of issue I have spent four hours (and more) in handing the books over to my helpers and taking their accounts in return. But the most arduous task has been the posting and packing of parcels. Nearly 7,000 wrappers have been addressed—for S. Africa, and friends at home—prior to receipt of books from the printers, by my daughter, and it was found to be a day's work almost to fold, enclose and stamp the booklets. The packets for parcel post necessitated counting, weighing, tying and stamping ; and this has been done by another member of my home—no small job—and well

KHAKI OFFICE WORK—*continued*.

done; my portion in this particular branch being the writing of bills, answering questions, and filling in receipts for remittances received, &c. Special forms were printed for this, and no fewer than 800 receipts have been made out. Specially addressed wrappers were also printed for the Boys out yonder.

Envelopes. I have done my best to encourage my colleagues at home to write to Our Boys, believing it would cheer them, and in order to secure delivery of letters, designed a special envelope for the purpose. No fewer than 6,250 have been sold. It is therefore reasonable to suppose that plenty of letters have been sent to South Africa.

In Memoriam Cards. Splendid cards have been printed, giving the photo reproduction of some of our fallen friends, together with various particulars upon them, and a verse or so. Some 1,500 have been disposed of among our readers.

Stationery, &c. Various articles have been required to run the concern. A pair of scales for book packets and letters (the household scales being used for big parcels), stamp-box, letter files, letter cases, &c., &c. All total up. Printed notices, order forms, note headings, copy paper, circulars, Hektograph requisites, packing paper, envelopes, and other little items—all cost money.

"My Colleagues in South Africa." Some 3,000 have been printed, but not sold. Unfortunately the calling up of more men entirely stopped the sale of one edition. "We will wait until you print one with *all* the fresh names on it." Result, *that* lot was a loss.

Postage and Carriage. Many friends in the provinces have paid either all the postage on their parcels, or part of it. Others have paid none. Some have caught the spirit of K.L.'s, others have not; and when I have paid 3d. on a parcel of 12 I have always failed to see a profit on the transaction, and certainly failed to get one. But that does not matter; those friends *believed* me, they have noticed my remarks that K.L. was not intended to be a money-making concern, and they have said, "Just so," but in the fact that they have *believed* me, I must thank them for their patronage. The postage item is a large one, amounting altogether to over £33.

A number of men have tried to guess the amount of cash necessary to meet the work of K.L. Although some have posed as judges, and with knitted brows have stood and thought (I've never interfered with them then—it's rather rare for some people to *think*), their calculations have been wide of the mark. The actual outlay for everything in connection with KHAKI LETTERS is as follows:—

		£ s. d.	£ s. d.
A.	Printing the book, from No. 1 to 21	277 1 6	
	Photo blocks for the same ..	12 3 4	
	Envelopes (printed for S. Africa), including my own	3 1 6	
	"My Colleagues" List of Names ..	4 10 0	
	Wrappers—with headings and addresses ..	2 18 7	
	In Memoriam Cards and Enlargements ..	7 18 0	
	Memos., Order Forms, Note Headings, Circulars, and General Stationery, &c.	4 13 0	
	Circulars announcing advent of KHAKI LETTERS ..	3 0 0	
	Paid to Messrs. Berryman & Sons		315 5 11
B.	Postage on KHAKI LETTERS (and letters in connection therewith)	33 10 0	
	Letter-balance, Stamp-box, Letter-files, String and other items purchased at various Establishments	1 17 9	35 7 9
C.	To Rudd Fund, £1; *Daily Telegraph* Fund, £20 ..	21 0 0	21 0 0
	Total Expenditure		**£371 13 8**

It will thus be seen that the work has greatly exceeded the anticipations of almost everybody in matters financially. And as regards the clerical portion of it, no one can conceive what it has meant. In addition to the work of the book, I have answered enquiries as far as my information has permitted me to do so, regarding the movements of the men, &c., &c. In fact, the whole of my time has been entirely given up to the work I so ardently undertook, for it is no use playing at it if success is to be achieved.

Bad Debts. It is not to be expected that even such a project as this should be without its shadowy side. I am sorry to say there are several bad debts, amounting in the aggregate to a pound or two; but I will not say more of this.

From the Khaki Letter-Box.

KENSINGTON, W.
25th December, 1900.

"DEAR COLOUR-SERGEANT KEMP,

"I understand the next issue of KHAKI LETTERS is likely to be the last, and therefore I write to tell you how highly I appreciate your undertaking. It has been a friendly link between our absent comrades and ourselves, and the letters have had for me a very deep interest. I greatly admire the cheerful spirit shown by all the writers, and the repeatedly expressed hope that they might do credit to the 24th. These KHAKI LETTERS have been supplemented by many private letters to myself from N.C.O. and men of 'L' Company, all expressing the same kindly feeling and the same cheerfulness under hardship; and what is very gratifying to me, they, as well as their comrades in the Army Post Office Corps, all utter the same longing to be back in the old 24th once more. I hope it may be my good fortune to be still in the regiment when all our comrades return home and to share in that warm and heartfelt welcome which awaits them here.

"The grievous thought at this glad season is the large number of well-loved comrades whom we can see no more in this world, and the touching kindness with which these 'who have gone before' are alluded to in your booklet has struck a tender chord in many a heart.

"I sincerely wish we could expect the others to return shortly, but at present the aspect of affairs in South Africa does not give much encouragement to this expectation; but whether their return be sooner or later, they may rest assured that our thoughts and sympathies are with them, and have been so especially to-day.

"Your booklet has been most interesting to me as well as to many others, and I know I am only giving utterance to the feelings of all who have read it when I say that its production is most creditable to you and most beneficial to the Company. It must have cost much time and trouble, and its success is I am sure very pleasing to you. When reading it I have sometimes regretted that the Army Post Office Company had no one standing in the same relation to it that you do to the Telegraph Company, for I think the many letters which I have received from N.C.O. and men of 'M' Company would bear comparison in point of interest with those of 'L' Company; but as there was apparently no one in the position to undertake for the 'M' Company what you have so enthusiastically and kindly done for 'L' Company, I can only thank you for the references to the Army Post Office Corps which have now and then appeared in your booklet. I enclose a cutting from a Johannesburg paper, which shows that their services are not unappreciated.

"The excellent spirit shown in the regiment when volunteers were needed for service in South Africa, when so many more than were required were anxious to go and keenly disappointed at being left behind, was a sign that the regiment's heart is in the right place. This is proved by the fact that some of our officers and men were to be found not only in the Royal Engineer Telegraph Battalion and in the Army Post Office Corps, but also in the Yeomanry and the City of London Imperial Volunteer Regiment.

"If you should think of putting this letter in KHAKI LETTERS, I would like to avail myself of the opportunity of conveying to all our comrades still in South Africa my most hearty good wishes for a Happy New Year.

"Yours faithfully,
(Signed) "S. RAFFLES THOMPSON, *Colonel.*"

FROM THE KHAKI LETTER-BOX—*continued.*

It was indeed a pleasure to receive the foregoing letter from my Commanding Officer, who takes so much interest in the men on Active Service, as well as those at home. With reference to the A.P.O.C. being represented, it may not be out of place to say that several receivers of letters from them suggested that theirs might find a place in our book. The idea was accepted, and not only were pages set apart for them, but reminders were sent, but no "copy" has ever been received; thus our comrades have lost their opportunity. We would have found their experiences of much interest, and gladly have accorded them "a look-in" in the book that was essentially the Telegraphists' own.

The Honoured Friend who runs the R.E.'s regimental paper sends the following letter :—

"*The Sapper* Offices, School of Military Engineering, Chatham,
"DEAR SIR, 28*th December*, 1900.

" We would not that the last issue of KHAKI LETTERS should appear without a few lines of congratulation concerning the admirable work you have done.

" We understand that you were prompted to publish this booklet chiefly for the following reasons :—

" 1—To keep the 24th Middlesex Post Office Rifle Volunteers (Royal Engineer Reserves) in touch with each other, and their friends at home.

" 2—To cause a closer relationship, and better feeling to exist, between the R.E. Regulars and their Telegraph Reserves.

" We congratulate you on the highly successful result of this self-imposed, and in some respects thankless, task.

" We have noted, with no small amount of interest, how keenly you have watched the interests of, and ungrudgingly and unremittingly devoted so much time in bringing about 1 and 2.

" You have stood by KHAKI LETTERS in all weathers! Courageous in the midst of discouragements! Sanguine of ultimate success in the face of apparent failure! Receiving at times worrying and trivial communications, yet ever and anon replying to them with infinite tact and discretion! In short, although there have been many ups and downs, many disappointments, and considerable anxiety, you have stood to your purpose throughout.

" Again we congratulate you.

" We understand that the chief reasons for discontinuing the publication of KHAKI LETTERS are :—

" (*a*) That of late you have experienced a difficulty in obtaining interesting copy, due chiefly to 'The Boys' being, to use a regimental—very regimental—expression, 'fed up.'

" (*b*) That the large amount of extra clerical labour involved in connection with the editing of KHAKI LETTERS is likely to interfere with your manifold usual office duties.

" Regarding (*a*), this is not at all surprising. We can assure readers of KHAKI LETTERS that the '24th' are not, by a very long way, the only ones 'down south' who are suffering from 'fed-upedness.'

" Regarding (*b*), this is easily understood. None but those who have taken part in a venture of this nature can conceive the immense amount of work entailed in connection with the publication of a paper, even so small as KHAKI LETTERS. We sincerely trust the day is not far distant when you will obtain the well-merited advancement you so richly deserve.

" Before concluding, we would take this opportunity of thanking you for the many kindly references you have from time to time made to *The Sapper* and the Royal Engineers generally, also we would tender our best thanks to the numerous readers of KHAKI LETTERS who so kindly contribute and subscribe to *The Sapper.*

" Should an occasion ever again arise in which it is desirable that the doings of the '24th' be chronicled, as in this instance, we hope and trust that, notwithstanding the many rebuffs you have received, you will be courageous enough to again assume the reins by publishing a booklet on similar lines to that which you are now about to relinquish.

" Adieu. With the kindest regards to yourself and the many readers of KHAKI LETTERS, we beg to subscribe ourselves, Yours faithfully,

"S. W. HURST, Qr.-Mr.-Sergt., R.E.,
" To The Editor KHAKI LETTERS. "Editor *The Sapper.*',

FROM THE KHAKI LETTER-BOX—*continued.*

Yet another, one of a very large number received, and from a gentleman in the *Civil* Service who is well known to most of us:—

"Post Office, Radcliffe, Manchester,
3rd December, 1900.

"MY DEAR KEMP,

"Small amount for your disposal herewith.

"I suppose '21' is to be 'finis.' Well, I can only say I have greatly appreciated your efforts. The work has been well done, and must have been satisfactory to those bearing the brunt of the fray, and to those who have only watched and prayed.

"To me, knowing so many of the Middlesex men, it has been an epitome of my old colleagues' doings, and it is indeed pleasant reading to know that they have acquitted themselves like men, and, *vide* Commander-in-Chief's despatch, 'have done good work under exceptionally difficult circumstances.'

"The best traditions of the Civil Service have been honourably upheld by them, and we are proud that the scientific branch has justified our ideas of its loyalty, and has furnished an important arm—an arm which has made itself conspicuous by the rendering of excellent services.

"In perusing the letters, I have found some light and some shadow. The shadows fell when reading of the death of some of my old colleagues, and the thoughts evoked by the photos of their graves in the lonely veldt.

"Your work has been thorough—well conceived and well carried out; and the wide-spread interest taken in the publication is evidence of the need of such an organ during such times as we have experienced in South Africa.

"My office is represented by a Seaforth Highlander—a Postman—and he has had varied experiences.

"Thanking you for your work, and with every good wish for the prosperity of the Corps of which you are an excellent representative,

"I am, Yours truly,
"D. SCOTT."

Thus we have, as it were, the Trinity again—the 24th Middlesex Rifle Volunteers, the Royal Regiment they have the honour to serve in, and the Service they are recruited from. A happy trio, a very special blend, spontaneously sent in.

Khaki Flashes.

In the first issue, articles on suitable subjects were asked for, also newspaper cuttings, in order to brighten the pages of K.L.; but very, very few have been received of the latter, and certainly none of the former. My own articles on Army Signalling I have never written, but I will just touch upon those means of communication that have often been referred to in the daily papers, *i.e.*, the flag, lamp and heliograph.

There are now two codes of Signalling in the Army—the Morse and the Semaphore. The latter system requires the use of two small flags, or two arms of a semaphore. We will bear in mind the Morse system only.

The flags used for signalling are of two colours, and each of two sizes. The large flag is 3-ft. square, mounted on a pole 5-ft. 6-in. in length, tapering from 1-in. in diameter at the butt to ½-in. at the point. The small flags are 2-ft. square, and are used on a pole 3-ft. 6-in. long, ¾-in. at the butt and tapering to ½-in. at the point. The flags are made of muslin. One is all dark blue and would be used when the background is of a light nature, or when the signaller is on the sky-line. The other flag is white with a blue horizontal stripe, and would be used when the background is dark; in other words, the flag to be used is the one that contrasts most with the surroundings of the sender as seen by the receiver, the latter giving the former the tip as to which he can read from best. With the large flag and a suitable atmosphere on well chosen positions, the distance signals may be read in this country by the aid of the service telescope is five to seven miles. In countries where the atmosphere is clearer than ours, greater distances have been recorded where it is possible for visual signalling to be successfully carried on. The photographer knows this, for the views he is enabled to take in England rarely define the distant hills or horizon with the cleanness and sharpness attained by his more favoured friends abroad. The lens is a good tester of distances discernible in varying atmospheres, fuzziness being more or less prominent in most landscapes

KHAKI FLASHES—*continued*.

taken at home. The large flag is used for long distances, the small for short. The small flag is more rapid in consequence of its lightness, and is always used when it can be well seen. Its range, under the same conditions as its bigger brother, is between three and four miles. It may be well to note that the horizontal blue stripe distinguishes the white flag from a flag of truce. The normal position of a flag, when ready to make a letter, will be understood from the position of the hands, *i.e.* :—with the large flag the butt of the pole is held by the left hand near the buckle of the belt and with the right hand grasps the pole at the point of the left shoulder. To make a dot the flag is brought over to a corresponding position on the right side and taken back again to the "normal" position. This is where the inability comes in : a good number of telegraphists try to read it as a single needle, dots one side, dashes the other. To make a dash the flag is brought right over until its point is about 18 inches from the ground, right arm extended, left wrist upturned, and back again to the "normal." Thus it will be seen a dash is—as it should be—three times the length of a dot. Some have asked, "Why is the flag taken back to the normal every time?" Well, you can't start a second dot, or dash, until it is. To keep the flag unfurled, you describe an elongated figure 8 in the air with the point of the pole, otherwise when "returning" from a smart signal you would meet the muslin with the pole and tie it up, preventing its being seen by the distant reader. Qualifying rate of working, large flag, 10, small flag, 12 words per minute, but much higher rates are attainable, especially with the small.

Lamps. These are large bullseye lamps, with a metal disc working behind the glass to shut off the light. The disc is fixed to a lever or key on the right side of the lamp. Depressing the key shews the light, and signals are thus made. It is fixed upon a tripod. The limelight is worked upon similar lines, but of course is much more powerful—also requires more transport and preparation. The hand lamp can be read at 3 or 4 miles, the limelight at from 10 to 15, in England. Qualifying rate of reading, 12 words per minute.

Heliographs.—Another misunderstood instrument. A week or two ago I heard it fully explained in a railway carriage on the Slow, Easy and Cautious-Riding Company's line. The instructor was profuse, and knew his subject well. "He gits yer angle with 'is eeligrarf and shews yer 'is light, then yer gets 'is angle and shews 'im your light, and so yer work on angles ; it's all angles, nothing but angles ; it's a fine bit o' work, but yer *must* get 'is angle." Further explanation is, therefore, unnecessary ; but in case you are no wiser, let us briefly go on. Take a mirror into the sunlight and let it flash on the wall some dozen yards in front of you. Notice that the smallest movement causes the light to dance away in various directions—high, low, right, or left. The heliograph is on the same principle, with an arrangement to keep it fixed on one spot, or direction—that of the distant station ; and as we see a sparkle from a small piece of china or glass in a ploughed field, or a window of a house a long way off, when the sun is on it, so the signaller sees the flash from the 5-inch mirror that is aligned on him. It is mounted on a tripod, at the head of which is a socket and tangent screw to give the **U** frame that supports the reflector a horizontal movement. Another screw gives the mirror a vertical motion within its **U** frame. From the socket a jointed arm extends some fourteen inches, at the end of which is a piece of silvered metal called a sighting vane ; on this vane is a mark and cross lines. In the centre of the mirror is an unsilvered spot ; this throws a shadow. Now, if the sighting vane mark and the unsilvered spot are brought into sight-line with the distant station (which can be seen by looking into the mirror, and seeing both reflected), it only remains for the reflector to be adjusted by the vertical and horizontal screws until the shadow in the centre of the reflected rays falls on the mark on the sighting vane, and you are then certain the distant signaller can see your light. If the key at the back of the mirror is depressed while this is being done, the light will be seen ; but on releasing the key the flash will disappear from view, as in the case of the reflection on the wall. When the sun is at such an angle that a flash cannot be sent in the desired direction, a second mirror replaces the vane and transmits the reflections from the sending mirror. This is called the duplex mirror, and does not mean duplex working, as in the case of wires. Twelve words per minute is the qualifying rate. Short and long flashes—same as Morse key work. Distance readable—according to atmosphere, &c. In one of our expeditions—the Waziri, in 1881—efficient communication was kept up, direct, at a distance of 70 miles. The instrument requires constant readjustment "as the earth goes merrily round."

It was my intention to give a par or two on air-line and cable-cart practice, as well as the formation of general signalling stations in the field, but space forbids,

⊸ Khaki Closes. ⊷

With this issue we arrive at our "Majority," and it is certainly not a pleasure to drop the pen and spring smartly to attention when work ought to be going on. As the book was started, so it has continued, in the very best of health, uncanny perhaps, but admired withal. You have overlooked my many failings, you have recognised for yourselves I was no expert journalist—I haven't got the cut of one, and never shall have; but you have entered into the spirit of the thing and I thank you for your support, and the honour you have done me in continuing to bestow your patronage upon this labour of love. I have tried to give you value for your money. I think I have done so. I have never been in a position to command copy, or to constrain my comrades to contribute their correspondence. If letters ceased, the book ceased: I knew that at the commencement. They have virtually ceased, and the book honourably closes.

I thank you, dear readers, most sincerely for the magnificent manner in which you have stood by me. I won't say I didn't want any more like you; the more the merrier. But we can congratulate each other on our short acquaintance, and the work WE have done—I in supplying, you in the buying, and both in the trying to keep up a means of fashioning and fostering a friendship with the Boys while away on Service.

My Distributors! You who have so zealously and untiringly assisted me in scattering the books far and wide, I sincerely thank you, and I know you have been proud of your position as a helper in the work.

No lengthy epistle of mine would be adequate to express the feelings I have towards all those who, in any way, have assisted in the work that has been accomplished, and I can say no more than that I tender every one of you my most grateful thanks.

I have had confidence in you, and that confidence has also been returned. You did not expect great things, you did not get them. You have been satisfied in some measure, I have been gratified also; and in severing our connection, as it were (at least in the relationship that has lately existed between us), I will remind you that we have helped *one* fund a trifle, and I take my leave, wishing you all "A Happy, Bright, and Prosperous New Year."

Yours heartily, "COLOURS."

❈ FINIS. ❈

"KHAKI LETTERS," One Penny. By post, Three Halfpence.

www.ingramcontent.com/pod-product-compliance
Lightning Source LLC
Chambersburg PA
CBHW031130160426
43193CB00008B/86